THE COMPLETE WORKS OF
FRANCIS A. SCHAEFFER
A CHRISTIAN WORLDVIEW

VOLUME FIVE

A Christian View of the West

THE COMPLETE WORKS OF

FRANCIS A. SCHAEFFER

A CHRISTIAN WORLDVIEW

VOLUME FIVE
A Christian View of the West
Second Edition

CROSSWAY BOOKS • WESTCHESTER, ILLINOIS
A DIVISION OF GOOD NEWS PUBLISHERS

First printing: hardback, first edition, 1982
Fifth printing: paperback, second edition, 1985
Eighth printing: paperback, second edition, 1988

Printed in the United States of America
Library of Congress Catalog Card Number: 84-72681
ISBN: 0-89107-336-1

The Complete Works of Francis A. Schaeffer.
Trade paper: 0-89107-331-0
   Volume 1   0-89107-332-9
   Volume 2   0-89107-333-7
   Volume 3   0-89107-334-5
   Volume 4   0-89107-335-3
   Volume 5   0-89107-336-1

Second edition, hardbound: 0-89107-347-7
   Volume 1   0-89107-348-5
   Volume 2   0-89107-349-3
   Volume 3   0-89107-350-7
   Volume 4   0-89107-351-5
   Volume 5   0-89107-352-3

THE COMPLETE WORKS OF
FRANCIS A. SCHAEFFER
A CHRISTIAN WORLDVIEW

Preface to Volumes I–V

We are reediting and republishing the twenty-one books written by me between 1968 and 1981. Various people asked for this, so that they would be available in permanent form. I agreed to the work involved in it because we have found that all the books are contemporary for the 1980s. We think they are more contemporary now than when they were first published.

These books are now published as five hardback volumes. Thus, all my printed work which is in book form will be available in five companion volumes.

Much reediting has gone into this. They are the same books, yet brought up to date and clarified where time has shown they need clarification.

A section of *The God Who Is There* which seems to have been rather widely discussed and, it seems to me, at times misunderstood and misstated has been what is sometimes called "Schaeffer's apologetics." This section is enlarged as an added appendix on pages 175-187 of Volume I of this series.

All the books are to be read and understood together (along with my wife Edith's books). They together are a unit.

They were written to be read and useful to both Christians and non-Christians. Time has proved this to be the case far beyond our hopes.

They were not written to be only used on the academic scene, though they have been used there, but also for the less academic— though, of course, we realize that they do take care and study and are not popular reading to be pursued while dozing in an armchair. Some have thought the terminology difficult, but I have letters from many parts of the world saying that it was the use of this terminology that for them showed that Christianity has something to say to twentieth-century people, and that it was this terminology which was the bridge which caused them to study the books and to be helped by them. We have tried to make the terminology easier where possible.

The Bible translations have been maintained as they were in the original editions: that is, the *King James* in the earlier books, and the *New International Version* in *Whatever Happened to the Human Race?* and *A Christian Manifesto*.

Another choice to be made was whether to leave the word *man*, as designating men and women, or go to the recent usage of indicating in each case that *she* or *he* is meant. When the earlier books were written, this was not a problem. In my later books the newer way of speaking and writing has been used. However, bringing the earlier books in line in this regard would have been a horrendous task. Please therefore forgive me, anyone who would be disturbed, and please read the usage in the older accepted way. I would be overwhelmingly sorry if anyone would be "put off." Please read it as "man" equaling a human being and all human beings—whoever you are—women and men, children and adults.

The basic trilogy has been: *The God Who Is There, Escape from Reason,* and *He Is There and He Is Not Silent.* All the others fit into these as spokes of the wheel fit into the hub.

The early books broke ground in calling for the Lordship of Christ in the arts—art, literature, cinema, philosophy and so on. *How Should We Then Live?, Whatever Happened to the Human Race?* and *A Christian Manifesto* bring this body of thought forward into the area of a Christian's duty, under the Lordship of Christ, in the whole of life as a citizen, especially in the area of law, government, and standing for a high view of human life.

We have been overwhelmed at the way these books have been used over such a wide spectrum of kinds of people and geographically. I can truly say it has brought us to awe and worship. These new five volumes are now published in the hope that they too will be so used.

To make these present volumes more useful for some, at the end of each volume there is a list of translations in the various countries and the publishers for the books in that volume.

This venture would not have been possible without the hard work and wisdom of Dr. Jeremy Jackson and Ranald Macaulay who gave me their suggestions. I thank them profoundly.

Francis A. Schaeffer, 1982

Contents

BOOK ONE: POLLUTION AND THE DEATH OF MAN

BOOK TWO: HOW SHOULD WE THEN LIVE?

POLLUTION AND THE DEATH OF MAN

CHAPTER ONE

"What Have They Done to Our Fair Sister?"

Some time ago when I was in Bermuda for a lecture, I was invited to visit the work of a young man well-known in the area of ecology. His name was David B. Wingate. He was especially known for his efforts to save the cahow bird from extinction. The cahow is a little larger than a pigeon and breeds only on a very few islands near Bermuda, just off the main island. Wingate struggled for many years to increase the number of these birds.

As we went around visiting the nests, we were talking together about the whole problem of ecology. He told me that he was losing ground in his battle, because the chicks were not hatching in the same proportion as before. If they had continued at the previous rate, he would have been well on his way to success. Instead, he found that fewer and fewer were hatching. What was the reason? To find out, he took an embryo chick from the egg and dissected it. Its tissues were found to be filled with DDT. Wingate was convinced that this accounted for the drop in the hatching rate.

The startling thing about this is that the cahow is a sea-feeding bird; it does not feed anywhere near land—only in the middle of the ocean. So it is obvious that it was not getting its DDT close to shore, but far out in the Atlantic. In other words, the use of DDT on land was polluting the whole area. It was coming down through the rivers, out into the ocean, and causing the death ot sea-feeding birds.[1]

When Thor Heyerdahl made his famous voyage in the Kon Tiki, he was able to use the ocean water quite freely; but he later said when he tried to cross the Atlantic in a papyrus boat, the ocean water was unusable because of the large amount of rubbish.

A man in California very vividly pointed up this serious problem. He erected a tombstone at the ocean-side, and on it he has carved this epitaph:

> The ocean born— [he gives hypothetical date]
> The oceans died—A.D. 1979
> The Lord gave; man hath taken away
> Cursed be the name of man.

The simple fact is that if man is not able to solve his ecological problems, then man's resources are going to die. It is quite conceivable that man will be unable to fish the oceans as in the past, and that if the balance of the oceans is changed too much, man will even find himself without enough oxygen to breathe.

So the whole problem of ecology is dumped in this generation's lap. *Ecology* means "the study of the balance of living things in nature." But as the word is currently used, it means also the problem of the destruction man has brought upon nature. It is related to such factors as water pollution, destructive noise levels, and air pollution in the great cities of the world. We have been reading and hearing of this on every side from all over the world.

Near the end of his life, Darwin acknowledged several times in his writings that two things had become dull to him as he got older. The first was his joy in the arts and the second his joy in nature. This is very intriguing. Darwin offered his proposition that nature, including man, is based only on the impersonal plus time plus chance, and he had to acknowledge at the end of his life that it had had these adverse effects on him. I believe that what we are seeing today is the same loss of joy in our total culture as Darwin personally experienced—in the area of the arts and general life, and in the area of nature. The distressing thing about this is that orthodox Christians often really have had no better sense about these things than unbelievers. The death of "joy" in nature is leading to the death of nature itself.

In the 1960s and early 1970s when there was a profound interest in the philosophic basis for life and the problems of life, this sort of anxiety was even being expressed in the area of "pop" music. The Doors had a song called "Strange Days" in which they said:

> What have they done to the earth?
> What have they done to our fair sister?
> Ravaged and plundered,
> And ripped her and bit her,
> Stuck her with knives in the side of the dawn,
> And tied her with fences and dragged her down.[2]

At any rate, people everywhere began to discuss what could be done about it. An intriguing article by Lynn White, Jr., on "The Historical Roots of Our Ecologic Crisis," was published in *Science* magazine.[3] White was a professor of history at the University of California at Los Angeles.

In his article he argued that the crisis in ecology is Christianity's fault. It is a brilliant article in which he argued that although we no longer are a Christian world, but a post-Christian one, nevertheless we still retain a "Christian mentality" in the area of ecology. He said Christianity presents a bad view of nature, and so this is carried over into the present-day post-Christian world. He based his allegations of a "bad view of nature" on the fact that Christianity taught that man had dominion over nature and so man has treated nature in a destructive way. He saw that there is no solution to ecological problems—any more than there is to sociological problems—without a "base." The base of man's thinking must change.

In ecology in the 1980s there is not much writing or discussion on the basic philosophies underlying the consideration of ecology. This is parallel to the lack of philosophic pornography, philosophic drug taking, philosophic films, etc. However, in ecology, as in these other areas, the thought-forms of the 1980s were laid in the earlier period of the 1960s. At that time there was much serious consideration, writing, discussion and expression concerning the world-views underlying all these areas.

People are now functioning on the ideas formulated in that earlier period—even though those so functioning do not consciously realize it.

As Christians, we should know the roots in order to know why those who speak and act against Christianity are doing so, and in order to know the strength of the Christian answer in each area. If we do not do this, we have little understanding of what is occurring about us. We also do not know the strength of what, as Christians, we have to say across the whole spectrum of life.

The articles of Lynn White and Richard Means, from the later part of the 1960s are, I think, still the classic ones concerning the area of ecology.

Modern man's viewpoint in the post-Christian world (as I have dealt with in my previous writings) is without any categories, and without any base upon which to build. Lynn White understood the need of a base in the area of ecology. To quote him: "What people do about their ecology depends on what they think about themselves in relation to things around them. Human ecology is deeply conditioned by beliefs about our nature and our destiny— that is, by religion." Here I believe he is completely right. Men *do* what they *think*. Whatever their world-view is, this is the thing which will spill over into the external world. This is true in every area, in sociology, in psychology, in science and technology, as well as in the area of ecology.

White's solution was to ask, "Why don't we go back to St. Francis of Assisi?" He contrasts St. Francis with what he saw as the "orthodox view" of men having the "right" to despoil nature. "The greatest spiritual revolutionary in Western history, St. Francis proposed what he thought to be an alternative Christian view of nature in man's relationship to it. He tried to substitute the idea of the equality of all creatures, including men, for the idea of man's limitless rule of creation."

Both our present science and our present technology, according to White, are so tinctured with orthodox Christian arrogance toward nature that no solution for our problem of ecology can be expected from them alone. He said that technology is not going to solve the problem because it is powered with its view of dominion over nature, which equals limitless exploitation. "Since the roots of our trouble are so largely religious, the remedy must also be essentially religious, whether we call it that or not. We must re-think and refeel our nature and destiny. The profoundly religious, but heretical, sense of the primitive Franciscans for the spiritual autonomy of all parts of nature may point out a direction. I propose Francis as the patron saint for ecologists."

The discussion of this was picked up and carried further, and aroused much interest. In the *Saturday Review* of December 2,

1967,[4] Richard L. Means, who was associate professor of sociology at the College of Kalamazoo, Michigan, quoted White and extended White's concept and asked: "Why not begin to find a solution to this in the direction of Pantheism?" In fact, he tied this call for a solution based upon pantheism into what he called the "cool cats" of the generation in their interest in Zen Buddhism. He is saying here, "Wouldn't it be a solution if we just said, 'We're all of one essence?' "

So here pantheism is proposed as an answer to our ecological dilemma. But is it an answer at all? That is a question we must now consider.

CHAPTER TWO

Pantheism: Man Is No More Than the Grass

Why not try to find a solution to this in the direction of pantheism? Here we find a use of the concept of pantheism by a Western scientist, a sociologist, in his effort to solve modern man's problem in relationship to the saving of nature—i.e., the ecological problem. This man seemed to be trying to use pantheism in a very specific way—not as a real, religious answer at all, but merely in a sociological or a scientific, pragmatic way.

Richard Means' article was entitled "Why Worry About Nature?" Means begins the article by quoting Albert Schweitzer: "The great fault of all ethics hitherto has been that they believed themselves to have to deal only with the relation of man to man." He thus quoted Schweitzer as saying ecology is a problem of ethics, but that man's only concept of ethics has been "man to man." Later Means said, "The notion that man's relation to nature is a moral one finds very few articulate champions, even among contemporary religious writers." He proceeded to refer to Harvey Cox's book, *The Secular City*. Cox, of course, is a very liberal theologian and at that time a proponent of the God-is-dead theology. Means said that even with Cox, "the city is taken for granted and the moral dimensions of Cox's analysis are limited to man's relations to man within this urban world, and not with the animals, the plants, the trees, and the air—that is, the natural habitat." It should be remembered that much modern theology is in the direction of pantheism, and thus Means' suggestion of a pragmatic pantheistic base for solving our ecological problems fits naturally into the climate which reaches all the way from the vague pantheism in much popular thinking today to the theological faculties.

Means went on to refer, interestingly enough, to Eric Hoffer, who was a popular American folk philosopher. He was a longshoreman who said many really profound things and had become very popular indeed with intellectuals. "Eric Hoffer, one of the few contemporary social critics who have met head-on the issue of man's relationship to nature, has warned in these pages of the danger of romanticizing nature" ("A Strategy for the War with Nature" in *Saturday Review,* February 5, 1966). Romanticizing means that one looks at nature and projects into it man's reaction. So one would look at a cat and think of it as though it were reacting as a man reacts. Hoffer very properly warned against this. However, his solution (according to Means) ends like this: "The great accomplishment of man is to transcend nature, to separate himself from the demands of instinct. Thus, according to Hoffer, a fundamental characteristic of man is to be found in his capacity to free himself from the restrictions of the physical and the biological." In other words, Hoffer was really not proposing that we should come to terms with nature (not as far as Means understood him anyway). What Hoffer was saying is that man has to transcend nature.

It should be said that it is correct to reject the romanticizing of nature as an answer or a solution. First, nature, as it now is, is not always benevolent; and second, to project our feelings and thoughts into a tree would mean that we would have no base upon which to justify cutting down and using the tree as a shelter for man.

Those who are familiar with Koestler's *The Man and The Machine* will recognize Hoffer's ideas to be merely a more poetic form of his concept. Koestler, along with Adler (*The Difference in Man and the Difference It Makes*) and Michael Polanyi of Oxford, attacks the classical view of evolution, at least pragmatically; these men were united as far as saying that it is leading us in the wrong direction. But Koestler in *The Man and The Machine* came up with the final solution by pleading with science to make a pill to bring together the upper and the lower brain. For Koestler, the lower brain deals with the instincts and the emotions, and the upper brain deals with the intellect and reasoning. According to Koestler, the real problem lies in the separation of the two. The point to be made here is that Hoffer's idea of man's "getting on top of" his nature in order to free himself from the restrictions of the physical and the biological is, interestingly enough, in the direction of Koestler's concept.

Reverting to Means' article, he went on to ask and answer an important question. Remembering that he was proposing the thesis that man's relationship to nature is a moral and not just a scientific crisis, his question and his immediate answer provide a brilliant snapshot of modern man: "What, then, is the moral crisis? It is, I think, a pragmatic problem."

Here was a remarkable combination of phrases; the moral dissolved into the pragmatic. He started off with a moral crisis, but suddenly all one is left with is a pragmatic problem. "It involves the actual social consequences of a myriad of unconnected acts. The crisis comes by combining the results of a mistreatment of our environment. It involves the negligence of a small businessman on the Kalamazoo River, the irresponsibility of a large corporation on Lake Erie, the impatient use of insecticides by a farmer in California, the stripping of land by Kentucky mine operators. Unfortunately there is a long history of unnecessary and tragic destruction of animal and natural resources on the face of this continent." Of course the pressure becomes greater on a world scale, and he was certainly right in pointing out that there is a serious problem. But that does not change his problem of dealing with the problem! He wanted a moral base on which to deal with the ecological problem, but soon all he had is the word *moral*. And what he was left with was the pragmatic and technological.

As one faces the growth of population, the ecological problem becomes even greater. In Switzerland, an excellent example was beautiful Lake Geneva and the difference since we came to Switzerland thirty-two years ago—a major difference. Happily, the Swiss have, at great expense, begun to clear up Lake Geneva, but the growth of population on its shores required a major effort. Left to itself, the lake could not have cared for the population growth.

As the pressure gets greater worldwide, upon what basis, different from the one we have employed in the past, are we to treat the nature which is our environment and upon which our life in this world depends? As the Sierra Club calendar for 1970 put it, "The moon, Mars, Saturn . . . nice places to visit, but you wouldn't want to live there." Human life depends on the uniquely balanced environment of this world.

Means went on to talk about the passenger pigeons, of which there were once many in the United States; but they had become extinct. The same could be said about the seal industry. "The trouble is, however, we do not seem to learn very much from these sad happenings for (to the anguish of men who have thrilled to the images created by Herman Melville and the great white whale) such marine scientists as Scott McVay believe that commercial fishing is endangering the whale, the last abundant species in the world. For those more inclined towards the cash nexus, there goes a profitable industry." He continued that it is not only an economic loss, but that "for those of us who have a respect for nature—in particular, for our mammalian kinsmen—the death of these great creatures will leave a void in God's creation, and in the imagination of men for generations to come." The use of Means' phrase "in God's creation," which for many Christians would inspire hope as to the kind of answer he might give us, must not be misunderstood, as I will point out later.

Then Means touched on the other basic issues, referring to the mighty Hudson River and the Great Lakes and the state of the air we breathe. Because of these matters and hundreds like them we can see why men are wrestling, in a way that they have never wrestled before, with the problem of ecology. There is a true dilemma. Modern man has seen that we are upsetting the balance of nature and the problem is drastic and urgent. It is not just a matter of aesthetics, nor is the problem only future; the quality of life has already diminished for many modern men. For the future, many thinking men see the ecological threat as greater than that of nuclear warfare.

Means proceeded to offer his solutions to this dilemma. These were presented as first a negative, and then later a positive side. It is worth considering Means' thinking in detail, because it is representative of what, with various modifications, we have heard from a multitude of sources—and will be hearing in the next years. Indeed, Aldous Huxley, in his last novel, *Island*,[1] pictured a "utopian" future in which the first lessons given to school children will be in ecology. He then went on to observe: "Elementary ecology leads straight to elementary Buddhism."

There was a conference in Buck Hill Falls, Pennsylvania, called "The Conference on Environment and Population." There was a light-show presenting the modern problems of ecology. Then the proposition was made that the answer must be in the direction of pantheism. We are going to hear more of this. Pantheism will be pressed as the only answer to ecological problems and will be one more influence in the West's becoming increasingly Eastern in its thinking.

What is man's relation to nature? Means asked, "Why is man's relation to nature a moral crisis? It is a moral crisis because it is a historical one involving man's history and culture, expressed at its roots by our religious and ethical view of nature—which have been relatively unquestioned in this context." Up to this point one could agree with his diagnosis. But then he went on to make a negative statement: "The historian in medieval culture, Lynn White, Jr., brilliantly traced the origin and consequences of this expression in an insightful article in *Science* last March: 'The Historical Roots of Our Ecologic Crisis.' He argues that the Christian notion of a transcendent God, removed from nature and breaking into nature only through revelation, removed spirit from nature and allows, in an ideological sense, for an easy exploitation of nature.

"On the American scene the Calvinistic and the deistic concepts of God were peculiarly alike at this point. Both envisioned God as absolutely transcendent, apart from the world, isolated from nature and organic life. As to the contemporary implications of the dichotomy between spirit and nature Professor White says: '. . . To a Christian a tree can be no more than a physical fact. The whole concept of the sacred grove is alien to Christianity and to the ethos of the West. For nearly two millennia Christian missionaries have been chopping down sacred groves, which are idolatrous because they assume spirit in nature.' "

Means' answer to his question ("What is man's relation to nature?") must be found in his proposition that our ecological problem exists because of Christianity. He laid the blame squarely on Christianity as such, which has, in its intrinsic nature (on his premise), created and sustained the ecological problem.

In contrast to this, we can agree with the first part of the next paragraph in Mean's article: "Perhaps, as Lynn White suggests, the persistence of this as a moral problem is illustrated in the protest of the contemporary generation of beats and hippies."

Our agreement with Means at this point centers on the fact that the hippies of the 1960s did understand something. They were right in fighting the plastic culture, and the church should have been fighting it too, a long, long time ago, before the counterculture ever came onto the scene. More than this, they were right in the fact that the plastic culture—modern man, the mechanistic world-view in university textbooks and in practice, the total threat of the machine, the establishment technology, the bourgeois upper middle-class—*is* poor in its sensitivity to nature. This is totally right. As a utopian group, the counterculture understands something very real, both as to the culture as a culture, but also as to the poverty of modern man's concept of nature and the way the machine is eating up nature on every side. At that point, I would side with the counterculture.

However, Means went on to suggest that the hippies had what was perhaps a good solution. We may differ with him here, but undoubtedly he did understand what the counterculture's solution was. He says, "There may be a 'sound instinct' involved in the fact that some of these so-called beats have turned to Zen Buddhism. It may represent an overdue perception of the fact that we need to appreciate more fully the religious and moral dimensions of the relation between nature and the human spirit." This showed a quite proper discernment of the counterculture direction, which was, and is, toward pantheism. He would not need to limit it to Zen because it is pantheism in general. Thus, after having given a negative statement, saying we must get rid of Christianity, we have a suggested solution which is in the direction of the drift of our culture. For, as I have said, almost all the new theologians are drifting toward pantheism in company with the often present vague pantheism which comes in many forms today.

Much of the surrounding culture undoubtedly is moving in the direction of the West's becoming the East. And Means offered this solution with regard to the problem of ecology. This is undoubtedly why he quoted Schweitzer in the first sentence of his article. At the end of his life Schweitzer was a pantheist, laying great emphasis on "reverence for life," by which he meant: all that is is of one essence. Means started with Schweitzer as a man well-known in the West, but who was a pantheist.

This is why I questioned Means' statement about "God's creation." He is really using a Western term for a completely different concept. The term "God's creation" has no real place in pantheistic thinking. One simply does not have a *creation,* but only an extension of God's essence. In pantheistic thinking any such term as "God's creation"—as though He were a personal God who created, whose creation was external to Himself (all of which is wrapped up in our Western phrase "God's creation")—has no place.

It is clear that Means was talking about a real pantheism when he went on: "On the other hand, the refusal to connect the human spirit to nature may reflect the traditional thought patterns of Western society wherein nature is conceived to be a separate substance—a material—mechanical, and, in a metaphysical sense, irrelevant to man." What he was trying to do was link up the fact that all that is, is the same substance with nature. In this way he hoped to get a reverence for nature that would cause us to treat nature more gently.

He said toward the end of the article: "Such a view should help destroy egoistic, status politics, for it helps unmask the fact that other men's activities are not just private, inconsequential, and limited in themselves; their acts, mediated through changes in nature, affect my life, my children, and the generations to come."

What is interesting here is to see, as noted earlier, that his use of the word *moral* leaves us with only the pragmatic. The only reason we are called upon to treat nature well is because of its effects on man and our children and the generations to come. So in reality, in spite of all Means' words, man is left with a completely egoistic position in regard to nature. No reason is given—moral or logical—for regarding nature as something in itself. We are left with a purely pragmatic issue.

Means ended his article: ". . . Our contemporary moral crisis, then, goes much deeper than questions of political power and law, of urban riots and slums. It may, at least in part, reflect American society's almost utter disregard for the value of nature." Here we must agree with him. We have mistreated nature—not just the Americans, but other people throughout the world.

But notice—he gave no answer; and the "no-answer" falls into three different levels. First of all, the moral only equals the pragmatic, and this, of course, is related to the fact that a modern man in this position has no basis for morals because he has no absolutes to which to appeal. One can have a basis for something else—a social contract, a hedonism—but one can never have real morals without absolutes. We may call them morals, but it always ends up as "I like," or social contract, neither of which are morals. The latter is a majority vote, or the arbitrary absolutes of an elite in society, by which one can decide anything. And having no absolutes, modern man has no categories. One cannot have real answers without categories, and these men can have no categories, beyond pragmatic, technological ones.

This can be seen in Means' article when he talks about cutting down the sacred groves. He has no categories whereby he could cut down a sacred grove when it is an idol and yet not be against trees as trees. As far as he is concerned, these categories do not exist. For him, the fact that a Christian would cut down a sacred grove when it has become an idol proves that Christians are against trees. It is rather like arguing concerning the Bible and art. The Bible is not "against" art. But supposing somebody argues that the Jews broke the brazen serpent which Moses had made (2 Kings 18:4). Here one has a serpent made of brass which the godly king broke; therefore, God is "against" art. Of course, from the biblical viewpoint, it is not a statement against art at all. They were against the brazen serpent, which God had originally commanded to be made, *only when it became an idol*. God commanded this work of art to be made, but when it became an idol it was to be destroyed. This means that one has categories.

In contrast, modern man has no categories. This brings us back to the first point. The moral equals the pragmatic on a very crude level, in spite of all this nice terminology. So we must not think that Means (and other people like him) is a man giving a moral answer, a higher answer; he is not. It is a very low answer indeed.

The second thing is that Means uses these religious words (*moral* for *pragmatic*) over and over again as religious connotation words for the purpose of motivation. He is also using the word *pantheism* as a motivation word. This is something we must always be careful of. Words have two meanings, the definition and the connotation. The connotation goes on no matter what you do with the definition. Modern man destroys the definition of religious words, but nevertheless likes to cash in on their connotation/ motivation force. This is precisely what Means was doing. By using these words, he hoped (even though he has indicated in his definition that *moral* equals *pragmatic*) that people would treat nature a little better because of the religious connotations of the words. It is one more illustration of a type of manipulation that is all about us.

The third thing to notice is that what one had was sociological religion and sociological science. It is important to note that

Means was a sociologist. One does not have religion as religion; nor does one have science as science. What one has is both religion and science being used and manipulated for sociological purposes.

Edmund Leach, the Cambridge anthropologist, in an article in the *New York Review of Books* (February 1966), chose a certain scientific solution, not because it had anything to do with objective science, but very clearly because it led to the sociological answer that he wanted. Edmund Leach was at this point the very opposite of a scientist. Here was a scientist using science for sociological manipulation. With this, then, a parallel can be found between Edmund Leach in his article and Richard Means in his. The latter was also using science and religion for purely sociological ends. With it, science dies, religion dies, and all you have left is sociological manipulation.

Remember what I have emphasized before—it is worth considering this article by Richard Means in detail because the thoughts presented in this article are representative of those which will be sounded by many voices, with a multitude of variations and subtleties. This is true about the theoretical and practical discussions in general, and the ecological discussion of the relationship of man to nature in particular. And the same basic factors are involved, whether the unity of everything that is is expressed with some form of the religious connotation word *pantheism,* or with purely secular terms, in reducing everything to energy particles.

Let us examine the reasons why pantheism in any form does not give a sufficient answer. Pantheism eventually gives no meaning to any particulars. In true pantheism unity has meaning, but the particulars have no meaning, including the particular of man. Also, if the particulars have no meaning, then nature has no meaning, including the particular of man. A meaning to particulars does not exist philosophically in any pantheistic system, whether it is the pantheism of the East or the "paneverything-ism" in the West, beginning everything only with the energy particles. In both cases, eventually the particulars have no meaning. Pantheism gives you an answer for unity, but it gives no meaning to the diversity. Pantheism is not an answer.

This is not just a theoretical dilemma—that the particulars have no meaning in pantheism. It is not just a vague philosophical objection. It leads to important conclusions. First, any "results" one does get from pantheism are obtained only by projecting *man's* feelings into *nature*. And that is simply the romanticism concerning which Hoffer warned, an endowing of the lower creation with a human reaction. So when we see a chicken, we endow its love-life with human qualities. But that is to evade the *reality* of the chicken. This kind of an answer can get results from these motivation words only by projecting human feelings into nature, and Hoffer was right to reject this.

What I am saying is that a pantheistic answer is not just a theoretically weak answer, but it is also a weak answer in *practice*. A man who begins to take a pantheistic view of nature has no answer for the fact that nature has two faces: it has a benevolent face, but it may also be an enemy. The pantheist views nature as normal. In this view, there is no place for abnormality in nature.

This was a very practical problem in Camus' *The Plague* where Camus comments on the dilemma facing Orion the recatcher: "Well, if he joins with the doctors and fights the plague, he is fighting against God, or if he joins with the priest and does not fight God by not fighting the plague, he is not being humanitarian." Camus never resolved this problem. If we accept this romantic and non-Christian mysticism, the difficulty is that we have no solution for the fact that nature is often not benevolent. If everything is one, and a part of one essence with no basic distinction, how does one explain nature when it is destructive? What is the theoretical answer? And as Camus understood, it isn't just a theoretical problem. Rather, how do I fight the plague?

The Christian *can* fight it. When Christ stood in front of the tomb of Lazarus (John 11), He was claiming to be divine and yet He was furious. The Greek makes it plain that He was *furious*. He could be furious with the plague *without being angry with Himself*. This turns upon the historic, space-time Fall. Consequently, the Christian does not have Camus' difficulty. But if one is putting forth a pantheistic, mystical answer, there is no solution to the fact that nature is not always benevolent. One has no way to understand the origin of this double fact of nature; one has no real way to "fight the plague." There may be much high-sounding talk, but eventually this is true of all pantheism, either Eastern or modern Western—either any of the vague forms of pantheism which are all about us or the modern theologian.

Again, a pantheistic stand always brings man to an impersonal and low place rather than elevating him. This is an absolute rule. Whether the pantheistic answer is the modern scientism which relates everything back to the energy particle, or whether it is Eastern, eventually nature does not become high, but man becomes low. This can be seen over and over again. Schweitzer spoke much of reverence for life, but a doctor who worked with him said that he wished Schweitzer had had less reverence for life and more love for it and for people. At the end of his life Schweitzer's pantheism, instead of going toward a higher view of those among whom he worked, went toward a lower view.

The Eastern pantheism leads to this same thing. In the Eastern countries there is no real base for the dignity of man. Thus, it must be pointed out that *idealistic* Marxism could only have come as a Christian heresy; it could never have originated in the East, because there is no place for a genuine dignity of man in the pantheistic East. Idealistic Marxism is a Judeo-Christian heresy.

The same is true even in the realm of economics. The economic dilemma of India is complicated by their pantheistic system in which the rats and cows are allowed to eat up food that the people need. Instead of man's being raised, in reality he is lowered. The rats and cows are finally given preference to man himself, and man begins to disappear into the woodwork in economics as well as in the area of personality and love.[2]

Those who propose the pantheistic answer ignore this fact—that far from raising nature to man's height, pantheism must push both man and nature down into a bog. Without categories, there is eventually no reason to distinguish bad nature from good nature. Pantheism leaves us with the Marquis de Sade's dictum, "What is, is right" in morals, and man becomes no more than the grass.

CHAPTER THREE

Other Inadequate Answers

Pantheism is not the answer. If the West turns to pantheism to solve its ecological problems, the human will be even more reduced, and impersonal technology will reign even more securely. But having said that, let us quickly add that a poor Christianity is not the answer either. There is a "Christianity" which gives no better answer than pantheism: Byzantine, pre-Renaissance Christianity, for instance. This Byzantine concept was that the only truly valuable thing is heavenly—so high, so lifted up, so holy that only symbols were used. For example, they never painted a real picture of Mary; the icons and mosaics are only symbols of her. The only thing that really mattered in life was the heavenly. This kind of Christianity will never give an answer to the problem of nature, for in this view nature has no real importance. So there is indeed a form of Christianity that has no *proper* emphasis upon nature.

At a certain point in history, as the medieval died and Renaissance man was born, Van Eyck began to paint nature. Likewise, in the marvelous Carmine Chapel in Florence, Masaccio went beyond Giotto and began to paint nature as real nature. At that point they could have gone toward a truly Christian art, because

21

there is a real place for nature in true Christianity. Those who followed Van Eyck and his backgrounds, and Masaccio painting in the round with the proper light and so on, could have gone either way—toward a truly Christian art, in which nature had a proper place, or toward humanism.

Pantheism is no answer for a proper view of nature, but one must understand that just any kind of Christianity is no answer either; not a Byzantine Christianity, nor a Christianity based on a nature/grace dichotomy. Neither will produce an answer. Nor is there any answer in the concept of nature and freedom held by Jean-Jacques Rousseau or Kant.[1] In all these areas one searches in vain for the Christian answer, or any real answer (even if Christian terms are used), and this includes any real answer for a proper view of nature.

But of course there exists a different kind of Christianity. The Christianity of the Reformation does give a unified answer, and this answer has meaning not only in speaking about heavenly things, but also about nature. God has spoken; and because of this, there is a unity. This gave the unity of the Reformation, in contrast to the nature/grace nonunity of the Renaissance. It turns upon the fact that God has spoken and told us something about both heavenly things and nature. On the basis of God's speaking, we know something truly of both universals and particulars, and this includes the meaning and proper use of the particulars.

This unity has not come from a rationalism, a humanism, in which man is generating something out of himself, gathering and looking at the particulars and then trying to make a universal, whether it be a philosophic universal, or Leonardo da Vinci trying to paint the "soul."[1] The Reformation believed what the Bible says: that God has revealed truth about Himself and the cosmos, and that therefore there is a unity. The Westminister Confession of Faith (of the seventeenth century) said that God has revealed His attributes, and these are true not only to us *but to Him*. We have a knowledge which is true both to us and to God. To us it is true but not exhaustive knowledge, as God is infinite and we are finite. But it *is* true, since God has spoken about Himself and about the cosmos and about history. This is the kind of Christianity that has an answer, including an answer about nature and man's relationship to it.

One feels this already in the paintings of Dürer, who in fact was painting a few years before Luther spoke out. As the late Professor

Rookmaaker of the Free University in Amsterdam pointed out, Dürer went through a humanistic period, and then he rejected the humanistic answer and came up with the biblical answer, and in that answer he knew what to do with nature.

One can also think of the post-Reformation Dutch painters, who painted nature beautifully and in its proper place. Without question, the greatest Dutch painting is that in which nature, the world as it is, had a tremendously important place. With the following of Van Eyck in the north (prior to the Reformation) and Masaccio in the south, Renaissance painting did not go in the right direction; it went into humanism that came to a dead end in modern man. Modern man does not have any answer for nature either in his painting or his use of nature in life—just as he does not have any answer for man. But the Dutch painters after the Reformation were able to give nature its proper place, the Reformation having restored a unity on the basis of the revelation of God.

It is well to stress, then, that Christianity does not automatically have an answer; it has to be the right kind of Christianity. Any Christianity that rests upon a dichotomy—some sort of Platonic concept—does not have an answer to nature; and we must say with sorrow that much orthodoxy, much evangelical Christianity, is rooted in a Platonic concept. In this kind of Christianity there is only interest in the "upper story," in the heavenly things—only in "saving the soul" and getting it to Heaven. In this Platonic concept, even though orthodox and evangelical terminology is used, there is little or no interest in the proper pleasure of the body or the proper uses of the intellect. In such a Christianity, there is a strong tendency to see nothing in nature beyond its use as one of the classic proofs of God's existence. "Look at nature," we are told; "look at the Alps. God must have made them." And that is the end. Nature has become merely an academic proof of the existence of the Creator, with little value in itself. Christians of this outlook do not show an interest in nature *itself*. They use it simply as an apologetic weapon, rather than thinking or talking about the real value of nature.

An extreme example of this attitude can be found in what the Dutch Christians have called the Black Stocking Calvinists in Holland. These have a tradition that they may treat their animals cruelly because the animals do not have a soul and are not going to Heaven. They would claim to be very, very orthodox, but actually they are not orthodox. Theirs is Christianity in a perverted form. As far as creedalism is concerned, they may be very strong, but they will actually beat and kick their animals because in their view the animals do not have souls or a heavenly destiny. Thus they are not worthy of kind treatment. This is a sub-Christian view concerning nature.

One can find deficient concepts in less extreme forms in many places. Some years ago I was lecturing in a certain Christian school. Just across a ravine from the school there was what they called a "hippie community." On the far side of the ravine one saw trees and some farms. Here, I was told, they had pagan grape stomps. Being interested, I made my way across the ravine and met one of the leading men in this "Bohemian" community.

We got on very well as we talked of ecology, and I was able to speak of the Christian answer to life and ecology. He paid me the compliment (and I accepted it as such) of telling me that I was the first person from "across the ravine" who had ever been shown the place where they did, indeed, have grape stomps and to see the pagan image they had there. This image was the center of these rites. The whole thing was set against the classical background of Greece and Rome.

Having shown me all this, he looked across to the Christian school and said to me, "Look at that; isn't that ugly?" And it was! I could not deny it. It was an ugly building, without even trees around it.

It was then that I realized what a poor situation this was. When I stood on Christian ground and looked at the Bohemian people's place, it was beautiful. They had even gone to the trouble of running their electricity cables under the level of the trees so that they couldn't be seen. Then I stood on pagan ground and looked at the Christian community and saw ugliness. Here you have a Christianity that is failing to take into account man's responsibility and proper relationship to nature.

So pantheism is not going to solve our international ecological problem. Lynn White's position is not going to solve it because it is obvious in practice that man really does have a special role in nature that nothing else has. And, third, a Platonic view of Christianity is not going to solve it. Here, unhappily, Lynn White is right. He looks back over the history of Christianity and sees that there is too much Platonic thinking in Christianity where nature is concerned.

Now, what is the genuine, biblical view that *will* give a sufficient base for solving the ecological problem? What should be our attitude to and our treatment of nature? What is the biblical view of nature? Let us now consider that question.

CHAPTER FOUR

The Christian View: Creation

The beginning of the Christian view of nature is the concept of creation: that God was there before the beginning of the space-time continuum and God created everything out of nothing. From this, we must understand that creation is not an extension of the essence of God. Created things have an objective existence in themselves. They are really there.

Whitehead, Oppenheimer, and others have pointed out that modern science was only born out of a surrounding consensus of historic Christianity. Why? Because, as Whitehead has emphasized, Christianity believes that God has created an external world that is really there; and because He is a reasonable God, one can expect to be able to find the order of the universe *by reason*. Whitehead was absolutely right about this. He was not a Christian, but he understood that there would never have been modern science without the biblical view of Christianity.

It is the same in the area of nature. It is the biblical view of nature that gives nature a value *in itself*: not to be used merely as an argument in apologetics, but of value in itself because God made it.

Jean-Paul Sartre stated that the basic philosophic problem is that

27

something exists. And nature *is* there—even if man doesn't know why. Christians know why it is there: because God created it out of nothing, and it is in its place! Created things are not an extension of God's essence. They are not a "dream of God," as some Eastern philosophies claim; they are really there. That may sound naive and obvious, but it is not; it is a profound concept with profound consequences. Think of Hume's arguments against cause and effect. They were demolished in Hume's day-by-day experience because nature is really there, and it exists because God made it to exist; and existing, the particulars of nature affect other particulars of nature which are there.

It is intriguing to note, as we did in the preceding chapter, that after the Reformation the Dutch painters began to paint nature, no longer feeling any necessity to restrict themselves to religious subjects. In fact, from that time on religious subjects were relatively rarely painted. Most artists had suddenly found that nature was worth painting, and that it is properly Christian to paint it.

Now it follows that if we return to the Reformation's biblical view that nature is worth painting, so the nature which we paint is also worth something in itself. This is the true Christian mentality. It rests upon the reality of creation out of nothing by God. But it also follows that *all* things are equally created by God. *All* things were equally created out of nothing. *All things, including man, are equal in their origin,* as far as creation is concerned.

All of this depends, of course, on the nature of God. What kind of God exists? The Judeo-Christian God is different from all the other gods in the world. The Judeo-Christian God is the personal-infinite God. The gods of the East are infinite by definition, in that they contain everything including the male and female equally, the cruel and the noncruel equally, and so on. But they are not personal. In contrast, the gods of the West—the Greek and the Roman gods, the great god Thor and the Anglo-Saxon gods—were personal but were always limited and finite.

So the Judeo-Christian God is unique: He is infinite and He is, at the same time, personal.

Now how did He create? On the side of His infinity there is the great chasm. He creates all things, and He alone is Creator. Everything else is created. Only He is infinite, and only He is the Creator; everything else is dependent. So man, the animal, the flower, and the machine, in the biblical viewpoint, are equally separated from God in that He created them all. On the side of infinity man is as separated from God as is the machine.

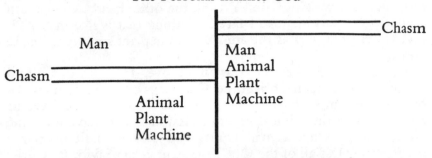

The Personal-Infinite God

So on the side of the infinite the chasm is between God and everything else, between the Creator and all created things.

But there is another side—the personal. Here the animal, the flower, and the machine are below the chasm. On the side of God's infinity everything else is finite and equally separated from God; but on the side of His personality, God has created man in His own image. Therefore, man's relationship is upward rather than downward—a tremendous factor that opens door after door for the comprehension of confused modern man.

Man is separated, as personal, from nature because he is made in the image of God. That is, he has personality, and as such he is unique in the creation; but he *is* united to all other creatures as being *created*. Man is separated from everything else, but that does not mean that there is not also a proper relationship downward on the side of man's being created and finite.

But his relationship is not *only* downward. Albert Schweitzer related himself to the hippopotamus coming through the bush, because Schweitzer had no sufficient relationship upward. But man is made in the image of God, who is personal; thus he has two relationships—upward and downward. Of course, if he does not find his relationship upward he will have to find this relationship (or integration point) downward. Christians reject this totally because we know who man is; we are not threatened by the machine as modern man is, because we know who we are. This is not said proudly, but humbly and reverently; we know we are made in the image of God. We reject an attitude that makes our integration point downward. Christians reject the view that there is no distinction—or only a quantitative distinction—between man and other things; *and* they reject the view that man is totally separated from all other things.

As a Christian I say, "Who am I?" Am I only the hydrogen

atom, the energy particle extended? No, I am made in the image of God. I know who I am. Yet, on the other hand, when I turn around and I face nature, I face something that is like myself. I, too, am created, just as the animal and the plant and the atom are created.

There is a parallel here to our call to love. The Christian is told to love as brothers in Christ other Christians only. All men are not our brothers in Christ, as the liberal theologian would have us believe. From the biblical point of view, brothers have the same father. Only when a man comes and casts himself upon the prophesied Messiah of the Old Testament as the Savior (as Christ has come in His substitutionary work) does God become his Father. This is clear from the teaching of Jesus. Therefore, not all men are our brothers in Christ.

However, just because the Bible says that not all men are our brothers, it does not follow that we are not to love *all* men as our neighbors. So one has the tremendous impact of the teaching of Jesus about the good Samaritan: I am to love on the basis of my neighborliness all that which is one blood with myself. And the New Testament uses that expression, "one blood" to indicate the unity of all people by God's creation. We are people who know we have one common origin with all races, all languages, and all people.

But only the Christian knows why he has a common origin. The evolutionist, the "modern" man, has no real reason to understand a common origin or a common relationship among men, except a biological one: people breed. That is all with which they are left.

The Christian, however, understands that people are all from one origin. We are all of one flesh; we are of one blood. One can say that from the biblical viewpoint, there are *two* humanities: one, the humanity that stands in revolt against God, and the other, the humanity that used to be in revolt against God (because none of us came into this second humanity by natural birth). The members of this second group, having believed on Christ, have cast themselves upon God and have become the sons of God.

Yet one must never forget there is only one humanity, and this is no paradox. There are orthodox Christians who will not let it be said that there is only one humanity, because they so strongly reject the liberal emphasis upon the one humanity at the expense of justification, but this is shortsighted. There are two, but one.

The Christian is called to understand that there are two humanities, and to love his brothers in Christ especially; and yet Christ also lays upon us the love of all men, as our neighbors, because we *are* one.

It is the same in regard to nature. On a very different level, we are separated from that which is the "lower" form of creation, yet we are united to it. One must not choose; one must say both. I am separated from it because I am made in the image of God; my integration point is upward, not downward; it is not turned back upon creation. Yet at the same time I am united to it because nature and man are both created by God.

This is a concept that no other philosophy has. Among other things, it explains the machine functions of man. For example, we have a common lung system with dogs and cats. This is not surprising. Both man and these other creatures have been created by God to fit a common environment. There is a common relationship in these mechanical functions, which relates man downward. There *are* machine functions to man. Psychologically there is a conditioning, not only in the animals but also, to a more limited extent, in man. This is to be expected, in view of our relationship both downward and upward. Nevertheless, this is not my *basic* relationship. I am not afraid of the machine. I am not overwhelmed or threatened, because I know I am made in the image of God. I can see why I have mechanical functions and some conditioning, because I have this downward relationship to "lower" things (though, as we shall see, the term "lower" is not ideal). Therefore, intellectually and psychologically, I look at these animals, plants, and machines, and as I face them I understand something of the attitude I should have toward them. I begin to think differently about life. Nature begins to look different. I am separated from it, yet related to it.

Notice the phrase "intellectually and psychologically." This is a very important distinction. I can say, "Yes, the tree is a creature like myself." But that is not all that is involved. There ought to be a psychological insight, too. Psychologically I ought to "feel" a relationship to the tree as my fellow-creature. It is not simply that we ought to feel a relationship intellectually to the tree, and then turn this into just another argument for apologetics, but that we should realize, and train people in our churches to realize, that on the side of creation and on the side of God's infinity and our finiteness we really *are* one with the tree!

This relationship should be not only for aesthetic reasons—though that would be enough reason in itself, because beautiful things are important—but we should treat each thing with integrity because it is the way God has made it. So the Christian treats "things" with integrity because we do not believe they are autonomous. Modern man has fallen into a dilemma because he has made things autonomous from God. Simone Weil's statement that modern man lives in a decreated world is acutely perceptive. Everything is decreated; everything is autonomous. But to Christians it is not autonomous, because God made it, and He made things on their own level. The value of the things is not in themselves autonomously, but that God made them—and thus they deserve to be treated with high respect. The tree in the field is to be treated with respect. It is not to be romanticized, as the old lady romanticizes her cat (that is, she reads human reactions into it). This is wrong because it is not true. When you drive the axe into the tree when you need firewood, you are not cutting down a person; you are cutting down a tree. But while we should not romanticize the tree, we must realize God made it and it deserves respect because He made it *as a tree*. Christians who do not believe in the complete evolutionary scale have reason to respect nature as the total evolutionist never can, because we believe God made these things specifically in their own areas. So if we are going to argue against the evolutionists intellectually, we should show the results of our belief in our attitudes. The Christian is a man who has a reason for dealing with each created thing with a high level of respect.

We warned earlier against allowing Platonic concepts to color our Christian thinking. Platonism regards the material as low. But we certainly cannot think the material low when we realize that God created it. We can think of things being created in different orders, but that is a very different concept from thinking things are low in the sense of base, as opposed to high. God made everything, and any sense of lowness (with its poor connotations) has no place here. To think of them as low is really to insult the God who made them.

The second reason why the material is not low is that Christ's body was raised from the dead. This really is a very important point. The resurrection of the body should be held as a doctrinal reality, and further as a truth that gives us an attitude toward life.

Christ's body really was raised from the dead. It could be

touched, and He could eat. And this resurrected body is now somewhere. We would reject Tillich's view of Heaven as a "philosophic other." I think that John Robinson, in *Honest to God,* was right, from his viewpoint, in making the ascension, rather than the resurrection, the crucial point. I think he really understood the implications. A physical resurrection might happen somehow or other in the modern theologian's world, but what you could not have is a body that could eat ascending into "the philosophic other." To the modern theologian, that is an unthinkable concept. In contrast to this, we believe in the ascension; the Bible tells us that the physically resurrected body of Jesus is somewhere in the unseen world.

The resurrection and ascension prove there is no reason to make a false dichotomy between the spiritual and the material. That is a totally nonbiblical concept. The material and the spiritual are not opposed. The fact that our bodies are going to be raised also speaks of this.

Another thing to notice from the biblical viewpoint is God's covenant of creation. God has given us certain written covenants in the Scripture. He has made tremendous promises—for example, the covenant promise to Abraham and to the Jewish people. And He has given the promise to the individual in the New Testament: "He that believeth on the Son hath everlasting life." But with God's written covenants there is also the covenant of creation. The covenant in the Scriptures is a propositional, verbalized covenant; the covenant of creation rests upon the way God made things. God is going to deal with them *as He made them.* God will not violate either covenant. He will always deal with a plant as a plant, with an animal as an animal, with a machine as a machine, and with a man as a man, not violating the orders of creation. He will not ask the machine to behave like a man, neither will He deal with man as though he were a machine.

Thus God treats His creation with integrity: each thing in its own order, each thing the way He made it. If God treats His creation in that way, should we not treat our fellow-creatures with a similar integrity? If God treats the tree like a tree, the machine like a machine, the man like a man, shouldn't I, as a fellow-creature, do the same—treating each thing in integrity in its own order? And for the highest reason: because I love God—I love the One who has made it! Loving the Lover who has made it, I have respect for the thing He has made.

Let us emphasize—this is not pantheistic; nevertheless, this respect for all created things must be consciously exercised. *Consciously* we are to treat each thing in its own order and on its own level. Like so many things in the Christian life, this attitude does not come mechanically, because God is treating us like man and expects us to choose and act like man. Thus we must *consciously* deal with the integrity of each thing that we touch.

The good modern architect struggles to use materials with integrity. Consequently, for example, if he is using poured concrete, he wants it to look like poured concrete and not like brick. Another area of integrity for the architect was emphasized by the great architect Wright, who put forward the concept of the integrity of the building to the integrity of the terrain. So there is this desire in our own day to treat material honestly. If we are to have something beautiful, a landscaping that is going to stand with strength, we shall have to keep in mind the integrity of the terrain and the integrity of the material used. Although this concept is true for all men (since they are made in the image of God, even if they do not know it), yet Christians have a special understanding of it because of their special relationship with God. And our conscious relationship with God is enhanced if we treat all the things He has made in the same way as He treats them.

In sociological things modern man deals only with sociological "averages." But in the modern field of ecology he begins to scream, "I am dying in my city and my ocean is dying." This goes far beyond sociological "averages." His inner attitude to nature is involved. How is he treating it? Modern man has no real "value" for the ocean. All he has is the most crass form of egoist, pragmatic value for it. He treats it as a "thing" in the worst possible sense, to exploit it for the "good" of man. The man who believes things are there only by chance cannot give things a real intrinsic value. But for the Christian, there is an intrinsic value. The value of a thing is not in itself autonomously, but because God made it. It deserves this respect as something which was created by God, as man himself has been created by God.

It is true, as Lynn White points out, that many "Christians" are worse off in the area of ecology than animists, who think there are spirits in the trees and so they don't cut down the trees carelessly. However, although this is true, it is not because Christianity does not have the answer, but because we have not acted on the answer; not because Christianity does not have a view that gives a greater value to the tree than the animist can give it, but because we haven't acted on the value that we know, or should know, it has as a creature of God.

This is an extension of Abraham Kuyper's sphere concept. He saw each of us as many men: the man in the state, the man who is the employer, the man who is the father, the elder in the church, the professor in the university—each of these in a different sphere. But even though they are in different spheres at different times, Christians are to act like Christians *in each of the spheres.* The man is *always* there and he is always a Christian under the norms of Scripture, whether in the classroom or at home.

Now, here is the extension: I am a Christian, but not only a Christian. I am also the creature, the one who has been created; the one who is not autonomous, dealing with these other things that equally are not autonomous. As a Christian, I am consciously to deal with every other created thing with integrity, each thing in *its proper sphere* by creation.

To summarize this chapter, let us reiterate the fundamental fact that God has made all men and all things. He has made my body as well as my soul. He has made me as I am, with the hungers of my spirit and my body. And he has made all things, just as He has made me. He has made the stone, the star, the farthest reaches of the cosmos. He has done all this!

To think of any of these things as intrinsically low is really an insult to the God who made it. Why do Christians lose their way when it seems so clear and so definite? Why should I say my body is lower than my soul when God made both my body and my soul?

Second, Christ's incarnation teaches us that the body of man and nature is not to be considered as low. After all, Jesus took on a real body because God had made man with a body. So, in the incarnation the God of creation took on a human body. More than that, after the resurrection Jesus Christ could eat and be touched. The Bible insists on the real, historic, space-time resurrection of Jesus, so that there was a resurrected body that could eat and that could be touched. This body was not just an apparition or a "ghost." And this same body ascended into Heaven and went into the unseen world. The body that can eat is still in the unseen world, and will one day in future history be visible in the seen world again.

Our resurrection is of the same kind. When Christ comes back again, our bodies are going to be raised from the dead. It is going to be a real physical resurrection, and consequently whether it is Jesus' body or our body the emphasis is the same: God has made the body, and the body is not to be despised and considered as low.

The same sort of emphasis is found explicitly in God's covenant of creation at the time of Noah. In Genesis 9:8-17 we have God's covenant within the relationship to creation. "And I, behold, I establish my covenant with you (mankind), and with your seed after you; and with every living created thing." So God says this, His covenant, was with mankind, but equally with all creation. Then again, in the thirteenth verse, He says: "I do set my bow in the cloud . . . for a token of the covenant between me and the *earth.*" God makes a promise here that embodies *all* creation. God is interested in creation. He does not despise it. There is no reason whatsoever, and it is absolutely false biblically, for the Christian to have a Platonic view of nature. What God has made, I, who am also a creature, must not despise.

CHAPTER FIVE

A Substantial Healing

In Romans 8 Paul looks ahead to what is going to happen when Jesus Christ comes back again. He writes: "For the earnest expectation of the creation waiteth for the manifestation of the sons of God (the Christians). For the creation was made subject to vanity (i.e., frustration), not willingly, but by reason of him who hath subjected the same in hope. Because the creation itself also shall be delivered from the bondage of corruption into the glorious liberty of the children of God. For we know that the whole creation groaneth and travaileth in pain together until now. And not only they, but ourselves also, who have the first fruits of the Spirit (the Christians), even we ourselves groan within ourselves, waiting for the adoption, that is, the redemption of our body."

What Paul says there is that when our bodies are raised from the dead, at that time nature too will be redeemed. The blood of the Lamb will redeem man and nature together. There is a parallel here to the time of Moses in Egypt when the blood applied to the doorposts saved not only the sons of the Hebrews, but also their animals.

As we stressed in the last chapter, the Bible has no place at all for Platonic distinctions about nature. As Christ's death redeems

37

men, including their bodies, from the consequences of the Fall, so
His death will redeem all nature from the Fall's evil consequences
at the time when we are raised from the dead.

In Romans 6 Paul applies this future principle to our present
situation. It is the great principle of Christian spirituality. Christ
died, Christ is our Savior, Christ is coming back again to raise us
from the dead. So by faith—because this is true to what has been
in Christ's death and to what will be when He comes again, by
faith, in the power of the Holy Spirit—we are to live this way
substantially now. "Now if we be dead with Christ, we believe that
we shall also live with him. . . . Likewise, reckon ye also yourselves to be dead indeed unto sin, but alive unto God through
Jesus Christ, our Lord." So we look forward to this, and one day
it will be perfect. But we should be looking now, on the basis of
the work of Christ, for substantial healing in every area affected
by the Fall.

We must understand that even in our relationship with God, a
distinction has to be made here. By justification our guilt was
completely removed, in a forensic way, as God declared our guilt
gone when we accepted Christ as our Savior. But in practice, in
our lives between becoming a Christian and the second coming of
Christ or our death, we are not in a perfect relationship to God.
Therefore, real spirituality lies in the existential, moment-by-
moment looking to the work of Christ—seeking and asking God
in faith for a substantial reality in our relationship with Him at the
present moment. I must be doing this so that substantially, in
practice, at this moment, there will be a reality in my relationship
with the personal God who is there.

This is also true in other areas, because the Fall, as the Reformation theology has always emphasized, not only separated man
from God, but also caused other deep separations. It is interesting
that almost the whole "curse" in Genesis 3 is centered upon the
outward manifestations. It is the *earth* that is going to be cursed for
man's sake. It is the woman's *body* that is involved in the pain of
childbirth.

So there are other divisions. Man was divided from God, first;
and then, ever since the Fall, man is separated from himself. These
are the psychological divisions. I am convinced that this is the
basic psychosis: that the individual man is divided from himself as
a result of the Fall.

The next division is that man is divided from other men; these are the sociological divisions. And then man is divided from nature, and nature is divided from nature. So there are these multiple divisions, and one day, when Christ comes back, there is going to be a complete healing of all of them, on the basis of the "blood of the Lamb."

But Christians who believe the Bible are not simply called to say that "one day" there will be healing, but that by God's grace, upon the basis of the work of Christ, substantial healing can be a reality here and now.

Here the church—the orthodox, Bible-believing church—has been really poor. What have we done to heal sociological divisions? Often our churches are a scandal; they are cruel not only to the man "outside," but also to the man "inside."

The same thing is true psychologically. We load people with psychological problems by telling them that "Christians don't have breakdowns," and that is a kind of murder.

On the other hand, what we should have, individually and corporately, is a situation where, on the basis of the work of Christ, Christianity is seen to be not just "pie in the sky," but something that has in it the possibility of substantial healings now in every area where there are divisions because of the Fall. First of all, my division from God is healed by justification, but then there must be the "existential reality" of this moment by moment. Second, there is the psychological division of man from himself. Third, the sociological divisions of man from other men. And last, the division of man from nature, and nature from nature. In all of these areas we should do what we can to bring forth substantial healing.

I took a long while to settle on that word "substantially," but it is, I think, the right word. It conveys the idea of a healing that is not *perfect*, but nevertheless is real and evident. Because of past history and future history, we are called upon to live this way now by faith.

When we carry these ideas over into the area of our relationship to nature, there is an exact parallel. On the basis of the fact that there is going to be total redemption in the future, not only of man but of all creation, the Christian who believes the Bible should be the man who—with God's help and in the power of the Holy Spirit—is treating nature now in the direction of the way nature will be then. It will not now be perfect, but there should be something substantial or we have missed our calling. God's calling to the Christian now, and to the Christian community, in the area of nature (just as it is in the area of personal Christian living in true spirituality) is that we should exhibit a substantial healing here and now, between man and nature and nature and itself, as far as Christians can bring it to pass.

In *Novum Organum Scientiarum* Francis Bacon wrote: "Man by the fall fell at the same time from his state of innocence and from his dominion over nature. Both of these losses, however, even in this life, can in some part be repaired; the former by religion and faith, the latter by the arts and sciences." It is a tragedy that the church, including the orthodox, evangelical church, has not always remembered that. Here, in this present life, it is possible for the Christian to have some share, through sciences and the arts, in returning nature to its proper place.

But how is this to be achieved? First, as we have seen, by the emphasis upon creation. Then, second, by a fresh understanding of man's "dominion" over nature (Genesis 1:28). Man has dominion over the "lower" orders of creation, but he is not sovereign over them. Only God is the Sovereign Lord, and the lower orders are to be used with this truth in mind. Man is not using his own possessions.

A parallel is the gift of economic possessions. They are to be used as God means them to be used. In the parable of the talents, told by Jesus (Matthew 25:15ff.), the talents or money did not belong to the man with whom they were left. He was a servant and a steward, and he held them only in stewardship for the true Owner.

It is the same when we have dominion over nature: *it is not ours.* It belongs to God, and we are to exercise our dominion over these things not as though entitled to exploit them, but as things borrowed or held in trust. We are to use them realizing that they are not ours intrinsically. Man's dominion is under God's dominion.

Whenever anything is made autonomous, as I stressed in *Escape from Reason,* nature "eats up" grace, and soon all meaning is gone. And that is true here. When nature is made autonomous, either by the materialist or by the Christian when he slips over and sits in the wrong place, soon *man eats up nature.* That is what we are seeing today. Suddenly man is beginning to scream, and I am convinced God is permitting these things to come to pass. The problem is not the growth of population alone, nor technical growth alone—those could be handled. The problem, as White correctly points out, is the philosophy with which man has looked on nature.

An essential part of a true philosophy is a correct understanding of the pattern and plan of creation as revealed by the God who made it. For instance, we must see that each step "higher"—the machine, the plant, the animal, and man—has the use of that which is lower than itself. We find that man calls upon and utilizes the animal, the plant, and the machine; the animal eats the plant. The plant utilizes the machine portion of the universe. Each thing in God's creation utilizes the thing that God has made under it.

We must also appreciate that each thing is limited by what it is. That is, a plant is limited by being a plant, but it is also limited by the properties of those things under it that it uses. So the plant can only use the chemicals on the basis of the boundary condition of the chemicals' properties. There is nothing else it can do.

But this is true also for man. We cannot make our own universe; we can only use what is under us in the order of creation. But there is a difference, and that is that the animal, for example, must use the lower *as what it is*. Man has to accept some necessary limitations of what is under him, but he can *consciously* act upon what is there. That is a real difference. The animal simply eats the plant. He cannot change its situation or properties. The man, on the other hand, has to accept limitations, but nevertheless is called upon in his relationship to nature to treat the thing that is under him *consciously,* on the basis of what God has made it to be. The animal, the plant *must* do it; the man *should* do it. We are to use it, but we are not to use it as though it were nothing in itself.

Now let us look at it in another way. Man was given dominion over creation. This is true. But since the Fall man has exercised this dominion wrongly. He is a rebel who has set himself at the center of the universe. By creation man has dominion, but as a fallen creature he has used that dominion wrongly. Because he is fallen, he exploits created things as though they were nothing in themselves, and as though he has an autonomous right to them.

Surely then, Christians who have returned, through the work of the Lord Jesus Christ, to fellowship with God and have a proper place of reference to the God who is there should demonstrate a proper use of nature. We are to have dominion over it, but we are not going to use it as fallen man uses it. We are not going to act as though it were nothing in itself, or as though we will do to nature everything we can do.

A parallel is man's dominion over woman. At the Fall man was given dominion in the home over the woman. But fallen man takes this and turns it into tyranny and makes his wife a slave. So first in the Judaic teaching—the Old Testament law—and then later and more specifically in the New Testament, man is taught to exercise dominion without tyranny. The man is to be the head of the home, but the man is also to love his wife as Christ loves the church. Thus everything is back in its right place. There is to be order in the midst of a fallen world, but in love.

So fallen man has dominion over nature, but he uses it wrongly. The Christian is called upon to exhibit this dominion, but exhibit it rightly: treating the thing as having value in itself, exercising dominion without being destructive. The church should always have taught and done this, but it has generally failed to do so, and we need to confess our failure. Francis Bacon understood this, and so have other Christians at different times; but by and large we must say that for a long, long time Christian teachers, including the best orthodox theologians, have shown a real poverty here.

As a parallel example, what would have happened if the church at the time of the Industrial Revolution had spoken out against the economic abuses which arose from it? This is not to suggest that the Industrial Revolution was wrong, or that private property as such is wrong, but that the church at a point in history when it had the consensus failed (with some notable exceptions) to speak against the abuse of economic dominion. So also the church has not spoken out as it should have done throughout history against the abuse of nature.

But when the church puts belief into practice, in relationship to man *and to nature,* there is substantial healing. One of the first fruits of that healing is a new sense of beauty. The aesthetic values are not to be despised. God has made man with a sense of beauty no animal has; no animal has ever produced a work of art. Man as made in the image of God has an aesthetic quality, and as soon as he begins to deal with nature as he should, beauty is preserved in nature. But also, economic and human value accrue, for the problems of ecology that we have now will diminish.

Christians should be able to exhibit individually and corporately that on the basis of the work of Christ, dealing with things according to the world-view and basic philosophy of the Bible, they can produce something that the world has tried, but failed, to produce. The Christian community should be a living exhibition of the truth that in our present situation it is possible to have substantial sociological healings—healings that humanism longs for, but has not been able to produce. Humanism is not wrong in its cry for sociological healing, but humanism is not producing it. And the same thing is true in regard to a substantial healing where nature is concerned.

So we find that when we begin to deal on a Christian basis, things begin to change—not just in theory but in practice. Man is not to be sacrificed, as pantheism sacrifices him, because after all he was made in the image of God and given dominion. And yet nature is to be honored, each thing on its own level. In other words, there is a balance here. Man has dominion; he has a right by choice, because he is a moral creature, a right by choice to have dominion. But he is also by choice to exercise it rightly. He is to honor what God has made, up to the very highest level that he can honor it, without sacrificing man.

Christians, of all people, should not be the destroyers. We should treat nature with an overwhelming respect. We may cut down a tree to build a house, or to make a fire to keep the family warm. But we should not cut down the tree just to cut down the tree. We may, if necessary, bark the cork tree in order to have the use of the bark. But what we should not do is to bark the tree simply for the sake of doing so, and let it dry and stand there a dead skeleton in the wind. To do so is not to treat the tree with integrity. We have the right to rid our houses of ants; but what we have not the right to do is to forget to honor the ant as God made it, in its rightful place in nature. When we meet the ant on the sidewalk, we step over him. He is a creature, like ourselves; not made in the image of God, but equal with man as far as creation is concerned. The ant and the man are both creatures.

In this sense Saint Francis' use of the term "brothers to the birds" is not only theologically correct, but a thing to be intellectually thought of and practically practiced. More, it is to be psychologically felt as I face the tree, the bird, the ant. If this was what the The Doors meant when they spoke of "our fair sister," it would have been beautiful. Used correctly in the Christian framework, that expression is magnificent. Why have orthodox, evangelical Christians produced few hymns putting such a beautiful concept in a proper theological setting?

One does not deface things simply to deface them. After all, the rock has a God-given right to be a rock as He made it. If you must move the rock in order to build the foundation of a house, then by all means move it. But on a walk in the woods do not strip the moss from it for no reason, and then leave the moss to lie by the side and die. Even the moss has a right to live. It is equal with man as a creature of God.

Hunting game is another example of the same principle. Killing of animals for food is one thing, but on the other hand they do not exist simply as things to be slaughtered. This is true of fishing, too. Many men fish and leave their victims to rot and stink. But what about the fish? Has it no rights—not to be romanticized as though he were a man—but real rights? On the one hand, it is wrong to treat the fish as though it were a human baby; on the other hand, neither is it a chip of wood or a stone.

When we consider the tree, which is "below" the fish, we may chop it down, so long as we remember it is a tree, with its own value *as a tree*. It is not a zero. Some of our housing developments demonstrate the practical application of this. Bulldozers have gone in to flatten everything and clear the trees before the houses are begun. The end result is ugliness. It would have cost another thousand dollars to bulldoze *around* the trees, so they are simply bulldozed down without question. And then we wonder, looking at the result, how people can live there. It is less human in its barrenness, and even economically it is poorer as the topsoil washes away. So when man breaks God's truth, in reality he suffers.

The hippies of the 1960s were right in their desire to be close to nature, even walking in bare feet in order to feel it. But they had no sufficient philosophy, and so it drifted into pantheism and soon became ugly. But Christians, who should understand the creation principle, have a reason for respecting nature, and when they do, it results in benefits to man. Let us be clear: it is not just a pragmatic attitude; there is a basis for it. We treat it with respect because God made it. When an orthodox, evangelical Christian mistreats or is insensible to nature, *at that point* he is more wrong than the hippie who had no real basis for his feeling for nature and yet sensed that man and nature should have a relationship beyond that of spoiler and spoiled. You may or may not want to walk barefoot to feel close to nature, but as a *Christian* what relationship have you thought of and practiced toward nature as your fellow-creature?

Why do I have an emotional reaction toward the tree? For some abstract or pragmatic reason? Not at all. Secular man may say he cares for the tree because if he cuts it down, his cities will not be able to breathe. But that is egoism, and egoism will produce ugliness, no matter how long it takes or what fine words are used. On this basis technology will continue to take another twist on the garrote of both nature and man. But the Christian stands in front of the tree and has an emotional reaction toward it, because the tree has a real value in itself, being a creature made by God. I have this in common with the tree: we were made by God and not just cast up by chance.

Suddenly then we have real beauty. Life begins to breathe. For us the world begins to breathe as it never breathed before. We can love a man for his own sake, for we know who the man is—he is made in the image of God. And we can care for the animal, the tree, and even the machine portion of the universe, each thing in its own order—for we know it to be a fellow-creature with ourselves, both made by the same God.

CHAPTER SIX

The Christian View: The "Pilot Plant"

So we have seen that a truly biblical Christianity has a real answer to the ecological crisis. It offers a balanced and healthy attitude to nature, arising from the truth of its creation by God. It offers the hope here and now of substantial healing in nature of some of the results of the Fall, arising from the truth of redemption in Christ. In each of the alienations arising from the Fall, Christians, individually and corporately, should consciously in practice be a healing redemptive factor—in the separation of man from God, of man from himself, of man from man, of man from nature, and of nature from nature.

A Christian-based science and technology should consciously try to see nature substantially healed, while waiting for the future complete healing at Christ's return. In this final chapter, we must ask how the Christian church, believing these truths, can apply them practically to the question of ecology.

For here is our calling. We must exhibit that on the basis of the work of Christ, the church can achieve partially, but substantially, what the secular world wants and cannot get. The church ought to be a "pilot plant," where men can see in our congregations and missions a substantial healing of all the divisions, the alienations which man's rebellion has produced.

Let me explain that phrase "pilot plant." When an industrial company is about to construct a big factory, they first of all make a pilot plant. This is to demonstrate that the full-scale plant will work. Now the church, I believe, ought to be a pilot plant in regard to the healing of man and himself, of man and man, and man and nature. Indeed, unless something like this happens, I do not believe the world will listen to what we have to say. For instance, in the area of nature, we ought to be exhibiting the very opposite of the situation I described earlier, where the pagans who had their wine stomps provided a beautiful setting for the Christians to look at, while the Christians provided something ugly for the pagans to see. That sort of situation should be reversed, or our words and our philosophy will, predictably, be ignored.

So the Christian church ought to be this "pilot plant," through individual attitudes and the Christian community's attitude, to exhibit that in this present life man can exercise dominion over nature without being destructive. Let me give two illustrations of what this might involve. The first is open-face or strip mining.

Why has strip mining usually turned the area where it has been used into desert? Why is the "Black Country" in England's Midlands black? What has brought about the ugly destruction of the environment? There is one reason: man's greed.

If the strip miners would take bulldozers and push back the topsoil, rip out the coal, then replace the topsoil, in ten years after the coal was removed there would be a green field, and in fifty years a forest. But as it has usually been practiced, for an added profit above what is reasonable in regard to nature, man turns these areas into deserts and then cries out that the topsoil is gone, grass will not grow, and there is no way to grow trees for hundreds of years!

It is always true that if you treat the land properly, you have to make two choices. The first is in the area of economics. It costs more money, at least at first, to treat the land well. For instance, in the case of the school I have mentioned, all they had to do to improve the place was to plant trees to shield the building they built. But it costs money to plant trees, and somebody decided that instead of planting trees they would prefer to do something else with the money. Of course, the school needs money for its important work; but there is a time when planting trees *is* an important work.

The second choice involved is that it usually takes longer to treat the land properly. These are the two factors that lead to the destruction of our environment: money and time—or to say it another way, greed and haste. The question is, or seems to be, are we going to have an immediate profit and an immediate saving of time, or are we going to do what we really should do as God's children?

Apply this to strip mining. There is no reason why strip mining had to leave western Pennsylvania or eastern Kentucky in its present condition. Strip mines, as we have seen, do not have to be left this way; the top soil can be bulldozed back. What we, the Christian community, have to do is to refuse men the right to ravish our land, just as we refuse them the right to ravish our women; to insist that somebody accept a little less profit by not exploiting nature. And the first step is exhibiting the fact that as individual Christians and as Christian communities we ourselves do not ravish our fair sister for the sake of greed in one form or another.

We can see the same sort of thing happening in Switzerland. Here is a village up in the mountains. It has never had electricity. The people have managed well for a thousand years without electricity. Now suddenly "civilization" comes, and everybody knows that you cannot have "civilization" without electricity, so the decision is made to give the village electrical power.

This can be done in one of two ways. They can have their electricity in about three months: just chop off everything, tear the forest in pieces, run big, heavy wires over the whole thing, and create ugliness out of what was beautiful. Or they can wait a couple of years for their electricity; they can handle the cables and the forests with more care, hiding what they need to hide and considering the integrity of the environment, and end up with something infinitely preferable. They have their electricity *and* the village has its beauty, and the only cost is to add two years to the thousand years that they have been without electricity. There would be some economic factors here, but the largest one is that of sheer haste.

Happily, in Switzerland in the last few years in certain places more things are being done in this direction. For example, in our village all the telephone wires have been put under the ground. This has made a very different impression: one now sees an uncluttered village in the Alps. This is so, even if the person now arriving at the village for the first time did not know the contrast to what it was previously.

One can also think of the highways—the asphalt jungle in the United States. Think, if you will, of the way the bulldozers are often used across the Swiss mountains. *Almost always* the scars and the ugliness are the result of hurry. And whether it is hurry or greed, these things eat away at nature.

What can be done was shown in the highway built near Castle Chillon in Switzerland. Both care and money were taken in building a bridgelike construction, high, behind and away from the castle, and the beauty of the site was not destroyed.

As Christians we have to learn to say "Stop!" because after all, greed is destructive of nature at this point, and there is a time to take one's time.

Now all this does not come about automatically. Science today treats man as less than man, and nature as less than nature. And the reason for this is that modern science has the wrong sense of *origin;* and having the wrong sense of origin, it has no category sufficient to treat nature as nature any more than it has to treat man as man.

Nevertheless, we who are Christians must be careful. We must confess that we missed our opportunity. We have spoken loudly against materialistic science, but we have done little to show that in practice we ourselves as Christians are not dominated by a technological orientation in regard either to man or nature. We should have been stressing and practicing for a long time that there is a basic reason why we should not do all that with our technology we can do. We have missed the opportunity to help man save his earth. Not only that, but in our generation we are losing an evangelistic opportunity because when modern people have a real sensitivity to nature, many of them turn to the pantheistic mentality. They have seen that most Christians simply do not care about nature as such.

So we have not only missed our opportunity to save the earth for man, but this also partly accounts for the fact that we have largely missed the opportunity of reaching the twentieth century. These are reasons why the church seems irrelevant and helpless in our generation. We are living in and practicing a sub-Christianity.

There is a parallel between man's misuse of nature and man's misuse of man. We can see this in two areas.

First of all, let us think of the sex relationship. What is man's attitude towards the girl? It is possible, and common in the modern setting, to have a "playboy" attitude, or rather a "plaything" attitude, where the "playmate" becomes the "plaything." Here, the girl is no more than a sex object.

But what is the Christian view? Somebody may offer at this point the rather romantic notion, "You shouldn't look for any pleasure for yourself; you should just look for the other person's pleasure." But that is not what the Bible says. We are to love our neighbor *as ourselves*. We have a right to pleasure, too. But what we do not have a right to do is to forget that the girl is a person and not an animal, or a plant, or a machine. We have the right to have our pleasure in a sexual relationship, but we have no right whatsoever to exploit a partner as a sex object.

There should be a conscious limitation upon our pleasure. We impose a limit—a *self-imposed* limit—in order to treat the wife fairly as a person. So although a husband *could* do more, he does not do everything he could do, because he must treat her also as a person and not just as a thing with no value. And if he does so treat her, eventually he loses, because love is gone, and all that is left is just a mechanical, chemical sexuality; humanity is lost as he treats her as less than human. Eventually not only her humanity is diminished, but his as well. In contrast, if he does less than he could do, eventually he has more, for he has a human relationship; he has love and not just a physical act. It is like the principle of the boomerang—it can come full circle and destroy the destroyer. *And that is exactly what happens with nature.* If we treat nature as having no intrinsic value, our own value is diminished.

A second parallel may be found with man in business. We have all kinds of idealists today who cry, "No profit! Down with the profit motive!" But men do not work this way. Even communism is learning the need to reinstate the profit motive. And certainly the Bible does not say that the profit motive is wrong.

But I am to treat the man I deal with in business *as myself*. I am to "love" him as my neighbor, and as myself. It is perfectly right that I should have some profit, but I must not get it by treating him (or exploiting him) as a consumer object. If I do this, eventually I shall destroy not him alone, but myself as well, because I shall have lowered the real value of myself.

So, just as the girl is not to be treated as a sex object but as a person, so again I must, if I am a businessman functioning on a Christian basis, realize I am dealing with another man made in the image of God, and I must impose some conscious limitation on myself. The Christian businessman will take profit, but he will not do everything he could do in exacting all the profit he could exact.

The Old Testament is very plain at this point: "If you take a man's cloak for a collateral, be sure to give it back to him every night, because he might be cold at night . . ." (Exodus 22:26). Again: "No man shall take a man's life to pledge" (Deuteronomy 24:6). That shows a very different mentality from that which often marks Christian businessmen. It may be properly called the right of private property, but it is a very different kind of right of private property. It realizes that if we treat other men in business or in industry as machines, we make ourselves machines, because we are not more than they are. Indeed, if we make other men and ourselves machines in commercial relationships, gradually this will penetrate every area of life and the wonder of humanity will begin to disappear.

Thus again, the Christian does not do all he can do. He has a limiting principle; and in doing less, he has more, for his own humanness is at stake. A girl should not be treated as a sex object to be used simply for pleasure. A man should not be treated as a consumer object simply for bigger profit. In the area of sex, and in the area of business, to treat persons as they should be treated, on the basis of the creation of God, is not only right in itself, but produces good results, because our own humanity begins to bloom.

In the area of nature it is exactly the same. If nature is only a meaningless particular, is "decreated," to use Simone Weil's evocative word, with no universal to give it meaning, then the wonder is gone from it. Unless there is a universal over the particulars, there is no meaning.

Jean-Paul Sartre picked this up: "If you have a finite point and it has no infinite reference point, then that finite point is absurd." He was right, and unhappily that is where he himself was—an absurd particular in the midst of only absurd particulars.

So if nature and the things of nature are only a meaningless series of particulars in a decreated universe, with no universal to give them meaning, then nature is become absurd, the wonder is gone from it. And wonder is equally gone from me, because I too am a finite thing.

But Christians insist that we do have a universal. God is there! The personal-infinite God is the universal of all the particulars, because He created all the particulars; and in His verbalized, propositional communications in the Scripture He has given us categories within which to treat everything within His creation: man to man, man to nature, the whole lot.

Now both the thing that He has made and I, who am also made by Him, have wonder, awe, and real value. But we must remember that the value I consciously put on a thing will finally be my own value, for I too am finite. If I let the wonder go from the thing, soon the wonder will go from mankind and me. And this is where people live today. The wonder is all gone. Man sits in his autonomous, "decreated" world, where there are no universals and no wonder in nature. Indeed, in an arrogant and egoistic way, nature has been reduced to a "thing" for man to use or exploit.

And if modern man speaks of protecting the ecological balance of nature, it is only on the pragmatic level for man, with no basis for nature's having any real value in itself. And thus man too is reduced another notch in value, and dehumanized technology takes another turn on the vise.

On the other hand, in the Christian view of things nature is restored. Suddenly the wonder returns.

But it is not enough merely as a matter of theory to believe that there is a real meaning in nature. The truth has to be practiced consciously. We have to begin to treat nature the way it *should* be treated.

We have seen in regard to the pleasure of sex, and in the making of profit in industry and business, that man must voluntarily limit himself. He must not be driven either for greed or haste to remove all the self-limitations. Or we can put it in another way: we must not allow ourselves individually, nor our technology, to do everything we or it can do.

The animal can make no conscious limitation. The cow eats the grass—it has no decision to make; it cannot do otherwise. Its only limitation is the mechanical limitation of its "cowness." I who am made in the image of God can make a choice. I am able to do things to nature that I should not do. So I am to put a *self-*limitation on what is possible. The horror and ugliness of modern man in his technology and in his individual life is that he does everything he can do, without limitation. Everything he *can* do, he *does*. He kills the world, he kills mankind, and he kills himself.

I am a being made in the image of God. Having a rational-moral limitation, not everything man can do is right to do. Indeed, this is the problem all the way back to the Garden of Eden. From the point of view of body structure, Eve could eat the fruit; Adam could eat the fruit. But on the basis of the second boundary condition of the moral command of God, and the character of God, it was wrong for them to eat the fruit. The call was for Eve to limit herself: to refrain from doing something she could do.

Technologically, modern man does everything he can do; he functions on this single boundary principle. Modern man, seeing himself as autonomous, with no personal-infinite God who has spoken, has no adequate universal to supply an adequate second boundary condition; and man, being fallen, is not only finite, but sinful. Thus man's pragmatic choices have no reference point beyond human egotism. It is dog eat dog, man eat man, man eat nature. Man with his greed has no real reason not to rape nature and treat it as a reverse "consumer object." He sees nature as without value or rights.

In conclusion, then, we may say that if things are treated only as autonomous machines in a decreated world, they are finally meaningless. But if that is so, then inevitably so am I—man—equally autonomous and also equally meaningless. But if individually and in the Christian community I treat the things which God has made with integrity and treat them this way lovingly, because they are His, things change.

If I love the Lover, I love what the Lover has made. Perhaps this is the reason why so many Christians feel an unreality in their Christian lives. If I don't love what the Lover has made—in the area of man, in the area of nature—and really love it because He made it, do I really love the Lover?

It is easy to make professions of faith, but they may not be worth much because they have little meaning. They may become merely a mental assent that means little or nothing.

But I must be clear that I am not loving the tree or whatever is standing in front of me for a pragmatic reason. It will have a pragmatic *result,* the very pragmatic results that the men involved in ecology are looking for. But as a Christian I do not do it for the practical or pragmatic results; I do it because it is right and because God is the Maker. And then suddenly things drop into place.

There are things before me which I now face, not as a cow would face the buttercup—merely the mechanical situation—but facing it by choice. I look at the buttercup, and I treat the buttercup the way it should be treated. The buttercup and I are both created by God; but beyond this, I can treat it properly by personal choice. I act personally, and I am a person! Psychologically I begin to breathe and live. Psychologically I am now dealing on a personal level, not only with men and women, but also with the things in nature that God has made which are less than personal in themselves, and the old hang-ups begin to crumble. My humanness grows, and the modern technological pit and pendulum is no longer closing in on me.

As a result, then, there is beauty instead of a desert. The question of aesthetics is also in place. This surely is something that has importance in itself and is not to be despised. Beauty does not have to have pragmatic reasons to have value. So if we did nothing else in our Christian view of nature than to save and enjoy beauty, it would be of value and worthwhile.

But it is not only that, as we have seen. The balance of nature will be more nearly what it should be, and there will be a way to utilize nature for man and yet not destroy the resources which man needs. But none of this will happen if it is only a gimmick. We have to be in the right relationship with Him in the way He has provided, and then, as Christians, have and practice the Christian view of nature.

When we have learned this—the Christian view of nature—then there can be a real ecology; beauty will flow, psychological freedom will come, and the world will cease to be turned into a desert. Because it is right, on the basis of the whole Christian system— which is strong enough to stand it all because it is true—as I face the buttercup, I say: "Fellow-creature, fellow-*creature*, I won't walk on you. We are both creatures together."

The Historical Roots of Our Ecologic Crisis

Lynn White, Jr.

A conversation with Aldous Huxley not infrequently put one at the receiving end of an unforgettable monologue. About a year before his lamented death he was discoursing on a favorite topic: man's unnatural treatment of nature and its sad results. To illustrate his point he told how, during the previous summer, he had returned to a little valley in England where he had spent many happy months as a child. Once it had been composed of delightful grassy glades; now it was becoming overgrown with unsightly brush because the rabbits that formerly kept such growth under control had largely succumbed to a disease, myxomatosis, that was deliberately introduced by the local farmers to reduce the rabbits' destruction of crops. Being something of a Philistine, I could be silent no longer, even in the interest of great rhetoric. I interrupted to point out that the rabbit itself had been brought as a domestic animal to England in 1176, presumably to improve the protein diet of the peasantry.

All forms of life modify their contexts. The most spectacular and benign instance is doubtless the coral polyp. By serving its own ends, it has created a vast undersea world favorable to thousands of other kinds of animals and plants. Ever since man

became a numerous species he has affected his environment notably. The hypothesis that his fire-drive method of hunting created
the world's great grasslands and helped to exterminate the mon-
ster mammals of the Pleistocene from much of the globe is plausi-
ble, if not proved. For six millennia at least, the banks of the lower
Nile have been a human artifact rather than the swampy African
jungle which nature, apart from man, would have made it. The
Aswan Dam, flooding 5,000 square miles, is only the latest stage
in a long process. In many regions terracing or irrigation, over-
grazing, the cutting of forests by Romans to build ships to fight
Carthaginians or by Crusaders to solve the logistics problems of
their expeditions have profoundly changed some ecologies.
Observation that the French landscape falls into two basic types,
the open fields of the north and the *bocage* of the south and west,
inspired Marc Bloch to undertake his classic study of medieval
agricultural methods. Quite unintentionally, changes in human
ways often affect nonhuman nature. It has been noted, for example, that the advent of the automobile eliminated huge flocks of
sparrows that once fed on the horse manure littering every street.

The history of ecologic change is still so rudimentary that we
know little about what really happened, or what the results were.
The extinction of the European aurochs as late as 1627 would seem
to have been a simple case of overenthusiastic hunting. On more
intricate matters it often is impossible to find solid information.
For a thousand years or more the Frisians and Hollanders have
been pushing back the North Sea, and the process is culminating
in our own time in the reclamation of the Zuider Zee. What, if
any, species of animals, birds, fish, shore life, or plants have died
out in the process? In their epic combat with Neptune, have the
Netherlanders overlooked ecological values in such a way that the
quality of human life in the Netherlands has suffered? I cannot
discover that the questions have ever been asked, much less answered.

People, then, have often been a dynamic element in their own
environment, but in the present state of historical scholarship we
usually do not know exactly when, where, or with what effects
man-induced changes came. As we enter the last third of the twentieth century, however, concern for the problem of ecologic backlash
is mounting feverishly. Natural science, conceived as the effort to
understand the nature of things, had flourished in several eras and
among several peoples. Similarly there had been an age-old accu-
mulation of technological skills, sometimes growing rapidly,

sometimes slowly. But it was not until about four generations ago that Western Europe and North America arranged a marriage between science and technology, a union of the theoretical and the empirical approaches to our natural environment. The emergence in widespread practice of the Baconian creed that scientific knowledge means technological power over nature can scarcely be dated before about 1850, save in the chemical industries, where it is anticipated in the eighteenth century. Its acceptance as a normal pattern of action may mark the greatest event in human history since the invention of agriculture, and perhaps in nonhuman terrestrial history as well.

Almost at once the new situation forced the crystallization of the novel concept of ecology; indeed, the word *ecology* first appeared in the English language in 1873. Today, less than a century later, the impact of our race upon the environment has so increased in force that it has changed in essence. When the first cannons were fired, in the early fourteenth century, they affected ecology by sending workers scrambling to the forests and mountains for more potash, sulfur, iron ore, and charcoal, with some resulting erosion and deforestation. Hydrogen bombs are of a different order: a war fought with them might alter the genetics of all life on this planet. By 1285 London had a smog problem arising from the burning of soft coal, but our present combustion of fossil fuels threatens to change the chemistry of the globe's atmosphere as a whole, with consequences which we are only beginning to guess. With the population explosion, the carcinoma of planless urbanism, the now geological deposits of sewage and garbage, surely no creature other than man has ever managed to foul its nest in such short order.

There are many calls to action, but specific proposals, however worthy as individual items, seem too partial, palliative, negative: ban the bomb, tear down the billboards, give the Hindus contraceptives and tell them to eat their sacred cows. The simplest solution to any suspect change is, of course, to stop it, or, better yet, to revert to a romanticized past: make those ugly gasoline stations look like Anne Hathaway's cottage or (in the Far West) like ghost-town saloons. The "wilderness area" mentality invariably advocates deep-freezing an ecology, whether San Gimignano or the High Sierra, as it was before the first Kleenex was dropped. But neither atavism nor prettification will cope with the ecologic crisis of our time.

What shall we do? No one yet knows. Unless we think about

fundamentals, our specific measures may produce new backlashes more serious than those they are designed to remedy.

As a beginning we should try to clarify our thinking by looking, in some historical depth, at the presuppositions that underlie modern technology and science. Science was traditionally aristocratic, speculative, intellectual in intent; technology was lower-class, empirical, action-oriented. The quite sudden fusion of these two, towards the middle of the nineteenth century, is surely related to the slightly prior and contemporary democratic revolutions which, by reducing social barriers, tended to assert a functional unity of brain and hand. Our ecologic crisis is the product of an emerging, entirely novel, democratic culture. The issue is whether a democratized world can survive its own implications. Presumably we cannot unless we rethink our axioms.

The Western Traditions of Technology and Science

One thing is so certain that it seems stupid to verbalize it: both modern technology and modern science are distinctively *Occidental*. Our technology has absorbed elements from all over the world, notably from China; yet everywhere today, whether in Japan or in Nigeria, successful technology is Western. Our science is the heir to all the sciences of the past, especially perhaps to the work of the great Islamic scientists of the Middle Ages, who so often outdid the ancient Greeks in skill and perspicacity: al-Razi in medicine, for example; or ibn-al-Haytham in optics; or Omar Khayyam in mathematics. Indeed, not a few works of such geniuses seem to have vanished in the original Arabic and to survive only in medieval Latin translations that helped to lay the foundations for later Western developments. Today, around the globe, all significant science is Western in style and method, whatever the pigmentation or language of the scientists.

A second pair of facts is less well recognized because they result from quite recent historical scholarship. The leadership of the West, both in technology and in science, is far older than the so-called Scientific Revolution of the seventeenth century or the so-called Industrial Revolution of the eighteenth century. These terms are in fact outmoded and obscure the true nature of what they try to describe—significant stages in two long and separate developments. By A.D. 1000 at the latest—and perhaps, feebly, as much as 200 years earlier—the West began to apply water power to industrial processes other than milling grain. This was followed in the late twelfth century by the harnessing of wind power. From simple beginnings, but with remarkable consistency of style, the West rapidly expanded its skills in the development of power machinery, labor-saving devices, and automation. Those who doubt should contemplate that most monumental achievement in the history of automation: the weight-driven mechanical clock, which appeared in two forms in the early fourteenth century. Not in craftsmanship but in basic technological capacity, the Latin West of the later Middle Ages far outstripped its elaborate, sophisticated, and aesthetically magnificent sister cultures, Byzantium and Islam. In 1444 a great Greek ecclesiastic, Bessarion, who had gone to Italy, wrote a letter to a prince in Greece. He is amazed by the superiority of Western ships, arms, textiles, glass. But above all he is astonished by the spectacle of waterwheels sawing timbers and pumping the bellows of blast furnaces. Clearly, he had seen nothing of the sort in the Near East.

By the end of the fifteenth century the technological superiority of Europe was such that its small, mutually hostile nations could spill out over all the rest of the world, conquering, looting, and colonizing. The symbol of this technological superiority is the fact that Portugal, one of the weakest states of the Occident, was able to become, and to remain for a century, mistress of the East Indies. And we must remember that the technology of Vasco da Gama and Albuquerque was built by pure empiricism, drawing remarkably little support or inspiration from science.

In the present-day vernacular understanding, modern science is supposed to have begun in 1543, when both Copernicus and Vesalius published their great works. It is not derogation of their accomplishments, however, to point out such structures as the *Fabrica* and the *De revolutionibus* do not appear overnight. The distinctive Western tradition of science, in fact, began in the late eleventh century with a massive movement of translation of Arabic and Greek scientific works into Latin. A few notable books— Theophrastus, for example—escaped the West's avid new appetite for science, but within less than 200 years effectively the entire corpus of Greek and Muslim science was available in Latin, and was being eagerly read and criticized in the new European universities. Out of criticism arose new observation, speculation, and increasing distrust of ancient authorities. By the late thirteenth century Europe had seized global scientific leadership from the faltering hands of Islam. It would be as absurd to deny the profound originality of Newton, Galileo, or Copernicus as to deny that of the fourteenth century scholastic scientists like Buridan or Oresme on whose work they built. Before the eleventh century, science scarcely existed in the Latin West, even in Roman times. From the eleventh century onward, the scientific sector of Occidental culture has increased in a steady crescendo.

Since both our technological and our scientific movements got their start, acquired their character, and achieved world dominance in the Middle Ages, it would seem that we cannot understand their nature or their present impact upon ecology without examining fundamental medieval assumptions and developments.

Medieval View of Man and Nature

Until recently, agriculture has been the chief occupation even in "advanced" societies; hence, any change in methods of tillage has much importance. Early plows, drawn by two oxen, did not normally turn the sod but merely scratched it. Thus, cross-plowing was needed and fields tended to be squarish. In the fairly light soils and semiarid climates of the Near East and Mediterranean, this worked well. But such a plow was inappropriate to the wet climate and often sticky soils of northern Europe. By the latter part of the seventh century after Christ, however, following obscure beginnings, certain northern peasants were using an entirely new kind of plow, equipped with a vertical knife to cut the line of the furrow, a horizontal share to slice under the sod, and a moldboard to turn it over. The friction of this plow with the soil was so great that it normally required not two but eight oxen. It attacked the land with such violence that cross-plowing was not needed, and fields tended to be shaped in long strips.

In the days of the scratch-plow, fields were distributed generally in units capable of supporting a single family. Subsistence farming was the presupposition. But no peasant owned eight oxen: to use the new and more efficient plow, peasants pooled their oxen to form large plow-teams, originally receiving (it would appear) plowed strips in proportion to their contribution. Thus, distribution of land was based no longer on the needs of a family but, rather, on the capacity of a power machine to till the earth. Man's relation to the soil was profoundly changed. Formerly man had been part of nature; now he was the exploiter of nature. Nowhere else in the world did farmers develop any analogous agricultural implement. Is it coincidence that modern technology, with its ruthlessness toward nature, has so largely been produced by descendants of these peasants of northern Europe?

This same exploitive attitude appears slightly before A.D. 830 in Western illustrated calendars. In older calendars the months were shown as passive personifications. The new Frankish calendars, which set the style for the Middle Ages, are very different: they show men coercing the world around them—plowing, harvesting, chopping trees, butchering pigs. Man and nature are two things, and man is master.

These novelties seem to be in harmony with larger intellectual patterns. What people do about their ecology depends on what they think about themselves in relation to things around them. Human ecology is deeply conditioned by beliefs about our nature and destiny—that is, by religion. To Western eyes this is very evident in, say, India or Ceylon. It is equally true of ourselves and of our medieval ancestors.

The victory of Christianity over paganism was the greatest psychic revolution in the history of our culture. It has become fashionable today to say that, for better or worse, we live in "the post-Christian age." Certainly the forms of our thinking and language have largely ceased to be Christian, but to my eye the substance often remains amazingly akin to that of the past. Our daily habits of action, for example, are dominated by an implicit faith in perpetual progress which was unknown either to Greco-Roman antiquity or to the Orient. It is rooted in, and is indefensible apart from, Judeo-Christian teleology. The fact that Communists share it merely helps to show what can be demonstrated on many other grounds: that Marxism, like Islam, is a Judeo-Christian heresy. We continue today to live, as we have lived for about 1,700 years, very largely in a context of Christian axioms.

What did Christianity tell people about their relations with the environment?

While many of the world's mythologies provide stories of creation, Greco-Roman mythology was singularly incoherent in this respect. Like Aristotle, the intellectuals of the ancient West denied that the visible world had had a beginning. Indeed, the idea of a beginning was impossible in the framework of their cyclical notion of time. In sharp contrast, Christianity inherited from Judaism not only a concept of time as nonrepetitive and linear but also a striking story of creation. By gradual stages a loving and all-powerful God had created light and darkness, the heavenly bodies, the earth and all its plants, animals, birds, and fishes. Finally, God had created Adam and, as an afterthought, Eve to keep man from being lonely. Man named all the animals, thus establishing his dominance over them. God planned all of this explicitly for man's benefit and rule: no item in the physical creation had any purpose save to serve man's purposes. And, although man's body is made of clay, he is not simply part of nature: he is made in God's image.

Especially in its Western form, Christianity is the most anthropocentric religion the world has seen. As early as the second century both Tertullian and Saint Irenaeus of Lyons were insisting that when God shaped Adam he was foreshadowing the image of the incarnate Christ, the Second Adam. Man shares, in great measure, God's transcendence of nature. Christianity, in absolute contrast to ancient paganism and Asia's religions (except, perhaps, Zoroastrianism), not only established a dualism of man and nature, but also insisted that it is God's will that man exploit nature for his proper ends.

At the level of the common people this worked out in an interesting way. In Antiquity every tree, every spring, every stream, every hill had its own *genius loci,* its guardian spirit. These spirits were accessible to men, but were very unlike men; centaurs, fauns, and mermaids show their ambivalence. Before one cut a tree, mined a mountain, or dammed a brook, it was important to placate the spirit in charge of that particular situation, and to keep it placated. By destroying pagan animism, Christianity made it possible to exploit nature in a mood of indifference to the feelings of natural objects.

It is often said that for animism the Church substituted the cult of saints. True; but the cult of saints is functionally quite different from animism. The saint is not *in* natural objects; he may have special shrines, but his citizenship is in heaven. Moreover, a saint is entirely a man; he can be approached in human terms. In addition to saints, Christianity of course also had angels and demons inherited from Judaism and perhaps, at one remove, from Zoroastrianism. But these were all as mobile as the saints themselves. The spirits *in* natural objects, which formerly had protected nature from man, evaporated. Man's effective monopoly on spirit in this world was confirmed, and the old inhibitions to the exploitation of nature crumbled.

When one speaks in such sweeping terms, a note of caution is in order. Christianity is a complex faith, and its consequences differ in differing contexts. What I have said may well apply to the medieval West, where in fact technology made spectacular advances. But the Greek East, a highly civilized realm of equal Christian devotion, seems to have produced no marked technological innovation after the late seventh century, when Greek fire was invented. The key to the contrast may perhaps be found in a difference in the tonality of piety and thought which students of comparative theology find between the Greek and the Latin Churches. The Greeks believed that sin was intellectual blindness, and that salvation was found in illumination, orthodoxy—that is, clear thinking. The Latins, on the other hand, felt that sin was moral evil, and that salvation was to be found in right conduct. Eastern theology has been intellectualist. Western theology has been voluntarist. The Greek saint contemplates; the Western saint acts. The implications of Christianity for the conquest of nature would emerge more easily in the Western atmosphere.

The Christian dogma of creation, which is found in the first clause of all the Creeds, has another meaning for our comprehension of today's ecologic crisis. By revelation, God had given man the Bible, the Book of Scripture. But since God had made nature, nature also must reveal the divine mentality. The religious study of nature for the better understanding of God was known as natural theology. In the early Church, and always in the Greek East, nature was conceived primarily as a symbolic system through which God speaks to men: the ant is a sermon to sluggards; rising flames are the symbol of the soul's aspiration. This view of nature was essentially artistic rather than scientific. While Byzantium preserved and copied great numbers of ancient Greek scientific texts, science as we conceive it could scarcely flourish in such an ambience.

However, in the Latin West by the early thirteenth century natural theology was following a very different bent. It was ceasing to be the decoding of the physical symbols of God's communication with man and was becoming the effort to understand God's mind by discovering how His creation operates. The rainbow was no longer simply a symbol of hope first sent to Noah after the Deluge: Robert Grosseteste, Friar Roger Bacon, and Theodoric of Freiberg produced startlingly sophisticated works on the optics of the rainbow, but they did it as a venture in religious understanding. From the thirteenth century onward, up to and including Leibnitz and Newton, every major scientist, in effect, explained his motivations in religious terms. Indeed, if Galileo had not been so expert an amateur theologian he would have got into far less trouble: the professionals resented his intrusion. And Newton seems to have regarded himself more as a theologian than as a scientist. It was not until the late eighteenth century that the hypothesis of God became unnecessary to many scientists.

It is often hard for the historian to judge, when men explain why they are doing what they want to do, whether they are offering real reasons or merely culturally acceptable reasons. The consistency with which scientists during the long formative centuries of Western science said that the task and the reward of the scientist was "to think God's thoughts after him" leads one to believe that this was their real motivation. If so, then modern Western science was cast in a matrix of Christian theology. The dynamism of religious devotion, shaped by the Judeo-Christian dogma of creation, gave it impetus.

An Alternative Christian View

We would seem to be headed toward conclusions unpalatable to many Christians. Since both *science* and *technology* are blessed words in our contemporary vocabulary, some may be happy at the notions, first, that, viewed historically, modern science is an extrapolation of natural theology and, second, that modern technology is at least partly to be explained as an Occidental, voluntarist realization of the Christian dogma of man's transcendence of, and rightful mastery over, nature. But, as we now recognize, somewhat over a century ago science and technology—hitherto quite separate activities—joined to give mankind powers which, to judge by many of the ecologic effects, are out of control. If so, Christianity bears a huge burden of guilt.

I personally doubt that disastrous ecologic backlash can be avoided simply by applying to our problems more science and more technology. Our science and technology have grown out of Christian attitudes toward man's relation to nature which are almost universally held not only by Christians and neo-Christians but also by those who fondly regard themselves as post-Christians. Despite Copernicus, all the cosmos rotates around our little globe. Despite Darwin, we are *not,* in our hearts, part of the natural process. We are superior to nature, contemptuous of it, willing to use it for our slightest whim. The newly elected Governor of California, like myself a churchman but less troubled than I, spoke for the Christian tradition when he said (as is alleged), "when you've seen one redwood tree, you've seen them all." To a Christian a tree can be no more than a physical fact. The whole concept of the sacred grove is alien to Christianity and to the ethos of the West. For nearly two millennia Christian missionaries have been chopping down sacred groves, which are idolatrous because they assume spirit in nature.

What we do about ecology depends on our ideas of the man-nature relationship. More science and more technology are not going to get us out of the present ecologic crisis until we find a new religion, or rethink our old one. The beatniks, who are the basic revolutionaries of our time, show a sound instinct in their affinity for Zen Buddhism, which conceives of the man-nature relationship as very nearly the mirror image of the Christian view. Zen, however, is as deeply conditioned by Asian history as Christianity is by the experience of the West, and I am dubious of its viability among us.

Possibly we should ponder the greatest radical in Christian history since Christ: Saint Francis of Assisi. The prime miracle of Saint Francis is the fact that he did not end at the stake, as many of his left-wing followers did. He was so clearly heretical that a General of the Franciscan Order, Saint Bonaventura, a great and perceptive Christian, tried to suppress the early accounts of Franciscanism. The key to an understanding of Francis is his belief in the virtue of humility—not merely for the individual but for man as a species. Francis tried to depose man from his monarchy over creation and set up a democracy of all God's creatures. With him the ant is no longer simply a homily for the lazy, flames a sign of the thrust of the soul toward union with God; now they are Brother Ant and Sister Fire, praising the Creator in their own ways as Brother Man does in his.

Later commentators have said that Francis preached to the birds as a rebuke to men who would not listen. The records do not read so: he urged the little birds to praise God, and in spiritual ecstasy they flapped their wings and chirped rejoicing. Legends of saints, especially the Irish saints, had long told of their dealings with animals but always, I believe, to show their human dominance over creatures. With Francis it is different. The land around Gubbio in the Apennines was being ravaged by a fierce wolf. Saint

Francis, says the legend, talked to the wolf and persuaded him of the error of his ways. The wolf repented, died in the odor of sanctity, and was buried in consecrated ground.

What Sir Steven Runciman calls "the Franciscan doctrine of the animal soul" was quickly stamped out. Quite possibly it was in part inspired, consciously or unconsciously, by the belief in reincarnation held by the Cathar heretics who at that time teemed in Italy and southern France, and who presumably had got it originally from India. It is significant that at just the same moment, about 1200, traces of metempsychosis are found also in western Judaism, in the Provencal *Cabbala*. But Francis held neither to transmigration of souls nor to pantheism. His view of nature and of man rested on a unique sort of pan-psychism of all things animate and inanimate, designed for the glorification of their transcendent Creator, who, in the ultimate gesture of cosmic humility, assumed flesh, lay helpless in a manger, and hung dying on a scaffold.

I am not suggesting that many contemporary Americans who are concerned about our ecologic crisis will be either able or willing to counsel with wolves or exhort birds. However, the present increasing disruption of the global environment is the product of a dynamic technology and science which were originating in the Western medieval world against which Saint Francis was rebelling in so original a way. Their growth cannot be understood historically apart from distinctive attitudes toward nature which are deeply grounded in Christian dogma. The fact that most people do not think of these attitudes as Christian is irrelevant. No new set of basic values has been accepted in our society to displace those of Christianity. Hence we shall continue to have a worsening ecologic crisis until we reject the Christian axiom that nature has no reason for existence save to serve man.

The greatest spiritual revolutionary in Western history, Saint Francis, proposed what he thought was an alternative Christian view of nature and man's relation to it: he tried to substitute the idea of the equality of all creatures, including man, for the idea of man's limitless rule of creation. He failed. Both our present science and our present technology are so tinctured with orthodox Christian arrogance toward nature that no solution for our ecologic crisis can be expected from them alone. Since the roots of our trouble are so largely religious, the remedy must also be essentially religious, whether we call it that or not. We must rethink and refeel our nature and destiny. The profoundly religious, but heretical, sense of the primitive Franciscans for the spiritual autonomy of all parts of nature may point a direction. I propose Francis as a patron saint for ecologists.

Why Worry About Nature?

Richard L. Means

Albert Schweitzer once wrote, "The great fault of all ethics hitherto has been that they believed themselves to have to deal only with the relation of man to man." Modern ethical discussion does not seem to have removed itself very far from this fallacy. Joseph Fletcher's *Situation Ethics: The New Morality,* for instance, deals piecemeal with man's relations to his fellows without even suggesting that man's relation to nature—to the physical and biological world—raises questions of moral behavior. Perhaps this oversight is due to the general psychological and subjective tone of much current social criticism. Or, even more likely, it represents the "revolt against formalism," the eschewing of the abstract and sweeping interpretations of man and nature once the passion of American social scientists.

It is true that the Thoreau-like comments of Joseph Wood Krutch or the aggressive naturalistic interpretations of the Austrian scientist, Konrad Lorenz, find a grudging response among some social scientists. But contemporary social scientists have so completely separated conditions of culture from nature that it will take some intellectual effort to overcome this dichotomy. Moreover, although the relations of man and nature may be envisioned

in various ways—all the way from control to passive obedience—
the notion that man's relation to nature is a moral one finds very
few articulate champions, even among contemporary religious
writers. Harvey Cox's book, *The Secular City,* for example, is set
in an urban world in rather extreme isolation from the surrounding problems of resources, food, disease, etc. The city is taken for
granted and the moral dimensions of Cox's analysis are limited to
man's relations to man within this urban world, and not with the
animals, the plants, the trees, the air—that is, the natural habitat.

Eric Hoffer, one of the few contemporary social critics who
have met head-on the issue of man's relationship to nature, has
warned in these pages of the danger of romanticizing nature. ["A
Strategy for the War with Nature," *SR,* February 5, 1966.] Longshoreman, dishwasher, student of human tragedy, and exposer
of the corruptions and perversions of power, Mr. Hoffer says
that the great accomplishment of man is to transcend nature, to
separate one's self from the demands of instinct. Thus, according
to Hoffer, a fundamental characteristic of man is to be found
in his capacity to free himself from the restrictions of the physical
and biological.

In a way, Hoffer is correct. Surely the effects on man of flood,
famine, fire, and earthquake have been great and hardly indicate a
beneficence in nature which is ready and willing to rush headlong
to the succor of man. But Hoffer's attack is basically political. It is
an attack on "romantic individualism"—a special interpretation of
man's relation to nature. Hoffer knows full well that romantic
individualism leads easily to a kind of egoism and antirationalism
which can pervert and destroy democratic institutions.

One is reminded of Hitler's call to neglect reason and to "think
with one's blood." Values—tradition, home soil, nationalism, and
race—have often been legitimized on the basis of a vague nature
mysticism. Such a nature mysticism is the very essence of romantic individualism (though, of course, there may be other types of
nature romanticism which do not advocate egotist striving).
Perhaps the problem lies in the focus on the "individual" as deline-
ated by Hoffer. He assumes that the response to nature couched in
the terms of a naive faith in nature's bountiful, miracle-working
properties is an individual response. And, of course, it always is,
to a degree, but, by failure to consider the collective or social side
of man's relation to nature, the true moral dimensions of the
problem are obscured.

It may be that *man* is at war with nature, but *men* are not (or, at least, cannot be). The reason is that certain individual attitudes and actions, when taken collectively, have consequences for nature, and these consequences may be most clearly understood under the stark realities of social survival itself. Take the problems of radioactive wastes, Strontium 90 contamination, etc. Man does not just do battle with the natural world; he may, in the act of cooperating with it, also shape and change it. Men join in a chain of decisions which facilitate the emergence of a new symbiotic relationship to nature—that is, we create civilization and culture. This crucial assumption strikes at the very roots of romantic individualism. One man, totally alone, acting before nature and using nature to satisfy needs of warmth, comfort, and creativity, is very difficult to imagine. Even Robinson Crusoe had his man Friday!

Hoffer seems to neglect the possibility that man's cooperation in the subjection of nature need not be conceptualized simply on the basis of brute force. Physical work, mechanical and otherwise—from the labor of the Chinese masses to the works of a sophisticated high-tower steeplejack—depends on the intrusion of human ideas into the natural world. Aided by machines, cranes, bulldozers, factories, transportation systems, computers, and laboratories, man does force nature's hand. This does not, however, force us to acceptance of metaphysical materialism, the naive belief that matter and physical force are the only realities. The power of ideas, of values, provides the presuppositions which in the first place create a particular web of human interaction between nature and man. The power of the contemplative idea, the chain of speculative reason, the mathematician's art, and the philosopher's dreams must also be considered. If this point of view is accepted, then the question of man's relation to nature is a much more crucial moral issue than Eric Hoffer seems to suggest.

What, then, is the moral crisis? It is, I think, a pragmatic problem—that is, it involves the actual social consequences of myriad and unconnected acts. The crisis comes from the combined results of a mistreatment of our environment. It involves the negligence of a small businessman on the Kalamazoo River, the irresponsibility of a large corporation on Lake Erie, the impatient use of insecticides by a farmer in California, the stripping of land by Kentucky mine operators. Unfortunately, there is a long history of unnecessary and tragic destruction of animal and natural resources on the face of this continent.

One might begin the indictment with the classical case of the passenger pigeon which once flew across America in tremendous numbers, and then end with the destruction of the seal industry. The trouble is, however, we do not seem to learn very much from these sad happenings, for (to the anguish of men who have thrilled to the images created by Herman Melville and the great white whale) such marine scientists as Scott McVay believe that commercial fishing is endangering the whale, the last abundant species in the world. For those more inclined toward a cash nexus, there goes a profitable industry. For those of us who have a respect for nature—in particular, for our mammalian kinsmen—the death of these great creatures will leave a void in God's creation and in the imagination of men for generations to come.

Another case in point is the attempt to dam and flood mile after mile of the Grand Canyon in order to produce more electricity—a commodity we seem to have in great abundance. The Grand Canyon, of course, is not a commodity; it is truly, in popular parlance, a "happening." Uncontrolled by man, created by nature, it cannot be duplicated. Any assault on its natural state is an equal attack on man's capacity to wonder, to contemplate his environment and nature's work. In short, such activities seem to belittle and diminish man himself. Thus the activities of those who suggest such destruction assume a restricted view of man and his capacity for joy in nature. In this sense, such activities are immoral. We could lengthen the list, but it should be clear that destruction of nature by man's gratuitous "busyness" and technological arrogance is the result of a thoughtless and mindless human activity.

A second basic issue is the growing biological pollution of the environment. Discussions of the pollution in just one river, the mighty Hudson, in financial terms stagger the imagination. The economic costs just to keep the river in its present undesirable state are immense—and to make any progress back toward a less polluted river will cost billions of dollars. The same is true of other great bodies of water.

And consider the state of the air we breathe. Air pollution has demonstrable ill effects on man, as many reports confirm. But in addition, for the economically minded, A. J. Haagen-Smit, a leading expert on air pollution, notes that a largely ignored breakdown in standards of efficiency and technology also is involved:

From all the emissions of an automobile, the total loss of fuel energy is about 15 percent; in the U.S. that represents a loss of about $3 billion annually. It is remarkable that the automobile industry, which has a reputation for efficiency, allows such fuel waste.

Perhaps an issue becomes most moral when it is personal, existential—appeals to our own experience. Scientists vary in estimates of the time when the Great Lakes will be largely polluted, but the day of reckoning may be much too near. When I was a boy in Toledo, Ohio, summer after summer many of my neighbors and playmates went to cottages along the shores of Lake Erie. Today, visiting these cottages is anything but a happy event, and some owners are attempting desperately to sell their properties to any bidder. An analysis by Charles F. Powers and Andrew Robertson on "The Aging Great Lakes" [*Scientific American,* November, 1966] is not at all comforting for those of us who love the miles of sandy beach of Lake Michigan or the rugged, cold, wind-whipped shores of Lake Superior. Although Lake Michigan will not immediately turn into a polluted wasteland like Lake Erie, with dark spots of water without aeration where only worms can live, pollution is growing in the southern end of Lake Michigan. And these problems, as Powers and Robertson point out, are beginning to touch even relatively unspoiled Lake Superior.

Why is man's relation to nature a moral crisis? It is a moral crisis because it is a historical one involving man's history and culture, expressed at its roots by our religious and ethical views of nature—which have been relatively unquestioned in this context. The historian of medieval culture, Lynn White, Jr., brilliantly traced the origin and consequences of this expression in an insightful article in *Science* last March: "The Historical Roots of Our Ecologic Crisis." He argues that the Christian notion of a transcendent God, removed from nature and breaking into nature only through revelation, removed spirit from nature and allows, in the ideological sense, for an easy exploitation of nature.

On the American scene, the Calvinistic and the deistic concepts of God were peculiarly alike at this point. Both envisioned God as absolutely transcendent, apart from the world, isolated from nature and organic life. As to the contemporary implications of this dichotomy between spirit and nature, Professor White says:

> The newly elected Governor of California, like myself a churchman but less troubled than I, spoke for the Christian tradition when he said (as is alleged), "When you've seen one redwood tree, you've seen

them all." To a Christian a tree can be no more than a physical fact. The whole concept of the sacred grove is alien to Christianity and to the ethos of the West. For nearly two millennia Christian missionaries have been chopping down sacred groves, which are idolatrous because they assume spirit in nature.

Perhaps, as Lynn White suggests, the persistence of this as a moral problem is illustrated in the protest of the contemporary generation of beats and hippies. Although the kind of "cool cat" aloofness expressed by this generation grates on the nerves of many of us, and more than a few "squares" find difficulty in "digging" the new hair styles (not to mention Twiggy), there may be a "sound instinct" involved in the fact that some of these so-called beats have turned to Zen Buddhism. It may represent an overdue perception of the fact that we need to appreciate more fully the religious and moral dimensions of the relation between nature and the human spirit.

Why do almost all of our wisest and most exciting social critics meticulously avoid the moral implications of this issue? Perhaps, in the name of political realism, it is too easy to fear the charge that one anthropomorphizes or spiritualizes nature. On the other hand, the refusal to connect the human spirit to nature may reflect the traditional thought pattern of Western society wherein nature is conceived to be a separate substance—a material—mechanical, and, in a metaphysical sense, irrelevant to man.

It seems to me much more fruitful to think of nature as part of a system of human organization—as a variable, a changing condition—which interacts with man and culture. If nature is so perceived, then a love, a sense of awe, and a feeling of empathy with nature need not degenerate into a subjective, emotional bid for romantic individualism. On the contrary, such a view should help destroy egoistic, status politics, for it helps unmask the fact that other men's activities are not just private, inconsequential, and limited in themselves; their arts, mediated through changes in nature, affect my life, my children, and the generations to come. In this sense, justification of a technological arrogance toward nature on the basis of dividends and profits is not just bad economics—it is basically an immoral act. And our contemporary moral crisis, then, goes much deeper than questions of political power and law, of urban riots and slums. It may, at least in part, reflect American society's almost utter disregard for the value of nature.

HOW SHOULD WE THEN LIVE?

Author's Note

In no way does this book make a pretense of being a complete chronological history of Western culture. It is questionable if such a book could even be written. This book is, however, an analysis of the key moments in history which have formed our present culture, and the thinking of the people who brought those moments to pass. This study is made in the hope that light may be shed upon the major characteristics of our age and that solutions may be found to the myriad of problems which face us as we look toward the end of the twentieth century.

CHAPTER ONE

Ancient Rome

There is a flow to history and culture. This flow is rooted and has its wellspring in the thoughts of people. People are unique in the inner life of the mind—what they are in their thought-world determines how they act. This is true of their value systems and it is true of their creativity. It is true of their corporate actions, such as political decisions, and it is true of their personal lives. The results of their thought-world flow through their fingers or from their tongues into the external world. This is true of Michelangelo's chisel, and it is true of a dictator's sword.

People have presuppositions, and they will live more consistently on the basis of these presuppositions than even they themselves may realize. By *presuppositions* we mean the basic way an individual looks at life, his basic world-view, the grid through which he sees the world. Presuppositions rest upon that which a person considers to be the truth of what exists. People's presuppositions lay a grid for all they bring forth into the external world. Their presuppositions also provide the basis for their values and therefore the basis for their decisions.

"As a man thinketh, so is he," is really most profound. An individual is not just the product of the forces around him. He has a mind, an inner world. Then, having thought, a person can bring forth actions into the external world and thus influence it. People are apt to look at the outer theater of action, forgetting the actor who "lives in the mind" and who therefore is the true actor in the external world. The inner thought-world determines the outward action.

Most people catch their presuppositions from their family and surrounding society the way a child catches measles. But people with more understanding realize that their presuppositions should be chosen after a careful consideration of what world-view is true. When all is done, when all the alternatives have been explored, "not many men are in the room"—that is, although world-views have many variations, there are not many basic world-views or basic presuppositions. These basic options will become obvious as we look at the flow of the past.

To understand where we are in today's world—in our intellectual ideas and in our cultural and political lives—we must trace three lines in history, namely, the philosophic, the scientific, and the religious. The philosophic seeks intellectual answers to the basic questions of life. The scientific has two parts: first, the makeup of the physical universe, and then the practical application of what it discovers in technology. The direction in which science will move is set by the philosophic world-view of the scientists. People's religious views also determine the direction of their individual lives and of their society.

As we try to learn lessons about the primary dilemmas which we now face, by looking at the past and considering its flow, we could begin with the Greeks, or even before the Greeks. We could go back to the three great ancient river cultures: the Euphrates, the Indus, and the Nile. However, we will begin with the Romans (and with the Greek influence behind them), because Roman civilization is the direct ancestor of the modern Western world. From the first conquests of the Roman Republic down to our own day, Roman law and political ideas have had a strong influence on the European scene and the entire Western world. Wherever Western civilization has gone, it has been marked by the Romans.

In many ways Rome was great, but it had no real answers to the basic problems that all humanity faces. Much of Roman thought and culture was shaped by Greek thinking, especially after Greece came under Roman rule in 146 B.C. The Greeks tried first to build their society upon the city-state, that is, the *polis*. The city-state, both in theory and fact, was comprised of all those who were accepted as citizens. All values had meaning in reference to the *polis*. Thus, when Socrates (469?-399 B.C.) had to choose between death and exile from that which gave him meaning, he chose death. But the *polis* failed since it proved to be an insufficient base upon which to build a society.

The Greeks and later the Romans also tried to build society upon their gods. But these gods were not big enough because they were finite, limited. Even all their gods put together were not infinite. Actually, the gods in Greek and Roman thinking were like men and women larger than life, but not basically different from human men and women. As one example among thousands, we can think of the statue of Hercules, standing inebriated and urinating. Hercules was the patron god of Herculaneum which was destroyed at the same time as Pompeii. The gods were amplified humanity, not divinity. Like the Greeks, the Romans had no infinite god. This being so, they had no sufficient reference point intellectually; that is, they did not have anything big enough or permanent enough to which to relate either their thinking or their living. Consequently, their value system was not strong enough to bear the strains of life, either individual or political. All their gods put together could not give them a sufficient base for life, morals, values, and final decisions. These gods depended on the society which had made them, and when this society collapsed the gods tumbled with it. Thus, the Greek and Roman experiments in social harmony (which rested on an elitist republic) ultimately failed.

In the days of Julius Caesar (100-44 B.C.), Rome turned to an authoritarian system centered in Caesar himself. Before the days of Caesar, the senate could not keep order. Armed gangs terrorized the city of Rome, and the normal processes of government were disrupted as rivals fought for power. Self-interest became more significant than social interest, however sophisticated the trappings. Thus, in desperation the people accepted authoritarian government. As Plutarch (A.D. 50?-120) put it in *Lives of the Noble Greeks and Romans,* the Romans made Caesar dictator for life "in the hope that the government of a single person would give them time to breathe after so many civil wars and calamities. This was indeed a tyranny avowed, since his power now was not only absolute, but perpetual, too."

After Caesar's death, Octavian (63 B.C.-A.D. 14), later called

Caesar Augustus, grandnephew of Caesar, came to power. He had become Caesar's son by adoption. The great Roman poet Virgil (70-19 B.C.) was a friend of Augustus and he wrote the *Aeneid* with the object of showing that Augustus was a divinely appointed leader and that Rome's mission was to bring peace and civilization to the world. Because Augustus established peace externally and internally and because he kept the outward forms of constitutionality, Romans of every class were ready to allow him total power in order to restore and assure the functioning of the political system, business, and the affairs of daily life. After 12 B.C. he became the head of the state religion, taking the title *Pontifex Maximus* and urging everyone to worship the "spirit of Rome and the genius of the emperor." Later this became obligatory for all the people of the Empire, and later still, the emperors ruled as gods. Augustus tried to legislate morals and family life; subsequent emperors tried impressive legal reforms and welfare programs. But a human god is a poor foundation and Rome fell.

It is important to realize what a difference a people's worldview makes in their strength as they are exposed to the pressure of life. That it was the Christians who were able to resist religious mixtures, syncretism, and the effects of the weaknesses of Roman culture speaks of the strength of the Christian world-view. This strength rested on God's being an infinite-personal God and His speaking in the Old Testament, in the life and teaching of Jesus Christ, and in the gradually growing New Testament. He had spoken in ways people could understand. Thus the Christians not only had knowledge about the universe and mankind that people cannot find out by themselves, but they had absolute, universal values by which to live and by which to judge the society and the political state in which they lived. And they had grounds for the basic dignity and value of the individual as unique in being made in the image of God.

Perhaps no one has presented more vividly to our generation the inner weakness of imperial Rome than has Fellini (1920-) in his film *Satyricon*. He reminded us that the classical world is not to be romanticized, but that it was both cruel and decadent as it came to the logical conclusion of its world-view.

A culture or an individual with a weak base can stand only when the pressure on it is not too great. As an illustration, let us think of a Roman bridge. The Romans built little humpbacked bridges over many of the streams of Europe. People and wagons went over these structures safely for centuries, for two millennia. But if people today drove heavily loaded trucks over these bridges, they would break. It is this way with the lives and value systems of individuals and cultures when they have nothing stronger to build on than their own limitedness, their own finiteness. They can stand when pressures are not too great, but when pressures mount, if *then* they do not have a sufficient base, they crash—just as a Roman bridge would cave in under the weight of a modern six-wheeled truck. Culture and the freedoms of people are fragile. Without a sufficient base, when such pressures come only time is needed—and often not a great deal of time—before there is a collapse.

The Roman Empire was great in size and military strength. It reached out over much of the known world. Its roads lead over all of Europe, the Near East, and North Africa. The monument to Caesar Augustus at Turbi (just above modern Monte Carlo) marks the fact that he opened the roads above the Mediterranean and defeated the proud Gauls. In one direction of Roman expansion the Roman legions passed the Roman city Augusta Praetoria in northern Italy which today is called Aosta, crossed the Alps, and came down the Rhone Valley in Switzerland past the peaks of the Dents du Midi to that place which is now Vevey. For a time the Helvetians, who were Celtic and the principal inhabitants of what is now Switzerland, held them in check and made the proud Romans pass under the yoke. The Swiss painter Charles Gleyre (1806-1874), in a painting which now hangs in the art museum in Lausanne, has shown the conquered Roman soldiers, hands tied behind their backs, bending to pass under a low yoke. All this, however, was temporary. Not much could hold back the Roman legions, neither difficult terrain nor enemy armies. After the Romans had passed what is now St. Maurice and the peaks of the Dents du Midi, and as they flowed around Lake Geneva to modern Vevey, they marched over the hills and conquered the ancient Helvetian capitol, Aventicum, today called Avenches.

I love Avenches. It contains some of my favorite Roman ruins north of the Alps. Some have said (although I think it is a high figure) that at one time 40,000 Romans lived there. Today the ruins of Roman walls rise from the blowing wheat in the autumn. One can imagine a Roman legionary who had slogged home from the vastness of the north, mounting the hill and looking down on Avenches—a little Rome, as it were, with its amphitheater and its theater and temple. The opulence of Rome was at Avenches, as one sees by the gold bust of Marcus Aurelius which was found there. Gradually Christianity came to Roman Avenches. We know this by studying the cemetery of that time—the Romans burned their dead, the Christians buried theirs. One can find many monuments and towns similar to Turbi, Aosta, and Avenches all the way from Emperor Hadrian's wall, which the Romans built to contain the Scots (who were too tough to conquer), to the forts of the Rhine and North Africa, the Euphrates River, and the Caspian Sea.

Rome was cruel, and its cruelty can perhaps be best pictured by the events which took place in the arena in Rome itself. People seated above the arena floor watched gladiator contests and Christians thrown to the beasts. Let us not forget why the Christians were killed. They were *not* killed because they worshiped Jesus. Various religions covered the whole Roman world. One such was the cult of Mithras, a popular Persian form of Zoroastrianism which had reached Rome by 67 B.C. Nobody cared who worshiped whom so long as the worshiper did not disrupt the unity of the state, centered in the formal worship of Caesar. The reason the Christians were killed was because they were rebels. This was especially so after their growing rejection by the Jewish synagogues lost for them the immunity granted to the Jews since Julius Caesar's time.

We may express the nature of their rebellion in two ways, both of which are true. First, we can say they worshiped Jesus as God and they worshiped the infinite-personal God only. The Caesars would not tolerate this worshiping of the one God *only*. It was counted as treason. Thus their worship became a special threat to the unity of the state during the third century and during the reign of Diocletian (284-305), when people of the higher classes began to become Christians in larger numbers. If they had worshiped Jesus *and* Caesar, they would have gone unharmed, but they rejected all forms of syncretism. They worshiped the God who had revealed Himself in the Old Testament, through Christ, and in the New Testament which had gradually been written. And they worshiped Him as the *only* God. They allowed no mixture: All other gods were seen as false gods.

We can also express in a second way why the Christians were killed: No totalitarian authority nor authoritarian state can tolerate those who have an absolute by which to judge that state and its actions. The Christians had that absolute in God's revelation. Because the Christians had an absolute, universal standard by which to judge not only personal morals but the state, they were counted as enemies of totalitarian Rome and were thrown to the beasts.

As the Empire ground down, the decadent Romans were given to a thirst for violence and a gratification of the senses. This is especially evident in their rampant sexuality. For example, in Pompeii, a century or so after the Republic had become a thing of the past, the phallus cult was strong. Statues and paintings of exaggerated sexuality adorned the houses of the more affluent. Not all the art in Pompeii was like this, but the sexual representations were unabashedly blatant.

Even though Emperor Constantine ended the persecution of the Christians and Christianity became first (in 313) a legal religion, and then (in 381) the official state religion of the Empire, the majority of the people went on in their old ways. Apathy was the chief mark of the late Empire. One of the ways the apathy showed itself was in a lack of creativity in the arts. One easily observed example of the decadence of officially sponsored art is that the fourth-century work on the Arch of Constantine in Rome stands in poor contrast to its second-century sculptures which were borrowed from monuments from the period of Emperor Trajan. The elite abandoned their intellectual pursuits for social life. Officially sponsored art was decadent, and music was increasingly bombastic. Even the portraits on the coins became of poor quality. All of life was marked by the predominant apathy.

As the Roman economy slumped lower and lower, burdened with an aggravated inflation and a costly government, authoritarianism increased to counter the apathy. Since work was no longer done voluntarily, it was brought increasingly under the authority of the state, and freedoms were lost. For example, laws were passed binding small farmers to their land. So, because of the general apathy and its results, and because of oppressive control, few thought the old civilization worth saving.

Rome did not fall because of external forces such as the invasion by the barbarians. Rome had no sufficient inward base; the barbarians only completed the breakdown—and Rome gradually became a ruin.

CHAPTER TWO

The Middle Ages

With the breakdown of Roman order and the invasions came a time of social, political, and intellectual turmoil. The artists of the Middle Ages forgot many technical things, such as the use of that type of perspective which the Romans employed in their paintings and mosaics. Roman painting had been full of life. In the early days Christian art was also full of life. One can think of the catacombs where the figures on the walls were realistically though simply portrayed. For all the limitations of the visual means, the people were real people in a very real world.

A parallel can be drawn between the "living" quality of this early Christian art and the living Christianity of the early church. Leaders like Ambrose of Milan (339-397) and Augustine (354-430) strongly emphasized a true biblical Christianity. Later in the church there was an increasing distortion away from the biblical teaching, and there also came a change in art. Interesting examples of a carry-over of the earlier, more living Christian art are the mosaics in the Arian Church of St. Lorenzo in Milan. These mosaics are probably from the mid-fifth century. The Christians portrayed in these mosaics were not symbols but real people.

Michael Gough in *The Origins of Christian Art* (1973) writes of the change from "the acceptance of an element of naturalistic realism to a preference for the fantastic and unreal." He also points out that by the mid-sixth century "the last vestiges of realism were abandoned." The Byzantine art became characterized by formalized, stylized, symbolic mosaics and icons. In one way there was something good here—in that the artists made their mosaics and icons as a witness to the observer. Many of those who made these did so with devotion, and they were looking for more spiritual values. These were pluses. The minuses were that in the portrayal of their concept of spirituality they set aside nature and the importance of the humanity of people.

Since A.D. 395 the Roman Empire had been divided into eastern and western portions. The Byzantine style developed in the east and gradually spread to the west. This art had a real beauty, but increasingly only religious themes were given importance, and people were depicted not as real people but as symbols. This came to its climax in the ninth, tenth, and eleventh centuries. The portrayal of nature was largely abandoned, and even more unhappily, the living, human element was removed. This, we should stress once more, was in contrast to the early Christian catacomb paintings in which, though simply portrayed, real people lived in a real world which God had made.

Ravenna was a center of the Byzantine mosaics in the west, a center brought to its greatness by the eastern Emperor Justinian, though he never visited it. Justinian, who ruled from 527 to 565, built many churches in the east, the most famous being Hagia Sophia in Constantinople, which was consecrated in 537. These new churches of the east stressed the interior, placing an emphasis on light and color.

During this time there was a decline in learning in the west, though the growing monastic orders, gradually organized around the rule of Benedict (480?-547?), provided a depository for many of the things of the past. Benedict himself had built a monastery on Monte Cassino near the main road from Naples to Rome. In the monasteries the old manuscripts were copied and recopied. Thanks to the monks, the Bible was preserved—along with sections of Greek and Latin classics. The old music, too, was sometimes kept alive by constant repetition. Some of the music came from Ambrose, who had been bishop of Milan from 374 to 397 and who had introduced to his people antiphonal psalmody and the singing of hymns.

Nevertheless, the pristine Christianity set forth in the New Testament gradually became distorted. A humanistic element was added: increasingly, the authority of the church took precedence over the teaching of the Bible. And there was an ever-growing emphasis on salvation as resting on man's meriting the merit of Christ, instead of on Christ's work alone. While such humanistic elements were somewhat different in content from the humanistic elements of the Renaissance, the concept was essentially the same in that it was man taking to himself that which belonged to God. Much of Christianity up until the sixteenth century was either reaction against or reaffirmation of these distortions of the original Christian, biblical teaching.

These distortions generated cultural elements which mark a clear alternative to what we could otherwise call a Christian or biblical culture. Part of the fascination of medieval studies is to trace the degree to which different aspects of the complex Western cultural inheritance were emphasized or deemphasized according to the moral and intellectual response of people to the Christian God they claimed to worship. It would be a mistake to suppose that the overall structure of thought and life was not Christian. Yet it would be equally mistaken to deny that into this structure were fitted alien or half-alien features—some of Greek and Roman origin, others of local pagan ancestry—which at times actually obscured the outlines of the Christianity underneath.

This was not and is not a peculiarly medieval problem. From the earliest days of the Christian church, when Christianity was a small minority movement, believers had struggled with their personal and corporate response to Christ's prayer that they be *in* the world but not *of* it. On one level, this challenged Christians in their attitude toward material possessions and style of living. Not only in the time of Peter and Paul but for generations after, believers were noted for openhanded generosity. Even their enemies admitted it.

On another level, this raised the issue of God's law as against the will of the state, especially when the two came into conflict. During the persecutions of the Christians under the Roman emperors, the action of the Roman military commander Maurice is a good example of a possible response. When he received an order to direct a persecution of Christians, he handed his insignia to his assistant in order to join the Christians and be killed as a fellow believer. This action took place in the Rhone valley in Switzerland about A.D. 286, against a giant cliff just under the peaks of the Dents du Midi. It is for him that the little town of St. Maurice is now named.

Finally, on the intellectual level, Christ's prayer posed the problem of whether or not it was edifying to read or quote the non-Christian classical authors. Tertullian (160-240) and Cyprian (200?-258) decided not, but they proved to be in the minority. It is interesting that in the area of music a strict view did prevail. The reason for the disappearance of the traditions of Roman musical practices in the beginning of the Middle Ages was that the church looked with indignation on the social occasions and pagan religious exercises connected with them. And thus the old Roman musical traditions disappeared.

In the Middle Ages proper, which everyone defines his own way but which we will call the period from about 500 to 1400, we can trace in general terms the continuing response to these same issues. Concerning material possessions, the pendulum swung back and forth between utter disregard of the command to live modestly (caring for the poor, orphaned, and widowed) and a razor-sharp application of these same injunctions (the early monastic ideal to have no money). Thus, at one extreme one could have a papal court popularly rebuked for its material lust. The twelfth-century *Gospel According to the Mark of Silver* pictured the pope egging on his cardinals to fleece litigants at the papal court, using phrases deliberately mimicking Christ's teachings: "For I have given you an example, that ye also should take gifts, as I have taken them," and "Blessed are the rich, for they shall be filled; blessed are they that have, for they shall not go away empty; blessed are the wealthy, for theirs is the Court of Rome." John of Salisbury (1115?-1180), friend of Thomas à Becket and no enemy of the church hierarchy, told a pope to his face that people thought that "the Roman Church, which is the Mother of all Churches, behaves more like a stepmother than a mother. The Scribes and Pharisees sit there placing on men's shoulders burdens too heavy to be borne. They load themselves with fine clothes and their tables with precious plate; a poor man can seldom gain admittance. . . ." In the midst of all this, Saint Francis (1182?-1226), recognizing the corrupting effect of this emphasis on wealth, forbade his followers to receive money at all.

Even if its upper echelon was far from pure, the church did make an effort to control the destructive effects of exorbitant money-lending by first prohibiting it and later trying to limit the interest rate on loans to an accepted market level. With further support of secular rulers, the church also sought to enforce just prices, by which it meant prices which did not exploit human beings through selfish manipulation or through hoarding goods during scarcity. However much one may argue about the success of these attempts at economic control in the name of love for one's neighbor, it would be false to assume no difference between a society which at least makes repeated public efforts to control greed and economic cruelty and a society which tends to glorify the most expert economic manipulators of their fellow-citizens.

Even beyond this, the medieval economic teaching was not wholly negative. It exalted the virtue of honest, well-executed work. This is no better illustrated than in the beautiful late-medieval Books of Hours, private prayer books in which typical occupations are depicted as month succeeds month. The most famous of such books belonged to Jean, duc de Berry, and was executed by the Limbourg brothers in 1415. An earlier illustration of the same thing was the series of reliefs from the early fourteenth century on the Campanile in Florence. And if age or infirmity precluded work, the church provided society with an impressive network of hospitals and other charitable institutions. One in Siena is still in working order. The downstairs women's ward, just through the main entrance, has a fifteenth-century display of frescoes illustrating what went on in a medieval hospital. If twentieth-century patients are grateful for modern medical advances, they can at the same time admire the superior artistic taste of the old Sienese interior decorators. Nowadays we expect the state to provide hospitals or deal out charity, and this expectation underlines a vast change in the powers of the modern state as against its medieval counterpart. But the state, strong or weak, has always posed a problem to the church, especially when it concerns questions of moral principle. To this area we must now turn.

The medieval situation was at the same time easier and more complex than it had been for the Roman officer Maurice. It was easier insofar as Europe was regarded as Christ's kingdom—Christendom. Thus, Christian baptism was not only spiritually but socially and politically significant: it denoted entrance into society. Only a baptized person was a fully accepted member of European society. A Jew was a nonperson in this sense, and for this reason he could engage in occupations (such as moneylending) which were otherwise forbidden. But if the church baptized or consecrated the state, this only made more complex the problem of conscience, because a government which is to all appearances in tune with society can, for that very reason, betray society with the greatest impunity. This, of course, was and is true of the church as an organization, too.

Probably the greatest artistic study of this subject produced in the medieval era is Ambrogio Lorenzetti's (c. 1290-1348) *Allegory of Good and Bad Government,* painted in 1338 and 1339 for the council chamber in the great Palazzo Pubblico (town hall) in Siena. Lorenzetti clearly distinguishes between good and bad government, showing on one side the devil presiding over all those vices which destroy community, and on the other side the Christian virtues from which flow all those activities—including honest toil—which manifest oneness between men under God. Considering our own day, it is interesting that one of the marks which is shown characterizing good government is that it is safe for a woman to walk alone in the streets, while under bad government she is subject to being attacked, raped, or robbed. However, as the painter knew well enough from Siena's own turbulent city politics, if the sources of good and evil were distinct, the effects were humanly mixed together in a more or less jumbled heap of good and bad intentions.

Looking at medieval reality, one observes the same mixed record with respect to state power in financial matters. The church, though often indeed furnishing models of effective economic and political management, was so involved with other medieval institutions that it was frequently difficult for it to be salt to its society. For example, estate management and various types of agricultural pioneering were most notably enterprised by the self-same monastic orders which, in their infancy, were dedicated not to profit but to poverty. Also, if we are looking for a model of effective centralizing monarchy guided by an efficient bureaucratic apparatus, we need travel no farther than the church court in Rome. The pope—who was called the Servant of Servants—was, by a choice irony, the most effective medieval monarch at the height of papal power between 1100 and 1300.

To leave off the discussion here, however, would be to caricature the church-state situation. For, if the church provided a model for absolute power, it also generated an impressive though eventually thwarted challenge to personal monarchy. Many people are familiar with the parliamentary assemblies in the Middle Ages; most are less aware that the Conciliar Movement in the late-medieval church was another potent force for decentralization. The Conciliar Movement stood for a revival of the idea that real authority in the church is vested not in one bishop, the pope, but in all the bishops together—in a council. Thus the Council of Constance (1414-1418) deposed three rival popes, thereby ending a scandalous epoch in church history, while at the same time declaring that the council's authority came directly from Christ and that all men, including the pope, were subject to its authority in questions of faith and church reform. The Conciliar Movement, however, was destined to wither and disappear; the principle of monarchy rather than of representative government would triumph within the Roman church.

Meanwhile, paradoxical as it may seem, the church, through its frequent tussles with secular rulers over the boundary between church power and state power, had encouraged the evolution of a tradition of political theory which emphasized the principle of governmental limitation and responsibility. There was, in other words, a limit—in this case, an ecclesiastical one—on worldly power; and the theme of kingship balanced by priesthood and prophetic office is important in the statuary of Chartres and many of the great Gothic cathedrals.

To complete our analysis we must also consider the relationship between Christian and classical thought in the Middle Ages. The writings of Greek and Roman thinkers who had such an impact upon Renaissance and post-Renaissance culture were in many cases available to be read because their works had been preserved, read, and discussed by medieval intellectuals. So how did the Middle Ages handle its pagan culture heritage? It is important to assert that although early Christians like Cyprian (d. 258) and Tertullian (d. c. 230) had a strictly negative attitude toward classical Greek and Roman learning, Paul had not been so inhibited. When it was to his purpose, he cited Greek authors just as he at other times employed the subtle rabbinic lines of reasoning which he had mastered as a pupil of the great Rabbi Gamaliel (d. pre-A.D. 70), grandson of the yet greater Rabbi Hillel (70 B.C.?-A.D. 10). Ambrose (339-397), Jerome (347-419) and Augustine (354-430), following Paul rather than Tertullian, learned to appreciate and utilize classical learning. Indeed, they set out thoroughly to domesticate it within the context of a majestic curriculum of

Christian education which became the general model followed right up to the Renaissance. But if a robust Christian faith could handle non-Christian learning without compromising, it was all too easy for Greek and Roman thought-forms to creep into the cracks and chinks of a faith which was less and less founded on the Bible and more and more resting on the authority of church pronouncements. By the thirteenth century the great Aquinas (1225-1274) had already begun, in deference to Aristotle (384-322 B.C.), to open the door to placing revelation and human reason on an equal footing.

We will consider this in detail later, but first we must conclude this whirlwind tour through the medieval centuries by looking at some of its most outstanding artistic achievements—achievements, in the main, of the church. Remembering that this church was universal in its European context, we should not be surprised that it worked along with society as a whole, particularly the leaders of society, to produce its greatest artistic monuments. This is very well emphasized in one of the founder-figures of the Middle Ages, Charlemagne (742-814), and in Carolingian culture as a whole.

Charlemagne, son of Pippin, became king of the Franks in 768 and was crowned emperor by Pope Leo III in Rome on Christmas Day of 800. He was a formidable man with colossal energy. He was also a great warrior and constantly on campaign. After he gained control over much of the western European territory formerly in the Roman Empire, his coronation by the pope as a Roman-style emperor followed easily. In return he strengthened the church in many ways, giving the pope a strong land base in Italy and also supporting the Anglo-Saxon missionaries in the areas he conquered, especially among the Germanic tribes. Charlemagne made tithing compulsory, and this supplied funds for the establishment of church administration. He also built impressive churches, including the Palatine Chapel, consecrated in 805 at Aachen (located in what is now West Germany), the home of his old age.

Under Charlemagne, the church became a more general cultural force. Church power became coextensive with state power, and culturally the two spheres fed one another. Scholars were encouraged, and though their work was not very original, there was a restirring through sheer industry, enthusiasm, and systematic propagation. Scholars came from all over Europe to Charlemagne's court; for example, Alcuin (735-804) came all the way from York in northern England when he was fifty years old. He became Charlemagne's advisor, head of the palace school at Aachen, and attracted a constellation of scholars to join him there. Charlemagne invited singers from Rome to his court and founded a school of song which he personally supervised. In short, Charlemagne and his scholar-courtiers laid a base for the unity of ideas throughout western Europe. This unity was certainly aided by the invention of the beautiful Carolingian minuscule script, a handwriting which was widely copied. But, note carefully, all of Charlemagne's scholars were clergy. Learning was not general. We still remember those days in our English language—our word *clerk* is related to the word *cleric,* that is, a member of the clergy. It seems that though Charlemagne himself learned to read, he never learned to write.

With the scholarly revival of the Carolingian Age, there also came an artistic revival. People in later centuries wondered at the costly and exquisite jewels, religious objects, and books. Most of these—like a talisman of Charlemagne which contained a relic, and an ivory bookbinding of the crucifixion—emphasize the religious orientation of the artistic revival of that time.

In considering the culture of the Middle Ages, we must not overlook its music. Pope Gregory I (pope from 590 to 604) brought the music of the western church into a systematic whole. This impersonal, mystical, and other-worldly music is named after him: the Gregorian chant or plainsong, a monophony. From about 1100 to 1300 there were the *troubadours,* a title which means "inventors" or "finders." They were mainly aristocratic poet-musicians of southern France who inaugurated a flowering of secular music. From 1150 to 1300 was the period of a distinct epoch of music called *ars antiqua*—which developed various forms of polyphonic compositions. The instruments of the Middle Ages were psalteries, flutes, shawms (a double-reed wind instrument of the oboe family), trumpets, and drums. The universal folk instrument was the bagpipe. There were also the great organs in the churches, and smaller, portable organs. With the rise of *ars nova* in the fourteenth century in France and Italy, for the first time composers began to be known by name. Guillaume de Machaut (c. 1300-1377), a canon at the cathedral at Rheims, is the outstanding representative of French *ars nova* music. In Italy, Francesco Landini (1325-1397) of Florence was the foremost Italian musician of the fourteenth century.

When we think of the artistic achievements of the Middle Ages, we usually think of architecture. It would be impossible to speak of the gradually awakened cultural thought of the Middle Ages and not consider the developments in architecture in some detail. Let us start with the first great medieval style—the eleventh-century Romanesque, whose essential distinguishing marks are the rounded arch, thick walls, and dim interiors. With the original developments in Romanesque architecture came a leap forward. Because Romanesque, as the name suggests, looked back to Roman styles, it owed a lot to Carolingian churches, such as the Palatine Chapel (ninth century) modeled on San Vitale at Ravenna (sixth century) and such early Christian churches as St. Paul's-Outside-the-Walls in Rome (fourth century). But whereas in Italy architects remained slavishly tied to the old Roman style, as in Romano-Byzantine San Marco in Venice whose plan was from the eleventh century, one can see in French and English churches the creative adaptation which made the style Roman-*esque*, rather than just Roman. In France the abbey churches of Vézelay from the eleventh and twelfth centuries, and Fontevrault from the twelfth century exemplify this.

The crucial moment in England came with the Norman invasion in 1066. The Chapel of St. John in the White Tower of the Tower of London was built about 1080. Winchester Cathedral was built between 1079 and 1093, and Durham Cathedral was begun in 1093. The latter is one of the primary sources of the rib-vault—as our eyes follow the columns upwards, our gaze is carried to ribs in the ceiling. This prepared the ground for the later Gothic architecture.

Then, in 1140, Abbot Suger supervised the building of the abbey of Saint-Denis. Now surrounded by a rather depressing suburb of Paris, it is one of the places of wonder of the world, for here the Gothic style was born and the awakened cultural patterns of the Middle Ages took another great leap forward. Whoever designed the choir of Saint-Denis invented the Gothic style. Here the Gothic was born, with its pointed arches, the lightness supplied by its many large high windows, and its clerestory (the windows set high in the walls which allow light to stream down from above). Out of the Gothic also came the wonder of the rose window as well as the flying buttress, which, by taking the weight of the outward thrust of the walls caused by the weight of the roof, enabled the walls to be thinner and the windows larger. When we see the Cathedral of Chartres, begun in 1194, we see the

Gothic in all its purity: the pointed arch, the flying buttress, and the rib-vault. At Chartres, too, we have fine examples of advance in sculpture, for instance in the west facade. One could date the early or classic Gothic from 1150 to 1250, and the late Gothic (which was more ornate, especially in England) from 1250 to 1500.

Florence showed marks of the Gothic in its art from the thirteenth century onward. Arnolfo (1232-1302), who worked on the old palace beginning at 1266 and began the cathedral in Florence, in 1294, worked in the Gothic style. Although the Florentine Gothic was never a fully developed Gothic, the earlier Gothic of northern Europe did have its influence. Santa Trinita (second half of the thirteenth century), Santa Maria Novella (1278-1360), Santa Croce (commenced 1295) were all built in the Gothic style, and the Loggia (1376-1382) is late Gothic. Although the Baptistry itself is Romanesque, the panels of the bronze South Door (1330-1336)—done by Andrea Pisano (c. 1290-1348), who was a friend of Giotto—are Gothic. In Lorenzo Ghiberti's (1378-1455) North Door, which he made between 1403 and 1424, Ghiberti still used the Gothic panel frames, though the subject matter within the panels was much more free. By the time Ghiberti reached the wonder of the eastern portal (1425-1452)—called by Michelangelo the Golden Gate of Paradise—the Gothic frames were completely gone and the Renaissance was in bloom. The transition from the Gothic period to the Renaissance period can be seen and felt most clearly at the wonderful doors of the Baptistry.

During the change from the Romanesque to the Gothic, Mariology began to grow in the church. The Romanesque churches were not dedicated to the Virgin, but the Gothic churches of France were overwhelmingly dedicated to her. Here again we see and feel a growing tension: the birth pangs of the Middle Ages were characterized by an awakened cultural and intellectual life and an awakened piety. Yet at the same time the church continued to move away from the teaching of early Christianity as distortions of biblical doctrine increased. Soon European thought would be divided into two lines, both of which have come down and influenced our own day: first, the humanistic elements of the Renaissance, and second, the Bible-based teaching of the Reformation.

When we approach the Renaissance we must not make either of two mistakes. First, as we have seen, we must not think that everything prior to the Renaissance had been completely dark. This false concept grew from the prejudice of the humanists (of the Renaissance and the later Enlightenment) that all good things began with the birth of modern humanism. Rather, the later Middle Ages was a period of slowly developing birth pangs. Second, while the Renaissance was a rich and wonderful period, we must not think that all which it produced was good for man.

In the last half of the eleventh century and into the twelfth century came a surge of activity which laid an economic foundation for the thirteenth-century peak of medieval culture. The population rose; integrated villages appeared, which increased the efficiency of agriculture; towns were planned on a convenient grid pattern. Even the Crusades became vehicles of economic expansion. By 1100 the heavy plow had become common, central to a process which historians regard as a revolution in cultivation. By the twelfth century water mills and windmills were common. This was a step forward in passing from the use of human and animal energy alone. The Greeks and Romans had never made this step. So with the heavy plow, the use of water and wind become a great leap forward. Italian towns became wealthy with oriental trade, and Flemish towns became rich through textiles. Gradually, the towns freed themselves from feudal restraints to achieve varying amounts of political freedom, expressed in the proud town halls erected in the fourteenth and fifteenth centuries.

The early universities also began to emerge. By the late thirteenth century there were universities at Paris, Orléans, Toulouse, Montpellier, Cambridge, Oxford, Padua, Bologna, Naples, Salerno, Salamanca, Coimbra, and Lisbon. These universities offered a rival education to one which was purely clerical. The vernacular languages began to be used in written form; for example, portions of the Bible were translated into French. In the tenth and eleventh centuries, the proclamations of "the peace of God" and later "the truce of God," while of doubtful success, were at least attempts to limit the wars between the nobles. And, of course, Romanesque and later Gothic architecture were great breakthroughs in the annals of human thought and achievement.

Having said all that, we must recognize that there eventually came a change which does merit the name *Renaissance*. But we should realize that it was not the rebirth of man; it was the rebirth of an idea about man. There was a change in thinking about man, a change which put man himself in the center of all things, and this change was expressed in the arts. The word *Renaissance,* taken to mean "rebirth," has less obvious meaning if applied at this time to political, economic, or social history, although changes of mentality do have an impact in all areas of life. But even where the word can be used without qualification, it should not be taken to imply that every aspect of the rebirth was a gain for mankind.

The Renaissance is normally dated at the fourteenth, fifteenth, and early sixteenth centuries, but to understand it we must look at events which led up to this, especially its philosophical antecedents during the Middle Ages. And that means considering in a bit more detail the thought of Thomas Aquinas (1225-1274). Aquinas was a Dominican. He studied at the universities of Naples and Paris, and later he taught in Paris. He was the outstanding theologian of his day and his thinking is still dominant in some circles of the Roman Catholic Church. Aquinas's contribution to Western thought is, of course, much richer than we can discuss here, but his view of man demands our attention. Aquinas held that man had revolted against God and thus was fallen, but Aquinas had an incomplete view of the Fall. He thought that the Fall did no affect man as a whole but only in part. In his view the will was fallen or corrupted but the intellect was not affected. Thus people could rely on their own human wisdom, and this meant that people were free to mix the teachings of the Bible with the teachings of the non-Christian philosophers.

This is well illustrated by a fresco painted in 1365 by Andrea da Firenze (?-1377) in the Spanish Chapel in Santa Maria Novella in Florence. Thomas Aquinas sits on a throne in the center of the fresco, and on the lower level of the picture are Aristotle, Cicero (106-43 B.C.), Ptolemy (active A.D. 121-151), Euclid (active around 300 B.C.) and Pythagoras (580?-? B.C.), all placed in the same category as Augustine. As a result of this emphasis, philosophy was gradually separated from revelation—from the Bible— and philosophers began to act in an increasingly independent, autonomous manner.

Among the Greek philosophers, Thomas Aquinas relied especially on one of the greatest, Aristotle (384-322 B.C.). In 1263 Pope Urban IV had forbidden the study of Aristotle in the universities. Aquinas managed to have Aristotle accepted, so the ancient non-Christian philosophy was reenthroned.

To understand what result this had, it is worthwhile to look at Raphael's (1483-1520) painting *The School of Athens* (c. 1510) to comprehend some of the discussions and influences which followed in the Renaissance period. The fresco is in the Vatican. In *The School of Athens* Raphael painted Plato with one finger pointed upward, which means that he pointed toward absolutes or ideals. In contrast, he pictured Aristotle with his fingers spread wide and thrust down toward the earth, which means that he emphasized particulars. By particulars we mean the individual things which are about us; a chair is a particular, as is each molecule which makes up the chair, and so on. The individual person is also a particular and thus you are a particular. Thomas Aquinas brought this Aristotelian emphasis on individual things—the particulars—into the philosophy of the late Middle Ages, and this set the stage for the humanistic elements of the Renaissance and the basic problem they created.

This problem is often spoken of as the nature-versus-grace problem. Beginning with man alone and only the individual things in the world (the particulars), the problem is how to find any ultimate and adequate meaning for the individual things. The most important individual thing for man is man himself. Without some ultimate meaning for a person (for me, an individual), what is the use of living and what will be the basis for morals, values, and law? If one starts from individual acts rather than with an absolute, what gives any real certainty concerning what is right and what is wrong about an individual action? The nature-and-grace tension or problem can be pictured like this:

Grace, the higher: *God the Creator;* heaven and heavenly things; the unseen and its influence on the earth; *unity,* or universals or absolutes which give existence and morals meaning.

Nature, the lower: *the created;* earth and earthly things; the visible and what happens normally in the cause-and-effect universe; what man as man does on the earth; *diversity,* or individual things, the particulars, or the individual acts of man.

Beginning from man alone, Renaissance humanism—and humanism ever since—has found no way to arrive at universals or absolutes which give meaning to existence and morals.

Aquinas's teaching had a *positive* side in that before his time there was little emphasis on the normal, day-to-day world, that is, the world and our relationship to it. These things do have importance be ause God has created the world. By the mid-thirteenth century, certain Gothic sculptors had begun to fashion leaves and flowers and birds, and had given these figures a more natural appearance. Thanks to Thomas Aquinas, the world and man's place in the world was given more prominence than previously. The *negative* result of his teaching was that the individual things, the particulars, tended to be made independent, autonomous, and consequently the meaning of the particulars began to be lost. We can think of it as the individual things, the particulars, gradually and increasingly becoming everything and thus devouring all meaning until meaning disappears.

Two things, then, laid the foundation for what was now to follow: first, the gradually awakened cultural thought and awakened piety of the Middle Ages; and second, an increasing distortion of the teaching of the Bible and the early church. Humanist elements had entered. For example, the authority of the church took precedence over the teaching of the Bible; fallen man was considered able to return to God by meriting the merit of Christ; and there was a mixture of Christian and ancient non-Christian thought (as Aquinas's emphasis on Aristotle). This opened the way for people to think of themselves as autonomous and the center of all things.

The unfortunate side of the Renaissance was the reaffirmation of the distortions. But soon there would be steps in another direction—a reaction against the distortions. There were earlier stirrings in this direction, but an important step came when an Oxford professor named John Wycliffe (c. 1320-1384) taught that the Bible was the supreme authority and produced his English translation of the Bible, raising a voice which had influence throughout Europe. John Huss (1369-1415) was influenced by Wycliffe. He also spoke out, affirming the Bible as the only final authority, emphasizing a return to the teaching of Scripture and the early church, and insisting that man must return to God through the work of Christ only. These teachings of Wycliffe and Huss moved away from the humanism which had gradually but increasingly entered the church. Thus the way was now open for two movements which were to have their influence down into our own day: the humanistic elements of the Renaissance and the scriptural Christianity of the Reformation.

CHAPTER THREE

The Renaissance

The positive side of Thomas Aquinas's thinking was soon felt in art. Before Giotto (1267?-1337), Florentine painting was merely a less polished form of Byzantine art—flat and without depth. For example, Mary and Christ were not portrayed realistically; they were not so much *pictured,* as represented by symbols. Five hundred years had made no real change in Florentine art.

With Giotto, whose teacher was Cimabue (1240-1302), came a radical change. Giotto gave nature a more proper place, and his people were real people. Giotto's first great work, produced in Padua in 1304, was a picture of the Last Judgment. In this he painted a genuine likeness of Enrico Scrovegni, the man who had commissioned the picture. Giotto's work did, however, have some technical flaws. For one thing, he never mastered the technique of having people's feet fastened on the earth. His figures all seem to stand on tiptoe. And his people are much larger in scale than the world around them—hills, houses, and trees are too small for the size of the people. Nevertheless, Giotto took a huge step toward giving nature its rightful place. That is proper, for, because God made the world, nature is indeed important—and nature was now being portrayed more like it actually is. Giotto also began to show the versatility which was to characterize Renaissance man. At the end of his lifetime he designed the bell tower, the Campanile, next to the cathedral in Florence (1334-1337).

The positive drift toward an art in which nature had more emphasis occurred not only in painting but also in writing. The writers wrote the way the painters painted. Specifically Dante (1265-1321), who may have known Giotto and who refers to him in *The Divine Comedy* (1300-1320), wrote in the way Giotto painted. A native of Florence, exiled in 1302 because of his political activity, Dante was one of the first men to write important works in the vernacular. His writing has a deep and profound beauty and is a work of genius on its highest level. But in the development of the humanistic elements of the Renaissance, Dante followed the unfortunate side of Thomas Aquinas in mixing the Christian and the classical pagan world in allusions throughout his work. To mention two examples from *The Divine Comedy:* first, Dante's guide through hell is the Roman poet Virgil, who was to Dante what Aristotle was to Aquinas; second, the worst sinners in hell are Judas who betrayed Christ and Brutus and Cassius who betrayed Caesar.

It is interesting that the nature-versus-grace problem is clearly reflected in the contrast in Dante's writing between Beatrice and Dante's wife. All his life Dante loved Beatrice (whom he actually only saw a couple of times), and he held up their love as a romantic ideal. For example, in about 1293 he wrote *La Vita Nuova,* celebrating his love for Beatrice: "Seeing her face is so fair to see . . . love sheds such perfect sweetness over me." On the other hand, the wife he married in 1285 never had a place in his poetry. She was only for doing his cooking and rearing his children. Those in this school of thinking saw a strong contrast between two views of love—one totally sensual, the other totally spiritual. They understood that sensual love needs the spiritual to give it any real meaning beyond a physical response at the passing moment, but instead of keeping this as a unity, they allowed it to be separated into a kind of *upper* and *lower story.* The sensual love of the novelists and poets was the lower story; the spiritual, supposedly ideal love of the lyric poets was the upper story. This situation did not produce beauty but ugliness. The wife was a dray horse; the idealized woman, a disembodied phantom.

Other writers followed in Dante's train. Petrarch (1304-1374) is rightly called "the father of the new humanism." He had a deep enthusiasm for the classical Roman writers, such as Cicero, and a deep love for ancient Rome. Boccaccio (1313-1375), author of *The Decameron,* learned Greek in order to study the classics better. His translation of Homer was one of the foundation stones of the Renaissance, reviving Greek literature after 700 years of neglect. From Petrarch came a line of professional humanists. These paid men of letters translated Latin, wrote speeches, and acted as secretaries. They were largely laymen, like the Florentine chancellors Salutati (1331-1406) and Bruni (1370-1444). Their humanism meant, first of all, a veneration for everything ancient and especially the writings of the Greek and Roman age. Although this past age did include the early Christian church, it became increasingly clear that the sort of human autonomy that many of the Renaissance humanists had in mind referred exclusively to the non-Christian Greco-Roman world. Thus Renaissance humanism steadily evolved toward modern humanism—a value system rooted in the belief that man is his own measure, that man is autonomous, totally independent.

The enthusiasm for the Greek and Roman classics was further stimulated by two events. First, a church council in Florence in 1439 discussed relations with the Eastern Orthodox Church and so opened the way for contacts with Greek scholars. Second, the fall of Constintinople in 1453 resulted in an exodus of Greek scholars who brought manuscripts with them to Florence and other northern Italian cities. It was the humanists of that time who, under the enthusiasm for the classics, spoke of what had immediately preceded them as a "Dark Age" and talked of a "rebirth" in their own era. Harkening back to the pre-Christian era, they visualized man as taking a great forward leap. The concept of autonomous man was growing. In other words, humanism in the form it took in the Renaissance (and after the Renaissance) was being born.

There was indeed a positive side to all that was occurring: a new and proper emphasis on nature and the enjoyment of it. About 1340 Petrarch climbed a mountain, Mont Ventoux, in the south of France just to climb it—something brand-new. Though this ascent may seem trivial, it was a parallel in life to Giotto's painting of nature.

A bit later, in the early fifteenth century, architecture was beginning to change dramatically with Brunelleschi (1377-1446). His architecture shifted the emphasis from the Gothic back to the classical. His churches in Florence of San Lorenzo (1421-1434) and Santo Spirito (built in 1445-1482 from his designs) show his use of the classical form. In 1421 he began work on the Foundling Hospital, which can be said to be the first Renaissance building. His dome of the cathedral in Florence (1434) was an immense architectural breakthrough: it brought together great artistic triumph with an overwhelming feat of engineering. It was and is one of the wonders of the world in architectural engineering. It was not only an artistic expression, but it showed the high state of his grasp of mathematics. In this dome Brunelleschi went beyond any dome ever built before—including the Pantheon of ancient Rome.

To see the interplay of the arts in the Renaissance period, it is interesting to note that the musician Guillaume Dufay (c. 1400-1474) wrote a motet especially for the consecration of the dome built by Brunelleschi. Later, Michelangelo used Brunelleschi's dome as the model for the dome of St. Peter's. All this is especially impressive when one realizes that Brunelleschi was trained not as an architect but as a goldsmith, which again emphasizes the versatility of the men of the Renaissance. The Renaissance architects emphasized the simple geometrical forms of the square and circle. And Leonardo da Vinci (1452-1519) made drawings that fitted man himself into these simple forms. Brunelleschi worked out perspective, as did Ghiberti and Donatello (1386-1466), while Leone Battista Alberti (1404-1472) wrote the first treatise on its theory and technique. Perspective made possible a new way of depicting space. Brunelleschi, the master of space, also greatly influenced the painters and sculptors of his day by making open space an important factor in their artistic concepts.

But for the men of the Renaissance the new view of perspective was also something more: it placed man in the center of this space, and space became subordinated to mathematical principles spun out of the mind of man. The emphasis on man was coming out in other new ways. For example, we know very little about those who built the cathedrals in the Gothic era or about those who wrote the Gregorian chants. By contrast, Brunelleschi's biography was written in detail by a friend, and Cellini (1500-1571) later wrote about his own life in a swaggering autobiography in which he assumed that ordinary morality did not apply to a genius like himself. Now, too, for the first time, portraits became a generally accepted art form. The architect Alberti even made self-portraits.

Now we come to the next big step forward in the flow of the art of the Renaissance. Masaccio (1401-1428), who died as a young man of twenty-seven, has been called the father of Renaissance painting. He knew Brunelleschi and, in turn, his work influenced Ghiberti's work on the North Door of the Baptistry. The best place to see Masaccio's work is in the Brancacci Chapel, Church of the Carmelite Order in Florence. He seemed to have had a special relationship with the Carmelite Order, for he had already worked in one of their churches in Pisa. In the panels of this chapel where Masaccio and his master, Masolino (1383?-1447?), labored together, his work far surpassed his master's in its lifelikeness. When Masaccio left some work unfinished in the chapel, Filippino Lippi (1457-1504) was brought in fifty years later to complete it. Even though Lippi's contribution was so much later, Masaccio's work was still far superior to Lippi's. In Masaccio's work many faces were clearly portraits. He made studies from life and was able to give his work a true-to-life quality. Nature had thus now truly come to its proper place.

Masaccio was the first painter who consistently used central perspective, though Donatello's earlier relief *St. George and the Dragon* also showed some knowledge of this. The Romans never knew central, one-point perspective, though they used a kind of perspective, seen for example in the wall paintings of Pompeii. So in painting (as in Brunelleschi's dome in architecture) the men of the Florentine Renaissance surpassed the ancients. Masaccio also was the first to bring light into his paintings from the naturally correct direction. He painted so that his figures looked "in the round" and in the midst of a realized space. One can feel the atmosphere about Masaccio's figures, this sense of true atmosphere being caused by the combination of perspective plus light. In addition, his work had real composition; there was a balance to the total work in the relationship of the figures and the whole. Vasari (1511-1574), who was also an architect and painter, in *The Lives of the Painters, Sculptors and Architects* (1550), wrote that Masaccio was the first artist who painted people with their feet actually standing on the ground. One can see this by comparing Masolino's and Masaccio's *Adam and Eve* on two walls facing each other in the Carmine chapel. In short, in the painting of Masaccio there were a massive number of breakthroughs and firsts.

In the north of Europe, the same techniques were wrestled with by the Flemish painters, of whom Jan van Eyck was the greatest (c. 1390-1441). Van Eyck in the north worked at the same time as

Masaccio in the south in Italy. Van Eyck mastered light and air and placed a strong emphasis on nature. He also used a new technique of oil plus tempera. In this he preceded the painters in Italy. By 1420—earlier than the Italians—the Flemish painter Campin (1378?-1444) had made real portraits, and van Eyck followed. The painting by van Eyck of Rolin in *Madonna with Chancellor Rolin* (about 1436), for example, is a true portrait.

At an earlier period in the north than in the south, painters also were interested in landscapes. Van Eyck, who was doing landscapes as early as 1415-1420, was the first great master of this subject, the first great landscape artist. A number of paintings show this early interest, but let us examine just one: his *Adoration of the Lamb* (1432) in the Cathedral of St. Bavon in Ghent, Belgium. It is an altarpiece containing wonderful pictures of Eve, Adam, and singing angels. But most impressive is the central theme: the rich, the poor—people of all classes and backgrounds—coming to Christ. And who is this Christ? Van Eyck comprehended the biblical understanding of Christ as the Lamb of God who died on the cross to take away the moral guilt of those who accept Him as Savior. But this Christ is not now dead. He stands upright and alive on the altar, symbolizing that He died as the substitute, sacrificed, but He now lives! As van Eyck painted this, almost certainly he had Jesus' own words in mind, as Christ speaks in the Apocalypse, the last book in the Bible: "I am the living one that became dead, and behold, I am alive for evermore, Amen; and I have the keys of death and hades."

The background of this painting is marvelous, a real landscape. Soon the Flemish painters' work in natural backgrounds was copied in the south—for example, in the background of Piero della Francesca's (c. 1416-1492) *Duke of Urbino,* now in the Uffizi Gallery in Florence.

In passing, we should note that the north influenced the south in music as well as in painting. Josquin des Prez (1450-1521) was a Fleming who came to Italy and served in the court of Milan. He excelled in his music as a "tone painter." He was one of the great composers of all time, and had considerable influence on the development of Renaissance music in the south. Music in the Renaissance made both technical and artistic advances. Technically, for example, the first printer of music, Ottaviano Petrucci (1466-1539), worked in Venice and printed music with movable type in 1501. Artistically, perhaps the most significant innovation was the art of orchestration. The main instruments were the lute (the most popular solo instrument), sackbut (like a trombone), shawm, viol, drum, and krumhorn (a curved horn), along with an extraordinary variety of wind instruments, all built in sets so that one uniform timbre was available throughout the entire range from bass to soprano. This was in keeping with the Renaissance ideal of homogeneous sound. Music was important in the Renaissance, and popular interest in music soon led to the rise of opera in Florence.

It is crucial to notice that with Masaccio and the others up to this point, art could still have moved toward either a biblical or a nonbiblical concept of nature and the particulars (that is, the individual things, including the individual man). Up to this time it could have gone either way. It was good that nature was given a proper place. And there could have continued an emphasis on real people in a real world which God had made—with the particulars, the individual things, important because God made the whole world. Masaccio, as we have noted, pictured Adam and Eve as the Bible portrays them—as real people in a real world. Or at this point humanism could take over, with its emphasis on things being autonomous. Immediately after Masaccio, the die was cast and the movement went in this direction. Man made himself increasingly independent and autonomous, and with this came an increasing loss of anything which gave meaning, either to the individual things in the world or to man. With this we begin to see the dilemma of humanism which is still with us today.

This position and its dilemma is strikingly shown in a shift in art. In France, one sees this with Fouquet (c. 1416-1480) in his painting *The Red Virgin* (1450?). The word *red* refers to the overall color used in part of the picture. The girl was shown with one breast exposed, and everybody who knew the situation knew that this was a picture of the king's mistress, Agnès Sorel. Was this the Madonna about to feed her baby? No, the painting might be titled *The Red Virgin*, but the girl was the king's mistress; and when one looked at the painting one could see what the king's mistress's breast looked like. Prior to this time, Mary was considered very high and holy. Earlier she was considered so much above normal people that she was painted as a symbol. When in the Renaissance Mary was painted as a real person, this was an advance over the representations of Mary in the earlier age, because the Bible tells us that Mary was a real girl and that the baby Jesus was a real baby. But now not only was the king's mistress painted as Mary with all of the holiness removed, but the meaning, too, was being destroyed. At first it might have seemed that only the religious aspect was threatened. But, as we can see in retrospect, gradually the threat spread to all of knowledge and all of life. All meaning to all individual things or all particulars was removed. Things were being viewed as autonomous, and there was nothing to which to relate them or to give them meaning.

Let us now look at another aspect of art to show that humanism had taken over. In the Academy in Florence is Michelangelo's (1475-1564) great room. Here we see on either side Michelangelo's statues of men "tearing themselves out of the rock." These were sculpted between 1519 and 1536. They make a real humanistic statement: Man will make himself great. Man as Man is tearing himself out of the rock. Man by himself will tear himself out of nature and free himself from it. Man will be victorious.

As the room in the Academy is arranged, it strikingly sets forth humanistic thought. As we go past these men tearing themselves out of the rock, we come finally, at the focal point of the room, to the magnificent statue of *David* (1504). As a work of art it has few equals in the world. Michelangelo took a piece of marble so flawed that no one thought it could be used, and out of it he carved this overwhelming statue. But let us notice that the *David* was not the Jewish David of the Bible. *David* was simply a title. Michelangelo knew his Judaism, and in the statue the figure is not circumcised. We are not to think of this as the biblical David but as the humanistic ideal. Man is great!

The statue was originally planned to stand forty feet above the street on one of the buttresses of the cathedral, but was placed outside the city hall in Florence, where a copy now stands. The Medicis, the great banking family which had dominated Florence since 1434, had run the city by manipulating its republican constitution. A few years before *David* was made, the Medicis had been thrown down by the people and a more genuine republic restored (1494). Thus, as the statue was raised outside the city hall, though Michelangelo himself had been a friend of the Medicis, his *David* was seen by the populace as the slayer of tyrants. Florence was looking with confidence toward a great future.

The *David* was the statement of what the humanistic man saw himself as being tomorrow! In this statue we have man waiting with confidence in his own strength for the future. Even the disproportionate size of the hands says that man is powerful. This statue is idealistic and romantic. There was and is no man like the *David*. If a girl fell in love with the statue and waited until she found such a man, she would never marry. Humanism was standing in its proud self and the *David* stood as a representation of that. But there are signs that by the end of his life Michelangelo saw that humanism was not enough. Michelangelo in his later years was in close touch with Vittoria Colonna (1490-1547), a woman who had been influenced by Reformation thought. Some people feel they see some of that influence in Michelangelo's life and work. However that may be, it is true that his later work did change. Many of his early works show his humanism, as does his *David*. In contrast stand his later *Pietàs* (statues of Mary holding the dead Christ in her arms) in the cathedral in Florence and in the castle in Milan, which was probably his last. In the *Pietà* in the cathedral in Florence, Michelangelo put his own face on Nicodemus (or Joseph or Arimathea—whichever the man is), and in both of these *Pietàs* humanistic pride seems lessened, if not absent.

Another giant of the Renaissance, equal to Michelangelo, is Leonardo da Vinci (1452-1519) who historically stood at a crucial place. He was a chemist, musician, architect, anatomist, botanist, mechanical engineer, and artist. He was the embodiment of the true Renaissance man: he could do almost everything and do it well. The classic work *Leonardo da Vinci,* published in Italy and translated into English in 1963, contained a section by Giovanni Gentile (1875-1944) on Leonardo's thought-forms. He spells out the fact that Leonardo really grasped the problem of modern man. Leonardo anticipated where humanism would end.

Leonardo is generally accepted as the first modern mathematician. He not only knew mathematics abstractly but applied it in his *Notebooks* to all manner of engineering problems. He was one of the unique geniuses of history, and in his brilliance he perceived that beginning humanistically with mathematics one *only* had particulars. He understood that man beginning from himself would never be able to come to meaning on the basis of mathematics. And he knew that having only individual things, particulars, one never could come to universals or meaning and thus one only ends with mechanics. In this he saw ahead to where our generation has come: everything, including man, is the machine. Realizing this, Leonardo thought that perhaps the painter, the sensitive man, could come to meaning, so he tried to paint "the soul"—not the soul as a Christian thinks of it, but rather the universal. He attempted to paint one thing that would include all of that class of things.

As you will remember, Thomas Aquinas emphasized Aristotelian thought. Think back to Raphael's fresco in the Vatican, *The School of Athens*. There Plato pointed upward, Aristotle downward. Aristotelian thought was directed toward the particulars and led through Thomas Aquinas to all the subsequent problems of an emphasis on the particulars at the expense of meaning. But in Florence the emphasis gradually shifted to Plato (427?-347? B.C.). The western interest in Plato accelerated as Greek scholars fled after the fall of Constantinople in 1453 and brought their texts with them. Marsilio Ficino (1433-1499) taught neo-Platonic thinking to Lorenzo the Magnificent (1449-1492), and this thinking became important in Florence. He was an influence on Michelangelo and other artists such as Sandro Botticelli (1444-1510), as well as on Lorenzo and the thinkers surrounding him. As Aristotelian thought emphasized the particulars, neo-Platonic thought emphasized the universals. The early men of the Renaissance had tried to syncretize Christianity and Aristotelian thought, but had failed. Thereafter, men of the Renaissance tried to syncretize Christianity and Platonism—and likewise failed.

In the midst of these crosscurrents of thought, Leonardo tried to paint the universal, thinking that a painter might be able to achieve what the mathematicians could not. But he never was able to paint the universal on a humanistic basis, any more than the mathematician could provide a mathematical universal on a humanist basis. Leonardo, the humanistic man (beginning only from himself), failed both as the mathematician and also as the artist who tried to paint the universal out of his observation of the particulars. The humanists had been sure that man starting from himself could solve every problem. There was a complete faith in man. Man starting from himself, tearing himself out of the rock, out of nature, could solve all. The humanistic cry was, "I can do what I will; just give me until tomorrow." But Leonardo, in his brilliance, saw at the end of his life humanism's coming defeat.

There was a split between Leonardo's theory and the way it worked out in practice. He could not bring forth the universal or meaning in either mathematics or painting, and when King Francis I of France (1494-1547) brought Leonardo to the French court as an old man, Leonardo was in despondency. *As a man thinketh so is he*—and humanism had already begun to show that pessimism was its natural conclusion. Actually, we could say that we went to Renaissance Florence and found modern man!

CHAPTER FOUR

The Reformation

While the men of the Renaissance wrestled with the problem of what could give unity to life and specifically what universal could give meaning to life and to morals, another great movement, the Reformation, was emerging in the north of Europe. This was the reaction we mentioned at the end of our study of the Middle Ages—the reaction against the distortions which had gradually appeared in both a religious and a secular form. The High Renaissance in the south and the Reformation in the north must always be considered side by side. They dealt with the same basic problems, but they gave completely opposite answers and brought forth completely opposite results.

As we have seen, there had been forerunners of the Reformation. John Wycliffe (c. 1320-1384), whose life overlapped Giotto's, Dante's, Petrarch's and Boccaccio's, emphasized the Bible as the supreme authority, and he and his followers produced an English translation which had wide importance throughout Europe. John Huss of Bohemia (the heartland of modern Czechoslovakia) was a professor of the University of Prague (the Charles University). He lived between about 1369 and 1415. Thus his life overlapped Brunelleschi's, Masaccio's and van Eyck's. In contrast to

119

the humanistic elements which had come into the church—and which led to the authority of the church being accepted as equal to, or greater than, the authority of the Bible and which emphasized human work as a basis for meriting the merit of Christ—Huss returned to the teachings of the Bible and of the early church and stressed that the Bible is the only source of final authority and that salvation comes only through Christ and His work. He further developed Wycliffe's views on the priesthood of all believers. Promised safe conduct to speak at the Council of Constance, he was betrayed and burned at the stake there on July 6, 1415. Wycliffe's and Huss's views were the basic views of the Reformation which came later, and these views continued to exist in parts of the north of Europe even while the Renaissance was giving its humanist answers in the south. The Bohemian Brethren, the antecedents of the Moravian Church, were founded in 1457 by Huss's followers, and, like Luther's doctrines later, their ideas were spread not only by their teaching but by their emphasis on music and use of hymns. Huss himself wrote hymns which are still sung today. Another voice was the Dominican monk, Girolamo Savonarola, who drew large audiences in Florence between 1494 and 1498. He was not as clear as Wycliffe and Huss, but he did see some of the growing problems and spoke out against them until he was hanged and then his body burned in the square before the town hall in Florence.

Martin Luther (1483-1546) nailed his Ninety-five Theses to the church door in Wittenberg on October 31, 1517. To put this into historical perspective, we should remember that Leonardo da Vinci lived from 1452 to 1519. Thus, Luther's Theses were set forth just two years before Leonardo's death. Calvin was born in 1509, ten years before Leonardo's death, and the year Leonardo died Luther had his disputation in Leipzig with Dr. Eck. Francis I, who in 1516 took Leonardo to France (where Leonardo died), is the same Francis I to whom Calvin (1509-1564) addressed his *Institutes of the Christian Religion* in 1536.

One must understand that these two things were happening almost simultaneously: first, in the south, much of the High Renaissance was based on a humanistic ideal of man's being the center of all things, of man's being autonomous; second, in the north of Europe, the Reformation was giving an opposite answer. In other words, the Reformation was exploding with Luther just as the High Renaissance was coming to its close. As we have said,

Luther nailed his Theses to the door in Wittenberg in 1517. Zwingli led Zürich to its break with Rome in 1523. Henry VIII of England broke with Rome in 1534. (This was at first political rather than religious, but it did lead later to a Protestant England.) Then, as we have mentioned, Calvin's *Institutes* were written in 1536.

But while the Reformation and the Renaissance overlapped historically and while they dealt with the same basic questions, they gave completely different answers. You will remember that to Thomas Aquinas the *will* was fallen after man had revolted against God, but the *mind* was not. This eventually resulted in people believing they could think out the answers to all the great questions, beginning only from themselves. The Reformation, in contrast to Aquinas, had a more biblical concept of the Fall. For the people of the Reformation, people could *not* begin only from themselves and on the basis of human reason alone think out the answers to the great questions which confront mankind.

The men of the Reformation did learn from the new knowledge and attitudes brought forth by the Renaissance. A critical outlook, for example, toward what had previously been accepted without question was helpful. And while the Reformers rejected the scepticism of Lorenzo Valla (c. 1409-1457), they gladly learned from his study of language. But from the critical attitude toward the traditions which had been accepted without question, the Reformers turned not to man as beginning only from himself, but to the original Christianity of the Bible and the early church. Gradually they came to see that the church founded by Christ had since been marred by distortions. However, in contrast to the Renaissance humanists, they refused to accept the autonomy of human reason, which acts as though the human mind is infinite, with all knowledge within its realm. Rather, they took seriously the Bible's own claim for itself—that it is the only final authority. And they took seriously that man needs the answers given by God in the Bible to have adequate answers not only for how to be in an open relationship with God, but also for how to know the present meaning of life and how to have final answers in distinguishing between right and wrong. That is, man needs not only a God who exists, but a God who has spoken in a way that can be understood.

The Reformers accepted the Bible as the Word of God in all that it teaches. Luther translated the Bible into German, and translations of the Bible began to be available for the people in the languages they could understand. To the Reformation thinkers, authority was not divided between the Bible and the church. The church was *under* the teaching of the Bible—not above it and not equal to it. It was *sola scriptura*, the Scriptures only. This stood in contrast to the humanism that had infiltrated the church after the first centuries of Christianity. *At its core, therefore, the Reformation was the removing of the humanistic distortions which had entered the church.*

It is worth reiterating the ways in which the infiltration by humanistic thought—growing over the years but fully developed by 1500—showed itself. First, the authority of the church was made equal to the authority of the Bible. Second, a strong element of human work was added to the work of Christ for salvation. Third, after Thomas Aquinas there had come an increasing synthesis between biblical teaching and pagan thought. This synthesis was not just a borrowing of words but actually of content. It is apparent in many places and could be illustrated in many ways. For example, Raphael in one of his rooms in the Vatican balanced *The School of Athens* (which represents Greek non-Christian philosophic thought) with his pictoral representation of the church, putting them on opposite walls. This representation of the church is called the *Disputà*, for it deals with the nature of the mass. Raphael was par excellence the artist of the synthesis. But Michelangelo, on the ceiling of the Sistine Chapel in the Vatican, also combined biblical teaching and non-Christian pagan thought; he made the pagan prophetesses equal to the Old Testament prophets. Dante's writings show the same mixture.

When in Basel, Guillaume Farel (1489-1565), the Reformer in French-speaking Switzerland before Calvin, showed plainly that there was a second kind of humanism that he stood against, as well as that which had come into the church. This kind of humanism was exemplified most clearly by Erasmus of Rotterdam (1466?-1536). Erasmus helped the Reformers by editing the New Testament in the original Greek (1516) and by urging in the preface that the New Testament be translated into all the vernacular languages. Some have called the view of Erasmus and those with him *Christian humanism,* but it was less than consistent Christianity. Erasmus and his followers wanted only a limited reform of the church, in contrast to the Reformers who wanted to go back to the church as it originally was, with the authority being the Bible only. Thus Farel thoroughly cut himself off from Erasmus to make plain that he stood on principle against either form of humanism. The various branches of the Reformation had differences among themselves, but together they constituted one system—a unity—in contrast to the humanism which had come into the church on one side and to the Erasmian humanism on the outside.

The Reformation was certainly not a golden age. It was far from perfect, and in many ways it did not act consistently with the Bible's teaching, although the Reformers were trying to make the Bible their standard not only in religion but in all of life. No, it was not a golden age. For example, such overwhelming mistakes were made as Luther's unbalanced position in regard to the peasant wars, and the Reformers showed little zeal for reaching people in other parts of the world with the Christian message. Yet though they indeed had many and serious weaknesses, in regard to religious and secular humanism, they did return to the Bible's instruction and the example of the early church.

Because the Reformers did not mix humanism with their position, but took instead a serious view of the Bible, they had no problem of meaning for the individual things, the particulars; they had no nature-versus-grace problem. One could say that the Renaissance centered in autonomous man, while the Reformation centered in the infinite-personal God who had spoken in the Bible. In the answer the Reformation gave, the problem of meaning for individual things, including man, was so completely answered that the problem—as a problem—did not exist. The reason for this is that the Bible gives a unity to the universal and the particulars.

First, the Bible tells men and women true things about God. Therefore, they can know true things about God. One can know true things about God because God has revealed Himself. The word *God* was not contentless to Reformation man. God was not an unknown "philosophic other" because God had told man about Himself. As the Westminster Confession (1645-1647) says, when God revealed His attributes to people, the attributes are not only true to people but true to God. That is, when God tells people what He is like, what He says is not just relatively true but absolutely true. As finite beings, people do not have exhaustive truth about God, but they can have truth about God; and they can know, therefore, truth about that which is the ultimate universal. And the Bible speaks to men and women concerning meaning, morals, and values.

Second, the Bible tells us true things about people and about nature. It does not give men and women *exhaustive* truth about the world and the cosmos, but it does give truth about them. So one can know many true things about nature, especially *why* things exist and why they have the form they have. Yet, because the Bible does not give exhaustive truth about history and the cosmos, historians and scientists have a job to do, and their work is not meaningless. To be sure, there is a total break between God and His creation, that is, between God and created things; God is infinite—and created things are finite. But man can know both truth about God and truth about the things of creation because in the Bible God has revealed Himself and has given man the key to understanding God's world.

So, as the Reformation returned to biblical teaching, it gained two riches at once: It had no particulars-versus-universals (or meaning) problem, and yet at the same time science and art were set free to operate upon the basis of that which God had set forth in Scripture. The Christianity of the Reformation, therefore, stood in rich contrast to the basic weakness and final poverty of the humanism which existed in that day and the humanism which has existed since.

It is important that the Bible sets forth true knowledge about mankind. The biblical teaching gives meaning to all particulars, but this is especially so in regard to that particular which is the most important to man, namely, the individual himself or herself. It gives a reason for the individual being great. The ironic fact here is that humanism, which began with Man's being central, eventually had no real meaning for people. On the other hand, if one begins with the Bible's position that a person is created by God and created in the image of God, there is a basis for that person's dignity. People, the Bible teaches, are made in the image of God— they are nonprogrammed. Each is thus Man with dignity.

That Man is made in the image of God gives many important answers intellectually, but it also has had vast practical results, both in the Reformation days and in our own age. For example, in the time of the Reformation it meant that all the vocations of life came to have dignity. The vocation of honest merchant or housewife had as much dignity as king. This was strengthened further by the emphasis on the biblical teaching of the priesthood of all believers—that is, that all Christians are priests. Thus, in a very real sense, all people are equal as persons. Moreover, the government of the church by lay elders created the potential for democratic emphasis.

The Bible, however, also says that man is fallen; he has revolted against God. At the historic space-time Fall, man refused to stand in the proper relationship with this infinite reference point which is the personal God. Therefore, people are now abnormal. The Reformation saw all people as equal in this way, too—all are guilty before God. This is as true of the king and queen as the peasant. So, in contrast to the humanism of the Renaissance, which never gave an answer to explain that which is observable in people, the Bible enabled people to solve the dilemma facing them as they look at themselves: they could understand both their greatness and their cruelty.

The Bible gives a different way to come to God from that teaching which had grown up in the church through the previous centuries. The Reformers went back to the teaching of the Bible and the early church and removed the humanistic elements which had been added. The individual person, they taught, could come to God directly *by faith* through the finished work of Christ. That is, Christ's sacrifice on the cross was of infinite value, and people cannot do and need not do anything to earn or add to Christ's work. But this can be accepted as an unearned gift. It was *sola gratia,* grace only.

Previously, those who came into the churches were separated from what to them was the center of worship—the altar in the chancel—by a high grill of iron or wood. This was the *rood screen,* so called from the rood, or crucifix, which it often supported or which was hung above it. But with the Reformation, when the Bible was accepted in all its unique authority, these screens were often removed. In some churches the Bible was placed exactly where the screen had been, to show that the teaching of the Bible opened the way for all the people to come directly to God. One such church is in Ollon, Switzerland. You can still see where the rood screen had fit into the wall but was removed; the pulpit was then placed so that the Bible is where the rood screen had previously been.

Guillaume Farel, the early French-Swiss Reformer, preached in this church, and from there and nearby Aigle the Reformation began in French-speaking Switzerland. Later, after ministries in Geneva and Lausanne, Farel preached for many years in the cathedral in Neuchâtel. The statue outside that cathedral could well be taken as the mark of the Reformation and of Christianity. This statue has Farel holding the Bible aloft. Thus it is *sola scriptura,* the Bible and the Bible only. This is what made all the difference to the Reformers, both in understanding the approach to God and in having the intellectual and practical answers needed in this present life.

Because of their tendency toward purifying religion from an overemphasis on visual symbols, the Reformers are often accused of being antagonistic to the arts. But the Reformation was not against art as art. To some of us the statues and paintings of the Madonna, saints, and so on may be art objects, and perhaps we wish that the people of the Reformation had taken these works and put them in a warehouse for a hundred years or so. Then they could have been brought out and put in a museum. But at that moment of history this would have been too much to ask! To the men and women of that time, these were images to worship. The men of the Reformation saw that the Bible stressed that there is only one mediator between God and man, Christ Jesus. Thus, in the pressure of that historic moment, they sometimes destroyed the images—not as works of art but as religious images which were contrary to the Bible's emphasis on Jesus as the only mediator.

We should note, however, that the Reformers usually distinguished between *cult images* and other works of art, the former alone falling under condemnation. But not even all of the cult images were destroyed. All over Europe in cathedrals and churches we can see thousands of statues which were not destroyed. The reason why some statues were destroyed is pointed out by Bernd Moeller (1931-) in *Imperial Cities and the Reformation* (1962; English translation, 1972). He shows that in certain cases the actual donors of the images smashed them because they represented religiously that which they now rejected as unbiblical. He writes, "Those who donated an image did not merely venerate that image; those who broke an image did not merely hate it. Both the donor and the breaker of images were concerned with eternal salvation." Image-breaking parallels in the area of ecology the early Christians' cutting down the sacred groves of trees which were related to the worship of pagan gods. These believers did not cut down the trees because they minimized trees or despised nature; they cut down these specific trees because of their anti-Christian religious significance. Equally, the people of the Reformation did not destroy art objects as art objects. Unlike modern man, the men of that day did not live in a splintered world. Art was an intimate part of life. What is represented had more than an aesthetic value divorced from considerations of truth and religious significance.

The proof that the Reformation was not against art *as* art is seen in the effects of the Reformation on culture. We should not forget that Lucas Cranach (1472-1553), the German painter and engraver, was a friend of Luther and painted Luther and his wife many times. Cranach also painted Luther's father. The vocal parts of the 1524 hymnbook were probably engraved by Cranach. Luther and Cranach were even the godfathers of each other's children. There is no indication at all that Luther disapproved of Cranach's painting in all the varied forms that it took.

Then, too, we can think of the music which the Reformation brought forth. There was the lively Geneva Psalter, the 1562 hymnbook made up of the Psalms. The tunes were so vivacious that some people in derision called them "Geneva Jigs." The great Theodore Beza (1519-1605), who followed Calvin as leader of the Reformation in Geneva, translated the Psalms' texts, and these were set to melodies selected or composed by Louis Bourgeois (1510-1570). Later this Psalter was used in England, Germany, the Netherlands, and Scotland, as well as in Switzerland. But it was in Luther's Germany where the effects of the Reformation on music are best seen.

Luther himself was a fine musician. He was a singer with a good tenor voice as well as an instrumentalist with skill and verve. In 1524 his choirmaster, Johann Walther (1496-1570), put out a hymnbook (*Wittenberg Gesangbuch*) which was a tremendous innovation. Walther and his friend Conrad Rupff worked on these hymns in Luther's home. Luther himself played out the tunes on his fife. The collection contained Luther's own great hymn "A Mighty Fortress Is Our God," to which he wrote both words and music. As the rood screen was removed in the churches—because with an open Bible the people had direct access to God—so also in a direct approach to God the congregations were allowed to sing again for the first time in many centuries.

We are swept back in this, as in other things, to the practice as well as the teaching of the early church. We are carried back to Ambrose (339-397), bishop of Milan, and his antiphonal psalmody, as he, like Luther, wrote hymn texts and taught his congregations to sing them. Luther said in the preface to the *Wittenberg Gesangbuch,* "I wish that the young men might have something to rid them of their love ditties and wanton songs and might instead of these learn wholesome things and thus yield willingly to the good; also, because I am not of the opinion that all the arts shall be crushed to earth and perish through the Gospel, as some bigoted persons pretend, but would willingly see them all, and especially music, servants of Him who gave and created them."

Hymnwriters who later brought forth more complicated forms were Hans Leo Hassler (1564-1612) and Michael Praetorius (1571-1621). Heinrich Schütz (1585-1672) and Dietrich Buxtehude (1637-1707) should also be noted. Schütz was influenced by the baroque music of Giovanni Gabrieli (c. 1557-1612) from Venice, but in the Reformation this style took on its own character and direction. Buxtehude, the organist at Lübeck, had a profound influence on Bach. It is interesting to note that, two years before Bach came to hear Buxtehude at Lübeck, Handel (1685-1759) came there, not only intending to hear Buxtehude, but hoping to inherit Buxtehude's post. In the contract was a clause saying that the new organist was to marry Buxtehude's daughter. Handel did not take the position! The so-called *Abendmusiken* (late Sunday afternoon sacred concerts) were begun by Buxtehude, and both Handel and Bach went to hear them. The Reformation's influence on culture was not just for a favored elite but for all the people. There were also less-remembered men of the period who did remarkable work. We could think of Bach's predecessor as organist at Leipzig, Johann Kuhnau (1660-1722), who wrote biblical sonatas for the harpsichord in 1700.

Johann Sebastian Bach (1685-1750) was certainly the zenith of the composers coming out of the Reformation. His music was a direct result of the Reformation culture and the biblical Christianity of the time, which was so much a part of Bach himself. There would have been no Bach had there been no Luther. Bach wrote on his score initials representing such phrases as: "With the help of Jesus"—"To God alone be the glory"—"In the name of Jesus." It was appropriate that the last thing Bach the Christian wrote was "Before Thy Throne I Now Appear." Bach consciously related both the form and the words of his music to biblical truth. Out of the biblical context came a rich combination of music and words and a diversity with unity. This rested on the fact that the Bible gives unity to the universal and the particulars, and therefore the particulars have meaning. Expressed musically, there can be endless variety and diversity without chaos. There is variety yet resolution.

We must, of course, remember Handel who also stood in the same tradition. One naturally thinks of Handel's *Messiah* (1741), which was in the tradition of the restored Christianity in both its music and its message. Handel's religious music included not only the *Messiah* but *Saul* (c. 1738), *Israel in Egypt* (c. 1738) and *Samson* (1743). The *Messiah* could only have come forth in a setting where the Bible stood at the center. Even the order of the selections follows with extreme accuracy the Bible's teaching about the Christ as the Messiah. For example, Handel did not put the "Hallelujah Chorus" at the end, but in its proper place in the flow of the past and future history of Christ. Many modern performances often place it at the end as a musical climax, but Handel followed the Bible's teaching exactly and placed it at that future historic moment when the Bible says Christ will come back to rule upon the earth—at that point where the Bible prophetically (in the Book of Revelation) puts the cry of "King of kings and Lord of lords!" Handel probably knew Charles Wesley (1707-1788) and wrote the music for a hymn to original words by Wesley, "Rejoice, the Lord Is King."

In passing, we should note that English church music followed the same emphasis found in the early music of Reformation Germany. A demand arose for a simplified style which would permit the words to be understood. We could mention here Thomas Tallis (c. 1505-1585) and Orlando Gibbons (1583-1625). In England as in Germany the stress was on content. Music was not incidental to the Reformation's return to biblical teaching; it was a natural outcome, a unity with what the Bible taught. What the Reformation produced musically gives us a clear affirmation that the Reformation was indeed interested in culture. As this was true in music, it was also true in visual art. We have already mentioned Cranach. We must also notice Dürer (1471-1528), Altdorfer (1480-1538), Hans Baldung-Grien (c. 1484-1545), and the Beham brothers: Hans (1500-1550) and Barthel (1502-1540).

Some of the work of Albrecht Dürer was done before the Reformation; yet he must be considered a Reformation artist. In 1521 he was in the Netherlands. (You will remember that Luther nailed his Ninety-five Theses to the door at Wittenberg on October 31, 1517.) There Dürer heard tidings that Luther had been taken captive. The rumor was false. Luther's friends had hidden him to protect his life, but most people thought he was a prisoner. Dürer was keeping a diary which he did not mean to have published.

This diary is worth quoting at length (as translated by Udo Middelmann):

On Friday before Pentecost (17th of May) in the year 1521 the news reached Antwerpen, that Martin Luther had been so treacherously taken prisoner. For when the herald of the emperor Charles had been ordered to accompany him with the emperial guard, he trusted this. But when the herald had brought him near Eisenach to an inhospitable place, he told him that he had no further need of him and rode off. Pretty soon ten riders on horseback appeared; they treacherously led away this deceived, pious man, who was illumined by the Holy Spirit and professed the true Christian faith. And is he still alive? Or have they murdered him?—which I do not know—in that case he has suffered it for the sake of the Christian truth in that he chastized the unchristian papacy, which resists the liberation by Christ with its heavy burdens of human laws; and also for this reason has he suffered it, that we should even longer as until now be deprived and completely disrobed of all that is the fruit of our blood and sweat, and that this fruit should shamefully and blasphemously be consumed by idle folk while the thirsty, parched people die because of it.

And especially, the hardest factor for me is that God might possibly want to keep us under their false and blind teaching, which has only been composed and compiled by people whom they call fathers. Because of this, the delicious Word of God is wrongly exegeted or not at all taught in many places.

Oh God in heaven, have mercy on us. Oh Lord Jesus Christ, pray for your people, deliver us at the right time, preserve in us the right, true Christian faith, gather your widely scattered sheep by your voice, which is called the Word of God in Scripture. Help us that we might recognize this your voice and would not follow another tempting call, that would only be human imagination, so that we might never leave you, Lord Jesus Christ! . . . Oh God! You have never burdened a people so horribly with human laws as we are under the Roman chair, who desire daily to be free Christians, redeemed by your blood. Oh highest, heavenly Father! Pour into our hearts by your son Jesus Christ such light, that we might recognize which messenger we are constrained to obey, so that we might reject the burden of the others in good conscience and be able to serve you, eternal heavenly Father, with a glad and cheerful heart.

And should we have lost this man, who has written more clearly than any other that has lived in the last 140 years and to whom you have given such an evangelical spirit, we pray you, Oh heavenly Father, that you would give your Holy Spirit again to someone who would gather your holy Christian Church so that we might live together again in a Christian manner and that because of our good works all unbelievers, as there are Turks, heathen, and Kalicutes, would desire after us of themselves and would accept the Christian faith. . . . Oh Lord! Present us afterwards with the new, decorated Jerusalem that descends from heaven, of which it is written in the Apocalypse, the holy pure gospel, which has not been darkened by human doctrine.

Anyone, after all, who reads Martin Luther's books, can see how his teaching is so clear and transparent when he sets forth the holy gospel. Therefore these are to be honored and ought not to be burned; unless one would throw his opponents, who combat the truth at all times, into the same fire together with their opinions, which want to make Gods out of men; and one should then proceed in this way that new printings of Luther's books would again be available. Oh God, if Luther is dead, who will henceforth proclaim the holy gospel with such clarity? Oh God! What would he not have still been able to write for us in ten or twenty more years?

In a letter to George Spalatin in 1520 Dürer wrote:

In all subservience may I ask your grace to recommend to you the praiseworthy Dr. Luther, for the sake of the Christian truth, for which we care more than all riches or power of this world, for all this passes with time, only the truth remains eternally. And help me God, that I might get to Dr. Martinus Luther, so that I might diligently picture him and etch him in copper for a lasting memorial of this Christian man who has helped me out of great anxieties. And I ask you, your honor, that if Dr. Martinus produces something new in German, you would send it to me against my money.

There are a number of things to notice in these quotations. Dürer says Luther has written more clearly than anyone for 140 years. John Wycliffe had lived from 1320 to 1384, John Huss from 1369 to 1415. Dürer's diary was written in 1521. When we subtract 140 years from this date, we arrive at 1381, which falls in the lifetime of both Wycliffe and Huss. Dürer may have had both men in mind, but probably he was thinking of Huss, for Huss's influence had remained strong in southern Germany. One thing is clear: Dürer was in the line of these men before the Reformation who had set forth many of the Reformation's basic ideas, especially the Bible as the only final authority. Notice how this fits in with what Dürer wrote about Martin Luther. A second prominent idea of Huss—that salvation did not come through the addition of man's works but through Christ and His work only—is also found echoed in the diary.

Thus Dürer was indeed a man in the stream of the Reformation when he did his great woodcuts illustrating the *Apocalypse* (1498) and his copperplate engravings of *The Knight, Death, and the Devil* (1513) and *St. Jerome in His Cell* (1514), even if he did them before Luther nailed his Theses to the door. Further, notice how he twice quotes from the Apocalypse (the last book in the Bible). This clearly ties in with his previous woodcuts and shows that even when he did them these thoughts were involved. His art is as much a cultural result of the Reformation as is Bach's music. Dürer lived at the same time as Raphael, Michelangelo and Leonardo. When he was thirteen years old, he already took nature seriously. His beautiful watercolors of flowers, rabbits, and so on were a clear exhibition that God's world has value, a real value.

I am not at all saying that the art which the Reformation produced was in every case greater as art than the art of the south. *The point is that to say that the Reformation depreciated art and culture or that it did not produce art and culture is either nonsense or dishonest.*

It is not only Christians who can paint with beauty, nor for that matter only Christians who can love or who have creative stirrings. Even though the image is now contorted, people are made in the image of God. This is who people are, whether or not they know or acknowledge it. God is the great Creator, and part of the unique mannishness of man, as made in God's image, is creativity. Thus, man as man paints, shows creativity in science and engineering, and so on. Such activity does not require a special impulse from God, and it does not mean that people are not alienated from God and do not need the work of Christ to return to God. It does mean that man as man, in contrast to non-man, is creative. A person's world-view almost always shows through in his creative output, however, and thus the marks on the things he creates will be different. This is so in all fields—for example, in the art of the Renaissance compared to that of the Reformation, or in the direction man's creative stirrings in science will assume, and whether and how the stirring will continue. In the case of the Reformation the art showed the good marks of its biblical base.

It was not only in Germany that the Reformation affirmed painting. The clearest example of the effects of the Reformation culture on painting is Rembrandt (1606-1669). Rembrandt had flaws in his life (as all people do), but he was a true Christian; he believed in the death of Christ for him personally. In 1633 he painted the *Raising of the Cross* for Prince Frederick Henry of

Orange. It now hangs in the museum Alte Pinakothek in München. A man in a blue painter's beret raises Christ upon the cross. That man is Rembrandt himself—a self-portrait. He thus stated for all the world to see that his sins had sent Christ to the cross.

Rembrandt shows in all his work that he was a man of the Reformation; he neither idealized nature nor demeaned it. Moreover, Rembrandt's biblical base enabled him to excel in painting people with psychological depth. Man was great, but man was also cruel and broken, for he had revolted against God. Rembrandt's painting was thus lofty, yet down to earth. There was no need for him to slip into the world of illusion, as did much of the baroque painting which sprang out of the Catholic Counter-Reformation. Nature to this Dutch Reformation artist was a thing to be enjoyed as a creation of God. We can think of Rembrandt's painting *Danae* (1636) in the museum in Leningrad. This is a picture of Rembrandt's nude wife waiting in bed for him. Rembrandt himself is not in the picture. And yet as she waits for him to come from the left side, though still hidden, he is the center of the picture. There is love and gentleness here. Rembrandt understood that Christ is the Lord of all of life. As a Christian, he lived in the midst of God's world and did not need to make himself God. Rather, he could use God's world and its form in his painting.

Many other Dutch artists stood firmly in the stream of Reformation culture. There were portrait painters, landscape painters, and still-life artists; for all of them, everyday reality was seen as God's creation and thus as important. This was the right direction, a proper view of nature. Up to a certain point the development of the Renaissance in the south could have gone in a good direction or a poor one. But humanism took over—all was made autonomous and meaning was lost. In the Reformation, the right direction was regained, and nature and the whole of life were things of dignity and beauty.

In 1860 Jacob Burckhardt (1818-1897) in *The Civilization of the Renaissance in Italy* pointed out a crucial difference between the Renaissance and the Reformation. While no one now would follow Burckhardt exactly, his discussion of the contrast between the Renaissance and the Reformation is still the most remarkable one we have and seems to me to be still valid. He indicated that freedom was introduced both in the north by the Reformation and in the south by the Renaissance. But in the south it went to license; in the north it did not. The reason was that in Renaissance humanism man had no way to bring forth a meaning to the particulars of life and no place from which to get absolutes in morals. But in the north, the people of the Reformation, standing under the teaching of Scripture, had freedom and yet at the same time compelling absolute values.

CHAPTER FIVE

The Reformation–Continued

We have seen that the Reformation was neither against culture nor against art as art. Let us also note the political freedom which the return to biblical Christianity gradually brought forth. The accent here is on the word *gradually,* for all the results did not come at once. Let us emphasize again that the Reformation was no golden age; and our eyes should not turn back to it as if it were to be our perfect model. People have never carried out the biblical teaching perfectly. Nonetheless, wherever the biblical teaching has gone, even though it has always been marred by men, it not only has told of an open approach to God through the work of Christ, but also has brought peripheral results in society, including political institutions. Secondary results are produced by the preaching of the gospel in both the arts and political affairs.

The Reformation did not bring social or political perfection, but it did gradually bring forth a vast and unique improvement. What the Reformation's return to biblical teaching gave society was the opportunity for tremendous freedom, but without chaos. That is, an individual had freedom because there was a consensus based upon the absolutes given in the Bible, and therefore real values within which to have freedom, without these freedoms leading to chaos. The world had not known anything like this before. In northern Europe, this view was seen in the form of society that resulted. The conveniently small Greek city-states for a short period of time attempted to have social and political participation for carefully defined segments of the population. And Roman law secured certain freedoms for Roman citizens—as we learn, for example, from the Apostle Paul's experiences. Yet these never approached what the Reformation produced.

The basis for freedom without chaos is exhibited by Paul Robert's (1851-1923) mural which he entitled *Justice Lifts the Nations* (1905). To make his point so that it could not be missed, he painted the title on the mural itself. It is on the stairway in the old Supreme Court Building in Lausanne where the judges had to pass each time before going up to try a case. Robert wanted to remind them that the place which the Reformation gave to the Bible provided a basis not only for morals but for law. Robert pictured many types of legal cases in the foreground and the judges in their black robes standing behind the judges' bench. The problem is neatly posed: How shall the judges judge? On what basis shall they proceed so that their judgment will not be arbitrary? Above them Robert painted Justice standing unblindfolded, with her sword pointed not vertically upward but downward toward a book, and on the book is written "The Law of God." This painting expressed the sociological base, the legal base, in northern Europe after the Reformation. Paul Robert understood what the Reformation was all about in the area of law. It is the Bible which gives a base to law.

Robert was expressing at a later date what some men in the flow of the Reformation had already understood and had expressed verbally. Alexandre Vinet (1797-1847) was professor of theology at the Academy of Lausanne (now the university). He was the thinker in the canton of Vaud who stood in the stream of the Reformers who had preceded him in Switzerland. He was the foremost representative of French Protestantism in the French-speaking world of his day. He said, "Christianity is the immortal seed of freedom of the world." Switzerland's unique freedoms rest on this base. Vinet did not just talk and write about these things, but was the outspoken leader for both freedom of religious worship and freedom of the conscience in relationship to the state. A statue of Vinet with the above quote on it is situated only a few hundred feet from the old Supreme Court Building in which Robert painted his mural.

In the Anglo-Saxon world, England showed clearly the results of the Reformation, as did Holland and in varying degrees the other Reformation countries. Too often we think of law, however, only in the context of civil and criminal conduct, forgetting that law is related to the entire structure of a society, including its government. Here the return to the Bible in the Reformation had an important and beneficial influence. The exact impact in any one place or country varied according to circumstance and opportunity. But, in general, the constitutionalist ideas of a Martin Bucer (1491-1551), who was a leader of the Reformation in Strasbourg and important throughout all the Reformation countries, or a John Calvin produced results because—unlike the moribund contract ideas of the late Middle Ages—they did not lose contact with daily life.

Bucer was one of the most levelheaded and charitable Reformers and had the strongest personal influence on Calvin's deep-rooted conciliatory views in church affairs at Geneva and in church-state relations. The constitutionalist model, implicit in Presbyterian church government, was not just an example but an education in the principle of political limitation. And where, as in England, Presbyterianism as such did not triumph, its political ideas were communicated through the many complex groups which made up the Puritan element in English public life and played a creative role in trimming the power of the English kings. As a result, the ordinary citizen discovered a freedom from arbitrary governmental power in an age when in other countries the advance toward absolutist political options was restricting liberty of expression.

Thus the biblical insistence on the responsibility of people—even of monarchs—to God's law turned the political tide in those countries where the Reformation emphasis on the Bible as the only final authority took root. Elsewhere, it was natural politically for the centralizing monarchs to welcome the aid of the monarchical Roman Church in controlling political (as well as religious) heterodoxy. In England the threat of absolutism was thwarted. Here was a country where increasingly men lived without fear of arbitrary revenge.

Many good things in England came from Scotland. The clearest example of the Reformation principle of a people's political control of its sovereign is a book written by a Scot, Samuel Rutherford (1600-1661). The book is *Lex Rex: Law Is King*. When it was published in 1644, Rutherford was one of the Scottish commissioners at the Westminster Assembly in London. Later he became rector of St. Andrew's University in Scotland. What Paul Robert painted for the justices at the Supreme Court Building Samuel Rutherford had already laid down in writing in this book. Here was a concept of freedom without chaos because there was a form. Or, to put it another way, here was a government of law rather than of the arbitrary decisions of men—because the Bible as the final authority was there as the base. This went beyond the Conciliar Movement and the early medieval parliaments, for these had no base beyond inconsistent church pronouncements and the changing winds of political events.

Samuel Rutherford's work and the tradition it embodied had a great influence on the United States Constitution, even though modern Anglo-Saxons have largely forgotten him. This influence was mediated through two sources. The first was John Witherspoon (1723-1794), a Presbyterian who followed Samuel Rutherford's *Lex Rex* directly and brought its principles to bear on the writing of the Constitution and the laying down of forms and freedoms. Witherspoon, educated at Edinburgh University, became president of the College of New Jersey (now Princeton University) in 1768. He was a member of the Continental Congress from 1776 to 1779 and from 1780 to 1782. The only clergyman to sign the Declaration of Independence, he played an important role on a number of the committees of the Congress.

The second mediator of Rutherford's influence was John Locke (1632-1704), who, though secularizing the Presbyterian tradition, nevertheless drew heavily from it. He stressed inalienable rights, government by consent, separation of powers, and the right of revolution. But the biblical base for these is discovered in Rutherford's work. Without this biblical background, the whole system would be without a foundation. This is seen by the fact that Locke's own work has an inherent contradiction. His empiricism, as revealed in his *Essay Concerning Human Understanding* (1690), really leaves no place for "natural rights." Empiricism would rest everything on experience. But "natural rights" must either be innate to the nature of man and not based on experience (thereby conflicting with the concept of empiricism) or they must have an adequate base other than man's experience. Locke's difficulty was that he did not have Samuel Rutherford's Christian base. He stated the results which come from biblical Christianity without having the base which produced them. That is, he secularized Christian teaching.

Thomas Jefferson (1743-1826) picked up the secularized form, often tying it into classical examples. Not all the individual men who laid down the foundation for the United States Constitution were Christians; some, in fact, were deists. But we should realize that the word *Christian* can legitimately be used two ways. The primary meaning is: an individual who has come to God through the work of Christ. The second meaning must be kept distinct but also has validity. It is possible for an individual to live within the circle of that which a Christian consensus brings forth, even though he himself is not a Christian in the first sense. This may be true in many areas—for example, in the arts or political thought. Some of the men who laid the foundation of the United States Constitution were not Christians in the first sense, and yet they built upon the basis of the Reformation either directly through the *Lex Rex* tradition or indirectly through Locke. To whatever degree a society allows the teaching of the Bible to bring forth its natural conclusions, it is able to have form and freedom in society and government.

So the Reformation's preaching of the gospel brought forth two things which were secondary to the central message of the gospel but nonetheless were important: an interest in culture and a true basis for form and freedom in society and government. The latter carries with it an important corollary, namely, that 51 percent of the vote never becomes the final source of right and wrong in government because the absolutes of the Bible are available to judge a society. The "little man," the private citizen, can at any time stand up and, on the basis of biblical teaching, say that the majority is wrong. So, to the extent to which the biblical teaching is practiced, one can control the despotism of the majority vote or the despotism of one person or group.

The Reformation in northern Europe also contributed to checks and balances in government. This idea was, of course, not new in the sixteenth century. Some form of checks and balances was implicit in some medieval political thought, as we saw earlier, and a particular form of it is central to so-called Polybian republicanism, which supposedly exemplified the best elements in Greek and Roman practice. Polybian republicanism is named for Polybius (c. 198-c. 117 B.C.), a Greek who wrote a history of the growth of the Roman Republic in terms which were designed to cause his fellow Greeks to accept Roman rule. Polybian republicanism—which Niccolò Machiavelli (1469-1527) embraced—was, however, economically and politically elitist. Since Machiavelli had witnessed the destruction of Florentine republicanism, he was interested in the Polybian theory of political cycles, which involved a cyclical view of history. Machiavelli therefore wrote *The Prince,* advocating firm autocratic rule, because in his view only the dictatorial regime of the "ideal" prince could push along the cycle of political history; only the exercise of ruthlessness could improve the cycles. Machiavelli already showed in his day that ultimately the humanist Renaissance had no more of a universal in political morals than it had in personal morals. Machiavelli's *The Prince*—destined to become a handbook of political practice used by heads of state as remote in time as Benito Mussolini (1883-1945) and Adolf Hitler (1889-1945)—stands in sharp contrast to the checks-and-balances tradition encouraged by the Reformation.

The Reformers were not romantic about man. With their strong emphasis on the Fall, they understood that since every person is indeed a sinner there is a need for checks and balances, especially on people in power. For this reason, Calvin himself in Geneva did not have the authority often attributed to him. As we have seen, Calvin had been greatly influenced by the thinking of Bucer in regard to these things. In contrast to a formalized or institutional authority, Calvin's influence was moral and informal. This was so not only in political matters (in which historians recognize that Calvin had little or no direct say), but also in church affairs. For example, he preferred to have the Lord's Supper given weekly, but he allowed the will of the majority of the pastors in Geneva to prevail. Thus the Lord's Supper was celebrated only once every three months.

Each Reformation country showed the practice of checks and balances in different forms. Switzerland (whose national political life was shaped by the Reformation tradition even though not all its cantons followed the Reformation) is especially interesting in this regard. Since the mid-nineteenth century, the Swiss have separated geographically the legislative and executive parts of government from the judiciary, placing the former in Bern, the latter in Lausanne. In Great Britain came the checks and balances of a king, two Houses of Parliament, and the courts. Today the monarch has less authority than when the division of power was made, but the concept of checks and balances continues. The United States has a slightly different arrangement, but with the same basic principle. The White House covers the executive administration; Congress, in two balanced parts, is the legislature; the

Supreme Court embodies the judiciary. In the Reformation countries, there was a solution to the "form" or "chaos" problem in
society.

We must repeat that when Christians who came out of the
Reformation tradition had more influence than they do now on
the consensus in the northern European culture (which would
include the United States, Canada, Australia, New Zealand, and
so on), this did not mean that they achieved perfection. Even
when the Reformation had more influence on generally accepted
thinking than is the case today, as the centuries passed, weaknesses
definitely existed and certain specific weaknesses gradually developed. At certain points the people in the stream of the Reformation were inconsistent with the biblical teaching they claimed
to follow. There were many areas where the Bible was not followed as it should have been, but two are outstanding: first, a
twisted view of race, and second, a noncompassionate use of
accumulated wealth.

In the area of race there were two types of abuse. The first was
slavery based on race; the second, racial prejudice as such. Both
practices were wrong, and often both were present when Christians had a stronger influence on the consensus than they now
have. And yet the church, as the church, did not speak out suffi-
ciently against them.

The conditions on the slave ships—in which thousands died
crossing the seas, the treatment slaves often received, and, in a
special way, slavery based on skin color cannot be just passed
over. For complex reasons still debated by historians, English-
men, continental Europeans, and Americans indulged in the fiction that the black man was not a person and could therefore be
treated as a thing. This fiction covered their hypocrisy. Actually
they harked back to Aristotle's definition of a slave as a living tool
and were far removed from the biblical teaching. And in this
situation the church *as* the church was all too often silent.

Today's Christians, by identification with their forebears, must
acknowledge these inconsistencies in regard to a twisted view of
race. We can use no lesser word than *sin* to describe those instances
where the practice was (or is) so far from what the Bible directs.
The most effective acknowledgment is for Christians to strive in
the present to follow the Bible at these points. Of course, slavery
was not only practiced in these Christian countries. In fact, in
some Moslem countries, black slavery continues to the present

day. But that does not lessen the wrongness of a twisted view of race in the countries where churches out of the Reformation tradition could have done more about it.

The lack of a compassionate use of accumulated wealth, especially following the Industrial Revolution, must also be faced squarely. We must not, of course, forget all the good things industrialization brought forth. The age belonged to the inventors and the engineers who harnessed first the power of water and then the power of steam. And out of that time came a steady stream of better things (one small example would be better pottery for the use of working people), and the base was laid for a greater flow of goods for people in general. If industrialization had been accompanied by a strong emphasis on the compassionate use of accumulated wealth and on the dignity of each individual, the Industrial Revolution would have indeed been a revolution for good. But all too often in England and other countries the church was silent about the Old and the New Testament's emphasis on a compassionate use of wealth. Individual efforts of charity did not excuse this silence. Following industrialization, the noncompassionate use of accumulated wealth was particularly glaring.

It was not that the majority of the people were worse off than under the previous agrarian situation, but rather that the wealth produced by the Industrial Revolution was not used with compassion. This resulted in the growth of the slums in London and other cities and industrial towns, the exploitation of children and women (who suffered especially), and the general discrepancy between the vast wealth of the few and the misery of the many (whose average working day was between twelve and sixteen hours). Seldom did the church, as the church, lift its voice against such "utilitarianism" (the teaching that utility is the ultimate appeal on all ethical questions).

It is significant that the evils of slavery and the noncompassionate use of wealth merged at this point, as slave owners used the arguments of utilitarianism to plead their cause. It must be said in fairness to Jeremy Bentham (1748-1832), the father of utilitarianism, that he himself proposed that the government should intervene to protect working children and improve housing and working conditions. But when utilitarianism is made the standard—if there is no absolute standard to judge it by or if the standard existing in the Bible is not courageously applied—then the concept of "the greatest happiness for the greatest number" is easily manipulated.

It is often forgotten that Thomas Robert Malthus (1766-1834), whose warnings about population growth in *An Essay on the Principle of Population* (1798) are much quoted today, also advocated a hands-off policy in regard to social reforms. To him, poverty is inevitable, and social reforms only increase the problems. Some of his followers today take the same position, saying, for example, that medical care for all people is an evil rather than a good. The same note came from David Ricardo (1772-1823), who in 1817 wrote the first real economics textbook, *The Principles of Political Economy and Taxation.* A tragic example of the acceptance of these views was the attitude toward the Irish potato famine held by Charles Edward Trevelyan (1807-1886), who was in charge of government relief in Ireland. He withheld government assistance from the Irish on the grounds that they should help themselves and that to do otherwise would encourage them to be lazy. It was not that he lacked compassion or a social conscience (his later career shows otherwise), but that at a crucial point a sub-Christian prejudice stifled the teaching of Christ and the Bible, and sealed Ireland's doom.

These views were *not* the product of the Christian consensus, but the churches of that time must be criticized for not shouting loudly enough against these abuses. The churches could have changed things in that day if they had spoken with clarity and courage. The central reason the church should have spoken clearly and courageously on these issues is that the Bible commands it. Had the church been faithful to the Bible's teaching about the compassionate use of wealth, it would not later have lost so many of the workers. And if it had spoken clearly against the use of wealth as a weapon in a kind of "survival of the fittest," in all probability this concept as it came into secularized science would not have been so automatically accepted. Of course, the church's silence was not only a problem in England. It was equally a problem in the United States. And in the area of slavery, the United States must bear special criticism, since slavery based on race continued there until such a late date.

To keep the matter in balance: in the first place it must be said that many non-Christian influences were also at work in the culture. Likewise, many influential people who automatically called themselves Christians were not Christian at all; it was merely socially acceptable to bear the name and go through the outward forms. In the second place, many Christians *did* take a vital and vocal lead in the fight against these abuses. Many Christians struggled to bring into being the social realities that should accompany a Christian consensus. Pastors and others spoke out as prophets, often at great personal cost to themselves. The Bible makes plain that there should be effects in society from the preaching of the gospel, and voices were raised to emphasize this fact and lives were given to illustrate it.

John Howard (1726-1790), John Wesley's friend, labored indefatigably for the reform of the prisons. A Quaker, Elizabeth Fry (1780-1845), had a profound and practical compassion for the prisoners at Newgate. The better-known Lord Shaftesbury (1801-1885) carried on an endless battle to prevent the exploitation of women and children in the mines and factories; he well understood the meaning of a compassionate use of wealth. John Wesley (1703-1791) was himself a strong critic of slavery, and he spoke his mind bluntly, including very frank statements against the slavery he observed in the United States. John Newton (1725-1807), after he became a Christian, not only was no longer a slave trader but turned against the trade. Thomas Clarkson (1760-1846), who spoke out so clearly against the slave trade, was the son of a clergyman in the Church of England and was an admirer and historian of the Quakers.

William Wilberforce (1759-1833) was able to utilize Clarkson's pioneer work. Wilberforce fought for many years in Parliament against the slave trade, battling for the basic recognition of the black man's humanity under God. Wilberforce the Christian—and because he was Christian—was the outstanding voice in England against the slave trade. Finally slave trade was prohibited in England in 1807, and as Wilberforce was dying, slavery itself was abolished there. Slavery was forbidden throughout the British colonies in a bill passed in 1833, to be effective in 1834. The British taxpayers paid twenty million pounds sterling as compensation to the owners of the slaves. One could wish that the United States had had some outstanding Christian as consistent as Wilberforce, someone in a position of influence who could have produced the same result in the United States at the same date, or better, much before! Or better still, to have kept slavery out of the United States entirely.

The black church in the United States cannot, of course, be included in our criticism about the silence of the churches. It was giving much to the United States in many ways, including its cultural heritage—of which the wonder of its music was a part—

but it had no way to speak effectively about slavery. This was especially so in those states where black slavery was practiced. Anyone with a tendency to minimize the brutality of the slavery which existed in the United States should read Charles Dickens's (1812-1870) *American Notes* (1842). He begins this portion of the book by saying, "The upholders of slavery in America—of the atrocities of which system I shall not write one word for which I have not ample proof and warrant. . . ." He then goes on to quote pages of newspaper ads which speak profoundly for themselves. Here are four examples out of the dozens which Dickens quotes: "Ran away, a negro boy about 12 years old. Had round his neck a chain dog-collar with 'De Lampert' engraved on it." "Detained at the police jail, the negro wench, Myra. Has several marks of lashing, and has irons on her feet." "One hundred dollars reward for a negro fellow, Pompoy, 40 years old. He is branded on the left jaw." "Ran away, a negro woman and two children. A few days before she went off, I burned her with a hot iron, on the left side of her face. I tried to make the letter M."

In the United States some groups did speak out. The Reformed Presbyterian Church in the United States decreed as a denomination as early as 1800 that no slave holder should be retained in their communion, and after that date no slave holder was admitted.

We should also mention the impact of the George Whitefield (1714-1770)-John Wesley revivals and the early Methodists and others who emerged from the revivals, from whom came so much emphasis on political, educational, and economic reform. In fact, the Cambridge historian J. H. Plumb (1911-) indicated that it is not too much to say that, without the influence which the Whitefield-Wesley revivals had at the grass roots, it is doubtful whether England would have avoided its own version of the French Revolution.

CHAPTER SIX

The Enlightenment

In the area of political reform, the results of the Reformation are impressive. One can think of Dickens's *Tale of Two Cities* (1859)—with Paris given over to the goddess of Reason, and London with all its inconsistencies—as having a Reformation base.

The change in England in 1688 could be and *was* bloodless. We must not discount the earlier civil wars, but the decisive change in England in 1688 was bloodless—so much so that among historians it is called the "Bloodless Revolution." At that time William III of Orange and Mary became monarchs, and it was made clear that Parliament was not a junior partner but an equal partner with the crown. This arrangement brought about the deliberate control of the monarchy within specific legal bounds.

The French philosopher Voltaire (1694-1778), often called "father of the Enlightenment," was greatly influenced by the results of this bloodless revolution in England during his time of exile there (1726-1729). The impact of the Bloodless Revolution and the ensuing freedom of public expression is shown in Voltaire's *Letters Concerning the English Nation* (1733). He wrote, "The English are the only people upon earth who have been able to prescribe limits to the power of Kings by resisting them, and who, by a series of struggles, have at last established . . . that wise government where the prince is all powerful to do good, and at the same time is restrained from committing evil . . . and where the people share in the government without confusion."

While Voltaire is sometimes overflattering about English conditions, he may be excused because of the terrible contrast in France. There were indeed vast areas in France which needed righting, but when the French Revolution tried to reproduce the English conditions without the Reformation base, but rather on Voltaire's humanist Enlightenment base, the result was a bloodbath and a rapid breakdown into the authoritarian rule of Napoleon Bonaparte (1769-1821).

The utopian dream of the Enlightenment can be summed up by five words: reason, nature, happiness, progress, and liberty. It was thoroughly secular in its thinking. The humanistic elements which had risen during the Renaissance came to flood tide in the Enlightenment. Here was man starting from himself absolutely. And if the humanistic elements of the Renaissance stand in sharp contrast to the Reformation, the Enlightenment was in total antithesis to it. The two stood for and were based upon absolutely different things in an absolute way, and they produced absolutely different results.

To the Enlightenment thinkers, man and society were perfectible. And the French romantically held to this view even in the midst of the Reign of Terror. Voltaire sketched out four epochs of history, of which his own was the apex. Marquis de Condorcet (1743-1794), a mathematician, who was one of the philosophers of Voltaire's circle and who was the author of *Sketch for a Historical Picture of the Progress of the Human Mind* (1793-1794), could talk of nine stages of progress as he hid in a garret in Paris while hiding from the Terror! While hiding for his very life from Robespierre's secret police, he wrote: "We have witnessed the development of a new doctrine which is to deliver the final blow to the already tottering structure of prejudice. It is the idea of the limitless perfectibility of the human species. . . ." Later he managed to escape from Paris, was recognized, arrested, and imprisoned, dying in custody while awaiting his turn at the guillotine.

If these men had a religion, it was deism. The deists believed in a God who had created the world but who had no contact with it now, and who had not revealed truth to men. If there was a God, He was silent. And Voltaire demanded no speech from Him—save when, after the Lisbon earthquake in 1755, Voltaire illogically complained of His nonintervention. The men of the French Enlightenment had no base but their own finiteness. They looked across the Channel to a Reformation England, tried to build without the Christian base, and ended with a massacre and Napoleon as authoritarian ruler.

In June 1789, the first phase of the liberal bourgeois plan of the French Revolution was at its height. Jacques-Louis David (1748-1825) depicted this in his painting *The Oath of the Tennis Court.* Here the members of the National Assembly swore to establish a constitution. Their base, consciously, was purely a humanist theory of rights. On August 26, 1789, they issued the Declaration of the Rights of Man. It sounded fine, but it had nothing to rest upon. In the Declaration of the Rights of Man what was called "the Supreme Being" equaled "the sovereignty of the nation"— that is, the general will of the people. Not only was there a contrast to England's Bloodless Revolution, but a sharp contrast with what resulted in the United States from the Declaration of Independence which was made thirteen years earlier. One had the Reformation base, the other did not.

It took two years for the National Constituent Assembly to draft a constitution (1789-1791). Within a year it was a dead letter. By that time what is often known as the Second French Revolution was in motion, leading to a bloodbath that ended with the revolutionary leaders themselves being killed.

To make their outlook clear, the French changed the calendar and called 1792 the "year one," and destroyed many of the things of the past, even suggesting the destruction of the cathedral at Chartres. They proclaimed the goddess of Reason in Notre-Dame Cathedral in Paris and in other churches in France, including Chartres. In Paris, the goddess was personified by an actress, Demoiselle Candeille, carried shoulder-high into the cathedral by men dressed in Roman costumes.

Like the humanists of the Renaissance, the men of the Enlightenment pushed aside the Christian base and heritage and looked back to the old pre-Christian times. In Voltaire's home in Ferney the picture he hung (in such a way on the wall at the foot of his bed that it was the first thing he saw each day) was a painting of the goddess Diana with a small new crescent moon on her head and a very large one under her feet. She is reaching down to help men.

How quickly all the humanist ideals came to grief! In September 1792 began the massacre in which some 1,300 prisoners were killed. Before it was all over, the government and its agents killed 40,000 people, many of them peasants. Maximilien Robespierre (1758-1794), the revolutionary leader, was himself executed in July 1794. This destruction came not from outside the system; it was produced by the system. As in the later Russian Revolution, the revolutionaries on their humanist base had only two options—anarchy or repression.

The parallels between the course of the French Revolution and the later Russian Revolution, both resting on the same base, are striking. Sometimes the French Revolution is likened to what occurred in the United States at a slightly earlier date. This is incorrect. While there were some historic crosscurrents between the United States and France, the similarities are in the Bloodless Revolution in England and the Revolution in the United States. In sharp contrast to both of these are the likenesses in the French Revolution and the later Russian Revolution. A factor in the parallel between the French Revolution and the Russian is that by 1799 Napoleon had arrived as the elite to govern France—as later Lenin, also as the elite, took over the rule of Russia.

Mention of the later Russian Revolution evokes the observation that a quite different dynamic was involved in the political fortunes of those parts of Europe structurally influenced by the restoration of biblical Christianity in the sixteenth century as compared to those not so influenced. In crude geopolitical terms, there is a contrast between the north of Europe and the south and east. Allowing for local influences, it would seem that the inspiration for most revolutionary changes in the south of Europe was a copy, but often in contorted form, of the freedoms gained from the Reformation in the north. In Italy, Giuseppe Garibaldi (1807-1882) gleaned his ideals from the north of Europe and had to carry them into the peninsula by force. In Spain, where the Inquisition continued into the eighteenth century, persecution and lack of freedom lasted in one form or another up to our own day.

And what the Reformation produced—by native growth as in England or by borrowing as in Italy—is all in gigantic contrast to what Communist countries continue to produce. Marxist-Leninist Communists have a great liability in arguing their case because so far in no place have the Communists gained and continued in power, building on their materialistic base, without repressive policies. And they have not only stifled political freedom but freedom in every area of life, including the arts. To mention only early examples in the field of music, Igor Stravinsky (1882-1971) and Sergei Rachmaninoff (1873-1943) left Russia in order to have liberty while Sergei Prokofiev (1891-1953) and Dmitri Shostakovich (1906-) chose to stay, only to meet with constant repression.

It should not be forgotten that the Leninists, the Bolsheviks, did not make the break for freedom in Russia. That came with the "February Revolution" of 1917. Prince Georgi Lvov (1861-1925) became prime minister of the provisional government and was succeeded by Aleksandr Kerensky (1881-1970) in July. Kerensky was a social reformer but not a Leninist. Vladimir Ilyich Lenin (1870-1924), Leon Trotsky (1879-1940), and Joseph Stalin (1879-1953) did not even return to Russia until after the victory of the February Revolution. Lenin returned from Switzerland in April, Trotsky from New York in May. Stalin returned from Siberia in March. In October 1917 they took over a revolution that had been made by others, and from the beginning under Lenin they built a regime of repression.

Solzhenitsyn says in *Communism: A Legacy of Terror* (1975), "I repeat, this was March 1918—only four months after the October Revolution—all the representatives of the Petrograd factories were cursing the Communists, who had deceived them in all their promises. What is more, not only had they abandoned Petrograd to cold and hunger, themselves having fled from Petrograd to Moscow, but had given orders to machine gun the crowds of workers in the courtyards of the factories who were demanding the election of independent factory committees."

The Bolsheviks were only a small percentage of the Russian people and made up only one-fourth of the constituent assembly which had been elected in November. When the assembly met for the first time in January 1918, the Bolshevist troops dispersed it by force. That was the first and last free election in Russia. Before the Leninists took over in October, Lenin wrote a book called *The Lessons of the Paris Commune*. There he analyzed why the Paris Commune was defeated in 1871. His principal conclusion was that the Commune had not killed enough of its enemies. When Lenin came to power he acted according to this analysis and set up all the machinery for oppression.

Communists speak about "socialism" and "communism," maintaining that socialism is only the temporary stage, with a utopian communism ahead. Over a half-century has passed and not only have they not achieved the goal of "communism" anywhere, they have not even come to a free socialism. The "temporary dictatorship of the proletariat" has proven, wherever the Communists have had power, to be in reality a dictatorship by a small elite—and not temporary but permanent. No place with a communistic base has produced freedom of the kind brought forth under the Reformation in northern Europe.

Communists have had to function on the basis of *internal* repression. We can think of the repression begun under Lenin, as well as the Stalin purges, the Berlin Wall built in 1961 to confine the people of East Germany by force, or the disappearance of freedom in China. *Externally* they hold their "allies" by coercion— the clearest examples being the secret execution of thousands of Polish officers buried in Katya Forest as the Communist prepared to make Poland their "ally," and the Russian tanks in East Germany in 1953, in Hungary in 1956, and in Czechoslovakia in 1968. In Czechoslovakia the repression did not end with the tanks; later half a million followers of Alexander Dubček (1921-) were purged from the Communist party. In 1981 the Soviet Union used their surrogates in Poland to crush the freedom growing there.

Seeing the contrast between the Reformation countries and the Communist and southern European countries, we must not minimize the riches in government and society which came forth from the Reformation. Even in those places where the Reformation consensus was less consistent than it should have been, on the basis of the biblical view there were absolutes on which to combat injustice. Men like Shaftesbury, Wilberforce, and Wesley could say that the evils and injustices which they fought were absolutely wrong. And even if we must say with sorrow that all too often Christians were silent when they should have spoken out, especially in the areas of race and the compassionate use of accumulated wealth, the Christians who were silent were inconsistent with their position.

In contrast to this, humanism has no final way of saying certain things are right and other things are wrong. For a humanist, the final thing which exists—that is, the impersonal universe—is neutral and silent about right and wrong, cruelty and noncruelty. Humanism has no way to provide absolutes. Thus, as a consistent result of humanism's position, humanism in private morals and political life is left with that which is arbitrary.

A good illustration is that at first in Russia, on the basis of Karl Marx's (1818-1883) teaching in the 1848 *Manifesto of the Communist*

Party, marriage was considered a part of capitalism (private prostitution, as he expressed it) and the family was thus minimized. Later, the state decreed a code of strict family laws. This was simply an "arbitrary absolute" imposed because it worked better. There is no base for right or wrong, and the arbitrary absolutes can be reversed for totally opposite ones at any time. For the Communists, laws always have a ground only in the changing historic situation brought about by the ongoing of history.

On the biblical basis, there *are* absolutes, and therefore we can say that certain things are right or wrong, including racial discrimination and social injustice. Consider Jesus standing in front of the tomb of Lazarus. The New Testament records that Jesus not only wept but was angry. The one who claimed to be God could be angry at the abnormality of death without being angry at Himself. To a Christian on the basis of what the Bible teaches, not only is death abnormal, so is the cruelty of man to man. These things did not exist as God made the world. A Christian can fight the abnormality which has resulted from man's rebellion against God without fighting the final reality of what is—that is, without fighting God. Therefore, because God exists and there are absolutes, justice can be seen as absolutely good and not as merely expedient.

These matters are not just theoretical but eminently practical, as can be seen from the results produced in England and the United States in contrast to those produced in France at the time of the Enlightenment, and later in Russia.

CHAPTER SEVEN

The Rise of Modern Science

Two eras in history came almost simultaneously: the High Renaissance and, in contrast to it, the Reformation. A third phenomenon which we must deal with began at approximately the same time. It is often called the Scientific Revolution.

We can date the rise of modern science with Copernicus (1475-1543), the Polish astronomer, and Vesalius (1514-1564), who was Italian. But this is not to say that nothing that could be called science preceded them. The Greeks, the Arabs, and the Chinese had a deep knowledge of the world. The Chinese, however, developed few general scientific theories based on their knowledge, and medieval science largely accepted Aristotle as the ultimate authority. In the Arabic world there was much discussion in this area, but it would seem that the principles by which they comprehended the world were formed under the combined influence of Aristotelianism and Neoplatonism. The Arabic scholars did remarkable work, especially in mathematics—in trigonometry and algebra, for example, and in astronomy. Omar Khayyam (c. 1048-c. 1122)—who is better known for his *Rubaiyat,* in which he carries to its logical conclusion the Islamic concept of fate—calculated the length of the solar year and carried algebra further than it had been taken before. But with the Arabs, as with medieval Europeans, science was considered one aspect of philosophy, with the traditions of the philosophers, especially Aristotle, ruling supreme. That is, medieval science was based on authority rather than observation. It developed through logic rather than experimentation, though there were notable exceptions.

The foundation for modern science can be said to have been laid at Oxford when scholars there attacked Thomas Aquinas's teaching by proving that his chief authority, Aristotle, made certain mistakes about natural phenomena. Roger Bacon (1214-1294) was a part of this Oxford group, but the most important man was Robert Grosseteste (c. 1175-1253), who laid the philosophical foundations for a departure from Aristotelian science. Of course other factors were involved as well, but the challenge to the authority of Aristotle opened the doors for less restricted thought. This challenge to the concepts of Aristotle developed fruitfully at the University of Padua in the fifteenth and sixteenth centuries.

When the Roman Church attacked Copernicus and Galileo (1564-1642), it was not because their teaching actually contained anything contrary to the Bible. The church authorities thought it did, but that was because Aristotelian elements had become part of church orthodoxy, and Galileo's notions clearly conflicted with them. In fact, Galileo defended the compatibility of Copernicus and the Bible, and this was one of the factors which brought about his trial.

Let us return to the fact that the Renaissance and Reformation overlap the Scientific Revolution. Let me emphasize that I am not implying that the Reformation caused the rise of modern science. All I am pointing out at this point is that the High Renaissance, the Reformation, and the Scientific Revolution were simultaneous at that point in history. To put the temporal relationship into perspective, let us consider a few dates: Leonardo da Vinci lived between 1452 and 1519. Luther's Ninety-five Theses were hammered to the church door in 1517. Calvin's *Institutes* were published in 1536. In 1546 Luther died. Copernicus, the astronomer, lived from 1473 to 1543 and gave a preliminary outline of his theory in 1530—that is, that the earth went around the sun, and not the sun around the earth. In the 1540s, three things happened: first, *On the Revolutions of the Heavenly Spheres* by Copernicus was published posthumously; second, Vesalius published his book *On the Structure of the Human Body* (this book is often spoken of as *De*

Fabrica); third, the first edition of a Latin translation of the collected works of Archimedes (c. 287-212 B.C.) was published in 1544 in Basel. This introduced some of the mathematical methods essential to the development of modern science.

Francis Bacon lived from 1561 to 1626. He was a lawyer, essayist, and Lord Chancellor of England. Though historians now do not give him as important a place as they used to, he did, nevertheless, fight a battle against the old order of scholasticism with its slavish dependence on accepted authorities. He stressed careful observation and a systematic collection of information "to unlock nature's secrets." In 1609 Galileo began to use the newly invented telescope, and what he saw and wrote about indicated that Aristotle had been mistaken in his pronouncements about the makeup of the universe. Galileo was not the first to rely on experimental evidence. Danish Tycho Brahe (1546-1601) had come to similar conclusions from observation, but Galileo articulated his findings publicly in his lifetime and in his native tongue so that all could read what he wrote. Condemned by the Roman Inquisition in 1632, he was forced to recant; but his writings continued to testify not only that Copernicus was right, but also that Aristotle was wrong.

The rise of modern science did not conflict with what the Bible teaches; indeed, at a crucial point the Scientific Revolution rested upon what the Bible teaches. Both Alfred North Whitehead (1861-1947) and J. Robert Oppenheimer (1904-1967) have stressed that modern science was born out of the Christian world-view. Whitehead was a widely respected mathematician and philosopher, and Oppenheimer, after he became director of the Institute for Advanced Study at Princeton in 1947, wrote on a wide range of subjects related to science, in addition to writing in his own field on the structure of the atom and atomic energy. As far as I know, neither of the two men were Christians or claimed to be Christians; yet both were straightforward in acknowledging that modern science was born out of the Christian world-view.

Oppenheimer, for example, described this in an article, "On Science and Culture" in *Encounter* in October 1962. In the Harvard University Lowell Lectures entitled *Science and the Modern World* (1925), Whitehead said that Christianity is the mother of science because of "the medieval insistence on the rationality of God." Whitehead also spoke of confidence "in the intelligible rationality of a personal being." He also says in these lectures that because of the rationality of God, the early scientists had an "inexpugnable belief that every detailed occurrence can be correlated with its antecedents in a perfectly definite manner, exemplifying general principles. Without this belief the incredible labors of scientists would be without hope." In other words, because the early scientists believed that the world was created by a reasonable God, they were not surprised to discover that people could find out something true about nature and the universe on the basis of reason.

This is a good place to emphasize some things I am *not* saying. First, the reasonableness of the created order on the basis of its creation by a reasonable God was not a distinctive emphasis of the Reformation, but was held in common by both the pre-Reformation church and the Reformers. The belief Whitehead describes would have been common to both: the heavens and earth had been created by God, and God is a reasonable God, as the Bible says He is.

Second (as was stressed when considering the art which flowed from the Reformation but should be repeated here), it is not only a Christian who can paint beauty or who has creative stirrings in the area of science. These creative stirrings are rooted in the fact that people are made in the image of God, the great Creator, whether or not an individual knows or acknowledges it, and even though the image of God in people is now contorted. This creativeness—whether in art, science, or engineering—is a part of the unique mannishness of man as made in the image of God. Man, in contrast to non-man, is creative. A person's world-view, however, does show through. This includes what happens to people's creative stirrings in science. The world-view determines the direction such creative stirrings will take, and how—*and whether the stirrings will continue or dry up.*

Third, not all the scientists to be considered in this section were individually consistent Christians. Many of them were, but they were all living within the thought-forms brought forth by Christianity. And in this setting man's creative stirring had a base on which to continue and develop. To quote Whitehead once more, the Christian thought-form of the early scientists gave them "the faith in the possibility of science."

Living within the concept that the world was created by a reasonable God, scientists could move with confidence, expecting to be able to find out about the world by observation and experimentation. This was their epistemological base—the philosophical foundations with which they were sure they could know. (*Episte-*

mology is the theory of knowledge—how we know, or how we know we can know.) Since the world had been created by a reasonable God, they were not surprised to find a correlation between themselves as observers and the thing observed—that is, between subject and object. This base is normative to one functioning in the Christian framework, whether he is observing a chair or the molecules which make up the chair. Without this foundation, Western modern science would not have been born.

Here one must consider an important question: did the work of the Renaissance play a part in the birth of modern science? Of course it did. More than that, the gradual intellectual and cultural awakenings in the Middle Ages also exerted their influence. The increased knowledge of Greek thought—at Padua University, for example—opened new doors. Certainly, Renaissance elements and those of the Greek intellectual traditions were involved in the scientific awakening. But to say theoretically that the Greek tradition would have been in itself a sufficient stimulus for the Scientific Revolution comes up against the fact that it was not. It was the Christian factor that made the difference. Whitehead and Oppenheimer are right. Christianity is the mother of modern science because it insists that the God who created the universe has revealed Himself in the Bible to be the kind of God He is. Consequently, there is a sufficient basis for science to study the universe. Later, when the Christian base was lost, a tradition and momentum had been set in motion, and the pragmatic necessity of technology, and even control by the state, drives science on, but, as we shall see, with a subtle yet important change in emphasis.

Francis Bacon, who could be called the major prophet of the Scientific Revolution, took the Bible seriously, including the historic Fall, the revolt of man in history. He said in *Novum Organum Scientiarum* (1620), "Man by the Fall fell at the same time from his state of innocence and from his dominion over creation. Both of these losses, however, can even in this life be in some parts repaired; the former by religion and faith, the latter by the arts and sciences." Notice that Bacon did not see science as autonomous. Man, including science, is not autonomous. He is to take seriously what the Bible teaches about history and about that which it teaches has occurred in the cosmos. Yet, upon the base of the Bible's teaching, science and art are intrinsically valuable before both men and God. This gave a strong impetus for the creative stirrings of science to continue rather than to be spasmodic.

To continue with the founders of modern science: Johannes

Kepler, a German astronomer, lived between 1571 and 1630, the same time as Galileo. He was the first man to show that the planets' orbits are elliptical, not circular. Sir Isaac Newton (1642-1727), while a young professor in his twenties at Cambridge University, came to the conclusion that there is a universal force of attraction between every body in the universe and that it must be calculable. That force he called *gravity*. He set this forth later in *The Mathematical Principles of Natural Philosophy* (1687). This became one of the most influential books in the history of human thought. By experimenting in Neville's Court in Trinity College at Cambridge University, he was also able to work out the speed of sound by timing the interval between the sound of an object which he dropped, and the echo coming back to him from a known distance.

Throughout his lifetime, Newton tried to be loyal to what he believed the Bible teaches. It has been said that seventeenth-century scientists limited themselves to the *how* without interest in the *why*. This is not true. Newton, like other early scientists, had no problem with the *why* because he began with the existence of a personal God who had created the universe.

In his later years, Newton wrote more about the Bible than about science, though little was published. Humanists have said that they wish he had spent all of his time on his science. They think he wasted the hours he expended on biblical study, but they really are a bit blind when they say this. As Whitehead and Oppenheimer stressed, if Newton and others had not had a biblical base, they would have had no base for their science at all. That is not to say that one must agree with all of Newton's speculations on either metaphysics or doctrine. But the point is that Newton's intense interest in the Bible came out of his view that the same God who had created the universe had given people truth in the Bible. And his view was that the Bible contained the same sort of truth as could be learned from a study of the universe. Newton and these other scientists would have been astonished at a science obsessed with *how* the universe functions, but professionally failing to ask the question "Why?"

Though later he became disillusioned with science, Blaise Pascal (1623-1662) made the first successful barometer and did important work on the equilibrium of fluids. He was not content to work only in a laboratory, but took a tube of mercury up the mountain Puy de Dôme (in central France) and thus recorded the changes in the mercury level according to altitude. He was also a mathematician of note whose work hastened the development of differential calculus. By some he is also considered the greatest writer of French prose who ever lived. An outstanding Christian, he emphasized that he did not see people lost like specks of dust in the universe (which was now so much larger and more complicated than people had thought), for people—as unique—could comprehend something of the universe. People could comprehend the stars; the stars comprehend nothing. And besides this, for Pascal, people were special because Christ died on the cross for them.

René Descartes (1596-1650) was important for his emphasis on mathematical analysis and theory of science. I personally would reject his philosophic views. But he regarded himself as a good Catholic, and it was his religion which, in light of his philosophic views, saved him from solipsism—that is, from living in the cocoon of himself.

In the early days of the Royal Society of London for Improving Natural Knowledge, founded in 1662, most of its members were professing Christians. George M. Trevelyan (1876-1962) in *English Social History* (1942) writes, "Robert Boyle, Isaac Newton and the early members of the Royal Society were religious men, who repudiated the sceptical doctrines of Hobbes. But they familiarized the minds of their countrymen with the idea of law in the Universe and with scientific methods of enquiry to discover truth. It was believed that these methods would never lead to any conclusions inconsistent with Biblical history and miraculous religion; Newton lived and died in that faith." We must never think that the Christian base hindered science. Rather, the Christian base made modern science possible.

The tradition of Bacon and Newton and the early days of the Royal Society was strongly maintained right through the nineteenth century. Michael Faraday (1791-1867) made his great contributions in the area of electricity. His crowning discovery was the induction of electric current. Faraday was also a Christian. He belonged to a group whose position was: "Where the Scriptures speak, we speak; where the Scriptures are silent, we are silent." In the conviction that knowledge concerning God's creation is for all people to enjoy, and not just a professional elite, he gave famous public demonstrations of his pioneering work in electricity. James Clerk Maxwell (1831-1879), who, like Faraday, worked with electricity, was also a believer in a personal God. Indeed, the majority of those who founded modern science, from Copernicus to Maxwell, were functioning on a Christian base. Many of them were personally Christians, but even those who were not, were living within the thought-forms brought forth by Christianity, especially the belief that God as the Creator and Lawgiver has implanted laws in His creation which man can discover.

But we may ask, "Isn't science now in a new stage, one in which the concept of an orderly universe is passé?" It is often said that relativity as a philosophy, as a world-view, is supported by Albert Einstein's (1879-1955) theory of relativity. But this is mistaken because Einstein's theory of relativity assumes that everywhere in the universe light travels at a constant speed in a vacuum. In other words, we must say with the utmost force that nothing is less relative philosophically than the theory of relativity. Einstein himself stood implacably against any such application of his concepts. We can think of his often quoted words from the *London Observer* of April 5, 1964: "I cannot believe that God plays dice with the cosmos."

One may then ask if Einstein's views have not been proven old-fashioned by Werner Heisenberg's (1901-1976) principle of uncertainty, or indeterminacy principle (1927), and by the wide acceptance of the concept of quantum. The answer again is *no*. The principle of indeterminacy has to do with a certain area of observation, namely, the *location* of an object and its *velocity*. For example, if we try to establish the exact position and speed of two atomic particles which are going to collide, we will never be able to determine exactly how they will rebound. The physicist cannot have an accurate *observation* of both their location and their velocity simultaneously. The quantum theory of either light or particles does not lead to the concept of chance or random universe either. For example, whether viewed as a wave or a particle, light does not function at random and it is an effect which brings forth causes. Even the far-out theoretical existence of "black holes" in space, as set forth by John G. Taylor (1931-), is based on the concept of an orderly universe and calculations resting on that concept.

If an airplane is to fly, it must be constructed to fit the order of the universe that exists. People, no matter what they have come to believe, still look for the explanation of any happening in terms of other earlier happenings. If this were not possible, not only would explanations cease, but science could not be used reliably in technology. It is possible to so function in our universe that, because there is a uniformity of natural causes, a man may travel hundreds of thousands of miles to the moon and land within a few feet of his planned destination, or he may aim an atomic weapon at a target on the other side of our planet and land it within ten feet of that target. We know we live in a universe that is much more complex than people, including scientists, once thought it to be, but that is much different from the concept of a random universe.

On the Christian base, one could expect to find out something true about the universe by reason. There were certain other results of the Christian world-view. For example, there was the certainty of something "there"—an objective reality—for science to examine. What we seem to observe is not just an extension of the essence of God, as Hindu and Buddhist thinking would have it. The Christian world-view gives us a real world which is there to study objectively. Another result of the Christian base was that the world was worth finding out about, for in doing so one was investigating God's creation. And people were free to investigate nature, for nature was not seen as full of gods and therefore taboo. All things were created by God and are open for people's investigation. God Himself had told mankind to have dominion over nature, and as we saw from the quotation from Francis Bacon, to him science had a part in this. There was a reason for continuing one's interest and pressing on.

In this setting, people's creative stirrings had a base from which to develop and to continue. To quote Bacon again, "To conclude, therefore, let no man out of weak conceit of sobriety, or in ill applied moderation, think or maintain, that a man can search too far or be too well studied in the book of God's word, or in the book of God's works." "The book of God's word" is the Bible; "the book of God's works" is the world which God has made. So, for Bacon and other scientists working on the Christian base, there was no separation or final conflict between what the Bible teaches and science.

The Greeks, the Moslems, and the Chinese eventually lost interest in science. As we said before, the Chinese had an early and profound knowledge of the world. Joseph Needham (1900-), in his book *The Grand Titration* (1969), explains why this never developed into a full-fledged science: "There was no confidence that the code of Nature's laws could ever be unveiled and read, because there was no assurance that a divine being, even more rational than ourselves, had ever formulated such a code capable of being read." But for the scientists who were functioning on a Christian base, there was an incentive to continue searching for the objective truth which they had good reason to know was there. Then, too, with the biblical emphasis on the rightness of work and the dignity of all vocations, it was natural that the things which were learned should flow over into the practical side and not remain a matter of mere intellectual curiosity and that, in other words, technology, in the beneficial sense, should be born.

What was the view of these modern scientists on a Christian base? They held to the concept of the uniformity of natural causes in an *open system,* or, as it may also be expressed, the uniformity of natural causes in a limited time span. God has made a cause-and-effect universe; therefore we can find out something about the causes from the effects. *But* (and the *but* is very important) it is an *open* universe because God and man are *outside* of the uniformity of natural causes. In other words, all that exists is not one big cosmic machine which includes everything. Of course, if a person steps in front of a moving auto, the cause-and-effect universe functions upon him; but God and people are not a part of a total cosmic machine. Things go on in a cause-and-effect sequence, but at a point of time the direction may be changed by God or by people. Consequently, there is a place for God, but there is also a proper place for man.

This carries with it something profound—that the machine, whether the cosmic machine or the machines which people make, is neither a master nor a threat—because the machine does not include everything. There is something which is "outside" of the cosmic machine, and there is a place for man to be man.

CHAPTER EIGHT

The Breakdown in Philosophy and Science

The point was made in Chapter One that to understand where we are today in our intellectual ideas and in our day-to-day lives (including our culture and political lives), we must trace three lines: the philosophic, the scientific, and the religious. We have done this through the preceding chapters and now have arrived at the era of modern man. As we go on to what I call *The Breakdown,* we will here consider the philosophic and scientific sides and their interrelation.

Alfred North Whitehead has remarked that the entire history of European philosophy is a series of footnotes to Plato. That goes too far. Nevertheless, Plato did understand something crucial—not only in theoretical thought but in practical life. He saw that if there are no absolutes, then the individual things (the particulars, the details) have no meaning. By particulars we mean the individual things which are about us. The individual stones on a beach are particulars. The molecules that make up the stones are particulars. The total beach is a particular. I am made up of molecules and the molecules are particulars. And I as an individual and you as an individual are particulars.

Plato understood that regardless of what kind of particulars one talks about, if there are no absolutes—no universal—then particulars have no meaning. The universal or absolute is that under which all the particulars fit—that which gives unity and meaning to the whole. We can apply this in language. Apples come in many varieties, but we do not verbalize each time by running through the names of all the varieties of apples. We sum them up by the word *apples*. Likewise, there are many kinds of pears, and we sum them up with the word *pears*. On a higher level of generality there are many other varieties of fruit. But again we do not run through all these, we simply say *fruit*.

The problem, however, is not only in language but in reality: What will unify and give meaning to everything there is? Jean-Paul Sartre (1905-1980), the French existential philosopher, emphasized this problem in our own generation. His concept was that a finite point is absurd if it has no infinite reference point. This concept is most easily understood in the area of morals. If there is no absolute moral standard, then one cannot say in a final sense that anything is right or wrong. By *absolute* we mean that which always applies, that which provides a final or ultimate standard. There must be an absolute if there are to be *morals,* and there must be an absolute if there are to be real *values*. If there is no absolute beyond man's ideas, then there is no final appeal to judge between individuals and groups whose moral judgments conflict. We are merely left with conflicting opinions.

But it is not only that we need absolutes in morals and values; we need absolutes if our existence is to have *meaning*—my existence, your existence, Man's existence. Even more profoundly, we must have absolutes if we are to have a solid epistemology (a theory of knowing—how we know, or how we know we know). How can we be sure that what we think we know of the world outside ourselves really corresponds to what is there? And in all these layers, each more profound than the other, unless there is an absolute these things are lost to us: morals, values, the meaning of existence (including the meaning of man), and a basis for knowing.

Non-Christian philosophers from the time of the Greeks until just before our modern period had three things in common. First, they were rationalists. That is, they assumed that man (though he is finite and limited) can begin from himself and gather enough particulars to make his own universals. Rationalism rejects any knowledge outside of man himself, especially any knowledge from God.

The second point they had in common was that they took reason seriously. They accepted the validity of reason—that the mind thinks in terms of antithesis. That is, with their minds people can come to the conclusion that certain things are true while certain other things are not true, that certain things are right in contrast to other things that are wrong. The first lessons in classical logic were: A is A, and A is not non-A.

Third, in addition to being rationalists who believed in the validity of reason, non-Christian philosophers prior to the eighteenth century also were optimistic. They thought they could and would succeed in their quest to establish by reason alone a unified and true knowledge of what reality is. When that happened, satisfying explanations would be on hand for everything people encountered in the universe and for all that people are and all that they think. They hoped for something which would unify all knowledge and all of life.

But three shifts came, and it was these shifts that made modern man what he is and our modern societies what they are. First, we will look at the shift in science, then the shift in philosophy, and later at the shift in theology. We have already seen that the Scientific Revolution rested on a Christian base. The early modern scientists believed in the concept of the uniformity of natural causes in an *open* system. God and man were outside the cause-and-effect machine of the cosmos, and therefore they *both* could influence the machine. To them all that exists is *not* one big cosmic machine which includes everything. The shift from modern science to what I call *modern modern science* was a shift from the concept of the uniformity of natural causes in an *open system* to the concept of the uniformity of natural causes in a *closed system*. In the latter view nothing is outside a total cosmic machine; everything which exists is a part of it.

Scientists in the seventeenth and eighteenth centuries continued to use the word *God,* but pushed God more and more to the edges of their systems. Finally, scientists in this stream of thought moved to the idea of a completely closed system. That left no place for God. But equally it left no place for man. Man disappears, to be viewed as some form of determined or behavioristic machine. Everything is a part of the cosmic machine, including people. To say this another way: prior to the rise of modern modern science (that is, naturalistic science, or materialistic science), the laws of cause and effect were applied to physics, astronomy, and chemistry. Today the mechanical cause-and-effect perspective is applied equally to psychology and sociology.

Notice especially that the scientists who gave birth to the earlier great breakthroughs of science would not have accepted this concept. It arose not because of that which could be demonstrated by science, but because the scientists who took this new view *had accepted a different philosophic base*. The findings of science, as such, did not bring them to accept this view; rather, their world-view brought them to this place. They became naturalistic or materialistic in their presuppositions.

The German philosopher Ludwig Feuerbach (1804-1872) was an early exponent of a philosophy of materialism, as was German physician Ludwig Büchner (1824-1899), whose book *Force and Matter* (1855) went into twenty-one editions and was translated into all the major languages. It is of more than passing interest that Richard Wagner (1813-1883), the German composer of opera, was reading Feuerbach as early as 1848. Wagner at this period of his life was deeply influenced by Feuerbach, and it was Wagner who encouraged Ludwig II of Bavaria to read Feuerbach. Thus the work of Feuerbach had its influence not only in abstract thought but also on the arts and on the state. Ernst Haeckel (1834-1919), a biologist at the University of Jena, wrote *The Riddle of the Universe at the Close of the 19th Century* (1899), and it became a best-seller, too. In this work Haeckel posited that matter and energy are eternal and also assumed that the human mind or soul is to be explained on the basis of materialism. He saw where this would lead and accepted that people have no freedom of will.

When people began to think in this way, there was no place for God nor for man as man. When psychology and social science were made a part of a closed cause-and-effect system, along with physics, astronomy and chemistry, it was not only God who died. Man died. And within this framework love died. There is no place for love in a totally closed cause-and-effect system. There is no place for morals in a totally closed cause-and-effect system. There is no place for the freedom of people in a totally closed cause-and-effect system. Man becomes a zero. People and all they do become only a part of the machinery.

In the humanism of the High Renaissance, flowing on to maturity through the Enlightenment, man was determined to make himself autonomous. This flow continues, and by the time we come to modern modern science man himself is devoured: man as man is dead. Life is pointless, devoid of meaning.

Büchner and Haeckel had said that matter and energy are eternal. Now the world-view of materialism went on to try to explain *man* by the uniformity of cause and effect in a closed system. Charles Lyell (1797-1875), in his *Principles of Geology* (1830-1833), was the one who especially opened the door to this by emphasizing the uniformity of natural causes in the field of geology. His idea was that there were no forces in the past except those that are active now.

Charles Darwin (1809-1882) extended Lyell's concepts to the origin of biological life. In his book *The Origin of Species by Means of Natural Selection or the Preservation of Favoured Races in the Struggle for Life* (1859), Darwin set forth the concept that all biological life came from simpler forms by a process called "the survival of the fittest." Questions still exist in regard to this concept. Darwinism, Neo-Darwinism, and reductionism all have their problems explaining *how* the processes they postulate actually work. There are statistical problems as well, as has been pointed out by Murray Eden (1920-) in the 1967 article "Heresy in the Halls of Biology—Mathematicians Question Darwin" (*Scientific Research,* November 1967). This problem was also dealt with in a more technical way in Eden's article "Inadequacies of Neo-Darwinian Evolution as a Scientific Theory" which appeared in *Mathematical Challenges to the Neo-Darwinian Interpretation of Evolution* (1967). Statistical studies indicate that pure chance (randomness) could not have produced the biological complexity in the world out of chaos, in any amount of time so far suggested. "Has there been enough time for natural selection, as it is seen through the eyepieces of Darwinism or Neo-Darwinism to operate and give rise to the observed phenomena of nature? No, say these mathematicians." In fact, we can go further; the study of statistics raises the question of whether pure chance could ever produce *an ongoing increased complexity.* If chance alone operates, *why* should that which exists (including biological structure) move toward a consistent increase of complexity?

Most importantly, no one has yet shown how man could have been brought forth from non-man solely by time plus chance. This position ends either in man's being made non-man, or in a sudden romantic explosion into a flood of words. For example, Jacob Bronowski (1908-1974) ends his book *The Ascent of Man* (1973) with such a romantic outpouring of sentences as: "We are nature's unique experiment to make the rational intelligence prove itself sounder than the reflex. Knowledge is our destiny. Self-knowledge, at last bringing together the experience of the arts and the explanation of science, waits ahead of us." The humanist thinkers, beginning from themselves autonomously, either come to the conclusion that there are no values and meaning or suddenly try to produce values and meaning out of rhetoric. Thus, there are problems of both the *how* and the *why*. The concept of an unbroken line from molecule to man, on the basis of only time plus chance, leaves these crucial questions of *how* and *why* unanswered.

Darwin's idea was popularized by Thomas Huxley (1825-1895). Herbert Spencer (1820-1903), who actually coined the phrase "survival of the fittest," extended the theory of biological evolution to all of life, including ethics. Spencer said, "The poverty of the incapable . . . starvation of the idle and those shoulderings aside of the weak by the strong . . . are the decrees of a large, far-seeing benevolence." There was no necessity to extend biological evolution to "social Darwinism." But it was natural for these men to do this because of their desire to find a unifying principle that would enable autonomous man to explain everything through naturalistic science, that is, on the basis of the uniformity of natural causes in a closed system. This had become the frame of reference by which they attempted to give unity to individual things, the particulars, to the details of the universe and to the history of man. In *Physics and Politics: Thoughts on the Application of Principles of Natural Selection and Inheritance to Political Science* (1872) Walter Bagehot (1826-1877) went even further than Spencer in applying these concepts to the advance of groups. Thus these concepts opened the door for racism and the noncompassionate use of accumulated wealth to be sanctioned and made respectable in the name of "science."

Later, these ideas helped produce an even more far-reaching yet logical conclusion: the Nazi movement in Germany. Heinrich Himmler (1900-1945), leader of the Gestapo, stated that the law of nature must take its course in the survival of the fittest. The result was the gas chambers. Hitler stated numerous times that Christianity and its notion of charity should be "replaced by the ethic of strength over weakness." Surely many factors were involved in the rise of National Socialism in Germany. For example, the Christian consensus had largely been lost by the undermining from a rationalistic philosophy and a romantic pantheism on the secular side, and a liberal theology (which was an adoption of rationalism in theological terminology) in the universities and many of the churches. Thus biblical Christianity was no longer giving the consensus for German society. After World War I came political and economic chaos and a flood of moral permissiveness in Germany. Thus, many factors created the situation. But in that setting the theory of the survival of the fittest sanctioned what occurred.

The Nazi movement was not the last result of this way of thinking. In a quieter way, and yet just as importantly, some of today's advocates of genetic engineering use the same arguments to support the position that the weak should not be kept alive through medical advances to produce a *weaker* next generation. Rather, they argue, genetic engineering should be used to propagate the fittest. Humanism had set out to make man autonomous; but its results have not been what the advocates of humanism idealistically visualized.

Having seen the shift that came in science, let us now examine the shift that came in philosophy. We have already noted that the older philosophic views were optimistic, for they assumed that people would be able through reason alone to establish a unified and true knowledge of what reality is, and that when this happened they would have satisfying explanations for everything encountered in the universe and for all that people are and think.

The history of this train of non-Christian philosophers could be pictured like this: One man would say, "Here is a circle which will give the unified and true knowledge of what really is:" ◯. The next man would say, "No!" and cross out the circle: ⊗. Then he would say, "Here is the circle:" ◯. A third would say, "No!," cross out that circle: ⊗ and say, "Here is the circle:" ◯. And so on through the centuries. Each one showed that the previous philosophers had failed and then tried to construct his answer, which future thinkers would again show to be inadequate to contain all of knowledge and all of life.

The older philosophers did not find the circle, but they optimistically believed someone would. Then the line of crossed-out circles was broken, and a drastic shift came. It is this shift that causes modern man to be modern man.

Many scholars name René Descartes (1596-1650) as the father of modern philosophy, and no one should minimize his importance. Yet it seems to me that he should be placed among the *older* philosophers for two reasons. First, he was supremely confident that by human thought alone one could doubt all notions based on authority and could begin from himself with total sufficiency ("I think, therefore I am"). Second, he believed that mathematics would provide a unity—as a model—for all kinds of investigation. He was optimistic that mathematics and mathematical analysis, with careful deductions from these, would provide a factor which would give a unity to all knowledge. Philosophical thought is a flowing stream, and certainly Descartes had an important part in preparing for what was to follow; but in my opinion the shift came in the next century, the eighteenth.

Four men directed the shift from this older optimistic view to the modern outlook in which this optimistic hope is lost. The shift came because the humanistic ideal had failed. After all the centuries of suggested circles, the humanistic expectation of autonomous man's providing a unity to all of knowledge and all of life had stalled. People had gone round and round variations of the same answers—like going around and around a large, dark, circular room looking for a way out—and it was slowly dawning on them that there was no exit. That realization came in the eighteenth century, and with it the stance of humanistic man changed from optimism to pessimism. He gave up the hope of a unified answer.

The relative importance of these four men is open to question, but when the influence of these four together (with the extensions made by their followers) had been exerted, the old optimism of a unified and true knowledge on the basis of reason alone was gone. This has had an enormous effect on Western culture and society, down to the simplest man in the street. The four crucial men were Jean-Jacques Rousseau, Immanuel Kant, George Wilhelm Hegel, and Søren Kierkegaard.

The first, Jean-Jacques Rousseau (1712-1778), was a French-speaking Swiss from Geneva. You will remember that the humanism of the High Renaissance ran into problems because, with man's beginning only from himself, there is tension between the individual things, the particulars, and any meaning for them. We could think of it like this:

UNIVERSALS which give meaning to the particulars

PARTICULARS, including each of us as a person

By the time of Rousseau, this humanist problem developed further. With Rousseau the same problem was worded differently and may be expressed like this:

AUTONOMOUS FREEDOM

AUTONOMOUS NATURE

There were two parts to this new formulation of the old humanist problem. First, there were those who were aware that in the area of reason people were increasingly coming to the place where everything was seen as a machine, even people. At the end of his life Leonardo da Vinci had foreseen that beginning humanistically with mathematics one has only particulars and will never come to universals or meaning, but will end only with mechanics. It took humanistic thought 250 years to arrive at the place which Leonardo had foreseen, but by the eighteenth century it had arrived. Everything is the machine, including people.

Second, Rousseau himself viewed the tension specifically at the point of society, political life, and culture. He viewed primitive man, "the noble savage," as superior to civilized man. He wrote, "If man is good by nature, as I believe to have shown him to be, it follows that he stays like that as long as nothing foreign to him corrupts him." He had a kind of "conversion" in 1749 when he concluded that the Enlightenment, with its emphasis on reason and the arts and sciences, had caused people to lose more than they had gained. So he gave up his faith in "progress."

Rousseau and his followers began to play down reason, and they saw the restraints of civilization as evils: "Man was born free, but everywhere he is in chains!" Rousseau saw the primitive as innocent and autonomous freedom as the final good. We must understand that the freedom he advocated was not just freedom from God or the Bible but freedom from any kind of restraint—freedom from culture, freedom from any authority, an absolute freedom of the individual—a freedom in which the individual is the center of the universe.

Theoretically this individual freedom would be perfectly reflected in the "general will" through the *social contract*. The utopianism of this concept was shown by the French Revolution's Reign of Terror, during which the purification of the general will meant not only the loss of freedom for the individual but the reign of the guillotine. Actually, one did not have to wait for the Reign of Terror to see the problem. It was already in Rousseau's own writing.

Rousseau's concept of autonomous freedom clashed with his own presentation when he moved from the individual to society.

In *The Social Contract* (1762) he writes, "In order that the social compact may not be an empty formula, it tacitly includes the undertaking, which alone can give force to the rest, that whoever refuses to obey the general will shall be compelled to do so by the whole body. This means nothing less than that he will be forced to be free." Once more a humanistic utopianism ends in tyranny, whether in Rousseau's writing or in the Reign of Terror which carried his position to its conclusion. Robespierre, the "King of the Terror," was a doctrinaire disciple of Rousseau and rationalized his actions on Rousseau's base. It is interesting to note in this relationship of the Enlightenment and the French Revolution to Rousseau that in Voltaire's château in Ferney two life-sized statues stand perfectly balanced on the two sides of the main doorway— statues of Voltaire and Rousseau.

Rousseau's concept of freedom showed itself in many forms. For example, in his *Confessions* (1782) he argued that the best education is virtually the absence of education. This had an impact on the later education theories of self-expression which are influential in our own day. We all have our inconsistencies, but it must be mentioned that while he wrote much on education, Rousseau sent the five children born to his mistress off to orphanages. His concepts were as utopian personally as they proved to be politically. Rousseau's influence was carried not only by his prose tracts but by the operas he composed. *Le Devin du Village* (1752) played an important role in forming the style of French *opéra comique,* while his later work *Pygmalion* (produced in 1775) laid the foundation for melodrama. With his cry of "Let us return to nature," Rousseau exerted a lasting influence on the music of his time as well as on the new movements in writing and painting.

In *Rousseau and Revolution* (1967) by Will and Ariel Durant, Rousseau is portrayed as the most important influence on modern thought, and thus their book commences with him. In this instance I think they are correct. Rousseau had a profound effect on the thoughts and the lives of those who followed him. His thinking influenced that of our own day in many ways. For this reason I will spend more time on his concepts and influence than on Kant, Hegel, and Kierkegaard.

Rousseau's concept of autonomous freedom led to the Bohemian ideal, in which the hero is the man who fights all of society's standards, values, and restraints. Giacomo Puccini (1858-1924) gave this operatic expression in his most popular opera, *La Bohème* (1896). And in our own recent past this Bohemian ideal was a factor leading expressly to the genuine part of the hippie world of the 1960s.

But Rousseau did not stand alone. In Britain the Scottish philosopher David Hume (1711-1776) was working at exactly the same time. He, too, criticized reason as a method of knowing truth and defended the centrality of human experience and feeling. In his criticism of reason as a method of knowing, Hume questioned the existence of the cause-and-effect concept itself. Hume had a wide influence both on British philosophy and on the German philospher Immanuel Kant, whom we will discuss below.

Returning to those standing in the flow of Rousseau we should consider the German poet-philosopher Johann Wolfgang von Goethe (1749-1832). Goethe equated nature and truth. Goethe did not just substitute nature for the Bible; for him nature was God. Here we have the vague pantheism which dominated so much of the stream of thinking at this time. Goethe became pantheistic in a conscious attempt to find a universal for all observed particulars in reality, even though those particulars were often contradictory. For example, the atrocities of the French Revolution were committed in an especially good wine year! In his naturalism—which took a vaguely pantheistic direction instead of an open materialism—Goethe romantically hoped to leave a place for man. As Goethe expressed it, nature is the ultimate sanction for all man's judgments.

Influenced by Rousseau, romanticism was born in Germany with Goethe, Johann Christoph Friedrich von Schiller (1759-1805), and Gotthold Lessing (1729-1781). All three of these men were at first followers of the Enlightenment before they turned aside to follow Rousseau. Reason was the hero of the Enlightenment; emotion became the hero of romanticism. Schiller's line, "All creatures drink in joy from nature's breast," aptly sums up this school of thought.

Beethoven (1770-1827) followed in this stream, carrying its expression into music. Beethoven's music, more than that of any composer before him, gives the impression of being a direct outpouring of his personality. In it we already feel the emphasis of modern man on self-expression. Beethoven's last quartets (1825-1826) opened the door to twentieth-century music.

The English romantic poets William Wordsworth (1770-1850) and Samuel Taylor Coleridge (1772-1834) were in the same stream. Wordsworth found his values in man's instincts rather than in learning. The English painter John Constable (1776-1837) not only painted the trees and clouds, but in some way related the nature he saw to a concept of the *moral* grandeur of the universe, thus echoing Wordsworth who wrote in "The Tables Turned,"

> One impulse from a vernal wood
> May teach you more of man,
> Of moral evil and of good,
> Than all the sages can.

It also echoes Rousseau's concept of the noble savage: That which is "natural" is morally good.

The attempt to make nature the basis of *morals* was also taken into the area of *civil law,* where it was called the Natural Law School of Jurisprudence. Its influence is still strongly felt in jurisprudence. It was an attempt in this eighteenth-century period to have principles of law, "even if there is no God." These jurists thought that a complete and perfect system of law could be constructed upon principles of natural law. But there was a serious problem in trying to construct a system of law upon nature. Nature is cruel as well as *non*cruel.

Consider the dilemma faced by Rousseau's follower Gauguin (1848-1903), the French painter who, in his hunt for total freedom, deserted his family and went to Tahiti where he tried to find it in the noble savage. After he had lived in Tahiti for a while, he found that the ideal of the noble savage was illusory. In his last great painting—*Whence Come We? What Are We? Whither Do We Go?* (1897 and 1898), which hangs in the Bostom Museum of Fine Arts—he showed that man in himself has no answer to the ultimate questions—and this applies as much to primitive man as to civilized man. He painted the title directly on this painting so that no one could miss its meaning. He wrote about this painting as he was working on it, and he called it a philosophical work, comparable to the gospel.

But what a "gospel"! In the picture is a primitive old woman dying. And Gauguin himself writes in a letter to Daniel de Montfreid, "Whither? Close to the death of an old woman, a strange stupid bird concludes: What? O sorrow, thou art my master. Fate how cruel thou art, and always vanquished. I revolt." What he found in Tahiti (where he went to find the uninhibited freedom of man, which to Rousseau and Gauguin was the "ought"), turned out to be death and cruelty. When he finished this painting, he tried to commit suicide, though he did not succeed.

Or, to illustrate in another way the problem of taking nature as the moral standard, we can consider Marquis de Sade (1740-1814), who well understood the logical conclusion of this deification of nature. He knew that if nature is all, then what *is* is right, and nothing more can be said. The natural result of this was his "sadism," his cruelty, especially to women. He wrote in *La Nouvelle Justine* (1791-1797): "As nature has made us (the men) the strongest, we can do with her (the woman) whatever we please." There are no moral distinctions, no value system. What *is* is right. Thus there is no basis for either morals or law.

It was one thing for the Dutch Reformation painters rejoicingly to paint the simple things of life, for they painted in a framework which had two parts: first, the creation of nature by a personal and a good God; second, the present abnormality of nature because of the Fall. But it was quite another thing to take nature as it is now and make it the measure of goodness. For if nature as it exists is the standard for men to live by, cruelty becomes equal to non-cruelty.

It should be said again that Rousseau's concept of autonomous freedom ran head-on into a conclusion which was to become increasingly dominant as time went on. It became clear that those who held the rationalistic position on the sole basis of their own reason increasingly were forced to conclude that everything, including man, is a machine. But one could not hold simultaneously the concept of everything's being a machine and the ideal of a person's having freedom. Thus, the concept of a unified knowledge of what reality is (on the basis of reason alone)—which almost all previous thinkers had as their aspiration—was under great strain. By the time of Rousseau and his followers there was a tendency for the concepts (*everything as a machine* and *man's autonomous freedom*) to split apart and go marching off in divergent directions.

The second of the four crucial men who directed the shift from the older optimistic view of philosophy to the modern outlook where hope is lost was the German philosopher Immanuel Kant (1724-1804). His books which were so important in the thought of his day and ever since are *Critique of Pure Reason* (1781), *Critique of*

Practical Reason (1788), and *Critique of Judgment* (1790). He worded the problem of his age differently from Rousseau, but it is still the same problem:

NOUMENAL WORLD—the concepts of meaning and value

PHENOMENAL WORLD—the world which can be weighed and measured, the external world, the world of science

Kant also tried to keep these two worlds together. In fact, much of the three books mentioned tried to solve this problem (this is especially so in *Critique of Judgment*), but he, like Rousseau, never found any way to produce unity. With his work, the hope of a unified knowledge was on the threshold of splitting into two parts, neither having a relationship with the other. The humanist dilemma which arose in the Renaissance—of the individual things, the particulars, versus meaning and values—was now ready to explode. There was no way beginning from man alone to bring the noumenal and phenomenal worlds together.

Romanticism, which had begun with the followers of Rousseau, now developed further with a strengthened desire to believe in something—to escape—even if to do so necessitated giving up the old non-Christian philosophers' hope that people starting from themselves could by their reason find a unified answer to everything.

The third of the four significant men was another German, Georg Wilhelm Friedrich Hegel (1770-1831). His most important books are *The Phenomenology of Mind* (1807), *Science of Logic* (1812-1816), *Encyclopaedia of the Philosophical Sciences* (1817), and *Philosophy of Right* (1821). From his writings it is clear that he understood the need for unity between the noumenal and phenomenal worlds. He struggled with this in a complex series of religious concepts, but he left us in reality only a flow of religious words. We can think of his words as given us by Walter Kaufmann (1921-) in his book *Hegel: Reinterpretation, Texts, and Commentary* (1965): "Not the Concept but the ecstasy, not the coldly progressing necessity of the subject matter but fermenting enthusiasm is held to be the best attitude and guide to the spread-out riches of the substance."

Hegel's intricate system puts great emphasis on the centrality of the state and the flow of history. In *The Universe Next Door* (1976) James W. Sire (1933-) summarizes Frederick Copleston's (1907-) study of Hegel in Volume 7 of *A History of Philosophy* (1963). This summary is so succinct that I will quote it, insofar as Copleston's treatment is too lengthy to quote in full: "According to Hegel, the universe is steadily unfolding and so is man's understanding of it. No single proposition about reality can truly reflect what is the case. Rather, in the heart of the truth of a given proposition one finds its opposite. This, where recognized, unfolds and stands in opposition to the thesis. Yet there is truth in both thesis and antithesis, and when this is perceived a synthesis is formed and a new proposition states the truth of the newly recognized situation. But this in turn is found to contain its own contradiction and the process goes on ad infinitum. Thus the universe and man's understanding of it unfolds dialectically. In short the universe with its consciousness—man—evolves."

The result is that all possible particular positions are indeed relativized. While it is an oversimplification of Hegel's complete position, this has led to the idea that truth is to be sought in synthesis rather than antithesis. Instead of antithesis (that some things are true and their opposite untrue), truth and moral rightness will be found in the flow of history, a synthesis of them. This concept has not only won on the other side of the Iron Curtain; it has won on this side as well. Today not only in philosophy but in politics, government, and individual morality, our generation sees solutions in terms of synthesis and not absolutes. When this happens, truth, as people had always thought of truth, has died.

The last of the four crucial men was Søren Kierkegaard (1813-1855), a Dane. He wrote both devotional and philosophical books. The later include *Either/Or* (1843), *Philosophical Fragments* (1844), and *The Concluding Unscientific Postscript* (1846). There can and will be a continuing discussion among scholars as to whether the secular and religious thinkers who built on Kierkegaard did him justice. However, what in these can be called secular and religious Kierkegaardianism did bring to full tide the notion that reason will always lead to pessimism. That is, one must try to find optimistic answers in regard to meaning and values on an "upper level" outside of reason. Through a "leap of faith" one must try to find meaning without reason.

You will remember that in the High Renaissance, humanistic man, starting only from himself, had problems concerning the meaning or value of things and of absolutes for morals. With Rousseau it became an AUTONOMOUS FREEDOM/AUTONOMOUS NATURE problem. With Kant it was NOUMENAL WORLD/PHE-

NOMENAL WORLD. With Kierkegaardianism it went a step further and now became:

NONREASON = FAITH/OPTIMISM

REASON = PESSIMISM

So optimism will now always be in the area of nonreason.

Modern man is a man of dichotomy. By *dichotomy* we mean a total separation into two reciprocally exclusive orders, with no unity or relationship between them. The dichotomy here is the total separation between the area of meaning and values, and the area of reason. Reason leading to despair must be kept totally separate from the blind optimism of nonreason. This makes a lower and an upper story, with the lower story of reason leading to pessimism and men trying to find optimism in an upper story devoid of reason. At this point the older rationalistic thinkers (with their optimistic hope of maintaining unity between the world of reason and that of meaning and values) were left behind. This is the mark of modern man.

In our day, humanistic reason affirms that there is only the cosmic machine, which encompasses everything, including people. To those who hold this view everything people are or do is explained by some form of determinism, some type of behaviorism, some kind of reductionism. The terms *determinism* or *behaviorism* indicate that everything people think or do is determined in a machinelike way and that any sense of freedom or choice is an illusion. In one form of reductionism, man is explained by reducing him to the smallest particles which make up his body. Man is seen as being only the molecule or the energy particle, more complex but not intrinsically different.

I have never heard this expressed more clearly than when I was lecturing in Acapulco, Mexico. George Wald (1906-), a chemistry professor from Harvard University, was also there lecturing to the same group. He expressed with great force the modern concept that all things, including man, are merely the product of chance. After he had stressed over and over again that all things, beginning from the molecule and ending with man, are only a product of chance, he said, "Four hundred years ago there was a collection of molecules named Shakespeare which produced *Hamlet*." According to these theories, that is *all* that man can be. Man beginning with his proud, proud humanism, tried to make himself autonomous, but rather than becoming great, he had found himself ending up as only a collection of molecules—and nothing more.

All this is related to the question of origins: what was the beginning of everything? Ultimately, there are not many possible answers to this question. First, we could say that everything came from nothing—that is, from *really* nothing, what I call *nothing-nothing*. This means that once there was no mass, no energy, no motion, and no personality. This is theoretically a possibility, but I have never heard anyone hold this view, for it seems to be unthinkable. It follows that if we do not hold that everything has come of nothing-nothing, then something has always existed.

Second, there is the possibility of a personal beginning—that everything else was made by a personality who could bring forth the universe (the space-time continuum) when it had not existed previously in *any* form. This is not out of nothing-nothing, but the personality would have existed previously.

Third, there is the possibility of an impersonal beginning—that some form of the impersonal has existed forever, even if in a form vastly different from that which we now know. This idea of an impersonal beginning has many variations, including the use of the word *God* to mean the ultimate impersonal, as in the case of pantheism. A more accurate word than *pantheism* to describe this position is *pan-everythingism*. The word *pantheism* slips in the connotation of personality, even though, by definition, the concept excludes it. In much modern thought, all begins with the impersonality of the atom or the molecule or the energy particle, and then everything—including life and man—comes forth by chance from that.

This is really very curious because Louis Pasteur (1822-1895), the French chemist, demonstrated the impossibility of the then-accepted concept of the spontaneous generation of life—that is, life springing from nonliving things. Pasteur showed in 1864 that if the nonliving things were pasteurized, then life could not come forth. In other words, what was previously considered spontaneous generation of life from nonliving things was mistaken— life always came from living things. When pasteurization killed all the elements of life, life never came forth from the nonliving things. But then the men of that same era returned to the concept of the spontaneous generation of life by adding a new factor: long reaches of time.

This equation of the impersonal plus time plus chance producing the total configuration of the universe and all that is in it, modern people hold by faith. And if one does in faith accept this, with what final value is he left? In his lecture at Acapulco, George Wald finished with only one final value. It was the same one with which English philosopher Bertrand Russell (1872-1970) was left. For Wald and Russell and for many other modern thinkers, the final value is the biological continuity of the human race. If this is the only final value, one is left wondering why this then has importance.

Now having traveled from the pride of man in the High Renaissance and the Enlightenment down to the present despair, we can understand where modern people are. They have no place for a personal God. But equally they have no place for man as man, or for love, or for freedom, or for significance. This brings a crucial problem. Beginning only from man himself, people affirm that man is only a machine. *But those who hold this position cannot live like machines!* If they could, there would have been no tensions in their intellectual position or in their lives. But even people who believe they are machines cannot live like machines, and thus they must "leap upstairs" against their reason and try to find something which gives meaning to life, even though to do so they have to deny their reason.

This was a solution Leonardo da Vinci and the men of the Renaissance never would have accepted, even if, like Leonardo, they ended their thinking in despondency. They would not have done so, for they would have considered it intellectual suicide to separate meaning and values from reason in this way. And they would have been right. Such a solution is intellectual suicide, and one may question the intellectual integrity of those who accept such a position when their starting-point was pride in the sufficiency of human reason.

CHAPTER NINE

Modern Philosophy and Modern Theology

Modern people have put various things "upstairs" in the area of nonreason in a desperate attempt to find some optimism about meaning and values. We will consider first those things the secular existential philosophers have put there, in their attempt to find meaning to life.

The existentialist who is probably best known is Jean-Paul Sartre (1905-1980). He held that in the area of reason everything is absurd, but nonetheless a person can authenticate himself by an act of the will; everyone should abandon the pose of spectator and act in a purposeless world. But because, as Sartre saw it, reason is separated from this authenticating, the will can act in any direction. On the basis of his teaching, you could authenticate yourself either by helping a poor old lady along the road at night or by speeding up your auto and running her down. Reason is not involved, and nothing can show you the direction which your will should take.

Albert Camus (1913-1960) was always named jointly with Sartre as one of the two leaders of French existentialism. However, Camus was never as consistent as Sartre with the presuppositions which they both held. Being less consistent, he was more human and therefore better liked by the young who were following French existentialism.

But Sartre could not live consistently with his position either. By signing the Algerian Manifesto (1960) which declared the Algerian War a dirty war—that is, by making a value judgment that was not just a leap of nonreason—he destroyed his own position. This action said that man can use his reason to conclude that some things are right and some things are wrong. Sartre's later left-wing political views did the same.

Martin Heidegger (1889-1976), a German philosopher, was an existentialist who set forth basically the same idea: that answers are separated from reason. His early books are *Being and Time* (1927) and *What Is Metaphysics?* (1929). As a young man, Heidegger introduced the term *angst* (roughly meaning "anxiety") as a word defining modern man's stance before the world. This *angst* is not to be confused with fear. As Heidegger defined it, fear has an object, while *angst* is the general feeling of anxiety one experiences in the universe. It is fear without a definite object. In Heidegger's view this mood of anxiety gives people certainty of existence, and in so doing there is laid upon them a call for decision. Thus out of this mood comes meaning to life and to choice, even against one's reason. But notice: this rests on nothing more than a vague feeling of anxiety, so nebulous it does not even have a specific object. We shall see that later this view was too weak for Heidegger, and as an older man he changed his position.

Karl Jaspers (1883-1969) was a German existentialist, but he is usually thought of as Swiss because he lived and taught in Basel for so long. In some ways he has had the greatest impact on the thought and the life forms which have followed the avenue of existential thought. Jaspers suggested that we may have a "final experience" in life. To him *final experience* was a technical term. By it he meant that even though our mind tells us life is absurd, we may have some huge experience that encourages us to believe that there is a meaning to life.

The dilemma of Jasper's existentialism can be understood clearly by an example. A young man from Holland who followed Jaspers came to study with me in Switzerland. He had had an experience in Amsterdam one night at the theater as he watched the play *Green Pastures*. Reason had played no part, but it had been a very emotional experience, and it had given him the *hope* of some meaning to life that he had not had before. Weeks and months passed, and because no reason was involved in the experience, he could not give any words or content to it, neither to others nor to himself. To put the experience into words is impossible, for in the existential system reason is excluded from the experience. Thus, by definition, content is excluded and the possibility of putting it into words is excluded. One can only say to others or to oneself, "I had an experience." All this young man could keep on saying was, "So many months ago, I had an experience." He was gradually overwhelmed and ready to commit suicide; the feeling of meaning which had no basis in his reason gradually slipped through his fingers and, being sensitive, he was left in despair. A bitter thing indeed!

As a formal philosophical position, existentialism is now not influential. But more and more among people generally this frame of thinking is increasing. This is so even if the people thinking this way do not know the word *existentialism*. They talk about or act upon the idea that reason leads only to pessimism. They say or act upon the concept (with varying degrees of understanding), "Let us try to find an answer in something totally separated from reason." Humanistic man tried to make himself self-sufficient and demanded that one start from himself and the individual details and build his own universals. His great hope that he could begin from himself and produce a uniformity of knowledge led him, however, to the sad place where his mind told him that he was only a machine, a bundle of molecules. Then he tried desperately to find meaning in the area of nonreason, until, with those following Jaspers, the problem became how one could be sure he would ever have a big enough *final experience* (or, even if he had one, how he could ever have another) and there was no way to be sure.

The man who followed on from that point was English— Aldous Huxley (1894–1963). He proposed drugs as a solution. We should, he said, give healthy people drugs and they can then find truth inside their own heads. They can then have the final experience any time they wish; they do not need to wait, hoping that something will happen. He first suggested this as a theoretical concept in *Brave New World* (1932), calling the all-important drug *soma*. He chose this name with care, for in Eastern Hindu myths, *soma* was the drug which kept the gods contented. Thus, in tying into Eastern thought his hope of finding a meaning for life in the area of nonreason, Aldous Huxley was already opening the door for what would be the next step.

Later Huxley went beyond the theoretical concept in *Brave New World* and openly advocated the use of drugs in *The Doors of Perception* (1956) and *Heaven and Hell* (1956). And in *The Humanist Frame* (1961), edited by his brother Julian Huxley (1887-1975), Aldous contributed the last chapter, "Human Potentialities," still pushing for first-order experiences through drugs. He held this view up to the time of his death. He made his wife promise to give him LSD when he was ready to die so that he would die in the midst of a trip. All that was left for Aldous Huxley and those who followed him was truth inside a person's own head. With Huxley's idea, what began with the existential philosophers—man's individual subjectivity attempting to give order as well as meaning, in contrast to order being shaped by what is objective or external to oneself—came to its logical conclusion. Truth is in one's own head. The ideal of objective truth was gone.

This emphasis on hallucinogenic drugs brought with it many rock groups—for example, Cream, Jefferson Airplane, Grateful Dead, Incredible String Band, Pink Floyd, and Jimi Hendrix. Most of their work was from 1965 to 1968. The Beatles' *Sergeant Pepper's Lonely Hearts Club Band* (1967) also fits here. This disc is a total unity, not just an isolated series of individual songs, and for a time it became the rallying cry for young people throughout the world. It expressed the essence of their lives, thinking, and feeling. As a whole, this music was the vehicle to carry the drug culture and the mentality which went with it across frontiers which were almost impassable by other means of communication.

The next accepted version in the West of life in the area of nonreason was the religious experience of Hinduism and Buddhism. This grasping for a nonrational meaning to life and values is the central reason that these Eastern religions are so popular in the West today. Goethe, Wagner, and others had opened the door to Eastern thinking with their vague pantheism. But it came flood-like into the West with Huxley and the emphasis on drugs, for it followed naturally in the line of what people had been putting into the area of nonreason in the hope of finding meaning and values. Young people (and older ones) tried the drug trip and then turned to the Eastern religious trip. Both seek truth inside one's own head and both negate reason.

In this flow there was also the period of psychedelic rock, an attempt to find this experience without drugs, by the use of a certain type of music. This was the period of the Beatles' *Revolver*

(1966) and *Strawberry Fields Forever* (1967). In the same period and in the same direction was *Blonde on Blond* (1966) by Bob Dylan.

We are seeing that many things can be put in the area of non-reason to provide an optimistic hope. Indeed it can be a highly sophisticated cultural concept. André Malraux (1901-1976) of France argued that art will give us the hope of some meaning to life—not the content of the art, but simply the fact that art exists. In *The Voices of Silence* (1953) Malraux showed that he understood very well that modern man is the man of no absolutes. Yet he offered art as a hope, a hope of nonreason.

Heidegger in his later years changed from his existential philosophy. His earlier existentialism had proved too weak and so he tried a new approach. His later books were *An Introduction to Metaphysics* (1953), *Essays in Metaphysics* (1957), *The Question of Being* (1956), *What Is Philosophy?* (1956), and *Discourse on Thinking* (1959). His new emphasis was clearly exhibited in his little book *What Is Philosophy?* According to the later Heidegger, because there is a being (that is, man) who speaks, who verbalizes, one can hope that the universe (that is, *Being*) has meaning. For him, this was his final cause for optimism. "Listen to the poet," he tells us in *What Is Philosophy?* It is not the content of what the poet says which is important, because the poets may contradict each other, but just the fact that poets exist.

We have also seen a tremendous rash of the occult appearing as an *upper-story* hope. Though demons do not fit into modern man's concepts on the basis of his reason, many moderns would rather have demons than be left with the idea that everything in the universe is only one big machine. People put the occult in the upper story of nonreason in the hope of having some kind of meaning, even if it is a horrendous one.

Another example of what can be put in the area of nonreason is found in the thought and the art of Salvador Dali (1904-). At first Dali was a Surrealist. *Surrealism* is the uniting of Freud's concept of the existence of the unconscious with Dada—an art and life form in which all was seen as absurd. The founding group chose its very name in Zürich by opening a French dictionary at random and putting a finger down on a chance word, which happened to be the French word for rocking horse, *dada*.

Eventually, Salvador Dali abandoned Surrealism—with its acceptance of absurdity—and began his mystical paintings in which Gala, his wife, became the focal point in his leap into the area of nonreason in a hope for meaning. The final breakthrough in this period was his painting *A Basket of Bread*. He had painted in 1926 and 1945 other works with this same title; these depicted baskets of rough Spanish bread. But in 1945, he used this title for a painting of Gala with one breast exposed. He wrote her name on the picture; there is no mistaking who she is. He made her his mystical center. In some of his paintings he would portray her three or four times, often where Mary would have appeared in Roman Catholic paintings. There are a number of such paintings in the New York Cultural Center in New York City. From this time on, many of his pictures show his mystical leap into the area of nonreason.

This was the period of *Christ of Saint John of the Cross* (1951), now in the Glasgow Art Gallery, and *The Sacrament of the Last Supper* (1955), now in the National Gallery of Art in Washington. These were not paintings of the Christ of history. Rather, in them Christ is an upper-story, mystical figure. They were the leap of Kierkegaardianism expressed in painting. The Christ in the *Last Supper* is a shadowy figure through whom we may look at the landscape behind. The little ships are visible through his body. This is not a body of flesh and blood in space and time. This intangible Christ which Dali painted is in sharp contrast to the bodies of the apostles who are physically solid in the picture.

Dali explained in his interviews that he had found a mystical meaning for life in the fact that things are made up of energy rather than solid mass. Because of this, for him there was a reason for a vault into an area of nonreason to give him the hope of meaning. Whether in his interviews or in these paintings, that which causes him to escape the absurdity which Surrealism presented is not reason, and it is not Christianity either; it is a blind leap into the area of nonreason.

One must understand that from the advent of Kierkegaardianism onward there has been a widespread concept of the dichotomy between reason and nonreason, with no interchange between them. The *lower-story* area of reason is totally isolated from the optimistic area of nonreason. The line which divides reason from nonreason is as impassable as a concrete wall thousands of feet thick, reinforced with barbed wire charged with 10,000 volts of electricity. There is no interchange, no osmosis between the two parts. So modern man now lives in such a total dichotomy, wherein reason leads to despair. "Downstairs" in the area of humanistic reason, man is a machine, man is meaningless. There are no values. And "upstairs" optimism about meaning and values is totally separated from reason. Reason has no place here at all; here reason is an outcast.

This division into these two areas is the *existential methodology*. This methodology (and the existence of the dichotomy) is the hallmark of the modern stream of humanistic thinking. Once people adopt this dichotomy—where reason is separated totally from nonreason—they must then face the fact that many types of things can be put in the area of nonreason. And it really does not matter what one chooses to put there, because reason gives no basis for a choice between one thing or another.

In addition to the secular existentialism of Sartre, Camus, Jaspers, and Heidegger, Kierkegaardianism brought forth another form of existentialism: the *theological* existentialism which began with Karl Barth (1886-1968), especially with his first commentary (1919) on ·the New Testament book entitled *The Epistle to the Romans*. We must have profound admiration for Karl Barth in that he, as a Swiss teaching in Germany, made a public stand against Nazism in the Barman Declaration of 1934. For many years he taught at the University of Basel, was a prolific writer, and has had a profound effect on the general flow of theology and intellectual thought in this generation. But in his theology Karl Barth made his own kind of dichotomy and brought the existential methodology into theology.

Back in the Middle Ages we saw that certain humanistic elements entered the church. The essence of the Reformation was the removal of these from the church's teaching. On the other hand, humanistic thinking developed in the Renaissance and again went further in the Enlightenment. The teachings of the Enlightenment became widespread in the various faculties of the German universities, and *theological* rationalism became an identifiable entity in the eighteenth century. Then gradually this came to full flood through the German theological faculties during the nineteenth century. Thus, though the Reformation had rid the church of the humanistic elements which had come into it in the Middle Ages, a more total form of humanism entered the Protestant church, and has gradually spread to all the branches of the church, including the Roman Catholic. The concept of man beginning from himself now began to be expressed in theology and in theological language. Or we can say that these theologians accepted the presuppositions of rationalism. As the Renaissance had tried to synthesize Aristotle and Christianity and then Plato and Christianity, these men were attempting to synthesize the rationalism of the Enlightenment and Christianity. This attempt has often been called *religious liberalism*.

The rationalistic theological liberalism of the nineteenth century was embarrassed by and denied the supernatural, but still tried to hold on to the historic Jesus by winnowing out of the New Testament all the supernatural elements. Let us notice, though, that they were functioning as the older *secular* thinkers had functioned: either a thing was true or it was not. It could not be true and untrue at the same time. For example, either Christ was raised from the dead or He was not.

This came to its climax with Albert Schweitzer's (1875-1965) book *The Quest for the Historical Jesus* (1906) in which he tried to hold on to the Jesus of history. We should remember Schweitzer as an expert on Bach and a genius on the organ, and we certainly should not forget his humanitarianism in Africa, but unhappily we must also remember his place in the theological stream. *The Quest for the Historical Jesus* (especially the conclusion of the second edition which was never translated into English) showed the impossibility of ridding the New Testament of the supernatural and yet keeping any historical Jesus. The rationalistic theologians could not separate the historic Jesus from the supernatural events connected with Him. History and the supernatural were too interwoven in the New Testament. If one retained any of the historical Jesus, one had to keep some of the supernatural. If one got rid of all the supernatural, one had no historical Jesus. Albert Schweitzer himself was left with what has often been called a poetic ethical pantheism.

Ever since theology accepted the presupposition of rationalism, it has followed, always a few years later, the shifting form of humanistic thought. Thus, as humanistic thought in general was first optimistic about finding out the answers to life by reason starting from man alone (but with Kierkegaardianism shifted to pessimism and accepted the *existential methodology* and its dichotomy), so liberal theology did the same. With Karl Barth the existential methodology and the dichotomy were accepted in theology. After the older theological liberalism had failed, Barth stepped into the vacuum with his Kierkegaardian theology.

Karl Barth held until the end of his life the "higher critical" views of the Bible which the nineteenth-century liberal theologians held, and thus he viewed the Bible as having many mistakes. But he then taught that a religious "word" breaks through from it. This was the theological form of existentialism and the dichotomy. In other words, the existential methodology was applied to theology. This meant that theology has now been added to all the other things which had been put into the area of nonreason.

Following the advent of the existential methodology there arose the neo-orthodox existential theology, which says that the Bible in the area of reason has mistakes but nonetheless can provide a religious experience in the area of nonreason. Neo-orthodox theologians do not see the Bible as giving truth which can be stated in contentful propositions, especially regarding the cosmos and history, that is, as making statements which are open to any verification. And for many of them the Bible does not give moral absolutes either. For these theologians, it is not faith in something; it is faith in faith.

But this finally brings them to the place where the word *God* merely becomes the *word* God, and no certain content can be put into it. In this many of the established theologians are in the same position as George Harrison (1943-) (the former Beatles guitarist) when he wrote "My Sweet Lord" (1970). Many people thought he had come to Christianity. But listen to the words in the background: "Krishna, Krishna, Krishna." Krishna is one Hindu name for God. This song expressed no content, just a feeling of religious experience. To Harrison, the words were equal: Christ or Krishna. Actually, neither the word used nor its content was of importance.

Many of the established theologians also came to the place where the word *God* had no certain content; but one can use the word *God* and other religious words as the basis for a contentless religious experience within which reason has no place. J. S. Bezzant (1897-), a Cambridge don, in the volume *Objections to Christian Belief* (1964) gave his opinion of the neo-orthodox position (though he himself was an old-fashioned liberal): "When I am told that it is precisely its immunity from proof which secures the Christian proclamation from the charge of being mythological, I reply that immunity from proof can 'secure' nothing whatever except immunity from proof, and call nonsense by its name." He understood neo-orthodoxy very well.

The new liberal theology, because it says that the Bible does not touch the cosmos or history, has no real basis for applying the Bible's values in a historic situation, in either morals or law. Everything religious is in the area of nonreason, and since reason has no place there, there is no room for discussion; there are only arbitrary pronouncements. Immanuel Kant could not bring together the noumenal and the phenomenal worlds, and the new theologian has no way logically to bring his personal arbitrary values into a historic situation. Or to say it another way: Sartre said that in an absurd world we can authenticate ourselves by an act of the will; but, as we saw, because reason has no place in this we can help people or hurt them. Similarly, because the pronouncements of these theologians about morals or law are arbitrary, in a different mood they, too, can be totally reversed.

The new theologians also have no way to explain why evil exists, and thus they are left with the same problem the Hindu philosophers have; that is, they must say that finally everything that *is* is equally in God. In Hindu thought one of the manifestations of God is Kali, a feminine representation of God with fangs and skulls hanging about her neck. Why do Hindus picture God this way? Because to them everything that exists now is a part of what has always been, a part of that which the Hindus would call "God"—and therefore cruelty is equal to noncruelty. Modern humanistic man in both his secular and his religious forms has come to the same awful place. Both have no final way to say what is right and what is wrong, and no final way to say why one should choose noncruelty instead of cruelty.

Paul Tillich (1886-1965) of Harvard Divinity School was one of the outstanding neo-orthodox theologians. A student related to me that when Tillich was asked just before his death in Santa Barbara, California, "Sir, do you pray?" he answered, "No, but I meditate." He was left only with the word *God,* with no certainty that there was anything more than just the word or that the word equaled anything more than the pantheistic pan-everythingism. The God-is-dead theology which followed Tillich concluded logically that if we are left only with the word *God,* there is no reason not to cross out the word itself.

But for many modern liberal theologians (even if they do not say that God is dead), certain other things *are* dead. Because they do not accept that God in the Bible and in the revelation in Christ has given man truth which may be expressed in propositions, for them all *content* about God is dead and all assurance of a *personal*

God is dead. One is left with the connotation of religious words without content, and the emotion which certain religious words still bring forth—and that is all.

The next step is that these highly motivating religious words out of our religious past, but separated from their original content and context in the Bible, are then used for manipulation. The words became a banner for men to grab and run with in any arbitrary direction—either shifting sexual morality from its historic Christian position based on the Bible's and Christ's teaching, or in legal and political manipulation.

Modern people and modern theology, in trying to start from man alone, are left where the brilliant German philosopher Friedrich Nietzsche (1844-1900) found himself. Nietzsche in the 1880s was the first one who said in the modern way that God is dead, and he understood well where people end when they say this. If God is dead, then everything for which God gives an answer and meaning is dead. And this is true whether it is a secular man or a modern theologian who says, "God is dead." It is also equally true whether the modern theologian says, "God is dead," or whether he reacts against those theologians who say that God is dead, but he continues to use an existential methodology. He himself is left with all *content* about God being dead and all assurance of God as *personal* being dead. The final result is the same.

I am convinced that when Nietzsche came to Switzerland and went insane, it was not because of venereal disease, though he did have this disease. Rather, it was because he understood that insanity was the only philosophic answer if the infinite-personal God does not exist.

I know well the beautiful village of Sils Maria in the Swiss Engadine, where Nietzsche spent his summers and did much work from 1881 to 1888. His house is still there. And on the lovely peninsula of Chasté a quotation from Nietzsche is inscribed on a plaque on a great rock. The following is an English translation from the German (by Udo Middelmann):

> Oh man! Take heed
>   of what the dark midnight says:
> I slept, I slept—from deep dreams I awoke:
> The world is deep—and more profound than day
>   would have thought.
> Profound in her pain—
> Pleasure—more profound than pain of heart,

Woe speaks; pass on.
But all pleasure seeks eternity—
a deep and profound eternity.

Surrounded by some of the most beautiful scenery in the world, Nietzsche knew the tension and despair of modern man. With no personal God, all is dead. Yet man, being truly man (no matter what he says he is), cries out for a meaning that can only be found in the existence of the infinite-personal God, who has not been silent but has spoken, and in the existence of a personal life continuing into eternity. Thus Nietzsche's words are profound: "But all pleasure seeks eternity—a deep and profound eternity."

Without the infinite-personal God, all a person can do, as Nietzsche points out, is to make "systems." In today's speech we would call them "game plans." A person can erect some sort of structure, some type of limited frame, in which he lives, shutting himself up in that frame and not looking beyond it. The game plan can be one of a number of things. It can sound high and noble, such as talking in an idealistic way about the greatest good for the greatest number. Or it can be a scientist concentrating on some small point of science so that he does not have to think of any of the big questions, such as why things exist at all. It can be a skier concentrating for years on knocking one-tenth of a second from a downhill run. Or it can as easily be a theological word game within the structure of the *existential methodology*. That is where modern people, building only on themselves, have come, and that is where they are now.

CHAPTER TEN

Modern Art, Music, Literature, and Films

Modern pessimism and modern fragmentation have spread in three different ways to people of our own culture and to people across the world. *Geographically,* it spread from the European mainland to England, after a time jumping the Atlantic to the United States. *Culturally,* it spread in the various disciplines from philosophy to art, to music, to general culture (the novel, poetry, drama, films), and to theology. *Socially,* it spread from the intellectuals to the educated and then through the mass media to everyone.

In spreading socially, modern pessimism left isolated a certain age group of the middle class which still thought in the old ways. Though many in the group had no sufficient base for doing so, nevertheless through inertia they continued to act as though values did exist for them. But as their children were educated, the children were injected with the new thought, and the *generation gap* came into being. Members of the new generation saw that many of their parents had no base for the values that they said they held. Many of their parents were governed only by a dead tradition; they acted largely out of habit from the past.

As time has gone on, people in Western culture have become

surrounded by an almost monolithic consensus. That is to say, the same basic dichotomy—in which reason leads to pessimism and all optimism is in the area of nonreason—surrounds us on every side and comes to us from almost every quarter. In the various disciplines, the first place this perspective was taught was in philosophy, of which we have already spoken at length. Then it was presented through art, then through music, then through general culture, and finally through theology.

After philosophy proper, the second vehicle was art. In art the way was prepared by a curious twist in the way naturalists were painting. The viewer comes to the painting and in one way sees what the artist pictures, but in another way asks himself, "Is there any meaning to what I am looking at?" The art had become sterile.

The breakthrough came with the Impressionists Claude Monet (1840-1926) and Pierre Auguste Renoir (1841-1919), who were soon followed by Camille Pissarro (1830-1903), Alfred Sisley (1839-1899), and Edgar Degas (1834-1917), all of them great artists. These men painted *only* what their eyes brought them, but this left the question as to whether there was a reality behind the light waves reaching the eyes. They called it "following nature." After 1885 Monet carried this to its logical conclusion, and reality tended to become a dream. We could think of Monet's series of poplar trees, for example, *Poplars at Giverney, Sunrise* (1888), now in the Museum of Modern Art in New York, and *Poplars at Epte* (1890), now in the Tate Gallery in London. As reality tended to become a dream, Impressionism as a movement fell apart. With Impressionism the door was opened for art to become the vehicle for modern thought.

Then came the post-Impressionists who attempted to solve the problem by trying to find the way back to reality, to the absolute behind the individual things. They felt the loss of universals, tried to solve the problem, and in the end they failed. It is not that these painters were always consciously painting their philosophy of life, but rather that in their work as a whole their world-view was often reflected. The great post-Impressionists were Paul Cézanne (1839-1906), Vincent Van Gogh (1853-1890), Paul Gauguin (1848-1903), and Georges Seurat (1859-1891).

These men had great talent as painters, and some of their paintings have great beauty. To read the letters of Vincent Van Gogh is to weep for the pain of this sensitive man. But we must also stress their place in culture, as art became the vehicle for modern man's view of the fragmentation of truth and life.

As philosophy had moved from unity to a fragmentation, this fragmentation was also carried into the field of painting. The fragmentation shown in post-Impressionist paintings was parallel to the loss of a hope for a unity of knowledge in philosophy. It was not just a new technique in painting. It expressed a world-view. Cézanne reduced nature to what he considered its basic geometric forms. In this he was searching for a universal which would tie all kinds of particulars in nature together. Nonetheless, this gave nature a fragmented, broken appearance. In *Bathers* (c. 1905, now in the National Gallery in London), there is much freshness and vitality, much in the balance of the picture as a whole. However, in this painting Cézanne brought the appearance of fragmented reality not only to his painting of nature but to man himself. Man, too, was presented as fragmented.

From this point onward one could either move to the extreme of an ultranatural naturalism, such as the photo-realists, or to the extreme of freedom, whereby reality becomes so fragmented that it disappears, and man is left to make up his own personal world. In 1912 abstract Expressionist painter Wassily Kandinsky (1866-1944) wrote an article entitled "About the Question of Form" in *The Blue Rider* saying that, since the old harmony (a unity of knowledge) had been lost, only two possibilities remained—extreme naturalism or extreme abstraction. Both, he said, were equal.

Gertrude Stein (1874-1946), an American author living in Paris, was important at this time. It was at her home that many artists and writers met and talked of these things, hammering out in talk the new ideas—many of them long before they personally became famous. Picasso initially met Cézanne at her home.

Pablo Picasso (1881-1973) brought together the fragmentation of Cézanne along with Gauguin's concept of the noble savage, and he added the form of the African masks which had just become popular in Paris. With this mixture he painted *Les Demoiselles d'Avignon* (1906-1907). This painting, now in the Museum of Modern Art in New York, marked the birth of "modern art."

In great art the technique fits the world-view being presented, and this new technique of fragmentation fits the world-view of modern man. The technique expressed well the concept of a fragmented world and fragmented man. What David Douglas Duncan

(1916–) says in his book *Picasso's Picassos* (1961) about a certain set of Picasso's pictures in Picasso's private collection is in a way a summing up of much of Picasso's work: "Of course, not one of these pictures was actually a portrait but his prophecy of a ruined world." It was a complete break with the art of the Renaissance which had been founded on man's humanist hope. In *Les Demoiselles d'Avignon* people were made to be less than people; the humanity had been lost.

But it is fascinating that Picasso could not really live with this loss. When he fell in love with Olga, and later Jacqueline, Picasso did not consistently paint them in a fragmented way. Rather, at crucial points in their relationship, he painted them with all his genius as they really were with all their humanity. He had many mistresses, but these were the two women he married. It is interesting that Jacqueline kept one of these paintings in her private sitting room. Duncan says of this lovely picture, "Hanging precariously on an old nail driven high into one of La Californie's [Picasso and Jacqueline's home] second floor sitting room walls, a portrait of Jacqueline Picasso reigns supreme. The room is her domain. . . . Painted in oil with charcoal, the picture has been at her side since shortly after she and the maestro met. . . . She loves it and wants it nearby." Then, too, when Picasso painted his children when they were young, he also often departed from his broken, fragmented technique.

Note that I am not saying that humanity or gentleness is never present in the techniques of modern art, but that as these techniques advanced, humanity was increasingly fragmented—as we shall see, for example, with Marcel Duchamp. The artists carried the idea of a fragmented reality onto the canvas. But at the same time, being sensitive men, the artists realized where this fragmented reality was taking man, that is, to the absurdity of all things.

Hans Arp (1887-1966), an Alsatian sculptor, wrote a poem which appeared in the final issue of the magazine *De Stijl* (The Style) which was published by the *De Stijl* group of artists led by Piet Mondrian and Theo van Doesburg. Mondrian (1872-1944) was the best-known artist of this school. He was not of the Dada school which accepted and portrayed absurdity. Rather, Mondrian was hoping to paint the absolute. Hans Arp, however, was a Dadaist artist connected with *De Stijl*. His poem "Für Theo Van Doesburg," translated from the German, reads:

the head downward
the legs upward
he tumbles into the bottomless
from whence he came

he has no more honour in his body
he bites no more bite of any short meal
he answers no greeting
and is not proud when being adored

the head downward
the legs upward
he tumbles into the bottomless
from whence he came

like a dish covered with hair
like a four-legged sucking chair
like a deaf echotrunk
half full half empty

the head downward
the legs upward
he tumbles into the bottomless
from whence he came.
(translated by Ina Kohrer)

Dada carried to its logical conclusion the notion of all having come about by chance; the result was the final absurdity of everything, including humanity.

The man who perhaps most clearly and consciously showed this understanding of the resulting absurdity of all things was Marcel Duchamp (1887-1969). He carried the concept of fragmentation further in *Nude Descending a Staircase* (1912), one version of which is now in the Philadelphia Museum of Art—a painting in which the human disappeared completely. The chance and fragmented concept of what *is* led to the devaluation and absurdity of all things. All one was left with was a fragmented view of a life which is absurd in all its parts. Duchamp realized that the absurdity of all things includes the absurdity of art itself. His "ready-mades" were any object near at hand, which he simply signed. It could be a bicycle wheel or a urinal. Thus art itself was declared absurd.

The historical flow is like this: the philosophers from Rousseau, Kant, Hegel and Kierkegaard onward, having lost their hope of a unity of knowledge and a unity of life, presented a fragmented concept of reality; then the artists painted that way. It was the artists, however, who first understood that the end of this view was the absurdity of all things. Temporally these artists followed the philosophers, as the artists of the Renaissance had followed Thomas Aquinas. In the Renaissance it was also philosophy, followed by the painters (Cimabue and Giotto), followed by the writers (Dante). This was the same order in which the concept of fragmented reality spread in the twentieth century. The philosophers first formulated intellectually what the artists later depicted artistically.

Jackson Pollock (1912-1956) is perhaps the clearest example in the United States of painting deliberately in order to make the statement that all is chance. He placed canvases horizontally on the floor and dripped paint on them from suspended cans swinging over them. Thus, his paintings were a product of chance. But wait a minute! Is there not an order in the lines of paint on his canvases? Yes, because it was not really chance shaping his canvases! The universe is not a random universe; it has order. Therefore, as the dripping paint from the swinging cans moved over the canvases, the lines of paint were following the order of the universe itself. The universe is not what these painters said it is.

The third way the idea spread was through music. This came about first in classical music, though later many of the same elements came into popular music, such as rock. In classical music two streams are involved: the German and the French.

The first shift in German music came with the last Quartets of Beethoven, composed in 1825 and 1826. These certainly were not what we would call "modern," but they were a shift from the music prior to them. Leonard Bernstein (1918-) speaks of Beethoven as the "new artist—the artist as priest and prophet." Joseph Machlis (1906-) says in *Introduction to Contemporary Music* (1961), "Schoenberg took his point of departure from the final Quartets of Beethoven." And Stravinsky said, "These Quartets are my highest articles of musical belief (which is a longer word for love, whatever else), as indispensable to the ways and meaning of art, as a musician of my era thinks of art and has to learn it, as temperature is to life."

Beethoven was followed by Wagner (1813-1883); then came Gustav Mahler (1860-1911). Leonard Bernstein in the *Norton Lectures* at Harvard University in 1973 says of Mahler and especially Mahler's Ninth Symphony, "Ours is the century of death and Mahler is its musical prophet. . . . If Mahler knew this [personal

death, death of tonality, and the death of culture as it had been]
and his message is so clear, how do we, knowing it too, manage to
survive? Why are we still here, struggling to go on? We are now
face to face with the truly ultimate ambiguity, which is the human
spirit—the most fascinating ambiguity of all. . . . We learn to
accept our mortality; yet we persist in our search for
immortality. . . . All this ultimate ambiguity is to be heard in the
finale of Mahler's Ninth." Notice how closely this parallels Nietzsche's poem on page 193. This is modern man's position. He has
come to a position of the death of man in his own mind, but he
cannot live with it, for it does not describe what he is.

Then came Schoenberg (1874-1951), and with him we are into
the music which was a vehicle for modern thought. Schoenberg
totally rejected the past tradition in music and invented the "12-
tone row." This was "modern" in that there was perpetual varia-
tion with *no resolution*. This stands in sharp contrast to Bach who,
on his biblical base, had much diversity but always resolution.
Bach's music had resolution because as a Christian he believed that
there will be resolution both for each individual life and for history. As the music which came out of the biblical teaching of the
Reformation was shaped by that world-view, so the world-view
of modern man shapes modern music.

Among Schoenberg's pupils were Alban Berg (1885-1935),
Anton Webern (1883-1945), and John Cage (1912-). Each of these
carried on this line of nonresolution in his own way. Donald Jay
Grout (1902-) in *A History of Western Music* speaks of Schoenberg's
and Berg's subject matter in the modern world: ". . . isolated,
helpless in the grip of forces he does not understand, prey to inner
conflict, tension, anxiety and fear." One can understand that a
music of nonresolution is a fitting expression of the place to which
modern man has come.

In *Introduction to Contemporary Music* Joseph Machlis says of
Webern that his way of placing the weightier sounds on the off-
beat and perpetually varying the rhythmic phrase imparts to his
music its indefinable quality of "hovering suspension." Machlis
adds that Karlheinz Stockhausen (1928-), and the German Co-
logne school in general, take up from Webern with the formation
of electronic music which "generates, transforms and manipulates
sounds electronically." Stockhausen produced the first published
score of electronic music in his *Electronic Studies*. A part of his
concern was with the element of chance in composition. As we

shall see, this ties into the work of John Cage, whom we will study in more detail below. But first let us look at the French stream.

The French shift began with Claude Debussy (1862-1918). His direction was not so much that of nonresolution but of *fragmentation*. Many of us enjoy and admire much of Debussy's music, but he opened the door to fragmentation in music and has influenced most of the composers since, not only in classical music but in popular music and rock as well. Even the music which is one of the glories of America—black jazz and black spirituals—was gradually infiltrated.

It is worth reemphasizing that this fragmentation in music is parallel to the fragmentation which occurred in painting. And again let us say that these were not just changes of technique; they expressed a world-view and became a vehicle for carrying that world-view to masses of people which the bare philosophic writings never would have touched.

John Cage provides perhaps the clearest example of what is involved in the shift in music. Cage believed the universe is a universe of chance, and to express this he produced music by chance. He tried carrying this out with great consistency. For example, at times he flipped coins to decide what the music should be. At other times he erected a machine that led an orchestra by chance motions so that the orchestra would not know what was coming next. Thus there was no order. Or again, he placed two conductors leading the same orchestra, separated from each other by a partition, so that what resulted was utter confusion. There is a close tie-in again to painting; in 1947 Cage made a composition he called *Music for Marcel Duchamp*. But the sound produced by Cage's chance music always turned out to be sheer noise. Some of his music was composed only of silence (interrupted only by random environmental sounds), but as soon as he used his chance methods sheer noise was the outcome.

But Cage also showed that one cannot live on such a base, that the chance concept of the universe does not fit the universe as it is. Cage is an expert in mycology, the science of mushrooms. And he himself said, "I became aware that if I approached mushrooms in the spirit of my chance operation, I would die shortly." Mushroom picking must be carefully discriminative. His theory of the universe does not fit the universe that exists.

All of this music by chance, which results in noise, makes a strange contrast to the airplanes sitting in our airports or slicing through our skies. An airplane is carefully formed; it is orderly (and many would also think it beautiful). This is in sharp contrast to the intellectualized art which states that the universe is chance. Why is the airplane carefully formed and orderly, and what Cage produced utter noise? Simply because an airplane must fit the orderly flow lines of the universe if it is to fly!

Sir Archibald Russel (1905-) was the British designer for the Concorde airliner. In a *Newsweek:* European Edition interview (February 16, 1976) he was asked: "Many people find that the Concorde is a work of art in its design. Did you consider its esthetic appearance when you were designing it?" His answer was, "When one designs an airplane, he must stay as close as possible to the laws of nature. You are really playing with the laws of nature and trying not to offend them. It so happens that our ideas of beauty are those of nature. Every shape and curve of the Concorde is arranged so it will conform with the natural flow as conditioned by the laws of nature. That's why I doubt that the Russian supersonic airplane is a crib of ours. The Russians have the same basic phenomena imposed on them by nature as we do."

Cage's music and the world-view for which it is the vehicle do not fit the universe that is. Someone might here bring in Einstein, Werner Heisenberg's principle of uncertainty and quantum, but we have considered them on page 162, and so will not repeat the discussion here. The universe is not what Cage in his music and Pollock in his painting say it is. And we must add that Cage's music does not fit what people are, either. It has had to become increasingly spectacular to keep interest; for example, a nude cellist has played Cage's music under water.

A further question is: Is this art really art? Is it not rather a bare philosophic, intellectual statement, separated from the fullness of who people are and the fullness of what the universe is? The more it tends to be only an intellectual statement, rather than a work of art, the more it becomes anti-art.

The fourth vehicle for these ideas is what I will call general culture. By this, I mean poetry, the novel, drama, and cinema. In the Anglo-Saxon world, the introduction in poetry came with T. S. Eliot's (1888-1965) "The Waste Land," which was published in 1922. Here he matched a fragmented message to a fragmented form of poetry. The end of the fifth (and last) section of "The Waste Land" reads:

Le Prince d' Aquitaine à la tour abolie.
These fragments I have shored against my ruins
Why then Ile fit you.
Hieronymo's mad againe.
Datta. Dayadhvam. Damyata.
Shantih shantih shantih.

In this poem he opened the door to modern poetry the way Picasso opened the way to a fragmented concept of life in his painting *Les Demoiselles d'Avignon.* It is interesting that later when Eliot became a Christian, his form of writing, although it did not become "old-fashioned," did change. We will pick up elements of general culture later in this chapter, especially the uniquely twentieth-century art form—the cinema. Popular music, such as some elements of rock, brought to the young people of the entire world the concept of a fragmented world—and optimism only in the area of nonreason. And poetry, drama, the novel, and especially films carried these ideas to the mass of people in a way that went beyond the other vehicles we have considered.

All of this gives us today an almost monolithic consensus, an almost unified voice shouting at us a fragmented concept of the universe and of life. And as it comes at us from every side and with many voices, it is difficult not to be infiltrated by it. We and our children now get this message from every side—from art, music, general culture, modern theology, the mass media, and often even comic books. Perhaps cinema, especially in the sixties, proclaimed this message in a way that spread it most widely. But in order to understand its unique contribution we must first consider other developments in philosophy.

Formal philosophy, as such, has tended to sicken, if not die, for modern people. As we have seen, modern modern science put aside the epistemological base of early science—this early base being that, because the world was created by a reasonable God, man can find out about the universe by reason. Then, when this Christian base was abandoned, scientists tried to make the philosophy of *positivism* their philosophic base for knowing.

Positivism had been worked out in the first half of the nineteenth century by the French philosopher Auguste Comte (1798-1857) and was developed as the base for science by Herbert Spencer (1820-1903). Related to John Locke's (1632-1704) empiricism, positivism is a naive philosophy which basically says that you look at an object and there it is. The data which reaches you through your senses enables you to know the object in a straight-forward and uncomplicated way.

But some years ago people began to realize that science did not really look at an object with total objectivity. In the *Journal of the Franklin Institute* (1936) Albert Einstein pointed out that man makes choices out of the multitude of sense data which comes to him. In other words, there is a subjective element involved in the scientific process. Michael Polanyi (1891-1976), who retired from Manchester University in 1958 and since that time had taught in many universities, in his book *Personal Knowledge: Towards a Post-Critical Philosophy* (1958) destroyed the naive view of positivism. Polanyi pointed out that the observer is always there and always makes the conclusions, and he is never entirely neutral.

And with this, positivism is no longer a viable base for knowing. In science a man arranges the experiment; he has a grid in his thinking into which he fits his observations and makes the conclusions. The positivism I knew when I was younger, which was so very, very strong in the universities of Europe and America, is now dead. No longer are those holding this view so sure of the relationship between themselves and the object they are observing.

There is another profound objection to positivism, namely, that on the basis of this philosophic system there is no reason for certainty that the data reaching the observer is really data and not just illusion. This was no problem when Christianity was the basis, with a view of the universe as created by a God of reason, and people created by the same reasonable God to live in that universe. But without the Christian base, what assurance do people have that what reaches them through the senses corresponds to what is "out there"? Humanism in the Renaissance had not been able to find a way to impart meaning and value to the individual things, the particulars. By the time of the death of positivism, humanism had no base for certainty in knowing.

Interestingly, the artists had seen the problem before the philosophers and scientists, for positivism was parallel to Impressionism. As we have said, the Impressionists painted what they saw, but this left the question of whether there was reality behind the light waves reaching their eyes. Monet took the next step in 1885 and reality tended to be obscured. Thus there was a time when the artists were ahead of both philosophers and scientists. Without the Christian base, neither artists nor philosophers nor scientists had a base which would bear the needed weight in the area of how we can be sure we can know.

What then has happened to science? In brief, science, as it is now usually conceived, has no epistemological base—that is, no base for being sure that what scientists think they observe corresponds to what really exists. It should be noted, however, that even though they have no such base in their own system, yet in both science and day-by-day knowing, there *is* a correspondence between the external world and ourselves, for God indeed made the subject and object to be in a proper relationship, just as our lungs fit this atmosphere on the earth. Thus, men can go on learning about the universe. But the point is that the humanist has no base for knowing *within his own philosophic system*. His optimism about knowing the external world is weakened.

In this setting modern modern science tends increasingly to become one of two things: either a high form of technology, often with a goal of increasing affluence, or what I would call *sociological science*. By the latter I mean that, with a weakened certainty about objectivity, people find it easier to come to whatever conclusions they desire for the sociological ends they wish to see attained.

One example is Edmund Leach (1910-), a Reith Lecturer and well-known teacher of anthropology at Cambridge University. In *The New York Review of Books* Leach said that in the past there have been two views of evolution: either that all men came from the same starting place, or that there were different starting places and different starting times from prehuman biological forms. This second concept usually carries with it the idea that the races which are the oldest are the most advanced. Leach said that he chose the first concept because the second led to racism. Speaking of this second concept, he said that "this view of race is utterly useless for any purpose whatsoever except for ammunition for deplorable political causes." This is what I would call *sociological science:* choices being made on the basis of the sociological consequences which would result. With the weakening of certainty about knowing the objective, external world, the ideal of *objectivity* in science is weakened.

This is parallel to a change among the news makers. As their concept of truth becomes more relative, the ideal of *objectivity* in the news columns in contrast to the editorial pages is increasingly diminished. Thus, the loss of a philosophic base for truth and the certainty of knowing has the practical result of making for a *socio-*

logical science and a *sociological news medium*—both available for use by manipulators. And this is especially potent with science because of the almost "religious" belief which people have developed about the objectivity—and thus the certainty—of the results of science.

Returning to philosophy as such, after positivism, came *linguistic analysis*. This is a philosophy that deals with the analysis of language. Two philosophies were then dominant: existentialism and linguistic analysis. But to me neither are philosophies; both are antiphilosophies.

Existentialism deals with the big questions, but separates the attempted answers from reason, placing them in the area of nonreason. By contrast, linguistic analysis examines language on the basis of reason—only to discover gradually that analysis of language leads neither to values nor to facts. Language leads only to language, and linguistic analysis thus never gets to the big questions. Consequently, existentialism and linguistic analysis are both antiphilosophies in that neither gives the basis people need for the answers to the big and fundamental questions. Not only do they not give the answers people need, but each in its own way generates confusion about meaning and values. There were other less influential philosophies as well, but they gave no more definitive answers. Formal philosophy had left a vacuum.

The important concepts of philosophy increasingly began to come not as formal statements of philosophy but rather as expressions in art, music, novels, poetry, drama, and the cinema—those things we spoke of as general culture earlier in the chapter. As an example, Sartre's and Camus' existentialism came not so much through formal philosophical statements as in their novels. Consider Sartre's *Nausea* (1938), and Camus' *The Stranger* (1942) and *The Plague* (1947), and also Simone de Beauvoir's (1908-) *L'Invitée* (1943).

Especially in the sixties the major philosophic statements which received a wide hearing were made through films. These philosophic movies reached many more people than philosophic writing or even painting and literature. Among these films were *The Last Year at Marienbad* by Alain Resnais (1961), *The Silence* by Ingmar Bergman (1963), *Juliet of the Spirits* by Federico Fellini (1965), *Blow-Up* by Michaelangelo Antonioni (1966), *Belle de Jour* by Luis Buñuel (1967), and *The Hour of the Wolf* by Ingmar Bergman (1967). They showed pictorially (and with great force) what it is like if man is a machine and also what it is like if man tries to live in the area of nonreason. In the area of nonreason man is left without categories. He has no way to distinguish between right and wrong, or even between what is objectively true as opposed to illusion or fantasy.

A good example is Antonioni's *Blow-Up*. The advertisement for the film read: "Murder without guilt, love without meaning." Antonioni was portraying how, in the area of nonreason, there are no certainties concerning moral values, and no human categories either. *Blow-Up* had no hero. Compare this with Michelangelo's *David*—that statement of humanist pride in the Renaissance. Man had set himself up as autonomous, but the end result was not Michelangelo's *David*, but Antonioni's nonhero. All there is in the film is the camera which goes "click, click, click," and the human has disappeared. The main character snaps pictures of individual things, particulars. One might point out, for example, the models he snaps; all their humanity and meaning are gone.

After a scene in which clowns play tennis without a ball, there is at the end of the film a reverse zoom shot in which the man who is the central character disappears entirely, and all that remains is the grass. Man is gone. Modern people, on their basis of reason, see themselves only as machines. But as they move into the area of nonreason and look for their optimism, they find themselves separated from reason and without any human or moral values.

Some of the films of this period went even further as, for example, *Juliet of the Spirits, The Last Year at Marienbad, The Hour of the Wolf* and *Belle de Jour*. They were saying something even more profound: For modern people, as they leap into the area of nonreason to try to find optimism without reason, not only are there no human or moral categories but there is no certainty, no categories upon which to distinguish between reality and illusion.

Bergman provides a clear case here. In 1963 he directed *The Silence*. In a filmed interview he said he had come to conclude that God is dead; therefore there is only silence in the universe. Thus, he made this film. Then followed *The Hour of the Wolf* (1967) where one cannot tell the difference between what is real and what is fantasy. Was what was presented really happening or was it in the mind of one of the characters? This same problem was involved in the films *Juliet of the Spirits, The Last Year at Marienbad,* and *Belle de Jour*. One could view these films a hundred times and there still would be no way to be sure what was portrayed as objectively true and what was part of a character's imagination. If people begin only from themselves and really live in a universe in which there is no personal God to speak, they have no final way to be sure of the difference between reality and fantasy or illusion.

But Bergman (like Sartre, Camus, and all the rest) cannot really live with his own position. Therefore in *The Silence* the background music is Bach's Goldberg Variations. When he was asked in the filmed interview about music, he said that there is a small holy part of the human being where music speaks. He added that as he was writing *The Silence* he had the Goldberg Variations playing in his house and that this music interfered with what was being set forth in that film.

On the Christian base it is possible to know why music speaks. Man is not the product of chance. Man is made in the image of God, and on this basis, it is understandable why music *is* music to man. On the basis of revelation—the Bible and the revelation of God through Christ—there is not ultimate silence in the universe, and there are certainties of human values and moral values and categories to distinguish between illusion and fantasy. And there is a reason why man is man. But not for these modern people with a humanist position.

These philosophic films have spoken clearly about where people have come. Modern people are in trouble indeed. These things are not shut up within the art museums, the concert halls and rock festivals, the stage and movies, or the theological seminaries. People function on the basis of their world-view. Therefore, society has changed radically. This is the reason—and not a less basic one—that it is unsafe to walk at night through the streets of many of today's cities. As a man thinketh, so is he.

CHAPTER ELEVEN

Our Society

Gradually that which had become the basic thought-form of modern people became the almost totally accepted viewpoint, an almost monolithic consensus. And as it came to the majority of people through art, music, drama, theology, and the mass media, values died. As the more Christian-dominated consensus weakened, the majority of people adopted two impoverished values: *personal peace* and *affluence.*

Personal peace means just to be let alone, not to be troubled by the troubles of other people, whether across the world or across the city—to live one's life with minimal possibilities of being personally disturbed. Personal peace means wanting to have my personal life pattern undisturbed in my lifetime, regardless of what the result will be in the lifetimes of my children and grandchildren. Affluence means an overwhelming and ever-increasing prosperity—a life made up of things, things, and more things—a success judged by an ever-higher level of material abundance.

For several generations the fragmented concept of knowledge and life which had become dominant was taught to the young by many of the professors in universities around the world. All too often when the students of the early sixties asked their parents and others, "Why be educated?" they were told, by implication, if not in words, "Because statistically an educated person makes so much more money a year." And when they asked, "Why make more money?" they were told, "So that you can send *your* children to the university." According to this kind of spoken or implied answer, there was no meaning for man, and no meaning for education.

Much of the mass media popularized these concepts, pouring them out in an endless stream so that a whole generation from its birth has been injected with the teaching that reason leads to pessimism in regard to a meaning of life and with reference to any fixed values. This had been that generation's atmosphere. It had no personal memory of the days when Christianity had more influence on the consensus. Those in the universities saw themselves as little computers controlled by the larger computer of the university, which in turn was controlled by the still-larger computer of the state.

The work ethic, which had meaning within the Christian framework, now became ugly as the Christian base was removed. Work became an end in itself—with no reason to work and no values to determine what to do with the products of one's work. And suddenly, in 1964 at the University of California at Berkeley, the students carried these ideas about the meaninglessness of man out into the streets. Why should anybody have been surprised? Many of the teachers taught the ultimate meaninglessness of man and the absence of absolutes, but they themselves lived inconsistently by depending on the memory of the past. Was it not natural that one generation would begin to live on the basis of what they had been taught? And at Berkeley in 1964 the results were visible, full blast.

Because the only hope of meaning had been placed in the area of nonreason, drugs were brought into the picture. Drugs had been around a long time, but, following Aldous Huxley's ideas, many students now approached drug-taking as an ideology, and some as a religion. They hoped that drugs would provide meaning "inside one's head," in contrast to objective truth, concerning which they had given up hope. Psychologist Timothy Leary (1920-), Gary Snyder (1930-), author-philosopher Alan Watts (1915-1973), and poet Allen Ginsberg (1926-) were all influential in making drugs an ideology. Timothy Leary, for example, said that drugs were the sacraments for the new religion. Of course, as we have seen in a previous chapter, this drug-taking was really only one more leap, an attempt to find meaning in the area of nonreason.

Charles Slack (1929-), writing of his long relationship with Leary, reported in *Timothy Leary, the Madness of the Sixties and Me* (1974) that Leary had said to him, "Death to the mind, that is the goal you must have. Nothing else will do."

The utopian dream of the turned-on world was that if enough people were on drugs, the problems of modern civilization would be solved. With this in mind there was talk of introducing LSD into the drinking water of the cities. This was not vicious, for the people suggesting it really believed that drugs were the door to Paradise. In 1964 and for some years after, the hippie world really believed this ideological answer.

At Berkeley the Free Speech Movement arose simultaneously with the hippie world of drugs. At first it was politically neither left nor right, but rather a call for the freedom to express any political views on Sproul Plaza. Then soon the Free Speech Movement became the Dirty Speech Movement, in which freedom was seen as shouting four-letter words into a mike. Soon after, it became the platform for the political New Left which followed the teaching of Herbert Marcuse (1898-). Marcuse was a German professor of philosophy related to the neo-Marxist teaching of the "Frankfurt School," along with Theodor Adorno (1903-1969), Max Horkheimer (1895-) and Jürgen Habermas (1929-). When he became the inspiration of the New Left, he was teaching at the University of California at San Diego.

For some time, young people were fighting against their parents' impoverished values of personal peace and affluence— whether their way of fighting was through Marcuse's New Left or through taking drugs as an ideology. The young people wanted more to life than personal peace and affluence. They were right in their analysis of the problem, but they were mistaken in their solutions.

The peak of the drug culture of the hippie movement was well symbolized by the movie *Woodstock*. Woodstock was a rock festival held in northeastern United States in the summer of 1969. The movie about that rock festival was released in the spring of 1970. Many young people thought that Woodstock was the beginning of a new and wonderful age. The organizer claimed, "This is the beginning of a new era. It works!" But the drug world was already ugly, and it was approaching the end of its optimism, although the young people did not yet know it. Jimi Hendrix (1942-1970) himself was soon to become a symbol of the end.

Black, extremely talented, inhumanly exploited, he overdosed in September 1970 and drowned in his own vomit, soon after the claim that the culture of which he was a symbol was a new beginning. In the late sixties the ideological hopes based on drug-taking died.

At Altamont, California, in December 1969, the Rolling Stones had a festival. They brought in the Hell's Angels to police the grounds in return for a certain amount of beer. But a man was killed, and *Rolling Stone* magazine in its next issue reported, "Our age of innocency is gone." Soon afterward (August 1970) 250,000 people came to a music festival on the Isle of Wight in the English Channel. It, too, ended in utter ugliness, and from that time on drug-taking changed.

Unhappily, the result was not that fewer people were taking drugs. The sixties drew to a close, and in the seventies and eighties probably more people are taking some form of drug, and at an ever-younger age. But taking drugs is no longer an ideology. That is finished. Drugs simply are the escape which they have been traditionally in many places in the past.

In the United States the New Left also slowly ground down, losing favor because of the excesses of the bombings, especially in the bombing of the University of Wisconsin lab in 1970, where a graduate student was killed. This was not the last bomb that was or will be planted in the United States. Hard-core groups of radicals still remain and are active, and could become more active, but the violence which the New Left produced as its natural heritage (as it also had in Europe) caused the majority of young people in the United States no longer to see it as a hope. So some young people began in 1964 to challenge the false values of personal peace and affluence, and we must admire them for this. Humanism, man beginning only from himself, had destroyed the old basis of values, and could find no way to generate with certainty any new values. In the resulting vacuum the impoverished values of personal peace and affluence had come to stand supreme. And now, for the majority of the young people, after the passing of the false hopes of drugs as an ideology and the fading of the New Left, what remained? Only *apathy* was left. In the United States by the beginning of the seventies, *apathy* was almost complete. In contrast to the political activists of the sixties, not many of the young even went to the polls to vote, even though the national voting age was lowered to eighteen. Hope was gone.

After the turmoil of the sixties, many people thought that it was so much better when the universities quieted down in the early seventies. I could have wept. The young people had been right in their analysis, though wrong in their solutions. How much worse when many gave up hope and simply accepted the same values as their parents—personal peace and affluence. Now drugs remain, but only in parallel to the older generation's alcohol, and an excessive use of alcohol has become a problem among the young people as well. Promiscuous sex and bisexuality remain, but only in parallel to the older generation's adultery. In other words, as the young people revolted against their parents, they came around in a big circle—and often ended an inch lower—with only the same two impoverished values: their own kind of personal peace and their own kind of affluence.

In some places the Marxist-Leninist line or the Maoist line took over. This was not so true in the United States, but these ideologies have become a major factor in Europe, South America, and other parts of the world. But Marxist-Leninism is another leap into the area of nonreason—as idealistic as drug-taking was in its early days. The young followed Marxism in spite of clear evidence that oppression was not an excess of Stalin, but was and is an integral part of the system of communism.

No one has made this more clear than Alexander Solzhenitsyn (1918-) in *The Gulag Archipelago* (Vol. I, 1974). He takes great pains to point out that the foundations of lawless expediency were firmly established by Lenin. Summarizing the trials up through 1922 and looking ahead to the famous "showcase trials" of 1937, Solzhenitsyn asks, "What, then, were they surprised at in 1937? Hadn't all the foundations of lawlessness been laid?" But if this preceded Stalin, it is clear that it also survived him. Solzhenitsyn says that the salamander, by which he means the prison-camp network, is still alive. In *The Gulag Archipelago* (Vol. II, 1975) he says that the prison camps held up to fifteen million inmates at a time, and he estimated that from the Revolution to 1959 a total of sixty-six million prisoners died.

Even if this salamander is not so obviously voracious now, Solzhenitsyn is not appeased. He correctly identifies the root cause of the lawless expediency as the willingness to assure internal security at any cost. And he sees that when his contemporaries now urge him to "let bygones be bygones" they are making the same choice. "Dwell on the past and you'll lose an eye," they say.

Solzhenitsyn adds, "But the proverb goes on to say: 'Forget the past and you'll lose both eyes.' "

Tellingly, he contrasts the West German effort since World War II to track down and punish major, known Nazi criminals (of which 86,000 had been convicted by 1966) with the total absence of such a procedure both in East Germany as regards Nazis and in Russia as regards the active agents of the officially condemned crimes of Stalin. He selects Molotov as a symbol of this mentality—a man who lives on comfortably, "a man who has learned nothing at all, even now, though he is saturated with our blood and nobly crosses the sidewalk to seat himself in his long, wide automobile." Reflecting upon these facts, Solzhenitsyn writes, "From the most ancient times justice has been a two-part concept: virtue triumphs and vice is punished." In contrast, Solzhenitsyn concludes about Russia, "Young people are acquiring the conviction that foul deeds are never punished on earth, that they always bring prosperity." He then adds, "It is going to be uncomfortable, horrible, to live in such a country!" And this is the case not only in Russia but wherever communism has attained power. China probably had less internal freedom than Russia.

Communists have also used external oppression: think of Hungary, Czechoslovakia, and Poland. I'll never forget the day—November 4, 1956—when Hungary was taken over. Listening in Switzerland to my shortwave radio, I heard the students repeatedly pleading in the English language for help, hoping the outside world would listen. I have a newspaper picture of one of the girls arrested in Hungary. It is a portrait of a lovely Hungarian girl on trial. Her name was Ilond Troth. She was hanged in July 1957. I keep her picture to remember: "Forget the past and you will lose both eyes."

How romantic, in a negative sense, is the leap into the area of nonreason to Marxist-Leninism! It is a different kind of leap from that of the existentialist and others we considered in the previous chapters, but it, too, is without a base in reason. Materialism, the philosophic base for Marxist-Leninism, gives no basis for the dignity or rights of man. Where Marxist-Leninism is not in power it attracts and converts by talking much of dignity and rights, but its materialistic base gives no basis for the dignity or rights of man. Yet it attracts by its constant talk of idealism.

To understand this phenomenon we must understand that Marx reached over to that for which Christianity *does* give a base—the dignity of man—and took the words as words of his own. The only understanding of idealistic sounding Marxist-Leninism is that it is (in this sense) a Christian heresy. Not having the Christian base, until it comes to power it uses the words for which Christianity does give a base. But wherever Marxist-Leninism has had power, it has at no place in history shown where it has not brought forth oppression. As soon as they have had the power, the desire of the majority has become a concept without meaning.

As we said in the first chapter, men have presuppositions and will live more consistently with these presuppositions than even they themselves know. People's presuppositions rest upon that which they consider to be the truth of what exists. With a whole state consciously resting upon philosophic materialism, there is no base for "communism with a human face," for which have pleaded some of the reformers in Poland, Czechoslovakia, and other Communist controlled countries (and some Communists in non-Communist controlled countries).

In 1975 when André Malraux was asked if there really can be communism with a human face, he pondered a while and then replied, "Historical experience suggests that there can't be." With no base for the dignity of the individual, only arbitrary expediency gives whatever dignity is given. And being only arbitrary, expediency can twist and turn at will. Men tend to act ultimately with remarkable consistency to their presuppositions, their worldview. To forget this in regard to a system which consciously rests on the philosophic base of materialism will be to lose not only two eyes, but also one's head.

Countries which have a different base, for example a Christian one (or at least one with the memory of a Christian foundation), may indeed act most inconsistently and horribly. But when a state with a materialistic base acts arbitrarily and gives no dignity to man, internally or externally, it is being consistent to its basic presuppositions and principles. To accept Marxist-Leninism is indeed a leap into the area of nonreason. It is its own kind of Nietzsche game plan, a setting of limits as to what one will observe, and a refusal to look outside of these boundaries lest the system be brought down like a house of cards. This does not make Marxist-Leninism less of a danger, and it is necessary to take into account the resurgence of the old-line Communist parties, and also the Russian-financed terrorist groups.

There are two streams of Marxist-Leninism: first, those who

hold it in an idealistic form as a leap against all reason—listening to the words which have been lifted as a Christian heresy, the words of dignity and rights—and who close their eyes to the intrinsic oppression of the system as a system; second, the old-line Communists who hold an orthodox communistic ideology. "Danny the Red" (Daniel Cohn-Bendit), who led the student riots in France in May 1968 and who is still a Marxist, in an interview in 1975 made the distinction between these two groups. He spoke of the old-line Communists in terms of "orthodox communist ideology" and "bureaucratic structure of the type existing in the Soviet Union."

If personal peace and affluence would seem available under communism, no one can be sure what many of the young people and older ones, too, will do. The two streams of Marxist-Leninism of which we have spoken could flow together at a crucial point and produce political results which would be irreversible.

In the United States many other practical problems developed as man's desire to be autonomous from God's revelation—in the Bible and through Christ—increasingly reached its natural conclusions. Sociologically, *law is king* (Samuel Rutherford's *Lex Rex*) was no longer the base whereby one could be ruled by law rather than the arbitrary judgments of men and whereby there could be wide freedoms without chaos. Any ways in which the system is still working is largely due to the sheer inertia of the continuation of the past principles. But this borrowing cannot go on forever.

As we have seen, there is a danger that without a sufficient base modern modern science will become *sociological science;* so civil law has moved toward being *sociological law.* Distinguished jurist and Supreme Court Justice Oliver Wendell Holmes, Jr. (1841-1935) took a long step in this direction. In *The Common Law* (1881) Holmes said that law is based on experience. Daniel H. Benson (1936-), assistant professor of law at the Texas Tech University School of Law, quotes Holmes: "Truth is the majority vote of that nation that could lick all others." In a 1926 letter to John C. H. Wu, Holmes wrote, "So when it comes to the development of a *corpus juris* the ultimate question is what do the dominant forces of the community want and do they want it hard enough to disregard whatever inhibitions may stand in the way." This is very different from Samuel Rutherford's biblical base and from Paul Robert's painting in which Justice points to "The Word of God."

Frederick Moore Vinson (1890-1953), former Chief Justice of the United States Supreme Court, spelled out this problem by saying, "Nothing is more certain in modern society than the principle that there are no absolutes." All is relative; all is experience. In passing, we should note this curious mark of our age: the only absolute allowed is the absolute insistence that there is no absolute.

Roscoe Pound (1870-1964) wrote in *Jurisprudence* (1959): "The Greek philosophers sought to find some assured basis of social control other than tradition and the habit of obedience on the one hand, or the will of the politically supreme for the moment on the other hand. They conceived they had found such a basis in the analogy of the constant and universal phenomena of physical nature." In the days of Rousseau, Goethe, and Constable, when nature was being venerated, there was a concerted attempt to make nature the base for law. It is called Natural Law or the Law-of-Nature School of Jurisprudence. Roscoe Pound writes about the men identified with this approach: "Jurists of the eighteenth century Law-of-Nature School conceived that a complete and perfect system of law might be constructed upon principles of natural (i.e., ideal) law which were discoverable by reason." This was a part of Enlightenment optimism.

But, as we have seen, nature provides no sufficient base for either morals or law, because nature is both cruel and noncruel. Gradually, the hope that nature would give a fixed value in law was abandoned, and instead (as Pound quotes French jurist and legal philosopher Joseph Charmont [1859-1922]) by the start of the twentieth century, law rooted in nature only had a variable content. A Jewish-Christian lawyer once wrote to me that as he considered the serious meaning of the Nuremburg war-crimes trials, "I knew then that no moral law was written on a blade of grass, in a drop of water, or even in the stars. I realized the necessity of the Divine Immutable Law as set forth in the Sacred Torah, consisting of definite commandments, statutes, ordinances and judgments."

Man has failed to build only from himself autonomously and to find a solid basis in nature for law, and we are left today with Oliver Wendell Holmes's "experience" and Frederick Moore Vinson's statement that nothing is more certain in modern society than that there are no absolutes. Law has only a variable content. Much modern law is not even based on precedent; that is, it does not necessarily hold fast to a continuity with the legal decisions of the past. Thus, within a wide range, the Constitution of the United States can be made to say what the courts of the present want it to say—based on a court's decision as to what the court feels is sociologically helpful at the moment. At times this brings forth happy results, at least temporarily; but once the door is opened, anything can become law and the arbitrary judgments of men are king. Law is now freewheeling, and the courts not only interpret the laws which legislators have made, but make law. *Lex Rex* has become *Rex Lex*. Arbitrary judgment concerning current sociological good is *king*.

As arbitrary absolutes characterize communistic rule, so there is a drift in this direction on our side of the Iron Curtain as well. *This means that tremendous changes of direction can be made and the majority of the people tend to accept them without question—no matter how arbitrary the changes are or how big a break they make with past law or past consensus.*

It is worth considering at length, as an example, the United States Supreme Court ruling concerning the human fetus, the unborn baby. On January 22, 1973, the United States Supreme Court ruled that every woman in the United States has the right to an abortion during the first three months of pregnancy, with no discussion. In the second three months abortion is allowed if the state agrees it is healthy for the mother to have the abortion. During the second three months, as in the first three months, the fetus does not enter into consideration. Even during the last three months the fetus does not have effective protection under the law, because the word *health* (of the mother) has been given a very wide meaning.

To quote Joseph P. Witherspoon (1916-), professor of jurisprudence at the University of Texas School of Law, in the *Texas Tech Law Review*, Volume six, 1974-1975: "In this 1973 decision the Court . . . held that the unborn child is not a person within the meaning and protection of the term 'person' utilized in the fourteenth amendment so as to strip all unborn children of all constitutional protection for their lives, liberty, and property." In Britain the law allows pregnancies to be terminated up to the twenty-eighth week. There are several things to notice here.

This is totally arbitrary. First, it is *medically* arbitrary. *Our Future Inheritance: Choice or Chance?* (1974) is a book put out in England to inform the public about the questions of genetics which are immediately before us at this point of history. It is based on a series of working papers produced with the cooperation of scientists in a number of fields, including some scientists from the United States. It is in favor of abortion. However, the book says that the question about when human life begins is open: "It [abortion] can be carried out before the foetus becomes 'viable'— although when that is, is in itself an arguable point." It further states that "a biologist might say that human life started at the moment of fertilization when the sperm and the ovum merge."

The arbitrary nature of the decision *medically* is underlined by the fact that one section of the book accepts the destruction of the fetus by abortion, yet another section focuses on the question of whether it is ethical to fertilize the ovum with a sperm *in vitro* (in the laboratory) when at that stage of technology it was certain to live for only a very limited number of days. The problem is that after fertilization it has "the full genetic potential for becoming a human being and will become one if implantation [in the womb] and gestation are successful. At what stage of development should the status of a patient be attributed to the embryo or foetus?" Here the question is raised whether the six-day-old fetus should be considered "a patient." In another place the book argues for fertilization in the laboratory on the basis that, since we help a baby who is prematurely born, should we not be willing to help "the complete development of a baby outside the body"? This is preceded by the sentence: "Assistance for the premature baby would, by most, be considered one of the basic duties of society." And in the argument for a total development outside the body the concept of the *premature baby* is carried back to the time of fertilization. What does this make the abortion of a five-and-one-half-month-old baby? It certainly has "the full genetic potential for becoming a human being."

I am making only one point here: both the ruling by the United States Supreme Court and the British law were purely arbitrary *medically*. They established an arbitrary absolute which affects millions of embryos, when *medically* the matter is so open that the asking of ethical questions about a fertilized ovum of only seven days is considered valid, and when *medically* the question concerning the seven-day-old fertilized ovum rests on the fact that it has "the full genetic potential for becoming a human being." So when the official *Supreme Court Reporter* (Vol. 410) says that the unborn are not recognized in the law as persons, here is a *medical* arbitrary absolute with a vengeance—and at the point of human life.

Second, it is not only arbitrary medically but *legally*. The ruling set up an arbitrary absolute by disregarding the intent of the Thirteenth and Fourteenth Amendments of the Constitution. Quoting Professor Witherspoon again:

Thus, the failure of the Court in Roe v. Wade [the abortion case] to have examined into the actual purpose and intent of the legislature in framing the fourteenth amendment and the thirteenth amendment to which it was so closely related and supplementary thereof when it was considering the meaning to be assigned to the concept of "person" was a failure to be faithful to the law or to respect the legislature which framed it. Careful research of the history of these two amendments will demonstrate to any impartial investigator that there is overwhelming evidence supporting the proposition that the principal, actual purpose of their framers was to prevent any court, and especially the Supreme Court of the United States, because of its earlier performance in the *Dred Scott* case, or any other institution of government, whether legislative or executive, from ever again defining the concept of person so as to exclude any class of human beings from the protection of the Constitution and the safeguards it established for the fundamental rights of human beings, including slaves, peons, Indians, aliens, women, the poor, the aged, criminals, the mentally ill or retarded, and children, including the unborn from the time of their conception.

Supreme Court Justice White in his dissent to the Court's action stated, "As an exercise of raw judicial power, the Court perhaps has authority to do what it does today; but in my view its judgment is an improvident and extravagant exercise of the power of judicial review that the Constitution extends to this Court." Upon this arbitrary ruling *medically* and *legally,* the Supreme Court invalidated the law on this subject of abortion of almost every one of the states in the Union.

Further, this arbitrary decision is at complete variance with the past Christian consensus. In the pagan Roman Empire, abortion was freely practiced, but Christians took a stand against it. In 314 the Council of Ancyra barred from the taking of the Lord's Supper for ten years all who procured abortions or made drugs to further abortions. Previously the Synod of Elvira (305-306) had specified excommunication till the deathbed for these offenses. The arbitrary absolutes of the Supreme Court are accepted against the previous consensus of centuries, as well as against past law. *And (taking abortion as an example) if this arbitrary absolute by law is accepted by most modern people, bred with the concept of no absolutes but rather relativity, why wouldn't arbitrary absolutes in regard to such matters as authoritarian limitations on freedom be equally accepted as long as they were thought to be sociologically helpful?* We are left with *sociological law* without any certainty of limitation.

By the ruling of the Supreme Court, the unborn baby is not counted as a person. In our day, quite rightly, there has been a hue and cry against some of our ancestors' cruel viewing of the black slave as a nonperson. This was horrible indeed—an act of hypocrisy as well as cruelty. But now, by an arbitrary absolute brought in on the humanist flow, millions of unborn babies of every color of skin are equally by law declared nonpersons. Surely this, too, must be seen as an act of hypocrisy.

The door is open. In regard to the fetus, the courts have arbitrarily separated "aliveness" from "personhood," and if this is so, why not arbitrarily do the same with the aged? So the steps move along, and euthanasia may well become increasingly acceptable. And if so, why not keep alive the bodies of the so-called neo-morts (persons in whom the brain wave is flat) to harvest from them body parts and blood, when the polls show that this has become acceptable to the majority? Dr. Willard Gaylin (1925-) discussed this possibility in *Harper's* (September 1974) under the title, "Harvesting the Dead." Law has become a matter of averages, just as the culture's sexual mores have become only a matter of averages.

As the Christian consensus dies, there are not many sociological alternatives. One possibility is hedonism, in which every man does his own thing. Trying to build a society on hedonism leads to chaos. One man can live on a desert island and do as he wishes within the limits of the form of the universe, but as soon as two men live on the island, if they are to live in peace, they cannot both do simply as they please. Consider two hedonists meeting on a narrow bridge crossing a rushing stream: each cannot do his own thing.

A second possibility is the absoluteness of the 51 percent vote. In the days of a more Christian culture, a lone individual with the Bible could judge and warn society, regardless of the majority vote, because there was an absolute by which to judge. There was an absolute for both morals and law. But to the extent that the Christian consensus is gone, this absolute is gone as a social force. Let us remember that on the basis of the absoluteness of the 51 percent vote, Hitler was perfectly entitled to do as he wished if he had the popular support. On this basis, law and morals become a matter of averages. And on this basis, if the majority vote supported it, it would become "right" to kill the old, the incurably ill, the insane—and other groups could be declared nonpersons. No voice could be raised against it.

Alfred Charles Kinsey (1894-1956), a biologist-sociologist at the Institute for Sex Research at Indiana University, produced his influential *Sexual Behavior of the Human Male* (1948) and *Sexual Behavior of the Human Female* (1953). These were based on 18,500 interviews. Kinsey made that which is "right" in sex a matter of statistics. Many people read his books because at that date they were far more titillating than other books accepted as respectable. However, their real impact was the underlying conception that sexual right and wrong depend only on what most people are doing sexually at a given moment of history. This has become the generally accepted sexual standard in the years since. Modern man has done the same thing in law.

As we saw in the first chapter, the Greeks found that society— the *polis*—was not a strong enough final authority to build upon, and it is still not strong enough today. If there are no absolutes, and if we do not like either the chaos of hedonism or the absoluteness of the 51 percent vote, only one other alternative is left: one man or an elite, giving authoritative arbitrary absolutes.

Here is a simple but profound rule: *if there are no absolutes by which to judge society, then society is absolute.* Society is left with one man or an elite filling the vacuum left by the loss of the Christian consensus which originally gave us form and freedom in northern Europe and in the West. In communism, the elite has won its way, and rule is based upon arbitrary absolutes handed down by that elite. Absolutes can be *this* today and *that* tomorrow. If Mao equaled the law, then the concept of a continual cultural revolution, "The Great Leap Forward," may be in order one year and very much out of order the next. Arbitrary absolutes can be handed down and there is no absolute by which to judge them.

So far, two elites put themselves forward, offering to fill the vacuum in our culture. The first was Marcuse's New Left, which has waned in influence. It no longer provides the live possibility for action which it did for a time. Then John Kenneth Galbraith (1908-) offered his form of the elite. Like the students at Berkeley, this economist has said that we live in a poor culture. Galbraith suggested an elite composed of intellectuals (especially the academic and scientific world) plus the government. In June 1975, 2,000 "futurists" met for the Second General Assembly of the World Future Society in Washington, D.C. Socioeconomist Robert Theobald (1929-) endorsed the concept of "sapientary authority," a social structure in which wise men selected by merit would be deeply involved in the governmental decision-making process. "It's naive," declared Theobald, "to deny the necessity for some kind of competent elite."

Daniel Bell (1919-), professor of sociology at Harvard University, sees an elite composed of select intellectuals. He writes in *The Coming of Post-Industrial Society* (1973), in the chapter entitled "Who Will Rule," that "the university—or some other knowledge institute—will become the central institution of the next hundred years because of its role as the new source of innovation and knowledge." He says that crucial decisions will come from government, but more and more the decisions of both business and government will be predicated on government-sponsored research, and "because of the intricately linked nature of their consequences, [the decisions] will have an increasingly technical character." Society thus turns into a technocracy where "the determining influence belongs to technicians of the administration and of the economy." Bell sees that in the final analysis the whole state— its business, its education, its government, even the daily pattern of the ordinary man's life—becomes a matter of control by the technocratic elite. They are the only ones who know how to run the complicated machinery of society and they will then, in collusion with the government elite, have all the power necessary to manage it.

Bell's most astute warning concerns the ethical implications of this situation: "A post-industrial society cannot provide a transcendent ethic. . . . The lack of a rooted moral belief system is the cultural contradiction of the society, the deepest challenge to its survival." He adds that in the future men can be remade, their behavior conditioned, or their consciousness altered. The constraints of the past vanish. To the extent that Bell's picture of this future is fulfilled, Galbraith's form of the elite will be the actuality.

Humanism has led to its natural conclusion. It has ground down to the point Leonardo da Vinci visualized so long ago when he realized that, starting only from man, mathematics leads us only to particulars—and particulars lead only to mechanics.

Humanism had no way to find the universal in the areas of meaning and values. As my son, Franky, put it, "Humanism has changed the Twenty-third Psalm:

> They began—I am my shepherd
> Then—Sheep are my shepherd
> Then—Everything is my shepherd
> Finally—Nothing is my shepherd."

There is a death wish inherent in humanism—the impulsive drive to beat to death the base which made our freedoms and our culture possible.

In ancient Israel, when the nation had turned from God and from His truth and commands as given in Scripture, the prophet Jeremiah cried out that there was death in the city. He was speaking not only of physical death in Jerusalem but also a wider death. Because Jewish society of that day had turned away from what God had given them in the Scripture, there was death in the *polis*— that is, death in the total culture and the total society.

In our era, sociologically man destroyed the base which gave him the possibility of freedoms without chaos. Humanists have been determined to beat to death the knowledge of God and the knowledge that God has not been silent, but has spoken in the Bible and through Christ—and they have been determined to do this even though the death of values has come with the death of that knowledge.

We see two effects of our loss of meaning and values. The first is degeneracy. Think of New York City's Times Square—Forty-second and Broadway. If one goes to what used to be the lovely Kalverstraat in Amsterdam, one finds that it, too, has become equally squalid. The same is true of lovely old streets in Copenhagen. Pompeii has returned! The marks of ancient Rome scar us: degeneracy, decadence, depravity, a love of violence for violence's sake. The situation is plain. If we look, we see it. If we see it, we are concerned.

But we *must* notice that there is a second result of modern man's loss of meaning and values which is more ominous, and which many people do not see. This second result is that the elite will exist. Society cannot stand chaos. Some group or some person will fill the vacuum. An elite will offer us arbitrary absolutes, and who will stand in its way?

Will the silent majority (which at one time we heard so much about) help? The so-called silent majority was, and is, divided into a minority and a majority. The *minority* are either Christians who have a real basis for values or those who at least have a memory of the days when the values were real. The *majority* are left with only their two poor values of personal peace and affluence.

With such values, will men stand for their liberties? Will they not give up their liberties step by step, inch by inch, as long as their own personal peace and prosperity is sustained and not challenged, and as long as the goods are delivered? The life-styles of the young and the old generations are different. There are tensions between long hair and short, drugs and non-drugs, whatever are the outward distinctions of the moment. But they support each other sociologically, for both embrace the values of personal peace and affluence. Much of the church is no help here either, because for so long a large section of the church has only been teaching a relativistic humanism using religious terminology.

I believe the majority of the silent majority, young and old, will sustain the loss of liberties without raising their voices as long as their own life-styles are not threatened. And since personal peace and affluence are so often the only values that count with the majority, politicians know that to be elected they must promise these things. Politics has largely become not a matter of ideals—increasingly men and women are not stirred by the values of liberty and truth—but of supplying a constituency with a frosting of personal peace and affluence. They know that voices will not be raised as long as people have these things, or at least an illusion of them.

Edward Gibbon (1737-1794) in his *Decline and Fall of the Roman Empire* (1776-1788) said that the following five attributes marked Rome at its end: first, a mounting love of show and luxury (that is, affluence); second, a widening gap between the very rich and the very poor (this could be among countries in the family of nations as well as in a single nation); third, an obsession with sex; fourth, freakishness in the arts, masquerading as originality, and enthusiasms pretending to be creativity; fifth, an increased desire to live off the state. It all sounds so familiar. We have come a long road since our first chapter, and we are back in Rome.

CHAPTER TWELVE

Manipulation and the New Elite

As we consider the coming of an elite, an authoritarian state, to fill the vacuum left by the loss of Christian principles, we must not think naively of the models of Stalin and Hitler. We must think rather of a *manipulative* authoritarian government. Modern governments have forms of manipulation at their disposal which the world has never known before. We will examine a number of these methods and theories of manipulation, concentrating first on the psychological techniques, then on techniques associated with biological science, and finally on the new ways in which some of the media are influencing behavior.

First, one could mention the determinists, who say man has no freedom in his choices. For example, we can think of Sigmund Freud's (1856-1939) *psychological determinism,* B. F. Skinner's (1904-) *sociological determinism* through conditioning, and Francis Crick's (1916-) *chemical,* that is, *genetic determinism.*

Freud's determinism rests upon the child's relationship to its mother during the early portion of its life. He taught that this sets the pattern of the child's psychological makeup.

The ideas of sociological determinism, primarily involving conditioning (behaviorism), were widely discussed after B. F. Skinner published *Beyond Freedom and Dignity* (1971). His thesis was that all that people are can be explained by the way their environment has conditioned them. Since society plays a specially important role in that environment, society can and should use positive stimuli to bring about the society it wants. That this was meant not only to be a theory but to be put into use is shown by his earlier book, *Walden Two* (1948), a novel.

In *Walden Two* Skinner's utopia was a totally conditioned society. The director, T. E. Frazier, manipulated everyone to control all the details of the society. He made the people think that they wanted what he had decided they and society itself should be. In this and all other forms of determinism, man dies. In fact, Skinner himself acknowledged that what is being abolished is man. He says, "To man qua [as] man we readily say good riddance."

Skinner (like Bertrand Russell and George Wald) retains only the value of biological continuity: "Survival is the only value according to which a culture is eventually to be judged, and any practice that furthers survival has survival value by definition." But like other people we have considered, Skinner cannot live on the basis of his own system. He lives inconsistently on the memory of Christian values for which his system has no place.

The Christian position is *not* that there is no element of conditioning in human life, but rather that by no means does conditioning explain what people are in their totality. To a determinist, however, if one removed all the bundle of conditioning in man, there would be no man *as* man. Christianity rejects this. It insists that each individual person exists as a being created in the image of God, and that therefore each person is an ongoing entity with dignity. To proud, humanist man, who demands to be autonomous, technology of one kind or another is to be used to get rid of the limitations of nature, *including human nature,* which autonomous man finds insufferably confining. There is here a tension in modern people, especially perhaps among students: modern people want to be free to shape their own destiny, and yet they think they know they are determined.

The sadism of Marquis de Sade is the specter standing behind any determinist because the basis of de Sade's sadism was his concept of determinism. De Sade's position was that what is, is right; and if a person holds *any* form of determinism, he must agree that de Sade's conclusion is the only logical one. This is not to say that the determinists always carry their position to de Sade's logical conclusion, but it is the conclusion. In any form of determinism, what is considered right or acceptable is arbitrary. Modern determinists have not presented only abstract theories. Rather, there have been two practical results. First, and most important, as their ideas about what people are have been increasingly accepted, people consciously or unconsciously have opened themselves to being treated as machines and treating other people as machines. Second, each theory of determinism has carried with it a method of manipulation. So even though many—even most—people may reject the concept that man is totally a product of psychological, sociological, or chemical conditioning, manipulation by these methods is still very much a live possibility. In fact, these techniques are all at the disposal of authoritarian states, and they are in some degree already being used.

Some people might say that these deterministic ideas are only science fiction, but this is not so. T. George Harris (1924-), who reviewed Skinner's book in *Psychology Today* (August 1971), said, "Nobody would panic at Skinner's attack upon our idea of freedom if he were only talking. But he has a program, and followers to push it." Voices have been raised against Skinner's views and against behaviorism in general. For example, Noam Chomsky's (1928-) 1959 article in *Language* spoke out against one of Skinner's earlier books, *Verbal Behavior* (1957). But the behaviorists are numerous and, as Harris said, they have a program and followers to push it. Those who hold behavioristic concepts are often in positions of influence. For example, they often control education down to the lowest grades. Articles in the press constantly remind us that behaviorism dominates various university psychology departments. This professor or writer or then another comes into fashion and later becomes less important, but behaviorism is an ongoing and progressing factor in society.

The pressure toward the development of manipulative techniques comes through strongly in current biological research and development. We see this clearly in the outlook of Francis Crick (1916-), who received the 1962 Nobel Prize in Physiology and Medicine—along with James D. Watson and Maurice Wilkins—for breaking the DNA code. The Spring 1971 issue of *Washington University Magazine* carries an article by Crick entitled "Why I Study Biology." He gives a call for full genetic engineering at once and tells us what is his basic motive for studying biology:

My own motivation, which I have only touched on up to now, is rather elsewhere. It is difficult to say it in a few words. If you had to find a simple description of why I do biological research, it is for philosophical and what you might call religious reasons.

A crucial part of the view of life that he expounds, as we can clearly see from what he writes, is the idea that man can be essentially reduced to the chemical and physical properties that go to make up the DNA template. Philosophically, therefore, Francis Crick is a reductionist, that is, one who would reduce man to an electrochemical machine. Such a view soon leads to the idea that man can and should be manipulated and even controlled.

In this article he mentions the fact that, when he was in California visiting a university, he met a charming girl who asked him about his birthdate and talked to him about astrology and the Age of Aquarius. He also noted that the bookstores were heavily stocked with books on the occult. Here is his reaction:

> . . . I think one has to say that scientifically, astrology really is complete nonsense. I have tried very hard to think of a way in which it could make some sense and it's too much. I wonder whether people who feel that way should be at a university.

Who, then, is going to be allowed in the universities? What he is suggesting is not just that the content of astrology is wrong or meaningless, but he raises the question as to whether people with such views should be in a university.

Francis Crick continues:

> The major conclusion which one draws from present-day biology is the importance of natural selection. The essence of natural selection, and this is the thing that people find very hard to accept, is that it's motivated by chance events. It is not pre-programmed but is driven by chance events. You can make an argument that chance is the only real source of true novelty.

Natural selection is not programmed; it is generated by chance. A little further on in the article, however, Dr. Crick says, "You cannot lay down a general trend [for the course of evolution]; natural selection is cleverer than that. It will think of combinations and ways of doing things which haven't been foreseen." The language here is interesting because it attributes personality to natural selection.

In *The Origin of the Genetic Code* (1968) Crick begins to spell *nature* with a capital *N* about halfway through the book, and in *Of*

Molecules and Men (1967) he refers to nature as "she." In other words, he personalizes what by definition is impersonal according to his own system. Why? Because he can't stand the implications of impersonality, and because this kind of semantic mysticism gives relief to people caught in the web of the impersonal. By his own definition Crick lives in an impersonal universe, but by the connotation of the language he uses, Crick personalizes the impersonal universe and calls natural selection "clever" and says it will "think." Such language takes the pressure off, and people fail to understand what they have read.

Dr. Crick says that his scientific enterprise is governed by a basic religious stance. And while he recognizes that the particular stance he takes is antireligious in conventional terms, ". . . it is a religious attitude because it's concerned with religious problems." He is right. What Crick is doing is bringing forth a faith system based on the prestige of science—even though the suggestions being made have no logical relationship to that on which the prestige rests.

Later in the article Crick turns to the area of mental behavior and how it is determined. He says, "We'd like to know more about mental health—how much is genetically determined and how much depends on the environment. We'd also like to know the same thing for intelligence and creativity." Is it not clear here how man suddenly disappears? There are only two factors: (1) heredity and (2) environment. Is it ninety percent of one and ten of the other? Or the other way around? It makes no difference. Either factor or both together are mechanical. Man has a genetic code. He has an environment which influences that which comes as a product of the genetic code. That's all people are.

In the last section of the article, he begins a new topic: "This leads us to the area of which I'm least at home in because it is not my particular temperament: the question of biology and politics." What is the state to do about biology? Crick tells us:

> . . . We all know, I think, or are beginning to realize, that the future is in our own hands, that we can, to some extent, do what we want.
>
> Now what is happening at the moment? What is happening is that we know that with technology we can make life easier for human beings; we can make changes. What we are really doing is learning to tinker with the system. But there is very little thinking at the fundamental level as to what sort of people we would like to have. In the long term, that is the question you are bound to come up with. I think

that you have to realize that in many contexts what will happen if we go on in the present way is not what people actually want.

. . . It's the aim of medical research to try to cure as many diseases as possible, in particular cancer and heart conditions. Those are probably the major killers. But what is going to happen under that situation? What is going to happen essentially is that you can easily work out the age distribution, under a stable population, from the death rate. It means that gradually the population is going to become very old. What medical research is aiming for at the moment is to make the world safe for senility.

Crick is really saying: Let's adjust the humanitarian concept of medicine. Furthermore, let's begin now. The article continues:

. . . It's going to be the people now between fifteen and twenty-five who are going to have to face it, so they may as well start thinking about it now.

. . . We've just seen that the discussion as to how many people there should be in the world has now, as it were, become quite acceptable. It is not acceptable, at the moment, to discuss who should be the parents of the next generation, who should be born, and who should have children. There's a general feeling that if we are all nice to each other and if everybody has 2.3 children, everything will pan out. I don't think that is true. For good genetic reasons, even though you have more medical care, transplantation of organs, and all these things, it would be an unhealthy biological situation. Some group of people should decide that some people should have more children and some should have fewer. . . . You have to decide who is to be born.

Biology is indeed a revolutionary subject when you look at it in this way. It is, in fact, *the* major revolutionary subject. It is the one that's going to make the new concepts which will come into social thinking. Biology is not simply, as it were, what you can do with herds of cattle. There are much more intricate things involving people at the psychological level interacting in society, but I don't think you're going to solve all these problems by just tinkering with the genetic material. I think it will turn out that thinking along these lines will have to take place, and if you don't do it in this country, it will start in another country.

Francis Crick closes "Why I Study Biology" in this way:

This comes to probably the basic thing that I would say. That really what is wanted is education—an education at the level of younger people. It's nice to read articles in *Time* and *Life,* but if you learn something when you're in school, you're forced to learn it in a more regular way. You absorb it, to some extent, at a more impressionable period; you're made to do exercise on it. And I think really there should be some thinking if we're to take this new view of looking at man.

Crick obviously wishes to bring the subject of the biological nature of man and the acceptability of human engineering down into the education of even the lower grades.

If man is what Francis Crick says he is, then he is only the sum of the impersonal *plus* time *plus* chance; he is nothing more than the energy particle extended and more complex. Our own generation can thus disregard human life. On the one end we kill the embryo through abortion—and on the other end we will introduce euthanasia for the old. The one is already here and the door is opened for the other.

Thus, Francis Crick is one of those who put a strong emphasis on the immediate use of the full range of "genetic engineering"— with some group of people deciding who should be the parents of the next generation, who should be born, and who should have children. Too often the subject of genetic engineering is approached in an atmosphere of spectacularism, in a "Sunday Supplement" frame of mind. But men like Crick must be taken seriously as an influence in the area of biological manipulation. Crick is not alone in his view that modern medicine is a menace since it keeps the weak alive to breed a less-than-best next generation. A chancellor of one of the Swiss universities took this for the theme of his inaugural speech some years ago.

The question of genetic engineering, however, must be seen in a balanced way, for by no means are all those involved as extreme as those to whom I have referred. The British book I mentioned before, *Our Future Inheritance: Choice or Chance?* (1974), tries to set forth a balanced view, though it seems to me that the title itself is slanted toward accepting genetic engineering: *choice* sounds so much better than *chance*. The book has special importance because of the many scientists whose working papers were the basis for it. The following few pages are largely based on material from this book or issues which are raised by the material in it.

As we evaluate genetic engineering, it must be said first that certain things are *not* immediately at hand—for example, a baby grown *entirely outside the body (in vitro)* or the making of endless duplicates of one individual without male and female elements (cloning). However, these phenomena may be possible later, and so are part of the whole question, ethically and practically. Some things, for example, transplants, *are* immediately at hand. The most successful have been kidney transplants.

This surely is a breakthrough for which we can be glad, but even this medical achievement creates problems. In order to justify the early taking of the needed kidneys and other organs, the criterion for death is now generally accepted as a flat brain wave over a twenty-four-hour period. This is not an ethical problem in itself, but as we have seen, the door is opened for keeping bodies alive indefinitely (where there is a flat brain wave but where the organs all continue to function) to harvest their blood and organs for transplants and experimentation. The problem is clear: without the absolute line which Christianity gives for the distinctiveness of people, even things which can be good in themselves lead to humanness being increasingly lost.

Another example of this problem is the curing of childlessness which is caused by an infertile husband. Such childlessness often can be cured by artificial insemination using the husband's sperm (A.I.H.). Surely this is a help to many couples. But what about A.I.D. (sperm by a donor, another man)? Where is the boundary condition? *Our Future Inheritance: Choice or Chance?* says that under present laws in Britain the child born is illegitimate, and in the United States judges in some divorce cases have ruled A.I.D. children the illegitimate products of adultery, denying custody rights to the husband or relieving him of financial-support obligations. And what is the next step? The book answers, "Perhaps the most sensible suggestion made is that the concept of legitimacy be removed entirely." If this suggestion were followed, morals would be shifted, and once more humanness would be weakened. What the family is, is weakened. What will be the relationship of parents and children? In the book this change in morals and laws is to be made upon the basis of "social hindrance." This is what I have called *sociological law*.

Any of us would be glad for methods of genetic changes which would cure genetic disease and help individuals. However, removing these things from the uniqueness which Christianity gives to people, and from the Christian absolutes, tends to lead to an increasing loss of humanness, even in the milder forms. In the call for full genetic engineering the door is wide open for the most far-reaching manipulation. The call concerns who should have children and what kind of children they should have. It is a call for a group in society to determine what kind of people is wanted, and a call to set out to make them genetically. It is striking that James D. Watson (1928-), who along with Francis Crick received the Nobel Prize in 1962 for breaking the DNA code, spoke out for exercising the greatest caution. He warned a congressional committee of the dangers of experiments in these areas and sounded the same note of warning in *The Atlantic* (May 1971) under the title "Moving Towards the Clonal Man, Is That What We Want?"

On every side people are taught that people are only machines, and as they are so taught their resistance to manipulation in all these ways is weakened, step by step. Modern man has no real boundary condition for what he *should* do; he is left only with what he *can* do. Moral "oughts" are only what is sociologically accepted at the moment. In this setting will today's unthinkable still be unthinkable in ten years?

Man no longer sees himself as qualitatively different from nonman. The Christian consensus gave a basis for people being unique, as made in the image of God, but this has largely been thrown away. Thus there tends, even with the good things, to be a progressive fracturedness in the practice of life as human life. Remember, too, that for a long time in philosophy, and popularly in some of the mass media, people have been taught that truth as objective truth does not exist. All morals and law are seen as relative. Thus people gradually accept the *idea* of manipulation, and a bit more gradually open themselves to accept the *practice* of the varying forms of manipulation.

We can also mention Jacques Monod's (1910-1976) *Chance and Necessity* (1971). Here all values are up for grabs. Monod's theory that everything is a product of chance did not rest on his scientific work, but rather on the fact that he followed the philosophy of Camus. With Monod science blurs into speculation, thus giving his work, for many people, the authority of his proper scientific prestige, when in reality no necessary relationship exists between the book's speculative and scientific portions. Monod argues correctly that on the basis of nature there is no way man can derive the *ought* from the *is*. For him the *is* is merely what is naturally there, what has willy-nilly come by chance. Therefore, since what *is* gives no clue to what ought to be, we must choose our values arbitrarily. Once people accept this mentality, it is much easier to impose arbitrary absolutes.

Arthur Koestler (1905-) suggested that a chemical element be developed to bring man into a place of tranquility (*Horizon Magazine*, Spring 1968). Based on his view of evolution, he postulates that man has three brains from his past: the brain of the reptile, the brain of the horse, and the unique human brain. Koestler urges the discovery of a chemical that will somehow bring peace between these brains and thus rid man of aggression. Essentially, he is calling for a supertranquilizer. He suggests the possibility that some community would put this in its drinking water, thus forcing all people to accept it. This actually is little different from the suggestion made by those who held the idealistic drug-taking concept of using the drinking water to give LSD to the residents of large cities. The principle involved is no different.

Newspapers reported that Kermit Krantz (1923-), head of the Gynecology and Obstetrics Department of the University of Kansas, urged in October 1969 that the pill to control birth be put into the world's drinking supplies to control population. Some others have suggested that the government could then dispense as it chose another drug to nullify what was in the water, so the state could decide who would be able to have babies. It all sounds very much like the ugliness portrayed in C. S. Lewis's (1898-1963) *That Hideous Strength* (1945). But this is not fiction; it is today's news, as is evidenced by news stories on the work of such men as José M. Delgado, Kenneth B. Clark, and Russel V. Lee.

José M. Delgado (1915-) of Yale University has been one of the men using sensors in the brains of monkeys and human epileptics to control their behavior. In a speech to the UNESCO Committee on Human Aggression, Delgado said that we will see a revolution in medicine's treating aggressiveness by these means in the next few years—a revolution which will be as great as the revolution in the treatment of infectious diseases with antibiotics a few years ago. The future society, he says, will be psycho-civilized with E.S.B. (Electrical Stimulating of the Brain).

Kenneth B. Clark (1914-), the American social psychologist, when president of the American Psychological Association in 1971, suggested that all political leaders should have to take anti-aggression pills. Then the leaders *could not* be aggressive. More recently he has advocated "psychotechnology," that is, experiments with brain control.

Newspapers reported that Clinical Professor Emeritus Russel V. Lee (1895-), of Stanford University Medical School, suggested that all public officials should be required to have a comprehensive psychological test each year. Then, in the case of high federal officials, when the testers decided it was necessary, the finding should be transmitted to a committee of Congress which could recommend that the official be removed from office. Both Clark and Lee were forgetting a small thing—that the man who dispensed the pills or who controlled the psychological testing would be king.

In the light of this discussion about social manipulation, three questions arise. First, who will control the controllers? Second, what will happen now that people have no boundary condition indicating what they *should* do in contrast to what they *can* do? Third, if mankind is only what modern people say it is, why does man's biological continuation have value?

Stories on all these techniques for manipulation have been given important space in the mass media. And the more these are absorbed without analysis, the more they open the way for men to think of themselves differently, and the more manipulation becomes acceptable. It is no secret from many articles and from Valeriy Tarsis's (1900-) book *Ward 7: An Autobiographical Novel* (1965) that in Russia political prisoners are put in mental wards to be "reconditioned." A person who does not agree with the social order is declared "ill" and becomes a nonperson, lost in the mental hospital and no longer possessing civil rights. But let us not assume that conditioning must be as crude as that of Ward 7. As we have seen, there are suggestions for the emergence of an elite to manipulate society on this side of the Iron Curtain. And the technical breakthroughs necessary to make this possible have largely been accomplished. Any modern authoritarian government has almost endless means of manipulation.

We can think of subliminal influence as a further example. It is possible to flash something over and over again on a TV or movie screen at such a fast rate that, while a viewer doesn't know he has seen it, it still has a strong influence upon him. In one experiment an audience was told, subliminally, to purchase a certain soft drink. People did not know they had seen these repeated messages, and yet when the film was over the supplies of this soft drink in the neighborhood were soon exhausted. This technique is banned by law in Western countries, but in totalitarian states why should it not be used? Even in the Western world only a law stands between us and its use; and we must not forget the drift in law toward that which is considered the sociological good at that moment. There would be no way of knowing if subliminal TV messages were beginning to be used.

Actually, TV manipulates viewers just by its normal way of operating. Many viewers seem to assume that when they have seen something on TV, they have seen it with their own eyes. It makes the viewer think he has actually been on the scene. He *knows,* because his own eyes have seen. He has the impression of greater direct objective knowledge than ever before. For many, what they see on television becomes more true than what they see with their eyes in the external world.

But this is not so, for one must never forget that every television minute has been edited. The viewer does not see the event. He sees an edited form of the event. It is not the event which is seen, but an *edited symbol* or an *edited image* of the event. An aura and illusion of objectivity and truth is built up, which could not be totally the case even if the people shooting the film were completely neutral. The physical limitations of the camera dictate that only one aspect of the total situation is given. If the camera were aimed ten feet to the left or ten feet to the right, an entirely different "objective story" might come across.

And, on top of that, the people taking the film and those editing it often do have a subjective viewpoint that enters in. When we see a political figure on TV, we are not seeing the person as he necessarily is; we are seeing, rather, the image someone has decided we should see. And if Leni Riefenstahl's (1902-) *Triumph of the Will,* a documentary on the 1934 Nazi rally at Nuremberg, could be a terrifyingly effective propaganda vehicle as it was for that authoritarian government, what can a properly managed TV schedule, with its edited illusion of reality, be as it enters every home and is watched for endless hours by both young and old?

With an elite providing the arbitrary absolutes, not just TV but the general apparatus of the mass media can be a vehicle for manipulation. There is no need for collusion or a plot. All that is needed is that the world-view of the elite and the world-view of the central news media coincide. One may discuss if planned collusion exists at times, but to be looking only for the possibility of a clandestine plot opens the way for failing to see a much greater danger: that many of those who are in the most prominent places of influence and many of those who decide what is news do have the common, modern, humanist world-view we have described at length in this book. It is natural that they act upon this viewpoint, with varying degress of consciousness of what they are doing, and even varying degrees of consciousness of who is using whom. Their world-view is the grid which determines their presentation.

A good example is that much of the press (and many diplomats, too) saw and spoke against Hitler's repressions much sooner (in fact, years sooner) than Stalin's repressions were acknowledged. This is not because the press was communistic, for most members of the press certainly were not; rather they had a world-view, a set of presuppositions, which caused them to look at what was happening in Hitler's Germany and what was happening in Russia through two entirely different sets of glasses. Edward Behr (1926-), *Newsweek's* European regional editor—in reviewing Oliver Todd's *The Ducks of Camau* in 1975—sets forth the problem well: ". . . the liberal dilemma: how to be against injustice . . . and yet remain lucid enough to combat the authoritarian forms of government that, through the revolutionary process, replace such injustice with tyranny of a different order."

And not all the media need to be involved in order for manipulation to be effective. In fact, rarely would all the media be involved. *It is always unfair to say simply "the press" or "the media" do this or that.* They are never to be all lumped together as though they were a monolithic whole. Nonetheless, the media can be a vehicle of manipulation.

There are certain news organizations, newspapers, news magazines, wire services, and news broadcasts which have the ability to generate news. They are the *news makers,* and when an item appears in them it *becomes* the news. This ability to generate news rests upon a kind of syndrome or psychology or mind-set, not only in the journalistic fraternity but also in influential circles comprised of congressmen, other government officials, and professors. The influence is not necessarily based on circulation, but rather on its reputation with the right people. This is at times consciously cultivated; for example, certain news outlets release their big stories to the wires and the radio and TV networks before the "big story" hits the newsstands.

Not only do these news makers make certain things news—in contrast to that which gets "lost"—but the color they put on the news tends to be picked up as well. Often this tone is set by starting off with what is called a "hard lead," the first sentence of a news article which is supposed to sum up the story in an eye-catching way. If this is subtly slanted, the tone of the whole story tends to be set, and it becomes the stained-glass window through which that story and perhaps even related stories are comprehended.

To put this in terms we have used before, just as we now tend to have *sociological science* and *sociological law*, we tend to have *sociological news*. Here, too, objectivity tends to be lost. One of the old ideals of journalism was objectivity, but, as White House correspondent Forrest Boyd (1921-) of Mutual Broadcasting remarked to me, "Objectivity has taken a beating in recent years." The distinction between the news columns and the editorial page has, in many of the most influential papers, become much less clear. An ideological position that has nothing to do with the item under review can even be dragged into the society section or into the movie reviews. The news makers obviously have tremendous power, and if either the elite captures them or if because of their world-view they and the elite coincide, then the media is a ready vehicle for manipulative authoritarianism.

Finally we must not forget the manipulative capacity of the high-speed computer. As a tool it is useful but neutral. It can be used for good purposes or equally for harm. It is not only helpful in scientific and business procedures but even now is useful in medicine to make more rapid diagnoses.

Yet the possibility of information storage, beyond what men and governments ever had before, can make available at the touch of a button a man's total history (including remarks put on his record by his kindergarten teacher about his ability and character). And with the computer must be placed the modern scientific technical capability which exists for wholesale monitoring of telephone, cable, Telex, and microwave transmissions which carry much of today's spoken and written communications. The combined use of the technical capability of listening in on all these forms of communications with the high-speed computer literally leaves no place to hide and little room for any privacy.

And as in the case with subliminal TV, what will happen as the pressures on society mount? What will protect us from computer control? To say it another way, what use will the present totalitarian countries make of the high-speed computers being made available to them at the present time?

The question, however, is not limited to the use to which present totalitarian regimes will put the computer. The question is what will all these available manipulating techniques mean in our own countries? We must not think of an overnight change, but rather of a subtle trend by the leadership toward greater control and manipulation of the individual. Of course, some might feel uncomfortable about this increased control and manipulation in a relativistic age, but where would they draw a line? Many who talk of civil liberties are also committed to the concept of the state's responsibility to solve all problems; so in a time of overwhelming pressures (and with the modern loss of any qualitative distinction between man and non-man) at some point the feeling of uncomfortableness will be submerged.

What of tomorrow? In the United States, for example, a manipulating authoritarian government could come from the administrative side or from the legislative side. A public official in the United States serving at the highest level wisely said, "Legislative dictatorship is no better than executive tyranny." And one would have to add that with the concept of variable law and with the courts making law, it could come from the judicial side as well. The Supreme Court has the final voice in regard to both administrative and legislative actions, and with the concept of variable law the judicial side could become more and more the center of power. This could well be called "the imperial judiciary." Cut away from its true foundation, the power of the Court is nothing more than the instrument of unlimited power. This is especially so when it is tied into what Oliver Wendell Holmes called "the dominant forces of the community" (*see* page 218).

And as a thinkable possibility, control could be imposed by a foreign power in the "right" mix of strength on their side and weakness on the other.

Of course, the makeup of the government in other countries is different. But that is only a minor detail and does not change the basic thrust of the possibility of a manipulative, authoritarian government arising from some part of the government in that particular country. As the memory of the Christian consensus which gave us freedom within the biblical form increasingly is forgotten, a manipulating authoritarianism will tend to fill the vacuum.

The central message of biblical Christianity is the possibility of men and women approaching God through the work of Christ. But the message also has secondary results, among them the unusual and wide freedoms which biblical Christianity gave to countries where it supplied the consensus. When these freedoms are separated from the Christian base, however, they become a force of destruction leading to chaos. When this happens, as it has today, then, to quote Eric Hoffer (1902-), "When freedom destroys order, the yearning for order will destroy freedom."

At that point the words left *or* right *will make no difference. They are only two roads to the same end. There is no difference between an authoritarian government from the right or the left: the results are the same.* An elite, an authoritarianism as such, will gradually force form on society so that it will not go on to chaos. And most people will accept it—from the desire for personal peace and affluence, from apathy, and from the yearning for order to assure the functioning of some political system, business, and the affairs of daily life. That is just what Rome did with Caesar Augustus.

CHAPTER THIRTEEN

The Alternatives

Overwhelming pressures are being brought to bear on people who have no absolutes, but only have the impoverished values of personal peace and prosperity. The pressures are progressively preparing modern people to accept a manipulative, authoritarian government. Unhappily, many of these pressures are upon us now.

Economic breakdown. Modern society's inability to find a solution to the problem of inflation without causing economic recession opens the door wide for economic breakdown. Each cycle of inflation, attempted control, the threat of economic recession, and finally, released control has increased inflation; yet *politically,* with most people dominated by the concept of an ever-expanding affluence, it is difficult or impossible to face the danger of economic recession. Thus, each threat of economic recession opens the door for the next higher state of inflation. At a certain point economic breakdown seems all too possible.

I cannot get out of my mind the uncomfortable parallel to the Germans' loss of confidence in the Wiemar Republic just before Hitler, which was caused by unacceptable inflation. History indicates that at a certain point of economic breakdown people cease being concerned with individual liberties and are ready to accept regimentation. The danger is obviously even greater when the two main values so many people have are personal peace and affluence.

War or the serious threat of war—between the expansionist, imperialistic, communistic countries and the West. Alistair Cooke (1908-) in *America* (1973) has said it well: "What is fiercely in dispute between the Communist and non-Communist nations today is the quality and staying power of American civilization." I would only add that not only America but the West in general is involved. Will the West be able to stand against the totalitarian nations now that the Christian base of the Western freedoms is largely gone? Obviously this could be related to point one—the possibility of economic breakdown in the West.

Pressure from the communistic countries could come in any of several ways or a combination of them: *militarily* by a strong East acting against a less militarily strong West over a crisis arising somewhere in the world; *economically* in the event of breakdown in the West; or *politically* through the takeover of some European countries by the old-line Communist parties in those countries. The latter could come suddenly with open collusion with Russia and its military power, or it could come subtly and slowly with apparent reasonableness, until a time of crisis and showdown. There is a surge by the old-line Communist parties in southern Europe, and it is important to note that these are the countries which never had the biblical base which the northern countries had after the Reformation. The freedoms in these countries were imported, not homegrown.

In this mix the threat of war, especially atomic war, would cause those who have only the values of personal peace and prosperity to be ready for almost any kind of authoritarian government which would be able to remove the threat of war, particularly if (as Augustus did in ancient Rome) it was brought in while seemingly keeping the outward forms of constitutionality. The atomic bomb is a special threat to a generation that has so largely turned away from the existence of an objective God and which therefore believes that only man exists to watch with intelligence the sun set or the birds fly.

Nevil Shute's (1899-1960) novel *On the Beach* (1952) still speaks with relevance. In it he envisions a time after the atom bombs have fallen, when no person is left alive. Lights will be left burning for a time in the cities, but no person will be there to see them. Not long ago, men thought there might be conscious life on Mars. It has been said that when Charlie Chaplin, speaking not as a clown but as a philosopher, heard that there is no conscious life there he said, "I'm lonely." And to the many thinkers for whom the only final value is the biological survival of the human race, the atom bomb brings a special pressure to give up almost anything in order for the threat of war to be even slightly minimized.

The chaos of violence—especially random or political violence and indiscriminate terrorism, in an individual nation or in the world. Both in individual nations and in the overall world the widespread use of political terrorism has become one of the phenomena of the age. Random and indiscriminate terrorism is even more frightening. Similarly alarming are the indications that terrorist organizations from all over the world have in some way coordinated their efforts. We have already seen indications of how people give up liberties when they are faced with the threat of terrorism.

The radical redistribution of the wealth of the world. Redistributing the world's wealth would be accompanied by at least two things. First, there would be a lowering of prosperity and affluence among those individuals and countries which have come to take an ever-increasing level of prosperity for granted. Recent history has shown us how quickly nations and individuals change their principles toward other nations and other individuals when this becomes a threat. Second would come a redistribution of power in the world. In a descending spiral of prosperity and world power, a manipulating authoritarian government might be easily welcomed, in the hope that such a government would somehow soften the unpleasant results caused by a lessening of prosperity and world power.

A growing shortage of food and other natural resources in the world. This last point is apt to become increasingly important. As the Christian consensus dies in countries where it has previously existed, we must expect that it will make a difference not only within the nations themselves but also in their compassion for others. What will be left will be not compassion but only utilitarianism. Not that the record has ever been perfect, but we can expect open pragmatism increasingly to take the place of the partial compassion which has existed. A growing food shortage is apt to constitute an increasing pressure to cause people to drift along with a growing authoritarianism which promises solutions. As insecurity grows, greed—with the goals of personal peace and affluence at any price—grows.

If these pressures do continue to mount, which seems probable, do you think people, young or old, will at great cost to themselves, at the cost of their present personal peace and affluence, stand up for liberty and for the individual? Countries that have never had a Christian Reformation base will be the first to bow to authoritarianism. Already a growing number in Asia and Africa have gone this way. Men in the Western governments, who were themselves often modern men, did not understand that freedom without chaos is not a magic formula which can be implanted anywhere. Rather, being modern men, it was their view that because the human race had evolved to a certain level by some such year as 1950, democracy could be planted anywhere from outside. They had carefully closed their eyes to the fact that freedom without chaos had come forth from a Christian base. They did not understand that freedom without chaos could not be separated from its roots.

And when these outward forms are imposed on a world-view that would have never produced freedom without chaos in the first place, people will not stand when the pressures increase. Reports in the newspapers remind us that in many countries where democracy has been imposed from outside or from the top downward authoritarianism has increasingly become the rule of the day. One could make a long list of such countries.

Jiro Tokuyama, managing director of the Nomuro Research Institute, the largest interdisciplinary research organization in Japan, wrote in *Newsweek:* "Whereas Western religions are based on beliefs in an everlasting, absolute God, the Japanese . . . did not perceive the presence of such a permanent being. Instead they believed that what is right changes with the times and changing situations." Tokuyama well understood that the world-view of a people will determine its private morals and its form of society.

Furthermore, when these nations which have no base for democratic procedures in their own countries gather in international organizations and form a majority in them, we are foolish to think that they will not function in the way they do in their own countries, even if this means functioning illegally against the constitutions or the charters of those organizations. This is true not only of the United Nations but of the whole range of such bodies. We can expect the tyranny of the majority in the midst of the winds of political change.

Let us hasten to say that freedom of the individual is not magic in the countries with a Reformation background either. As the memory of the Christian base grows ever dimmer, freedom will disintegrate in these countries as well. The system will not simply go on, divorced from its founding roots. And the drift will tend to be the same, no matter what political party is voted in. When the principles are gone, there remains only expediency at any price.

Most of the leaders of the countries which used to have a Christian base are now "modern" men. Happily there are notable exceptions, but they are exceptions. The attempt to be autonomous—to be independent from God and from what He has taught in the Bible and from the revelation of God in Christ—affects the political leaders as well as the university professors and the common people. Most of these leaders, too, think in terms of synthesis instead of fixed standards and absolutes, and this shows in political actions both at home and in foreign affairs.

Synthesis has won on both sides of the Iron Curtain: people see no fixed, final right or wrong, but only a mixture in public dealing as well as in private morals, in foreign affairs as well as in internal matters. This is especially so in the intellectuals who have understandingly carried the abandonment of the Christian base toward its logical conclusion. But it is also true of those who have been influenced by this thought without analyzing it. Pragmatism, doing what seems to work without regard for fixed principles of right or wrong, is largely in control. In both international and home affairs, expediency—at any price to maintain personal peace and affluence at the moment—is the accepted procedure. Absolute principles have little or no meaning in the place to which the decline of Western thought has come.

But we must have a disquieting memory—the memory of British Prime Minister Neville Chamberlain signing the Münich Pact with Hitler on September 30, 1938, at the cost of Czechoslovakia and at the cost of all that followed, in the illusion of attaining "peace in our time." Winston Churchill's (1874-1965) words in the House of Commons after the Münich Pact was signed now sound prophetic: "[The people] should know that we have sustained a defeat without a war . . . they should know that we have passed an awful milestone in our history . . . and that the terrible words have for the time being been pronounced against the Western democracies: 'Thou art weighed in the balance and found wanting.' And do not suppose this is the end. This is only the beginning of the reckoning. This is only the first sip, the first foretaste of a bitter cup which will be proffered to us year by year unless, by a supreme recovery of moral health and martial vigor, we arise again and take our stand for freedom as in the olden times."

It is unfortunate that no leader of vision was available after the crisis of war to warn the West that the moral battle was being lost in a new way. After the war thousands of Cossacks were forcibly thrust back into Russia against their wishes, to be killed and imprisoned by Stalin. Solzhenitsyn asked in *Gulag Archipelago*, "What military or political reason can there have been for the delivery to death at Stalin's hands of these hundreds of thousands?" In *Communism: A Legacy of Terror* Solzhenitsyn said that one and a half million Soviet citizens who did not want to return to Communist Russia were turned over by force to Stalin to be exterminated. And in *The Last Secret* (1974) by Nicholas Bethell (1938-), a British senior staff officer who supervised the handover of the Cossacks is said to have told Bethell, "There is nothing we can do to help these poor wretches now, but we can at least learn something from their fate."

But the years that have passed show no sign that such a lesson has been learned. Without the base for right and wrong, but only a concept of synthesis, pragmatism, and utilitarianism, what will *not* be given up, both inside of nations or in foreign affairs, for the sake of *immediate* peace and affluence? The weak humanistic ideals are not and will not be enough in our own generation or for the future. Remember from the first chapter the little Roman bridge that would stand when people walked over it, but would break under the weight of a truck? If further economic recessions come, if fear of the loss of personal peace and prosperity increases, if wars and threats of wars intensify, if violence and terrorism spread, if food and other resources in the world become ever scarcer—and all of these are more than possible—then the trend is speeded up. As these things come upon people who have only the values of personal peace and affluence, they will crush them as a six-wheeled truck will crush the little bridge.

In such circumstances, it seems that there are only two alternatives in the natural flow of events: first, imposed order or, second, our society once again affirming that base which gave freedom without chaos in the first place—God's revelation in the Bible and His revelation through Christ. We have seen in the previous chapters many of the implications of an imposed order. But rather than throwing up our hands and giving in, we should take seriously the second alternative.

Christian values, however, cannot be accepted as a superior utilitarianism, just as a means to an end. The biblical message is truth and it demands a commitment to truth. It means that everything is not the result of the impersonal plus time plus chance, but that there is an infinite-personal God who is the Creator of the universe, the space-time continuum. We should not forget that this was what the founders of modern science built upon. It means the acceptance of Christ as Savior and Lord, and it means living under God's revelation. Here there are morals, values, and meaning, including meaning for people, which are not just a result of statistical averages. This is neither a utilitarianism, nor a leap away from reason; it is the truth that gives a unity to all of knowledge and all of life. This second alternative means that individuals come to the place where they have this base, and then they influence the consensus. *Such Christians do not need to be a majority in order for this influence on society to occur.*

In about A.D. 60, a Jew who was a Christian and who also knew the Greek and Roman thinking of his day wrote a letter to those who lived in Rome. Previously, he had said the same things to Greek thinkers while speaking on Mars Hill in Athens. He had spoken with the Acropolis above him and the ancient marketplace below him, in the place where the thinkers of Athens met for discussion. A plaque marks that spot today and gives his talk in the common Greek spoken in his day. He was interrupted in his talk in Athens, but his Letter to the Romans gives us without interruption what he had to say to the thinking people of that period.

He said that the integration points of the Greek and Roman world-view were not enough to answer the questions posed either by the existence of the universe and its form, or by the uniqueness of man. He said that they deserved judgment because they knew that they did not have an adequate answer to the questions raised by the universe or by the existence of man, and yet they refused, they suppressed, that which is the answer. To quote his letter: "The retribution of God is revealed from heaven against all ungodliness and unrighteousness of men, who suppress the truth in unrighteousness. Because that which is known of God is evident within them [that is, the uniqueness of man in contrast to non-man], for God made it evident to them. For the invisible things of

him since the creation of the world are clearly seen, being perceived by the things that are made [that is, the existence of the
universe and its form], even his eternal power and divinity; so that
they are without excuse."

Here he is saying that the universe and its form and the mannishness of man speak the same truth that the Bible gives in greater detail. That this God exists and that He has not been silent but
has spoken to people in the Bible and through Christ was the basis
for the return to a more fully biblical Christianity in the days of
the Reformers. It was a message of the possibility that people
could return to God on the basis of the death of Christ alone. But
with it came many other realities, including form and freedom in
the culture and society built on that more biblical Christianity.
The freedom brought forth was titanic, and yet, with the forms
given in the Scripture, the freedoms did not lead to chaos. And it
is this which can give us hope for the future. It is either this or an
imposed order.

As I have said in the first chapter, people function on the basis of
their world-view more consistently than even they themselves
may realize. The problem is not outward things. The problem is
having, and then acting upon, the right world-view—the world-
view which gives men and women the truth of what is.

A Special Note

This special note is primarily for Christians. First, let us remember what is the hallmark of the present generation of humanistic thinking. It is the acceptance of the dichotomy, the separation of optimism about meaning and values from the area of reason. Once this separation is accepted, what an individual puts in the area of non-reason is incidental. The mark of the present form of humanistic thinking is this *existential methodology*.

As Christians, we must not slip into our own form of existential methodology. We do this if we try to keep hold of the value system, the meaning system, and the "religious matters" given in the Bible, while playing down what the Bible affirms about the cosmos, history, and specific commands in morals. We are following our own form of existential methodology if we put what the Bible says about the cosmos, history, and absolute commands in morals in the realm of the culturally oriented. If we do this, the generation which follows will certainly be undercut as far as historic Christianity is concerned. But also, if we ourselves bear the central mark of our generation, we cannot at this moment in history be the voice we should be to our poor and fractured generation; we cannot be the restorative salt which Christians are supposed to be to their generation and their culture if in regard to the

Scriptures we, too, are marked by the existential methodology. If we are so marked, we then have no real absolute by which to help, or by which to judge, the culture, state, and society.

Second, as Christians we are not only to *know* the right world-view, the world-view that tells us the truth of what *is,* but consciously to *act* upon that world-view so as to influence society in all its parts and facets across the whole spectrum of life, as much as we can to the extent of our individual and collective ability.

Third, as we look back to the time of slavery and the time after the Industrial Revolution, we are thankful for Christians such as Elizabeth Fry, Lord Shaftesbury, William Wilberforce, and John Wesley who spoke out and acted publicly against slavery and against the noncompassionate use of accumulated wealth. I wonder if Christians of the future will be thankful that in our day we spoke out and acted against abuses in the areas of race and the noncompassionate use of wealth, *yet simultaneously and equally* balanced this in speaking out and acting also against the special sickness and threat of our age—the rise of authoritarian government? That is, will we resist authoritarian government in all its forms regardless of the label it carries and regardless of its origin? The danger in regard to the rise of authoritarian government is that Christians will be still as long as their own religious activities, evangelism, and life-styles are not disturbed.

We are not excused from speaking, just because the culture and society no longer rests as much as they once did on Christian thinking. Moreover, Christians do not need to be in the majority in order to influence society.

But we must be realistic. John the Baptist raised his voice, on the basis of the biblical absolutes, against the personification of power in the person of Herod, and it cost him his head. In the Roman Empire the Christians refused to worship Caesar along with Christ, and this was seen by those in power as disrupting the unity of the Empire; for many this was costly.

But let us be realistic in another way, too. If we as Christians do not speak out as authoritarian governments grow from within or come from outside, eventually we or our children will be the *enemy* of society and the state. No truly authoritarian government can tolerate those who have a real absolute by which to judge its arbitrary absolutes and who speak out and act upon that absolute. This was the issue with the early church in regard to the Roman Empire, and though the specific issue will in all probability take a different form than Caesar-worship, the basic issue of having an absolute by which to judge the state and society will be the same.

Here is a sentence to memorize: *To make no decision in regard to the growth of authoritarian government is already a decision for it.*

The title of this book and film series *How Should We Then Live?* comes from the watchman passage in Ezekiel 33:1-11, 19. The title is contained in verse 10.

> Again the word of the Lord came unto me, saying,
>
> Son of man, speak to the children of thy people, and say unto them, When I bring the sword upon a land, if the people of the land take a man of their coasts, and set him for their watchman:
>
> If when he seeth the sword come upon the land, he blow the trumpet, and warn the people;
>
> Then whosoever heareth the sound of the trumpet, and taketh not warning; if the sword come, and take him away, his blood shall be upon his own head.
>
> He heard the sound of the trumpet, and took not warning; his blood shall be upon him. But he that taketh warning shall deliver his soul.
>
> But if the watchman see the sword come, and blow not the trumpet, and the people be not warned; if the sword come, and take any person from among them, he is taken away in his iniquity; but his blood will I require at the watchman's hand.
>
> So thou, O son of man, I have set thee a watchman unto the house of Israel; therefore thou shalt hear the word at my mouth, and warn them from me.
>
> When I say unto the wicked, O wicked man, thou shalt surely die; if thou dost not speak to warn the wicked from his way, that wicked man shall die in his iniquity; but his blood will I require at thine hand.
>
> Nevertheless, if thou warn the wicked of his way to turn from it; if he do not turn from his way, he shall die in his iniquity; but thou hast delivered thy soul.
>
> Therefore, O thou son of man, speak unto the house of Israel; Thus ye speak, saying, If our transgressions and our sins be upon us, and we pine away in them, *how should we then live?*
>
> Say unto them, As I live, saith the Lord God, I have no pleasure in the death of the wicked; but that the wicked turn from his way and live: turn ye, turn ye from your evil ways; for why will ye die, O house of Israel?
>
> . . . But if the wicked turn from his wickedness, and do that which is lawful and right, *he shall live thereby.*

This book is written in the hope that this generation may turn from the greatest of wickednesses, the placing of any created thing in the place of the Creator, and that this generation may get its feet out of the paths of death and may live.

Chronological Index

Events and Periods (A.D.)		People (A.D.)	
		339–397	Ambrose of Milan
		347–419	Jerome
		354–430	Augustine
381	Christianity as state religion of Empire		
395	Empire split into East and West		
410, 455	Rome sacked by barbarians		
476	End of Roman Empire in West		
		480?–547	Benedict and monastic order
		527–565	Justinian, Emperor
537	Justinian builds Hagia Sophia		
		590–604	Gregory I, pope
600 (c.)	Gregorian chant		
		735–804	Alcuin of York
		751–768	Pippin of Franks
		768–814	Charlemagne, King of Franks, Emperor
800	Pope crowns Charlemagne Emperor in Rome		
805	Palatine Chapel, Aachen		
800–1000	Byzantine art climaxing		
1000s	Truce of God movements		
		1048–1122	Omar Khayyam
1066	Norman Conquest of England		
1000s–1100s	Economic advance		
	Romanesque architecture		
1095–1204	Epoch of major crusades		
		1115	Death of Ivo of Chartres
		c. 1115–1180	John of Salisbury
		c. 1119–1170	Thomas à Becket
1100–1300	Troubadours and *ars antiqua*		
	Height of papal power		
	Growth of Mariology		
	Attacks on papal excesses: *Gospel of Mark of Silver*, 12th cent.		
1140–1250	Gothic architecture: Abbot Suger and St. Denis [1140–] and Chartres [1194–]		
		c. 1175–1253	Robert Grosseteste
		c. 1181–1226	Francis of Assisi
		1214–1294	Roger Bacon
		1225–1274	Thomas Aquinas
1200s	Universities develop		
		1240–1302	Cimabue, Giotto's teacher
1263	Urban IV forbids teaching of Aristotle in universities		
1250–1450	Representative assemblies		
	Late Gothic and Florentine Gothic		
	Ars nova in France and Italy		
		1265–1321	Dante
		c. 1267–1337	Giotto

Events and Periods (A.D.)		People (A.D.)	
1300–21	Dante's *Divine Comedy*		
1304	Giotto's *Last Judgment*		
		1304–1374	Petrarch
		c. 1304–1377	Guillaume de Machaut
		1313–1375	Boccaccio
		c. 1320–1384	Wycliffe
		1325–1397	Landini
1338–39	Lorenzetti's *Allegory of Good and Bad Government*		
c. 1340	Petrarch climbs Mt. Ventoux		
c. 1350	Boccaccio's *Decameron*		
		1369–1415	John Huss
		1377–1446	Brunelleschi
1378–1417	Great Schism: rival popes and Conciliar Movement		
		1378–1455	Ghiberti
1380	Wycliffe's English New Testament		
1415	Huss betrayed and burned		
		1389–1469	Cosimo Medici
1375–1406–1444	Salutati and Bruni as successive Chancellors of Florence		
		c. 1400–1474	Guillaume Dufay
		1401–1428	Masaccio
		1404–1472	Alberti and perspective
		1409–1457	Valla and philology
1424–25	Masaccio's *Adam and Eve* in Carmine chapel		
1425–52	Ghiberti's East Door of Florence Baptistry		
1432	Van Eyck's *Adoration of the Lamb*		
1434	Brunelleschi's Cathedral dome consecrated		
c. 1436	Van Eyck's *Rolin Madonna*		
1439	Council of Florence		
		1444–1510	Botticelli
c. 1450	Fouquet's *Red Virgin*		
		1450–1521	Josquin des Prez
		1452–1519	Leonardo da Vinci
1453	Fall of Constantinople to Turks		
		c. 1466–1536	Erasmus
1469–92	Lorenzo the Magnificent Neo-Platonism of Ficino		
		1469–1527	Machiavelli
		1471–1528	Dürer
		1475–1543	Copernicus
		1475–1564	Michelangelo
		1483–1520	Raphael
		1483–1546	Martin Luther
		1489–1565	Guillaume Farel
1494–98	Savonarola's ascendancy		
		1494–1547	Francis I
		1500–1571	Cellini

Events and Periods (A.D.)		People (A.D.)	
1501	Petrucci and music printing at Venice		
1504	Michelangelo's David		
		1509–1564	John Calvin
1510	Raphael's School of Athens		
		1511–1574	Vasari: Lives of Great Painters
c. 1513	Machiavelli's Prince		
		1514–1564	Vesalius
1516	Erasmus's Greek New Testament		
1517	Luther's 95 Theses		
1519–36	Michelangelo's Prisoners		
		1519–1605	Theodore Beza
1523	Zwingli's Zürich reform		
1534	Henry VIII and English Reformation		
1536	Calvin's Institutes		
1543	Copernicus: De Revolutionibus Vesalius: De Fabrica		
		1546–1601	Tycho Brahe
		1561–1626	Francis Bacon
		1564–1642	Galileo
1564	Calvin dies Michelangelo dies Galileo born Beza succeeds Calvin		
		1571–1630	Johannes Kepler
		1583–1625	Orlando Gibbons
		1585–1672	Heinrich Schütz
		1596–1650	René Descartes
		1600–1661	Samuel Rutherford
		1606–1669	Rembrandt
1620	Bacon: Novum Organum		
		1623–1662	Pascal
		1627–1691	Robert Boyle
		1632–1704	John Locke
1632	Galileo condemned by Inquisition		
1633	Rembrandt's Raising of the Cross		
1637	Descartes: Discourse on Method		
		1637–1707	Dietrich Buxtehude
		1642–1727	Isaac Newton
1644	Rutherford's Lex Rex		
1643–47	Westminster Confession of Faith		
1648	Pascal and barometer		
1651	Hobbes: Leviathan		
1662	London Royal Society		
		1685–1750	J. S. Bach
		1685–1759	G. F. Handel
1687	Newton's Principia		
1688	England's Bloodless Revolution		
		1689–1702	William III, King of England
1690	Locke: Essay Concerning Human Understanding		

Events and Periods (A.D.)	People (A.D.)	
	1694–1778	Voltaire
	1703–1791	John Wesley
	1711–1776	David Hume
	1712–1778	Rousseau
	1714–1770	George Whitefield
	1723–1794	John Witherspoon
	1724–1804	Immanuel Kant
	1729–1781	Lessing
1733–4 Voltaire: *Letters Concerning the English Nation*		
1741 Handel's *Messiah*	1740–1814	Marquis de Sade
1730s– Religious awakening in Great Britain 1770s and America		
The Enlightenment		
	1743–1826	Thomas Jefferson
	1748–1832	Bentham and Utilitarianism
	1749–1832	Goethe
1755 Lisbon earthquake and Voltaire's poem		
	1758–1974	Robespierre
	1759–1833	W. Wilberforce
1762 Rousseau: *Social Contract*		
	1769–1821	Napoleon
	1770–1827	Beethoven
	1770–1831	Hegel
	1770–1850	W. Wordsworth
1776 Declaration of Independence Gibbon: *Decline and Fall of Roman Empire*		
1750– Classic phase of England's Industrial 1850 Revolution		
	1780–1845	Elizabeth Fry
1781 Kant's *Critique of Pure Reason*		
1787 U.S. Constitution		
1789–92 French Revolution		
1789 Declaration of Rights of Man and Citizen		
	1791–1867	Michael Faraday
1792 "Second" French Rev. Revolutionary Calendar		
1792–94 The Terror		
1794 Condorcet: *Sketch . . . Human Mind*		
1798 Malthus: *Essay on . . . Population*		
	1798–1857	Auguste Comte
1799– Napoleon: Consul, Emperor, Dictator 1815		
1800 U.S. Reformed Presb. Church excludes slavers		
	1801–1855	Lord Shaftesbury
	1804–1872	Feuerbach
1807 Slave trade abolished in Great Britain		
	1807–1882	Garibaldi
	1809–1882	Charles Darwin
	1813–1855	Kierkegaard

Events and Periods (A.D.)

1817	Ricardo's *Political Economy*
1830–33	Lyell's *Principles of Geology*
1833–34	Slavery abolished in British Empire
1840s	Irish potato famine and Trevelyan's policy
1848	Marx and Engels: *Communist Party Manifesto*
1855	Büchner: *Force and Matter*
1859	Darwin: *Origin of Species* Dickens: *Tale of Two Cities*
1860	Burckhardt: *Civilization of Renaissance in Italy*
1872	Bagehot: *Physics and Politics*
1881	Holmes: *Common Law*
1899	Haeckel: *Riddle of the Universe* . . .

People (A.D.)

1813–1883	Richard Wagner
1818–1883	Karl Marx
1820–1903	Herbert Spencer
1822–1895	Louis Pasteur
1825–1895	T. H. Huxley
1831–1879	J. C. Maxwell
1839–1906	Paul Cézanne
1840–1926	Claude Monet
1841–1935	Oliver Wendell Holmes
1844–1900	Nietzsche
1848–1903	Paul Gauguin
1856–1939	Sigmund Freud
1862–1918	Claude Debussy
1866–1944	W. Kandinsky
1870–1924	V. I. Lenin
1872–1970	Bertrand Russell
1874–1951	A. Schoenberg
1874–1965	Winston Churchill
1879–1953	Joseph Stalin
1879–1955	Albert Einstein
1881–1973	Pablo Picasso
1882–1971	I. Stravinsky
1883–1945	Anton Webern
1883–1969	Karl Jaspers
1886–1965	Paul Tillich
1886–1968	Karl Barth
1888–1965	T. S. Eliot
1889–1945	Adolf Hitler
1889–1976	M. Heidegger
1891–1953	S. Prokofiev
1893–1976	Mao Tse-tung
1894–1963	Aldous Huxley
1898–	Herbert Marcuse
1899–1963	C. S. Lewis
1901–1976	André Malraux
1904–	Salvador Dali
1904–	B. F. Skinner
1905–1980	Jean-Paul Sartre

Events and Periods A.D.)		People (A.D.)	
1904	Einstein: Relativity		
	Robert: *Justice Lifts the Nations*		
1906	Schweitzer: *Quest for the Historical Jesus*		
1906–07	Picasso: *Demoiselles d'Avignon*		
1912	Duchamp: *Nude Descending a Staircase*		
		1912–	John Cage
		1913–1960	Albert Camus
1914–18	World War I		
		1915–1973	Alan Watts
		1916–	Francis Crick
1917	Feb. and Oct. Revolution in Russia		
		1917–	A. Solzhenitsyn
1919	Barth: *Romans* commentary		
1922	Eliot: *Waste Land*		
1926	Whitehead: *Science and Modern World*		
		1926–	Allen Ginsberg
1922–43	Mussolini and Fascism in Italy		
1927	Heisenberg: principle of indeterminacy		
		1928–	K. Stockhausen
1932	Huxley: *Brave New World*		
1933	Hitler and Nazis come to power in Germany		
1934	Barth: Barman Declaration		
1938	Chamberlain: Munich Pact and "peace in our time"		
	Sartre's *Nausea*		
1942	Camus: *The Stranger*		
1945	C. S. Lewis: *That Hideous Strength*		
1945–46	Nuremberg Trials		
1947	Camus: *The Plague*		
1948	Kinsey: *Sexual Behavior in Human Male*		
1953	Russia intervenes in East Germany		
1958	Polanyi's *Personal Knowledge*		
1961	*The Humanist Frame*, ed. J. Huxley		
1964	Berkeley Free Speech Movement		
1965	Tarsis: *Ward 7*		
1967	Beatles: *Sergeant Pepper* album		
1968	Russia intervenes in Czechoslovakia		
1969	Woodstock and Altamont rock festivals		
		1970	Jimi Hendrix dies
1971	Skinner: *Beyond Freedom and Dignity*		
1972	Monod: *Chance and Necessity*		
1973	Supreme Court and abortion		
	Solzhenitsyn: *Gulag Archipelago*		
	Bell: *Coming of Post-Industrial Society*		
	Bronowski: *Ascent of Man*		
1974	*Our Future Inheritance: Choice or Chance?*		

Select Bibliography

As the heading suggests, the following list of books and articles is not intended as a complete bibliographical guide to the complex and multidimensional argument set forth in the text. Rather, in the spirit of a responsible declaration of one's immediate sources, it is, first of all and mainly, an alphabetical listing of works actually mentioned in the text and second, mention of other works which are related to the same areas of thought. Even so, for a subject as vast as the development of Western civilization—one in which I have been keenly absorbed for many years—it is impossible to remember, let alone do full justice to, all the writings which have helped to form my opinions.

Parentheses after a title indicate the original, primary date of publication where this date is of significance. Wherever possible, the publisher and date is supplied for an edition which is currently in print.

Alberti, Leone Battista. *On Painting and on Sculpture* (1435), New York: Phaidon, 1972.

Anderson, F. M., ed. *Constitutions and Other Select Documents Illustrative of the History of France, 1789–1907.* 2nd rev. & enl. ed. 1908. New York: Russell & Russell, 1967.

Anderson, J. N. D. *Christianity: The Witness of History.* Downers Grove, Ill.: InterVarsity, 1970.

Apel, Willi, ed. *Harvard Dictionary of Music.* Cambridge, Mass.: Harvard University Press, 1969.

Archimedes. *Opera* (1543).

Arp, Hans. "Für Theo Van Doesburg." *De Stijl,* January 1932.

Augustine, St. *The City of God* (413–426). 2 vols. New York: Dutton, 1945.

Ayer, A. J. *What I Believe*. 1966.

Bacon, Francis. *The New Organon* (1620). New York: Bobbs, 1960.

Bagehot, Walter. *Physics and Politics*. Thoughts on the Application of the Principles of Natural Selection and Inheritance to Political Science (1872). Lexington, Mass.: Gregg Intl. Pub. Ltd., 1971.

Balsdon, J. P. V. D. *Life and Leisure in Ancient Rome*. New York: McGraw-Hill, 1969.

Barth, Karl. *The Epistle to the Romans* (1919). New York: Oxford University Press, 1933.

Beauvoir, Simone de. *L'Invitée*. New York: French & European, 1943.

Bell, Daniel. *The Coming of Post-Industrial Society*. A Venture in Social Forecasting. New York: Basic Books, 1973.

Benda, Julien. *The Treason of the Intellectuals* (1928). Translated by Richard Aldington. New York: Norton, 1969.

Bernstein, Leonard. *Norton Lectures* at Harvard University, 1973.

Bethell, Nicholas. *The Last Secret*. New York: Basic Books, 1974.

Bezzant, J. S. "Intellectual Objections." *Objections to Christian Belief*. Vidler, ed. 1963.

Blamires, Harry. *The Christian Mind*. New York: Seabury, 1963.

Boccaccio, Giovanni. *The Decameron* (c. 1350). Translated by Richard Aldington. New York: Doubleday, 1949.

Bonjour, E.; Offler, H. S.; and Potter, G. R. *A Short History of Switzerland*. New York: Oxford University Press, 1952.

Boorstin, Daniel. *Image; or, What Happened to the American Dream*. New York: Atheneum, 1962.

Borsook, Eve. *Florence*. 1973.

Boyd, Forrest. *Instant Analysis: Confessions of a White House Correspondent*. Richmond, Va.: John Knox, 1974.

Brinton, Crane, ed. *Portable Age of Reason Reader*. New York: Viking, 1956.

Bronowski, Jacob. *The Ascent of Man*. Boston: Little, Brown, 1973.

Brown, Colin. *Philosophy and the Christian Faith*. Downers Grove, Ill.: InterVarsity, 1969.

Büchner, Ludwig. *Force and Matter* (1855).

Bulteau, L'Abbé. *Monographie de la Cathédrale de Chartres* (1887–92). Vol. I.

Burckhardt, Jacob. *The Civilization of the Renaissance in Italy* (1860). New York: Phaidon, 1952.

Burgess, Anthony. *The Clockwork Orange.* New York: Norton, 1963.

Calvin, John. *The Institutes of the Christian Religion* (1536, 1559). Edited by John T. McNeill. 2 vols. Philadelphia: Westminster, 1960.

Camus, Albert. *The Stranger.* New York: Knopf, 1946.

————. *The Plague.* New York: Knopf, 1948.

Canons of the Council of Ancyra. *Sacrorum Conciliorum Nova.* Vol. 2. Edited by Mansi.

Cellini, Benvenuto. *Autobiography* (1558f.). Translated by J. Bull. Baltimore: Penguin, 1956.

Chomsky, Noam. Review of *Verbal Behavior* by B. F. Skinner. *Language* 35 (Jan.–March, 1959):26–58.

Clark, Kenneth. *Civilisation: A Personal View.* New York: Harper & Row, 1969.

Condorcet, Marquis Antoine Nicolas de. *Sketch for a Historical Picture of the Progress of the Human Mind* (1793–4). Atlantic Highlands, N.J.: Humanities, 1955.

Constant, Pierre. *Les Hymnes et Chansons de la Révolution Française* (1901).

Cooke, Alistair. *Alistair Cooke's America.* New York: Knopf, 1973.

Copernicus, Nicholas. *De Revolutionibus Orbium Coelestium* (1543). New York: Johnson Reprint Corp., 1973.

Copleston, Frederick. *A History of Philosophy.* 8 vols. Paramus, N.J.: Paulist-Newman, 1946–1966.

Crick, Francis. *Of Molecules and Men.* Seattle: University of Washington Press, 1967.

————. *Origins of the Genetic Code.* 1968.

————. "Why I Study Biology." *Washington University Magazine,* Spring 1971, pp. 20–24.

Dante, Alighieri. *La Vita Nuova (The New Life)* (1293). Bloomington, Ind.: Indiana University Press, 1973.

————. *The Divine Comedy* (1300–1320). Translated by J. B. Fletcher. New York: Columbia University Press, 1951.

Darwin, Charles. *The Origin of Species by Means of Natural Selection or the Preservation of Favoured Races in the Struggle for Life* (1859). New York: Oxford University Press, 1963.

Darwin, Charles. *The Descent of Man* (1871). Philadelphia: R. West, 1902.

David, Hans T. and Mendel, Arthur, eds. *The Bach Reader*. A Life of Bach in Letters and Documents. New York: Norton, 1945.

Dickens, Charles. *American Notes* (1842). Baltimore: Penguin Books, 1972.

————. *A Tale of Two Cities* (1859). Gloucester, Mass.: Peter Smith, 1957.

Drew, Donald. *Images of Man*. Downers Grove, Ill.: InterVarsity, 1974.

Duncan, David B. *Picasso's Picassos*. New York: Harper & Row, 1961.

Durant, Will and Ariel. *The Age of Reason Begins*. New York: Simon & Schuster, 1961.

————. *Rousseau and Revolution*. New York: Simon & Schuster, 1967.

————. *Interpretations of Life*. New York: Simon & Schuster, 1970.

Dürer, Albrecht. *Diary* (1521). Translated by Udo Middelmann, 1975.

Eden, Murray. "Inadequacies of Neo-Darwinian Evolution As a Scientific Theory." *Mathematical Challenges to the Neo-Darwinian Interpretation of Evolution* (The Wistar Symposium Monograph No. 5, June 1967), pp. 5–12. "Discussion," of same, pp. 12–19.

————. "Heresy in the Halls of Biology—Mathematicians Question Darwin." *Scientific Research,* November 1967, pp. 59–66.

Eicher, D. L. *Geologic Time*. Englewood Cliffs, N.J.: Prentice-Hall, 1968.

Einstein, Albert. "Physics and Reality." *Journal of the Franklin Institute:* 221 (March 1936): 349–382.

Einstein, Alfred. *Mozart, His Character, His Work*. New York: Oxford University Press, 1945.

Eliot, T. S. *The Wasteland and Other Poems*. New York: Harcourt Brace Jovanovich, 1923.

Ellul, Jacques. *The Technological Society*. New York: Knopf, 1964.

Esslin, Martin. *The Theatre of the Absurd*. New York: Doubleday, 1961.

Fichtenau, Heinrich. *The Carolingian Empire*. Atlantic Highlands, N.J.: Humanities, 1957.

Flew, Anthony. "Must Morality Pay?" *The Listener*. 13 October 1966.

Galbraith, John Kenneth and Randhawa, M. S. *The New Industrial State*. Boston: Houghton Mifflin, 1967.

Garin, Eugenio. *Italian Humanism*. Philosophy and Civic Life in the Renaissance. Translated by P. Munz. New York: Harper & Row, 1966.

Gay, Peter, ed. *The Enlightenment*. A Comprehensive Anthology. New York: Simon & Schuster, 1973.

Gaylin, Willard. "Harvesting the Dead." *Harper's Magazine*, September 1974.

Geneva Psalter, 1562.

Gentile, Giovanni. *Leonardo da Vinci*. 1956.

Gibbon, Edward. *The Decline and Fall of the Roman Empire* (1776–1788). 6 vols. New York: Dutton, 1910.

————. Autobiography. Oxford University Press.

Gierke, Otto von. *Natural Law and the Theory of Society, 1500–1800*. New York: Cambridge University Press, 1934.

Gombrich, E. H. *The Story of Art*. New York: Oxford University Press, 1966.

Gospel According to the Mark of Silver (12th century).

Gough, Michael. *The Origins of Christian Art*. New York: Praeger, 1973.

Green, E. M. B. *Evangelism in the Early Church*. Grand Rapids: Eerdmans, 1970.

Grout, Donald J. *A History of Western Music*. New York: Norton, 1960.

Guinness, Os. *The Dust of Death*. Downers Grove, Ill.: Inter-Varsity, 1973.

Haeckel, Ernst. *The Riddle of the Universe at the Close of the Nineteenth Century* (1899). Saint Clair Shores, Mich.: Scholarly Press, 1900.

Harris, T. George. "All the World's a Box. An Introduction" (to B. F. Skinner). *Psychology Today* 5:3 (August 1971): 33–35.

Hartt, Frederick. *History of Italian Renaissance Art*. New York: Abrams, 1969.

Headlam, Cecil. *The Story of Chartres*. 1971.

Hegel, George W. F. *The Logic of Hegel* (1812–1816). New York: Oxford University Press, 1892.

Hegel, George W. F. *The Phenomenology of Mind* (1807). Atlantic Highlands, N.J.: Humanities, 1964.

————. *Encyclopaedia of the Philosophical Sciences* (1817).

————. *Lectures on the Philosophy of History* (1822–3). New York: Dover, 1956.

————. *Philosophy of Right* (1821). New York: Oxford University Press, 1942.

Heidegger, Martin. *Being and Time* (1927). New York: Harper & Row, 1962.

————. *What Is Metaphysics?* (1929).

————. *An Introduction to Metaphysics* (1953). New Haven, Conn.: Yale, 1959.

————. *What Is Philosophy?* (1956). Boston: Twayne, 1958.

————. *The Question of Being* (1956). Boston: Twayne, 1958.

————. *Essays in Metaphysics* (1957).

————. *Discourse on Thinking* (1959). New York: Harper & Row, 1966.

Heller, Erich. *The Disinherited Mind.* Chester Springs, Penna.: Dufour, 1953.

Hibbert, Christopher. *Garibaldi and His Enemies.* Boston: Little, Brown, 1966.

Hill, Christopher. *The Century of Revolution, 1603–1714.* New York: Nelson, 1961.

Holmes, Oliver Wendell. *The Common Law* (1881). Boston: Little, Brown, 1964.

Huizinga, Johann. *The Waning of the Middle Ages.* New York: St. Martins, 1924.

————. *Erasmus of Rotterdam* (1924). New York: Doubleday, 1953.

Hutchins, Farley K. *Dietrich Buxtehude* (1955).

Huxley, Aldous. *Brave New World.* New York: Harper & Row, 1932.

————. *The Doors of Perception.* New York: Harper & Row, 1954.

————. *Heaven and Hell.* New York: Harper & Row, 1956.

Huxley, Julian, ed. *The Humanist Frame.* New York: Harper & Row, 1962.

————. *The Human Crisis.* Seattle: University of Washington Press, 1963.

————. *Essays of a Humanist.* New York: Harper & Row, 1964.

Huxley, T. H. *Science and Hebrew Tradition.* Vol. 4 of *Collected Essays* (1902). Westport, Conn.: Greenwood, 1969.

Jaki, Stanley L. *Science and Creation: From Eternal Cycles to an Oscillating Universe.* New York: N. Watson, 1974.

Jaspers, Karl. *Man in the Modern Age.* New York: Doubleday, 1957.

————. *Nietzsche.* Tucson: University of Arizona Press, 1965.

————. *The Origin and Goal of History.* Translated by Michael Bullock. New Haven, Conn.: Yale University Press, 1953.

————. *Philosophical Faith and Revelation.* 1967.

————. *Philosophy.* Translated by E. B. Ashton. 3 vols. Chicago: University of Chicago Press, 1969–1970.

————. *Reason and Existenz.* Translated from German by William Earle. New York: Farrar Straus and Giroux, 1956.

Jones, Alun and Bodmer, Walter F. *Our Future Inheritance: Choice or Chance?* New York: Oxford University Press, 1974.

Kandinsky, Wassily. "About the Question of Form." *The Blue Rider* (1912).

Kant, Immanuel. *Critique of Pure Reason* (1781). New York: Dutton, 1934.

————. *Critique of Practical Reason* (1788). New York: Bobbs, 1956.

————. *Critique of Judgement* (1790). New York: Oxford University Press, 1952.

————. *Prolegomena to Any Future Metaphysics That Will Present Itself As a Science.* New York: Barnes & Noble, 1953.

————. *Religion Within the Limits of Reason Alone.* New York: Harper & Row, 1934.

Katzenellenbogen, Adolf. *The Sculptural Programs of Chartres Cathedral.* Baltimore: Johns Hopkins Press, 1959.

Kaufmann, Walter. *Hegel: Reinterpretation, Texts, and Commentary.* New York: Doubleday, 1965.

Khayyam, Omar. *Rubaiyat of Omar Khayyam.* Translated by Edward Fitzgerald. New York: Doubleday, 1930.

Kierkegaard, Søren. *Either/Or* (1843). Gloucester, Mass.: Peter Smith, 1959.

————. *Fear and Trembling* (1843), and *The Sickness Unto Death* (1849). Princeton, N.J.: Princeton University Press, 1974.

Kierkegaard, Søren. *Philosophical Fragments* (1846). Princeton, N.J.: Princeton University Press, 1974.

————. *Concluding Unscientific Postscript* (1846). Princeton, N.J.: Princeton University Press, 1941.

————. *Purity of Heart* (1847). New York: Harper & Row, 1956.

————. *Christian Discourses,* and *Lilies of the Field,* and *Birds of the Air,* and *Three Discourses at the Communion on Fridays.* New York: Oxford University Press, 1939.

————. *Training in Christianity* (1848). Princeton, N.J.: Princeton University Press, 1944.

Kinsey, Alfred. *Sexual Behavior of the Human Male.* Philadelphia: Saunders, 1948.

————. *Sexual Behavior of the Human Female.* Philadelphia: Saunders, 1953.

Klee, Paul. *Creative Confession* (1920).

Koestler, Arthur. *Darkness at Noon.* New York: Macmillan, 1941.

————. *The Ghost in the Machine.* New York: Macmillan, 1968.

————. "Is Man's Brain an Evolutionary Mistake?" *Horizon* X:2 (Spring 1968): 34–43.

Kristeller, P. O. "Thomism and the Italian Thought of the Renaissance." *Medieval Aspects of Renaissance Learning,* 1974, pp. 27–91.

Kunzle, David. *The History of the Comic Strip: Vol. 1: The Early Comic Strip: Picture Stories & Narrative Strips in the European Broadsheet, ca. 1450–1826.* Berkeley: University of California Press, 1973.

Latourette, Kenneth Scott. *A History of Christianity.* New York: Harper & Row, 1953.

Leach, Edmund. Review in *New York Review of Books,* 3 February 1966, pp. 13, 14.

Lefebvre, Georges. *The French Revolution.* 2 vols. New York: Columbia University Press, 1962–64.

Leff, Gordon. *Medieval Thought: St. Augustine to Ockham.* Santa Fe, N.M.: Gannon, 1958.

Lenin, V. I. and Marx, Karl. *Civil War in France: The Paris Commune* (1917). New York: International Publishing Co., 1968.

Leonardo da Vinci: A Definitive Study. New York: Reynal & Company, 1963.

Lewis, C. S. *That Hideous Strength.* New York: Collier, 1945.

———. *The Discarded Image*. New York: Cambridge University Press, 1964.

Locke, John. *Essay Concerning Human Understanding* (1690). Gloucester, Mass.: Peter Smith, 1973.

Luther, Martin. *Ninety-Five Theses* (1517). Philadelphia: Fortress, 1957.

———. *Luther's Primary Works* (1896).

———. German translation of the Bible (1534).

Lyell, Charles. *Principles of Geology* (1830–33). 3 vols. New York: Hafner Service, 1970.

MacKay, Donald. *The Clockwork Image*. Downers Grove, Ill.: InterVarsity, 1974.

Macquarrie, John. "History and the Christ of Faith." *The Listener*, 12 April 1962.

McCurdy, Edward, ed. *Notebooks of Leonardo Da Vinci* (1923). New York: Tudor, 1954.

McManners, John. *The French Revolution and the Church*. New York: Harper & Row, 1969.

McNeill, William H. *A World History*. New York: Oxford University Press, 1971.

Machen, J. Gresham. *Christianity and Culture* (1912). Republished 1969 by L'Abri Fellowship, Huémoz, Switzerland.

Machiavelli, Niccolo. *The Prince* (1513). New York: Penguin, 1961.

———. *The Discourses of Niccolo Machiavelli* (1517). 2 vols. Atlantic Highlands, N.J.: Humanities, 1950.

Machlis, Joseph. *Introduction to Contemporary Music*. New York: Norton, 1961.

Malraux, André. *The Voices of Silence*. New York: Doubleday, 1953.

Malthus, Thomas R. *Population: The First Essay* (1798). Ann Arbor, Mich.: University of Michigan Press, 1959.

Manetti, Antonio di Tuccio. *Vita di Filippo di ser Brunellesco* (15th century).

Manuel, Frank E. *The Prophets of Paris*. Boston: Harvard University Press, 1962.

Marcuse, Herbert. *One Dimensional Man*. Boston: Beacon Press, 1964.

———. *A Critique of Pure Tolerance*. 1969.

Markham, Felix. *Napoleon*. New York: Mentor Books. Imprint New American Library, 1963.

Marx, Karl and Engels, Friedrich. *The Manifesto of the Communist Party* (1848). San Francisco, Calif.: China Books, 1965.

Middelmann, Udo. *Pro-Existence*. Downers Grove, Illinois: Inter-Varsity, 1974.

Moeller, Bernd. *Imperial Cities and the Reformation*. Philadelphia: Fortress, 1972.

Molapoli, Bruno. *Florence*. New York: Holt, Rinehart & Winston, 1972.

Monod, Jacques. *Chance and Necessity*. New York: Knopf, 1971.

Muggeridge, Malcolm. *The Thirties*. 1940.

Muller, Herbert. *The Uses of the Past*. New York: New American Library, 1954.

Needham, Joseph. *The Grand Titration: Science & Society in East and West*. Buffalo, N.Y.: University of Toronto Press, 1970.

Newton, Isaac. *The Mathematical Principles of Natural Philosophy* (1687). 2 vols. 1729 ed. Atlantic Highlands, N.J.: Humanities, 1968.

New Cambridge Modern History. Vol. 2, *The Reformation (c. 1520–1559)*. New York: Cambridge University Press.

Oppenheimer, J. Robert. "On Science and Culture." *Encounter*, October 1962.

Packer, J. I. *Knowing God*. Downers Grove, Ill.: InterVarsity, 1973.

Panikkar, Raymond. *The Unknown Christ of Hinduism*. Atlantic Highlands, N.J.: Humanities, 1968.

Panofsky, Erwin. *Studies in Iconology: Humanistic Themes in the Art of the Renaissance*. Gloucester, Mass.: Peter Smith, 1962.

———. *The Life and Art of Albrecht Dürer*. 2 vols. Princeton, N.J.: Princeton University Press, 1955.

Pevsner, Nikolaus. *An Outline of European Architecture*. New York: Penguin, 1960.

———. *Pioneers of Modern Design: From William Morris to Walter Gropius*. Santa Fe, N.M.: Gannon, 1974.

Plato. *Timaeus* (c. 360–50 B.C.). New York: Dutton.

———. *Plato: Timaeus and Critias*. New York: Penguin, 1972.

Plumb, J. H. *England in the Eighteenth Century*. Santa Fe, N.M.: Gannon, 1950.

Plutarch. *Lives of the Noble Greeks and Romans.* New York: Dell, 1968.

Pocock, J. G. A. "Civic Humanism and Its Role in Anglo-American Thought." *Politics, Language and Time,* 1973, pp. 80–103.

Polanyi, Michael. *Personal Knowledge: Towards a Post-Critical Philosophy.* Chicago: University of Chicago Press, 1958.

Pound, Roscoe. *Jurisprudence.* Vol. 1, St. Paul, Minn.: West Pub., 1959.

Read, Herbert. *The Contrary Experience.* New York: Horizon, 1974.

―――. *The Philosophy of Modern Art.* Folcroft, Penna.: Folcroft, 1973.

Ricardo, David. *Principles of Political Economy and Taxation* (1817). New York: Dutton, 1933.

Richardson, Alan. "When Is a Word an Event?" *The Listener,* 3 June 1965.

Rivier, Louis. *Le Peintre Paul Robert* (1930).

Rookmaaker, H. R. *Art and the Public Today* (1968).

―――. *Modern Art and the Death of a Culture.* Downers Grove, Ill.: InterVarsity, 1970.

―――. *Synthetist Art Theories. The Ideas on Art of Gauguin and His Circle* (1959). Republished under the title *Gauguin and Nineteenth Century Art Theory.* Atlantic Highlands, N.J.: Humanities, 1972.

Rousseau, Jean-Jacques. *The Social Contract* (1762). New York: Oxford University Press, 1972.

―――. *Politics and the Arts: Letter to M. d'Alembert on the Theatre* (1758). Ithaca, N.Y.: Cornell University Press, 1968.

―――. *Emile* (1762). New York: Larousse, 1962.

―――. *Confessions* (1766–70). New York: French & European, 1782.

Rutherford, Samuel. *Lex Rex* (1644). (In *The Presbyterian Armoury* 1843).

Sade, Marquis de. *La Nouvelle Justine* (1791–1797). New York: French & European, 1960.

Sartre, Jean-Paul. *Nausea.* New York: French & European, 1938.

―――. *Existentialisme Est un Humanisme.* New York: French & European, 1947.

Scholes, Percy. *The Oxford Companion to Music* (1938). New York: Oxford University Press, 1970.

Schultz, William L. "The Father's Rights in the Abortion Decision." *Texas Tech Law Review,* VI (Spring, 1975):1075–1094.

Schweitzer, Albert. *The Quest for the Historical Jesus* (1906). New York: Macmillan, 1968.

———. *J. S. Bach.* New York: Macmillan, 1962.

Senghor, Léopold Ségar. *Selected Poems.* New York: Atheneum, 1964.

———. *On African Socialism.* New York: Praeger, 1964.

Seznec, Jean. *The Survival of the Pagan Gods.* Princeton, N.J.: Princeton University Press, 1972.

Shute, Nevil. *On the Beach.* New York: Morrow, 1957.

Sire, James W. *The Universe Next Door.* Downers Grove, Ill.: InterVarsity, 1976.

Skinner, B. F. *Walden Two* (1948). New York: Macmillan, 1960.

———. *Science and Human Behavior.* New York: Macmillan, 1953.

———. *Verbal Behavior.* Englewood Cliffs, N.J.: Prentice-Hall, 1957.

———. *Beyond Freedom and Dignity.* New York: Knopf, 1971.

Slack, Charles W. *Timothy Leary, the Madness of the Sixties and Me.* New York: Wyden, 1974.

Solzhenitsyn, Alexander. *The Gulag Archipelago* I & II. New York: Harper & Row, 1974, 1975.

———. *Communism: A Legacy of Terror.* 1975.

Southern, R. W. *The Making of the Middle Ages.* New Haven, Conn.: Yale, 1953.

Spencer, Herbert. *Principles of Biology* (1864–1867). 2 vols.

———. *Principles of Sociology* (1880–1897). 3 vols. Westport, Conn.: Greenwood, 1974.

———. *Principles of Ethics* (1892–1893). 2 vols.

Spengler, Oswald. *The Decline of the West* (1918–1922). 2 vols. New York: Knopf, 1945.

Sprigge, Sylvia. *Bernard Berenson: A Biography.* Boston: Houghton Mifflin, 1960.

Strayer, J. R.; Gatzke, H. W.; Harbison, E. H.; Dunbauh, E. *The Mainstream of Civilization.* New York: Harcourt Brace Jovanovich, 1969.

Tarsis, Valeriy. *Ward 7.* New York: Dutton, 1965.

Taylor, Gordon R. *The Biological Time-Bomb.* New York: New American Library, 1969.

Teilhard de Chardin, Pierre. *The Phenomenon of Man.* New York: Harper & Row, 1959.

Tillich, Paul. *The Courage To Be.* New Haven, Conn.: Yale, 1952.

————. *Dynamics of Faith.* New York: Harper & Row, 1957.

————. *Systematic Theology* (1951–1963). 3 vols. Chicago: University of Chicago Press.

Toynbee, Arnold. *A Study of History* (1934–1961). 12 vols. New York: McGraw-Hill, 1972.

Trevelyan, G. M. *English Social History* (1946). New York: Barnes & Noble, 1961.

Valla, Lorenzo. *Treatise of Lorenzo Valla on the Donation of Constantine* (1440). Reprint of 1922. New York: Russell & Russell, 1971.

Vasari, Giorgio. *The Lives of the Painters, Sculptors and Architects* (1550). 4 vols. New York: Dutton.

Vesalius, Andreas. *De Humani Corporis Fabrica* (1543).

Virgil. *The Aeneid* (29–19 B.C.). New York: St. Martins Press, 1964.

Voltaire, Francois Marie Arouet de. *Letters Concerning the English Nation* (1733). Buffalo, N.Y.: University of Toronto Press.

Walther, Johann. *Wittenberg Gesangbuch* (1524).

Watson, James D. "Moving Towards the Clonal Man." *The Atlantic* 227:5 (May 1971): 50–53.

Westminster Larger Catechism (1648). 1963.

Whitehead, Alfred North. *Science and the Modern World.* New York: Macmillan, 1926.

Windelband, Wilhelm. *A History of Philosophy* (1898). New York: Harper & Row, 1968.

Witherspoon, Joseph P. "Representative Government, the Federal Judicial and Administrative Bureaucracy, and the Right to Life." *Texas Tech Law Review,* VI (Symposium, 1975):363–384.

Wordsworth, William. "The Tables Turned." *The Complete Poetical Works of William Wordsworth* (1896). Boston: Houghton Mifflin, 1971.

Wycliffe, John. *The New Testament in English According to the Version by J. Wycliffe About A.D. 1380* (1879).

WHATEVER HAPPENED TO THE HUMAN RACE?

Coauthored with C. Everett Koop, M.D.

CHAPTER ONE

The Abortion of the Human Race

Cultures can be judged in many ways, but eventually every nation in every age must be judged by this test: *how did it treat people?* Each generation, each wave of humanity, evaluates its predecessors on this basis. The final measure of mankind's humanity is how humanely people treat one another.

The great dramatic moments of history have left us with monuments and memories of compassion, love, and unselfishness which punctuate the all-too-pervasive malevolence that dominates so much human interaction. That there is any respite from evil is due to some courageous people who, on the basis of personal philosophies, have led campaigns against the ill-treatment and misuse of individuals. Each era faces its own unique blend of problems. Our own time is no exception. Those who regard individuals as expendable raw material—to be molded, exploited, and then discarded—do battle on many fronts with those who see each person as unique and special, worthwhile, and irreplaceable.

The reason we are writing this book is that we feel strongly that we stand today on the edge of a great abyss. At this crucial moment choices are being made and thrust on us that will for many years to come affect the way people are treated. We want to try to help tip the scales on the side of those who believe that individuals are unique and special and have great dignity.

Yad Vashem is the monument in Jerusalem to the six million Jews and others who were killed in the Nazi Holocaust.[1] It is one of the many memorials that are scattered over the world in tribute to those who have perished in upheavals of rampant evil—evil that swirls in on people when they no longer have a basis for regarding one another as wonderful creatures worthy of special care. Yad Vashem is a fitting place to begin, for it reminds us of what, unhappily, is possible in human behavior. Those who were murdered were people just like all of us. More important to realize is that those who murdered them were also people just like all of us. We seem to be in danger of forgetting our seemingly unlimited capacities for evil, once boundaries to certain behavior are removed.

There are choices to be made in every age. And who we are depends on the choices we make. What will our choices be? What boundaries will we uphold to make it possible for people to say with certainty that moral atrocities are truly evil? Which side will we be on?

The Thinkable and the Unthinkable

There is a "thinkable" and an "unthinkable" in every era. One era is quite certain intellectually and emotionally about what is acceptable. Yet another era decides that these "certainties" are unacceptable and puts another set of values into practice. On a humanistic base, people drift along from generation to generation, and the morally unthinkable becomes the thinkable as the years move on. By "humanistic base" we mean the fundamental idea that men and women can begin from themselves and derive the standards by which to judge all matters. There are for such people no fixed standards of behavior, no standards that cannot be eroded or replaced by what seems necessary, expedient, or even fashionable.

Perhaps the most striking and unusual feature of our moment of history is the speed with which eras change. Looking back in history, we notice that cultures such as the Indus River civilization (the Harappa culture) lasted about a thousand years. Today the passing of eras is so greatly speeded up that the 1960s stand in sharp contrast to the 1970s. The young people of the seventies do not understand their older brothers and sisters of the sixties. What was unthinkable in the sixties is unthinkable no longer.

The ease and speed of communication has been a factor in this. A protest in South Africa, for example, can be echoed by sympathizers in New York in just a few hours. Social conventions appear and disappear with unprecedented rapidity.

The thinkables of the eighties and nineties will certainly include things which most people today find unthinkable and immoral, even unimaginable and too extreme to suggest. Yet—since they do not have some overriding principle that takes them beyond relativistic thinking—when these become thinkable and acceptable in the eighties and nineties, most people will not even remember that they were unthinkable in the seventies. They will slide into each new thinkable without a jolt.

What we regard as thinkable and unthinkable about how we treat human life has changed drastically in the West. For centuries Western culture has regarded human life and the quality of the life of the individual as special. It has been common to speak of "the sanctity of human life."

For instance, the Hippocratic Oath, which goes back more than 2,000 years, has traditionally been taken by the graduates of American medical schools at the time of their commencement.[2] The Declaration of Geneva (adopted in September 1948 by the General Assembly of the World Medical Organization and modeled closely on the Hippocratic Oath) became used as the graduation oath by more and more medical schools. It includes: "I will maintain the utmost respect for human life from the time of conception." This concept of the preservation of human life has been the basis of the medical profession and society in general. It is significant that when the University of Pittsburgh changed from the Hippocratic Oath to the Declaration of Geneva in 1971, the students deleted "from the time of conception" from the clause beginning: "I will maintain the utmost respect for human life." The University of Toronto School of Medicine has also removed the phrase "from the time of conception" from the form of the oath it now uses.[3]

Of course, the Hippocratic Oath takes us back to the time of the Greeks. But the fully developed concept of the sanctity of human life that we have known did not come from Greek thought and culture but from the Judeo-Christian world-view which dominated the West for centuries. This view did *not* come from *nowhere*. Biblical doctrine was preached not as *a* truth but as *the* truth. This teaching formed not only the religious base of society but the cultural, legal, and governmental bases as well. As a total world-view it answered the major questions people have always asked. It dealt not only with the questions *Who is God? What is He like?* It also gave answers to the questions of *Who are we as people? How ought we to live together? What meaning does human life have?* In this way, Judeo-Christianity formed a general cultural consensus. That is, it provided the basic moral and social values by which things were judged.

Judeo-Christian teaching was never perfectly applied, but it did lay a foundation for a high view of human life in concept and practice. Knowing biblical values, people viewed human life as unique—to be protected and loved—because each individual is created in the image of God. This stands in great contrast, for example, to Roman culture. The Roman world practiced both abortion and infanticide, while Christian societies have considered abortion and infanticide to be murder.

Until recently in our own century, with some notable and sorry exceptions, human beings have generally been regarded as special, unique, and nonexpendable. But in one short generation we have moved from a generally high view of life to a very low one.

Why has our society changed? The answer is clear: the consensus of our society no longer rests on a Judeo-Christian base, but rather on a humanistic one. Humanism makes man "the measure of all things." It puts man rather than God at the center of all things.

Today the view that man is a product of chance in an impersonal universe dominates both sides of the Iron Curtain. This has resulted in a secularized society and in a liberal theology in much of the church; that is, the Bible is set aside and humanism in some form (man starting from himself) is put in the Bible's place. Much of the church no longer holds that the Bible is God's Word in all it teaches. It simply blends with the current thought-forms rather than being the "salt" that judges and preserves the life of its culture. Unhappily, this portion of the church simply changes its standards as the secular, humanist standards sweep on from one loss of humanness to the next. What we are watching is the natural result of humanism in its secular and theological forms, and the human race is being increasingly devalued.

In our time, humanism has replaced Christianity as the consensus of the West. This has had many results, not the least of which is to change people's view of themselves and their attitudes toward other human beings. Here is how the change came about. Having rejected God, humanistic scientists, philosophers and professors began to teach that only what can be mathematically measured is real and that all reality is like a machine. Man is only one part of the larger cosmic machine. Man is more complicated than the machines people make, but is still a machine, nevertheless.

As an example, in 1968 Dr. Edmund R. Leach, Provost of Kings College, Cambridge, wrote in the *London Times:*

> Today when the molecular biologists are rapidly unravelling the genetic chemistry of all living things—while the radio astronomers are deciphering the programme of an evolving cosmos—all the marvels of creation are seen to be mechanisms rather than mysteries. Since even the human brain is nothing more than an immensely complicated computer, it is no longer necessary to invoke metaphysics to explain how it works. In the resulting mechanistic universe all that remains of the divine will is the moral consciousness of man himself.

How unsatisfactory this evaluation is can be seen in the fact that a decade later every point Edmund Leach made is still in question.

Nonetheless, even though the years pass and men like Leach do not prove their points, the idea of a purely mechanistic universe with people as only complicated machines infiltrates the thinking of many. By constant repetition, the idea that man is nothing more than a machine has captured the popular mind. This idea keeps being presented year after year in the schools and in the media, however unfounded and unproven the hypothesis. Gradually, after being generally unquestioned, it is blindly accepted— just as, after many years of teaching that the earth was flat, the notion was believed because of its sheer pervasiveness. Flawed and erroneous teachings about mankind, however, have far more serious effects. After all, they are talking about *us*.

For a while, Western culture—from sheer inertia—continued to live by the old Christian ethics while increasingly embracing the mechanistic, time-plus-chance view of people. People came more and more to hold that the universe is intrinsically and originally impersonal—as a stone is impersonal. Thus, *by chance,* life began on the earth and then, through long, long periods of time, *by chance,* life became more complex, until man with his special brain came into existence. By "chance" is meant that there was no reason for these things to occur; they just happened that way. No matter how loftily it is phrased, this view drastically reduces our view of self-worth as well as our estimation of the worth of others, for we are viewing ourselves as mere accidents of the universe.

Sociological Law and Personal Cruelty

Recently a generation has arisen that has taken these theories out of the lab and classroom and into the streets. Its members have carried the reduction of the value of human beings into everyday life. Suddenly we find ourselves in a more consistent but uglier world—more consistent because people are taking their low view of man to its natural conclusion, and uglier because humanity is drastically dehumanized.

To illustrate what it means to practice this low view of man, let us consider some present realities that only a few years ago would have been unthinkable—even on the base provided by a memory of the Christian consensus, let alone within the Christian consensus itself. The Christian consensus gave a basis and a framework for our society to have freedoms without those freedoms leading to chaos. There was an emphasis on the value of the individual person—whose moral choices proceed from judgments about man and society on the basis of the existence of the infinite-personal God and His teaching in the Bible.

The Bible teaches that man is made in the image of God and therefore is unique. Remove that teaching, as humanism has done on both sides of the Iron Curtain, and there is no adequate basis for treating people well. Let us now look at some of those related unthinkable realities. The loss of the Christian consensus has led to a long list of inhuman actions and attitudes which may seem unrelated but actually are not. They are the direct result of the loss of the Christian consensus.

First, the whole concept of law has changed. When a Christian consensus existed, it gave a base for law. Instead of this, we now live under arbitrary, or sociological, law. Supreme Court Justice Oliver Wendell Holmes took a big step in the change toward sociological law. Holmes said, "Truth is the majority vote of that nation that could lick all others." In other words, law is only what most of the people think at that moment of history, and there is no higher law. It follows, of course, that the law can be changed at any moment to reflect what the majority currently thinks.

More accurately, the law becomes what a few people in some branch of the government think will promote the present sociological and economic good. In reality the will and moral judg-

ments of the majority are now influenced by or even overruled by
the opinions of a small group of men and women. This means that
vast changes can be made in the whole concept of what should and
what should not be done. Values can be altered overnight and at
almost unbelievable speed.

Consider the influence of the United States Supreme Court.
Ralph Winter, reviewing *The Memoirs of Earl Warren,* said in the
Wall Street Journal of July 27, 1977, that a large body of academic
criticism has argued that the Warren Court was essentially anti-
democratic because it paid little heed to traditional legal criteria
and procedures and rewrote law according to the personal values
of its members. Winter summed up Supreme Court Justice Douglas's concept as, "If the Supreme Court does it, it's all right." The
late Alexander M. Bickel of Yale said that the Supreme Court was
undertaking "to bespeak the people's general will when the vote
comes out wrong." And Bickel caustically summed the matter up
by saying, "In effect, we must now amend the Constitution to
make it mean what the Supreme Court says it means."[4]

The shift to *sociological* law can affect everything in life, including who should live and who should die.

Those taking the lead in the changes involving who should live
and who should die increasingly rely on litigation (the courts)
rather than legislation and the election process. They do this because they can often accomplish through the courts changes they
could not achieve by the will of the majority, using the more
representative institutions of government.

The Christian consensus held that neither the majority nor an
elite is absolute. God gives the standards of value, and His absolutes are binding on both the ordinary person and those in all
places of authority.

Second, because the Christian consensus has been put aside, we
are faced today with a flood of personal cruelty. As we have
noted, the Christian consensus gave great freedoms without leading to chaos—because society in general functioned within the
values given in the Bible, especially the unique value of human
life. Now that humanism has taken over, the former freedoms run
riot, and individuals, acting on what they are taught, increasingly
practice their cruelties without restraint. And why shouldn't they?
If the modern humanistic view of man is correct and man is only a
product of chance in a universe that has no ultimate values, why
should an individual refrain from being cruel to another person, if
that person seems to be standing in his or her way?

Abusing Genetic Knowledge
Beyond the individual's cruelty to other individuals, why should society not make over humanity into something different if it can do so—even if it results in the loss of those factors which make human life worth living? New genetic knowledge could be used in a helpful way and undoubtedly will bring forth many things which are beneficial, but—once the uniqueness of people as created by God is removed and mankind is viewed as only one of the gene patterns which came forth on the earth by chance—there is no reason not to treat people as things to be experimented on and to make over the whole of humanity according to the decisions of a relatively few individuals. If people are not unique, as made in the image of God, the barrier is gone. Once this barrier is gone there is no reason not to experiment genetically with humanity to make it into what someone thinks to be an improvement socially and economically. The cost here is overwhelming. Should the genetic changes once be made in the individual, these changes will be passed down to his or her children, and they cannot ever be reversed.

Modern humanism has an inherent need to manipulate and tinker with the natural processes, including human nature, because humanism:

1. Rejects the doctrine of Creation.
2. Therefore rejects the idea that there is anything stable or "given" about human nature.
3. Sees human nature as part of a long, unfolding process of development in which everything is changing.
4. Casts around for some solution to the problem of despair that this determinist-evolutionist vision induces.
5. Can only find a solution in the activity of the human will, which—in opposition to its own system—it hopes can transcend the inexorable flow of nature and act upon nature.
6. Therefore encourages manipulation of nature, including tinkering with people, as the only way of escaping from nature's bondage. But this manipulation cannot have any certain criteria to guide it because, with God abolished, the only remaining criterion is nature (which is precisely what humanist man wants to escape from) and nature is both noncruel and cruel.

This explains why humanism is fascinated with the manipulation of human nature.

It is not only Christians who are opposed to the forms of genetic engineering which tinker with the structure of humanity. Others such as Theodore Roszak and Jeremy Rifkin of the People's Business Commission rightly see this genetic engineering as incompatible with democracy. Christians and other such people can raise their voices together against this threat. That does not, however, change the realization that the democracy such people are trying to save is a product of Reformation Christianity, and without Reformation Christianity the base for that democracy and its freedom is gone.

In sociological law, with the Christian consensus gone, the courts or some other part of government arbitrarily make the law. In the concept of genetic engineering, with the uniqueness of people as made in the image of God thrown away, mankind itself is in danger of being made over arbitrarily into the image of what some people think mankind ought to be. This will overwhelmingly be the case if such concepts as what has been called "sociobiology" are widely accepted.

According to these concepts, people do what they do because of the makeup of the genes, and the genes (in some mysterious way) know what is best for keeping the gene pool of the species flourishing. Regardless of what you think your reasons are for unselfishness, say the sociobiologists, in reality you are only doing what your genes know is best to keep your gene configuration alive and flourishing into the future. This happens because evolution has produced organisms that automatically follow a mathematical logic; they calculate the genetic costs or benefits of helping those who bear many of the same genes and act to preserve their own image. Thus, the reason why parents help their children live is that the genes of the parents make them act to preserve the future existence of like genetic forms.[5]

No one tells us how the genes got started doing this. The *how* is not known. And even if the *how* were demonstrated, the *why* would still be in total darkness. Yet with neither the *how* nor the *why* known, everything human is abandoned. Maternal love, friendships, law, and morals are all explained away. Those who hold the sociobiological view believe that conflict both in the family and with outsiders is the essence of life. This serves as a chilling reminder of Hitler's Germany, which was built on the social conclusions logically drawn from the Darwinian concept of the survival of the fittest.

Harvard zoologist Edward O. Wilson, who wrote *Sociobiology:*

The New Synthesis, says on page 562: "We may find that there is an overestimation of the nature of our deepest yearnings." He calls for "ethics to be removed temporarily from the hands of the philosophers and biologized."[6]

The humanistic philosophers tried to make ethics independent of biblical teaching; the present tragic result is the loss of humanness on every level. Now, Wilson argues, ethics and behavior patterns should be made independent of these humanistic philosophers and put into the realm of the purely mechanical, where ethics reflect only genes fighting for survival. This makes ethics equal no ethics.

Time said of sociobiology, "Indeed, few academic theories have spread so fast with so little hard proof." Why has it spread so fast with no hard proof? That is easy to explain: we have been prepared for it by all the humanistic materialism of past years. A constant barrage of authoritative, though unproven, statements comes from every side, and gradually people accept themselves and others as only machinelike things. If man is only a product of chance in an impersonal universe, and that is all there is, this teaching is a logical extension of that fact.[7]

To summarize: On the one hand, the idea that mankind is only a collection of the genes which make up the DNA patterns has naturally led to the concept of remaking all of humanity with the use of genetic engineering. On the other hand, it has led to the crime and cruelty that now disturb the very people whose teaching produces the crime and cruelty in the first place. Many of these people do not face the conclusion of their own teaching. With nothing higher than human opinion upon which to base judgments and with ethics equaling no ethics, the justification for seeing crime and cruelty as disturbing is destroyed. The very word *crime* and even the word *cruelty* lose meaning. There is no final reason on which to forbid anything—"If nothing is forbidden, then anything is possible."

If man is not made in the image of God, nothing then stands in the way of inhumanity. There is no good reason why mankind should be perceived as special. Human life is cheapened. We can see this in many of the major issues being debated in our society today: abortion, infanticide, euthanasia, the increase of child abuse and violence of all kinds, pornography (and its particular kinds of violence as evidenced in sadomasochism), the routine torture of political prisoners in many parts of the world, the crime explosion, and the random violence which surrounds us.

In communist countries, where materialism and humanistic thinking have been dominant for over several generations, a low view of people has been standard for years. This is apparent not only in the early legislation about abortion but also in the thousands of political prisoners who have been systematically oppressed, tortured, and killed as part of the very fabric of communism. Now, however, as humanism dominates the West, we have a low view of mankind in the West as well. Let us consider some more of the direct and indirect results that this low view of people has brought into our society in the noncommunist world.

Child Abuse

Dr. C. Henry Kempe, a pediatrician at the University of Colorado School of Medicine, first used the term *battered-child syndrome*. The term *child abuse* covers at least three separate entities: physical assault, physical neglect, and emotional abuse and neglect. In the first of these the child is a victim of an act of aggression.[8] These case histories are typical of thousands:

> *Case 1:* Police found a nine-year-old girl in a closet measuring twenty-three by fifty-two inches, where she had been locked for half of her life. She weighed only twenty pounds and stood less than three feet tall. Smeared with filth and scarred from parental beatings, this child had become irrevocably mentally damaged.

> *Case 2:* An eleven-year-old boy was brought to a San Francisco hospital suffering from severe malnutrition. He weighed forty-four pounds, had a body temperature of eight-four degrees, and was in coma. The suspicious marks on his wrists and ankles were related to his mother's and her boyfriend's immobilization of the boy for hours on end by means of handcuffs, chains and locks.

The second variety of child abuse, physical neglect, is probably many times more frequent than either the medical profession or the police can document. The third form, emotional abuse, is not only difficult to define but more difficult to detect and prove—after which comes the very difficult task of rehabilitative therapy.

So far it is children who have suffered the most from dehumanization. Nothing could illustrate better the dehumanization and exploitation of children than child pornography. Why doesn't public outcry demand that films depicting child pornography be withdrawn? Because the producers know that they will not be box-office failures. Dehumanization of both adults and children is taking quantum leaps. The unthinkable rapidly becomes not only thinkable but even welcome as entertainment—and being accepted as entertainment, it becomes powerful propaganda for ongoing personal and social practice, further dehumanizing young and old alike.

To begin to grasp the enormity of the problem, consider that in 1972 there were 60,000 child-abuse incidents which were brought to official attention in the United States. Just four years later, in 1976, the number that received official attention passed the half-million mark. *Reported* cases of child abuse probably represent only about half of what really occurs.

Child abuse is the fifth most frequent cause of death among children. In *U.S. News and World Report* (May 3, 1976) it was reported that Dr. Irwin Hedlener, investigating child abuse at Jackson Memorial Hospital in Miami, said: "If child abuse were polio, the whole country would be up in arms looking for a solution."

An especially alarming form of dehumanization is the apparent increase of incest. Dr. Harry Giarretto, director of the pioneering Child Sexual Abuse Treatment Center in San Jose, California, says that incest is an epidemic in America.[9] Dr. Amanat, who heads up the Sexual Abuse Committee in Saint Louis, believes that 40,000 of the 1,000,000 victims of sexual abuse a year are victims of incest. Some say that incest is the most frequent unrecorded crime in this country and much more common than general child abuse or child neglect.[10]

We believe that the increased use of children in sex films has contributed to the sexual abuse of children. When absolute sexual standards are replaced by relativistic ones, and this is coupled with the generally low view of people that modern humanists have been teaching, society is not left with many barriers against the sexual abuse of children. After you remove the psychological and moral barriers imposed by a high and sacred view of human life, child abuse of all kinds becomes very easy, given the stresses of child rearing, especially child rearing in the antifamily climate of today.[11] The Supreme Court ruling that legalized abortion and the arbitrariness of that decision regarding who is or is not a "person" have broken down barriers. There has been a drastic rise of crimes against children since abortion-on-demand became legal in the United States. We are convinced that this increase is caused in part by the liberalization of abortion laws and the resultant drastic lowering of the value placed on human life in general and on children's lives in particular.[12]

The forces of humanism have scoffed at Christian morality and ethics as well as at the Christian view of man. These theories of so-called liberation from the biblical absolutes are bearing their fruit. But humanists, far from reexamining the basis of their position now that the situation is souring, stubbornly propose (on the same old base) remedial action to the problems that humanist philosophy itself has created. This action is even more dehumanizing in its results, as we shall see later in this book.

Abortion

Of all the subjects relating to the erosion of the sanctity of human life, abortion is the keystone. It is the first and crucial issue that has been overwhelming in changing attitudes toward the value of life in general. The Supreme Court of the United States on January 22, 1973, in deciding *Roe* v. *Wade* and *Doe* v. *Bolton* declared that a new personal right or liberty existed in the Constitution—the right of a woman to procure an abortion at any time. The right of privacy was given a completely new interpretation.[13]

The Supreme Court went far beyond its own judicial function and invalidated the regulation of abortion in every state in the union. Professor John T. Noonan, Jr., professor of law at the University of California (Berkeley) said:

> Some of the legislation affected was old, going back to the mid-19th century, some was recent, reflecting the wisdom of the American Law Institute or containing explicit statements of intent to protect the fetus. Some of the legislation had been confirmed by recent popular referenda, as in Michigan and North Dakota; some of the legislation was in the process of repeal, as in New York. Old or new, compromise or complete protection from conception, passed by 19th-century males or confirmed by popular vote of both sexes, maintained by apathy or reaffirmed in vigorous democratic battle, none of the existing legislation on abortion conformed to the Court's criteria. By this basic fact alone, *Roe* v. *Wade* and *Doe* v. *Bolton* may stand as the most radical decisions ever issued by the Supreme Court.[14]

The decision of the Court went far beyond the expectation of the wildest dreams of the proabortion elite in the United States. Noonan summarized the situation this way: "By virtue of its opinions, human life has less protection in the United States today than at any time since the inception of the country. By virtue of its opinions, human life has less protection in the United States than in any country of the Western world."[15]

Archibald Cox of Watergate-prosecution fame said in his book *The Role of the Supreme Court in American Government:* "The decisions plainly . . . sweep away established law supported by the moral themes dominant in American life for more than a century in favor of what the Court takes to be the wiser view of a question under active public debate. . . . My criticism of [the decision] is that the Court failed to establish the legitimacy of decision . . . to lift the ruling above the level of political judgment."[16]

In 1977 what eventually became known as the Hyde Amendment, designed to ban the use of taxpayers' money to pay for abortion-on-demand, was repeatedly blocked by congressional technicalities. The debate on the Hyde Amendment was begun in June 1976, lasted until October, and then was passed in both houses, only to be halted by a single Brooklyn federal judge named John F. Dooling who decided that the Hyde Amendment was unconstitutional. In effect, the Supreme Court, by refusing to reverse Dooling, "gave a district court judge the power to frustrate the clearly expressed congressional will in a matter of appropriating tax funds [which] turns the doctrine of separation of powers on its head" (Congressman Hyde's words).

The Court had the opportunity to pull back from its position in a series of decisions in the summer of 1976, but instead confirmed its position and declared that a physician need not provide the same care for a living product of an abortion that would be required for a living baby delivered in a situation when the intent was to have a baby.[17]

The schizophrenic nature of our society became further evident as it became common practice for pediatricians to provide the maximum of resuscitative and supportive care in newborn intensive-care nurseries where premature infants were under their care—while obstetricians in the same medical centers were routinely destroying enormous numbers of unborn babies who were normal and frequently of larger size. Minors who could not legally purchase liquor and cigarettes could have an abortion-on-demand and without parental consent or knowledge.[18]

In our day, quite rightly, there has been great protest because society in the past viewed the black slave as a nonperson. Now, by an arbitrary absolute brought into the humanist flow, the law in similar fashion declares millions of unborn babies of every color of skin to be nonpersons. Abortion-on-demand is the law of the land, and with the erosion of society's belief in the sanctity of human life there has followed the killing of more than a million unborn babies a year.

We should say here that those who favor abortion argue that child abuse will decrease if abortion is practiced. It is supposed to be kinder to the unborn child to abort it than to allow it to be born and possibly suffer mistreatment. Those who fought for liberalized abortion policies have had their way, and since 1970 it is conservatively estimated in the United States that there are probably over ten million fewer children who would now be between the ages of one and seven. Since these ten million were "unwanted" and supposedly would have been prime targets for child abuse, it would seem reasonable to look for a sharp drop in child abuse in this same period. But in fact, since the legalization of abortion-on-demand, child abuse has grown remarkably, and it is not due to just more efficient reporting.

This is because nationwide abortion-on-demand has what might be called an "educational impact." The West German Federal Constitutional Court (West Germany's Supreme Court) in its February 1975 decision banning abortion-on-demand during the first twelve weeks of pregnancy stated this: "We cannot ignore the educational impact of abortion on the respect for life." The German court reasoned that if abortion were made legal for any and every reason during the first trimester, it would prove difficult to persuade people that second- and third-trimester fetuses deserve protection simply because they are a few weeks older. The court apparently feared that what would happen to older fetuses could also happen to children after birth.[19] As Harold O. J. Brown observes, parents, perhaps unconsciously, could reason, "I didn't have to have him. I could have killed him before he was born. So if I want to knock him around now that he is born, isn't that my right?"[20]

Is it not logical, after all, that if one can legally kill a child a few months before birth, one should not feel too bad about roughing him up a little bit (without killing him) after he is born? Parents who are apprehended for child abuse must feel that the system is somewhat unfair in that they can be arrested for beating their child, whereas people who kill their infant before birth (at an "earlier age") go scot-free—in fact, have society's approval.

There is further evidence that our society is schizophrenic on these matters. Consider our concern to provide special facilities for the handicapped in public places: restrooms that can be used by someone in a wheelchair, ramps instead of steps going into public buildings, lifts on public conveyances to get a handicapped individual onto a bus or train. Yet, while having proven that we do have compassion for the handicapped as well as the resources to care for them, at the same time we have a growing tendency to destroy the newborn baby who might have been one of those handicapped individuals.

A much more serious example of this schizophrenic mentality is that we will transport a newborn baby, who is premature and has a congenital defect incompatible with life, to a hospital a considerable distance away—so that a sophisticated team of doctors and nurses can correct that defect and plan for the rehabilitation of the youngster. Meanwhile, in a number of other hospitals within gunshot distance of that center, other medical personnel are destroying perfectly normal infants in the womb.

The Growth of Human Life

Our reasons against abortion are logical as well as moral. It is impossible for anyone to say when a developing fetus becomes viable, that is, has the ability to exist on its own. Smaller and smaller premature infants are being saved each year! There was a day when a 1000-gram preemie had no chance; now 50 percent of preemies under 1000 grams are being saved. Theoretically, there once was a point beyond which technology could not be expected to go in salvaging premature infants—but with further technological advances, who knows what the limits may be! The eventual possibilities are staggering.

The logical approach is to go back to the sperm and the egg. A sperm has twenty-three chromosomes; even though it is alive and can fertilize an egg, it can never make another sperm. An egg also has twenty-three chromosomes, and it can never make another egg. Thus, we have sperm that cannot reproduce and eggs that cannot reproduce unless they get together. Once the union of a sperm and an egg occurs and the twenty-three chromosomes of each are brought together into one cell that has forty-six chromosomes, that one cell has all the DNA (the whole genetic code) that will, if not interrupted, make a human being.[21]

Our question to a proabortion doctor who would not kill a *newborn* baby is this: "Would you then kill this infant a minute before he was born, or a minute before that, or a minute before that, or a minute before that?" At what point in time can one consider life to be worthless and the next minute precious and worth saving?

Having already mentioned the union of sperm and egg to give forty-six chromosomes, let us briefly review the development of a baby. At twenty-one days, the first irregular beats occur in the developing heart, long before the mother is sure she is pregnant. Forty-five days after conception, electroencephalographic waves can be picked up from the baby's developing brain.

By the ninth and tenth weeks, the thyroid and the adrenal glands are functioning. The baby can squint, swallow, and move his tongue. The sex hormones are already present. By twelve or thirteen weeks, he has fingernails; he sucks his thumb and will recoil from pain. His fingerprints, on the hands which have already formed, will never change throughout his lifetime except for size. Legally, it is understood that an individual's fingerprints distinguish him as a separate identity and are the most difficult characteristic to falsify.

In the fourth month the growing baby is eight to ten inches long. The fifth month is a time of lengthening and strengthening. Skin, hair, and nails grow. Sweat glands come into being; oil glands excrete. This is the month in which the mother feels the infant's movements.

In the sixth month the developing baby responds to light and sound. He can sleep and awaken. He gets hiccups and can hear the beat of his mother's heart. Survival outside the womb is now possible. In the seventh month the nervous system becomes much more complex. The infant is about sixteen inches long and weighs about three pounds. The eighth and ninth months see a fattening of the baby.

We do not know how anyone who has seen the remarkable films of the intrauterine development of the human embryo can still maintain that the product of an abortion consists of just some membranes or a part of the woman's body over which she has complete control—or indeed anything other than a human life within the confines of a tiny body. At the very least we must admit that an embryo is not simply an extension of another person's body; it is something separate and uniquely irreplaceable. Another good reason we should not view the unborn baby as an extension of the woman's body is that it did not originate only from the woman. The baby would not exist without the man's seed.

We are convinced that the reason the Supreme Court decision for abortion-on-demand never came to grips with the issue of the viability of the human fetus is that its viability (that is, ability to live outside the womb on its own) is really not the important point.

Viable or not, the single-celled fertilized egg will develop into a human being unless some force destroys its life. We should add that biologists take the uniform position that life begins at conception; there is no logical reason why the proabortionist should try to arrive at a different definition when he is talking about people, the highest form of all biological creatures. After conception, no additional factor is necessary at a later time. All that makes up the adult is present as the ovum and the sperm are united—the whole genetic code is present.

Abortion Techniques
There are three commonly used techniques for abortion. The technique used most often to end early pregnancies is called the D & C or *dilation and curettage*. In this procedure, usually carried out before the twelfth or thirteenth week of pregnancy, the uterus is approached through the vagina. The cervix is stretched to permit the insertion of a curette, a tiny hoelike instrument. The surgeon then scrapes the wall of the uterus, cutting the baby's body to pieces and scraping the placenta from its attachments on the uterine wall. Bleeding is considerable.

An alternate method which is used during the same period of pregnancy is called *suction abortion*. The principle is the same as in the D & C. A powerful suction tube is inserted through the dilated cervix into the uterus. This tears apart the body of the developing baby and the placenta, sucking the pieces into a jar. The smaller parts of the body are recognizable as arms, legs, head, and so on. More than two-thirds of all abortions performed in the United States and Canada apparently are done by this method.

Later in pregnancy, when the D & C or suction abortion might produce too much bleeding in the expectant mother, doctors employ the second most common abortion technique, called the *saline abortion,* or "salting out." This method is usually carried out after sixteen weeks of pregnancy, when enough amniotic fluid has accumulated in the sac around the baby. A long needle is inserted through the mother's abdomen directly into the sac, and a solution of concentrated salt is injected into the amniotic fluid. The salt solution is absorbed both through the lungs and the gastrointestinal tract, producing changes in the osmotic pressure. The outer layer of skin is burned off by the high concentration of salt. It takes about an hour to kill the baby by this slow method. The mother usually goes into labor about a day later and delivers a dead, shriveled baby.

If abortion is decided on too late to be accomplished by either a D & C, suction, or saline procedure, physicians resort to a final technique called *hysterotomy*. A hysterotomy is exactly the same as a Cesarean section with one difference—in a Cesarean section the operation is usually performed to save the life of the baby, whereas a hysterotomy is performed to kill the baby. These babies look very much like other babies except that they are small and weigh, for example, about two pounds at the end of a twenty-four-week pregnancy. They are truly alive, but they are allowed to die through neglect or sometimes killed by a direct act.

Hysterotomy gives the fetus the best chance for survival, but at a very high price in morbidity for the mother—fifteen times greater than that of saline infusion, the more commonly used alternative. In 1977 a Boston jury found Dr. Kenneth Edelin guilty of manslaughter for killing the product of this type of abortion.[22]

That children are often born alive after abortions is fact and not a new phenomenon. A brief in one case before the Supreme Court (*Markle* v. *Abele*) contained a table listing twenty-seven live births after abortions.[23] That was in 1972. In the first year of liberalized abortion laws in New York State, before the Supreme Court decision regarding abortion-on-demand, some of those "products of abortions" were eventually adopted.

Nothing is more embarrassing to an abortionist than to deliver a live baby. To show that this is so, the following is a quote from a publication of the International Correspondence Society of Obstetrics and Gynecologists (November 1974):

> At the time of delivery it has been our policy to wrap the fetus in a towel. The fetus is then moved to another room while our attention is turned to the care of the gravida [the former mother-to-be]. She is examined to determine whether placenta expulsion has occurred and the extent of vaginal bleeding. Once we are sure her condition is stable, the fetus is evaluated. Almost invariably all signs of life have ceased.

What a nice little piece of "how to" instruction! It was once thought that live births after abortions would be possible only after hysterotomies. Now it is obvious that babies are born alive after saline abortions as well. Dr. William G. Waddill, Jr., an obstetrician in California, was indicted and tried in January 1977 for allegedly strangling to death a baby born alive following a saline abortion.

An interminable trial got out of hand when the issue departed from whether or not Waddill had indeed attempted to strangle a living infant. The trial resulted in a hung jury when the judge introduced for deliberation new material concerning a California definition of death, which really had little bearing on this subject. The former mother-to-be of the allegedly strangled infant filed suit for $17,000,000 on grounds that she was not adequately informed of the possible outcome of the abortion and that she had suffered long-lasting physical and emotional pain as a result of the doctor's actions.[24]

If live babies as a result of saline abortions and hysterotomies cause problems for the abortionist, they are minor compared to the problems that have been introduced by the prostaglandin method of abortion. The use of prostaglandin has multiplied the number of embarrassing situations manifold. Prostaglandin is a hormone which has practically no other use except to induce abortions. Upjohn manufactures it in the United States, and in September 1977 the Food and Drug Administration approved it for use in hospitals. It is advertised in the pharmacy reports as "Prostin E. Upjohn abortion inducer." This warning was carried in the September 12, 1977, issue of Weekly Pharmacy Reports, pointing out the approved Prostin labeling notes that suppository form, unlike saline injection form, "does not appear to directly effect the integrity of the feto-placental unit and therefore, there exists a possibility that a live-born fetus may occur, particularly as gestational age approaches the end of the second trimester." So likely is a live birth after a prostaglandin abortion that a medical representative of Upjohn advises using Prostin E. "only in hospitals with certain intensive care facilities."[25]

Although technically the product of a legal abortion, each fetus expelled alive because of prostaglandin lives for several hours, later has to be pronounced dead by a physician, must receive both a birth and death certificate, and is sent to a funeral director for burial or cremation.

Live Births After Abortions

Physicians have been reluctant to reveal the number of second-trimester abortions (during the second three-month period of pregnancy) that result in live births. Of 607 such abortions done at Mount Sinai Hospital in Hartford, Connecticut, forty-five resulted in live births, including one set of twins. All of these forty-five babies were taken to the neonatal nursery for active resuscitation. Physicians there decided how long to consider resuscitation, according to the infant's weight, neurological maturity, and general condition. None of the babies survived more than thirteen hours, despite attempts to save them. These infants were born following an intra-amniotic injection of prostaglandin, and we would expect that the suppository form would produce more, not fewer, of these embarrassing situations for abortionists.

It could be said in passing that there were other complications in addition to the live births in the second-trimester abortions at Mount Sinai. Excessive blood loss occurred in 19.4 percent of the women; 41 percent had incomplete abortions, in which case the placenta had to be removed manually. The Mount Sinai series was reported by Dr. Wing K. Lee at an Atlanta meeting in 1977.[26]

Other presentations at that same clinical congress reported that hypertonic saline injections for mid-trimester abortions beyond twenty weeks produce a higher rate of other complications. In spite of that, at least the Nassau County Medical Center in East Meadow, New York, decided to return to that form of treatment rather than have the embarrassment of live births. Dr. Joel Robins of the Stony Brook branch of the State University of New York compared 700 prostaglandin with 170 saline abortions. He found it was not such a bad idea to switch back to saline, because the rates of complication were similar and there were seven live births with prostaglandin and none with saline.[27]

It remained for a Johns Hopkins University team to introduce an economic factor. They added hyperosmoler urea to augment the prostaglandin. The combined technique was reported to have a lower failure rate and a lower cost. Since the urea dilates the cervix, the Hopkins group found that it is easier to remove fetal parts than with a D & C and that the process carries a lower coagulation risk than saline.[28]

We would like to assume the role of prophet and say that since the FDA has approved Prostin E. by Upjohn as an abortion inducer, we think they will before long give Upjohn the approval to market a vaginal tampon with prostaglandin on its tip, which will be advertised as an inducer of menstruation. This would then bring to its logical conclusion Justice Blackmun's statement that the right of privacy covers his decision about abortion-on-demand. With such a menses inducer, any woman could use a vaginal tampon containing Prostin E. once a month and never know whether she was having a normal menstrual period or an abortion. Thus, abortion could become a totally private affair. The only good we can see coming out of that terrible situation is that at least it would eliminate the abortionist.

Inasmuch as the live product (i.e., a living baby, although not necessarily able to support itself outside the womb) of a prostaglandin abortion lives for several hours after the abortion—and so must be pronounced dead by a physician, receives both birth and death certificates, and needs management by a funeral director for burial or cremation—it is clear that there can be considerable consternation and emotional upset on the part of the hospital staff, particularly the nurses and paramedical attendants at the time of "delivery."

In 1977 the nurses and medical staff at Hollywood's Memorial Hospital (Florida) rebelled after several live fetuses were born during second-trimester abortions. Hospital Administrator Sal Mudano commented, "We've had preemies that have lived that were less developed than some of these abortions were. Our personnel are not in favor of working in that kind of situation, and the law says we can't force people to participate against their personal or religious beliefs." And he added, "It's not that we're preaching, and we don't have a bunch of religious fanatics on our staff. But our nurses are geared to saving lives and this is just the opposite."[29]

According to the Fort Lauderdale News, officials at Broward General Hospital in Fort Lauderdale feel as if they are forced to walk a tightrope between providing a legally sanctioned service demanded by the public and living up to their duty to save lives. "The law is not really clear on whether a publicly supported hospital can limit the type of abortions it offers," said a hospital spokesman.

The nursing supervisor at Hollywood Memorial, Joann Kopacka, said, "The use of prostaglandin was totally unacceptable. Philosophically, it was a very difficult thing to handle for the nurses. The live fetus is not an 'it,' or a thing, it is a life."

Mudano said the antiabortion feeling among the staff at Memorial is so strong that doctors generally take their second-trimester abortion cases elsewhere. "We're down to six or eight saline solution abortions a month, which is significantly less than when we started doing them," Mudano said. "That's the result of our philosophy of discouraging them."

Mrs. Jean Moore, supervisor of the obstetrical nurses at Broward General for seventeen years, said the nurses at the hospital have not reacted as emotionally as the nurses at Hollywood. "We can't see that they are reacting any differently when a live fetus is born," Mrs. Moore said. "The nurses who work in this area know what to expect. They feel that they are there to assist the physician. We really don't have any problems among the nurses."

A hospital spokesman said the lack of problems with the nurses at Broward General was due to good scheduling by Mrs. Moore. "She is careful not to put anyone with strong feelings about abortions in that area," he said. "We try to arrange the schedules so that those who prefer not to be involved are not, unless it is absolutely necessary."

A doctor said he has never seen any adverse reactions on the part of the Broward General staff when a live fetus is born. "When you have a ten-ounce fetus with spontaneous respiration or movement, it is more upsetting to the lay public than to anybody else. The hospital procedure is almost mechanical at this point. It kind of works very smoothly."[30]

As another example, a publication of Nurses Concerned for Life, Inc., considered these facts, reported in the *Pittsburgh Press* on November 1, 1974:

A 26-year-old woman requested an abortion of her 5-month fetus, claiming that she had been raped. The woman was first turned down by Magee Woman's Hospital because it was thought the pregnancy was too far advanced. The staff physician estimated the gestational age to be about 25 weeks. It was later established that she had not been raped.

The abortion was then performed by Dr. Leonard Laufe of West Penn Hospital in Pittsburgh, Pa., who decided to use the prostaglandin method. Prostaglandin is an abortifacient drug whose primary effect is stimulation of the uterine contractions. Its use frequently leads to a live birth. Nurse Monica Bright testified that the child gasped for breath for at least 15 minutes following the abortion and no attempts were made to help the child in any way. Ms. Bright is a circulating

nurse in Labor and Delivery. She further testified that she observed a
pulse in the upper chest, left neck area. Ms. Shirley Foust, R.N.,
testified she had seen the baby move and that one of the foreign
residents, who was observing, baptized the child. The Head Nurse,
Carol Totton, testified that the baby was gasping and a pulse was
visible. Both the nurse anaesthetist and Ms. Totton refused to admin-
ister a lethal dose of morphine to the baby despite the fact that "someone in the room had ordered it."

The nurse anaesthetist, Nancy Gaskey, testified that the abortion
was performed in a room where there were no resuscitative measures
available if the child was born alive.

The entire procedure was filmed for educational purposes and the
film showed the baby moving. Dr. Jules Rivkind, Chairman, Department of OB and Gyn, at Mercy Hospital, testified that this was indeed
"a live birth."

The original birth records indicate the baby girl weighed 3 lbs. 1
ounce and listed the length as 45 centimeters. Dr. Laufe later changed
the hospital records to read as follows: weight 2 lbs. 9 oz., length 29
centimeters. Lois Cleary, a staff nurse, witnessed this change, and
testified that in the 3,000 to 4,000 births she had assisted with there
had never been such changes made on original records to her knowledge. This change was also verified by an OB technician who was
present. Estimated gestational age 29 to 32 weeks.

John Kenny, a young medical student, testified that he had been
threatened by Dr. Laufe's attorney if he testified in court against Dr.
Laufe. The young man was told that he would be unable to get an
internship in any hospital in Pennsylvania if he testified. He was also
told he would be unable to get a license to practice medicine.

Editor's note [You Be the Judge]—Dr. Laufe was acquitted of the
charges because he claimed the baby's brain was dead due to damage
caused when he clamped the umbilical arteries in utero.[31]

Embryos "created" in the biologists' laboratories raise special
questions because they have the potential for growth and development if planted in the womb. The disposal of these live embryos
is a cause for ethical and moral concern. Dr. Leon Kass, a University of Chicago biologist, wonders:

Who decides what are the grounds for discard? What if there is
another recipient available who wishes to have the otherwise unwanted embryo? Whose embryos are they? The woman's? The couple's? The geneticist's? The obstetrician's? The Ford Foundation's?
Shall we say that discarding laboratory grown embryos is a matter
solely between a doctor and his plumber? . . . We have paid some
high prices for the technological conquest of nature, but none so high

as the intellectual and spiritual costs of seeing nature as mere material for our manipulation, exploitation and transformation. With the powers for biological engineering now gathering, there will be splendid new opportunities for a similar degradation of our view of man. Indeed, we are already witnessing the erosion of our idea of man as something splendid or divine, as a creature with freedom and dignity. And clearly, if we come to see ourselves as meat, then meat we shall become.[32]

There are many unpleasant spin-offs from the basic ugliness of the abortion scene. One is that fewer babies are available for adoption. More childless couples remain childless. This seems especially ironic when one considers that many abortions are being performed very late in term and that a prospective mother could, with little more physical trauma, wait to deliver a normal child at full term and give it up for adoption. That this is not done more often raises the question as to whether in certain cases the mother-to-be does not have an instinctive attachment to the unborn child. That she anticipates the sorrow the separation will bring—and would rather kill the child than lose it—testifies to the fact that the mother knows subconsciously that she has in her womb something more than the mere glob of protoplasm the abortionist would have her believe she is carrying.

Obviously, many more babies are unwanted early in pregnancy than is the case later in pregnancy or after birth. It is the ready availability of abortion-on-demand, when a pregnant woman first has that natural question about how well she can handle a pregnancy, that leads to the tremendous number of abortions. This can be put in personal terms by asking people, "If abortion-on-demand had been available to your mother when she first heard she was pregnant with you, would you be here today?"

Recently several local and state abortion regulations have stipulated that some time must elapse between the woman's decision to abort and the actual procedure. The Akron ordinance passed in March 1978 is the prototype for such legislation. Such legislation does not ban abortion (a ban that would be unconstitutional at the present time), but it does impose some controls. The Akron regulation requires that parents of pregnant girls under eighteen be notified before an abortion is performed. The ordinance also requires that a woman receive counseling by a physician about the results of abortion and that at least twenty-four hours must pass before the abortion can be performed. This provision of course gives a woman more time to think through a hasty decision, so that there will be less chance that she will regret it later.[33]

Current sexual mores, sexually permissive life-styles, and the breakdown of the family demand abortion. At the same time the availability of abortion contributes to a change in our sexual mores, our permissive life-styles, and general family break-down—truly a vicious cycle. The changes in the technical aspects of medicine are almost staggering. It is said that about 90 percent of the current body of medical knowledge has been learned in the last twenty-five years. We can only regret that ethical views of the medical profession, and of society in general, have not kept pace with the technological advances.

That over a million unborn children die each year at the hands of abortionists is sufficient reason for the ardor of those who oppose abortion. When one sees the potential of handicapped youngsters realized through surgery, sees the blessing they are to their families, sees how loved and loving they are themselves, it makes it impossible for some to stand by while millions of normal babies are being killed before birth and discriminated against on so large a scale. As individuals who have marveled at the unique personalities of even the tiniest infants, something basically human in us is revolted by the thought of wanton slaughter of the unborn.

Three Final Issues
First, why is it that so few abortion counselors are fair to the "whole person" of the pregnant woman? "Why didn't anyone tell me?" is a fair question from a girl suffering the aftereffects of a recommended abortion.[34] "Why didn't anyone tell me I would feel like a mother with empty arms?" "Why didn't anyone tell me I risked spoiling the possibility of having a normal pregnancy, because of the damage that might be done to my body by the abortion?" These are not just theoretical questions put forth in an abstract academic debate. Abortion counselors rarely talk about physical dangers, emotional results, and psychological consequences. They seldom tell the woman what is going to happen or what may be involved.[35]

We need to think seriously about the aborted human beings who have been deprived of a chance to live, but we also need to consider with sympathy and compassion the women being turned into "aborted mothers"—bereft mothers—bitter in some cases, hard in some cases, exceedingly sorrowful in other cases. It is unfair not to make the options clear. To tell a pregnant woman that a few hours or a day in the hospital or clinic will rid her of all her problems and will send her out the door a free person is to forget the humanness of women who are now mothers. With many of the women who have had abortions, their "motherliness" is very much present even though the child is gone.

Abortion does not end all the problems; often it just exchanges one set for another. Whether or not one believes in the reality of guilt is *not* the question at this point. One of the facts of being a human being is that in spite of the abnormality of human beings and the cruelty of their actions, there still exist the hopes and fears, the longings and aspirations, that can be bundled together in the word *motherliness*. To stamp out these feelings is to insure that many women will turn into the kind of hard people they may not want to be. For others, it is a bewildering nightmare to be overwhelmed with longings for the baby to be back in them and to be able to complete that which had begun. To assume that all women will want to abort—and to give flat advice without explaining the very real problems some aborted mothers have—is cruelty in the wrappings of blasé and glib kindness.

Second, abortion is not a "Roman Catholic issue." This must be emphasized. Those who favor abortion often try to minimize the arguments of those who oppose it by conveying the idea that only the Roman Catholic Church is against abortion. We must indeed be glad for the Roman Catholics who have spoken out, but we must not allow the position to be minimized as though it is a "religious" issue. It is not a religious issue.

This line of attack has been carried so far that some lawyers want to rule out the entrance of Congress and the courts into the discussion at all, on the basis that it is only a Roman Catholic issue and therefore a violation of the separation of church and state. The issue, however, is not "divided along religious lines," and it has nothing to do with the separation of church and state.[36]

The issue of the humanness of the unborn child is one raised by many people across a vast spectrum of religious backgrounds, and, happily, also by thousands who have no religion at all. A picture in the *International Herald Tribune* of January 25, 1978, showed a Washington protest march on the fifth anniversary of the Supreme Court decision that restricted the rights of states to regulate and thereby curtail the spread of abortion. The most outstanding sign being carried read: IF MY MOM DIDN'T CARE—I MIGHT NOT BE HERE—THANKS, MOM! The young girl carrying that sign did not have to be religious to paint and carry it; all she needed was to be glad she was not aborted. And the right of that girl to express her views on life and death to those who represent her in the democratic process and to be heard in the courts depends only on her being a citizen of the United States. Abortion is not a religious issue. It is a human issue!

Nor is abortion a feminist issue, any more than slavery was only a slave owners' issue. Abortion has been tacked onto the feminist issue, with the feminist issue being used to carry abortion. But there is no intrinsic relationship between them. The fate of the unborn is a question of the fate of the human race. We are one human family. If the rights of one part of that family are denied, it is of concern to each of us. What is at stake is no less than the essence of what freedom and rights are all about.[37]

Third, when the United States Supreme Court made its ruling about abortion on January 22, 1973, Mr. Justice Blackmun delivered the opinion of the Court. The first section in his opinion was titled "Ancient Attitudes." In it he referred back to pre-Christian law. He said, "Greek and Roman law afforded little protection to the unborn. If abortion was prosecuted in some places, it seems to have been based on a concept of a violation of the father's right to his offspring. Ancient religion did not bar abortion." Thus, as his first point, Mr. Justice Blackmun based his opinion on the practice of pre-Christian Greek and Roman law. Most people who read this did not realize the logical result concerning babies after their birth. Roman law permitted not only abortion but also infanticide. As we think this over, we ask ourselves, "Now that this door is open, how long will it be before infanticide is socially accepted and perhaps legalized?"

CHAPTER TWO

The Slaughter of the Innocents

Infanticide is not yet legalized, but the law is strangely silent about what amounts to public confessions in reputable scientific journals by medical doctors who admit that they are indeed practicing it. Infanticide is the killing of a born child—whether that killing is accomplished by a direct act on the part of someone, or whether ordinary care vital to the child's survival, such as feeding, is refused. It makes little difference whether infanticide is direct or indirect. Either way a child is killed.

The first effort we know of in this country to educate the medical profession in the art of infanticide was a documentary motion picture titled *Who Shall Survive?* Johns Hopkins Hospital and Medical School produced it in 1972. It shows a newborn infant with Down's syndrome (frequently called mongolism) who was permitted to die by "inattention." We suspect that "starving to death" would be a more accurate way of saying this.

People who have never had the experience of working with children who are being rehabilitated into our society after the correction of a congenital defect often say that infants with such defects should be allowed to die or even "encouraged" to die, because their lives can obviously be nothing but unhappy and miserable. Yet it is constantly to be observed that disability and unhappiness do not necessarily go together. Some of the most unhappy children have all of their physical and mental faculties, while some of the happiest youngsters have borne burdens which most of us would find very difficult to endure.

The obligation in such circumstances is to find alternatives for the problems such children and their parents face. Morally and logically, we do not consider infanticide an acceptable alternative. With today's technology and creativity, we are merely at the beginning of what we can do to help such youngsters with formal educational and leisure-time activities.

Who knows what constitutes "happiness" for another person? And what about the rewards and satisfactions that come to those who succeed in rehabilitating other-than-perfect children? Stronger character, compassion, deeper understanding of another's burden, creativity, and deeper family bonds—all these can and do result from the so-called social burden of raising a child with a congenital defect.

The Medical Profession Views Infanticide
Infanticide is being practiced right now in this country, and the saddest thing about it is that it is being carried on by the very segment of the medical profession which has always stood in the role of advocate for the lives of children. The fully developed view of the medical profession in the West grew out of the Christian consensus, and, as we have seen, stands in sharp contrast to old Roman customs. The traditional view of the medical profession has been well stated by J. Engelburt Dunphy, Robert D. Zachary, and Peter Paul Rickham. Dunphy is one of the great teachers of American surgery in this generation. Zachary is the senior pediatric surgical consultant at Children's Hospital of Sheffield, England. He has been in the forefront of developing operations for the correction of spina bifida and its complications: orthopedic defects and hydrocephalus (water on the brain). Rickham is professor of pediatric surgery at the University of Zurich and has been a pioneer in developing surgery and intensive care for the newborn.

Dunphy said in the annual oration before the Massachusetts Medical Society in 1976:

> We cannot destroy life. We cannot regard the hydrocephalic child as a nonperson and accept the responsibility for disposing of it like a sick animal. If there are those in society who think this step would be

good, let them work for a totalitarian form of government where, beginning with the infirm and incompetent and ending with the intellectually dissident, nonpersons are disposed of day and night by those in power.

History shows clearly the frighteningly short steps from "the living will" to "death control" to "thought control" and finally to the systematic elimination of all but those selected for slavery or to make up the master race. We physicians must take care that support of an innocent but quite unnecessary "living will" does not pave the way for us to be the executioners while the decisions for death are made by a panel of "objective experts" or by big brother himself. The year of 1984 is not far away!

Robert D. Zachary, on July 9, 1976, in the Forshall Lecture given before the British Association of Pediatric Surgeons in Sheffield, England, said:

> I believe that our patients, no matter how young or small they are, should receive the same consideration and expert help that would be considered normal in an adult. Just because he is small, just because he cannot speak for himself, this is no excuse to regard him as expendable, any more than we would do so on account of race or creed or color or poverty. Nor do I think we ought to be swayed by an argument that the parents have less to lose because he is small and newborn, and has not yet established a close relationship with them, or indeed because the infant himself does not know what he is losing, by missing out on life.

Zachary concluded his lecture with these comments:

> There are some ways in which modern society cares greatly about those who are less well off: the poor, the sick, and the handicapped, but it seems to me that newborn babies are often given less than justice. Our primary concern must be the well-being of the patient— as far as it is in our power to achieve it. In his battle at the beginning of life, it could well be that his main defense will be in the hands of pediatric and neonatal surgeons.[38]

At the hundredth anniversary of Children's Hospital in Sheffield, England, in an address titled "The Swing of the Pendulum," Professor Rickham said:

> How many normal newborn infants will live happily ever after, especially in our present time? It may be argued that by not selecting, we artificially increase the number of people with an unhappy future, but can we be sure of this in any given case? After all, doctors deal with single, individual patients and not with statistical possibilities. It

has also been pointed out that even a child with a grave physical and mental handicap can experience emotions such as happiness, fright, gratitude and love and that it may be therefore, in fact, a rewarding task to look after him. It has been further argued that, strictly speaking, selection implies a limitation of resources, because with an optimum of resources and care a great deal can be done for these children and their families. In underdeveloped countries these resources do not exist, but in developed countries, where such enormous sums are spent by governments on purposes which are of very doubtful benefit to humanity at large, the distribution of resources is a debatable subject. Finally, it can be argued that if selection is practiced, it may not be necessarily the fittest on whom the greatest effort should be expended.

The late Lord Cohen of Birkenhead, a man whose name is associated with the beginnings of the National Health Service in Great Britain, had this to say about the possibility of killing British children who are mentally defective or epileptic: "No doctor could subscribe to this view . . . who has seen the love and devotion which brings out all that is best in men when lavished on such a child."

In 1975 the Sonoma Conference (in California) on Ethical Issues in Neonatal Intensive Care produced a 193-page report titled "Ethics of Newborn Intensive Care." At the conference, seventeen members of a panel of twenty answered yes to this question: "Would it be right to directly intervene to kill a self-sustaining infant?" (A self-sustaining infant is a child who can live without technical assistance of any kind. That means he can survive with no help other than normal feeding.) One of the marks of our time is that many of the nonphysicians on the panel, including bioethicists, lawyers, a nurse, a social worker, a sociologist, an anthropologist, and a philosopher, could see no difference at all between not putting a child on a machine and not giving it food. Letting a dying child die and actually killing a living child by starvation were all the same to them. The physicians on the panel said they themselves would hesitate to kill such an infant directly, but would not prevent someone else from doing so. This is total relativism. Values are a purely subjective matter and could change with any circumstance.

A widely read monthly newspaper for pediatricians called *Pediatric News* posed questions to three physicians concerning the 1975 Sonoma Conference report. *Pediatric News* devoted a large portion of its April 1977 issue to the answers, which are most significant in a discussion of the implications of this problem—the wrong answers to which can shape the foundations of the futures for us all.

One of the physicians quizzed was Dr. George M. Ryan, Jr., of Boston Hospital for Women. He said:

> The most difficult question is obviously whether it would ever be right to intervene directly to kill a self-sustaining infant. It is relatively easy to conceive of ceasing to provide unnatural prolongation of meaningless life by technology, but to actively kill an infant that is living without this support is to me repugnant. I think this action is so in conflict with the concept of the physician as a "healer" that such a decision should not be thrust upon the medical profession. Clearly the physician can testify as to the physical and medical status of the patient and can even predict some of the elements of the general human potential of the individual, but beyond this point, the physician has no special talent or training not available to the rest of society that might provide him with the capability of making infallible decisions. I am not very sanguine about the wisdom of any one group in making such decisions.

We certainly agree with Dr. Ryan on how repugnant this situation is. We agree, too, that physicians have no corner on the market in making infallible decisions, even though they certainly have some knowledge that is not available to the average consumer of health care. The point is that no one should be making decisions to kill self-sustaining infants.

Another of the three physicians was asked his opinion about the Sonoma Conference findings. Dr. R. T. F. Schmidt of Cincinnati, at that time president-elect of the American College of Obstetrics and Gynecologists, answered from the point of view of traditional moral and ethical standards. He said, "The fact that seventeen of twenty expert panelists believe that some severely defective infants should be killed under certain conditions is deeply disturbing. This position is not only deeply disturbing to our traditional concept of the inherent value of human life but is potentially shattering to the foundations of Western civilization."

Dr. Schmidt was careful to point out that much of the Sonoma Conference represented sound deliberation, but he felt that the issue of infanticide is of such far-reaching importance that it deserves to be singled out. He concluded his remarks by saying:

> Finally, the issue was clouded by questions raised as to what state of

perfection or imperfection qualifies a human being as a person. The Supreme Court decision of 1973 has already severely limited this qualification. Under current law, the existence of every future member of our society may be terminated [within the uterus] according to the value judgment of one or, at the most, two private individuals. To extend this contingency of private value judgment to the newborn infant in either ethical standard or in law would be another ominous step backward.

The Decision to Kill

Although the following headline is unfair to Dr. Victor Vaughn, an ethical and reputable pediatrician and educator, once chief at St. Christopher's Hospital in Philadelphia, the fact that such a headline could appear in a medical newspaper in 1977 should jolt us to the very foundation of our being: M.D.-PARENT DECISION NEEDED TO KILL INFANT. One only has to read the article to see that it is considered unwise for a parent to decide by himself to kill his child, or for a physician to decide by himself to kill the parent's child, but that their consensus makes such a decision legitimate.

Dr. John A. Robertson of the University of Wisconsin Law School and Medical School spoke what seems to us a word of wisdom to bring this discussion down to earth. He said that "one must decide for whose benefit is the decision to withhold treatment from a child with severe birth defects. Is no life better than one of low quality? The person to ask is an individual who has a disabling birth defect." Let us emphasize: *The person to ask is an individual who has a disabling birth defect.*

In preparing for the writing of this book, we did just that and something more. Four patients of one of us—born with congenital defects incompatible with life (who had been operated upon on the first day or two of life)—were assembled with four other children who had developed lethal problems in early childhood. They were not coached in any way concerning what answers they were to give to questions. They were told that we were making some documentary movies and were writing a book on the general topic of "Whatever Happened to the Human Race?" We allowed them to talk with each other for about an hour, in order to feel comfortable before being asked to participate in our plans.

The patients at the time ranged in age from eleven to thirty years. One patient had been born with a number of major congenital defects down the midline of his body, requiring twenty-seven operative procedures for correction. Another was born without an esophagus, requiring a transplantation of the colon to replace the absent organ. Still another was born with a tumor of the tongue, necessitating almost total amputation of that structure in a series of operations. The final youngster with congenital defects was born with major defects of the esophagus, the lower bowel, and the bladder.

The other four children all had tumors. One was a benign tumor of the bones of the face, which had required a number of operations for correction and still had not achieved perfection. The other three had cancers of the adrenal gland, of the parotid gland, and of the uterus.

There can be no doubt about how such young people feel about the joy of living, despite the time-consuming and usually painful medical and surgical procedures they have endured to correct birth defects or those discovered in early childhood. Here is a sampling of their comments:

> Because the start was a little abnormal, it doesn't mean you're going to finish that way. I'm a normal, functioning human being, capable of doing anything anyone else can. . . .

> At times it got very hard, but life is certainly worth living. I married a wonderful guy and I'm just so happy. . . .

> At the beginning it was a little difficult going back to school after surgery, but then things started looking up, with a little perseverance and support. I am an anesthetist and I'm happily married. Things are going great for me. . . .

> I really think that all my operations and all the things I had wrong with me were worth it, because I really enjoy life and I don't really let the things that are wrong with me bother me. . . .

> If anything, I think I've had an added quality to my life—an appreciation of life. I look forward to every single morning. . . .

> Most of the problems are what my parents went through with the surgery. I've now been teaching high school for eight years and it's a great joy. . . .

> They spend millions of dollars to send men to the moon. I think they can spend any amount necessary to save someone's life. A human life is so important because it's a gift—not something that you can give, so you really don't have the right to take it either. . . .

> I really don't consider myself handicapped. Life is just worth living. What else can I say? . . .

One of our special friends is Craig, who was a student at L'Abri in Switzerland. He is a graduate in philosophy from Cal State and is now a theological student at Covenant Seminary. He was born without a left leg and without arms below the elbows. Today, in some hospitals, Craig might have been deliberately allowed to die at birth, on the mistaken assumption that life is not worth living for the seriously handicapped person. When we asked Craig what he thought about those who say that people born with such serious birth defects should be eliminated, this, in part, was his reply:

> They don't really see that what they are talking about is murder. I know, when I was born, the first thing my dad said to my mom was that "this one needs our love more." An individual with a handicap needs our love and needs us to help him grow into the being that God has made him to be. They are advocating that we destroy these children before they're even given a chance to live and to conquer their handicaps.
>
> I'm very glad to be alive. I live a full, meaningful life. I have many friends and many things that I want to do in life. I think the secret of living with a handicap is realizing who you are—that you're a human being, somebody who is very special—looking at the things that you *can* do in spite of your handicap, and maybe even through your handicap.

Those who graduated from medical school in the first half of this century probably came out of that experience with the idea that they had been trained to "alleviate suffering and save lives." The suffering to be relieved was the *patient's* suffering and the life to be saved was the *patient's* life. This has become distorted in the semantics of the euthanasia movement in the following way. Doctors are to save lives; that is part of their profession. If the life they are trying to save, however, is producing suffering on the part of the family, doctors are to allay that suffering by disposing of their patient. So, in a strange way, it can still be said that doctors are alleviating suffering and saving lives. But the practice of infanticide for the well-being of the family is a far cry from the traditional role of the pediatrician and more lately of the pediatric surgeon.

Abortion, infanticide, and euthanasia are not only questions for women and other relatives directly involved—nor are they the prerogatives of a few people who have thought through the wider ramifications. They are life-and-death issues that concern the whole human race and should be addressed as such. Putting pressure on the public and on legislators to accept a lower view of human beings, small groups of people often argue their case by using a few extreme examples to gain sympathy for ideas and practices that later are not limited to extreme cases. These then become the common practice of the day. Abortion, for example, has moved from something once considered unusual and now in many cases is an accepted form of "birth control."

Infanticide is following the same pattern. The argument begins with people who have a so-called vegetative existence. There then follows a tendency to expand the indications and eliminate almost any child who is unwanted for some reason.

The same movement can be seen with euthanasia. The arguments now being put forward center on the "miserable" person in old age—one dying of cancer, for instance. But once the doors are open, there is no reason why the aged, weak, and infirm will not find that as they become economic burdens they will be eliminated under one pretext or another.

At first we hear much talk of compassion for the unwanted. The discussion moves on to "rights," then to "my" rights and soon to pure "economics." The discussion of life must be brought back to where it belongs—not to emotional, extreme examples, not to selfish questions of rights, not to expedience, and certainly not to economics.[39] The matter should be discussed in terms of right and wrong.

How Should We Then Live? spoke of "sociological law"—that is, law based only on what the majority of society thinks is in its best interests at a given moment—and "sociological news," slanted to produce what some person thinks will produce a helpful sociological result. *Now arbitrary abortion has opened wide the door at the point of life and death for "sociological medicine"—not just for the yet unborn but for all human life.*

Treating Congenital Defects

The most challenging aspect of children's surgery is the treatment of those congenital defects that are incompatible with life, but nevertheless can be corrected by the proper surgical procedure carried out shortly after birth. We are talking about such defects as those in babies who are born without a connection between the throat and stomach, or with no rectum, perhaps with their abdominal organs out in the umbilical cord or up in the chest cavity, or infants with any one of a great many varieties of intestinal obstruction. Many of those babies are operated on as youngsters and grow into adult life, marry, and have children of their own.

Of course there are problems in raising some of these children, and they may on occasion constitute a burden for the rest of the family. One of us has had thirty-five years' experience in performing thousands of just such operations. No family has ever asked, "Why did you work so hard to save the life of my child?" No grown child or young adult has ever asked, "Why did you struggle so hard when you knew the outcome would not be perfect?"[40]

One of us operated at Philadelphia's Children's Hospital on young Christopher Wall, who was born with *ectopia cordis* (the heart outside the chest), actually performing fifteen different procedures over 1,117 days to get his heart repositioned without crowding and to permit his lungs to function adequately. Chris is the first patient who has ever survived after being born with this type of *ectopia cordis*. The case of Chris Wall raises a number of questions asked from time to time: "Why do you think it's right to spend that much money in caring for one child, when you could take the same amount of money and spread it over the treatment of many children?" Or, as some people asked, "What kind of life is the child living? He is on a respirator; he has never been home; his parents have almost no relationship with this son who is more emotionally tied to the nurses who have raised him during the past two years."[41] *Note:* Chris did go home after 1,117 days in the hospital and is off the respirator for as long as eight hours at a time and will eventually come off the respirator completely. A doctor is responsible to God for the manner in which he works to save a single human life. It is a matter of stewardship. The surgeon is accountable for the way he uses the gifts that God has given him. He is also responsible for the life entrusted to his care. It is a question of moral principle.

But even if we were pragmatists, we would still believe that doctors should work to save the Chris Walls of this world. For when a hospital is geared to save lives at any cost, this attitude affects health care down to the most mundane level.[42] On the other hand, when one set of patients can be eliminated at will, the whole spirit of struggling to save lives is lost, and it is not long before a doctor or nurse will say, "Why try so hard on anybody? After all, we deliberately fail to treat some patients and we kill others." Even if it were not expressed this blatantly, an erosion takes place, which over a number of years would undermine the care of all patients in any institution that kills any patient placed in its care.

Eventually, abortion must surely have this effect on the field of obstetrics. We do not understand how an obstetrician can destroy a 1000-gram fetus in one uterus and deliver a 1500-gram premature baby from out of another uterus, carrying it to the tender, loving care of the intensive-care nursery down the hall.

Just as child abuse has risen dramatically during the years of legalized abortion, the gradual brutalizing of society that is taking place has included doctors and legislators as well as ordinary citizens. If you doubt that we are becoming brutal, consider for a moment that many pediatric surgeons, highly skilled in surgery of the newborn and most knowledgeable about what can be accomplished by rehabilitation, choose not to operate on a given newborn with a given congenital defect. By making the decision of allowing him to die or acquiescing to the parents' wishes not to operate, they allow the baby to die.[43] Think of mothers who express the idea of "personal rights" by having dragged piecemeal from their wombs the child they have conceived. Think of legislators debating, as if they were talking about the price of coffee, what action they should take to eliminate economic burdens on society by opening the doors to a lack of protection for the weak, the old, the infirm, the young and the unborn—in fact, for all those our society traditionally has protected. Indeed, this protection was once a hallmark of our civilization. *Whatever happened to the human race?*

Advocates of Infanticide

It frightens us when we see the medical profession acquiesce to, if not lead in, a trend which in our judgment will carry us to destruction. The loss of humanness shown in allowing malformed babies to starve to death is not a thing of the future. It is being put forward as the accepted thing right now in many quarters. All that is left is for it to become totally accepted and eventually, for economic reasons, made mandatory by an increasingly authoritarian government in an increasingly selfish society.

In May 1973, James D. Watson, the Nobel Prize laureate who discovered the double helix of DNA, granted an interview to *Prism* magazine, then a publication of the American Medical Association. *Time* later reported the interview to the general public, quoting Watson as having said, "If a child were not declared alive until three days after birth, then all parents could be allowed the choice only a few are given under the present system. The doctor could allow the child to die if the parents so choose and save a lot of misery and suffering. I believe this view is the only rational, compassionate attitude to have."

In January 1978, Francis Crick, also a Nobel laureate, was quoted in the *Pacific News Service* as saying, ". . . no newborn infant should be declared human until it has passed certain tests regarding its genetic endowment and that if it fails these tests it forfeits the right to live."

In *Ideals of Life,* Millard S. Everett, who was professor of philosophy and humanities at Oklahoma A&M, writes, "My personal feeling—and I don't ask anyone to agree with me—is that eventually, when public opinion is prepared for it, no child should be admitted into the society of the living who would be certain to suffer any social handicap—for example, any physical or mental defect that would prevent marriage or would make others tolerate his company only from the sense of mercy." He adds, "This would imply not only eugenic sterilization but also euthanasia due to accidents of birth which cannot be foreseen."[44]

Perhaps the paper most outspokenly advocating infanticide was published in the prestigious 167-year-old *New England Journal of Medicine.* In October 1973, Dr. Raymond S. Duff and Dr. A. G. M. Campbell of the department of pediatrics at Yale University School of Medicine wrote, "Moral and Ethical Dilemmas in the Special-Care Nursery."[45]

Very few parents come of their own volition to a physician and say, "My baby has a life not worthy to be lived." Duff and Campbell say that the parents in such a case are not in a condition to give "informed consent" by themselves. But any physician in the emotional circumstances surrounding the birth of a baby with any kind of a defect can, by innuendo if not advice, prepare the family to make the decision the physician wants them to make. We do not consider this "informed consent."

Duff and Campbell acknowledge that the parents' and siblings' rights to relief from "seemingly pointless, crushing burdens were important considerations" in letting children die. Even Duff and Campbell use the word *seemingly* to modify *pointless,* and we are sure the burden would not be nearly as *crushing* as the guilt many of these parents will eventually feel.[46]

As partial justification for their point of view, Duff and Campbell say that "although some parents have exhibited doubts that the choices were correct, all appear to be as effective in their lives as they were before this experience. Some claim that their profoundly moving experience has provided a deeper meaning in life, and from this they have become more effective people." Some of the parents, the two doctors admit, had doubts that their choice to let the child die was correct. If these parents were seeking deeper meaning in life—and if Duff and Campbell were indeed interested in providing deeper meaning in life for the parents of their deformed patients—why not let the family find that deep meaning by providing the love and attention necessary to take care of an infant who has been given to them? We suspect that the deeper meaning would then be deeper still, that their effectiveness would be still more effective, and that they would be examples of courage and determination to others less courageous. Duff and Campbell say, "It seems appropriate that the profession be held accountable for presenting fully all management options and their expected consequences." We wonder how commonly physicians are willing to be held accountable for the consequences that may not be apparent in a family until years later?

There have been many times when one of us, having operated on a newborn younger who has subsequently died, has been inwardly relieved and has expressed honestly to the family that the tragic turn of events was indeed a blessing in disguise. But being able to look on such an occasion in retrospect as a blessing does not, we believe, entitle a doctor to distribute a "shower of blessings" by eliminating the problems that families might have to face in raising a child who is less than perfect—by eliminating the baby.

On the basis of interviews he has given and comments we have read in the press, we believe that Professor Duff is perfectly sincere in believing that he is moving in an ethical and moral direction when he advocates death as one of the options in the treatment of a defective newborn. It should not be thought that we are singling out Duff and Campbell. There are growing numbers of other physicians and surgeons who unfortunately, we believe, are advocating the same course of action. Anthony Shaw, a pediatric surgeon, has been in the forefront of these discussions from a neonatal surgeon's point of view. He says: "My ethic holds that all rights are not absolute all the time. As Fletcher points out, '. . . all rights are imperfect and may be set aside if human need requires it.' My ethic further considers quality of life as a value that must be balanced against the belief in the sanctity of life."[47]

We are moving from the state of mind in which destruction of life is advocated for children who are considered to be socially useless or deemed to have nonmeaningful lives to the stance that we should perhaps destroy a child because he is socially disturbing. One wonders if the advocates of such a philosophy would espouse a total blockade and "starving out" of urban slums as a solution to poverty—considering all the social and economic problems this would solve all at once!

The twentieth century has produced many monsters. One has been the idea of "built-in obsolescence," not only in material things but also in human matters such as marriage and the responsibilities of parenthood. One can picture a parent picking up one baby and, not being quite satisfied with it, trading it in for another one.

Medical science can now make a prenatal diagnosis of the sex of the expected offspring. In spite of the depravity of our society regarding abortion-on-demand, even abortionists recoil a little from eliminating an unborn child just because it is not the sex the family wants. There was a recent example involving a couple who wanted a boy but not a girl. Rather than make this crass request of their obstetrician, they claimed to be concerned about hemophilia in the wife's family. Amniocentesis was therefore undertaken to determine the sex of the baby, because only males are affected. When the obstetrician reported that there was no need for concern because the unborn child was a girl and could not have hemophilia, the parents responded, "That's what we wanted to know. We want a boy, so now we want an abortion."

One wonders what the chances are for someone who becomes a burden in a society that practices the concept of the survival of the fittest and has begun this practice by starting to eliminate its children. Most societies, recognizing the total dependency of children, have given their young a place of special protection. Since our society has begun by abusing and then killing children, we feel that for us the worst has come first. Where the destruction will end depends only on what a small scientific elite and a generally apathetic public will advocate and tolerate. Any hope of a comprehensive standard for human rights has already been lost.

Meaningful Humanhood
Joseph Fletcher, formerly of Harvard Divinity School and now at the University of Virginia in Charlottesville, talks about "mean-

ingful humanhood" in an article entitled "Indicators of Human-hood: A Tentative Profile of Man."[48] H. Tristam Engelhart, Jr., formerly clinical professor of physiology of medicine at the University of Texas and more recently professor of philosophy and medicine at the Kennedy Institute of Georgetown University in Washington, D.C., writes of "wrongful life."[49]

As soon as we let anyone, even a physician, make decisions about our "meaningful humanhood," about "wrongful life" or "rightful life," we have then invited others to make decisions about our worth. And our worth may be entirely different in the eyes of these men or their followers from what it would have been to anyone in our culture in the past. In fact, it might even be different from the view held by the majority of people today.

If we decide that a child with a chronic cardiopulmonary disease, short-bowel syndrome, or various manifestations of brain dramage should be permitted to die (some of Duff and Campbell's examples), what is to prevent us from eliminating an adult with chronic cardiopulmonary disease—who may be much more of a burden to his family than the child is? Or what about an adult with ulcerative colitis (with symptoms much the same as short-bowel syndrome) and some psychiatric problems as well? Are we to extend the slaughter to all those who in one way or another become a burden or nuisance, or who stop us from enjoying our rights as we perceive them? The word *rights* is meaningless outside the context of some moral framework that extends its protection to the whole human family.

Because a newborn child has the possibility or even the probability of problems in later life, does this give us the right to terminate his or her life now? If it does, then should we also do away with the people reading this book who have chronic shortness of breath, oxygen dependency, paralysis, a sexual handicap, or a psychological problem? The problems in the Duff and Campbell article all have their adult counterparts.

We think many miss the essential message in the Duff and Campbell paper. These authors first brought to public attention death as an option in newborn pediatric care. But it is not always understood that the death they presented as an option *was not the death of infants who could not possibly survive, but rather the death of infants who could live if treated—but whose lives would not be "normal."*

The physician's decision—not the infant's defect—becomes the lethal factor. In view of the fact that, to Duff and Campbell, the economic status of the family and the stability of the marriage are mitigating circumstances in deciding on treatment or nontreatment, it is clear that there has been introduced a discrimination just as deplorable as those based on race, creed, color, or sex. And, as is so often the case, not only is such immoral and discriminatory behavior propagated, but those who push for it do so with high and lofty pseudomoral language.

Duff and Campbell offer death as an option in health care, even though they say in one place in their article, "We recognize great variability and often much uncertainty in prognoses and in family capacities to deal with defective newborn infants. . . . Prognosis was not always exact and a few children with extensive care might live for months and occasionally years. *Some might survive and function satisfactorily*" (italics ours).

When the physician responsible for managing a newborn baby with a defect is committed to the thesis that there is some human life not worthy to be lived, and when he considers death as one of the options in treatment, the baby concerned does not have a chance. Obviously, the determining factor is not the baby's physical defect but the physician's decision.

The *Newsweek* (November 12, 1973) report of the Duff and Campbell article quotes Duff as saying, "The public has got to decide what to do with vegetated individuals who have no human potential." This was answered by a letter in *Newsweek* two weeks later:

"Life-and-Death Decisions"

I'll wager my entire root system and as much fertilizer as it would take to fill Yale University that you have never received a letter from a vegetable before this one, but, much as I resent the term, I must confess that I fit the description of a "vegetable" as defined in the article "Shall This Child Die?"

Due to severe brain damage incurred at birth, I am unable to dress myself, toilet myself, or write; my secretary is typing this letter. Many thousands of dollars had to be spent on my rehabilitation and education in order for me to reach my present professional status as a counselling psychologist. My parents were also told, 35 years ago, that there was "little or no hope of achieving meaningful 'humanhood' " for their daughter. Have I reached "humanhood"? Compared with Drs. Duff and Campbell, I believe I have surpassed it!

Instead of changing the law to make it legal to weed out us "vegetables," let us change the laws so that we may receive quality medical care, education and freedom to live as full and productive lives as our potentials allow.

Sondra Diamond
Philadelphia, Pa.

The medical profession has traditionally made its treatment of patients a reflection of our society's concern for those who are ill or helpless. Indeed, it has often acted as an advocate for those who had no one else to stand up for them. Thus it responded, in days gone by, with love and compassion toward the helpless child. Technical skills have increased rapidly and have produced dilemmas that doctors did not face a decade ago. But this does not give them any new expertise in deciding who shall live and who shall die, especially when so many nonmedical factors must be taken into account in making the decision. The new gadgetry of medical practice and the growing sophistication of technology do not give a doctor any more right than the rest of us to play God. Many in the medical profession are losing this viewpoint. They are setting the worth of the individual person aside. We would insist that if we cannot cure, we can care; and we do not mean ever to use the words *care* and *kill* as synonyms.

Infanticide and the Church

Mauthausen in Austria was a Nazi concentration camp where, between 1938 and 1945, over 110,000 people were brutally killed to help build the Nazis' idea of heaven on earth. There are monuments to the many Jews and non-Jews who died. What happened in Mauthausen shows the lowest possible view of human life. All conventions of war were put aside, as people of all nationalities were tortured and had pseudomedical experiments performed on them.

To the Nazis the Jews were an unwanted burden on society— parasites who consumed more than they gave. The young, the old, the aged, the weak, and the strong were all eliminated in an attempt to build a perfect race according to Nazi standards. Individuals were no longer perceived as special creatures created in the image of God. Regardless of their nationality or race, people were viewed as pawns to be exploited, and when they no longer fulfilled a function, they were eliminated.

Not so long ago, at the Charleston, South Carolina, slave market, black men, women, and children were sold as cattle. On a balcony they were paraded as so much merchandise before the prospective buyers standing down below. For economic convenience, they had been arbitrarily reclassified by a white society as nonhuman. The Supreme Court of the United States, in the Dred Scott Decision, upheld this fiction by declaring the black person to be chattel property.

These atrocities are not just a record in past history. There is in our own day a low view of human life, not only in the secular world but in certain religious groups as well. The Religious Coalition for Abortion Rights is a case in point. Among what the organization calls its "eleven major denominations" are the Unitarian Universal Association, the American Ethical Union, the American Jewish Congress, and the Union of American Hebrew Congregations. This group has attempted to use anti-Catholic thinking as a weapon by declaring that abortion is a Roman Catholic issue. Its position on abortion is weakened by ignorance—because it seeks the "legal option of abortion in accordance with sound medical practice." Actually, this "sound medical practice" is just the whim of the mother-to-be.

Dean J. Philip Wogaman of Wesley Theological Seminary has espoused the cause of the Religious Coalition for Abortion Rights by ignoring the right of the developing, unborn baby in favor of what he calls "God's loving intention for existing human beings."[50] That "loving intention" for an existing human being turns out to be supporting the mother-to-be in the murder of her unborn child.

Certain segments of the church are also not without a positive opinion on the subject of infanticide. A task force of the Anglican Church of Canada reached a conclusion in a 1977 report that it could be morally right to terminate the lives of newborn infants with severe brain damage. The callousness of the report is evident in its phraseology: "Our sense and emotions lead us to the grave mistake of treating human-looking shapes as if they were human, although they lack the least vestige of human behavior and intellect. In fact the only way to treat such defective infants humanely is not to treat them as human."[51]

The task force was made up of eleven people with backgrounds in medicine, nursing, law, and theology. It is astounding that the professions represented could have produced such a report. It is humanism producing inhumanity. The self-assured language of these individuals and people like them must surely remind us of the words and sentiments expressed by those who in another era were espousing and defending slavery and attempting to prove the nonhuman status of the black person.

Happily, the general synod of the Anglican Church in Canada did not approve the report, but that such a report came forth from an official group of a major denomination in our day says much about the direction taken by certain segments of the church in regard to infanticide.

That even the church is being used by the proponents of infanticide is particularly alarming. Those who have propagated these ideas or simply not bothered to think them through have had ample warning in history—if they would care to look. Doctors and nurses should be aware of how fallible these decisions are and how disastrous have been simplistic pop-science theories about human worth in the past. Lawyers should be frightened to let down the bars on the killing of any human being, when the decision is made on the arbitrary basis of the quality of life. And finally, these theologians have obviously forgotten God's view of the worth of every human being as made in the image of God. If these same theologians no longer believe in such a God, they should not use the church as a platform from which to propagate their discriminatory ideas.

In general, liberal theologians and church bodies (those who have tried to mix Christian and humanistic thought) support abortion and thus contribute to the subsequent slide into the loss of humanness. These religious groups have departed from the stand against abortion that the Christian church has taken from its earliest days. The *Didache,* or *The Teaching of the Twelve Apostles,* an early Christian document from the second century (or maybe even the late first century) clearly prohibits abortion. Tertullian, in his *Apologeticus* of A.D. 197 writes:

> For us murder is once for all forbidden; so even the child in the womb, while yet the mother's blood is still being drawn on to form the human being, it is not lawful for us to destroy. To forbid birth is only quicker murder. It makes no difference whether one take away the life once born or destroy it as it comes to birth. He is a man, who is to be a man; the fruit is always present in the seed.

Those in the church who have not made these questions a burning issue have forgotten the church's centuries-old tradition of social action on behalf of the weak and the unwanted. One remembers William Wilberforce, fighting the slave trade in the British Empire on the basis of his Christian faith, representative of the many down through the ages who have tried to practice what they preach.

What Chance for Humanity?

At a population-control conference in Washington, D.C., as reported by editor-writer Norman Podhoretz, one speaker saw "no reason why anyone who accepted abortion should balk at infanticide." Another urged certain medical qualifying tests for all newborns. These would determine their genetic characteristics and, thus, whether their right to life should be forfeited.[52] Of course, at present only a few hold these ideas, but unfortunately they are presenting these ideas again and again. Taken a little more seriously each time, they become just a little more thinkable each time.

Link this view with the abuse of genetic knowledge, the ever-expanding power of the government, and arbitrary law, and, indeed, the prospects for the right of the individual and for humanness are grim. Dr. James R. Sorenson, associate professor of socio-medical sciences at Boston University Medical Center, spoke at the symposium "Prenatal Diagnosis and Its Impact on Society" and said:

> [There is] a developing cultural or social attitude that . . . a couple ought to exercise control over their reproductive fate. While a couple should have as many children as they please (within cultural "limits"), increasingly our societal view is that they should not have unwanted children. I think that this developing societal attitude can very easily extend to encompass not just control of the number of children but . . . control of their quality as well. In short, I am suggesting that it may become culturally acceptable and perhaps even expected that parents ought to avoid the birth of a defective child, especially when we have a technology that can help avoid such events.

The matter does not stop with malformed babies, but leads naturally to limiting the number of babies a family may have. In 1971, at the National Conference on Population Education in Washington, D.C., Martha Willing, codirector of Population Dynamics of Seattle, Washington, first proposed tax disincentives for parents who have more than two children. Then the state should proceed "to penalize deliberate violations of a small family norm and set up controls which prevent such violations." The author continues:

After the third child is born, both mother and father will have to present themselves at a hospital to undergo sterilization procedures. If the couple does not appear, there will be no birth certificate issued to the third child, but instead a "third child paper." The mother can be tattooed or marked to signify a third birth to any subsequent doctor. Instead of the missing parent, the child can be sterilized on the spot, insuring that this undue share of the gene pool will not be carried forward.[53]

Without the Judeo-Christian base which gives every individual an intrinsic dignity as made in the image of the personal-infinite Creator, each successive horror falls naturally into place. Combine arbitrary law (in which a small group of people may decide what is good for society at that moment of history) with the Supreme Court ruling on arbitrary abortion and the gates are opened for many kinds of killing under the guise of social good. Nan Mizrachi, in "Eliminating the Medical Hazards of Delayed Abortions," says:

> Arguments that the fetus is only "human" at a particular stage of gestation violate biological reality. It attempts to oversimplify a complex issue. Whereas the reality that abortion is killing should not, in my view, remove abortion as a socially acceptable surgical procedure, I do think we should face up to the reality of what the decision to abort entails.[54]

In other words, abortion is killing, but it is nevertheless to be practiced. But if that kind of killing, why not others?

As much as we would differ with Professor Joseph Fletcher's views of ethics, we can agree that his logic is impeccable when he says in *The Humanist* (July-August 1974): "To speak of living and dying, therefore . . . encompasses the abortion issue along with the euthanasia issue. They are ethically inseparable."

Here we come to the next logical step that follows from abandoning the biblical perspective that mankind is unique, in that all men, women, and children are made in the image of God. The wide-open door of abortion-on-demand leads naturally to infanticide which leads naturally to euthanasia.

CHAPTER THREE

Death by Someone's Choice

Life is a continuum from conception until natural death. Since life is being destroyed before birth, why not tamper with it on the other end?

Will a society which has assumed the right to kill infants in the womb—because they are unwanted, imperfect, or merely inconvenient—have difficulty in assuming the right to kill other human beings, especially older adults who are judged unwanted, deemed imperfect physically or mentally, or considered a possible social nuisance?

The next candidates for arbitrary reclassification as nonpersons are the elderly. This will become increasingly so as the proportion of the old and weak in relation to the young and strong becomes abnormally large, due to the growing antifamily sentiment, the abortion rate, and medicine's contribution to the lengthening of the normal life span. The imbalance will cause many of the young to perceive the old as a cramping nuisance in the hedonistic lifestyle they claim as their right. As the demand for affluence continues and the economic crunch gets greater, the amount of compassion that the legislature and the courts will have for the old does not seem likely to be significant considering the precedent of the nonprotection given to the unborn and newborn.

How did the concept of euthanasia get such a head start in the seventies? We must keep referring back to abortion—because it is the Supreme Court decision on abortion that stated that "only viable human beings who have the capability for meaningful life may, but need not, be protected by the state." That statement could be a death warrant for many in a few years.

Euthanasia: "Death with Dignity"

The word *euthanasia* becomes a respectable part of our vocabulary and consciousness in a subtle way, via the phrase *death with dignity*. This term was first used, as far as we know, in a book published in Germany in 1920 by Karl Binding and Alfred Hoche: *The Release of the Destruction of Life Devoid of Value.*[55] There is no doubt about what the authors meant by the term. They made it the motto of the movement to legalize the killing of a person who had "the right to the complete relief of an unbearable life." *But, we have to ask, "unbearable" by whose definition?*

Starving to death a newborn infant with a congenital defect is given the name *passive euthanasia,* and somehow or other seems more acceptable in the minds of those who commit such an atrocity than taking an active step to kill the same child.

On occasion, a physician may decide to withhold extraordinary means in the management of a patient. Is there ever justification for this? First of all, one must define the term *extraordinary* as it refers to medical care. Things which are extraordinary today will not be extraordinary next year, and things which were extraordinary last year are ordinary now. There was a day when the administration of oxygen or the use of intravenous fluids was extraordinary—and so it has been with respirators, pacemakers, and heart-lung machines.

One of us has shown that newborns with severe congenital defects (those incompatible with life) upon whom he operates would *ordinarily* never survive—without extraordinary care. Yet, with that extraordinary care, most live and grow and do well without the continuation of any of the extraordinary measures. As a Christian, does this surgeon have any guidelines? For him it comes down to a matter of stewardship. He is answerable to society for the skills he exercises in the care of his patients. Yet, above that, he believes that he is also answerable to God for the skills he has been given, as well as for the care of the patients God has entrusted to him.

To use nonreligious terms, the issue is motivation. It is his motivation or intent that a physician must keep uppermost in his mind. He must constantly be aware of the wonderful uniqueness of human life. Of course, at times he faces difficult decisions. Once he believes that the technical gadgetry he is using is merely prolonging the experience of dying, rather than extending life, he can withdraw the extraordinary means and let nature take its course, while keeping the patient as comfortable as possible. This is what physicians have done for years, in the realm of trust between patient and physician or between the patient's family and physician. That is truly "death with dignity," and no mere manufactured euphemism for euthanasia.

This is not the question being debated today, however. It is not doctors with a biblical view of life who are debating the cases in which death is imminent and inevitable. Rather, it is a whole new breed of medical and paramedical personnel for whom the issues go much further. With these individuals, the intent is to advocate the death of a patient either by directly killing him, or by doing nothing when there could be given help and support that would result in life—even though the circumstances might be difficult. This, ironically, is called "mercy killing."

The next step is to destroy human individuals or groups of individuals because they are unwanted, imperfect, or socially embarrassing. Senility, infirmity, retardation, insanity, and incontinence are conditions that come to mind. Obviously, when one comes to that practice, he has gone far beyond even so-called mercy killing. He has entered the same realm as that of Nazi behavior during World War II. This is essentially what abortionists are doing with unborn babies—because many of these abortionists have no medical concern for whether the unborn babies live. To have those babies is merely inconvenient, uneconomical, or perhaps embarrassing. Carrying this practice to its logical conclusion, we come to death selection and genocide.

The Case of Karen Quinlan

When one discusses euthanasia, the case of Karen Quinlan comes to mind as probably the best-known medical-ethical dilemma of recent years. To summarize very briefly: Karen Quinlan was delivered to an emergency room of a community hospital by friends.

She was unconscious after having taken a combination of alcohol and drugs. If a thousand people were delivered to an emergency room in such a condition, the result would probably be a few survivors and a tremendous number of deaths, but Karen Quinlan lived on in an unconscious limbo between life and death.

Miss Quinlan was undoubtedly in a most deplorable physical state. She lost a great deal of weight and lay in a fetal position. Although she was unconscious, she was far from legally dead. She responded to pain and noise and withdrew her limbs when they were stroked. Expert medical witnesses from various parts of the country said that she would never recover and that her life was being sustained only by the mechanical respirator which breathed for her. Because of this "expert testimony," Karen's parents petitioned the court to direct the physicians caring for their daughter to "pull the plug" on the respirator. Judge Robert Muir, Jr., of the lower New Jersey court delivered a remarkable verdict, which ruled that to disconnect the respirator would be an act of homicide, because Karen would be unable to support her own respiratory effort and would die.[56]

Subsequently, Karen's family appealed this decision to the Supreme Court of New Jersey, which reversed the lower court's decision. These judges said that the plug *could* be pulled.[57] Accordingly, the respirator was disconnected, and—to everyone's amazement—Karen went right on breathing. This should be a lesson for all concerned. Medical opinion, no matter how learned and expert, is never infallible.[58]

If Judge Muir in Morristown, New Jersey, had ruled that the plug could be pulled in this case, it would have been legitimate for other patients in the same condition as Karen to be candidates for the same kind of treatment. At the time of Judge Muir's decision, one of us had under his care four children who did not match all the neurological criteria of Karen Quinlan, but who were unconscious, though responsive to loud noises and pain, and had all their respiratory needs cared for by mechanical respirators. If Judge Muir had said to remove Karen's respirator, it might have been logical for the hospital's administrator, medical staff, nursing personnel, or the parents of these patients to have said, "Look, there is now a legal precedent. Let's disconnect the machines and get this over with." But all these children eventually went home well. It is obvious that one cannot accept the same legal guidelines for all people, not even when there is a court trial, expert testimony, and every other indicator that says, "Do it this way and it will be all right."[59]

Does Anyone Want to Die?
The concern about euthanasia and the use of that term in our common vocabulary lead to a degradation of the elderly and, ultimately, to inferior health care for the elderly—as well as encouraging the thought that those who do not want to "shuffle off" quickly are somehow failing in their contribution to society. Economic considerations then creep in, and old folks are made to feel—in this crazy, schizophrenic society of ours—that they are in some way depriving younger and more deserving people of the medical care that is now being provided them at the same cost. For example, one of the undersecretaries of the Department of Health, Education and Welfare suggested in 1977 that the various states that did not enact living-will legislation be penalized by having withdrawn or curtailed the federal funds that would ordinarily supplement state funds allocated for certain major programs.[60]

Some people not only believe that men and women are only machines, but are acting on the idea that they are only so many digits in one big computer. Feelings that place warmth, love, and compassion—not to mention the beauty and reality of human relationships—above other considerations are often all put aside for the great god of efficiency, especially in the economic realm.

We must be careful not to be misled by the euthanasia forces. They are active as they have never been before. Consider, for example, the following statement under the heading "The Right to Choose Death" by Professor O. Ruth Russell (*The New York Times,* February 14, 1972): "Surely it is time to ask why thousands of dying, incurable and senile persons are being kept alive—sometimes by massive blood transfusions, intravenous feedings, artificial respiration and other heroic measures—who ummistakably want to die." There are thousands of "dying, incurable and senile persons" who are alive—not through any extraordinary means, but just plain "alive." When Dr. Russell says that some "unmistakably want to die," how does she know that if an appreciable number of these people could be helped to live, they would not be exceedingly grateful for all that had been done to keep them alive? Many of us have heard people say, "I want to die"—even those without great pain—and find that only a short time later they think completely differently about living.

There are put forward so many arguments, using such terms as "rights" and "compassion." These terms are borrowed from a more moral and compassionate age, and their use is purely manipulative and deceptive, because the words can cover the most barbarous ideas with a certain emotional respectability. When these ideas gain acceptance, the results are ugly. The original so-called ideal is soon forgotten and traded in for pragmatic, arbitrary, and economic factors. And the situation becomes more and more brutal and careless of life, people, individuality,. and humanness.

Dr. Malcolm Todd, president-elect of the American Medical Association in 1973, argued that physicians should not have to make the decisions on mercy killings by themselves, even if they are merely decisions to refrain from medical intervention. He suggested that the needed determinations be made by boards made up of diverse kinds of people. Do you see what this would bring to the scene? This board would be merely a way of spreading the decision-making responsibility to many so-called experts, who would each decide on the basis of the criteria of his own field.

Such a broad review does not establish a solid base for either objectivity or morality. All you would need is someone convinced that too much money is being spent on elderly people—and what started as a board to decide on extraordinary means could quickly become a death-selection committee, if it lacked objectivity and moral criteria.[61]

When Dr. Philip H. Addison was secretary of the Medical Defense Union in London, the British Medical Association Board of Science and Education told the Third World Congress on Medical Law, meeting in Ghent, Belgium, that dying patients seldom ask for euthanasia. Those knowing that they are dying usually welcome any prolongation of life. The report went on to say that the majority of deaths in the present day can be made peaceful, whatever the nature and character of the preceding illness. It has been said that modern medicine can now overcome pain without shortening life. If this is really so, the case for legalizing euthanasia is considerably weakened.[62]

Thus we find that the pragmatic arguments for euthanasia are often based on a world-view which holds a low opinion of life, rather than being grounded on facts. Even if some token willingness on the part of the prospective euthanasia victim is prescribed as a criterion—in this day of manipulation and the vast potential for the like-minded media to put pressure on people—what real choice will the potential victim have, especially if he or she is ill and in pain?

Another argument for euthanasia is given by Joseph Fletcher, the popularizer of "situational ethics," in his 1973 discussion of death with dignity in the *American Journal of Nursing*:

> It is ridiculous to give ethical approval to the positive ending of sub-human life in utero as we do in therapeutic abortions for reasons of mercy and compassion but refuse to approve of positively ending a sub-human life in extremis. If we are morally obliged to put an end to a pregnancy when an amniocentesis reveals a terribly defective fetus, we are equally obliged to put an end to a patient's hopeless misery when a brain scan reveals that a patient with cancer has advanced brain metastases.[63]

Fletcher declares without discussion that ethical approval has been given to ending the lives of babies out of "compassion." Then he puts that very questionable "ethical approval" in the form of an obligation and says that because we are obliged to do that, we are also morally obliged to put an end to the life of a patient who has cancer with advanced brain metastases. To argue otherwise, he says, is ridiculous.[64]

Thus, once again, the most deplorable sentiments are presented in the guise of some humanitarian gesture. One is reminded of the slaveholders who devoutly espoused the theory that slavery was really for the good of the black man and that in the end he would be thankful for the opportunity to share the white man's culture, even from the distance of the garden shed! The Nazis also argued that their victims were being sacrificed for the high end of the general good of society. We look upon such people as Joseph Fletcher as great meddlers in human lives. They are also meddlers in God's business.

Reports in the Press

With arbitrary abortion already declared legal, the speed with which the other forms of killing are being accepted must take even their advocates by surprise. The medical and scientific professions are not the only culprits. Popular apathy in general and small negatively active groups in particular have contributed much to the demise of the unique worth of humanity. Members of the government as well as the press have also shut their eyes or simply drifted along, having no firm moral base themselves. But the main culprit is the humanistic consensus, which declares man to be a machine and demotes his unique worth in his own eyes.

Let us examine a few of the discussions of euthanasia in the media. The Associated Press reports: DEBATE RAGES IN ENGLAND OVER "DEATH PILL FOR AGED." A British doctor, John Goundry, says that a "death pill" will be available and perhaps obligatory by the end of the century. He says that doctors should be able to give a "demise pill" to old people if they ask for it. He also says, "In the end I can see the state taking over and insisting on euthanasia."[65]

David Hobman, director of Help the Aged in Britain, has said that the suggestion of a death pill seems to him totally inconsistent with the Hippocratic Oath. This oath has already been changed (*see* note 3 for chapter 1), and as there is increasing loss of humanness we can expect to see it changed even more radically.

Swedish public-health physician Ragnar Toss wants to open a suicide clinic for the more than 2,000 Swedes who kill themselves each year—"not to treat them but to help them do it." Dr. Toss, writing in the respected *Swedish Medical Journal* of August 1977, says that this suggestion is related to the choice that women now have about abortions.

So you see, this is not just theory for the future. As people are confronted with the flow of ideas from arbitrary abortion to infanticide to euthanasia, "death by someone's choice" becomes increasingly thinkable. The case of a woman in Great Britain is an illustration of the drift to the thinkableness of abortion/infanticide/euthanasia—all part of the natural trend toward the loss of humanness. Yolande McShane urged her mother in a nursing home to take an overdose of sleeping pills that she had brought her. The mother, showing attitudes rooted in Christianity, resisted: "A dog hasn't got a soul. I'm so afraid of being punished after. It's a mortal sin." The daughter gave the answer which the erosion of the Christian base and the consequent loss of humanness would naturally produce: "People are doing it left, right and center. It's not a sin anymore—it's nothing nowadays."[66]

Of course, if a human being is *not* made in the image of God, why shouldn't the malformed young and the elderly be put out of the way for the good of society—once society and the courts separate life and personhood? "Right" or "wrong" is then only a matter of what the majority thinks at that given moment, or what the courts judge is for the benefit of society at that moment. The next turn of the screw comes quickly, when a noble-sounding phrase like "the good of society" is replaced by cold, hard economics. Yolande McShane's case is apt in this regard. She was in debt and, had her attempt at euthanasia been successful, would have inherited a considerable sum from her mother's will.

According to a news report, the doctor in England who advocated the "death pill"—and said that he could see the state's insisting on euthanasia—also built his argument on economics. "[Dr. John] Goundry said hundreds of British hospitals have been taken over to house the aged sick and that hotels once serving the rich now house the old. The economics are devastating."[67]

If you say that this is just the idea of one man, think again. What is the new element in the United States' debate regarding abortion? It is sheer economics. A *Newsweek* article was titled "Abortion: Who Pays?" This article dealt with a June 20, 1977, Supreme Court ruling on abortion funding. With the Christian consensus on abortion thrown out, the argument slides into the issue of which will cost society more—free abortions or caring for the babies who are born. *Newsweek* reports: "According to HEW estimates, the price of a Medicaid abortion in the first trimester is $150, while the first year cost to taxpayers of each unwanted child is $2,200."[68] This figure, of course, fails to take into consideration the fact that many children who are unwanted in the first months of pregnancy are wanted and loved after they are born, and thus do not become an economic burden on society. Justice Lewis Powell wrote one of the majority opinions on the 1977 Supreme Court ruling that stated that the individual states may not ban abortions, but that they do not necessarily have to pay for them. Powell also added a footnote: "Legitimate demographic concerns . . . could constitute a substantial reason for departure from a position of neutrality between abortion and childbirth." These "legitimate demographic concerns" mean that the government could give free abortions in one place and deny them in another, in order to increase population in the one location, while holding it down in the other.

Or it could mean that the government could give free abortions to one class of people or one race and deny it to another, in order to change the mix of the population. How could anyone read this footnote by a Supreme Court Justice and not be startled and incensed at the doors it opens for government manipulation and for a further thrust of dehumanization? Here again, with morals in law gone, we are left with the harsh and ugly linkage of economics and manipulation.

The Holocaust

Does all this still seem an extreme projection? The fork is three-pronged: first, arbitrary sociological law by the courts and legislators; second, the changed attitude of the medical profession; third, the general apathy and selfishness of the population, which in the name of "rights" grasps at a more and more hedonistic life-style.

Recent history has something to teach us about where we are. We think historians are becoming aware that a great number of the abnormal behavior patterns of man were concentrated in the Nazi experience. Richard L. Rubenstein, in his book *The Cunning of History: Mass Death and the American Future*, speaks of the Holocaust in this way:

> The destruction process required the cooperation of every sector of German society. The bureaucrats drew the definitions and decrees, the churches gave evidence of Aryan descent, the postal authorities carried the messages of definition, expropriation, denaturalization and deportation. A place [of execution was] made available to the Gestapo and the SS by the Wehrmacht. To repeat, the operation required and received the participation of every major social and political and religious institution of the German Reich.[69]

The important thing to remember is that the medical profession took a leading part in the planning of abortion and euthanasia. It seems likely that had it not been for the example and active role played by German physicians in the practice of euthanasia, Hitler's progress in the extermination programs would have been slowed if not stopped. The medical profession went along with Nazism in discouragingly large numbers. More than a few participated in the terror, genocide, extermination programs, and active and barbaric experimentation on the unfortunate minorities in the Nazi grip.[70]

In 1946 and 1947, Leo Alexander, a Boston psychiatrist, was consultant to the Secretary of War and on duty with the office of Chief of Counsel for War Crimes in Nuremberg. In a remarkable paper, "Medical Science Under Dictatorship," he outlined the problem. His concerns were vital when he first wrote about them in this country in 1949; they are of even greater concern to us today. Here are some of the highlights of Dr. Alexander's presentation:

Irrespective of other ideological trappings, the guiding philosophic principle of recent dictatorships, including that of the Nazis, has been Hegelian in that what has been considered "rational utility" and corresponding doctrine and planning has replaced moral, ethical and religious values. . . .

Medical science in Nazi Germany collaborated with this Hegelian trend particularly in the following enterprises: the mass extermination of the chronically sick in the interest of saving "useless" expenses to the community as a whole; the mass extermination of those considered socially disturbing or racially and ideologically unwanted; the individual, inconspicuous extermination of those considered disloyal within the ruling group; and the ruthless use of "human experimental material" for medico-military research. . . .

It started with the acceptance of the attitude basic in the euthanasia movement, that there is such a thing as life not worthy to be lived. . . .

[Before Hitler came to power in 1933] a propaganda barrage was directed against the traditional, compassionate, nineteenth-century attitudes towards the chronically ill, and for the adoption of a utilitarian, Hegelian point of view. Sterilization and euthanasia of persons with chronic mental illnesses was discussed at a meeting of Bavarian psychiatrists in 1931.[71]

Many people, including some in the medical profession, had accepted these principles before Hitler came on the scene.

Alexander says that Hitler exterminated 275,000 people "in these killing centers." Then he adds that those so killed were to be only "the entering wedge for extermination. . . . The methods used and the personnel trained in the killing centers for the chronically sick became the nucleus of much larger centers in the East, where the plan was to kill all Jews and Poles and to cut down the Russian population by 30,000,000." The first to be killed were the aged, the infirm, the senile and mentally retarded, and defective children. Eventually, as World War II approached, the doomed undesirables included epileptics, World War I amputees, children with badly modeled ears, and even bed wetters.

Physicians took part in this planning on matters of life and death to save society's money. Adults were propagandized, one outstanding example being a motion picture called *I Accuse,* which dealt with euthanasia. Commenting on this, Alexander reported:

This film depicts the life history of a woman suffering from multiple sclerosis. In it her husband, a doctor, finally kills her to the accompaniment of soft piano music rendered by a sympathetic colleague in an adjoining room. Acceptance of this ideology was implanted even in the children. A widely-used high school mathematics text, *Mathematics in the Service of Political Education,* Second Edition 1935, Third Edition 1936 . . . includes problems stated in distorted terms of the cost of caring for and rehabilitating the chronically sick and crippled. One of the problems asked, for instance, is how many new housing units could be built and how many marriage-allowance loans could be given to newly-wed couples for the amount of money it cost the state to care for "the crippled and the insane."[72]

The second and most widely used edition of this textbook was issued in 1935, soon after Hitler came to power. Alexander continues:

> The first direct order for euthanasia was issued by Hitler on Sept. 1, 1939. . . . All state institutions were required to report on patients who had been ill for five years or more or who were unable to work, by filling out questionnaires giving name, race, marital status, nationality, next of kin, whether regularly visited and by whom, who bore the financial responsibility and so forth. The decision regarding which patients should be killed was made entirely on the basis of this brief information by expert consultants, most of whom were professors of psychiatry in the key universities. These consultants never saw the patients themselves.[73]

There was an organization specifically for the killing of children, which was known by the euphemistic name of Realm's Committee for Scientific Approach to Severe Illness Due to Heredity and Constitution. Transportation of the patients to killing centers was carried out by The Charitable Transport Company for the Sick. In addition, Alexander notes that The Charitable Foundation for Institutional Care was "in charge of collecting the cost of the killings from the relatives without, however, informing them what the charges were for; in the death certificates the cause of death was falsified."

Alexander, under the heading "The Early Change in Medical Attitudes," gives his warning. *It all started with the acceptance of the attitude that there is such a thing as a life not worthy to be lived.* That is exactly what is being accepted today in the abortion, infanticide, and euthanasia movements.

Continuing his warning, Alexander adds: "But it is important to realize that the infinitely small wedged-in lever from which all this entire trend of mind received its impetus was the attitude towards the nonrehabilitable sick."

This attitude is very much with us today. The "small wedged-in lever" is opening doors to what would have been inconceivable before.[74] Alexander is quite correct in adding: "It is therefore this subtle shift in emphasis of the physicians' attitude that one must thoroughly investigate."

In our present climate, resulting from the humanistic base of society (with its attitude of all things being relative), it is instructive to consider how some of today's university students in the United States regard those days of Nazi rule. Dr. Richard M. Hunt, associate dean of Harvard University's Graduate School of Arts and Science, says:

I have taught courses at Harvard for many years. I used to teach these courses from a straight historical perspective. Recently, I tried a new approach and I call the course, "Moral Dilemma in a Repressive Society: Nazi Germany." Through case studies of issues and personalities I try to present the Nazi phenomenon from the inside, so to speak, from the experience and testimony of those who lived through the period as victims, victimizers, bystanders, true believers, and members of the resistance.

To make a long story short, I was greatly surprised with the reaction of the students. I had asked for personal interpretations of moral relevant dilemmas. In their end-of-term papers, it was not a matter of indifference to Nazi oppressions that I found. Nobody attempted to minimize or explain away Nazi excesses.

Rather what struck me most forcibly were the depressing fatalistic conclusions about major moral dilemmas facing the German people of that particular place and time in history.

Comments like these were frequent. "And with the ever present threat of Gestapo terror, who would dare to speak out and resist? Would you? Would I? Probably not!"

Most disturbing of all to me was the end of the line of such arguments. This point was reached by a few students who seemed somehow to realize the moral peril of such exculpatory judgments. Their way out was to lessen the responsibility of any individual person by dispersing the guilt among all.

Clearly some trends of our times seemed to be running towards a no-fault, that is, a guilt-free society. One might say the virtues of responsible choice, paying the penalty, taking the consequences, all appear at low ebb today.

Next time I teach this course, I hope to stress more strongly my own belief in the contingencies, the open-endedness of history. Somehow, I have got to convey the meaning of moral decisions and their relation to significant outcomes. Most important, I want to point out that single acts of individuals and strong stands of institutions at an early date do make a difference in the long run. I am through with teaching no-fault history.[75]

The attitudes expressed by Dr. Hunt's students become even more alarming when one stops to think that it is difficult to understand what is going on in one's own period of time with the same depth of perception that one has while looking back on history—as these students can do as they study Nazi Germany.

The euthanasia movement—that term is used in the broadest possible sense—is with us today in great strength and with great persuasive power. Many well-meaning people are attracted to what might seem to be the beneficial aspects of some sort of euthanasia program, because they think they can be free of the guilt of responsibility. Yet undoubtedly many have not thought about where this may lead us.

Do not dismiss contemptuously our concern about the wedge principle. When the camel gets his nose in the tent, he *will* soon be in bed with you! Historians and jurists are well aware of what we say. The first step is followed by the second. It is easy to see that if the first step is immoral, whatever follows it must be immoral. But even if the first step is moral, it does not necessarily follow that the second step will also be moral. We have to be consciously aware with each step as to what the next step is *likely* to be.

Semantic legerdemain can prepare us for accepting a horror. When the World Conference on Population Control in 1974 can refer to abortion as "a retrospective method of fertility control," we know that the euphemisms for infanticide and euthanasia can be many indeed![76] In England, some call starving a child with spina bifida (cleft spine) putting it on a "low calorie diet"!

Language itself is a subtle indicator and a powerful tool. Think of the deliberate changes in language that have been used to soften the stark impact of what is actually happening. Abortion is merely the "removal of fetal tissue," or "discontinuing" or "termination" of pregnancy. Childless couples are now "child free," a term that subtly establishes children as an unwanted burden. Language has power. The language we use actually forms the concepts we have and the results these concepts produce. Think of the Nazi use of the name *The Charitable Transport Company for the Sick* for the agency conveying people to the killing centers. But let us not be naive. Exactly the same language power is being used when the unborn baby is called "fetal tissue."[77]

We view what we are experiencing now as a critical situation which can accelerate month by month until the downhill momentum cannot be arrested. Times of monstrous inhumanity do not come about all at once; they are slipped into gradually. Often those who use certain emotional phrases or high-sounding moral tones about "freedom of the individual" and appeal to "rights" do not even know what they are starting. They see only some isolated condition they want to accomplish, but have not considered soberly the overall direction in which things are moving. At some later point they want to go backwards. But then it is too late. Mankind's selfishness and greed can be counted on to widen every breach, exploiting each to the fullest for selfish purposes.

Principal Concerns
Our concerns center around several aspects of this issue. First of all, we must say that we are proponents of the sanctity of human life—*all* human life—born and unborn; old and young; black, white, brown, and yellow. We fear the attitude of the medical profession in sanctioning abortion and in moving inexorably down the road from abortion to infanticide and finally further on to what might be unthinkable today but acceptable in a very few years—such as a widespread euthanasia program.

We are concerned that there is not more protest, outcry, or activism in regard to these issues of life and death. We can even recognize that there are people who are led to starve children to death, because they think they are doing something helpful for society. Lacking an absolute ethical standard, they have only the concept of what they think is beneficial for society to guide them. But we cannot understand why other people, those with a moral base—and we know there are many of them—do not cry out. We are concerned about this because, when the first German aged, infirm, and retarded were killed in gas chambers, there was likewise no perceptible outcry from the medical profession or from an apathetic population. It was not far from there to Auschwitz. Surely those who call themselves Christians, having a moral base, should make these things a principal issue and be willing, even at the risk of personal sacrifice, to strive privately and publicly for the dignity and sanctity of the individual.

Although at the moment the discussion is being conducted chiefly in terms of morals and ethics, another of our concerns is: What is going to happen with the addition of the economic factor?

If you are a social burden *and* an economic burden, no matter how precious life might be to you, there will be little chance of your surviving.

Let it never be said by historians in the latter days of this century that—after the Supreme Court decided on abortion in 1973 and the practice of infanticide began—there was no outcry from the medical profession and no outcry from many outside this profession. Let it never be said that the extermination program for various categories of our citizens could never have come about if the physicians of this country had stood for the moral integrity that recognizes the worth of every human life. And above everything else, let it never be said that there was no outcry from the Christians! All Christians know why people are different and have value as unique individuals—sick or well, young or old. People are unique because they are made in the image of God.

. What *has* happened to the human race? Why are we afraid of being people, of being human? Of enjoying the greatest blessings that life can bring—being alive and being people of love, tenderness, gentleness, care, and concern?

It is vital that we put first *not* economics or efficiency charts and plans, but being *people*—real flesh-and-blood people. We are not to be materialistic robots who think and act like machines and will even kill to maintain their life-styles. This attitude is as stupid as it is wrong. It is stupid because such people have traded in their beautiful humanity for sawdust and ashes—for broken homes, for abortions, for starved children, and for old people locked away and even destroyed. Being a person has infinitely greater rewards for those who will consciously concentrate on being people—warm and loving people—rather than on their personal peace and affluence.

We challenge you to be a person in this impersonal age. Be human in this inhuman age. Put the people in your life first—whether perfect or marred. This is your once-in-a-lifetime chance of being "people with people." Come to your senses. You and those around you *are* people, made in the image of the personal God who created all people in His image.

We have seen how a people's world-view affects how its individuals look at themselves and others. Your basic world-view matters. It will have enormous results. A mild revulsion at people's inhumanity to one another will not change anything. Outward actions against such horrors must begin with the inward action of each individual's evaluating the basis for his standards and then assessing the application of those standards to the world around him.

In Old Testament days, God expressed special abhorrence for the Canaanite practice of infant sacrifice. With heathenism, this was not confined to the Canaanites. For example, the ancient Europeans also offered up their offspring to the gods. These people killed their offspring *in order to purchase from the gods, they hoped, their own personal peace and affluence.*

Today, indiscriminate abortion, infanticide, and euthanasia are also performed *for the personal peace and affluence of individuals.* People who destroy their own children and others', so that they can maintain their life-styles, are also sacrificing to the gods—the gods of a materialistic world-view and practice, and the god of the "self" as the egotistic center and measure of all things.

In Nazi-occupied Holland, the Dutch people often distinguished themselves by the great personal sacrifices they made in defending, hiding, protecting, and *protesting for* their fellow citizens who were Jewish. Given a decree by the Nazis that they were to perform for Hitler as the German medical profession had done, Dutch physicians refused. As a result, the Dutch medical profession has no blot on its record of performance as physician-stewards. What would have happened if the *German* physicians had refused?

A resistance leaflet circulated by the Dutch underground at that time exhorted:

> Protest against the detestable persecution of Jews!!! Organize self-defense in the factories and districts!!! Solidarity with the hard-hit Jewish section of the working people!!!
> Snatch the Jewish children from Nazi violence—take them into your family!!!
> Strike!!! Strike!!! Strike!!!
> Solidarity!!! Courage!!!
> Fight proudly for the liberation of our country!!!

The Dutch resistance movement, armed only with great courage and a few typewriters, stood against the evil of its day. Let those of us who share a high view of people use wisely these days when we have influence and the freedom to strike a great blow for the humanity, dignity, and sanctity of individuals.

Alternatives

Christians and others who wish to see an end to inhumanities, in compassion and love must offer alternative solutions to the problems. What we are about to suggest does not by any means exhaust the inventory of practical proposals we must put forward—and for which we must sacrifice our own personal peace and affluence. Such a list would be impossible to complete, so we will just give examples.

Churches and other groups opposed to abortion must be prepared to extend practical help to both the unmarried woman who is pregnant and the married woman who may be faced with the question of abortion. Merely to say to either one, "You must not have an abortion"—without being ready to involve ourselves in the problem—is another way of being inhuman.

The unmarried woman may need a place to stay. Time should be taken to tell her about the many couples who cannot have babies and who long to have a child to adopt. She will certainly need counsel about how to care for her child if she decides to keep the baby. Pleasant institutions should be available for unmarried women awaiting the birth of a baby, but each person who does not believe that abortion is right should personally be prepared to offer hospitality, financial aid, or other assistance.

Have you ever welcomed an unwed mother in your home for the months before her baby was born? Are there babies now growing happily in homes that adopted them, or living with their mothers who have a changed outlook on life and death because of the months spent in your home? Hospitality, for a great number of us, should include some period of time in our lives when we care for a pregnant woman in her waiting months.

L'Abri has become known as an example of Christians practicing community over a wide spectrum of life—intellectually and practically. In its twenty-seven-year history, there has been a succession of unwed mothers cared for, encouraged, and helped in a variety of ways. Because it has been a part of L'Abri life to make people in need a part of the family, there has been participation in some eager moments at the hospital, when a new baby is welcomed into the world as a wanted human being. L'Abri is not a "work for unwed mothers," but in all its branches a community of open homes—limited, of course, in space and in the possibility of giving personal attention. Yet L'Abri workers have been able to help a number of women who have chosen not to abort their babies.

For married women facing the problems that prompt them to consider abortion, support from a church can be a critical factor. If a mother must work, why shouldn't the church provide for her child's care? Surely such an arrangement could be worked out as an expression of the community which the church is supposed to be. The church might provide a child-care center on its own premises (too many of our churches are only one-purpose buildings) or church members might take a child into their own families for a certain number of hours each week.

We are not trying to propose a universal formula, but to emphasize that saying that abortion is wrong immediately confronts us with a challenge to be willing to share in the consequences which our advice brings. For Christians who adhere to the truth of the Bible, the importance of doing what it teaches is imperative. We are to be compassionate about people's physical needs.

The same principle can be applied to infanticide. If a family resists letting a handicapped child die after birth, the church cannot just walk away from the family or the child. From the earliest days of the church, a part of its life and testimony has always been that its members care for one another in material ways as well as otherwise. Many of the best "homes for the handicapped" had Christian beginnings. But we should also consider the practical possibility of our church's setting up a plan (to be overseen by some loving person) which schedules different church members to help in the home of a handicapped person for definite periods during the week, sharing in the hard work of this type of care.

In one of the churches Francis Schaeffer pastored in the United States, there were a mongoloid child and a mentally retarded youngster. The parents, far from wealthy, had no hope of providing special education for their children. Public services were poor. He began to spend a certain number of hours each week with the two children together. The leap forward in their achievements was a thing of joy for the whole congregation. In all his Christian work, Francis Schaeffer has never had a more satisfying ministry. Similarly, C. Everett Koop has placed many pregnant girls with Christian families in Pennsylvania. During this sheltering, ruptured father-daughter relationships have been healed, girls have become Christians, and unwanted babies have eventually brought joy to childless couples.

Again, we are offering no universal formula. The concept of being involved in hard situations and the practical outworking of that concept are the important things. It takes effort, concern, work, and often money. Christian love and humanness mean not only saying, "Infanticide is wrong." They also mean giving part of our own personal peace and affluence to share in the results that morally correct decisions produce. That means not allowing the state to take all the responsibility. As Christians, we cannot slough off the whole burden on the state. In many cases, this means finding ourselves caring for handicapped people within the totality of the Christian community. Those in groups which are not Christian must likewise find ways of being human in the years following the birth of a handicapped child.

It is worth digressing here to insist that the positive aspects of the women's rights movement can be achieved without including abortion on the agenda. The linking of the women's movement with abortion is a deliberate strategem used by some to make this practice acceptable. This uses the women's rights movement as a vehicle to which abortion has no intrinsic relationship. Unhappily, at times the leadership of this movement has built an antihuman stance into its platform in regard to abortion-on-demand. This is hardly liberation, since—carried to its logical extreme—this arbitrary and inhuman stance can only lead to a further enslavement of women and of everyone else as well. Women cannot "liberate" themselves by aborting their babies or killing their infants. The rights of women are fundamentally rooted in the biblical view of the value of each individual human being and the sacredness of human life.

Moral obligations fall to those who stand by the principle that there is no such thing as a life not worthy to be lived. We also have a responsibility toward people with terminal illnesses and toward the dying aged. Saint Joseph's Hospice in London and The Hospice Home Care Team of New Haven, Connecticut (both institutions that had Christian beginnings) can show us some ways of dying that can affirm and enhance life. We do not know the New Haven work personally, but are familiar with a representative hospice through a friend who spent a certain number of hours there each week—reading, talking, speaking of Christian beliefs, and just *being* with the dying patients. At most such hospices, three things are done. First, all possible medical knowledge is employed to keep pain under control. Second, patients are visited, read to, and kept in almost constant contact with a loving human being, so that they are not alone and deserted in that time when, of all times, being human means not being deserted. Third, families are treated as units; the family and its needs and the individual in his need are kept together as a human unit. These hospices are not in the business of dying, but of *living* right up to the end. Is this not the natural and rightful outflow of what we Christians believe about the abnormality of death and about the future resurrection victory we will experience through Christ?

If we oppose euthanasia, we must also share the weight of caring for lonely or incapacitated older people who are not terminally ill. One of us has personal knowledge about sharing such a burden. Francis Schaeffer's mother lived in his home in Switzerland for the last seven years of her life. At first she could come down to meals, go out for rides in the mountains, attend church, and so on. Gradually this changed, and she needed constant care, especially after breaking her hip. All this was taking place in the midst of the pressures at L'Abri. Students and others took turns playing checkers with her, reading to her, talking with her, and just being with her. The family could not have done this alone—it would have been a crushing strain upon them as well as upon the work. But in the united community, not only was she well cared for, but the caring was a thing of beauty. We are sure that some of those who gave of themselves in this way are still seeing their lives enhanced by this experience, as they are scattered over the face of the earth.

Our concern is more than *not killing* the elderly and the ill. *It is giving them real life.* Of course, there must be some facilities that care for the terminally ill. In fact, Christians and others should see to it that places like St. Joseph's become models for many more such hospices. But, as long as possible and in spite of smaller apartments and the antifamily influences of our age, the old, infirm, and dying should be given the chance to be really alive in the midst of the whole spectrum of life. This includes being in relationship with the family and sharing in a Christian community. Christian doctors and others of the medical profession who stand for human life can make a special contribution in this whole area, but it is not their responsibility alone (and certainly not the responsibility of the state alone). It becomes *our* responsibility when we quite properly say, "Euthanasia is wrong."

We must be realistic. The alternatives we have discussed will demand a high price. They will cost each of us some of our personal peace and affluence. But we must do them—first of all, because they are right. This is taught in the whole of the Bible and especially in the teachings of Christ. And, second, it will be a sharing of the burdens of life, and one day it will be *our* turn to be helped—and we will be glad when we are.

The question is not the worth of the imperfect infant, the retarded child, the defective adult, and the aging individual with physical and mental signs of the aging process. The question is this: Are we worthy enough to extend ourselves to meet their needs?

If we in the second half of the twentieth century wish to be remembered well, we need to do something to stop all the evils we have been speaking about. If we sit back and do nothing, our mere passivity and apathy will lead to actively evil results by removing resistance to those who *are* active and nonapathetic. That so many are doing so little should encourage more than a mild commitment to some vague idea of doing the "right" thing, as opposed to the "wrong" thing. As people, we are only as good as our deep inner principles; we are only as good as our world-view.

In the chapters that follow, we will examine what to us is the ultimate basis for life, ethics, and an active moral stand against evil. We will look at biblical Christianity and the Bible itself. For, without a firm set of principles, without a firm world-view, there cannot and will not be any firm and continued resistance to evil—or even any cohesive unity to our own lives and private moral decisions.

CHAPTER FOUR

The Basis for Human Dignity

So far in this book we have been considering an evil as great as any practiced in human history. Our society has put to death its own offspring, millions upon millions of them. Our society has justified taking their lives, even claiming it a virtue to do so. It has been said this is a new step in our progress toward a liberated humanity.

Such a situation has not come out of a vacuum. Each of us has an overall way of looking at the world, which influences what we do day by day. This is what we call a "world-view." And all of us have a world-view, whether we realize it or not. We act in accordance with our world-view, and our world-view rests on what to us is the ultimate truth.

Materialistic Humanism: The World-View of Our Era
What has produced the inhumanity we have been considering in the previous chapters is that society in the West has adopted a world-view which says that all reality is made up only of matter. This view is sometimes referred to as philosophic materialism, because it holds that only *matter* exists; sometimes it is called naturalism, because it says that no supernatural exists. Humanism

which begins from man alone and makes man the measure of all things usually is materialistic in its philosophy. Whatever the label, this is the underlying world-view of our society today. In this view the universe did not get here because it was created by a "supernatural" God. Rather, the universe has existed forever in some form, and its present form just happened as a result of chance events way back in time.

Society in the West has largely rested on the base that God exists and that the Bible is true. In all sorts of ways this view affected the society. The materialistic or naturalistic or humanistic world-view almost always takes a superior attitude toward Christianity. Those who hold such a view have argued that Christianity is unscientific, that it cannot be proved, that it belongs simply to the realm of "faith." Christianity, they say, rests only on faith, while humanism rests on facts.

Professor Edmund R. Leach of Cambridge University expressed this view clearly:

> Our idea of God is a product of history. What I now believe about the supernatural is derived from what I was taught by my parents, and what they taught me was derived from what they were taught, and so on. But such beliefs are justified by faith alone, never by reason, and the true believer is expected to go on reaffirming his faith in the same verbal formula even if the passage of history and the growth of scientific knowledge should have turned the words into plain nonsense.[78]

So some humanists act as if they have a great advantage over Christians. They act as if the advance of science and technology and a better understanding of history (through such concepts as the evolutionary theory) have all made the idea of God and Creation quite ridiculous.

This superior attitude, however, is strange because one of the most striking developments in the last half-century is the growth of a profound pessimism among both well-educated and less-educated people. The thinkers in our society have been admitting for a long time that they have no final answers at all.

Take Woody Allen, for example. Most people know him as a comedian, but he has thought through where mankind stands after the "religious answers" have been abandoned. In an article in *Esquire* (May 1977), he says that man is left with:

> . . . alienation, loneliness [and] emptiness verging on madness. . . .
> The fundamental thing behind *all* motivation and *all* activity is the

constant struggle against annihilation and against death. It's absolutely stupefying in its terror, and it renders anyone's accomplishments meaningless. As Camus wrote, it's not only that *he* (the individual) dies, or that *man* (as a whole) dies, but that you struggle to do a work of art that will last and then you realize that *the universe itself* is not going to exist after a period of time. Until those issues are resolved within each person—religiously or psychologically or existentially— the social and political issues will never be resolved, except in a slap-dash way.

Allen sums up his view in his film *Annie Hall* with these words: "Life is divided into the horrible and the miserable."

Many would like to dismiss this sort of statement as coming from one who is merely a pessimist by temperament, one who sees life without the benefit of a sense of humor. Woody Allen does not allow us that luxury. He speaks as a human being who has simply looked life in the face and has the courage to say what he sees. If there is no personal God, nothing beyond what our eyes can see and our hands can touch, then Woody Allen is right: life is both meaningless and terrifying. As the famous artist Paul Gauguin wrote on his last painting shortly before he tried to commit suicide: "Whence come we? What are we? Whither do we go?" The answers are *nowhere, nothing,* and *nowhere.* The humanist H. J. Blackham has expressed this with a dramatic illustration:

> On humanist assumptions, life leads to nothing, and every pretense that it does not is a deceit. If there is a bridge over a gorge which spans only half the distance and ends in mid-air, and if the bridge is crowded with human beings pressing on, one after the other they fall into the abyss. The bridge leads nowhere, and those who are pressing forward to cross it are going nowhere. . . . It does not matter where they think they are going, what preparations for the journey they may have made, how much they may be enjoying it all. The objection merely points out objectively that such a situation is a model of futility.[79]

One does not have to be highly educated to understand this. It follows directly from the starting point of the humanists' position, namely, that everything is just matter. That is, that which has existed forever and ever is only some form of matter or energy, and everything in our world now is this and only this in a more or less complex form. Thus, Jacob Bronowski says in *The Identity of Man* (1965): "Man is a part of nature, in the same sense that a stone is, or a cactus, or a camel." In this view, men and women are by chance more complex, but not unique.

Within this world-view there is no room for believing that a human being has any final distinct value above that of an animal or of nonliving matter. People are merely a different arrangement of molecules. There are two points, therefore, that need to be made about the humanist world-view. First, the superior attitude toward Christianity—as if Christianity had all the problems and humanism had all the answers—is quite unjustified. The humanists of the Enlightenment two centuries ago *thought* they were going to find all the answers, but as time has passed, this optimistic hope has been proven wrong. It is their own descendants, those who share their materialistic world-view, who have been saying louder and louder as the years have passed, "There are no final answers."

Second, this humanist world-view has also brought us to the present devaluation of human life—not technology and not overcrowding, although these have played a part. And this same world-view has given us no limits to prevent us from sliding into an even worse devaluation of human life in the future.

So it is naive and irresponsible to imagine that this world-view will *reverse* the direction in the future. A well-meaning commitment to "do what is right" will not be sufficient. Without a firm set of principles that flows out of a world-view that gives an adequate reason for a unique value to all human life, there cannot be and will not be any substantial resistance to the present evil brought on by the low view of human life we have been considering in previous chapters. It was the materialistic world-view that brought in the inhumanity; it must be a different world-view that drives it out.

An emotional uneasiness about abortion, infanticide, euthanasia, and the abuse of genetic knowledge is not enough. To stand against the present devaluation of human life, a significant percentage of people within our society must adopt and live by a world-view which not only hopes or intends to give a basis for human dignity but which really does. The radical movements of the sixties were right to hope for a better world; they were right to protest against the shallowness and falseness of our plastic society. But their radicalness lasted only during the life span of the adolescence of their members. Although these movements claimed to be radical, they lacked a sufficient root. Their world-view was incapable of giving life to the aspirations of its adherents. Why? Because it, too—like the society they were condemning—had no sufficient base. So protests are not enough. Having the right ideals is not enough. Even those with a very short memory, those who can look back only to the sixties, can see that there must be more than that. A truly radical alternative has to be found.

But where? And how?

The Search for an Adequate World-View: A Question of Method
Before we consider various possibilities, we must settle the question of method. What is it we are expecting our "answer" to answer?

There are a number of things we could consider, but at this point we want to concentrate on just two. The first is what we will call "the universe and its form," and the second is "the mannishness of man." The first draws attention to the fact that the universe around us is like an amazing jigsaw puzzle. We see many details, and we want to know how they fit together. That is what science is all about. Scientists look at the details and try to find out how they all cohere. So the first question that has to be answered is: how did the universe get this way? How did it get this *form*, this pattern, this jigsawlike quality it now has?

Second, "the mannishness of man" draws attention to the fact that human beings are different from all other things in the world. Think, for example, of creativity. People in all cultures of all ages have created many kinds of things, from "High Art" to flower arrangements, from silver ornaments to high-technology supersonic aircraft. This is in contrast to the animals about us. People also fear death, and they have the aspiration to truly choose. Incidentally, even those who in their writings say we only *think* we choose quickly fall into words and phrases that only make sense if they are wrong and we do truly choose. Human beings are also unique in that they verbalize. That is, people put concrete and abstract concepts into words which communicate these concepts to other people. People also have an inner life of the mind; they remember the past and make projections into the future. One could name other factors, but these are enough to differentiate people from the other things in the world.

What world-view adequately explains the remarkable phenomenon of the distinctiveness of human beings? There is one world-view which can explain the existence of the universe, its form, and the uniqueness of people—the world-view given to us in the Bible. There is a remarkable parallel between the way scientists go about checking to see if what they think about reality does in fact correspond to it and the way the biblical world-view can be checked to see if it is true.

Many people, however, react strongly against this sort of claim. They see the problem—Where has everything come from and why is it the way it is?—but they do not want to consider a solution which involves God. God, they say, belongs to "religion," and religious answers, they say, do not deal with facts. Only science deals with facts. Thus, they say, Christian answers are not real answers; they are "faith answers."

This is a strange reaction, because modern people pride themselves on being open to new ideas, on being willing to consider opinions which contradict what has been believed for a long time. They think this is what "being scientific" necessitates. Suddenly, however, when one crosses into the area of the "big" and most basic questions (like those we are considering now) with an answer involving God, the shutters are pulled down, the open mind closes and a very different attitude, a dogmatic *rationalism,* takes over.[80]

This is curious—first, because few seem to notice that the humanist explanation of the big and most basic questions is just as much a "faith answer" as any could be. With the humanist worldview everything begins with only matter; whatever has developed has developed only within matter, a reordering of matter by chance.

Even though materialistic scientists have no scientific understanding of *why* things exist, nor any certain scientific understanding of *how* life began, and even though this world-view leaves them with vast problems—the problems Woody Allen has described of "alienation, loneliness [and] emptiness verging on madness"—many modern people still reject at once any solution which uses the word *God,* in favor of the materialistic humanist "answer" which answers nothing. This is simply prejudice at work.

We need to understand, however, that this prejudice is both recent and arbitrary. Professor Ernest Becker, who taught at the University of California at Berkeley and San Francisco State College, said that for the last half-million years people have always believed in two worlds—one that was visible and one that was invisible. The visible world was where they lived their everyday lives; the invisible world was more powerful, for the meaning and existence of the visible world was dependent on it. Suddenly in the last century and a half, as the ideas of the Enlightenment have spread to the whole of Western culture, we have been told quite arbitrarily that there *is* no invisible world. This has become dogma for many secular people today.

Christians try to answer prejudices like these by pointing out that the biblical system does not have to be accepted blindly, any more than the scientific hypotheses have to be accepted blindly. What a scientist does is to examine certain phenomena in the world. He then casts about for an explanation that will make sense of these phenomena. That is the hypothesis. But the hypothesis has to be checked. So a careful checking operation is set up, designed to see if there is, in fact, a correspondence between what has been observed and what has been hypothesized. If it does correspond, a scientist accepts the explanation as correct; if it does not, he rejects it as false and looks for an alternative explanation. Depending on how substantially the statement has been "verified," it becomes accepted as a "law" within science, such as the law of gravity or the second law of thermodynamics.

What we should notice is the method. It is rather like trying to find the right key to fit a particular lock. We try the first key and then the next and the next until finally, if we are fortunate, one of them fits. The same principle applies, so Christians maintain, when we consider the big questions. Here are the phenomena. What key unlocks their meaning? What explanation is correct?

We may consider the materialistic humanist alternative, the Eastern religious alternative, and so on. But each of these leaves at least a part of these most basic questions unanswered. So we turn to examine the Christian alternative.

Obviously, Christians do not look on the Bible as simply an alternative. As Christians we consider it to be objectively true, because we have found that it does give the answers both in knowledge and in life. For the purposes of discussion, however, we invite non-Christians to consider it as *an* alternative—not to be accepted blindly, but for good and sufficient reasons.

But note this—the physical scientist does something very easy, compared to those who tackle the really important and central questions for mankind. He examines a tiny portion of the real world—a leaf, a cell, an atom, a particle—and, because these things are not personal and obey very precise laws, he is able to arrive at explanations with relative ease. C. F. A. Pantin, who was professor of zoology at Cambridge University, once said: "Very clever men are answering the relatively easy questions of the natural examination paper." This is not to disparage physical science. It works consistently with its own principles of investigation, looking further and further into the material of the world around us. But it only looks at part of the world. As Professor W. H. Thorpe of Cambridge University says, it is "a deliberate restriction to certain areas of our total experience—a technique for understanding certain parts of that experience and achieving mastery over nature."

We are not then moving from definite things to indefinite things, when we look at those aspects of our experience which are more central than the study of an individual physical thing such as a leaf, a cell, an atom, or a particle. Rather, we are turning from a small part of reality to a larger part of reality. Picture a scientist for a moment: he is looking at a particular detail and carrying out his scientific investigation according to the recognized procedures. We have already discussed the method he uses to find the answers. Now we need to draw back and consider the whole phenomenon we are looking at, that is, the scientist carrying out his experiment. When the scientist is seated at his desk, he is able to find answers to his questions only *because* he has made two colossal assumptions about his situation, in fact about the entire world. He is assuming first of all that the things he is looking at do fit together somehow, even if some areas—such as particle physics—cannot at this time be fitted into a simple explanation. If the scientist did not assume that the things he is studying somehow fit together, he would not be trying to find an answer. Second, he is assuming that he as a person is able to find answers.

In other words, the *big* questions constitute the very framework within which the scientist is operating. To quote Thorpe again, "I recently heard one of the most distinguished theoretical scientists state that his own scientific drive was based on two fundamental attitudes: a conviction of his own responsibility and an awe at the beauty and harmony of nature." So we have to resist any suggestion that to be involved in answering the big questions is somehow to be getting further and further away from "the real world."

The opposite is the case. It is as we come to these big questions that we approach the real world that every one of us is living in twenty-four hours a day—the world of real persons who can think and so work out problems such as how to get to the other side of town, persons who can love, persons who can make moral decisions. These are, in other words, the phenomena which cry out for an adequate explanation. These are the things we know best about ourselves and the world around us. What world-view can encompass them?

C. S. Lewis pointed out that there are only two alternatives to the Christian answer—the humanist philosophy of the West and the pantheist philosophy of the East. We would agree. We agree, too, with his observation that Eastern philosophy is an "opposite" answer to the Christian system, but we shall look at that later. For the present our attention is directed toward the materialistic world-view of the West.

From time to time we read in the press or hear on the radio that an oil tanker has run aground on rocks and that the crude oil is being driven by the wind and currents onto an otherwise beautiful coast. We can picture the problem of humanism in that way. There is a rock on which all humanist philosophy must run aground. It is the problem of relative knowledge and relative morality or, to put it another way, the problem of finiteness or limitation. Even if mankind now had perfect moral integrity regarding the world, people would still be finite. People are limited. This fact, coupled with the rejection of the possibility of having answers from God, leads humanists into the problem of relative knowledge. There *has* been no alternative to this relativity for the past 200 years, and there can be no alternative within the humanist world-view. That is what we want to show now.

How Do We Know We Know?

During the early stages of modern philosophy (as distinguished from medieval philosophy)—that is, around the seventeenth century in Europe—the question that was troubling philosophers was this: *how do we know that we know?*

The early modern scientists had made advances in the physical sciences by rejecting previous human authority. For example, they rejected much of what had been inherited from the science of the Middle Ages. At that time, investigation had been governed and restrained by the concepts of Aristotle. In the field of astronomy, this had meant that the Ptolemaic system held sway. Suddenly, observations were made which cast doubt on that entire system of understanding the heavenly bodies. The result was, of course, the Copernican revolution: the discovery that the sun does not move around the earth but, rather, the earth around the sun. Thus, a general attitude was developed toward the ideas which had prevailed till then. The scientists said, "We must not accept the ideas passed down to us or derived from various previous authorities. We must start from scratch and simply observe the world and see how it works. Otherwise, we may be hampered from seeing what is there."

The early modern scientists did not, however, reject the knowledge that God gave in the Bible as they rejected previous human authority and opinion. For example, in *Novum Organum* (1620) Francis Bacon wrote: "To conclude, therefore, let no man out of weak conceit of sobriety, or an ill applied moderation, think or maintain that a man can search too far or be too well studied in the book of God's word, or in the book of God's works."[81] "The book of God's word" is the Bible. "The book of God's works" is the world which God has made.

Modern scientists in general lived, thought, and worked in the framework of rejecting human authority, while respecting what was taught in the Bible in regard to the cosmos—right up to the time of Michael Faraday and James Clerk Maxwell in the second half of the nineteenth century.

The *philosophers* (and later the materialistic scientists) went further. Their error was to confuse the escape from past human authority (which was indeed confining) with putting man at the center and rejecting God's authority as well. They wanted to reject all outside authority. They wanted to establish everything only on human observation. That was how the question of epistemology (how we know we know) became so important in modern philosophy. It has remained so right up to our own day.

The philosopher who first raised these questions was René Descartes (1596-1650). Descartes wrote in *Meditations on First Philosophy:*

> How often it happened to me that in the night I dreamt that I found myself on this particular place . . . whilst in reality I was lying on my bed! At this moment it does seem that it is with eyes awake that I am looking at this paper. . . . But in thinking over this I remind myself that on many occasions I have in sleep been deceived by similar illusions, and in dwelling carefully on this reflection I see so manifestly that there are no certain indications by which we may clearly distinguish wakefulness from sleep that I am lost in astonishment. And my astonishment is such that it is almost capable of persuading me that I now dream.[82]

Here is the modern epistemological problem expressed three centuries ago! All knowledge comes through the senses, but how can we rely on our own senses? Sometimes, as in dreaming, we seem to be experiencing things very really, yet the reality is only in our heads.

We are reminded of the 1966 film by Michelangelo Antonioni called *Blow-Up,* in which one of the central issues was this same question. A photographer had taken a picture of a murdered man in a park in London and then became uncertain whether this was, in fact, part of reality or an experience of fantasy similar to a drug trip. Within the humanist world-view there is no final way of telling. And Antonioni ends his film by making the point graphically. Tennis players play the game without a ball. The invisible "ball" goes back and forth and the spectators watch its "path" from side to side until finally the "ball" (which does not exist) goes out over the surrounding wire and "falls" at the photographer's feet. He pauses for a moment, uncertain about what he should do. (Is observation simply a matter of the majority? Does the reality of things come from the general agreement in society and nothing more?) Then the photographer stoops down, picks up the "ball," and throws it back onto the court. Here, depicted brilliantly, is the problem of any system which builds its epistemology on man alone. This film was a philosophic statement of the period in which we are living.

Take another example out of the history of this new approach in philosophy, that of David Hume (1711-1776). In 1732 he shocked the world with *A Treatise of Human Nature.* John Locke (1632-1704) had already denied the concept of "innate ideas" of right and wrong; that is, Locke denied that these ideas are inherent in the mind from birth. This had troubled many. Then Hume burst on the scene with a challenge which went further.

What was most startling was his progression beyond skepticism concerning God and other things of the "invisible world" to a skepticism about the visible world as well. Among other things, he questioned the concept of causality. That is, Hume challenged the notion that there is a reality in the external world which leads us to speak about one thing as being the cause of another. When we see a tree bending and swaying and its leaves falling to the ground and racing off across the field, we naturally speak of the wind as *causing* this phenomenon. Hume challenged this.

Following on from Locke, who said that all knowledge comes only from the senses, Hume argued that causality is *not* perceived by the senses. What we *perceive* are two events following closely upon each other. It was custom, he argued, which led us to speak in terms of causality, not any objective "force" working in the things themselves. Anyone can see where this thinking leads, and it was so understood at the time. If causality is not real, science becomes impossible—for what scientists are doing is tracing the path of cause and effect from one event to the next.

A modern British humanist, Kathleen Nott, has written perceptively about Hume in *Objections to Humanism* (1967): "Among great philosophers, Hume . . . hung his nose as far as any over the nihilistic abyss."[83] This is right. Hume was questioning the most basic elements of our experience. Yet he was trying to be consistent to his presuppositions (that is, his starting point). Where did this lead him? To a skepticism about knowledge itself. Hume wrote designedly against the Christian world-view which prevailed in England at the time. He wanted to dismantle the system of ideas which came out of the Bible, of a God before whom man was responsible, of people being more than matter, of a life after death which seemed to defy all natural law. Where he ended, though, was with uncertainty even about the ordinary things of life. As Kathleen Nott continues: "Hume's philosophizing was indeed a radical skepticism, which left no convincing logical grounds for believing that anything natural, let alone supernatural, was there at all."[84]

But there is something even more striking about Hume. Skepticism was the direction in which his philosophy led him; yet he was not able to live with it himself. He "hung his nose over the nihilistic abyss"—and we can picture him standing on the edge and peering over—but what then? Nott says he "withdrew it sharply when he saw the psychological risks involved." Hume himself said in *A Treatise of Human Nature* (Volume I):

> Should it be asked me whether I sincerely assent to this argument which I have been to such pains to inculcate, and whether I be really one of those skeptics who hold that all is uncertain . . . I . . . should reply . . . that neither I nor any other person was ever sincerely and constantly of that opinion. . . . I dine, I play backgammon, I converse and am merry with my friends; and when, after 3 or 4 hours amusement, I would return to these speculations, they appear so cold and strained and ridiculous that I cannot find in my heart to enter into them any further. Thus the skeptic still continues to reason and believe, though he asserts that he cannot defend his reason by reason;

and by the same rule, he must assent to the principle concerning the existence of body, though he cannot pretend, by any argument of philosophy, to maintain its veracity.[85]

We believe there are only two basic alternatives in the search for the source of knowledge. One is that a person attempts to find the answers to all his questions alone. The other is that he seeks revealed truths from God. We shall come to the second later. Now we are looking at the former, and we are suggesting that this is the basic problem with which all humanistic systems must wrestle: the problem of knowledge.

We could go into many other details concerning the subsequent history of the ideas we have dealt with, including in particular Immanuel Kant (1724-1804) and his own "Copernician revolution" in philosophy and also the developments surrounding Ludwig Wittgenstein (1889-1951) and linguistic philosophy in the twentieth century. We shall stop here, partly to keep the discussion of modern philosophy from becoming too technical, but mainly because the basic difficulties had already been expressed within a century of the birth of modern philosophy.

Starting with himself, a person cannot establish an adequate explanation for the amazing possibility that he can observe the world around him and be assured that his observations have a correspondence with reality. The problem is not just that a person cannot know everything. The need is not for exhaustive knowledge; the need is for a base for any knowledge at all. That is, even though we know we cannot exhaustively perceive even the smallest things in our experience, we want assurance that we have really perceived something—that is "perception" is not simply an "image" in our brain, a model or symbol of reality which we have projected out from ourselves. We want to know that we have had a *real* contact with reality. Even Hume had to admit that his philosophizing did not make sense, that it did not fit into his own experience of the world. On the humanist side this is the great tension—to have no reason for reason and yet at the same time to have to live continuously on the reality of reason.

At this point, someone is bound to ask, "But why is it necessary to have an 'adequate explanation' for knowledge?" Agreeing that Descartes, Hume, and others could find no theoretical base which tied in with their experience, isn't it sufficient to just *reason*? Probably many of you have been wanting to ask this, as you have followed along. It is a good question, for the bulk of the world never bothers about the issues which Locke, Hume, and others like them raised. Most people simply live, going about their daily lives, never troubling themselves about reality and fantasy, the subject and the object, and so on. And we are not suggesting that their experience *in itself* is invalid, as if to imply that they are not perceiving and knowing the universe around them. They are. What we *are* saying is that—whether they know it or not—their experience is possible only because they are living in the universe the Bible describes, that is, in a universe which was created by God. Their internal faculty of knowing was made by God to correspond to the world and its form which He made and which surrounds them.

If, however, we attempt to bypass the question, "Why is it possible for man to have knowledge in this way?" we must then remember the other two great problems of any system which starts only from man. Recall the illustration of the oil tanker and the rock. The rock is the problem of knowledge which we have been considering. That is the central problem. But there are two forms of pollution which flow from the broken ship of knowledge: first, the meaninglessness of all things and, second, the relativity of morals.

The Meaninglessness of All Things
An overwhelming number of modern thinkers agree that seeing the universe and man from a humanist base leads to meaninglessness, both for the universe and for man—not just mankind in general but for each of us as individuals. Professor Steven Weinberg of Harvard University and the Smithsonian Astrophysical Observatory has written a book entitled *The First Three Minutes: A Modern View of the Origin of the Universe* (1976). Here he explains, as clearly as probably anyone has ever done, the modern materialistic view of the universe and its origin.

But when his explanation is finished and he is looking down at the earth from an airplane, as Weinberg writes, "It is very hard to realize that this all is just a tiny part of an overwhelmingly hostile universe . . . [which] has evolved from an unspeakably unfamiliar early condition, and faces a future extinction of endless cold or intolerable heat. The more the universe seems comprehensible, the more it also seems pointless."[86]

When Weinberg says that the universe seems more "comprehensible," he is, of course, referring to our greater understanding of the physical universe through the advance of science. But it is an understanding, notice, within a materialistic framework, which considers the universe solely in terms of physics and chemistry—simply machinery. Here lies the irony. It is comprehension of a sort, but it is like giving a blind person sight, only to remove anything seeable. As we heard Woody Allen saying earlier, such a view of reality is "absolutely stupefying in its terror, and it renders anyone's accomplishments meaningless."

So, to the person who wants to be left alone without explanations for the big questions, we must say very gently, "Look at what you are left alone with." This is not merely rhetoric. As the decades of this century have slipped by, more and more have said the same thing as Steven Weinberg and Woody Allen. It has become an obvious thing to say. The tremendous optimism of the nineteenth century, which stemmed from the Enlightenment of the eighteenth century, has gradually ebbed away.

If everything "faces a future extinction of endless cold or intolerable heat," all things are meaningless. This is the first problem, the first form of pollution. The second is just as bad.

The Relativity of Morals

The material universe in itself gives no basis for values. Those who begin with the material universe can *describe* but they can never *define*. They can speak only in the indicative, never in the imperative. They can describe, for example, what physical strength involves and how it works physiologically, but from the material universe alone they cannot derive any idea as to how strength *ought* and *ought not* to be used. The most they can do is argue that certain moral systems have been worked out through the passage of time on the basis of "social contact." This is what we call the 51 percent view of morality—the majority has thought such and such is a good way to operate and so it becomes "morality." What confusion! What disaster! With this view any action can be justified, and our own very recent history has given us appalling examples.

Aldous Huxley said it all clearly in the thirties in his brilliant little novel *Brave New World*. In it he pictures a society which has reversed the morality of the present, especially in the area of sexual relationships. Faithfulness within a unique love relationship becomes "evil"; promiscuity becomes "good."[87]

Here then is the humanist dilemma. They have to generate the answers to the big questions, but out of their own limited experience they can know *nothing* with certainty. If we were to add up the thinking of *all* of mankind, we would still have only limited knowledge. *Truth* with a capital *T*—explanations which would be true for all time and all people—would be impossible.

What is left, therefore, is "relative" truth, and with relative truth, relative morality. Given time, even the "certainties" of our ethical systems can be undone—the bills of rights, the charters of freedom, the principles of justice, everything. Aleksandr Solzhenitsyn understands this not only as a theoretical problem of a humanistic philosophy. He has suffered under its implications. He writes:

> Communism has never concealed the fact that it rejects all absolute concepts of morality. It scoffs at good and evil as indisputable categories. Communism considers morality to be relative. Depending upon circumstances, any act, including the killing of thousands, could be good or bad. It all depends upon class ideology, defined by a handful of people. . . . It is considered awkward to use seriously such words as good and evil. But if we are to be deprived of these concepts, what will be left? We will decline to the status of animals.

We in the West must understand that it is not only Iron Curtain countries who operate on the basis of relative morality. Now the West does, too. The materialist world-view has dominated the thinking of the West just as much. Therefore we can expect to see the same inhumanity here, just as Solzhenitsyn has warned. We must not sit back and think, *It could never happen here.* Worse still, we must not be confused into thinking the issue is principally or only military or economic power. The issue is more subtle, more immediate, a cancerlike growth which is in our midst right now— the materialist philosophy which underlies the Western humanistic world-view. Marx may have proposed an economic system different from our own, but we have shared his basic world-view.

The greatest dilemma for those who hold this world-view, however, is that it is impossible to live consistently within it. We saw how this was true of David Hume. Likewise the playwright Samuel Beckett can "say" that words do not communicate anything—and that everything, including language, is absurd—yet he must use words to write his plays, even plays about meaninglessness. If the words that Beckett uses did not convey meaning to his hearers, he could not say that everything, including words, is meaningless.

The list of contradictions can be extended endlessly. The truth is that everyone who rejects the biblical world-view must live in a state of tension between ideas about reality and reality itself.

Thus, if a person believes that everything is only matter or energy and carries this through consistently, meaning dies, morality dies, love dies, hope dies. *Yet!* The individual does love, does hope, does act on the basis of right and wrong. This is what we mean when we say that everyone is caught, regardless of his world-view, simply by the way things are. No one can make his own universe to live in.

The reason for this, as we have said all along, is that the individual is confronted with two aspects of reality that do not basically change: the universe and its form and the mannishness of man. Humanists argue that everything is finally only matter or energy and end up with no answers to the big questions. They arrive at only meaninglessness, relative morality, relative knowledge. But humanists actually live as if there *is* meaning and real morality. They act, for example, as if cruelty is not the same as noncruelty, or justice the same as injustice. Also, humanists do have knowledge, knowledge of a world in which causality is real and science is possible.

Exactly the same dilemma exists with the other main alternative to Christianity: the philosophies of the East. Despite their many differences, all of these philosophies flow out of the view that ultimately everything is impersonal. The universe we are experiencing, the Eastern philosophers say, is simply an extension of God, but—and here we need to be careful—they do not mean that God is personal. "God" means the "impersonal everything," which has no final distinctions. So, within this view, the solution is to say we must get rid of those aspirations that are personal, those things that make us seem to be independent entities, entirely independent selves. Such an idea is *maya,* that is, "illusion."

In the Eastern thinking, the only reality is *one* beyond all distinctions and therefore impersonal: no "male" or "female," no "you" or "me," no "good" or "evil." It is important to note that Eastern thinkers come to exactly the same place as those who begin by saying that everything is matter or energy. At first the two positions sound very different, but they result in the same final position.

And so we ask again: Can a person espousing this Eastern world-view live consistently with it? In his 1974 book *Zen and the Art of Motorcycle Maintenance,* Robert M. Pirsig relates an interesting anecdote. The author, who calls himself Phaedrus in the story, studied philosophy at Benares University for about ten years. He tells how his time there came to an end.

> One day in the classroom the professor of philosophy was blithely expounding on the illusory nature of the world for what seemed the fiftieth time and Phaedrus raised his hand and asked coldly if it was believed that the atomic bombs that had dropped on Hiroshima and Nagasaki were illusory. The professor smiled and said yes. That was the end of the exchange.
>
> . . . Within the traditions of Indian philosophy that answer may have been correct, but for Phaedrus and for anyone else who reads newspapers regularly and is concerned with such things as mass destruction of human beings that answer was hopelessly inadequate. He left the classroom, left India and gave up.[88]

There are, then, only two main alternative world-views to Christianity, both of which begin with the impersonal. The West has a *materialistic* view and is nonreligious. The East has an *immaterialistic* view and is religious. *But both are impersonal systems.* This is the important point; by comparison, their differences pale into insignificance. The result is that, in both the West and the East, men and women are seen as abnormal aliens to the way things really are. In Eastern terms they are spoken of as *maya* or illusion; in Western terms, as absurd machines.

Relieving the Tension in the West
In both the East and the West, however, there are attempts to relieve the tension of seeming to be nothing, while in fact being something very real—a person in a real world which has a definite form. On the materialist side, Sir Julian Huxley (1887-1975) has clarified the dilemma by acknowledging, though he was an atheist, that somehow or other—against all that one might expect—a person functions better if he acts *as though God exists.* "So," the argument goes, "God does not in fact exist, but act as if He does!" As observed by the Norwegian playwright Henrik Ibsen (1828-1906) in *The Wild Duck:* "Rob the average man of his life-illusion, and you rob him of his happiness at the same stroke." In other words, according to Huxley, you can function properly only if you live your whole life upon a lie. You act as if God exists, which to the

materialist is false. At first this sounds like a feasible solution for relieving the tension produced by a materialistic world-view. However, a moment's reflection shows what a terrible solution it is. You will find no deeper despair than this for a sensitive person. This is no optimistic, happy, reasonable, brilliant answer. It is darkness and death.

Another way the tension is relieved is through the theory of evolution, the idea that *by chance* there is an increasing advance. People are given an impression of progress—up from the primeval slime and the amoeba, up through the evolutionary chain, with life developing by chance from the simple carbon molecule to the complex, right up to the pinnacle, mankind.

This is not the place to discuss evolutionary theory, but it surprises us how readily people accept it, even on the scientific side, as if it had no problems. There are problems, even if these are not commonly realized or discussed.[89] The primary point we are interested in, however, is not evolution itself but the illusion of "progress" which has been granted by it. By chance, this amazing complexity called "man" has been generated out of the slime. So, of course, there is progress! By this argument people are led into imagining that the whole of reality does have purpose even if, as we have said, there is no way that it really can have purpose within the humanistic world-view.

Evolution makes men and women feel superior and at the top of the pile, but in the materialistic framework, the whole of reality is meaningless; the concept of "higher" means nothing. Even if, within the humanist world-view, people are more complex than plants and animals, both "higher" and "lower" have no meanings. We are left with everything being sad and absurd.

Thus, the concept of progress is an illusion. Only some form of mystical jump will allow us to accept that personality comes from impersonality.[90] No one has offered to explain, let alone demonstrate it to be feasible, how the impersonal plus time plus chance can give personality. We are distracted by a flourish of words—and, lo, personality has appeared out of a hat.

Imagine a universe made up of only liquids and solids, one containing no free gases. A fish is swimming in this universe. This fish, quite naturally, is conformed to its environment so that it is able to exist quite happily. Let us suppose, then, that by blind chance (as the evolutionists would have us believe) this fish developed lungs as it continued swimming in this universe without any gases. This fish would no longer be able to function and to fulfill its position as a fish. Would it then be "higher" or "lower" in its new state with lungs? Obviously it would be lower, for it would drown.

In the same way, if a person has been kicked up from the impersonal by chance, those things that make him a person—hope of purpose and significance, love, notions of morality and rationality and beauty—are ultimately unfulfillable and are thus meaningless. In such a situation, is man higher or lower? Mankind would then be the lowest creature on the scale, the least conforming to what reality is. Thus we see how hopeless is the illusion of meaning or purpose as derived from evolutionary thought.

Relieving the Tension in the East

Within Eastern thinking, attempts to relieve the tension have been made by introducing "personal gods." To the uninitiated these gods seem to be real persons; they are said to appear to human beings and even have sexual intercourse with them. But they are not really personal. Behind them their souce is the "impersonal everything" of which they are simply emanations. We find a multitude of gods and goddesses with their attendant mythologies, like the *Ramayana,* which then give the simple person a "feeling" of personality in the universe. People need this, because it is hard to live as if there is nothing out there in or beyond the universe to which they can relate personally. The initiated, however, understand. They know that ultimate reality is impersonal. So they submit themselves to the various techniques of the Eastern religions to eliminate their "personness." Their goal is to achieve a state of consciousness not bounded by the body and the senses or even by such ideals as "love" or "good."

Probably the most sophisticated Eastern attempt to deal with the tension we are considering is the Bhagavad-Gita. This is a religious writing probably produced around 200 B.C. in India. It has been the inspiration for multitudes of Hindus through the centuries and most notably for Indian spiritual and political leader Mahatma Gandhi. In it the individual is urged to participate in acts of charity. At the same time, however, the individual is urged to enter into these acts in "a spirit of detachment." Why? Because the proper attitude is to understand that none of these experiences really matter. It is the state of consciousness that rises above personality which is important, for personality is, after all, an abnormality within the impersonal universe.

Alternatively, the East proposes a system of "endless cycles" to try to give some explanation for things which exist about us. This has sometimes been likened to the ocean. The ocean casts up waves for a time, but the waves are still a part of the ocean, and then the waves pull back into the ocean and disappear. Interestingly enough, the Western materialist also tries to explain the form of the universe by a theory of endless cycles. He says that impersonal material or energy always exists, but that this goes through endless cycles, taking different forms—the latest of which began with the "big bang" which spawned the present expanding universe. Previously, billions and billions of years ago, this eternal material or energy had a different form and had contracted into the heavy mass from which came the present cycle of our universe. Both the Eastern thought and the Western put forth this unproven idea of endless cycles because their answers finally answer nothing.

We have emphasized the problems involved in these two alternatives because they are real. It is helpful to see that the only serious intellectual alternatives to the Christian position have such endless difficulties that they actually are nonanswers. We do it, too, because we find people in the West who imagine that Christianity has nothing to say on these big issues and who discard the Bible without ever considering it. This superior attitude, as we said earlier, is quite unfounded. The real situation is very different. The humanists of the Enlightenment acted as if they would conquer all before them, but two centuries have changed that.

One would have imagined at this point that Western man would have been glad for a solution to the various dilemmas facing him and would have welcomed answers to the big questions. But people are not as eager to find the truth as is sometimes made out. The history of Western thought during the past century confirms this.

Reason Is Dead

The hallmark of the Enlightenment had been "Reason Is King." The leading thinkers had consciously rejected the need for revelation. As Paul Hazard in *European Thought in the Eighteenth Century* says, they put Christianity on trial.[91]

Gradually, however, the problems of this enthronement of human reason emerged. The reason of man was not big enough to handle the big questions, and what man was left with was relative knowledge and relative morality. This noose around the humanist's neck tightened with every passing decade and generation.

What would he do?

Ironically, even though the basis of the humanists' whole endeavor had been the central importance of man's reason, when faced with the problems of relative knowledge and relative morality they repudiated reason. Rather than admit defeat in front of God's revelation, the humanists extended the revolution further—and in a direction which would have been quite unthinkable to their eighteenth-century predecessors. Modern irrationalism was born.

We could go as far back as Immanuel Kant (1724-1804) in philosophy and to Friedrich Schleiermacher (1768-1834) in theology. Modern existentialism is also related to Søren Kierkegaard (1813-1855). However, our intention here is neither to go into the history of irrationalism, nor to examine the proponents of existentialism in our own century, but rather to concentrate on its main thesis. It is this that confronts us on all sides today, and it is impossible to understand modern man without understanding this concept.

Because we shall be using several terms a great deal now, we would ask the reader to attend carefully. When we speak of *irrationalism* or *existentialism* or *the existential methodology,* we are pointing to a quite simple idea. It may have been expressed in a variety of complicated ways by philosophers, but it is not a difficult concept.

Imagine that you are at the movies watching a suspense film. As the story unfolds, the tension increases until finally the hero is trapped in some impossible situation and everyone is groaning inwardly, wondering how he is going to get out of the mess. The suspense is heightened by the knowledge (of the audience, not the hero) that help is on the way in the form of the good guys. The only question is: *will the good guys arrive in time?*

Now imagine for a moment that the audience is slipped the information that there are no good guys, that the situation of the hero is not just desperate, but completely hopeless. Obviously, the first thing that would happen is that the suspense would be gone. You and the entire audience would simply be waiting for the axe to fall.

If the hero faced the end with courage, this would be morally edifying, but the situation itself would be tragic. If, however, the hero acted *as if* help were around the corner and kept buoying himself up with this thought ("Someone is on the way!"—"Help is at hand!"), all you could feel for him would be pity. It would be a means to keep hope alive within a hopeless situation. The hero's hope would change nothing *on the outside;* it would be unable to manufacture, out of nothing, good guys coming to the rescue. All it would achieve would be the hero's own mental state of hopefulness rather than hopelessness.

The hopefulness itself would rest on a lie or an illusion and thus, viewed objectively, would be finally absurd. And if the hero really knew what the situation was, but consciously used the falsehood to buoy up his feelings and go whistling along, we would either say, "Poor guy!" or "He's a fool." It is this kind of conscious deceit that someone like Woody Allen has looked full in the face and will have none of.

Now this is what the existential methodology is about. If the universe we are living in is what the materialistic humanists say it is, then with our reason (when we stop to think about it) we could find absolutely no way to have meaning or morality or hope or beauty. This would plunge us into despair. We would have to take seriously the challenge of Albert Camus (1913-1960) in the first sentence of *The Myth of Sisyphus:* "There is but one truly serious philosophical problem, and that is suicide."[92] Why stay alive in an absurd universe? Ah! But that is *not* where we stop. We say to ourselves—"There *is* hope!" (even though there is no help). "We shall overcome!" (even though nothing is more certain than that we shall be destroyed, both individually at death and cosmically with the end of all conscious life). This is what confronts us on all sides today: the modern irrationalism.

Long Live Experience!

Another way to understand all this is to say that modern man has become a mystic. The word *mystic* makes people think immediately of a religious person—praying for hours, using techniques of meditation, and so on. Of course, the word *mysticism* includes this, but modern mysticism is different in a profound way. As the late Professor H. R. Rookmaaker of the Free University of Amsterdam said, modern mysticism is "a nihilistic mysticism, *for God is dead.*"

The mystics within the Christian tradition (Meister Eckhart in the thirteenth century, for example) believed in an objective personal God. But, they said, though God is really there, the mind is not the way to reach Him. On the other hand, modern mysticism comes from a quite different background, and this we must be clear about.

When modern philosophers realized they were not going to be able to find answers on the basis of reason, they crossed over in one way or another to the remarkable position of saying, "That doesn't matter!" Even though there are no answers by way of the mind, we will find them without the mind. The "answer"—whatever that may be—is to be "experienced," for it cannot be thought. Notice, the answer is not to be the experience of an objective and supernatural God whom, as the medieval mystics thought, it was difficult to understand with the mind. The developments we are considering came *after* Friedrich Nietzsche (1844–1900) had celebrated the "death of God," *after* the materialist philosophy had worked its way throughout the culture and created skepticism about the supernatural.

The modern mystic, therefore, is not trying to "feel" his way to a God he believes is really there (but whom he cannot approach by way of the mind). The modern mystic does not know if *anything* is there. All he knows is that he cannot know anything ultimate through the mind. So what is left is *experience as experience*. This is the key to understanding modern man in the West: Forget your mind; just experience! It may seem extreme—but we say it carefully—this is the philosophy by which the majority of people in the West are now living. For everyday purposes the mind is a useful instrument, but for the things of meaning, for the answers to the big questions, it is set aside.

"Whatever Reality may be, it is beyond the conception of the finite intellect; it follows that attempts at descriptions are misleading, unprofitable, and a waste of time." That is a quotation from a modern Buddhist in the West. The secular existentialists may seem a long way from such an Eastern formulation about reality, but their rejection of the intellect as a means of finding answers amounts to the same thing. That is what the existentialist "revolt," as it has been called, is. It is a revolt against the mind, a passionate rejection of the Enlightenment ideal of reason. As Professor William Barrett of New York University has put it: "Existentialism is the counter-Enlightenment come at last to philosophic expression."[93]

The way to handle philosophy, according to the existential methodology, is not by the use of the mind that considers (impersonally and objectively) propositions about reality. Rather, the way to deal with the big questions is by relying only on the individual's experience. That which is being considered is not necessarily an experience of something that really exists. What is involved is the experience *as an experience,* whether or not any objective reality is being experienced. We are reminded of our imaginary hero who said, "Help is coming," and therefore kept himself going, even though he had no reason to think any help existed. It is the experience as the experience that counts, and that is the end of it.

There are, of course, some valuable insights in what the existentialists have said. For one, they were right to protest against scientism and the impersonalism of much post-Enlightenment thought. They were right to point out that answers have to be "lived" and not just "thought." (We will say more about this in Chapter 6.) But their rejection of the mind is no solution to anything. It *seems* like a solution but is in fact a counsel of despair.

Having started with the apparently different positions of the Buddhist and the secular existentialist, we should now look at culture at large. One of the "cultural breakpoints" was Haight-Ashbury in the sixties. There the counterculture, the drug culture, was born. Writing about the experience of Ken Kesey and his Merry Pranksters in the early days of Haight-Ashbury, Tom Wolfe says,

> Gradually the Prankster attitude began to involve the main things religious mystics have always felt, things common to Hindus, Buddhists, Christians, and for that matter Theosophists and even flying-saucer cultists. Namely, the experiencing of an Other World, a higher level of reality. . . .
> Every vision, every insight . . . came out of the *new experience.* . . . And how to get it across to the multitudes who have never had this experience for themselves? *You couldn't put it into words.* You had to create conditions in which they would *feel* an approximation of that *feeling,* the sublime kairos (*italics* added).

Do you see what is involved here? We can agree this represents a wild-fringe element of the counterculture which is already behind us. But we must understand that the central ideas and attitudes are now part of the air we breathe in the West. "Every insight . . . came out of the new experience." *Experience!*—that is the word! And how to tell it? "You couldn't put it into words."

The New Mysticism

What about the spread of Eastern religions and techniques within the West—things like TM, Yoga, the cults? We have moved beyond the counterculture of the sixties, but where to? These elements from the East no longer influence just the beat generation and the dropouts. Now they are fashionable for the middle classes as well. They are everywhere.

What has become important is not whether there is anything that causes an experience, but just the experience as such. What about modern theology in the churches? It is the same thing. Maybe the terminology is "Christian," but the ideas are on the other side—experience is the important thing, not propositions about reality, about God, about salvation and all the rest. It does not matter if anything exists that has caused or conforms to the experience.

What about the sudden growth of interest in UFOs and UFOlogy? Even though not a scrap of evidence exists to support Erich von Däniken's "scientific" theories about spacemen who visited earth in the distant past, millions of people have been taken with these assumptions. He has given his ideas an aura of scientific plausibility, plenty of technical jargon, photographs, and so forth, and because this is a "scientific age," people are impressed. But the real evidence is unconvincing. Is there conscious life in other parts of the cosmos? We do not know. If there is, it would pose no problem for Christianity. Still, at this time there is no proof at all that this is the case. Why then do people accept it? We suggest it is part of the swing to the irrational.

People are hungry for something which will give them hope in life. They are tired of the empty platitudes that politicians and many theologians have made: endless exhortations to be good, to be good, to be good! They are also afraid. Things really do seem hopeless, even on the level of everyday life with its threats of a lower standard of living, of a growing authoritarianism, of famine and ecological disaster, of devastating war. And they are looking for *any* answer. So the UFOs are messengers of a friendly race from another planet. "Do not fear—the Force is with you!"—to borrow from a current science-fiction film. And so people believe it irrationally. If they used their minds, they would see no evidence for friendly people from outside. But the feeling of experience as they read about this or see it on a screen is enough. It does not matter whether there is any reality to it.

What about the growth of occultism, witchcraft, astrology? Is it simply economics that has put the signs of the zodiac in shops from one end of our society to the other? In part it is economics, but, once again, the real reason is deeper. People are looking for answers—answers they can experience.

What about those who take drugs as a means of "expanding their consciousness"? This, too, is in the same direction. Your mind is a hindrance to you: "Blow it"! As Timothy Leary put it in *The Politics of Ecstasy* (1968): "Our favorite concepts are standing in the way of a flood tide two billion years building up. The verbal dam is collapsing. Head for the hills or prepare your intellectual craft to flow with the current." So we see again the rejection of the mind. The verbal dam, the concepts, the intellectual craft? These must be bypassed by the "new man."

Wherever we look, this is what confronts us: irrational experience. We must be careful not to be bewildered by the surface differences between these movements. We are not saying they are all the same. Of course there are differences. The secular existentialists, for example, disagree with one another. Then, too, secular existentialists differ with religious existentialists; the former tend to be pessimistic, the latter optimistic. Some of the movements are serious and command our respect. Some are just bizarre. There *are* differences. *Yet, all of them represent the new mysticism!*

The problem with mysticism of this sort is, interestingly enough, the same problem we considered earlier in relation to all humanistic systems. Who is going to say what is right?

As soon as one removes the checking mechanism of the mind by which to measure things, everything can then be "right" and everything can also be "wrong." Eventually, anything and everything can be allowed! Take a simple example from life: If you are asking for directions in a city, you first listen to the directions your guide is giving and then you set off. Let us say the directions are: "Take the first turn on the right, called Twenty-fourth Street; then the next turn on the left, called Kennedy Drive; and then keep going till you come to the park where you will see the concert hall just past a big lake on your right." Armed with these directions, you go along—checking up on what you have been told: "Yes, there is Twenty-fourth Street. Yes, there is Kennedy Drive," and so on.

In other words, you are not just told words; you are able to see if these words relate to the outside world, the world you have to operate in if you are going to get from *A* to *B*. This is where your mind is essential. You can check to see if the information you have been given is true or false.

Imagine, on the other hand, that someone said, in answer to your request for directions, "I don't know where or what *B* is. It is impossible to talk about a 'concert hall.' What is a 'concert hall' anyway? We can only say of it that it is the 'Unknowable.' " How completely ridiculous for you to be told, "Go *any* way—because this is the way"!

The trick in all these positions is to argue first of all that the End—Final Reality—cannot be spoken of (because it cannot be known by the mind) and yet to give the directions to find it. We should notice, however, that in this setting we can never ask questions ahead of time about the directions we receive. They are directions only for blindfolded experience, the blind "leap of faith."

We cannot ask, "How will I know that it is truth or that it is the divine I am experiencing?" The answer is always, "There is no way you can be told, for it is an answer beyond language, beyond categories, but take this path [or that one, or another one] anyway."

Thus, modern man is bombarded from all sides by devotees of this or that *experience*. The media only compound the problem. So does the commercialism of our highly technological societies. The danger of manipulation from these alone is overwhelming. In the absence of a clear standard, they are a force for the control of people's minds and behavior that is beyond anything in history. In fact, there are no clear standards in Western society now; and where there is an appearance of standards, very often there is insufficient motivation to lean against the enormous pressures. And why? In part, at least, because there is an inadequate basis for knowledge and for morality.

When we add to this that modern man has become a "mystic," we soon realize the seriousness of the situation. For in all these mystical solutions no one can finally say anything about right and wrong. The East has had this problem for thousands of years. In a pantheistic system, whatever pious statements may be made along the way, ultimately good and evil are equal in God, the impersonal God. So we hear Yun-Men, a Zen master, saying, "If you want to get the plain truth, be not concerned with right and wrong. Conflict between right and wrong is the sickness of the mind."

Society can have no stability on this Eastern world-view or its present Western counterpart. It just does not work. And so one finds a gravitation toward some form of authoritarian government, an individual tyrant or group of tyrants who takes the reins of power and rule. And the freedoms, the sorts of freedoms we have enjoyed in the West, are lost.

We are, then, brought back to our starting point. The inhumanities and the growing loss of freedoms in the West are the result of a world-view which has no place for "people." Modern humanistic materialism is an impersonal system. The East is no different. Both begin and end with impersonality.

We have looked at reasons for concluding not merely that these world-views are uncomfortable because they lead to inhumanity, but because they are false. They do not fit into what we know best about ourselves and our environment. Ours is a universe which contains real personality. Neither the universe nor this personality is illusory. We will turn now to the Bible's claim to be the reliable source of information about the universe and mankind. But first, there are two very important introductory comments.

The Unveiling of Truth

The famous Hindu writer and statesman Sarvepalli Radhakrishnan once wrote, "The altars erected to the unknown gods in the Graeco-Roman world were but an expression of man's ignorance of the divine nature. The sense of failure in man's quest for the unseen is symbolized by them. When asked to define the nature of God, the seer of the Upanishad sat silent, and when pressed to answer claimed that the Absolute is silence."

By contrast, the Apostle Paul, speaking in the context of the very same altars to unknown gods in Athens, said, ". . . Now what you worship as something unknown I am going to proclaim to you" (Acts 17:23). And again, writing to the Corinthians not far away, "However, as it is written: 'No eye has seen, nor ear has heard, no mind has conceived . . .' but God has revealed it to us . . ." (1 Corinthians 2:9, 10). This claim is common to the whole Bible. God has not waited for us to stumble to Him in the dark (which would be impossible anyway), but has revealed Himself to us. The word *revelation* in Greek is *apokalupsis* which means literally "unveiling"; so God has "unveiled" to us the things we could not know because of our finiteness and sin.

This revelation or unveiling to finite and sinful people is the

Bible as the *written Word*. This is the claim of the whole Bible. Moreover, through the Bible we learn of the life and teaching of the Second Person of the Trinity, who became man at a point in history and so became the *Living Word* of the Godhead: "For in Christ all the fullness of the Deity lives in bodily form" (Colossians 2:9).

In this claim the dilemma of all humanistic systems is overcome at a stroke. The *infinite* God has spoken. None of the many finite attempts to define truth, doomed to failure as we have seen, is necessary. God has communicated to man, the infinite to the finite. God has communicated, in addition, in words that are understandable to us. The One who made man capable of language in the first place has communicated to man in language. Also, God has communicated truth about both spiritual reality and physical reality, about both the nature of God and the nature of man, about both events in past history and events in the future. Where all humanistic systems of thought are unable to give an adequate explanation of things, the Bible as God's statement is adequate.

It is equally important to note that the Bible's answer does not have to be believed blindly. There are good and sufficient reasons for seeing that it is true. It is the key that fits into the lock of what we know best about ourselves and the universe around us.

To change the metaphor: Imagine a book which has been mutilated, leaving just one inch of printed matter on each page. Although it would obviously be impossible to piece together and understand the book's story, few people would imagine that the printing which was left on those one-inch portions had come together by chance. However, if the torn pieces of each page were found in a trunk and were added in the right places, then the story could be read and would make sense.

So it is with Christianity. The ripped pages remaining in the book correspond to the universe and its form and to the mannishness of man. The parts of the pages discovered in the trunk correspond to the Scriptures, which are God's propositional communication to mankind. Neither the universe nor personality can give the answer to the whole meaning of the created order. Yet both are important as a testimony in helping us know that the Scriptures, God's communication to man, are what they claim to be. The question is whether the communication given by God completes and explains the portions we had before and especially whether it explains what was open to observation before (though without an explanation), that is, that the existence of the universe and its form and the mannishness of man are not just chance configurations of the printer's scrambled type.

This illustration is important for several reasons. First, it emphasizes that Christians do not start out from themselves autonomously, as the humanists try to do. God gives the pages, and thus God gives the answers.

Second, it helps us see the proper place of man's reason. Just as a scientist does not create the order in the universe but does recognize it, so reason does not create the answer but simply recognizes it. Of course this does not mean that reason will necessarily *receive* the answer. Each person has to *choose* to receive God's truth. But God's truth is clear. The individual must acknowledge that he (and mankind) is not autonomous, not the center of all things, and he must acknowledge that he has many times done what he knows to be wrong and thus needs the work of Christ for himself. Those who refuse to back down from the position of autonomy make it impossible for themselves to receive the truth, even though there are good and sufficient reasons for knowing that it is the truth.

The Personal Origin of Man

The Scriptures tell us that the universe exists and has form and meaning because it was created purposefully by a personal Creator. This being the case, we see that, as we are personal, we are not something strange and out of line with an otherwise impersonal universe. Since we are made in the image of God, we are in line with God. There is a continuity, in other words, between ourselves, though finite, and the infinite Creator who stands behind the universe as its Creator and its final source of meaning.

Unlike the evolutionary concept of an impersonal beginning plus time plus chance, the Bible gives an account of man's origin as a finite person made in God's image, that is, like God. We see then how man can have personality and dignity and value. Our uniqueness is guaranteed, something which is impossible in the materialistic system. If there is no qualitative distinction between man and other organic life (animals or plants), why should we feel greater concern over the death of a human being than over the death of a laboratory rat? Is man in the end any higher?

Though this is the logical end of the materialistic system, men and women still usually in practice assume that people have some real value. All the way back to the dawn of our investigations in history, we find that man is still man. Wherever we turn, to the caves of the Pyrenees, to the Sumerians in Mesopotamia, and even further back to Neanderthal man's burying his dead in flower petals, it makes no difference: men everywhere show by their art and their accomplishments that they have been and have considered themselves to be unique. They *were* unique, and people today are unique. What is wrong is a world-view which fails to explain that uniqueness. All people are unique because they are made in the image of God.

The Bible tells us also, however, that man is flawed. We see this to be the case both within ourselves and in our societies throughout the world. People are noble and people are cruel; people have heights of moral achievement and depths of moral depravity.

But this is not simply an enigma, nor is it explained in terms of "the animal in man." The Bible explains how man is flawed, without destroying the uniqueness and dignity of man. Man is evil and experiences the results of evil, not because man is non-man but because man is fallen and thus is *abnormal*.

This is the significance of the third chapter of Genesis. Some time after the original Creation (we do not know how long), man rebelled against God. Being made in the image of God as persons, Adam and Eve were able to make real choices. They had true creativity, not just in the area we call "art" but also in the area of choice. And they used this choice to turn from God as their true integration point. Their ability to choose would have been equally validated if they had chosen not to turn away from God, as their true integration point, but instead they used their choice to try to make themselves autonomous. In doing this, they were acting against the moral absolute of the universe, namely, God's character—and thus evil among people was born.

The Fall brought not only moral evil but also the abnormality of (1) each person divided from himself or herself; (2) people divided from other people; (3) mankind divided from nature; and (4) nature divided from nature. This was the consequence of the choice made by Adam and Eve some time after the Creation. It was not any original deformity that made them choose in this way. God had not made them robots, and so they had real choice. It is man, therefore, and not God, who is responsible for evil.

We have to keep pointing out, because the idea is strange to a society by which the Bible has been neglected or distorted, that Christianity does not begin with a statement of Christ as Savior. That comes later in its proper setting. Genesis 1:1 says, "In the beginning God created. . . ." Christianity begins with the personal and infinite God who is the Creator. It goes on to show that man is made in God's image but then tells us that man is now fallen. It is the rebellion of man that has made the world *abnormal*. So there is a broken line as we look back to the creation of man by God. A chasm stands there near the beginning, the chasm which is the Fall, the choice to go against God and His Word.

What follows from this is that not everything that happens in the world is "natural." Unlike modern materialistic thought on both sides of the Iron Curtain, Christianity does not see everything in history as equally "normal." Because of the abnormality brought about by man, not everything which occurs in history should be there. Thus, not all that history brings forth is right just because it happens, and not all personal drives and motives are equally good. Here, then, is a marked difference between Christianity and almost all other philosophies. Most other philosophies do not have the concept of a present abnormality. Therefore, they hold that everything now is normal; things are now as they always have been.

By contrast, Christians do *not* see things as if they always have been this way. This is of immense importance in understanding evil in the world. It is possible for Christians to speak of things as absolutely wrong, for they are not original in human society. They are derived from the Fall; they are in that sense "abnormal." It also means we can stand against what is wrong and cruel without standing against God, for He did not make the world as it now is.

This understanding of the chasm between what mankind and history are now and what they could have been—and should have been, from the way they were made—gives us a real moral framework for life, one which is compatible with our nature and aspirations. So there are "rules for life," like the signs on cliff tops which read: DANGER—KEEP OUT. The signs are there to help, not hinder us. God has put them there because to live in this way, according to His rules, is the way for both safety and fulfillment. The God who made us and knows what is for our best good is the same God who gives us His commands. When we break these, it is not only wrong, it is also not for our best good; it is not for our fulfillment as unique persons made in the image of God.

Freedom Within Form

We should not allow ourselves to hurry past this point, because it is of tremendous importance in relation to the problems we outlined in the first three chapters of this book. Knowing what is right and wrong, we have a way to have order and freedom simultaneously. It is relatively easy to attain order in society and not have any freedom. There are plenty of examples of that today. Likewise, it is easy to practice freedom without any order. There are examples of that, too, in the Western societies most of us live in. But how do we get both together? That is the problem.

The Bible gives a world-view that provides order and yet at the same time freedom. God's rules are like a perimeter fence. We must stay within that fence if we are to avoid getting messed up. But inside the fence we have an almost endless *variety of possibilities for freedom*. These touch every area of human life.

A good example is the pursuit of science. The Christian world-view gives us a base for science, yet (since we are made in the image of God) a freedom to pursue science. The birth of modern science is generally conceded to be heavily indebted to the Christian world-view. The Bible tells us that the universe is ordered, because God made it to cohere in all sorts of amazing ways. At the same time it tells us that we are persons. We are able to know what is around us; the subject can know the object.

It may seem rather obvious to say we can know what is around us, for everyone lives like this, day in and day out. We drive the car, use the stove, and so forth. Even though we cannot completely know any single detail of what is around us, we can still have accurate knowledge. This is what makes science possible, too. But, for the materialistic philosophers, this is still a problem.

Why is it that the noises we make from our mouths, for example, "cat," "dog," "glass," "hand," have a correspondence with objects in the outside world? That is the problem with which modern philosophers are still struggling. But within the Christian view the answer is simple and obvious: the world was made that way in the first place. Without the Bible's answer of a personal God who has made the universe—and at the same time persons within it to have a relationship with what has been made—people can still know the objects, *but they do not know why they can know them.*

The Importance of Genesis
So the Bible is the key to understanding the universe and its form and the mannishness of man. Without this key our observations are out of perspective; we do not know what we are looking at.

This being the case, our conclusions about what we are seeing can be massively in error.

Unless we are told about our beginnings, we cannot make sense of our present history. And secular study is incapable of doing that. This is not to say that the study of history and science is irrelevant or useless, but when secular study is finished, the most important questions are left unanswered. It can tell us much of patterns and statistics, but not the reason or meaning or significance of it all. Twentieth-century people know something exists, but have no way of saying what that something amounts to.

This is where the early chapters of Genesis are so important. These chapters give the history that comes before anything that secular historians have been able to ascertain, and *it is this presecular history which gives meaning to mankind's present history*.

Some people mistakenly believe that one can "spiritualize" away the history of the first chapters of Genesis and that this will make no difference. They argue that these chapters are not history but something like parables. This type of thinking depreciates the factual content, which gives information about history and the cosmos. Those who do this sometimes imagine that doing this makes little or no difference. But it changes everything. For these chapters tell us the *why* (the significance and meaning) of all the subsequent history which historians can know through their investigations. These chapters tell us also the *why* of our own personal history.

For this reason we can say that in this sense the early chapters of Genesis are more important than anything else we could have. They are the very foundation on which *all* knowledge rests. So we learn from them that before the creation of the universe, the infinite-personal God existed and that He created the universe (the space-time continuum) by choice, out of nothing. The Creation was not without a cause.

The infinite-personal God was its cause. He chose to create, He willed to create, and "it was"—it came into being.

> You are worthy, our Lord and God,
>   to receive glory and honor and power,
> for you created all things,
>   and by your will they were created
>   and have their being.
>   Revelation 4:11

As we have seen already, we learn also about the fact that man was made "in the image of God," a person, and that then there was a space-time Fall.

All the information given by the Bible flows out of the information given in the early chapters of Genesis. If we are to understand the world as it is and ourselves as we are, we must know the flow of history given in these chapters. Take this away and the flow of history is lost. Take this away and even the death of Christ has no meaning.

So the Bible tells us who we are and who other people are. It tells us how people are differentiated from all other things. We do not need to be confused, as is much of modern mankind, about people's distinction from both animal life and the complicated machines of the second half of the twentieth century. Suddenly people have unique value, and we can understand how it is that each of us is different as a person.

Furthermore, we can see that *all* people are similarly to be distinguished from non-man and that therefore we ourselves must look on others as having great value. Anyone who kills a person is not killing just another member of the same biological species, but one of overwhelming value, one made in the image, the likeness, of God.

Any person, no matter who he or she is—a stranger or a friend, a fellow-believer or someone who is still in rebellion against God, anyone of any age, before or after birth—*any and every person is made after the likeness of God.*

Each man, woman, and child is of great value, not for some ulterior motive such as self-gratification or wealth or power or a sex object or "the good of society" or the maintenance of the gene pool—but simply because of his or her origin.

This flow of history that springs from Genesis has implications for every aspect of our lives. Each of us stands in the flow of history. We know our origin—a lineage more ancient than the Queen of England's or the Pilgrim Fathers'. As we look at ourselves in the flow of space-time reality, we see our origin in Adam and Eve, and we know that God has created every human being in His own image.

CHAPTER FIVE

Truth and History

In the previous chapter we saw that the Bible gives us the explanation for the existence of the universe and its form and for the mannishness of man. Or, to reverse this, we came to see that the universe and its form and the mannishness of man are a testimony to the truth of the Bible. In this chapter we will consider a third testimony: the Bible's openness to verification by historical study.

Christianity involves history. To say only that is already to have said something remarkable, because it separates the Judeo-Christian world-view from almost all other religious thought. It is rooted in history.

The Bible tells us how God communicated with man in history. For example, God revealed Himself to Abraham at a point in time and at a particular geographical place. He did likewise with Moses, David, Isaiah, Daniel and so on. The implications of this are extremely important to us. Because the truth God communicated in the Bible is so tied up with the flow of human events, it is possible by historical study to confirm some of the historical details.

It is remarkable that this possibility exists. Compare the information we have from other continents of that period. We know comparatively little about what happened in Africa or South America or China or Russia or even Europe. We see beautiful remains of temples and burial places, cult figures, utensils, and so forth, but there is not much actual "history" that can be reconstructed, at least not much when compared to that which is possible in the Middle East.

When we look at the material which has been discovered from the Nile to the Euphrates that derives from the 2500-year span before Christ, we are in a completely different situation from that in regard to South America or Asia. The kings of Egypt and Assyria built thousands of monuments commemorating their victories and recounting their different exploits. Whole libraries have been discovered from places like Nuzu and Mari and most recently at Ebla, which give hundreds of thousands of texts relating to the historical details of their time. It is within this geographical area that the Bible is set. So it is possible to find material which bears upon what the Bible tells us.

The Bible purports to give us information on history. Is the history accurate? The more we understand about the Middle East between 2500 B.C. and A.D. 100, the more confident we can be that the information in the Bible is reliable, even when it speaks about the simple things of time and place.[94]

Moses and Joshua
Mount Sinai is one of the most important sites of the entire Bible. It was here that the Hebrew people came shortly after their flight from Egypt. Here God spoke to them through Moses, giving them directions for their life as a newly formed nation and making a covenant with them.[95]

The thing to notice about this epochal moment for Israel is the emphasis on history which the Bible itself makes. Time and time again Moses reminds the people of what has happened on Mount Sinai:

> You came near and stood at the foot of the mountain while it blazed with fire to the very heavens, with black clouds and deep darkness. Then the LORD spoke to you out of the fire. You heard the sound of words but saw no form; there was only a voice.
>
> Deuteronomy 4:11, 12

Moses emphasizes that those alive at the time had actually heard God's direct communication in words. They also were eyewitnesses of what had occurred—they saw the cloud and the mountain burning with fire. They saw and they heard. In the same way they had been eyewitnesses of the remarkable events which had accompanied their escape from Egypt shortly before: "But it was your own eyes that saw all these great things the LORD has done" (Deuteronomy 11:7). Therefore, Moses says, on the basis of what they themselves have seen and heard in their own lifetime, they are not to be afraid of their present or future enemies.

> But do not be afraid of them; remember well what the LORD your God did to Pharaoh and to all Egypt. You saw with your own eyes the great trials, the miraculous signs and wonders, the mighty hand and outstretched arm, with which the LORD your God brought you out. The LORD your God will do the same to all the peoples you now fear.
> Deuteronomy 7:18, 19

On the same basis too, Moses urges them to obey God: "Only be careful, and watch yourselves closely so that you do not forget the things your eyes have seen . . ." (Deuteronomy 4:9).

Thus the people's confidence and trust in God and their obedience to Him are alike rooted in truth that is historical and observable. Therefore, the historical records are subject to factual study; the historical records are not only open to verification but to falsification as well. The relationship between God and His people was not based on an inward experience inside their own heads, but upon a reality which was seen and heard. They were called to obey God not because of a leap of faith, but because of God's real acts in history. For God is the *living* God. The universe within which man lives is not a "closed" system of natural causes. The universe is God's creation and it is "open" to Him. God has acted into history, into a history which is seeable.

"Religious truth" according to the Bible involves the same sort of truth which people operate on in their everyday lives. If something is true, then its opposite cannot also be true. For example, if the Israelites were slaves in Egypt under the Egyptian pharaohs at a particular moment in history, then it cannot also be true that at the same time the Israelites were *not* slaves in Egypt. Likewise, if Jesus was raised from the dead, His body will not be able to be found where He was buried near Jerusalem.

This is the Bible's view of truth: certain things are true whose opposites are not true. It is important to understand that this concept of truth did not begin with the Greeks, as some people suggest. God made the human mind itself so that we all act on this. Even those who deny the concept act on it in practice. If someone says that all truth is relative, he is saying absolutely that this is true. The necessities of everyday life give the lie to relativistic thought.

From the Bible's viewpoint, all truth finally rests upon the fact that the infinite-personal God exists in contrast to His not existing. This means that God exists objectively; He exists whether or not people say He does. The Bible also teaches that God is personal. That means, therefore, that the statements "God does *not* exist" and "God is *im*personal" are false.

Three things should be emphasized about the Hebrew (and biblical) view of truth.

1. In the Hebrew (and biblical) view, truth is grounded ultimately in the existence and character of God and what has been given to us by God in creation and revelation. Because people are finite, reality cannot be exhausted by human reason. Mankind, being limited, can know many things only through revelation. (Biblical truth is bountifully full. Thus, while what the Bible teaches can be put into words and discussed, it so gives things in balance that its teaching as a whole is often richer than any single statement quoted as a proof text.)

2. The biblical view of truth is not a lesser view of truth than the Greek view, but a far higher one. The Judeo-Christian world-view is not merely a philosophic system to be reasoned about abstractly as a nicely balanced system as the Greeks did. It is certainly a world-view, one that makes sense of our experience. But it is more; *it is a world-view related to history* and therefore at crucial points open to confirmation through what can be touched and seen.

3. It is a view of truth that involves the whole person; it is to be enjoyed; it is to be upheld through opposition and denial. It demands choice and commitment. Why? Because it is objectively true. It is truth both to God and to us. Thus, the Hebrew (and biblical) view of truth, rather than being similar to the modern relativistic (or dialetical or existential) concept of truth, is completely contrary to it.

It is within this Judeo-Christian view of truth that, by its own insistence, we must understand the Bible. Moses could appeal to real historical events as the basis for Israel's confidence and obedience into the future. He could even pass down to subsequent generations physical reminders of what God had done, so that the people could see them and remember. So, for example, he gave the Ten Commandments on the two tablets of stone to be kept in the Ark of the Covenant. Likewise he gave them a pot of manna (the food provided by God during the wilderness wanderings), and the rod belonging to Aaron, Moses' brother, which had been used in Egypt and later as a sign of God's power and presence. These were kept as silent witnesses of truth; they were observable in history from generation to generation within the Jewish sanctuary.

At the time of Joshua, who followed Moses in the leadership of the Jews, we find the same emphasis on historic testimony as in the writings of Moses: "Joshua set up the twelve stones that had been in the middle of the Jordan at the spot where the priests who carried the ark of the covenant had stood. And they are there to this day" (Joshua 4:9). God is not an abstract force or idea. Man's experience of God is not just within his head. God is active in history. And just as in the time of Moses God commanded various items to be kept as physical reminders of what He had done, so God did the same thing in the time of Joshua.

God temporarily dried up the Jordan River so that the Jews could pass. As a memorial of that fact—so that it could be observed through subsequent generations—two piles of twelve stones each were made. The first pile was made in the riverbed of the Jordan itself while the people were actually crossing. There they could be seen for centuries when the water in the Jordan was low. The second pile was made out of rocks which the Jews lifted from the river as they passed by and then piled on the dry land at their camp in Gilgal: "And Joshua set up at Gilgal the twelve stones they had taken out of Jordan" (Joshua 4:20).[96]

Abraham and Isaac
The Bible's account of Abraham's life also emphasizes historic events as real events. This becomes especially obvious—and important—in the account of Abraham's "sacrifice" of his son, Isaac.

The Bible sets this event in a definite framework. We are told, for example, that Abraham was directed by God to take Isaac to a particular mountain, Mount Moriah—a long three-day journey from where Abraham and Isaac were. This is important, not just an incidental detail. This was the site on which Solomon many years later built the temple. And the New Testament tells us that Jesus died not far from this same spot.

None of this is by chance. Jesus died as the promised Lamb of

God, as John the Baptist calls Him. He died to take away the sin of the world. As such He is the fulfillment of what was prefigured in the "almost sacrifice" of Isaac a bit less than 2,000 years earlier. And as such, too, Jesus is the fulfillment of all the sacrifices associated with the tabernacle and temple. God was indicating in "the sacrifice of Isaac" that it is not an animal which delivers people from their sins, but a Person.

This also helps us to understand why something which the rest of the Bible tells us is abhorrent to God, human sacrifice, could have been used as the supreme test of Abraham's trust in God's promises to him. It was not because God wished Isaac to die (and, of course, Isaac did not die), but because God wished to make clear that He Himself would provide the sacrifice and that that sacrifice would not be an animal but a very special *Person*.

Let us notice in particular that God did not ask Abraham for a "leap of faith," any more than He asked the people of Israel for a leap of faith at the time of Moses. Abraham had already been given many evidences of God's reality and of His reliability. God had spoken to him over and over again before this time:

> The Lord had said to Abram, "Leave your country, your people and your father's household and go to the land I will show you.

> "I will make you into a great nation
>   and I will bless you;
> I will make your name great,
>   and you will be a blessing.
> I will bless those who bless you,
>   and whoever curses you I will curse;
> and all peoples on earth
>   will be blessed through you."
>   Genesis 12:1-3

Then again, when Abraham came into Canaan: "The LORD said to Abram after Lot had parted from him, 'Lift up your eyes from where you are and look north and south, east and west. All the land that you see I will give to you and your offspring forever . . .' " (Genesis 13:14, 15).

God promised to give Abraham a new country and descendants. However, where was the son and heir? Abraham was old, and in his concern to provide an heir he had first chosen a servant called Eliezer who came from Damascus. Here are the key passages from Genesis which record Abraham's experience in getting a proper heir:

Then the word of the LORD came to him: "This man will not be your heir, but a son coming from your own body will be your heir." He took him outside and said, "Look at the heavens and count the stars—if indeed you can count them." Then he said to him, "So shall your offspring be."

Abram believed the LORD, and he credited it to him as righteousness.

Genesis 15:4-6

When Abram was ninety-nine years old, the LORD appeared to him and said, "I am God Almighty; walk before me and be blameless. I will confirm my covenant between me and you and will greatly increase your numbers."

Abram fell facedown, and God said to him, "As for me, this is my covenant with you: You will be the father of many nations. No longer will you be called Abram; your name will be Abraham, for I have made you a father of many nations."

Genesis 17:1-5

The LORD appeared to Abraham near the great trees of Mamre while he was sitting at the entrance to his tent in the heat of the day. Abraham looked up and saw three men standing nearby. When he saw them, he hurried from the entrance of his tent to meet them and bowed low to the ground.

He said, "If I have found favor in your eyes, my lord, do not pass your servant by. . . ."

"Where is your wife Sarah?" they asked him.

"There, in the tent," he said.

Then the LORD said, "I will surely return to you about this time next year, and Sarah your wife will have a son."

Now Sarah was listening at the entrance to the tent, which was behind him. Abraham and Sarah were already old and well advanced in years, and Sarah was past the age of childbearing. So Sarah laughed to herself as she thought, "After I am worn out and my master is old, will I now have this pleasure?"

Then the LORD said to Abraham, "Why did Sarah laugh and say, 'Will I really have a child, now that I am old?' Is anything too hard for the LORD? I will return to you at the appointed time next year and Sarah will have a son."

Genesis 18:1-3, 9-14

Thus, in this remarkable way Abraham came to have an heir, just as God had said. Abraham also saw God's remarkable deliverance of his nephew Lot from Sodom and Gomorroh.

Therefore, the certainty that God was both real and trustworthy had been established to Abraham through a number of revelations and events. He had heard God, he had talked with Him, he had received propositional revelation from God. He had seen God keep His promises, both in regard to a son (even though he and Sarah were old) and in regard to Lot's rescue. When we read the following account of the "sacrifice" of Isaac, we must keep these facts in mind. Abraham knew God was both real and trustworthy.

> Some time later God tested Abraham. He said to him, "Abraham!" "Here I am," he replied.
> Then God said, "Take your son, your only son Isaac, whom you love, and go to the region of Moriah. Sacrifice him there as a burnt offering on one of the mountains I will tell you about."
> Early the next morning Abraham got up and saddled his donkey. He took with him two of his servants and his son Isaac. When he had cut enough wood for the burnt offering, he set out for the place God had told him about. On the third day Abraham looked up and saw the place in the distance. He said to his servants, "Stay here with the donkey while I and the boy go over there. We will worship and then we will come back to you."
> Abraham took the wood for the burnt offering and placed it on his son Isaac, and he himself carried the fire and the knife. As the two of them went on together, Isaac spoke up and said to his father Abraham, "Father?"
> "Yes, my son?" Abraham replied.
> "The fire and wood are here," Isaac said, "but where is the lamb for the burnt offering?"
> Abraham answered, "God himself will provide the lamb for the burnt offering, my son." And the two of them went on together.
> When they reached the place God had told him about, Abraham built an altar there and arranged the wood on it. He bound his son Isaac and laid him on the altar, on top of the wood. Then he reached out his hand and took the knife to slay his son. But the angel of the LORD called out to him from heaven, "Abraham! Abraham!"
> "Here I am," he replied.
> "Do not lay a hand on the boy," he said. "Do not do anything to him. Now I know that you fear God, because you have not withheld from me your son, your only son."
> Abraham looked up and there in a thicket he saw a ram caught by its horns. He went over and took the ram and sacrificed it as a burnt offering instead of his son. So Abraham called that place "The LORD will provide." And to this day it is said, "On the mountain of the LORD it will be provided."
>
> Genesis 22:1-14

Far from Abraham being asked to make a blind leap of faith, the

Bible indicates that it would have been unreasonable and disobedient on Abraham's part for him not to obey God. He had previously had ample evidence of God's reliability. Therefore he had said to the servants, with real assurance, ". . . we will come back to you" (Genesis 22:5).

This is not to minimize his difficulty as a human father, as he stood there with his much loved son at his side. Nor is it to minimize the profound obedience he showed toward God as he followed along toward the sacrifice of that son until God stopped him. But any idea that Abraham's faith was contrary to reason overlooks all that had gone before.

Paul in Corinth

This emphasis—that faith is not contrary to reason—is presented in both the Old and the New Testaments. The entire Bible makes plain that the history it records is to be seen as real history. Consider the Apostle Paul in Greece. Paul visited Corinth and stayed there for a year and a half.

> There he met a Jew named Aquila, a native of Pontus, who had recently come from Italy with his wife Priscilla, because Claudius had ordered all the Jews to leave Rome. Paul went to see them, and because he was a tentmaker as they were, he stayed and worked with them. Every Sabbath he reasoned in the synagogue, trying to persuade Jews and Greeks. . . . So Paul stayed for a year and a half, teaching them the word of God.
>
> Acts 18:2-4, 11

We have now left far behind the great powers of Assyria and Babylon and Egypt. Alexander the Great has also come and gone. Though the Greek language is still used through the Mediterranean world, it is now Rome who rules and Claudius who is emperor. This is our setting; we are in a real moment of history and the people we read about in the Bible are as real as ourselves.[97]

There are a number of interesting things about Corinth. We learn from Acts 18:2 that while Paul was here he met a Jewish couple, Priscilla and Aquila, who had recently come from Italy, and he stayed with them and, in fact, supported himself financially by helping them in their craft of tentmaking. Priscilla and Aquila had had to leave Italy, Acts tells us, because Claudius had commanded all Jews to depart from Rome.

What we should notice is that the Book of Acts gives us here, in the midst of an account of Paul's preaching in Corinth and his trials and deliverances, a statement about the Roman Emperor Claudius and a decree of his against the Jews. We are immediately conscious that this is the same type of world-view we have become accustomed to throughout the Old Testament. This is real history again.

The Roman biographer Suetonius tells us more about that expulsion of the Jews, and the occasion can be dated from another source to the year A.D. 49. Acts tells us that the governor in Corinth while Paul was there was a man named Gallio. Now Gallio was a famous man, the brother of Seneca, who was a prominent Roman philosopher and writer and who later became tutor to the future emperor Nero. Seneca wrote about his brother Gallio, and some of his letters have been preserved down to the present. He mentioned, for example, Gallio's year of office in Corinth. This has also been attested by several fragments of an inscribed stone from Delphi (which is across the isthmus from Corinth). This gives the dates when Gallio held his governorship: the summer of A.D. 51 to the summer of A.D. 52. It also gives his title as "Proconsul of Achaia" (that is, southern Greece), which is exactly the title used of him in Acts 18:12.

Here, then, are a number of historical strands inside and outside the Bible which run together naturally and easily. Archaeology has even identified the governor's palace at Corinth, and we can see the very place where Paul is likely to have appeared before Gallio.[98]

Resurrection and History

Later we find Paul writing a letter to the church at Corinth. In it he presents what he preached and taught throughout the Roman Empire:

> Now, brothers, I want to remind you of the gospel I preached to you, which you received and on which you have taken your stand. By this gospel you are saved, if you hold firmly to the word I preached to you. Otherwise, you have believed in vain.
>
> For what I received I passed on to you as of first importance: that Christ died for our sins according to the Scriptures, that he was buried, that he was raised on the third day according to the Scriptures, and that he appeared to Peter, and then to the Twelve. After that, he appeared to more than five hundred of the brothers at the same time, most of whom are still living, though some have fallen asleep. Then

he appeared to James, then to all the apostles, and last of all he appeared to me also, as to one abnormally born.

For I am the least of the apostles and do not even deserve to be called an apostle, because I persecuted the church of God. But by the grace of God I am what I am, and his grace to me was not without effect. No, I worked harder than all of them—yet not I, but the grace of God that was with me. Whether, then, it was I or they, this is what we preach, and this is what you believed.

But if it is preached that Christ has been raised from the dead, how can some of you say that there is no resurrection of the dead? If there is no resurrection of the dead, then not even Christ has been raised. And if Christ has not been raised, our preaching is useless and so is your faith. More than that, we are then found to be false witnesses about God, for we have testified about God that he raised Christ from the dead. But he did not raise him if in fact the dead are not raised. For if the dead are not raised, then Christ has not been raised either. And if Christ has not been raised, your faith is futile; you are still in your sins. Then those who have fallen asleep in Christ are lost. If only for this life we have hope in Christ, we are to be pitied more than all men.

But Christ has indeed been raised from the dead, the firstfruits of those who have fallen asleep. For since death came through a man, the resurrection of the dead comes also through a man. For as in Adam all die, so in Christ all will be made alive. But each in his own turn: Christ, the firstfruits; then, when he comes, those who belong to him. Then the end will come, when he hands over the kingdom to God the Father after he has destroyed all dominion, authority and power.

1 Corinthians 15:1-24

In this section of his First Letter to the Corinthians, Paul asserts unequivocally that Jesus has been raised from the tomb and that we shall ourselves be raised like Him in the future. Jesus' body was placed in the tomb, but it did not remain there. Jesus rose from the dead. It was not simply a subjective experience by which the disciples were deceived. Jesus rose from the dead as a space-time fact and then He appeared to the disciples.

But we should notice particularly the other side of Paul's argument. He says, "Suppose that Jesus did *not* rise from the dead." That is not what he believes, of course, for he knows on objective grounds that Jesus has been raised; he himself had met Jesus and heard Him speak to him in the Hebrew language. And there were many other eyewitnesses to the resurrected Christ. Paul is saying, "Let us just suppose for the sake of seeing what follows that Jesus was not resurrected. What would happen then?" Paul is quick to reply: "If this did not happen, everything is finished from Christianity's point of view. We may as well 'eat and drink, for tomorrow we die.' If Christ did not rise from the dead as a historical fact, we have no Savior. Therefore we are 'still in our sins'; we shall have to face God's judgment and bear the penalty for our sin alone."

What he does *not* say is the sort of thing one hears all over the world today from churchmen who have been influenced by existential thought. They say, "Even if Jesus did *not* rise from the dead, Christianity is untouched." One such theologian said that the Resurrection took place—but if a television crew had visited the tomb that morning, it could not have recorded the event. In other words, the body of Christ was still there! But this is unthinkable to Paul. Either Christ rose from the dead as an objective fact of history, or He did not. If He did not, Christianity is finished.

When we examine the actual account of the Resurrection of Jesus in the Gospels, we find the same emphasis. The Garden Tomb in Jerusalem may not be the precise place where Jesus was buried, but certainly it must have been a tomb very like it and somewhere near that site. On the third day after the burial, Jesus rose from the dead. Here is how the Gospel of John records the events:

> Early on the first day of the week, while it was still dark, Mary of Magdala went to the tomb and saw that the stone had been removed from the entrance. . . . Then Simon Peter, who was behind him [the other disciple, John] arrived and went into the tomb. He saw the strips of linen lying there, as well as the burial cloth that had been around Jesus' head. The cloth was folded up by itself, separate from the linen.
>
> John 20:1, 6, 7

Notice that Mary Magdalene and Peter and John observed something *with normal observation*—the stone was rolled away; the linen cloth and the headcloth in which Jesus had been wrapped at His burial were still lying in the empty tomb. We read in Luke 24 that Jesus later appeared to all the disciples as they were gathered together. Evidently they were in some agitation, both from what they had witnessed at Christ's death and by the reports that Jesus had risen from the dead:

> While they were still talking about this, Jesus himself stood among them and said to them, "Peace be with you."

They were startled and frightened, thinking they saw a ghost. He said to them, "Why are you troubled, and why do doubts rise in your minds? Look at my hands and my feet. It is I myself! Touch me and see; a ghost does not have flesh and bones, as you see I have."

When he had said this, he showed them his hands and feet. And while they still did not believe it because of joy and amazement, he asked them, "Do you have anything here to eat?" They gave him a piece of broiled fish, and He took it and ate it in their presence.

Luke 24:36-43

The Resurrection of Christ is presented in the Gospels as verifiable history. It is given in the same frame of reference as applies in science—when Christ arose, He did not leave His body in the grave. The Resurrection was open to normal observation. There were the graveclothes. Jesus spoke to the disciples. He could be touched. He ate before them.

Thomas and the Resurrected Christ

Perhaps the most striking incident recorded involves Thomas:

Now Thomas (called Didymus), one of the Twelve, was not with the disciples when Jesus came. When the other disciples told him that they had seen the Lord, he declared, "Unless I see the nail marks in his hands and put my finger where the nails were, and put my hand into his side, I will not believe it."

A week later his disciples were in the house again, and Thomas was with them. Though the doors were locked, Jesus came and stood among them and said, "Peace be with you!" Then he said to Thomas, "Put your finger here; see my hands. Reach out your hand and put it into my side. Stop doubting and believe."

Thomas said to him, "My Lord and my God!"

Then Jesus told him, "Because you have seen me, you have believed; blessed are those who have not seen and yet have believed."

John 20:24-29

Just as Moses said, well over a thousand years before, "You saw, you heard," so the Gospels say, "You saw, you heard!" God acted in history, and this was observed and was able to be described in ordinary language.

If Jesus did not live, or if He did not rise from the dead, Christianity cannot continue. It cannot live on as a mere *idea,* because Christianity is about objective truth and not merely religious experiences. Both the Old Testament and the New Testament claim to be truth, in contrast to that which is not true, and this truth is rooted in history. We have only one hope, and it rests on a serious commitment to the existence of God and the reliability of His Word, the Bible, in all the areas in which it speaks.

There is truth that can be known and before which we can bow with joy—truth that in a very real way is climaxed in the physical Resurrection of Christ. If the tomb was not empty—so that a camera crew could have recorded the absence of Jesus' body at the same time that they could have filmed the linen strips and head-cloth in which His body had been wrapped—we have no hope.

Thomas should have believed on the basis of the evidence that he had from the other disciples and that was quite sufficient. Jesus rebuked him when He appeared to him and said, "Put your finger here; see my hands. Reach out your hand and put it into my side. Stop doubting and believe." After Thomas had said, "My Lord and my God!" Jesus said, "Because you have seen me, you have believed; blessed are those who have not seen and yet have believed."

Is Jesus saying by this that believing is a blind leap of ungrounded faith? Quite the opposite! Because Thomas insisted on seeing and touching Jesus in His resurrected body, we have been given in the Gospels an even clearer evidence of the Resurrection than we would otherwise have had. But Jesus is saying that Thomas should have believed without this additional evidence, because the evidence available to Thomas before was in itself sufficient. In other words, before Thomas saw and heard Jesus in this way, he was in the same position as we are today. Both he at that time and we today have the same sufficient witness of those who have seen and heard and who have had the opportunity to touch the resurrected Christ. In fact, in the light of this sufficient and sure witness we, like Thomas, are disobedient if we do not bow. We are without excuse.

After telling about Thomas, the Gospel of John then turns to another appearance of Jesus:

> Afterward Jesus appeared again to his disciples by the Sea of Tiberias. It happened this way: Simon Peter, Thomas (called Didymus), Nathanael from Cana in Galilee, the sons of Zebedee, and two other disciples were together. "I'm going out to fish," Simon Peter told them, and they said, "We'll go with you." So they went out and got into the boat, but that night they caught nothing.
>
> Early in the morning, Jesus stood on the shore, but the disciples did not realize that it was Jesus.

He called out to them, "Friends, haven't you [caught] any fish?" "No," they answered.

He said, "Throw your net on the right side of the boat and you will find some." When they did, they were unable to haul the net in because of the large number of fish.

Then the disciple whom Jesus loved said to Peter, "It is the Lord!" As soon as Simon Peter heard him say, "It is the Lord," he wrapped his outer garment around him (for he had taken it off) and jumped into the water. The other disciples followed in the boat, towing the net full of fish, for they were not far from the shore, about a hundred yards. When they landed, they saw a fire of burning coals there with fish on it, and some bread.

Jesus said to them, "Bring some of the fish you have just caught."

Simon Peter climbed aboard and dragged the net ashore. It was full of large fish, 153, but even with so many the net was not torn. Jesus said to them, "Come and have breakfast." None of the disciples dared ask him, "Who are you?" They knew it was the Lord. Jesus came, took the bread and gave it to them, and did the same with the fish. This was now the third time Jesus appeared to his disciples after he was raised from the dead.

John 21:1-14

The resurrected Jesus stood there on the beach of the Sea of Galilee. Before the disciples reached the store, He had already prepared a fire with fish cooking on it for them to eat. It was a fire that could be seen and felt; it cooked the fish, and the fish and bread could be eaten for breakfast.

When the fire died down, it left ashes on the beach; the disciples were well fed with bread and fish. There is no reason to suppose that Christ's footprints were not visible on the beach.

We must respond with Thomas: "My Lord and my God!"

CHAPTER SIX

Our Personal Response and Social Action

The relationship of Chapters 4, 5, and 6 to Chapters 1, 2, and 3 is direct and far-reaching. In the flood of the loss of humanness in our age—including the flow from abortion-on-demand to infanticide and on to euthanasia—the only thing that can stem this tide is the certainty of the absolute uniqueness and value of people. And the only thing which gives us this is the knowledge that people are made in the image of God. We have no other final protection. And the only way we know that people are made in the image of God is through the Bible and the Incarnation of Christ, which we know from the Bible.

If people are not made in the image of God, the pessimistic, realistic humanist is right: the human race is indeed an abnormal wart on the smooth face of a silent and meaningless universe. In this setting, abortion, infanticide, and euthanasia (including the killing of mentally deranged criminals, the severely handicapped, or the elderly who are an economic burden) are completely logical. Any person can be obliterated for what society at one moment thinks of as its own social or economic good. Without the Bible and without the revelation in Christ (which is only told to us in the Bible) there is nothing to stand between us and our children and the eventual acceptance of the monstrous inhumanities of the age.

In Chapters 4 and 5 we saw reasons why we can know that the Bible is truth. The existence of the universe and its form and the uniqueness of man testify to the truth of Scripture, and historical study likewise testifies to the truth of Scripture. The Bible gives us a solid and certain basis on which we can begin to act toward stemming the side of inhumanity. The solution to the inhuman drift begins, however, with each of us as individuals. It begins with you, with me—with each of us.

First Steps Toward Solving the Problem
First, Christianity must be acknowledged to be the truth. Christianity and Christ must not be accepted merely to change society and stop the drift of our culture toward the loss of humanness.

Unhappily, it is possible for people to reject the truth of Christianity and the claims of Christ and yet to hope that others will accept Christianity so that the drift of society will be halted. They think that some kind of Christian revival would be useful in order to affect human behavior and thus protect their own political and economic comfort, allowing them to keep their personal peace and affluence. Biblical Christianity and Christ will indeed stop the drift, but not if Christianity is only used for manipulation by those who think it is not true—but only useful.

In contrast to this attempted utilitarian use of Christianity, what must we do? First, we should see that, for what are good and sufficient reasons, Christianity is true. Then we should personally bow as finite creatures before our infinite-personal Creator. And then we should accept Christ as Savior to remove our personal moral guilt before God. We need that true moral guilt removed because there is the absolute of the Creator's character, and over and over again we have deliberately done what we know to be wrong.

God's promise of a solution to mankind's revolt against Him was first given in the third chapter of Genesis. This promise was expanded with increasing clarity right through the Old Testament. A Messiah, a Savior, was coming. He would take upon Himself the punishment of our sins. As Isaiah said, some 700 years before Christ came:

> We all, like sheep, have gone astray,
> each of us has turned to his own way;

and the Lord has laid on him
        the iniquity of us all.
                                    Isaiah 53:6

And we are told that the work of Christ as the dying and resurrected Lamb of God was sufficient to reconcile us to God, that we
do not have to add any "works" of our own, that we are saved by
the infinite value of what Christ has done—plus *nothing*. Salvation
is a gift that we receive with empty hands. This is what it means to
have faith in Christ, or to accept Christ as Savior.

The Lordship of Christ
But when we accept Christ as Savior, we must also acknowledge
and then act upon the fact that if He is our Savior, He is also our
Lord in *all* of life. He is Lord not just in religious things and not
just in cultural things such as art and music, but in our intellectual
lives and in business and our attitude toward the devaluation of
people's humanness in our culture. Acknowledging Christ's Lordship and placing ourselves under what is taught in the whole Bible
includes thinking and acting as citizens in relation to our government and its laws. We must know what those laws are and act
responsibly to help to change them if they do not square with the
Bible's concepts of justice and humanness. The biblical answers
have to be lived and not just thought.

We must live under the Lordship of Christ in all the areas of
life—at great cost, if need be. It is moving to think of the Christians in China, paying a great price for their loyalty to Christ, but
that does not relieve each of us from being under the Lordship of
Christ in regard to our own country.

Who is on the cutting edge here? The doctor who pays the price
of having certain hospitals closed to him because he will not perform abortions. The businessman who knows he is forfeiting advancement in his company because he will not go along with some
inhuman practice of his company. The professor of sociology who
is willing to lose his post because he will not teach sociology on
the basis of determinism. The pastor who loses his church rather
than follow the dictates of a liberal theology or a "trashy Christianity." Or the pastor who preaches the Bible, stressing that today's people are called to sacrificial action, rather than keeping his
congregation comfortable while death, spiritual and physical, is
built up year after year for their children and grandchildren. Examples could be endlessly multiplied.

Faithfulness to the Lordship of Christ means using the constitutional processes while we still have them. We live in a shrinking island of free constitutional practice. Only a small percentage of countries in the world still possess this. The Lordship of Christ means using these processes to speak and to act on the basis of the principles set forth in the Bible.

With Christ as Savior and Lord, we must do all we can to lead others to Christ. And simultaneously we must use every constitutional practice to offset the rise of authoritarian governments and the loss of humanness in our society. But there is no use in talking of offsetting the loss of humanness in society if we do not act humanly to all people about us in the contacts of our individual lives. We must practice the human alternatives set forth at the end of Chapter 3. We ourselves must act humanly, even when it is costly.

We implore those of you who are Christians to exert all your influence to fight against the increasing loss of humanness—through legislation, social action, and other means at your disposal, both privately and publicly, individually and collectively, in all areas of your lives.

Without the uniqueness and inherent dignity of each human being, no matter how old or young, sick or well, resting on the fact that each person is made in the image of God, there is no sufficient foundation to build on as we resist the loss of humanness in our generation. So we would say again to those of you who are Christians, do not allow your only base, your only hope to be able to stand—namely, the Bible—to be weakened by however subtle means. The Bible is truth in all its parts, and provides, if taken as a whole, the truth of salvation and also a base to work from in our daily lives, a base to stand on morally.

So we who are Christians must, on the one hand, fight with determination and sacrifice for the individual in society, and on the other, provide the loving care of people as individuals. Thus the world will truly feel our presence in its midst as the true salt of the earth. That salt will be a true preservative, both showing forth the beauty of care in the midst of utilitarian ugliness and also helping to remove the festering malignancy of evil that surrounds us.

The Challenge Before Us

As a result of being made in the image of God, each man and woman has a conscience. That built-in monitor, coupled with the advantages of being raised in a society that has had until recently a Judeo-Christian tradition, permits the understanding of the worth of human life to surface periodically, even subconsciously—as, for example, in the recent preoccupation with the special needs of the handicapped adult. But that memory will not last forever without the Judeo-Christian base. Recent history shows us that the conscience can be so corrupted and manipulated that today's unthinkable becomes tomorrow's thinkable with remarkable speed.

People are special and human life is sacred, whether or not we admit it. Every life is precious and worthwhile in itself—not only to us human beings but also to God. Every person is worth fighting for, regardless of whether he is young or old, sick or well, child or adult, born or unborn, or brown, red, yellow, black, or white.

If, in this last part of the twentieth century, the Christian community does not take a prolonged and vocal stand for the dignity of the individual and each person's right to life—for the right of each individual to be treated as created in the image of God, rather than as a collection of molecules with no unique value—we feel that as Christians we have failed the greatest moral test to be put before us in this century.

Future generations will look back, and many will either scoff or believe in Christ on the basis of whether we Christians of today took a sacrificial stand in our various walks of life on these overwhelmingly important issues. If we do not take a stand here and now, we certainly cannot lay any claim to being the salt of the earth in our generation. We are neither preserving moral values and the dignity of the individual nor showing compassion for our fellow human beings.

Will future generations look back and remember that—even if the twentieth century *did* end with a great surge of inhumanity—at least there was one group who stood consistently, whatever the price, for the value of the individual, thus passing on some hope to future generations? Or are we Christians going to be merely swept along with the trends—our own moral values becoming increasingly befuddled, our own apathy reflecting the apathy of the world around us, our own inactivity sharing the inertia of the masses around us, our own leadership becoming soft?

What can we do concerning these issues that we are not doing now?

On the basis of an unweakened Bible, we must teach and act, in our individual lives and as citizens, on the fact that every individual has unique value as made in the image of God. This is so from a child just conceived in the womb to the old with their last gasping breath and beyond; for death does not bring the cessation of life, but all people will spend eternity somewhere . . . with God or not, depending on their relationship to Christ as Savior.

If we ache and have compassion for humanity today in our own country and across the world, we must do all that we can to help people see the truth of Christianity and accept Christ as Savior. And we must stand against the loss of humanness in all its forms. It is God's life-changing power that is able to touch every individual, who then has a responsibility to touch the world around him with the absolutes found in the Bible. In the end we must realize that the tide of humanism, with its loss of humanness, is not merely a cultural ill, but a spiritual ill that the truth given us in the Bible and Christ alone can cure.

A CHRISTIAN MANIFESTO

Dedication

To all those who have said: "Here I stand" facing oppressive authoritarian civil and church power.

There were Peter and John who said to the Sanhedrin: "Judge for yourselves whether it is right in God's sight to obey you rather than God" (Acts 4:19).

There were the Reformers of the sixteenth century when they had to decide whether they were going to obey God or man.

And most of all, to Samuel Rutherford. He has meant much to me for many years, but especially so from the time I began working on the material for the book and films *How Should We Then Live?* At that time I understood increasingly that Samuel Rutherford's *Lex Rex* was an important trailmarker for our day. In the times I have spoken at St. Andrews University, the most outstanding thing for me was a feeling that Samuel Rutherford was not far away, that the old Rector was close by, and very contemporary!

Preface

This book is the natural outgrowth of the books which have gone before. The earliest books, *The God Who Is There, Escape from Reason,* and *He Is There and He Is Not Silent,* dealt with the Lordship of Christ over all of life—philosophy, theology and the church, art, music, literature, films, and culture in general. The books that followed dealt with and extended areas of Christ's total Lordship in all of life, and my wife Edith's books added to that extension and expansion.

With the most recent books and their accompanying film series, I, and all of us working together on these, carried the Lordship of Christ in the whole spectrum of life further. *How Should We Then Live?* dealt with the area of history and with the shifts which have come in society, government, and law. *Whatever Happened to the Human Race?,* written and filmed with Dr. C. Everett Koop, dealt with how modern, arbitrary law and modern and humanistic medicine have met at the crucial point of human life.

That led to the demand of the next legocal step: What is the Christian's relationship to government, law, and civil disobedience?

At that point, Jerry Nims, who with his family had come to

417

study at L'Abri, began to ask penetrating questions concerning these things. We had long talks and he urged me to put my answers into written form. Without that impetus there would have been no book.

Then Franky Schaeffer V entered and put together the basic publishing package as well as providing ideas and concepts in long times of talking and adding to the early draft of a possible text.

Duriing this same period Franky, Jim Buchfuehrer, Edith, and I had been working on a new film series, *Reclaiming the World* (Franky Schaeffer V Productions). As Franky, Dr. Jeremy Jackson, Edith, and I discussed the pressing questions of the day before the camera, ideas about the Christian's relationship to government and law (among many other subjects) were sharpened and focused.

Then John Whitehead, an attorney-at-law, gave certain invaluable suggestions and ideas for which I am deeply appreciative.

Finally, the skeleton of the book emerged on the basis of a talk I gave at a plenary session of the Christian Legal Society Conference in South Bend on April 24, 1981. The discussion period following the lecture with the attending lawyers stirred my thinking further. Since the talk I have read many legal briefs and records of specific cases. The talk I gave at the Conference is enlarged into the present form and includes all I have been reading and thinking about in the area for many years, the material I have been especially gathering over the last year, and the input I have spoken of above.

The book is written not as a theoretical exercise but as a *manifesto*.

For additional reading, do pursue the books and films mentioned in the text. They are listed at the end of this book. A film entitled *The Second American Revolution*, being made by Franky Schaeffer V Productions, will be a special help.

Of course, there are many helpful books, but I would especially suggest these:

The Second American Revolution by John W. Whitehead documents in detail the root causes of the humanist dominance in the West while focusing on the emergence of the judicial and governmental authoritarian elite in the United States. It also discusses Christian resistance in light of unbiblical state actions.

No Other Foundation by Jeremy Jackson offers a solid study of church history which is not a series of dry facts but which relates past history to lessons to be learned for the present problems facing the church.

Addicted to Mediocrity by Franky Schaeffer V speaks practically concerning the truncated view of culture which a false and unbiblical pietism has caused.

These last two books, and this volume as well, are published by Crossway Books. We appreciate Lane Dennis at Crossway, who has worked closely with us on format and design to produce books not only of beauty, but books that deal with the hard areas where Christians will or will not confront today's increasingly broken and inhuman world.

And I do want to say thank you to my wife, Edith, for her sensitivity concerning the many difficult balances involved in this present book; to Udo Middelmann for his positive criticism; to Jeremy Jackson for help concerning historical details; and to Jim and Gail Ingram, without whose help I never could have made the publisher's deadline.

Francis A. Schaeffer
Switzerland, 1981

The Communist Manifesto 1848
Humanist Manifesto I 1933
Humanist Manifesto II 1973

CHAPTER ONE

The Abolition of Truth and Morality

The basic problem of the Christians in this country in the last eighty years or so, in regard to society and in regard to government, is that they have seen things in bits and pieces instead of totals.

They have very gradually become disturbed over permissiveness, pornography, the public schools, the breakdown of the family, and finally abortion. But they have not seen this as a totality—each thing being a part, a symptom, of a much larger problem. They have failed to see that all of this has come about due to a shift in world view—that is, through a fundamental change in the overall way people think and view the world and life as a whole. This shift has been *away from* a world view that was at least vaguely Christian in people's memory (even if they were not individually Christian) *toward* something completely different— toward a world view based upon the idea that the final reality is impersonal matter or energy shaped into its present form by impersonal chance. They have not seen that this world view has taken the place of the one that had previously dominated Northern European culture, including the United States, which was at least Christian in memory, even if the individuals were not individually Christian.

These two world views stand as totals in complete antithesis to each other in content and also in their natural results—including sociological and governmental results, and specifically including law.

It is not that these two world views are different only in how they understand the nature of reality and existence. They also inevitably produce totally different results. The operative word here is *inevitably*. It is not just that they happen to bring forth different results, but it is absolutely *inevitable* that they will bring forth different results.

Why have the Christians been so slow to understand this? There are various reasons but the central one is a defective view of Christianity. This has its roots in the Pietist movement under the leadership of P. J. Spener in the seventeenth century. Pietism began as a healthy protest against formalism and a too abstract Christianity. But it had a deficient, "platonic" spirituality. It was platonic in the sense that Pietism made a sharp division between the "spiritual" and the "material" world—giving little, or no, importance to the "material" world. The totality of human existence was not afforded a proper place. In particular it neglected the intellectual dimension of Christianity.

Christianity and spirituality were shut up to a small, isolated part of life. The totality of reality was ignored by the pietistic thinking. Let me quickly say that in one sense Christians should be pietists in that Christianity is not just a set of doctrines, even the right doctrines. *Every* doctrine is in some way to have an effect upon our lives. But the poor side of Pietism and its resulting platonic outlook has really been a tragedy not only in many people's individual lives, but in our total culture.

True spirituality covers all of reality. There are things the Bible tells us as absolutes which are sinful—which do not conform to the character of God. But aside from these the Lordship of Christ covers *all* of life and *all* of life equally. It is not only that true spirituality covers all of life, but it covers all parts of the spectrum of life equally. In this sense there is nothing concerning reality that is not spiritual.

Related to this, it seems to me, is the fact that many Christians do not mean what I mean when I say Christianity is true, or Truth. They are Christians and they believe in, let us say, the truth of creation, the truth of the virgin birth, the truth of Christ's miracles, Christ's substitutionary death, and His coming again. But they stop there with these and other individual truths.

When I say Christianity is true I mean it is true to total reality—the total of what is, beginning with the central reality, the objective existence of the personal-infinite God. Christianity is not just a series of truths but *Truth*—Truth about all of reality. And the holding to that Truth intellectually—and then in some poor way living upon that Truth, the Truth of what is—brings forth not only certain personal results, but also governmental and legal results.

Now let's go over to the other side—to those who hold the materialistic final reality concept. They saw the complete and total difference between the two positions more quickly than Christians. There were the Huxleys, George Bernard Shaw (1856-1950), and many others who understood a long time ago that there are two total concepts of reality and that it was one total reality against the other and not just a set of isolated and separated differences. The *Humanist Manifesto I*,[1] published in 1933, showed with crystal clarity their comprehension of the totality of what is involved. It was to our shame that Julian (1887-1975) and Aldous Huxley (1894-1963), and the others like them, understood much earlier than Christians that these two world views are two total concepts of reality standing in antithesis to each other. We should be utterly ashamed that this is the fact.

They understood not only that there were two totally different concepts but that they would bring forth two totally different conclusions, both for individuals and for society. What we must understand is that the two world views really do bring forth with inevitable certainty not only personal differences, but also total differences in regard to society, government, and law.

There is no way to mix these two total world views. They are separate entities that cannot be synthesized. Yet we must say that liberal theology, the very essence of it from its beginning, is an attempt to mix the two. Liberal theology tried to bring forth a mixture soon after the Enlightenment and has tried to synthesize these two views right up to our own day. But in each case when the chips are down these liberal theologians have always come down, as naturally as a ship coming into home port, on the side of the nonreligious humanist. They do this with certainty because what their liberal theology really is is humanism expressed in theological terms instead of philosophic or other terms.

An example of this coming down naturally on the side of the nonreligious humanists is the article by Charles Hartshorne in the January 21, 1981, issue of *The Christian Century*, pages 42-45. Its title is, "Concerning Abortion, an Attempt at a Rational View." He begins by equating the fact that the human fetus is alive with the fact that mosquitoes and bacteria are also alive. That is, he begins by assuming that human life is not unique. He then continues by saying that *even after the baby is born* it is not fully human until its social relations develop (though he says the infant does have some primitive social relations an unborn fetus does not have). His conclusion is, "Nevertheless, I have little sympathy with the idea that infanticide is just another form of murder. Persons who are already functionally persons in the full sense have more important rights even than infants." He then, logically, takes the next step: "Does this distinction apply to the killing of a hopelessly senile person or one in a permanent coma? For me it does." No atheistic humanist could say it with greater clarity. It is significant at this point to note that many of the denominations controlled by liberal theology have come out, publicly and strongly, in favor of abortion.

Dr. Martin E. Marty is one of the respected, theologically liberal spokesmen. He is an associate editor of *The Christian Century* and Fairfax M. Cone distinguished service professor at the University of Chicago divinity school. He is often quoted in the secular press as the spokesman for "mainstream" Christianity. In a *Christian Century* article in the January 7-14, 1981, issue (pages 13-17 with an addition on page 31), he has an article entitled: "Dear Republicans: A Letter on Humanisms." In it he brilliantly confuses the terms "being human," humanism, the humanities and being "in love with humanity." Why does he do this? As a historian he knows the distinctions of those words, but when one is done with these pages the poor reader who knows no better is left with the eradication of the total distinction between the Christian position and the humanist one. I admire the cleverness of the article, but I regret that in it Dr. Marty has come down on the nonreligious humanist side, by confusing the issues so totally.

It would be well at this point to stress that we should not confuse the very different things which Dr. Marty did confuse. *Humanitarianism* is being kind and helpful to people, treating people humanly. The *humanities* are the studies of literature, art, music, etc.—those things which are the products of human creativity. *Humanism* is the placing of Man at the center of all things and making him the measure of all things.

Thus, Christians should be the most humanitarian of all people.

And Christians certainly should be interested in the humanities as the product of human creativity, made possible because people are uniquely made in the image of the great Creator. In this sense of being interested in the humanities it would be proper to speak of a Christian humanist. This is especially so in the past usage of that term. This would then mean that such a Christian is interested (as we all should be) in the product of people's creativity. In this sense, for example, Calvin could be called a Christian humanist because he knew the works of the Roman writer Seneca so very well.[2] John Milton and many other Christian poets could also be so called because of their knowledge not only of their own day but also of antiquity.

But in contrast to being humanitarian and being interested in the humanities Christians should be inalterably opposed to the false and destructive humanism, which is false to the Bible and equally false to what Man is.

Along with this we must keep distinct the "humanist world view" of which we have been speaking and such a thing as the "Humanist Society," which produced the *Humanist Manifestos I and II* (1933 and 1973). The Humanist Society is made up of a relatively small group of people (some of whom, however, have been influential—John Dewey, Sir Julian Huxley, Jacques Monod, B. F. Skinner, etc.). By way of contrast, the humanist world view includes many thousands of adherents and today controls the consensus in society, much of the media, much of what is taught in our schools, and much of the arbitrary law being produced by the various departments of government.

The term humanism used in this wider, more prevalent way means Man beginning from himself, with no knowledge except what he himself can discover and no standards outside of himself. In this view Man is the measure of all things as the Enlightenment expressed it.

Nowhere have the divergent results of the two total concepts of reality, the Judeo-Christian and the humanist world view, been more open to observation than in government and law.

We of Northern Europe (and we must remember that the United States, Canada, Australia, New Zealand and so on are extensions of Northern Europe) take our *form-freedom balance* in government for granted as though it were natural. There is form in acknowledging the obligations in society, and there is freedom in acknowledging the rights of the individual. We have form, we have freedom; there is freedom, there is form. There is a balance here which we have come to take as natural in the world. It is not natural in the world. We are utterly foolish if we look at the long span of history and read the daily newspapers giving today's history and do not understand that the form-freedom balance in government which we have had in Northern Europe since the Reformation and in the countries extended from it is unique in the world, past and present.

That is not to say that no one wrestled with these questions before the Reformation nor that no one produced anything worthwhile. One can think, for example, of the Conciliar Movement in the late medieval church and the early medieval parliaments.[3] Especially one must consider the ancient English Common Law. And in relation to that Common Law (and all English Law) there is Henry De Bracton. I will mention more about him in a moment.

Those who hold the material-energy, chance concept of reality, whether they are Marxist or non-Marxist, not only do not know the truth of the final reality, God, they do not know who Man is. Their concept of Man is what Man is not, just as their concept of the final reality is what final reality is not. Since their concept of Man is mistaken, their concept of society and of law is mistaken, and they have no sufficient base for either society or law.

They have reduced Man to even less than his natural finiteness by seeing him only as a complex arrangement of molecules, made complex by blind chance. Instead of seeing him as something great who is significant even in his sinning, they see Man in his essence only as an intrinsically competitive animal, that has no other basic operating principle than natural selection brought about by the strongest, the fittest, ending on top. And they see Man as acting in this way both individually and collectively as society.

Even on the basis of Man's finiteness having people swear in court *in the name of humanity,* as some have advocated, saying something like, "We pledge our honor before all mankind,"[4] would be insufficient enough. But reduced to the materialistic view of Man, it is even less. Although many nice words may be used, in reality law constituted on this basis can only mean brute force.

In this setting Jeremy Bentham's (1748-1842) Utilitarianism can be and must be all that law means. And this must inevitably lead to the conclusion of Oliver Wendell Holmes, Jr. (1841-1935): "The life of the law has not been logic: it has been experience."[5] That is, there is *no* basis for law except Man's limited, finite experience. And especially with the Darwinian, survival-of-the-fittest concept of Man (which Holmes held) that must, and will, lead to Holmes' final conclusion: law is "the majority vote of that nation that could lick all others."[6]

The problem always was, and is, What is an adequate base for law? What is adequate so that the human aspiration for freedom can exist without anarchy, and yet provides a form that will not become arbitrary tyranny?

In contrast to the materialistic concept, Man in reality is made in the image of God and has real humanness. This humanness has produced varying degrees of success in government, bringing forth governments that were more than only the dominance of brute force.

And those in the stream of the Judeo-Christian world view have had something more. The influence of the Judeo-Christian world view can be perhaps most readily observed in Henry De Bracton's influence on British Law. An English judge living in the thirteenth century, he wrote *De Legibus et Consuetudinibus* (c. 1250).

Bracton, in the stream of the Judeo-Christian world view, said:

> And that he [the King] ought to be under the law appears clearly in the analogy of Jesus Christ, whose vice-regent on earth he is, for though many ways were open to Him for His ineffable redemption of the human race, the true mercy of God chose this most powerful way to destroy the devil's work, he would not use the power of force but the reason of justice.[7],[8]

In other words, God in His sheer power could have crushed Satan in his revolt by the use of that sufficient power. But because of God's character, justice came before the use of power alone. Therefore Christ died that justice, rooted in what God is, would be the solution. Bracton codified this: Christ's example, because of who He is, is our standard, our rule, our measure. Therefore power is not first, but justice is first in society and law. The prince may have the power to control and to rule, but he does not have the right to do so without justice. This was the basis of English Common Law. The Magna Charta (1215) was written within thirty-five years (or less) of Bracton's *De Legibus* and in the midst of the same universal thinking in England at that time.

The Reformation (300 years after Bracton) refined and clarified this further. It got rid of the encrustations that had been added to the Judeo-Christian world view and clarified the point of authority—with authority resting in the Scripture rather than church *and* Scripture, or state *and* Scripture. This not only had meaning in regard to doctrine but clarified the base for law.

That base was God's written Law, back through the New Testament to Moses' written Law; and the content and authority of that written Law is rooted back to Him who is the final reality. Thus, neither church nor state were equal to, let alone above, that Law. The base for law is not divided, and no one has the right to place anything, including king, state or church, above the content of God's Law.

What the Reformation did was to return most clearly and consistently to the origins, to the final reality, God; but equally to the reality of Man—not only Man's personal needs (such as salvation), but also Man's social needs.

What we have had for 400 years, produced from this clarity, is unique in contrast to the situation that has existed in the world in forms of government. Some of you have been taught that the Greek city states had our concepts in government. It simply is not true.[9] All one has to do is read Plato's *Republic* to have this come across with tremendous force.

When the men of our State Department, especially after World War II, went all over the world trying to implant our form-freedom balance in government downward on cultures whose philosophy and religion would never have produced it, it has, in almost every case, ended in some form of totalitarianism or authoritarianism.

The humanists push for "freedom," but having no Christian consensus to contain it, that "freedom" leads to chaos or to slavery under the state (or under an elite). Humanism, with its lack of *any* final base for values or law, always leads to chaos. It then naturally leads to some form of authoritarianism to control the chaos. Having produced the sickness, humanism gives more of the same kind of medicine for a cure. With its mistaken concept of final reality, it has no intrinsic reason to be interested in the individual, the human being. Its natural interest is the two collectives: the state and society.

CHAPTER TWO

Foundations for Faith and Freedom

The Founding Fathers of the United States (in varying degrees) understood very well the relationship between one's world view and government. John Witherspoon (1723-1794) has always been important to me personally, and he is even more so since I have read just recently a biography of him by David Walker Woods.[1] John Witherspoon, a Presbyterian minister and president of what is now Princeton University, was the only pastor to sign the Declaration of Independence. He was a very important man during the founding of the country. He linked the Christian thinking represented by the College of New Jersey (now Princeton University) with the work he did both on the Declaration of Independence and on countless very important committees in the founding of the country. This linkage of Christian thinking and the concepts of government were not incidental but fundamental. John Witherspoon knew and stood consciously in the stream of Samuel Rutherford, a Scotsman who lived from 1600-1661 and who wrote *Lex Rex* in 1644. *Lex rex* means law is king—a phrase that was absolutely earthshaking. Prior to that it had been *rex lex,* the king is law. In *Lex Rex* he wrote that the law, and no one else, is king. Therefore, the heads of government are under the law, not a law unto themselves.

Jefferson, who was a deist, and others, knew they stood in the stream of John Locke (1632-1704), and while Locke had secularized *Lex Rex* he had drawn heavily from it. These men really knew what they were doing. We are not reading back into history what was not there. We cannot say too strongly that they really understood the basis of the government which they were founding. Think of this great flaming phrase: "certain inalienable rights." Who gives the rights? The state? Then they are not inalienable because the state can change them and take them away. Where do the rights come from? They understood that they were founding the country upon the concept that goes back into the Judeo-Christian thinking that there is Someone there who gave the inalienable rights. Another phrase also stood there: "In God we trust." With this there is no confusion of what they were talking about. They publicly recognized that law could be king because there was a Law Giver, a Person to give the inalienable rights.

Most people do not realize that there was a paid chaplain in Congress even before the Revolutionary War ended. Also we find that prior to the founding of the national congress all the early provincial congresses in all thirteen colonies always opened with prayer. And from the very beginning, prayer opened the national congress. These men truly understood what they were doing. They knew they were building on the Supreme Being who was the Creator, the final reality. And they knew that without that foundation everything in the Declaration of Independence and all that followed would be sheer unadulterated nonsense. These were brilliant men who understood exactly what was involved.

As soon as the war was over they called the first Thanksgiving Day. Do you realize that the first Thanksgiving Day to thank God in this country was called immediately by the Congress at the end of the war? Witherspoon's sermon on that day shows their perspective: "A republic once equally poised must either preserve its virtue or lose its liberty." Don't you wish that everybody in America would recite that, and truly understand it, every morning? "A republic once equally poised must either preserve its virtue or lose its liberty." Earlier in a speech Witherspoon had stressed: "He is the best friend of American liberty who is most sincere and active in promoting pure and undefiled religion." And for Witherspoon, and the cultural consensus of that day, that meant Christianity as it had come to them through the Reformation. This was the consensus which then gave religious freedom to all—including the "free thinkers" of that day and the humanists of our day.

This concept was the same as William Penn (1644-1718) had expressed earlier: "If we are not governed by God, then we will be ruled by tyrants." This consensus was as natural as breathing in the United States at that time. We must not forget that many of those who came to America from Europe came for religious purposes. As they arrived, most of them established their own individual civil governments based upon the Bible. It is, therefore, totally foreign to the basic nature of America at the time of the writing of the Constitution to argue a separation doctrine that implies a secular state.

When the First Amendment was passed it only had two purposes. The first purpose was that there would be no established, national church for the united thirteen states. To say it another way: there would be no "Church of the United States." James Madison (1751-1836) clearly articulated this concept of separation when explaining the First Amendment's protection of religious liberty. He said that the First Amendment to the Constitution was prompted because "the people feared one sect might obtain a preeminence, or two combine together, and establish a religion to which they would compel others to conform."[2]

Nevertheless, a number of the individual states had state churches, and even that was not considered in conflict with the First Amendment. "At the outbreak of the American Revolution, nine of the thirteen colonies had conferred special benefits upon one church to the exclusion of others."[3] "In all but one of the thirteen states, the states taxed the people to support the preaching of the gospel and to build churches."[4] "It was not until 1798 that the Virginia legislature repealed all its laws supporting churches."[5] "In Massachusetts the Massachusetts Constitution was not amended until 1853 to eliminate the tax-supported church provosions."[6]

The second purpose of the First Amendment was the very opposite from what is being made of it today. It states expressly that government should not impede or interfere with the free practice of religion.

Those were the two purposes of the First Amendment as it was written.

As Justice Douglas wrote for the majority of the Supreme Court in the United States v. Ballard case in 1944:

The First Amendment has a dual aspect. It not only "forestalls compulsion by law of the acceptance of any creed or the practice of any form of worship" but also "safeguards the free exercise of the chosen form of religion."

Today the separation of church and state in America is used to silence the church. When Christians speak out on issues, the hue and cry from the humanist state and media is that Christians, and all religions, are prohibited from speaking since there is a separation of church and state. The way the concept is used today is totally reversed from the original intent. It is not rooted in history. The modern concept of separation is an argument for a total separation of religion from the state. The consequence of the acceptance of this doctrine leads to the removal of religion as an influence in civil government. This fact is well illustrated by John W. Whitehead in his book *The Second American Revolution*.[7] It is used today as a false political dictum in order to restrict the influence of Christian ideas. As Franky Schaeffer V says in the *Plan for Action*:

> It has been convenient and expedient for the secular humanist, the materialist, the so-called liberal, the feminist, the genetic engineer, the bureaucrat, the Supreme Court Justice, to use this arbitrary division between church and state as a ready excuse. It is used, as an easily identifiable rallying point, to subdue the opinions of that vast body of citizens who represent those with religious convictions.[8]

To have suggested the state separated from religion and religious influence would have amazed the Founding Fathers. The French Revolution that took place shortly afterwards, with its continuing excesses and final failure leading quickly to Napoleon and an authoritative rule, only emphasized the difference between the base upon which the United States was founded and the base upon which the French Revolution was founded. History is clear and the men of that day understood it. Terry Eastland said in *Commentary* magazine:

> As a matter of historical fact, the Founding Fathers believed that the public interest was served by the promotion of religion. The Northwest Ordinance of 1787, which set aside federal property in the territory for schools and which was passed again by Congress in 1789, is instructive. "Religion, morality, and knowledge being necessary to good government and the happiness of mankind," read the act, "schools and the means of learning shall forever be encouraged." . . .

In 1811 the New York state court upheld an indictment for blasphemous utterances against Christ, and in its ruling, given by Chief Justice Kent, the court said, "We are Christian people, and the morality of the country is deeply engrafted upon Christianity." Fifty years later this same court said that "Christianity may be conceded to be the established religion."

The Pennsylvania state court also affirmed the conviction of a man on charges of blasphemy, here against the Holy Scriptures. The Court said: "Christianity, general Christianity is, and always has been, a part of the common law of Pennsylvania . . . not Christianity founded on any particular religious tenets; nor Christianity with an established church and tithes and spiritual courts; but Christianity with liberty of conscience to all men." . . .

The establishment of Protestant Christianity was one not only of law but also, and far more importantly, of culture. Protestant Christianity supplied the nation with its "system of values"—to use the modern phrase—and would do so until the 1920s when the cake of Protestant custom seemed most noticeably to begin crumbling.[9]

As we continue to examine the question of law in relation to the founding of the country, we next encounter Sir William Blackstone (1723-1780). William Blackstone was an English jurist who in the 1760s wrote a very famous work called *Commentaries on the Law of England*. By the time the Declaration of Independence was signed, there were probably more copies of his *Commentaries* in American than in Britain. His *Commentaries* shaped the perspective of American law at that time, and when you read them it is very clear exactly upon what that law was based.

To William Blackstone there were only two foundations for law, nature and revelation, and he stated clearly that he was speaking of the "holy Scripture." That was William Blackstone. And up to the recent past not to have been a master of William Blackstone's *Commentaries* would have meant that you would not have graduated from law school.

There were other well-known lawyers who spelled these things out with total clarity. Joseph Story in his 1829 inaugural address as Dane Professor of Law at Harvard University said, "There never has been a period in which Common Law did not recognize Christianity as laying at its foundation."[10]

Concerning John Adams (1735-1826) Terry Eastland says:

. . . most people agreed that our law was rooted, as John Adams had said, in a common moral and religious tradition, one that stretched back to the time Moses went up on Mount Sinai. Similarly almost everyone agreed that our liberties were God-given and should be exercised responsibly. There was a distinction between liberty and license.[11]

What we find then as we look back is that the men who founded the United States of America really understood that upon which they were building their concepts of law and the concepts of government. And until the takeover of our government and law by this other entity, the materialistic, humanistic, chance world view, these things remained the base of government and law.

CHAPTER THREE

The Destruction of Faith and Freedom

And now it is all gone!

In most law schools today almost no one studies William Blackstone unless he or she is taking a course in the history of law. We live in a secularized society and in secularized, sociological law. By sociological law we mean law that has no fixed base but law in which a group of people decides what is sociologically good for society at the given moment; and what they arbitrarily decide becomes law. Oliver Wendell Holmes (1841-1935) made totally clear that this was his position.[1] Frederick Moore Vinson (1890-1953), former Chief Justice of the United States Supreme Court, said, "Nothing is more certain in modern society than the principle that there are no absolutes."[2] Those who hold this position themselves call it sociological law.

As the new sociological law has moved away from the original base of the Creator giving the "inalienable rights," etc., it has been natural that this sociological law has then also moved away from the Constitution. William Bentley Ball,[3] in his paper entitled "Religious Liberty: The Constitutional Frontier," says:

> I propose that secularism militates against religious liberty, and indeed against personal freedoms generally, for two reasons: first, the

437

familiar fact that secularism does not recognize the existence of the "higher law"; second, because, that being so, secularism tends toward decisions based on the pragmatic public policy of the moment and inevitably tends to resist the submitting of those policies to the "higher" criteria of a constitution.

This moving away from the Constitution is not only by court rulings, for example the First Amendment rulings, which are the very reversal of the original purpose of the First Amendment (see pp. 433, 434), but in other ways as well. Quoting again from the same paper by William Bentley Ball:

Our problem consists also, as perhaps this paper has well enough indicated, of *more general* constitutional concepts. Let me refer to but two: the unconstitutional delegation of legislative power and *ultra vires*. The first is where the legislature hands over its powers to agents through the conferral of regulatory power unaccompanied by strict standards. The second is where the agents make up powers on their own—assume powers not given them by the legislature. Under the first, the government of laws largely disappears and the government of men largely replaces it. Under the second, agents' personal "homemade" law replaces the law of the elected representatives of the people.

Naturally, this shift from the Judeo-Christian basis for law and the shift away from the restraints of the Constitution automatically militates against religious liberty. Mr. Ball closes his paper:

Fundamentally, in relation to personal liberty, the Constitution was aimed at restraint of the State. Today, in case after case relating to religious liberty, we encounter the bizarre presumption that it is the other way around; that the State is justified in whatever action, and that religion bears a great burden of proof to overcome that presumption.

It is our job, as Christian lawyers, to destroy that presumption at every turn.

As lawyers discuss the changes in law in the United States, often they speak of the influence of the laws passed in relationship to the Mormons and to the laws involved in the reentrance of the southern states into the national government after the Civil War. These indeed must be considered. But they were not the reason for the drastic change in law in our country. This reason was the takeover by the totally other world view which would never have given the form and freedom in government we have had in Northern

Europe (including the United States). That is the central factor in the change.

It is parallel to the difference between modern science beginning with Copernicus and Galileo and the materialistic science which took over in the last century. Materialistic thought would never have produced modern science. Modern science was produced on the Christian base. That is, because an intelligent Creator had created the universe we can in some measure understand the universe and there is, therefore, a reason for observation and experimentation to be optimistically pursued.

Then there was a shift into materialistic science *based on a philosophic change* to the materialistic concept of final reality. This shift was based on no addition to the facts known. It was a choice, in faith, to see things that way.[4] No clearer expression of this could be given than Carl Sagan's arrogant statement on public television—made without any scientific proof for the statement—to 140 million viewers: "The cosmos is all that is or ever was or ever will be." He opened the series, *Cosmos,* with this essentially creedal declaration and went on to build every subsequent conclusion upon it.

There is exactly the same parallel in law. The materialistic-energy, chance concept of final reality never would have produced the form and freedom in government we have in this country and in other Reformation countries. But now it has arbitrarily and arrogantly supplanted the historic Judeo-Christian consensus that provided the base for form and freedom in government. The Judeo-Christian consensus gave greater freedoms than the world has ever known, but it also contained the freedoms so that they did not pound society to pieces. The materialistic concept of reality would not have produced the form-freedom balance, and now that it has taken over it cannot maintain the balance. It has destroyed it.

Will Durant and his wife Ariel together wrote *The Story of Civilization.* The Durants received the 1976 Humanist Pioneer Award. In *The Humanist* magazine of February 1977, Will Durant summed up the humanist problem with regard to personal ethics and social order: "Moreover, we shall find it no easy task to mold a natural ethic strong enough to maintain moral restraint and social order without the support of supernatural consolations, hopes, and fears."

Poor Will Durant! It is not just difficult, it is impossible. He should have remembered the quotation he and Ariel Durant gave from the agnostic Renan in their book *The Lessons of History*. According to the Durants, Renan said in 1866: "If Rationalism wishes to govern the world without regard to the religious needs of the soul, the experience of the French Revolution is there to teach us the consequences of such a blunder."[5] And the Durants themselves say in the same context: "There is no significant example in history, before our time, of a society successfully maintaining moral life without the aid of religion."[6]

Along with the decline of the Judeo-Christian consensus we have come to a new definition and connotation of "pluralism." Until recently it meant that the Christianity flowing from the Reformation is not now as dominant in the country and in society as it was in the early days of the nation. After about 1848 the great influx of immigrants to the United States meant a sharp increase in viewpoints not shaped by Reformation Christianity. This, of course, is the situation which exists today. Thus as we stand for religious freedom today, we need to realize that this must include a general religious freedom from the control of the state for all religion. It will not mean just freedom for those who are Christians. It is then up to Christians to show that Christianity is the Truth of total reality in the open marketplace of freedom.

This greater mixture in the United States, however, is now used as an excuse for the new meaning and connotation of pluralism. It now is used to mean that all types of situations are spread out before us, and that it really is up to each individual to grab one or the other on the way past, according to the whim of personal preference. What you take is only a matter of personal choice, with one choice as valid as another. Pluralism has come to mean that everything is acceptable. This new concept of pluralism suddenly is everywhere. There is no right or wrong; it is just a matter of your personal preference. On a recent *Sixty Minutes* program on television, for example, the questions of euthanasia of the old and the growing of marijuana as California's largest paying crop were presented this way. One choice is as valid as another. It is just a matter of personal preference. This new definition and connotation of pluralism is presented in many forms, not only in personal ethics, but in society's ethics and in the choices concerning law.

Now I have a question. In these shifts that have come in law, where were the Christian lawyers during the crucial shift from forty years ago to just a few years ago? These shifts have all come, or have mostly come, in the last eighty years, and the great, titanic shifts have come in the last forty years. Within our lifetime the great shifts in law have taken place. Now that this has happened we can say, surely the Christian lawyers should have seen the change taking place and stood on the wall and blown the trumpets loud and clear. A nonlawyer like myself has a right to feel somewhat let down because the Christian lawyers did not blow the trumpets clearly between, let us say, 1940 and 1970.

When I wrote *How Should We Then Live?* from 1974 to 1976 I worked out of a knowledge of secular philosophy. I moved from the results in secular philosophy, to the results in liberal theology, to the results in the arts, and then I turned to the courts, and especially the Supreme Court. I read Oliver Wendell Holmes and others, and I must say, I was totally appalled by what I read. It was an exact parallel to what I had already known so well from my years of study in philosophy, theology, and the other disciplines.

In the book and film series *How Should We Then Live?* I used the Supreme Court abortion case as the clearest illustration of arbitrary sociological law. But it was only the clearest illustration. The law is shot through with this kind of ruling. It is similar to choosing Fletcher's situational ethics and pointing to it as the clearest illustration of how our society now functions with no fixed ethics. This is only the clearest illustration, because in many ways our society functions on unfixed, situational ethics.

The abortion case in law is exactly the same. It is only the clearest case. Law in this country has become situational law, using the term Fletcher used for his ethics. That is, a small group of people decide arbitrarily what, from their viewpoint, is for the good of society at that precise moment and they make it law, binding the whole society by their personal arbitrary decisions.

But of course! What would we expect? These things are the natural, inevitable results of the material-energy, humanistic concept of the final basic reality. From the material-energy, chance concept of final reality, final reality is, and must be by its nature, silent as to values, principles, or any basis for law. There is no way to ascertain "the ought" from "the is."[7] Not only should we have known what this would have produced, but on the basis of this viewpoint of reality, we should have recognized that *there are no other conclusions that this view could produce*. It is a natural result of really believing that the basic reality of all things is merely material-energy, shaped into its present form by impersonal chance.

No, we must say that the Christians in the legal profession did not ring the bell, and we are indeed very, very far down the road toward a totally humanistic culture. At this moment we are in a humanistic culture, but we are happily not in a totally humanistic culture. But what we must realize is that the drift has been all in this direction. If it is not turned around we will move very rapidly into a *totally* humanistic culture.

The law, and especially the courts, is *the vehicle to force* this total humanistic way of thinking upon the entire population. This is what has happened. The abortion law is a perfect example. The Supreme Court abortion ruling invalidated abortion laws in all fifty states, even though it seems clear that in 1973 the majority of Americans were against abortion. It did not matter. The Supreme Court arbitrarily ruled that abortion was legal, and overnight they overthrew the state laws and forced onto American thinking not only that abortion was legal, but that it was ethical. They, as an elite, thus forced their will on the majority, even though their ruling was arbitrary both legally and medically. Thus law and the courts became the vehicle for forcing a totally secular concept on the population.

But I would say for the comfort of the Christian lawyers, it was not only the lawyers that did not blow the trumpet. Certainly the Bible-believing theologians were not very good at blowing trumpets either. In 1893 Dr. Charles A. Briggs had been put out of the Presbyterian ministry for teaching liberal theology. I would repeat that liberal theology is only humanism in theological terms. Then after Dr. Briggs was put out of the Presbyterian ministry there largely followed a tremendously great silence. Until the twenties and the thirties, few, if any, among the Bible-believing theologians blew a loud horn. By that time it was too late as most of the old line denominations had come under the dominance of liberal theology at the two power centers of the bureaucracies and the seminaries. By then voices were raised. But with rare exceptions, by that time it was too late. From then on, the liberal theologians would increasingly side with the secular humanists in matters of life style and the rulings of sociological law.

And those Bible-believing theologians who did see the theological danger seemed totally blind to what was happening in law and in the total culture. Thus the theologians did no better in seeing the shift from one world view to a totally different world view. Nor did Christian educators do any better either. The failed responsibility covers a wide swath. Christian educators, Christian theologians, Christian lawyers—none of them blew loud trumpets until we were a long, long way down the road toward a humanistically based culture.

But, while this may spread the problem of responsibility around, that does not help us today—except to realize that if we are going to do better we must stop being experts in only seeing these things in bits and pieces. We have to understand that it is one total entity opposed to the other total entity. It concerns truth in regard to final and total reality—not just religious reality, but total reality. And our view of final reality—whether it is material-energy, shaped by impersonal chance, or the living God and Creator—will determine our position on every crucial issue we face today. It will determine our views on the value and dignity of people, the base for the kind of life the individual and society lives, the direction law will take, and whether there will be freedom or some form of authoritarian dominance.

CHAPTER FOUR

The Humanist Religion

The humanists have openly told us their views of final reality. The *Humanist Manifesto I* (1933), page 8[1] says

> Religious humanists regard the universe as self-existing and not created.
>
> Humanism asserts that the nature of the universe depicted by modern science makes unacceptable any supernatural or cosmic guarantees of human values.

And Carl Sagan indoctrinated millions of unsuspecting viewers with this humanistic final view of reality in the public television show *Cosmos*: "The cosmos is all that is or ever was or ever will be." The humanist view has infiltrated every level of society.

If we are going to join the battle in a way that has any hope of effectiveness—with Christians truly being salt and the light in our culture and our society—then we must do battle on the entire front. We must not finally even battle on the front for freedom, and specifically not only *our* freedom. It must be on the basis of Truth. Not just religious truths, but the Truth of what the final reality is. Is it impersonal material or is it the living God?

The *Humanist Manifestos I and II* both state that humanism is a

445

religion, a faith. [*Manifesto I:* pages 3 and 7; *Manifesto II:* pages 13 and 24.] *Manifesto I,* page 9, very correctly says: "Nothing human is alien to the religious." Christians of all people should have known, taught, and acted on this. Religion touches all of thought and all of life. And these two religions, Christianity and humanism, stand over against each other as totalities.

The *Humanist Manifestos* not only say that humanism is a religion, but the Supreme Court has declared it to be a religion. The 1961 case of *Torcaso* v. *Watkins* specifically defines secular humanism as a religion equivalent to theistic and other nontheistic religions.

On page 19 the *Humanist Manifesto II* says: "It [the State] should not favor any particular religious bodies through the use of public monies. . . ." Ironically, *it is the humanist religion* which the government and courts in the United States favor over all others!

The ruling of the Supreme Court in the *Torcaso* v. *Watkins* case in 1961 is instructive in another way. It shows that within the span of twenty-eight years the Supreme Court turned radically from a Christian memory to the humanist consensus. In 1933 in the *United States* v. *MacIntosh* case about conscientious objection, Justice Hughes stated in his dissent:

> The essence of religion is belief in a relation to God involving duties superior to those arising from any human relation. . . . One cannot speak of religious liberty, with proper appreciation of its essential and historical significance, without assuming the existence of a belief in supreme allegiance to the will of God.

In 1965 in *United States* v. *Seeger,* also about conscientious objection, the Court held that the test of religious belief is a "sincere and meaningful belief which occupies in the life of its possessor a place parallel to that filled by the God of those admittedly qualifying for the exemption." This, of course, is a drastic change away from the position of 1933.

The case *Torcaso* v. *Watkins* in 1961 takes the final step. Here, theistic religions, nontheistic religions, and pure materialistic humanism as a religion are all equated. And the change was complete in twenty-eight years from 1933 to 1961.

We live in a democracy, or republic, in this country which was born out of the Judeo-Christian base. The freedom that this gives is increasingly rare in the world today. We certainly must use this freedom while we still have it. There was a poll done by a secular group a few years ago which looked across the world to determine where there were freedoms today out of the 150 or so nations. Less than twenty-five were rated as today having significant freedom. We still have it. And it is our calling to do something about it and use it in our democracy while we have it.

Most fundamentally, our culture, society, government, and law are in the condition they are in, *not because of a conspiracy, but because the church has forsaken its duty to be the salt of the culture*. It is the church's duty (as well as its privilege) to do now what it should have been doing all the time—to use the freedom we do have to *be* that salt of the culture. If the slide toward authoritarianism is to be reversed we need a committed Christian church that is dedicated to what John W. Whitehead calls "total revolution in the reformative sense."[2]

Some of us may perhaps have some questions about the Moral Majority and some of the things they have said. But I would say one thing we certainly must do is get our information about anything like the Moral Majority not from the secular media, which so largely have the same humanistic perspective as the rest of culture has today. If we are going to make judgments on any such subject we must not get our final judgments uncritically from media that see things from this perspective and see it that way honestly. Most of the media do not have to be dishonest to slide things in their own direction because they see through the spectacles of a finally relativistic set of ethical personal and social standards.

A good example of this lack of objectivity is public television. One of the public television program directors we approached in Washington, D.C., refused to watch the film *Whatever Happened to the Human Race?*, or even to consider it. As soon as she heard of the position it took concerning abortion, she made the excuse, "We can't program anything that presents only one point of view."

At that same time public television was running *Hard Choices*, a program totally slanted in favor of abortion. The Study Guide which accompanied the series *Hard Choices* speaks clearly for the total view of a materialistic final reality:

> The vast majority of people believe there is a design or force in the universe; that it works outside the ordinary mechanics of cause and effect; that it is somehow responsible for both the visible and the moral order of the world. Modern biology has undermined this

assumption. Even though it is often asserted that science is fully compatible with our Judeo-Christian ethical tradition, in fact it is not. . . .

To be sure, even in antiquity, the mechanistic view of life—that chance *was* responsible for the shape of the world—had a few adherents. But belief in overarching order was dominant; it can be seen as easily in such scientists as Newton, Harvey, and Einstein as in the theologians Augustine, Luther, and Tillich. But beginning with Darwin, biology has undermined that tradition. Darwin in effect asserted that all living organisms had been created by a combination of chance and necessity—natural selection.

In the twentieth century, this view of life has been reinforced by a whole series of discoveries. . . .

Mind is the only remaining frontier, but it would be shortsighted to doubt that it can, one day, be duplicated in the form of thinking robots or analyzed in terms of the chemistry and electricity of the brain.

The extreme mechanistic view of life, which every new discovery in biology tends to confirm, has certain implications. First, God has no role in the physical world. . . .

Second, except for the laws of probability and cause and effect, there is no organizing principle in the world, and no purpose. Thus, there are no moral or ethical laws that belong to the nature of things, no absolute guiding principles for human society. . . .

The mechanistic view of life has perhaps only one tangible implication for ethics: we should feel freer to adapt our morality to new social situations. But we are already fairly adept at that. . . . As a result, ethical choices are likely to become more difficult, not because people are less moral but because they will be unable to justify their choices with fairy tales.[3]

Here is public tax money being used not only in favor of abortion but to teach the whole view of a materialistic, mechanistic universe, shaped only by chance, with no final purpose and with morals (and law) purely a matter of social choice. The Judeo-Christian view is pushed into the category of "fairy tales."

How much this sounds like the *Humanist Manifesto II*, page 13, which said:

As in 1933 [the date of the *Humanist ManifestoI*] humanists still believe that traditional theism, especially faith in the prayer-hearing God, assumed to love and care for persons, to hear and understand their prayers, and to be able to do something about them, is an unproved and outmoded faith. Salvationism, based on mere affirmation, still appears as harmful, diverting people with false hopes of heaven hereafter. Reasonable minds look to other means for survival.

Once again we are reminded of public television's airing of *Cosmos* by Carl Sagan which teaches as dogma that the impersonal cosmos is all there is or ever was or ever will be.

In this setting we must indeed not expect objectivity from the media.

Even the most respected commentators are affected. On the eve of Walter Cronkite's retirement as anchorman on the CBS Evening News he gave an interview in Monte Carlo to Jeffrey Robinson of the *International Herald Tribune,* featured in the February 18, 1981 issue. In it, Walter Cronkite questions whether, with television, democracy is any longer a suitable political philosophy—whether we can still be sure that democracy can work. Reporting on the interview the *Tribune* observes:

> He [Cronkite] seriously suggests that under the high technology circumstances of today, there might be some questions as to whether or not democracy is a suitable political philosophy.

The article continues, quoting Cronkite directly:

> "I'm not saying that the answer should immediately come down on the side of no. I support democracy. I'm simply saying that there is a question. I think there is a hell of a lot of explaining to be done before we can be sure that democracy can work."

The media and especially television have indeed changed the *perception* of not only current events, but also of the political process. We must realize that things can easily be presented on television so that the *perception* of a thing may be quite different from fact itself. Television not only reports political happenings, it enters actively into the political process. That is, either because of bias or for a good story, television so reports the political process that it influences and becomes a crucial part of the political process itself. A good example was Walter Cronkite's part in orchestrating the Gerald Ford candidacy for Vice-President at the 1980 Republican Convention.

We must realize that the communications media function much like the unelected federal bureaucracy. They are so powerful that they act as if they were the fourth branch of government in the United States. Charles Peters, editor-in-chief of *The Washington Monthly,* in his book *How Washington Really Works,*[4] writes that the media, instead of exposing the "make believe" of the federal government, are "part of the show."

Television (and the communications media in general) thus are not only reporting news, but making it. Their ability to change our *perception* of any event raises serious questions concerning the democratic process.

The solution is not the one Cronkite gives in his interview—perhaps changing to a political philosophy different from democracy. The solution is to limit somehow television's power to use its bias in "the editorial" reporting of events,[5] and most specifically to keep it from shaping the political process.

In the midst of all this Christians must certainly not uncritically accept what they read, and especially what they see on television, as objective. This is especially the case when the subject under consideration is one we know to be different from that which their world view normally causes them to champion.

Returning to the Moral Majority, we must realize that regardless of whether we think the Moral Majority has always said the right things or whether we do not, or whether we think they have made some mistakes or whether we do not, they have certainly done one thing right: they have used the freedom we still have in the political arena to stand against the other total entity. They have carried the fact that law is king, law is above the lawmakers, and God is above the law into this area of life where it always should have been. And this is a part of true spirituality.

The Moral Majority has drawn a line between the one total view of reality and the other total view of reality and the results this brings forth in government and law. And if you personally do not like some of the details of what they have done, do it better. But you must understand that all Christians have got to do the same kind of thing or you are simply not showing the Lordship of Christ in the totality of life.

CHAPTER FIVE

Revival, Revolution, and Reform

As we turn to the evangelical leadership of this country in the last decades, unhappily, we must come to the conclusion that often it has not been much help. It has shown the mark of a platonic, overly spiritualized Christianity all too often. Spirituality to the evangelical leadership often has not included the Lordship of Christ over the whole spectrum of life. Spirituality has often been shut up to a very narrow area. And also very often, among many evangelicals, including evangelical leaders, it seems that the final end is to protect their own projects. I am not saying all, by any means, but all too often that has been the case. I am again asking the question, why have we let ourselves go so far down the road? And this is certainly one of the answers.

Now you must remember, this is a rather new phenomenon. The old revivals are spoken about so warmly by the evangelical leadership. Yet they seem to have forgotten what those revivals were. Yes, the old revivals in Great Britain, in Scandinavia, and so on, and the old revivals in this country did call, without any question and with tremendous clarity, for personal salvation. But they also called for a resulting social action. Read the history of the old revivals. Every single one of them did this, and there can be no greater example than the great revivals of John Wesley (1703-1791) and George Whitefield (1714-1770).

Concerning Wesley, Howard A. Snyder says:

> Migration to the cities had produced a new class of urban poor in Wesley's day. The Industrial Revolution was in full swing, fired by coal. When Wesley preached to the Kingswood colliers he was touching those most cruelly victimized by industrialization. Yet his response among the coal miners was phenomenal, and Wesley worked tirelessly for their spiritual and material welfare. Among other things, he opened free dispensaries, set up a kind of credit union, and established schools and orphanages. His ministry branched out to include lead miners, iron smelters, brass and copper workers, quarrymen, shipyard workers, farm laborers, prisoners and women industrial workers.
>
> To all these people—the victims of society—Wesley offered the Good News of Jesus Christ. But he did more. He formed them into close-knit fellowships where they could be shepherded and where leaders could be developed, and he worked to reform the conditions under which they lived. His efforts went beyond welfare to include creative economic alternatives. Through his pointed and prolific writings he agitated for major reforms. He was convinced that "the making an open stand against all the ungodliness and unrighteousness which overspreads our land as a flood, is one of the noblest ways of confessing Christ in the face of His enemies."[1]

The Wesley and Whitefield revivals were tremendous in calling for individual salvation, and thousands upon thousands were saved. Yet even secular historians acknowledge that it was the social results coming out of the Wesley revival that saved England from its own form of the French Revolution. If it had not been for the Wesley revival and its social results, England would almost certainly have had its own "French Revolution." We should sound the names of some of our Christian predecessors with a cry of pride and thankfulness to God: Lord Shaftesbury (1801-1855), who dared to stand for justice for the poor in the midst of the Industrial Revolution; William Wilberforce (1759-1833), who was the greatest single personal force in changing England from a slave-owning country to a country that turned away legally and totally from slavery long before the United States did. These men did not do these things incidentally, but because they saw it as a part of the Christian good news. God used those involved in the revivals to bring forth the results not only of individual salvation, but also social action.

Jeremy Rifkin, whom some of you will know as a leading counter-culture figure of the sixties, in 1980 wrote *Entropy*.[2] In this book he shows that he understands, far better than the evangelical leadership often has, that the old revivals resulted in social action. He quotes *Pollution and the Death of Man—The Christian View of Ecology*[3] at length in the chapter he calls "The Second Reformation," pointing out that there is a different possibility for a Christian answer in regard to ecology. He really understands something, though not as a Christian (for he continues in his pantheistic framework). But he really comprehends that in the days of the revivals and today there are Christian answers for social action and answers in areas such as ecology. Christianity does have answers.

Now when we come nearer to home, Wheaton College stands out as a great name in evangelical circles. In the old days Oberlin College was known as a great Bible-believing college. But it is no longer; it is liberal. Happily Wheaton is not. But what most people do not realize is that Jonathan Blanchard (1811-1892), who was the founder and president of Wheaton College, and Charles Finney (1792-1875), who was the president of Oberlin College, were tremendously interested in the question of social action concerning slavery. They were two great voices in America calling out for social action, and both of them said something very firmly: *If a law is wrong, you must disobey it*. Both of them call, when it is necessary, for civil disobedience.

Finney in his book *Systematic Theology* on page 158 has a heading: "I propose now to make several remarks respecting forms of government, the right and duty of revolution." Do note his phrase "The right and duty of revolution." On page 162 he says: "There can scarcely be conceived a more abominable and fiendish maxim than 'our country right or wrong.' " He then goes on to stress that not everything the government does is to be supported, and he includes the Mexican War and slavery. On page 157 he says: "Arbitrary legislation can never be really obligatory."[4]

And we must not forget that Jonathan Kaufman was right when he wrote in the *Wall Street Journal*: ". . . [it was the] Great Religious Awakening two and one half centuries ago that helped sow the seeds of the American Revolution. . . ."[5]

Our evangelical leadership seems to have forgotten its heritage. When the book and film series *Whatever Happened to the Human Race?* came out we observed something very instructive. The call for a public stand against abortion, infanticide, euthanasia, and against the general eradication of the unique dignity and worth of all human beings was not widely accepted at first. Many of the evangelical leadership either were totally silent about abortion, or qualified what they did say about abortion to such an extent that they really said nothing, or less than nothing, as far as the battle for human life was concerned.

The seminars for *Whatever Happened to the Human Race?* were marvelous seminars certainly. My wife and I both agree we have never seen people go out of seminars or meetings so committed to action. People went out from those seminars and there was a change. Prior to that, to our shame, across the United States and Great Britain as well, there were very, very few evangelicals involved in the movement against abortion. We had left it to the Roman Catholics to such an extent that the battle for human life was being lost by the simple tactic of its being called "a Roman Catholic issue." After this project, happily, there were more evangelicals who saw the importance of the issue of human life and bringing the Lordship of Christ concerning law into this very important area.

But often the seminars were not well attended. We found that it was often because much of the evangelical leadership did not want to become involved. With some it was the prison of their platonic spirituality, and this, of course, makes them incapable of engaging in any such warfare. Franky Schaeffer V writes in *Addicted to Mediocrity*:

> Either God is the Creator of the whole man, the whole universe, and all of reality and existence, or he is the Creator of none of it. If God is only the Creator of some divided platonic existence which leads to a tension between the body and the soul, the real world and the spiritual world, if God is only the Creator of some spiritual little experiential "praise the Lord" reality, then he is not much of a God. Indeed, he is not I AM at all. If our Christian lives are allowed to become something spiritual and religious as opposed to something real, daily applicable, understandable, beautiful, verifiable, balanced, sensible, and above all united, whole, if indeed our Christianity is allowed to become this waffling spiritual goo that nineteenth-century platonic Christianity became, then Christianity as truth disappears and instead we only have a system of vague experiential religious platitudes in its place.[6]

With some it was their desire not to have their own projects disturbed. There were cases where some not only did not urge people to come, but where other meetings were planned which hindered people from coming. A very unhappy thing. No, the Christian lawyers, theologians, and educators, indeed, much of the evangelical establishment, certainly have not been in there blowing the trumpet loud and clear.

We must understand that the question of the dignity of human life is not something on the periphery of Judeo-Christian thinking, but almost in the center of it (though not *the* center because the center is the existence of God Himself). But the dignity of human life is unbreakably linked to the existence of the personal-infinite God. It is because there is a personal-infinite God who has made men and women in His own image that they have a unique dignity of life as human beings. Human life then is filled with dignity, and the state and humanistically oriented law have no right and no authority to take human life arbitrarily in the way that it is being taken.

We must see then that indeed the cry has not been given. We must see that here, on such a central issue as abortion, the true nature of the problem was not understood: Christians failed to see that abortion was really a symptom of the much larger problem and not just one bit and piece. And beyond this as the material-energy-chance humanistic world view takes over increasingly in our country, the view concerning the intrinsic value of human life will grow less and less, and the concept of compassion for which the country is in some sense known will be further gone.

A girl who has been working with the Somalian refugees has just been in our home and told us their story and shown us their pictures. One million—and especially little children—in agony, pain, and suffering! Can we help but cry? But forget it! In the United States we now kill by painful methods one and a half times that many each year by abortion. In Somalia it is war. But we kill in cold blood. The compassion our country has been known somewhat for is being undermined. And it is not only the babies who are being killed; it is humanness which the humanist world view is beating to death.

The people in the United States have lived under the Judeo-Christian consensus for so long that now we take it for granted. We seem to forget how completely unique what we have had is a result of the gospel. The gospel indeed is, "accept Christ, the Messiah, as Savior and have your guilt removed on the basis of His death." But the good news includes many resulting blessings.

We have forgotten why we have a high view of life, and why we have a positive balance between form and freedom in government, and the fact that we have such tremendous freedoms without these freedoms leading to chaos. Most of all, we have forgotten that none of these is natural in the world. They are unique, based on the fact that the consensus was the biblical consensus. And these things will be even further lost if this other total view, the materialistic view, takes over more thoroughly. We can be certain that what we so carelessly take for granted will be lost.

CHAPTER SIX

An Open Window

What is ahead of us? I would suggest that we must have *Two Tracks* in mind.

The *First Track* is the fact of the conservative swing in the United States in the 1980 election. With this there is at this moment a unique window open in the United States. It is unique because it is a long, long time since that window has been open as it is now. And let us hope that the window stays open, and not on just one issue, even one as important as human life—though certainly every Christian ought to be praying and working to nullify the abominable abortion law. But as we work and pray, we should have in mind not only this important issue as though it stood alone. Rather, we should be struggling and praying that this whole other total entity—the material-energy, chance world view—can be rolled back with all its results across all of life. I work, I pray that indeed the window does stay open. I hope that will be the case.

Now the window is open and we must take advantage of it in every way we can as citizens, as Christian citizens of the democracy in which we still have freedom. We must try to roll back the other total entity. It will not be easy to roll it back because those

457

who hold the other total world view of reality have no intention
that it will be rolled back. Those who hold this view are deeply
entrenched, they have had their own way without opposition for a
long time, and they will use every means to see that the momentum they have achieved, and the results they have brought forth in
all fields, will be retained and enlarged.

For example, all you have to do is to consider the way the media
treated Dr. C. Everett Koop. Dr. Koop is one of the foremost
pediatric surgeons in the United States, and among other honors,
he was given the highest honor of the French government for his
pioneering work in pediatric surgery. But when he was nomin-
ated for the position of Surgeon General, he was attacked by the
secular media with total disregard for objective reporting—and
with total disregard for his brilliant humanitarian record as a
surgeon. Those in the media holding the humanist world view
could not tolerate Dr. Koop's voice to be heard—they could not
tolerate his articulate defense of the sanctity of human life to be
expressed.

We must understand that there is going to be a battle every step
of the way. They are determined that what they have gained will
not be rolled back. But it is our task to use the open window to try
to change that direction at this very late hour. And we must press
on, hoping, praying, and working that indeed the window can
stay open and the total entity will be pressed back rather than the
whole thing ending only in words.

Some of us, however, who have some position of leadership,
must unhappily be thinking of the possible *Second Track*.

The *Second Track* is, What happens in this country if the window does not stay open? What then?

Thinking this way does not mean that we stop doing all we can
to keep the window open. Nevertheless some people must be
thinking about what to do if the window closes And though we
hope it stays open, what happens if it does not?

Now let's ask ourselves where we are in the sociological atmosphere of our country. Think of the counter-culture people out of
the sixties. By the end of the sixties they had given up their hope
of an ideological solution on the basis of drugs or on the basis of
Marcuse's New Left. That is, by the end of the sixties they had
given up their two optimistic, ideological hopes.

As we consider those who came out of the sixties and the seventies we see there are not many anarchists around us in the United

States. In Europe, however, there are a growing number of young anarchists—in West Germany, especially West Berlin, Holland, Great Britain, and even Switzerland. These anarchists are there. They have a cry, "No power to nobody!" They paint a large A on the walls of beautiful cathedrals and beautiful old churches and government buildings. Anarchists! They are nihilists. I saw a graffito on the wall of a government building in Lausanne a few nights ago which read: "The State is the enemy. The Church is the collaborator." What they practice in their lives is exactly what the words of punk rock say. Most people do not listen to the words of punk rock, even if they listen to the music. The words of punk rock speak of nihilism, hopelessness, the meaninglessness of life, anarchy. This group in Europe is now living that way and in practice stands against the total society.

But that has not happened in the United States. In the seventies the counter-culture young people who had given up the hope of an *ideological solution* of drugs and of Marcuse's New Left began to join the system in order to get their part of the affluence and thus be able to live their own life style. That is what we find in the seventies and the beginning of the eighties. They may continue to use drugs but no longer as an ideological solution. If they use drugs it is now rather as the traditional use of drugs, for personal escape.

Now I want to add something to that. In the Nixon era we heard a lot about the Silent Majority, but most people did not realize that there were two parts to that Silent Majority among the older people. There was the *majority* of the Silent Majority and there was the *minority* of the Silent Majority.

The *majority* of the Silent Majority were those who had only two bankrupt values—personal peace and affluence. Personal peace means just to be let alone, not to be troubled by the troubles of other people, whether across the world or across the city. Affluence means an overwhelming and ever-increasing prosperity—a life made up of things and more things—a success judged by an ever-higher level of material abundance.

On the other hand, the *minority* of the Silent Majority were those who were standing on some kind of principle, and often with at least a memory of Christianity even if they were not individually Christians.

We must realize that if you take the join-the-system young people and the majority of the Silent Majority, though they may have very different life styles, they support each other completely sociologically. They are in exactly the same place. In this respect, we must remember that although there are tremendous discrepancies between conservatives and liberals in the political arena, if they are both operating on a humanistic base there will really be no final difference between them. As Christians we must stand absolutely and totally opposed to the whole humanist system, *whether it is controlled by conservative or liberal elements.* Thus Christians must not become officially aligned with either group just on the basis of the name it uses.

Terry Eastland in *Commentary* says:

> It is the style nowadays not only among the college-educated but also among many blue-collar workers to be economically conservative but socially and morally liberal. This, translated, means balance the budget but decriminalize marijuana and cocaine and let us have abortion on demand. If the liberalism of the sixties has a definite legacy, it is found in the far more liberalized and hedonistic lives many Americans, including many older Americans, and indeed many political conservatives, now lead.[1]

What percentage in the 1980 election voted out of principle and what percentage voted for a change of some sort in order to increase their own affluence? George F. Will is a columnist for 360 newspapers, including the *Washington Post,* and is a contributing editor for *Newsweek.* In a February 16, 1981, article entitled "Rhetoric and Reality" in the *International Herald Tribune,* he wrote: "In 1980, the electorate's mandate probably was about 20 percent for conservatism and 80 percent for improved economic numbers, no matter how produced." Notice the important phrase: "no matter how produced."

Long before I read that quote I said that was what had happened. I would not dare give such exact percentages, but I think what George Will is stating is exactly the case. And if the improved economic numbers are not forthcoming, then what? With the two sociological groups of the join-the-system young people and the affluence-centered older ones supporting each other, do you think the window that is open will stay open?

With the window that is open we must beware of letting a foolish triumphalism cause us to think that all is now won and certain. We hear: "There is a new wind blowing." True, but often those who say this, or something like it, then forget that this does not mean the new wind will automatically keep blowing. It does not mean we can return to the practice of false views of spirituality. And it does not mean we can withdraw from a struggle for continued reformation, even if it is at great cost to us personally and to our favorite projects.

And if the window does close, if people do not get their "economic numbers no matter how produced," I do not think there will be a return to the old liberalism of the last fifty years. Rather, my guess is that there will be some form of an elite authoritarianism just as I suggested at the conclusion of *How Should We ThenLive?*[2]

All that would be needed in much of the Western world is even an illusion of what George Will calls "improved economic numbers" to accept some form of an elite to give at least the illusion of these numbers. And as I said in *How Should We Then Live?* this will be especially so if it is brought in under the guise of constitutionality as it was under Caesar Augustus in the Roman Empire. If it could be brought in in that way I think there would be hardly a ripple.

What form of elite might take over? A number of thinkers have set forth their predictions. John Kenneth Galbraith (1908-   ) has suggested an elite composed of intellectuals (especially from the academic and scientific world) plus government. Daniel Bell (1919-   ), professor of sociology at Harvard University, saw an elite composed of select intellectuals made up of those who control the use of the technological explosion, a technocratic elite. Speaking more recently, Gerald Holton (1922-   ), Mallinckrodt Professor of physics and professor of the history of science at Harvard University, seems to agree with Bell. *The Chronicle of Higher Education,* May 18, 1981, quotes Holton in an article entitled, "Where is Science Taking Us? Gerald Holton Maps the Possible Routes."

> Therein lies the problem. More and more frequently, major decisions that profoundly affect our daily lives have a large scientific or technological content, he says. "By a recent estimate, nearly half the bills before the U.S. Congress have a substantial science-technology component," he says, and "some two-thirds of the District of Columbia Circuit Court's case load now involves review of action by federal administrative agencies; and more and more of such cases relate to matters on the frontiers of technology.
>
> "If the layman cannot participate in decision making, he will have to turn himself over, essentially blind, to a hermetic elite," Mr. Hol-

ton said in the interview last week. Then, he continued, the fundamental question becomes, "Are we still capable of self-government and therefore of freedom?

"Margaret Mead wrote in a 1959 issue of *Daedalus* about scientists elevated to the status of priests," Mr. Holton said.

"Now there is a name for this elevation, when you are in the hands of—one hopes—a benevolent elite, when you have no control over your political decisions. From the point of view of John Locke, the name for this is slavery."

For myself I think we should not rule out the courts, and especially the Supreme Court, as being such an elite for these reasons:

1. They are already ruling on the basis of sociological, arbitrary law.
2. They are *making* much law, as well as ruling on law.
3. They dominate the two other parts of government.

They rule on what the other two branches of government can and cannot do, and they usually go unchallenged. It has been said that in the last couple of years the Supreme Court has tended to defer to the other two branches of government. However, while one could hope this will set a trend toward self-restraint away from an "Imperial Court," the figures suggest otherwise. In the first 195 years of the existence of the United States the Supreme Court voided only ninety-one acts of Congress—that is, considerably less than one every two years. In the last ten years it has voided fifteen acts of Congress—that is, an average age of one and a half acts of Congress have been voided each year.

At the same time I would stress the fact that the main point is not trying to choose at this moment what the elite might be. Instead we must realize the possibility of such an elite if the masses do not get their "economic numbers." As I write this there are strikes in Britain—partially, at least, because of the price of rectifying fifty or so years of flagrant economic spending. The United States has also had its fifty years of spending, and this presents a painful problem. Indeed, the political price for solving the problem may be too high to make any solution possible.

I hope the window does not close. I hope those with a humanistic world view who have increasingly controlled our culture for the last twenty, thirty, forty years, something like this, cannot close the open window with all their efforts. But if they do, if they take over with increased power and control, will we be so foolish as to think that religion and the religious institutions will not be even further affected than they have been so far? I wonder how many of us are aware of the cases that the churches have faced in the last ten years in various places. The things that have been brought into courts of law should make our hair stand on end. Do you think that in such a case as I have portrayed (and may it not happen!) that the Christians and the Christian institutions will not be even further affected?

Robert L. Toms, an attorney-at-law, lists the issues pending this year and which are up for final adjudication during the coming decade before the United States' courts, administrative bodies, executive departments, and legislatures:

1. Is a minister of the gospel liable for malpractice to a counselee for using spiritual guidance rather than psychological or medical techniques?

2. Can a Christian residence house in a college have the same standing as a fraternity and sorority house for purposes of off-campus residency rules?

3. Can Christian high school students assemble on the public school campus for religious discussion?

4. Can Christian teachers in public schools meet before class for prayer?

5. Can Christian college students meet in groups on the state university campus?

6. Can HEW require a Bible college to admit drug addicts and alcoholics as "handicapped persons"?

7. Can a church build a religious school or a day-care center in an area zoned residential?

8. Can parents who send their children to religious schools not approved by a state board of education be prosecuted under the truancy laws?

9. Is an independent, wholly religious school entitled to an exemption from unemployment taxes as are church-owned schools?

10. Will the State enforce antiemployment discrimination laws against a church which in accordance with its stated religious beliefs fires a practicing homosexual staff member?

11. Can seminary trustees refuse to graduate a practicing homosexual?

12. Can a city continue its forty-year practice of having a nativity scene in front of the city hall?

13. Can zoning laws be used to prevent small group Bible studies from meeting in homes?

14. Can a court decide which doctrinal group in a church split gets the sanctuary?

15. Must a religious school accept as a teacher an otherwise qualified practicing homosexual?

16. Can a church be fined by a court for exuberant noise in worship?

17. Can a state department of health close a church-run juvenile home for policies that include spanking?

18. Can religious solicitation in public places be confined to official booths?

19. Is an unborn fetus a "person" and entitled to Constitutional protection?

20. Can The Ten Commandments be posted in a public classroom?

21. Can students in public education have a period of silent meditation and prayer?

22. Can Christmas carols be sung in the public schools?

23. Must an employee who believes he should worship on Saturday be permitted a work holiday on that day in order to worship?

24. Can the graduation ceremony of a public high school be held in a church?

25. Can a State official seize a church on allegations of misconduct by dissident members and run the church through a court-appointed receiver?

26. Can the State set minimum standards for private religious school curricula?

27. Is religious tax exemption a right or privilege, and, if it is a privilege, are the exemptions an unwarranted support of religion by the State?

28. Should churches be taxed like any other part of society?

29. Can Federal labor laws be used to enforce collective bargaining rights and unionization in religious enterprises?

30. Can the State require a license before a religious ministry may solicit funds for its work?

31. Are hospitals, schools, counseling groups, halfway houses, famine-relief organizations, youth organizations, homes for unwed mothers, orphanages, etc., run with religious motivations or are they secular and subject to all controls secular organizations are subject to?[3]

He further says:

. . . two U.S. trial courts have recently ruled that a group of college students who wish to discuss religion could not meet in the context of a public state university, that religious speech must go on elsewhere since it might "establish religion" on the campus. . . . The State must screen out religious speech from the otherwise free speech practiced on a university campus.[4]

We might differ as to what the ruling should be in some of these cases, but that does not change the weight of the whole. It should be said that it is not only Protestants who are facing the implications of the above list, but Roman Catholics and Jews as well.

And for Christians who are in the habit of drifting complacently, a case presently before the courts should be a loud-sounding alarm bell. As I write, Samuel E. Ericsson, an attorney-at-law, is defending Grace Community Church, the largest Protestant church in Los Angeles County, in a clergyman malpractice suit. This suit was brought by parents because the pastors of that church cared for their son (who had later committed suicide) instead of turning him over to professional psychiatric and psychological care.[5] Obviously if the church lost this case, all religions would be greatly affected. In fact, anyone who tried to help someone with questions or fears could be sued if he or she did not fall under the category of professional psychiatric and psychological competence! And to make matters more complicated, no one has thought how to set standards acceptably for professional psychiatric and psychological competence.

Samuel Ericsson has put the case in the proper perspective when in a letter to me dated May 1, 1981, he wrote: "I believe that clergyman malpractice, or more accurately spiritual counseling malpractice, is going to present the secular courts with a head-on clash between the two competing world views, secularism and Christianity."

Should not all of us be thinking what to do about it if the window does shut? The Christian theologians, the educators, the lawyers, the evangelical leadership, have not had a very good record in the past of seeing things as a whole. That is, they have not seen the contrast between the consensus which is based on there being a Law Giver and what that naturally brings forth, and the totally different material-energy, chance world view of reality and what that naturally brings forth. Now if we have not run very well in the past with the footmen when it has been so very easy, I wonder what is going to happen to us if we have to run with the horsemen? What will protect us from what is happening in most of the world today? Have we run with the footmen? Very, very poorly. What happens if we must run with the horsemen?

CHAPTER SEVEN

The Limits of Civil Obedience

The Founding Fathers and those in the thirteen states understood what they were building upon. We have reached a place today which is violently opposed to what the Founding Fathers of this country and those in the thirteen individual states had in mind when they came together and formed the union.

It is time to think to *the bottom line* as our forefathers did. What was *the bottom line* that our forefathers thought to that made it possible for them to act as they did?

First, what is the final relationship to the state on the part of anyone whose base is the existence of God? How would you answer that question?

You must understand that those in our present material-energy, chance oriented generation have *no reason* to obey the state except that the state has the guns and has the patronage. That is the only reason they have for obeying the state. A material-energy, chance orientation gives no base, no reason, except force and patronage, as to why citizens should obey the state.

The Christian, the God-fearing person, is not like that. The Bible tells us that God has commanded us to obey the state.

But now a second question follows very quickly. Has God set

up an authority in the state that is autonomous from Himself? Are we to obey the state no matter what? Are we? In this one area is indeed Man the measure of all things? And I would answer, not at all, not at all.

When Jesus says in Matthew 22:21: "Give to Caesar what is Caesar's, and to God what is God's," it is not:

GOD and CAESAR

It was, is, and it always will be:

GOD
and
CAESAR

The civil government, as all of life, stands under the Law of God. In this fallen world God has given us certain offices to protect us from the chaos which is the natural result of that fallenness. But when *any office* commands that which is contrary to the Word of God, those who hold that office abrogate their authority and they are not to be obeyed. And that includes the state.

Romans 13:1-4 says:

Everyone must submit himself to the governing authorities, for there is no authority except that which God has established. The authorities that exist have been established by God. Consequently, he who rebels against the authority is rebelling against what God has instituted, and those who do so will bring judgment on themselves. For rulers hold no terror for those who do right, but for those who do wrong. Do you want to be free from fear of the one in authority? Then do what is right and he will commend you. For he is God's servant to do you good. But if you do wrong, be afraid, for he does not bear the sword for nothing. He is God's servant, an agent of wrath to bring punishment on the wrongdoer.

God has ordained the state as a *delegated* authority; it is not autonomous. The state is to be an agent of justice, to restrain evil by punishing the wrongdoer, and to protect the good in society. When it does the reverse, *it has no proper authority*. It is then a usurped authority and as such it becomes lawless and is tyranny.

In 1 Peter 2:13-17 we read:

Submit yourselves for the Lord's sake to every authority instituted among men: whether to the king, as the supreme authority, or to governors, who are sent by him to punish those who do wrong and to commend those who do right. For it is God's will that by doing good you should silence the ignorant talk of foolish men. Live as free men, but do not use your freedom as a cover-up for evil; live as servants of God. Show proper respect to everyone: Love the brotherhood of believers, fear God, honor the king.

Peter says here that civil authority is to be honored and that God is to be feared. The state, as he defines it, is to punish those who do wrong and commend those who do right. If this is not so, then the whole structure falls apart. Clearly, the state is to be a ministry of justice. This is the legitimate function of the state, and in this structure Christians are to obey the state as a matter of "conscience" (Romans 13:5).

But what is to be done when the state does that which violates its legitimate function? The early Christians died because they would not obey the state in a civil matter. People often say to us that the early church did not show any civil disobedience. They do not know church history. Why were the Christians in the Roman Empire thrown to the lions? From the Christian's viewpoint it was for a religious reason. But from the viewpoint of the Roman State they were in civil disobedience, they were civil rebels. The Roman State did not care what anybody believed religiously; you could believe anything, or you could be an atheist. But you had to worship Caesar as a sign of your loyalty to the state. The Christians said they would not worship Caesar, anybody, or anything, but the living God. Thus to the Roman Empire they were rebels, and it was civil disobedience. That is why they were thrown to the lions.

Francis Legge in volume one of his book *Forerunners and Rivals of Christianity from 330 B.C. to A.D. 330* writes: "The officials of the Roman Empire in times of persecution sought to force the Christians to sacrifice, not to any heathen gods, but to the Genius of the Emperor and the Fortune of the City of Rome; and at all times the Christians' refusal was looked upon not as a religious but as a political offense."[1]

The bottom line is that at a certain point there is not only the right, but the duty, to disobey the state.

Through the ages Christians have taken the same position as did the early church in disobeying the state when it commanded what was contrary to God's Law. William Tyndale (c. 1490-1536), the English translator of the Bible, advocated the supreme authority of the Scripture over and against the state and the church. Government authorities continually sought to capture him, but Tyndale was successful in evading them for years. Tyndale was eventually condemned as a heretic, tried and executed on October 6, 1536. John Bunyan (1628-1688) was found guilty of breaking the king's law. Arrested three times for preaching without a state license and for failing to attend the Church of England, he spent twelve years in an English jail. He wrote many works from this jail cell, including *Pilgrim's Progress*.

In almost every place where the Reformation had success there was some form of civil disobedience or armed rebellion:

Netherlands: Catholic Spain had isolated the non-Catholic population both politically and geographically. Thus the Protestants concentrated in what is now Holland which became the last holdout against the Spanish power. The leaders of the revolt established Protestantism as the dominant religious form of the country. The turning point was the battle for Leyden in 1574. The Dutch Protestants fought a very hard and costly battle. When they finally won, the door was open not only for the subsequent political entity of Holland, but also for the successful Dutch Reformation with all its cultural as well as religious results.

Sweden: In 1527 the Vasa family broke away from Denmark as an act of rebellion and established Sweden as a Lutheran country. Later, in 1630, it was the Swedish king, Gustavus Adolphus, a sincere champion of Lutheranism, who marched his army out of Sweden and into Germany against the Emperor to protect Protestant Germany with his force of arms.

Denmark: In 1536 the Protestant party of nobles overthrew the Danish dynasty—an act of "civil disobedience" with accompanying strife. They then set up a new government and a new dynasty and established Lutheranism in the country.

Germany: Luther was protected by the Duke of Saxony against the political and military power of the Emperor. After many wars in which the Duke of Saxony and other German nobles kept the Emperor at bay, the Peace of Augsburg was signed in 1555. In this it was established that the ruler's religion would determine the religion of his geographical location. Thus the German Reformation won its right to exist. Later, with the rise of the Roman Catholic Counter-Reformation, the Thirty Years War was fought, and out of this came the Peace of Westphalia in 1648 which ratified the 1555 Peace of Augsburg. By this, German Protestantism was protected from the reprisals of the Counter-Reformation.

Switzerland: Bern established reform and Protestantism between 1523 and 1525 by Communal vote. Yet for what is now the Canton of Vaud (where I live), it was Protestant Bern's military control of this area at that time which gave William Farel his opportunity to preach the gospel in Aigle and Ollon, leading to reformation in French-speaking Switzerland.

Geneva: This area became Protestant by vote of the Common Council in 1533-1534. Calvin came to Geneva in 1536. There was no open war, but the Reformation was established despite the constant threat of war by the House of Savoy.

Because John Knox of Scotland is such a clear example I will give more detail concerning him. Knox was ordained to the priesthood in 1536 (the year William Tyndale was executed) after studying at St. Andrews University near Edinburgh where Samuel Rutherford later was Rector. Knox was also a lawyer and a bodyguard to the fiery evangelist George Wishart.

Shortly thereafter, Knox accepted a call to the ministry and began attacking the Roman Catholic Church. This was extremely dangerous since the Roman Catholic Church exerted a dominant influence over the Scottish State. Knox was prevented from preaching on Sundays (the dates were conveniently filled by priests). Knox held services on weekdays during which he refuted what was said by others on Sundays. So successful were his efforts that a majority of those in Edinburgh made an open profession of the Protestant faith by participating in the Lord's Supper as administered by Knox.

On June 30, 1547, Knox, along with others, was captured by French forces in the war with England. Disaster that this was, it was better than what would have happened if the Scottish government had apprehended him. Most likely, he would have been burned at the stake.

After almost two years as a galley slave, Knox gained his liberty. He landed as a refugee in England in 1549 and resumed preaching. He was so effective that Protestant families in Scotland, hearing of his ministry, crossed the border illegally and resettled in Berwick, England, so as to be near him.

Knox is rightly thought of as a radical reformer. There is, however, an important distinction to keep in mind concerning him. Throughout his ministry, Knox appealed for moderation and compromise whenever truly fundamental issues were not at stake.

Attempts to keep the English crown in Protestant hands failed and in August of 1553 the Roman Catholic Mary Tudor entered London. Many of the outspoken Protestants were taken captive and imprisoned. Knox was able to escape from the country to Geneva, Switzerland.

It was during this time that Knox developed a theology of resistance to tyranny. He began smuggling pamphlets into England. The most significant of these was the *Admonition to England* (for complete title see *References* in the back of this book), published in July of 1554. With this move, he had stepped into new territory, going further than any Reformer had previously gone. Within a few years, tens of thousands of Huguenots were offering armed resistance to the French government; and the year Knox died saw the beginning of the successful revolt and saving of Holland. Knox had shocked the world with his *Admonition to England*, but he had also been convincing. Jasper Ridley in *John Knox* writes, "The theory of the justification of revolution is Knox's special contribution to theological and political thought."[2]

Whereas Reformers such as Martin Luther and John Calvin had reserved the right to rebellion to the civil rulers alone, Knox went further. He maintained that the common people had the right and duty to disobedience and rebellion if state officials ruled contrary to the Bible. To do otherwise would be rebellion against God.

Knox was not against civil government *per se*. He knew well that civil government is ordained of God. Knox maintained, however, that state officials have the duty of obeying God's Laws. He wrote: "Kings then have not an absolute power in their regiment to do what pleases them; but their power is limited by God's word."[3] A ruler must consider that he is "Lieutenant to One whose eyes watch upon him."[4] All life and all actions, he reiterated, must have their base in God's Word.

Knox finally arrived back in Scotland on May 2, 1559. Scotland became a Protestant country. The effectiveness of the Presbyterian system there was so great that the persecutions of the following century were unable to root it out. The Reformation had come to stay. And it was John Knox, an exponent of godly resistance in the face of tyranny, who planted the seeds that were later nurtured by such men as Samuel Rutherford.

In contrast to the countries named above where there was success for the Reformation—in each case involving various forms of civil disobedience or armed rebellion—one can think of where the Reformation was exterminated by force because of the lack of such protection:

Hungary: The Reformation had great initial success. But when the Turks pulled out of the country, the Roman Catholic authorities had unchecked power and used it to eliminate the Reformation—largely by killing off just about all of the Protestants.

France: The Huguenots were most successful in numbers and position. But on St. Bartholomew's Day (1572), lacking protection, the Reformation was broken in France by the mass assassination of most of its leadership.

Spain: There was a small Reformation movement among the monks of Seville. Lacking any protection, they were totally eliminated by martyrdom.

Thus, in almost every place where the Reformation flourished there was not only religious noncompliance; there was civil disobedience as well.

It was in this setting that Samuel Rutherford (1600-1661) wrote his *Lex Rex: or The Law and the Prince* (1644). What is the concept in *Lex Rex?* Very simply: The law is king, and if the king and the government disobey the law they are to be disobeyed. And the law is founded on the Law of God. *Lex Rex* was outlawed in both England and Scotland. The parliament of Scotland was meeting in order to condemn Samuel Rutherford to death for his views, and the only reason he was not executed as a civil rebel is because he died first.

In his classic work, *Lex Rex,* Rutherford set forth the proper Christian response to nonbiblical acts by the state. Rutherford, a Presbyterian, was one of the Scottish commissioners at the Westminster Assembly in London (1643-1647) and later became Rector at St. Andrews University in Scotland. The book *Lex Rex,* in a society of landed classes and monarchy, created an immediate controversy.

The governing authorities were concerned about *Lex Rex* because of its attack on the undergirding foundation of seventeenth century political government in Europe—"the divine right of kings." This doctrine held that the king or state ruled as God's appointed regent and, this being so, the king's word was law. Placed against this position was Rutherford's assertion that the basic premise of civil government and, therefore, law, must be based on God's Law as given in the Bible. As such, Rutherford argued, all men, even the king, are *under* the Law and not above it. This concept was considered political rebellion and punishable as treason.

Rutherford argued that Romans 13 indicates that all power is from God and that government is ordained and instituted by God. The state, however, is to be administered according to the principles of God's Law. Acts of the state which contradicted God's Law were illegitimate and acts of tyranny. Tyranny was defined as ruling without the sanction of God.

Rutherford held that a tyrannical government is always immoral. He said that "a power ethical, politic, or moral, to oppress, is not from God, and is not a power, but a licentious deviation of a power; and is no more from God, but from sinful nature and the old serpent, than a license to sin."[5]

Rutherford presents several arguments to establish the right and duty of resistance to unlawful government. *First,* since tyranny is satanic, not to resist it is to resist God—to resist tyranny is to honor God. *Second,* since the ruler is granted power conditionally, it follows that the people have the power to withdraw their sanction if the proper conditions are not fulfilled. The civil magistrate is a "fiduciary figure"—that is, he holds his authority in trust for the people. Violation of the trust gives the people a legitimate base for resistance.

It follows from Rutherford's thesis that citizens have a *moral* obligation to resist unjust and tyrannical government. While we must always be subject to the *office* of the magistrate, we are not to be subject to the *man* in that office who commands that which is contrary to the Bible.

Rutherford offered suggestions concerning illegitimate acts of the state. A ruler, he wrote, should not be deposed merely because he commits a single breach of the compact he has with the people. Only when the magistrate acts in such a way that the governing structure of the country is being destroyed—that is, when he is attacking the fundamental structure of society—is he to be relieved of his power and authority.

That is exactly what we are facing today. The whole structure of our society is being attacked and destroyed. It is being given an entirely opposite base which gives exactly opposite results. The reversal is much more total and destructive than that which Rutherford or any of the Reformers faced in their day.

CHAPTER EIGHT

The Use of Civil Disobedience

Civil disobedience is, of course, a very serious matter and it must be stressed that Rutherford was the very opposite of an anarchist. In *Lex Rex* he does not propose armed revolution as an automatic solution. Instead, he sets forth the appropriate response to interference by the state in the liberties of the citizenry. Specifically, he stated that if the state deliberately is committed to destroying its ethical commitment to God then resistance is appropriate.

In such an instance, for *the private person*, the individual, Rutherford suggested that there are three appropriate levels of resistance: *First*, he must defend himself by protest (in contemporary society this would most often be by legal action); *second*, he must flee if at all possible; and, *third*, he may use force, if necessary, to defend himself. One should not employ force if he may save himself by flight; nor should one employ flight if he can save himself and defend himself by protest and the employment of constitutional means of redress. Rutherford illustrated this pattern of resistance from the life of David as it is recorded in the Old Testament.

On the other hand, when the state commits illegitimate acts against *a corporate body*—such as a duly constituted state or local body, or even a church—then flight is often an impractical and unrealistic means of resistance. Therefore, with respect to a corporate group or community, there are two levels of resistance: remonstration (or protest) and then, if necessary, force employed in self-defense. In this respect, Rutherford cautioned that a distinction must be made between a lawless uprising and lawful resistance.

For *a corporate body* (a civil entity), when illegitimate state acts are perpetrated upon it, resistance should be under the protection of the duly constituted authorities: if possible, it should be under the rule of the lesser magistrates (local officials). Rutherford urged that the *office* of the local official is just as much from God as is the *office* of the highest state official. Rutherford said, "When the supreme magistrate will not execute the judgment of the Lord, those who made him supreme magistrate, under God, who have under God, sovereign liberty to dispose of crowns and kingdoms, are to execute the judgment of the Lord, when wicked men make the law of God of none effect."

Samuel Rutherford and Bob Dylan would have understood each other. In "When You Gonna Wake Up" from the album *Slow Train Coming,*[1] Dylan has the lines:

> Adulterers in churches and pornography in the schools
> You got gangsters in power and lawbreakers making rules
>
> When you gonna wake up,
> When you gonna wake up,
> When you gonna wake up
> And strengthen the things that remain?

The difference in the centuries, and the difference in the language used, changes nothing.

In a similar way John Locke (1632–1704) approached the same problem. Locke took Rutherford's *Lex Rex* and secularized it. Locke, though secularizing *Lex Rex* and the Presbyterian tradition, nevertheless drew heavily from it. Locke made four basic points:

1. inalienable rights;
2. government by consent;
3. separation of powers;
4. the right of revolution (or you could word it, the right to resist unlawful authority).

These were the four points of Locke which were acted upon by the men among the American Founders who followed Locke.

Witherspoon certainly knew Samuel Rutherford's writing well. The other Founding Fathers may have known him. They certainly knew about Locke. And for both *Lex Rex* and Locke there comes a time when there must be civil disobedience *on the appropriate level*. One begins not on the highest level, but on the appropriate level at one's own point of history.

Many within the Christian community would agree that Christians can protest and take flight in the face of state oppression. However, force of any kind is a place where many Christians stop short.

Force, as used in this book, means *compulsion* or *constraint* exerted upon a person (or persons) or on an entity such as the state.

When discussing force it is important to keep an axiom in mind: always before protest or force is used, we must work for reconstruction. In other words, we should attempt to correct and rebuild society before we advocate tearing it down or disrupting it.

If there is a legitimate reason for the use of force, and if there is a vigilant precaution against its overreaction in practice, then at a certain point a use of force is justifiable. We should recognize, however, that overreaction can too easily become the ugly horror of sheer violence. Therefore, the distinction between force and violence is crucial. Os Guinness in *The Dust of Death* writes:

> Without such a distinction there can be no legitimate justification for authority or discipline of any kind, whether on a parental or on a presidential level. In a fallen world the ideal of legal justice without the exercise of force is naive. Societies need a police force, a man has the right to defend his wife from assault. A feature of any society which can achieve a measure of freedom within form is that responsibility implies discipline. This is true at the various structural levels of society—in the sphere of the state, business, the community, the school, respectively.[2]

In a fallen world, force in some form will always be necessary. We must not forget that every presently existing government uses and must use force in order to exist. Two principles, however, must always be observed. *First,* there must be a legitimate basis and a legitimate exercise of force. *Second,* any overreaction crosses the line from force to violence. And unmitigated violence can never be justified.

As Knox and Rutherford illustrate, however, the proper use of force is not only the province of the state. Such an assumption is born of naiveté. It leaves us without sufficient remedy when and if the state takes on totalitarian dimensions.

One factor today that is different from Rutherford's day is that due to the immense power of the modern state there may be no place to flee. The Pilgrims could escape tyranny by fleeing to America. But today this is often much more complicated and for many in the world today the frontiers are closed.

At this time in our history, protest is our most viable alternative. This is because in our country the freedom that allows us to use protest to the maximum still exists. However, we must realize that protest is a form of force. This is very much so with the so-called "nonviolent resistance." This was, and is, not a negation of force, but a choice of the kind of force to be used.

In our day an illustration for the need of protest is tax money being used for abortion. After all the normal constitutional means of protest had been exhausted, then what could be done? At some point protest could lead some Christians to refuse to pay some portion of their tax money. Of course, this would mean a trial. Such a move would have to be the individual's choice under God. No one should decide for another. But somewhere along the way, such a decision might easily have to be faced. Happily, at the present time in the United States the Hyde Amendment has removed the use of national tax money for abortions, but that does not change the possibility that in some cases such a protest would be the only way to be heard. One can think, for example, of the tax money going to Planned Parenthood which is openly a propaganda agency for abortion.

Another illustration would be Christian schools resisting the undue entanglement and interference of the state into their affairs. This same thing is equally true for other private schools. That might include resisting the Internal Revenue Service's use of its tax rulings if they were used to enforce such undue entanglement and interference. Again there would be trials and possibly jail for someone. But at a certain point there may be no other effective protest.

The problem in relation to a state public school system is not just an abstract possibility. As I write, a case of undue entanglement and interference is in the courts in a situation that corresponds exactly to Samuel Rutherford's concept of the proper procedure for a *corporate body* to resist.

The state of Arkansas has passed a law allowing creation to be taught in the public schools. The American Civil Liberties Union (ACLU) is trying to have this law revoked, saying it violates the separation of church and state. Here is a clear case fitting Rutherford's criteria. The state of Arkansas has passed a law. The courts are being used by the ACLU to try to nullify a state law which has the support of the original meaning of the First Amendment. The ACLU is arguing its case based upon a certain concept of the separation of church and state. But it must be stressed that this concept is entirely new and novel from the viewpoint of the original intent of the First Amendment and the total intent of the Founding Fathers. This new separation concept is a product of the recent humanist dominance in the United States and is being used in this case to destroy the power of a properly elected state legislature's "sovereign" ruling.

The ACLU is acting as the arm of the humanist consensus to force its view on the *majority* of the Arkansas state officials.

If there was ever a clearer example of the lower "magistrates" being treated with tyranny, it would be hard to find. And this would be a time, if the appeal courts finally rule tyrannically, for the state government to protest and refuse to submit. This fits Rutherford's proper procedures exactly.

It is a time for Christians and others who do not accept the narrow and bigoted humanist views rightfully to use the appropriate forms of protest.

In this case in Arkansas the ACLU has shown that it is the reverse of a civil liberties union. It is trying to make the schools totally secularistic, against the majority wishes of the Arkansas Legislature, and probably the majority of the citizens of the state of Arkansas. Under the guise of "civil liberties" it is tyranny and not only the individual states should resist but the people should resist. The humanist forces have used the courts rather than the legislatures because the courts are not subject to the people's thinking and expression by the election process—and especially they (the courts) are not subject to *reelection*. This is also related to the courts increasingly making law and thus the diminishing of the federal and state legislatures. The people must act against tyranny by returning these issues to themselves. The *Time* magazine article of January 18, 1982 reporting on the lower courts ruling against the Arkansas legislature spoke of "a poll showing that 76 percent of the United States public favors the teaching of both theories"—

i.e., evolution and creation. Thus if the poll is accurate, the lower court's ruling is openly contrary to the will of not only the legislature of Arkansas and the people of Arkansas but to 76 percent of the United States population. Any election figure getting such a percentage would consider this a mandate. Surely, the Founding Fathers would have considered this situation to be tyranny. It would be appropriate to remember the Boston Tea Party of December 16, 1773.

In a different area from the state schools: "undue entanglement" in the Christian schools makes an especially apt illustration. In Russia the state schools are geared to teach their form of state religion—the materialistic, humanistic world view—as the exclusive position. And simultaneously one of the outstanding issues in Russia concerning which Christians must disobey the state to be loyal to God is the state's laws against the parents' teaching their children concerning Christ and Christian truth.

In the United States the materialistic, humanistic world view is being taught exclusively in most state schools. But then, those holding the humanistic world view move to control (through the curricula and other ways) the Christian or other private schools—even though these schools were set up at private cost by the parents in order to give their children an education based on the world view of a universe created by a God who objectively exists.

There is an obvious parallel between this and the situation in Russia. And we really must not be blind to the fact that indeed in the public schools in the United States all religious influence is as forcibly forbidden as in the Soviet Union. Marxism usually is not taught here, but the total exclusive secularization is as complete. It should be noted that this is not only a problem for Christians but for other religious groups.

We must never forget that the humanistic position is an exclusivist, closed system which shuts out all contending viewpoints—especially if these views teach anything other than relative values and standards. Anything which presents absolute truth, values, or standards is quite rightly seen by the humanist to be a total denial of the humanistic position.

As a result the humanistic, material-energy, chance world view is completely intolerant when it presents itself through the political institutions and especially through the schools. In his book *Leftism,* Eric von Kuehnelt-Leddihn writes that as humanism begins to dominate the state "religion is then removed from the market place and the school, later from other domains of public life. The state will not tolerate any gods besides itself."[3] The school is their special target.

This is readily apparent in the Soviet Union. And it is carried forth in the name of religious freedom. For example, the Soviet Constitution provides:

> *Art* 124. In order to ensure to citizens freedom of conscience, the church in the U.S.S.R. is separated from the State, and the school from the church. Freedom of religious worship and freedom of anti-religious propaganda is recognized for all citizens.

Though this is clearly apparent in Russia in regard to its schools, it is also apparent in the public schools of the United States. The humanistic, material-energy, chance world view intolerantly uses every form of force at its disposal to make its world view the exclusive one taught in the schools.

One of the unhappy things in our country is that when states have objected to the continued encroachment of the original rights of the individual states, the objection has usually been motivated by some selfish end. However, if this could be put aside and the matter considered objectively, then we must realize that the individual states, in the origin of the United States, did not trust an overly powerful Federal Government, and the Constitution limited the Federal Government to definite areas. It was understood that powers not specifically granted to the Federal Government were not its prerogative.

James Madison (1751-1836) in *The Federalist,* no. 45, wrote: "The powers delegated by the proposed Constitution to the federal government are few and defined. Those which remain in the state governments are numerous and indefinite." In the intervening years this has been totally reversed.

Having lived in Switzerland for thirty-three years, I am especially sensitive to this. The individual Swiss cantons have courageously resisted the growth of Federal encroachment in Switzerland much more resolutely than the states have in the United States. Thus, the checks and balances in government between canton and Federal Government are functioning for governmental freedom in Switzerland much better than those between the individual states and the Federal Government in the United States. In our day, the checks and balances in government which resulted from the Reformation are functioning in this regard more consistently in Switzerland than they are in the United States. In Switzerland, federal statism has thus been somewhat restrained.

We must realize that the Reformation world view leads in the direction of government freedom. But the humanist world view with inevitable certainty leads in the direction of statism. This is so because humanists, having no god, must put something at the center, and it is inevitably society, government, or the state. Russia is the perfect example. But with the weakening or loss of the Christian consensus the Reformation countries have also become an example—including the United States. Thus, if the United States is to move back toward the original Reformation basis, this would mean severely limiting the scope of Federal State authority.

It is curious that the present Socialist Government in France, our of sheer pragmatism, is trying to dismantle its overly centralized government. It may be only pragmatic and "political," but it is instructive. This overcentralization is the outgrowth of Napoleon's Governmental Code. They are trying to dismantle the authoritarian result which was produced by the chaos caused by the French Revolution. These results of chaos and then Napoleon's resulting authoritarian regime with its network of administrative bureaucracy were the very opposite of that which was produced by the American Revolution on its base which placed God above the government.[4] It is worth repeating James Madison's statement concerning the purpose of the United States Constitution: "The powers delegated by the proposed Constitution to the federal government are few and defined. Those which remain in the state governments are numerous and indefinite." But as the Judeo-Christian consensus in the United States has weakened and all but disappeared, with lack of vision even from a pragmatic perspective, let alone principle, the United States federal government has continually taken over the very power the original government of the United States did its best to curtail, limit, and resist.

Again we must see that what we face is a totality and not just bits and pieces. It is not too strong to say that we are at war, and there are no neutral parties in the struggle. One either confesses that God is the final authority, or one confesses that Caesar is Lord.

CHAPTER NINE

The Use of Force

There does come a time when force, even physical force, is appropriate. The Christian is not to take the law into his own hands and become a law unto himself. But when all avenues to flight and protest have closed, force in the defensive posture is appropriate. This was the situation of the American Revolution. The colonists used force in defending themselves. Great Britain, because of its policy toward the colonies, was seen as a foreign power invading America. The colonists defended their homeland. As such, the American Revolution was a conservative counter-revolution. The colonists saw the British as the revolutionaries trying to overthrow the legitimate colonial governments.

A true Christian in Hitler's Germany and in the occupied countries should have defied the false and counterfeit state and hidden his Jewish neighbors from the German SS Troops. The government had abrogated its authority, and it had no right to make any demands.

This brings us to a current issue that is crucial for the future of the church in the United States—the issue of abortion. What is involved is the whole issue of the value of human life. A recent report indicates that for every three live births, one child is aborted. Christians must come to the children's defense, and Christians must come to the defense of human life as such.

This defense should be carried out on at least four fronts:

First, we should aggressively support a human life bill or a constitutional amendment protecting unborn children.

Second, we must enter the courts seeking to overturn the Supreme Court's abortion decision.

Third, legal and political action should be taken against hospitals and abortion clinics that perform abortions.

In order to operate, many hospitals and abortion clinics receive tax money in some form—at least from individual states. Our representatives must be confronted with political force (if they will not do so out of principle) into introducing legislation cutting off such funds. If this fails, then lawsuits should be initiated to stop such funds from flowing to such institutions.

Simultaneously with these steps, some Christians have picketed. I greatly admired Dr. William S. Barker, president of Covenant Theological Seminary in St. Louis, when he supported seminary students who had been arrested for picketing an abortion clinic in St. Louis. The Covenant Seminary students said:

"We feel we owe the Covenant community an explanation. First, we consulted a lawyer on what is the most effective way to combat this problem; according to him, it is through being arrested which most effectually draws attention to the situation.

"Second, we wanted to demonstrate to the media and to the courts that abortion is not primarily a Catholic issue.

"Third, we felt the need to demonstrate our commitment in the view of the media and the pro-life organizations. We felt our Christian testimony was at stake here.

"Finally, we wanted to get involved in the court system: our case will receive a trial and could possibly be taken to higher courts. If abortion is to be eradicated, it will have to be through the proper legal means.

"It was not an easy decision to be disobedient to the magistrates, but in light of the facts—the destroying of human life on a grand scale—we felt this was the most effective way to respond. It is an urgent situation which requires response now."[1]

Dr. Barker acknowledged some differences within the seminary community but explained that he personally supported the students:

"Such non-violent civil disobedience is proper, I believe, when other channels have been exhausted or will not serve to avoid or oppose the evil which one finds he cannot in obedience to God ignore or tolerate. At the same time one who violates man's law must be prepared to suffer the consequences."[2]

Fourth, the State must be made to feel the presence of the Christian community.

State officials must know that we are serious about stopping abortion, which is a matter of clear principle concerning the babies themselves and concerning a high view of human life. This may include doing such things as sit-ins in legislatures and courts, including the Supreme Court, when other constitutional means fail. We must make people aware that this is not a political game, but totally crucial and serious. And we must also demonstrate to people that there is indeed a proper *bottom line.* To repeat: *the bottom line* is that at a certain point there is not only the right, but the duty, to disobey the state.

Of course, this is scary. There are at least four reasons why.

First, we must make definite that we are in no way talking about any kind of a theocracy. Let me say that with great emphasis. Witherspoon, Jefferson, the American Founders had no idea of a theocracy. That is made plain by the First Amendment, and we must continually emphasize the fact that we are not talking about some kind, or any kind, of a theocracy.

In the Old Testament there was a theocracy commanded by God. In the New Testament, with the church being made up of Jews and Gentiles, and spreading over all the known world from India to Spain in one generation, the church was its own entity. There is no New Testament basis for a linking of church and state until Christ, the King returns. The whole "Constantine mentality" from the fourth century up to our day was a mistake. Constantine, as the Roman Emperor, in 313 ended the persecution of Christians. Unfortunately, the support he gave to the church led by 381 to the enforcing of Christianity, by Theodosius I, as the official state religion. Making Christianity the official state religion opened the way for confusion up till our own day. There have been times of very good government when this interrelationship of church and state has been present. But through the centuries it has caused great confusion between loyalty to the state and loyalty to Christ, between patriotism and being a Christian.

We must not confuse the Kingdom of God with our country.

To say it another way: "We should not wrap Christianity in our national flag."

None of this, however, changes the fact that the United States was founded upon a Christian consensus, nor that we today should bring Judeo-Christian principles into play in regard to government. But that is very different from a theocracy in name or in fact.

Second, it is frightening when we realize that our consideration of these things, and this book, will certainly get behind the Iron Curtain and into other tyrannical countries where Christians face these questions in practice every day of their lives, in prison or out of prison. Their position is very different from ours. We have freedom from physical oppression and they do not.

The early church carried out their civil disobedience in the only way available to them. They came to the clear issue of worshiping Caesar or not, and rebelled in refusing to do so, though they knew the cost.

It seems to me that in most of the Iron Curtain countries the Christians are in about the same position as the early church. They are not in a position to change the system because of their low numbers, because as Christians they are systematically shut out of places of influence, and because of the iron control. Thus they must resist, in the manner the early church did, when they are commanded to disobey God. An illustration would be the state's command not to give their children religious training. To do so is considered an act of civil disobedience under the Criminal Codes of the Soviet Union. Jan Pit in *Persecution: It Will Never Happen Here?* writes about one of the restrictions on religious freedom in Iron Curtain countries: "Christians are forbidden to teach religion to children; therefore Sunday schools and youth gatherings are not allowed. Even within the home, Christian training is not to take place."[3] That clearly disobeys God's commands—as well as the parents' deepest longings if indeed the parents believe Christ is the way of eternal life—and the law would have to be disobeyed. Civil disobedience in that case would be continuing the instruction and, if apprehended, paying the price of being sent to the labor camps in Siberia, which at times still means certain death, and certainly great suffering. The labor camps take the place of the lions.

In the communist countries and in other countries in Africa, etc., God's leading might be to further action as in Poland at the present time—or at some point to an even more violent action.

With their idea of the "Perfectibility of Man" the Soviet leaders expected the "New Man" to be brought forth by changed economic conditions. This, of course, has not happened. The Christians have the opportunity to show that Christ, and the Christian understanding of reality, can, and do, bring forth the "New Man"—not perfectly of course until Christ returns, but still in a substantial way, whereas the Soviets have failed. In order for Christians to show forth the New Man they must demonstrate a positive practice and exhibit a caring Christian community in the group and care beyond the Christian group. But showing forth the New Man also means a standing against the law of the state which would destroy the very things Christians should produce in society. The civil disobedience forced upon them by the tyranny of the state is an essential part of being the New Man, because to obey would destroy both what Christians should be and also what they should be producing in society.

Three things must be stressed for those in *all* totalitarian countries:

1. A platonic concept of spirituality which does not include all of life is not true biblical spirituality. True spirituality touches all of life, including things of government and law, and not just "religious things."

2. We who are outside of such countries must allow those in these countries to know what "the appropriate level" is in their time and place. We in our place of lesser physical danger must not heap guilt on them. That is not to say that some of them will not compromise, but that is their responsibility before God.

3. They should understand that there is *a bottom line* of civil disobedience on the appropriate level. They should recognize that this is biblical because any government that commands what contradicts God's Law abrogates its authority. It is no longer our proper legal government, and at that point we have the right, and the duty, to disobey it.

Third, speaking of civil disobedience is frightening because of an opposite situation from the second. That is, with the prevalence of Marxist thinking—and especially with the attempted synthesis of Marxism and Christianity in certain forms of liberation theology in South America and other places—what we are saying could become a Marxist and terrorist tool to bring anarchy. Or in a similar vein, it could become a tool to impose by force the humanist world view resulting in the loss of humanness and in some form of authoritarianism.

Much of liberation theology is built on the concept of Man

being basically good, linked with the idea that all people need is to be released from their economic chains. This is utopian, because Man is not basically good (bound only by social, economic, and political chains). Man is fallen. The Perfectibility of Man was the basis of much of the Enlightenment and of the French Revolution. Theoretically it was a basis of the Marxist-Lenin revolution in Russia. Each place this concept of the Perfectibility of Man has been acted on it has led to tragedy, to political chains, and to the loss of humanness.[4] Every attempt to put this utopian concept into practice has led to failure because it is false to what Man as he now is, really is. Man is not intrinsically unselfish, corrupted only by outward circumstances. He is fallen; he is not what he was created to be.

Even if some in this general stream of thought do not go as far as to be infiltrated by Marxism and the concept of the Perfectibility of Man, there is still the danger of confusing the Kingdom of God with the socialistic program. Those who have this tendency also could misuse this book.

Even as we say this, however, we must also say that the use of the freedoms we do have does not remove from us the duty of *making* and *using* our possessions with compassion. That is a Christian duty which the church has often not emphasized.[5] We can understand why some, reacting to the church's lack of emphasis concerning the proper compassionate use of possessions, then make the mistake of equating the Kingdom of God with a state program. Nevertheless, we should clearly recognize that those who do confuse the Kingdom of God with a socialistic program could misuse this book, and we must see that they do not do so.

And *fourth,* we must say that speaking of civil disobedience is frightening because there are so many kooky people around. People are always irresponsible in a fallen world. But we live in a special time of irresponsible people, and such people will in their unbalanced way tend to do the very opposite from considering the appropriate means at the appropriate time and place. Anarchy is never appropriate.

But these very real problems do not change the principle that the men of the Reformation and the Founding Fathers of the United States knew and operated on. This principle is that there is a *bottom line* that must be faced squarely if the state is not to become all-powerful and usurp God's primacy. We must recognize that there is a *bottom line if we are to have real freedom of thought and action at the present time—even if, happily, we never reach that bottom line.* If we have not faced the possibility of civil disobedience, if needed, our thinking and action at the present time will lack the freedom they should have. Locke understood that. Without the possibility of his fourth point—the right to resist unlawful authority—the other three would have been meaningless.

All the problems which do indeed exist do not change the need of thinking about the possibility of civil disobedience. Let us remind ourselves that Jonathan Blanchard and Charles Finney in their day thought through and taught this bottom line in regard to the need for the abolition of slavery. They taught this—facing the possibility that they might have to pay the price of going to jail, or more, if that was the result of civil disobedience.

The colonists followed Rutherford's model in the American Revolution. They elected representatives from every state who, by way of the Declaration of Independence, protested the acts of Great Britain. Failing that, they defended themselves by force.

The Declaration of Independence contains many elements of the Reformation thinking of Knox and Rutherford and should be carefully considered when discussing resistance. It speaks directly to the responsibility of citizens concerning oppressive civil government.

After recognizing man's God-given absolute rights, the Declaration goes on to declare that whenever civil government becomes destructive of these rights, "it is the right of the people to alter and abolish it, and institute new government, laying its foundation on such principles, and organizing its powers in such form, as to them shall seem most likely to effect their safety and happiness." The Founding Fathers, in the spirit of *Lex Rex,* cautioned in the Declaration of Independence that established governments should not be altered or abolished for "light and transient causes." But when there is a "long train of abuses and usurpations" designed to produce an oppressive, authoritarian state, "it is their right, it is their duty, to throw off such government . . ."

Simply put, the Declaration of Independence states that the people, if they find that their basic rights are being systematically attacked by the state, have *a duty* to try to change that government, and if they cannot do so, to abolish it.

Numerous historians have noted the strong religious influence on the American Revolution. One such historian was Harvard professor Perry Miller. Professor Miller was a convinced atheist, but he probably knew the primary sources of colonial history better than anyone of his generation. He concluded in *Nature's Nation:* "Actually, European deism was an exotic plant in America, which never struck roots in the soil. 'Rationalism' was never so widespread as liberal historians, or those fascinated by Jefferson, have imagined. The basic fact is that the Revolution had been preached to the masses as a religious revival, and had the astounding fortune to succeed."[6]

The importance of America's clergy has been too often ignored as a primary factor in the coming revolution and the support of it. They were called the "black regiment"—referring to their clerical robes—of the revolution. Professor Miller's words are vitally important:

> [We] still do not realize how effective were generations of Protestant preaching in evoking patriotic enthusiasm. No interpretation of the religious utterances as being merely sanctimonious window dressing will do justice to the facts or to the character of the populace. Circumstances and the nature of the dominant opinion in Europe made it necessary for the official statement [that is, Declaration of Independence] to be released in primarily "political" terms—the social compact, inalienable rights, the right of revolution. But those terms, in and by themselves, would never have supplied the drive to victory, however mightily they weighed with the literate minority. What carried the ranks of militia and citizens was the universal persuasion that they, by administering to themselves a spiritual purge, acquired the energies God has always, in the manner of the Old Testament, been ready to impart to His repentant children.[7]

And we must again remember the *Wall Street Journal's* statement about the place the earlier revivals had in America "that helped sow the seeds of the American Revolution."

The thirteen colonies concluded that the time had come and they disobeyed. We must understand that for Rutherford and Locke, and for the Founding Fathers, *the bottom line* was not an abstract point of conversation over a tea table; at a certain point it had to be acted upon. The thirteen colonies reached the bottom line: they acted in civil disobedience. That civil disobedience led to open war in which men and women died. And that led to the founding of the United States of America. There would have been no founding of the United States of America without the Founding Fathers' realization that there is *a bottom line*. And to them the basic *bottom line* was not pragmatic; it was one of principle.

Please read most thoughtfully what I am going to say in the next sentence: *If there is no final place for civil disobedience, then the government has been made autonomous, and as such, it has been put in the place of the Living God.* If there is no final place for civil disobedience, then the government has been put in the place of the Living God, because then you are to obey it even when it tells you in its own way at that time to worship Caesar. And that point is exactly where the early Christians performed their acts of civil disobedience even when it cost them their lives.

CHAPTER TEN

By Teaching, by Life, by Action

What does all this mean in practice to us today? I must say, I really am not sure all that it means to us in practice at this moment. To begin, however, it certainly means this: We have been utterly foolish in our concentration on bits and pieces, and in our complete failure to face the total world view that is rooted in a false view of reality. And we have not understood that this view of reality inevitably brings forth totally different and wrong and inhuman results in all of life. This is nowhere more certain than in law and government—*where law and government are used by this false view of reality as a tool to force this false view and its results on everyone.*

It is time we consciously realize that when *any office* commands what is contrary to God's Law it abrogates its authority. And our loyalty to the God who gave this law then requires that we make the appropriate response in that situation to such a tyrannical usurping of power. I would emphasize at this point that Samuel Rutherford was not wrong, he was right; it was not only in the seventeenth century in Scotland where he was right; it was not only in 1776 where he was right: he is right in our century.

All we have been saying is relevant for the present moment, and especially in such areas as abortion. You will remember, however, that the primary consideration we have been dealing with is the possibility that the window which is now open might close. But the *First Track* is based on the window being open at the moment and our taking advantage of it. *We must not be satisfied with mere words.* With the window open we must try to roll back the results of the total world view which considers material-energy, shaped by chance, as the final reality. We must realize that this view will with inevitable certainty always bring forth results which are not only relativistic, and not only wrong, but which will be inhuman, not only for other people, but for our children and grandchildren, and our spiritual children. It will always bring forth what is inhuman, for with its false view of total reality it not only does not have a basis for the uniqueness and dignity of the individual person, but it is totally ignorant as to what, and who, Man is.

As we think about these things, we must think about one other factor: Those who have the responsibility as Christians, as they live under Scripture, must not only take the necessary legal and political stands, but must practice all the possible Christian alternatives simultaneously with taking stands politically and legally. In *Whatever Happened to the Human Race?* we stress this in regard to abortion, infanticide, and euthanasia of the old—that Christians must not only speak and fight against these things, but then must show there are Christian alternatives. But it must not only be in regard to abortion, infanticide, and euthanasia that alternatives are practiced. They must be practiced in all areas. This is so, and especially so, even when it is extremely costly in money, time, and energy.

As a positive example, the Christian Legal Society has set up a service for mediating disputes. I would say that is a Christian alternative. In a number of places crisis pregnancy centers have been set up. That is a proper alternative. We should be practicing these alternatives in all areas even as we stand legally and politically against our present society's and government's wrong solutions for the ills of humanity. We indeed are to be humanitarians in living contrast to the inhumanity brought forth by materialistic humanism.

Now I must quickly say there are going to be people who say, "don't use the legal and political means, just show the Christian alternatives." That is absolutely utopian in a fallen world, and specifically in a world such as ours at the present moment. But while it is utopian to say, just use the Christian alternatives and do not use the political and legal means, on the other hand, it is also incomplete and wrong only to use the legal and political means without showing forth the Christian alternatives. It is incomplete in conviction and will be incomplete in results; and it is wrong to the reality of the God we say we are obeying.

If we do not practice the alternatives commanded in the Scripture we are not living under the Scripture. And if we do not practice *the bottom line* of civil disobedience on the appropriate level, when the state has abrogated its authority, we are equally not living under the Scripture.

I would conclude by summarizing this Manifesto as follows:

1. The Reformation in Northern Europe not only brought forth a clear preaching of the gospel, but also brought forth distinctive governmental and social results. Among these was a form-freedom balance in government with its series of checks and balances. There was great freedom without the freedom pounding the order of the society to pieces because it was contained by the Christian consensus.

2. In the middle of the last century, groups began to enter the United States in increasing number which did not have the Reformation base. These enjoyed the freedom, though their base would not have produced it.

3. The greatest shift came with the rise of the material-energy, chance view of final reality. This view was completely contrary to that which had produced the form-freedom balance in the United States with its resulting great freedom. This mistaken view of what final reality is leaves no room for meaning, purpose, or values in the universe and it gives no base for law. This view brings forth its natural results in all fields, and these results are the opposite of the natural results of the final reality being the personal God.

The humanistically based view of final reality began to be influential in the United States about eighty years ago. Its control of the consensus has become overwhelmingly dominant in about the last forty years. The shift has affected all parts of society and culture, but most importantly it has come largely to control government and law. These, then, have become the vehicle for forcing this view (with its natural results) on the public. This has been true in many areas—including, especially, the way it has been forced on students in the schools. Media which almost entirely hold the same world view have added to all this.

4. The world view which produced the founding of the United

States in the first place is increasingly now not allowed to exert its influence in government, in the schools, or in the public means of information.

The result of the original base in the United States gave the possibility of "liberty and justice for all." And while it was always far from perfect, it did result in liberty. This included liberty to those who hold other views—views which would not give the freedom. The material-energy, chance view has taken advantage of that liberty, supplanted the consensus, and resulted in an intolerance that gives less and less freedom in courts and schools for the view which originally gave the freedoms. Having no base for law, those who hold the humanist view make binding law whatever they personally think is good for society at the moment. This leads increasingly to arbitrary law and rulings which produce chaos in society and which then naturally and increasingly tend to lead to some form of authoritarianism. At that point what the country had in the first place is lost and dead.

5. What is now needed is to stand against that other total world view. We must see and make clear that it is not the truth of final reality; and we must understand and show that it is producing its own natural results which are opposite to those upon which the United States was founded. It is opposite to the great freedoms produced which everyone now enjoys. What is needed at this time is to take the steps necessary to break the authoritarian hold which the material-energy, chance concept of final reality has on government and law.

6. The result would be freedom for all and especially freedom for all religion. That was the original purpose of the First Amendment.

7. With this freedom Reformation Christianity would compete in the free marketplace of ideas. It would no longer be subject to a hidden censorship as it is now. It can and would give out the clear preaching of God's "good news" for individuals, and simultaneously it is also the view which gives the consistent base for the form-freedom balance in government and society—the base which brought forth this country with its freedoms. It is the responsibility of those holding this view to show it to be unique (the truth of total reality) for individual salvation and for society—by teaching, by life, and by action.

For our offenses are many in your sight,
    and our sins testify against us.
Our offenses are ever with us,
    and we acknowledge our iniquities:
rebellion and treachery against the Lord,
    turning our backs on our God,
fomenting oppression and revolt [against God],
    uttering lies our hearts have conceived.
So justice is driven back,
    and righteousness stands at a distance;
truth has stumbled in the streets,
    honesty cannot enter.
Truth is nowhere to be found,
    and whoever shuns evil becomes a prey.
The Lord looked and was displeased
    that there was no justice.
He saw that there was no one,
    and he was appalled that there was no one to intercede.[8]

Wake up! Strengthen the things which remain,
    that are about to die,
For I have not found your deeds complete in the sight of my God.[9]

References

Books, articles, films, and records mentioned in the text.

Ball, William Bentley, "Religious Liberty: The Constitutional Frontier," a paper given at the Christian Legal Society Conference, South Bend, Ind., April 1980.

Blackstone, William. *Commentaries on the Law of England.* Chicago: University Chicago Press, 1979.

Bracton, Henry De. *De Legibus et Consuetudinibus.* Cambridge, Mass.: Harvard-Belknap, 1968.

Bunyan, John. *Pilgrim's Progress.* (Many editions in print.)

Durant, Will and Ariel. *The Lessons of History.* New York: Simon and Schuster, 1968.

————. *The Story of Civilization,* 10 vols. New York: Simon and Schuster, 1935–1967.

Dylan, Bob. *Slow Train Coming* (record), New York: CBS, Inc., 1979.

Ericsson, Samuel E. *Clergy Malpractice: Constitutional and Political Issues.* Washington, D.C.: The Center for Law and Religious Freedom, 1981.

Finney, Charles. *Systematic Theology.* Minneapolis: Bethany Fellowship, 1976.

Fisk, James L. *The Law and Its Timeless Standard.* Washington, D.C.: Lex Rex Institute, 1981.

Guinness, Os. *The Dust of Death.* Downers Grove, Ill.: InterVarsity Press, 1973.

Humanist Manifestos I and II. New York: Prometheus Books, 1973.

Jackson, Jeremy. *No Other Foundation: The Church Through Twenty Centuries.* Westchester, Ill.: Crossway Books, 1979.

Knox, John. "A Godly Warning or Admonition to the Faithful in London, Newcastle, and Berwick," in *The Works of John Knox,* Vol. 3. New York: AMS Press, 1966.

Kuehnelt-Leddihn, Eric von. *Leftism: From de Sade and Marx to Hitler and Marcuse.* New Rochelle, N.Y.: Arlington House, 1974.

Legge, Francis. *Forerunners and Rivals of Christianity from 330 B.C. to A.D. 330.* New Hyde Park, N.Y.: University Books, 1964.

Miller, Perry, ed. *The Legal Mind in America: From Independence to the Civil War.* Cornell, N.Y.: Cornell University Press, 1962.

Miller, Perry. *Nature's Nation.* Cambridge, Mass.: Harvard-Belknap, 1967.

Monod, Jacques. *Chance and Necessity.* New York: Knopf, 1971.

Peters, Charles. *How Washington Really Works.* Reading, Mass.: Addison-Wesley, 1980.

Pit, Jan. *Persecution: It Will Never Happen Here?* Orange, Calif.: Open Doors With Brother Andrew, 1981.

Plato. *Republic.* (Many editions in print.)

Provine, William B. "The End of Ethics?" in *Hard Choices* (a magazine companion to the television series *Hard Choices*). Seattle, Wash.: KCTS-TV, channel 9, University of Washington, 1980.

Ridley, Jasper. *John Knox.* New York: Oxford, 1968.

Rutherford, Samuel. *Lex Rex: Or the Law and the Prince.*

Sagan, Carl. *Cosmos,* a public television series.

Schaeffer, Francis A. *Escape From Reason.* Downers Grove, Ill.: InterVarsity Press, 1968.

————. *He Is There and He Is Not Silent.* Wheaton, Ill.: Tyndale House, 1972.

————. *How Should We Then Live?* Old Tappan, N.J.: Revell, 1976.

————. *How Should We Then Live?* (film). Muskegon, Mich., 1976.

————. *Pollution and the Death of Man: The Christian View of Ecology.* Wheaton, Ill.: Tyndale House, 1970.

————. *The God Who Is There.* Downers Grove, Ill.: InterVarsity Press, 1968.

————, and Koop, C. Everett, M.D. *Whatever Happened to the Human Race?* Old Tappan, N.J.: Revell, 1979.

————, and Koop, C. Everett, M.D. *Whatever Happened to the Human Race?* (film). Los Gatos, Calif., 1979.

Schaeffer, Franky. *Addicted to Mediocrity.* Westchester, Ill.: Crossway Books, 1981.

————. *Plan for Action.* Old Tappan, N.J.: Revell, 1980.

————. *Reclaiming the World* (film). In process.

Snyder, Howard A. *The Radical Wesley.* Downers Grove, Ill.: InterVarsity Press, 1980.

Whitehead, John W. *The Second American Revolution.* Elgin, Ill.: David C. Cook, 1982.

Woods, David Walker. *John Witherspoon.* Old Tappan, N.J.: Revell, 1906.

Notes to Volume V

BOOK ONE: POLLUTION AND THE DEATH OF MAN

Chapter 1. "What Have They Done to Our Fair Sister?"
[1] For a technical study of Wingate's work, see *Science* magazine, March 1, 1968, pp. 979-981.
[2] From "Strange Days" by the Doors, Elektra EKS 74014. Copyright Polydon Records Ltd.
[3] This appears as an Appendix of this book.
[4] See Appendix, page 57.

Chapter 2. Pantheism: Man Is No More Than the Grass.
[1] Aldous Huxley, *Island*, (New York: Harper and Row, 1962; London: Penguin), pp. 219, 220.
[2] See "Wilful Waste, Woeful Want," by Max Kirschner, *The Listener*, January 26, 1967.

Chapter 3. Other Inadequate Answers
[1] For a detailed consideration of these points, only touched upon here, see the books *The God Who Is There* and *Escape from Reason*.

BOOK THREE: WHATEVER HAPPENED TO THE HUMAN RACE?

[1] The barbarism of the holocaust was not limited to European Jewry. Gypsies, Slavs, Russians, German dissidents for political and religious reasons, resistance leaders from occupied European countries, ordinary captives in the course of war, and even children of some of these former categories were eliminated. However, the Jews were especially slated for total elimination. Heinrich Himmler delivered an address on October 10, 1943, to an assembly of SS generals at Poznan. By this time both Himmler and his audience must have known that Germany could not win the war. Himmler stated: "Among ourselves it should be mentioned quite frankly, and yet we will never speak of it publicly . . . I mean . . . the extirpation of the Jewish race . . . this is a page of glory in our history which has never been written and is never to be written."
[2] The following is the standard form of the Oath of Hippocrates taken by those current medical students who take an oath. This so-called "original" form of the oath is the most widely used, although frequently the reference to Apollo, the Physician, and the other gods is omitted:

> I swear by Apollo, the Physician, and Aesculapius and health and all-heal and all the gods and goddesses that, according to my ability and judgment, I will keep this oath and stipulation:
> To reckon him who taught me this art equally dear to me as my parents,

to share my substance with him and relieve his necessities if required: to regard his offspring as on the same footing with my own brothers, and to teach them this art if they should wish to learn it, without fee or stipulation, and that by precept, lecture and every other mode of instruction, I will impart a knowledge of the art to my own sons and to those of my teachers, and to disciples bound by a stipulation and oath, according to the law of medicine, but to none others.

I will follow that method of treatment which, according to my ability and judgment, I consider for the benefit of my patients, and abstain from whatever is deleterious and mischievous. I will give no deadly medicine to anyone if asked, nor suggest any such counsel; furthermore, I will not give to a woman an instrument to produce abortion.

With Purity and with Holiness I will pass my life and practice my art. I will not cut a person who is suffering with a stone, but will leave this to be done by practitioners of this work. Into whatever houses I enter I will go into them for the benefit of the sick and will abstain from every voluntary act of mischief and corruption; and further from the seduction of females or males, bond or free.

Whatever, in connection with my professional practice, or not in connection with it, I may see or hear in the lives of men which ought not to be spoken abroad I will not divulge, as reckoning that all such should be kept secret.

While I continue to keep this oath unviolated may it be granted to me to enjoy life and the practice of the art, respected by all men at all times but should I trespass and violate this oath, may the reverse be my lot.

[3]Jaan Kangilaski writing in *Medical Forum* in May 1978 reported on an informal survey of 1977 commencement practices in reference to the Hippocratic Oath. One hundred and thirty-two medical schools were queried; ninety-two responded. Fifty-three schools used the "original" form of the Hippocratic Oath, twenty-six used the Declaration of Geneva, thirteen used the prayer of Maimonides, and seven others used various other pledges, sometimes student written.

Sometimes the oath is administered to the class; sometimes one student or one faculty member recites the pledge and others follow; sometimes the pledge is said by one person while the others stand silent; and at Yale the 1977 program allowed time so that those who wished to take the oath could do so in silence.

[4]George F. Will, *Newsweek*, April 4, 1977, p. 96.

[5]*Time*, August 1, 1977, p. 54.

[6]Edward O. Wilson wrote *Sociobiology: The New Synthesis* in 1975 (Belknap Press of Harvard University). His more recent book (1978)—*On Human Nature* (Harvard University Press)—applies his ideas specifically to human behavior.

[7]*Time*, August 1, 1977, p. 54.

[8]Joan Hutchison, writing in *Challenge* for May/June 1976, started her essay dealing with the history of child abuse in the following way: "Burned, bashed, beaten, stomped, suffocated, strangled, poisoned, choked, ripped, steamed, boiled, dismembered, bitten, raped, clubbed, banged, torn. Ignored, starved, abandoned, exploited, demeaned, ridiculed, treated with coldness and indifference or unreasonable demands."

[9]Gay Pauley, "Of Cries, Whispers, and Incest," *Philadelphia Evening Bulletin*, October 3, 1977.

[10]Gay Pauley, "Incest: Healing Taboos, Harsh Wounds," *Philadelphia Evening Bulletin,* October 4, 1977.

[11]A number of forces at work in America are antifamily. Among these are the constantly climbing divorce rate, the gay-liberation movement, extreme forms of women's lib, and abortion-on-demand. One child in six now lives in a single-parent family. Of every eight women giving birth to a child, one is not married (compared to one in twenty in 1960). More than half of American married women with children of ages six through seventeen are now in the labor force (double the 1948 rate). A third of unmarried women with children under three are in the work force.

[12]Mothers who have had several abortions are more likely than others to beat their children, according to a study conducted by Dr. Burton G. Schoenfeld, a child psychiatrist of Prince Georges County General Hospital in Maryland.

[13]In the National Right to Life *News* of January 1977, Jesse L. Jackson had this to say on the right of privacy: "There are those who argue that the right to privacy is of higher order than the right to life . . . that was the premise of slavery. You could not protest the existence or treatment of slaves on the plantation because that was private and therefore outside your right to be concerned. . . . The Constitution called us three-fifths human and the whites further dehumanized us by calling us 'niggers.' It was part of the dehumanizing process. . . . These advocates taking life prior to birth do not call it killing or murder, they call it abortion. They further never talk about aborting a baby because that would imply something human. . . . Fetus sounds less than human and therefore can be justified. . . .

"What happens to the mind of a person, and the moral fabric of a nation, that accepts the aborting of the life of a baby without a pang of conscience? What kind of a person and what kind of a society will we have twenty years hence if life can be taken so casually? It is that question, the question of our attitude, our value system, and our mind set with regard to the nature and worth of life itself that is the central question confronting mankind. Failure to answer that question affirmatively may leave us with a hell right here on earth."

[14]John T. Noonan, Jr., "Why a Constitutional Amendment?" *Human Life Review* 1:28 (1975).

[15]Ibid.

Did the Court really go so far? Here is what it held:

Until a human being is "viable" or "capable of meaningful life," a state has no "compelling interest" that justifies it in restricting in any way in favor of the fetus a woman's fundamental personal liberty of abortion. For six months, or "usually" for seven months (the Court's reckoning), the fetus is denied the protection of law by virtue of either the Ninth Amendment or the Fourteenth Amendment.

After viability has been reached, the human being is not a person "in the whole sense," so that even after viability he or she is not protected by the Fourteenth Amendment's guarantee that life shall not be taken without due process of law. At this point he or she is, however, legally recognizable as "potential life."

. . . The state may require that after the first trimester abortions be performed in licensed "facilities," and that after viability they be regulated so long as "health" abortions are not denied. The state is constitutionally barred, however, from requiring review of the abortion decision by a hospital committee or concurrence in the decision by two physicians other than the attending physician. The Constitution also prohibits a state from requiring that the abortion be in a hospital licensed by the Joint Committee on Accreditation of Hospitals or indeed that it be in a hospital at all.

[16]Archibald Cox, *The Role of the Supreme Court in American Government* (New York: Oxford University Press, 1976).

[17]It is interesting to note that while over a million unborn babies were being destroyed in the womb each year, the same Supreme Court which made that slaughter possible stopped the construction of the $116,000,000 Tellico Dam in Tennessee—because it might wipe out the snail darter, a three-inch fish. Since then, the threat to the lousewort plant has raised legal questions about building a power plant in Maine, and the orange-bellied mouse has complicated citing requirements for a power plant near San Francisco. A $340,000,000 dam on the Stanislaus River in California ran into legal difficulties because a ⅝-inch daddy-long-legs spider dwells there. There are quotas on whales and porpoises, but it is always open season on unborn babies. Although we can applaud the efforts to preserve our environment, it seems that we have confused our priorities.

[18]The organization Planned Parenthood, on the other hand, is flourishing. With millions and millions of dollars of taxpayers' money (plus substantial sums from private fund raising) and usually working with the American Civil Liberties Union, Planned Parenthood launched an all-out war against pro-life gains. This is a far cry from what its founder Margaret Sanger had in mind when the organization was an active proponent of "birth control." Mrs. Sanger always believed that abortion was killing.

Planned Parenthood-World Population describes itself as "the nation's foremost agent of social change in the area of reproductive health and well-being." In 1976 their audited statement reported $89,900,000 in income. In fact, when Title X funds are considered, Planned Parenthood is fueled with $300,000,000 annually from the United States Government at some level as it pursues its goal.

The law is clear concerning the use of Title X funds for abortion: *None of the funds appropriated under Title X may be used in programs where abortion is a method of family planning.* Planned Parenthood's Jeannie Rosoff contends: "There is no basis for believing that the prohibition of Title X funds for abortion as a method of family planning was intended to prohibit the use of such funds for abortion counseling and referral or even promotion or encouragement of abortion."

[19]Harold O. J. Brown, in comparing the action of the United States Supreme Court with that of the West German Federal Constitutional Court (in an action the latter took in June 1974) had this to say: "The West German Federal Constitutional Court dealt with the question of unlimited right to abortion on demand on the basis of an elevation of fundamental questions concerning the nature of man and the requirements of justice, which the courts held to be reflected in the German Federal Constitution. The decision of the American Court represents the deliberate avoidance of the larger moral, ethical, and anthropological questions to which the German court addressed itself. . . . The comparison between the American and German courts' thinking on the issue was especially disappointing. No one familiar with *Roe* v. *Wade* can fail to recognize that in it the

highest American court has evaded the basic moral issue and resolved a fundamental question only on the basis of technical legal construction." (*see* Harold O. J. Brown, "Abortion: Rights or Technicalities," *Human Life Review*, Vol. 1, No. 3, 1975, pp. 72, 73.)

[20]Harold O. J. Brown, "Abortion and Child Abuse," *Christianity Today*, October 7, 1977, p. 34.

[21]As recently as 1967, at the First International Conference on Abortion, a purely secular group of people said, "We can find no point in time between the union of sperm and egg and the birth of an infant at which point we can say that this is not a human life" (Washington, D.C.: conference sponsored by Harvard Divinity School and Joseph P. Kennedy, Jr., Foundation).

[22]According to nurses' testimony after the uterus was opened at the time of hysterotomy, Dr. Edelin purportedly cut off the blood supply of an allegedly viable fetus by detaching the placenta and waiting three minutes before removing the fetus from the uterus. A number of emotional factors were introduced by the media during this trial. One of these factors was that the trial was taking place in Roman Catholic Boston which obviously should be against abortion. A second of these factors was that Dr. Edelin was black and therefore the trial was seen to be racist. The final conclusion of the case was that a higher court reversed the lower court's decision and Dr. Edelin was not only free but went on to become the president of a national medical organization.

[23]*Markle* v. *Abele* (1972), Supreme Court of the United States, No. 72-56, 72-730, p. 72.

[24]The Waddill case raises a very serious difference between what the Supreme Court has called the woman's right to have an abortion-on-demand and what actually happens in cases of live births following abortion—and that is the destruction of the living baby. There is nothing even implied in the woman's "right" to abortion that says she also has the right to a dead child.

Waddill was charged with strangling a baby girl at Westminster Community Hospital, March 2, 1977, after an unsuccessful abortion attempt. At a preliminary hearing in April 1977 before the jury trial in January 1978, Dr. Ronald Cornelsen testified that Dr. Waddill throttled the infant's neck and complained about what would happen if the baby survived. According to Cornelsen's testimony, Waddill said that there would be lawsuits, that the baby would be brain damaged, and talked about stopping respiration by drowning or injecting potassium chloride.

At the trial in January 1978, Mrs. Joanne Griffith, a nurse at the hospital where the abortion was performed, testified that another nurse had quoted Dr. Waddill on the telephone as ordering everyone involved not to do anything, and to leave the baby alone. Dr. Cornelsen testified at the trial that when he first examined the baby, and the heart was beating sixty to seventy times a minute with a regular rhythm, there was some discoloration on the baby's neck (allegedly from the first attempt at strangling) and further testified that while he was examining the baby, Dr. Waddill ". . . stuck his hand back in [the isolette] and pressed the baby's neck again" (from *The Los Angeles Times*, January 26, February 8, 1978).

Dr. Waddill was brought to trial again on the same charges in the same case in 1979.

[25]*Medical World News*, November 14, 1977.

[26]Ibid.

[27]Ibid.

[28]Ibid.

[29]*Fort Lauderdale News*, November 13, 1977.

[30]Ibid.

[31]"You Be the Judge," *National Newsline*, February 1975 (Dayton, Ohio: Nurses Concerned for Life, Inc.).

[32]Leon Kass, as quoted by George F. Will in "Discretionary Killing," *Newsweek*, September 20, 1976.

[33]The Akron ordinance regulating abortion was put together and guided through City Council by a twenty-three-year-old Orthodox Jew named Marvin Weinberger, a Boston University law student. He took leave from Boston University Law School and formed a group called Citizens for Informed Consent and guided the ordinance from its original draft and early public hearings to a 7-to-6 City Council victory.

[34]Dr. Matthew Bulfin, onetime president of Pro-Life Obstetricians and Gynecologists, has done a study on more than 300 patients who previously had legal abortions and later saw him as gynecological patients. He developed a set of questions that he asked this selected group of patients. Here are some of the things he learned:

The vast majority of women would not have had an abortion if it were illegal to do so.

For 90 percent of the women, a physician apparently never entered into the decision to have an abortion.

The majority of women did not even know the name of the doctor who performed the abortion.

The great majority of patients did not seem to recall any discussion of the risks of the abortion itself or the possible risks of future childbearing.

Not one patient admitted to having any kind of thorough examination until the actual pelvic exam that was done as the abortion was about to be started.

When complications occurred after the abortion, most women reported they did not know the name of the doctor nor had they any confidence in him and therefore usually called their own gynecologist or went to the emergency room of the nearest hospital.

Dr. Bulfin used to ask this question: "Were you aware at any time that you might be destroying a human life when you had your abortion?" The reason he stopped asking the question is that too many patients either broke down in tears or became upset because they thought he might be about to impose a religious prejudice on them (*Newsletter:* Pro-Life Obstetricians and Gynecologists).

[35]It is very difficult to obtain statistics in the United States that illuminate the effects of abortion on the woman. The 1973 Supreme Court ruling, which made possible the establishment of free-standing clinics outside the scrutiny of accreditation groups, contributes to the loss of statistical data for these purposes. The Department of Health, Education and Welfare released an "interim report" in 1978, indicating that women who have had an abortion face an 85 percent higher "spontaneous fetal death ratio" in subsequent pregnancies.

The National Health Service in Great Britain keeps excellent records and has been in the abortion-on-demand business for several years longer than the United States. These records have revealed an increase in illegitimacy, venereal disease, prostitution, and pelvic inflammatory disease from gonorrhea, as well as sterility of previously aborted mothers and subsequent spontaneous abortions or miscarriages. Ectopic pregnancies—where the egg is implanted not in the uterus but in the Fallopian tube, requiring an emergency abdominal operation—have doubled since abortion has been liberalized. Prematurity in British women who have had a previous abortion is 40 percent higher than those who have not.

In May 1976, the *British Medical Journal* reported a paper by Richardson and Dickson entitled "The Effects of Legal Termination on Subsequent Pregnancy" (May 29, 1976, pp. 1303-04). Using the Richardson and Dickson statistics, Barbara J. Siska has done a study on what that means for the one million American woman who abort their babies in a given year (*Newsletter* of National Right to Life Committee, Summer 1976). Projecting from such a small sample as that given by Richardson and Dickson gives only a rough estimate, but close enough to reveal the magnitude of the problems induced by abortion. About 430,000 women who had abortions (out of the 1,000,000) would not now be pregnant a second time had they carried their babies to term, since there would be no time for them to get pregnant. Inasmuch as about 48 percent of all abortions are performed on women who have no living children, Siska had this to say about the 478,000 women (who aborted their first babies): "As many as 88,000 will lose their 'wanted' baby. Taking into account the normal infant mortality rate for 1974 (16.7 per 1,000), 26,000 infants would die solely because their mothers had abortions beforehand."

[36]Harold O. J. Brown has this to say about the separation of church and state: "No American historian would seriously contend that the phrase 'regarding an establishment of religion' in the First Amendment means anything other than what it says: it forbids the establishment of a national religion or church. . . ." (It did not in fact forbid the establishment of *state churches,* as both Massachusetts and Connecticut had them at the time of the amendment's adoption and retained them for many years to come. The limitations of federal power contained in the Bill of Rights have subsequently been extended to apply to the individual states as well. Yet even when applied to the states, the First Amendment means only that no state may establish a state church, just as the federal government may not establish a national church. It certainly did not mean, in its conception, that nothing in public law or policy may reflect the convictions or insights of any church or of the Christian religion [*see* Harold O. J. Brown, "The Passivity of American Christians," *Christianity Today,* January 16, 1976].)

[37]More and more feminists are disgusted with the realities of the abortion situation. One such group is known as Women Exploited. Their leader, Sandra Haun, testified before the Pennsylvania legislature as follows: "The members of our organization have all had abortions and have come to realize, too late, that our decision was wrong. We were encouraged and pushed into a hasty decision that now we find impossible to live with. We were lied to and deliberately misinformed."

[38]From the same Children's Hospital in Sheffield where Robert Zachary works, pediatrician John Lorber, discouraged with the results of surgery on spina bifida (cleft spine) and its complications, has in visits to this country been urging his American counterparts to consider not operating on at least the 20 percent of victims who are severely affected. Lorber claims that among 323 children treated vigorously from 1959 to 1963 only 7 percent were normal.

This view has been countered particularly by Dr. John M. Freeman at Johns

Hopkins University School of Medicine. Freeman quoted a series of 171 patients with spina bifida treated at the University of Pennsylvania between 1963 and 1968. Of the children with thoracolumbar lesions, 42 percent had IQs of 80 or better and were able to get around "albeit often with braces and crutches," said Dr. Freeman, "so the outlook does not have to be as bad as Dr. Lorber would have us believe."

Patients with spina bifida have been frequently reported to die quickly if unattended. This is not so. About 60 percent of untreated patients are alive at a month, 45 percent at two months, 19 percent at one year, and 16 percent at two years. Though these untreated children do not die quickly, they die slowly, over months and years and sometimes don't die at all.

[39]The term *cost containment* is the magic phrase in medical economics today. It did not seem to be the case when the right of every citizen to dialysis, pending kidney transplantation, was established by federal law. But in a few years the cost of intensive care is singled out as being too much for the American people to bear. One is considered an intolerable reactionary if he compares the cost of medical care with that of unnecessary luxuries such as alcohol or tobacco. Nevertheless, the figures invite comparison.

If we are social burdens in days to come, it seems fair to assume that our futures are somewhat limited. If, in addition to being social burdens, we are economic burdens as well, we don't stand a chance.

One is amazed that in the debates concerning the cost of intensive care for premature babies (or youngsters born with congenital defects requiring surgery) so little mention is made of the good news concerning newborn intensive care. The kind of intensive care we are talking about has cut the neonatal death rate in half in less than a generation, and the cost of saving most babies referred to newborn intensive-care units is far less than the figures usually cited for extreme cases. At the Children's Hospital of Philadelphia (where one of us works in neonatal surgery), it would be absolutely impossible to achieve the results that we do in presenting perfectly normal, healthy youngsters to their parents were it not for our absolute dependence upon the technology of intensive care, coupled with the dedication and skill of physicians, nurses, and paramedical personnel.

Jeffrey J. Pomerantz, M.D., of the Cedars-Sinai Medical Center in Los Angeles, studied seventy-five infants weighing less than 1000 grams during the period from 1973 through 1975. He found that thirty infants (40 percent) lived, and 70 percent of these were judged to be neurologically and developmentally normal (one to three years later). Thus the intact survival rate was 28 percent.

Pomerantz calculated the average daily cost for each survivor to be $450. By dividing the total cost for all the babies by the twenty-one intact survivors, he found an average cost per "normal" survivor of $88,058. Even with inflation adjustment, Pomerantz concluded, "It is our belief, that the outcome justifies this expense" (*Pediatrics,* June 1978, as reported in *American Medical News).*

[40]A study was done in 1977 on the impact of an abnormal child upon the parents. In summary, thirty families with a newborn mongoloid baby were matched with thirty families with a normal baby. Both groups were followed for eighteen months to two years and interviewed six times. Few differences could be found in the mental or physical health of the parents in the two groups.

Interestingly enough, a low rate of broken homes was found among the families of mongoloid children living at home. There was an increased incidence of divorce and separation in families of similar children in institutions.

Author Ann Gath reports, "Despite their grief, the parents of almost half the mongol children in the study felt drawn closer together and their marriage rather strengthened than weakened by their shared tragedy, a view similar to that expressed by parents of older mongol children in a survey of school age siblings of mongol children [done earlier]" (*British Journal of Psychiatry*, 1977, 130:405-10).

A study by Burton in 1975 revealed that 64 percent of mothers and 53 percent of fathers of children with fibrocystic disease also believed that their problems and distress had brought them closer to their spouses. (*See* L. Burton, *The Family Life of Sick Children*, London: Routledge and Keagan, 1975).

[41]One of the most remarkable medical achievements in the world today is to be found centered in the Parisian suburb of Garches. Here, after acute care at the Raymond Poincare Hospital, a private paramedical corporation is overseeing the care of 450 patients on respirators in their own homes. Some of these patients are on total respiratory support, others only on demand. Many have completed their higher education and some are employed in responsible consultant positions. It is a marvelous example of hospital personnel, paramedical technicians, the government's assisting private enterprise, and the will of individuals to succeed in spite of handicaps. The man whose vision this was is a paraplegic.

[42]Another factor that must always be considered in such cases, although one does not plan them that way, is that what is learned in one individual spectacular success eventually has benefit to untold thousands of subsequent patients.

About a decade ago we had a newborn patient whose entire small bowel was gangrenous, and in desperation one of our surgeons put the bowel together after removing the gangrenous portion in the only possible way—but one which was incompatible with eventual survival. It was on this diminutive patient that the first total parenteral (other than intestinal) nutritional program ever tried on an infant was carried out. Although that youngster tragically succumbed to sepsis well over a year after her initial operation, the knowledge gained in that instance has benefitted literally thousands upon thousands of children the world over, to say nothing of the adults who have benefitted as well. Total parenteral nutrition as worked out on this youngster is perhaps one of the four or five outstanding medical achievements of the past decade.

[43]A questionnaire mailed to members of the surgical section of the American Academy of Pediatrics in 1975 sought to explore the beliefs and practices of the surgical Fellows concerning ethical issues in the care of the newborn with a life-threatening defect which was correctable by a surgical procedure.

While acknowledging the difficulties inherent in interpreting a questionnaire, it was clear that a substantial number of this group of elite surgeons would acquiesce to parents' wishes in not treating a newborn, but rather allowing him or her to die with intestinal atresia (obstruction with excellent prognosis after operation) alone (7.9 percent) or accompanied by mongolism (76.8 percent).

[44]Millard Everett, *Ideals of Life: An Introduction to Ethics and the Humanities, With Readings* (New York: Wiley, 1954). *Note:* This was quoted in *The Way We Die* by David Dempsey.

[45]In response to the publication of "Moral and Ethical Dilemmas in the Special-

Care Nursery" in the *New England Journal of Medicine* by Duff and Campbell in October of 1973, there appeared among other letters to the editor in the same journal (February 28, 1974) one by Joan L. Venes, M.D., and Peter R. Huttenlocher, M.D., of the Yale University School of Medicine. They described themselves as some of the "specialists based in the medical center" referred to by Duff and Campbell. This is the final paragraph of that letter:

"As consultants to the Newborn Special Care Unit, we wish to dissociate ourselves from the opinions expressed by the authors. The 'growing tendency to seek early death as a management option' that the authors referred to has been repeatedly called to the attention of those involved and has caused us deep concern. It is troubling to us to hear young pediatric interns ask first, 'Should we treat?' rather than 'How do we treat?': we are fearful that this feeling of nihilism may not remain restricted to the Newborn Special Care Unit. To suggest that the financial and psychological stresses imposed upon a family with the birth of a handicapped child constitutes sufficient justification for such a therapy of nihilism is untenable and allows us to escape what perhaps after all are the real issues—i.e., the obligation of an affluent society to provide financial support and the opportunity for a gainful life to its less fortunate citizens."

[46]Here is a quotation from a pediatric surgeon, appended to a questionnaire on his attitude toward patients with Down's syndrome: "I have a fifty-three-year-old cousin with Down's syndrome. His father is a ninety-three-year-old arteriosclerotic, incontinent at night of urine and stool. He refuses to go to a nursing home. They live alone and the son with Down's syndrome provides most of the care."

[47]Anthony Shaw, "Dilemmas of Informed Consent in Children," *New England Journal of Medicine*, October 25, 1973, pp. 885-890.

[48]*The Hastings Center Report*, Vol. 2, No. 5 (November 1972).

[49]"Euthanasia and Children: The Injury of Continued Existence," *Journal of Pediatrics*, 83 (1973), pp. 170, 171.

[50]J. Philip Wogaman in *The Washington Post*, August 16, 1977.

[51]*The New York Times*, July 28, 1977.

[52]*Commentary*, 53:8 (May 1972).

[53]Martha Willing, *Beyond Conception: Our Children's Children* (Ipswich, Massachusetts: Gambit, 1971), p. 174.

[54]*Medical Tribune*, July 20, 1977, pp. 23, 29.

[55]This book was probably the beginning of the German rationale for what began as euthanasia programs and ended up as attempted genocide of specific groups.

[56]The Quinlan case should never have gone to court in the first place. The medical malpractice climate in the United States at the time (and still present) was probably the major factor which initiated the court proceeding. Many in the medical profession hailed the decision on the part of the Quinlans to go to court, when they should have been appalled at the implications for their own future practice of medicine.

What the Karen Quinlan case threatened was the disruption of the patient-family-doctor relationship. It foretold the day when the doctor would become a technical instrument in the hands of the court and a hospital ethics committee.

Richard A. McCormick, S.J., of the Kennedy Institute Center for Bioethics in Washington, D.C., said it very well this way: ". . . the abiding issue [in the Quinlan case] is . . . the very moral matrix of the healing profession. That matrix roots in the conviction that decision making within health care . . . must be controlled primarily within the patient-doctor-family relationship and these decisions must be tailor made to individual cases and circumstances. If technology and law were largely to usurp these prerogatives . . . impersonal consideration would replace personal ones and preprogram our treatment. . . ."

[57]The New Jersey Supreme Court overruled the lower court in a 7-0 decision on March 31, 1976. The decision was as follows: "Upon the concurrence of the guardian [the father] and family of Karen, should the responsible attending physicians conclude that there is no reasonable possibility of Karen's ever emerging from her present comatose condition in a cognitive sapient state and that the self-support apparatus now being administered to Karen should be discontinued, they shall consult with the hospital's 'ethics committee' or like body of the institution in which Karen is then hospitalized.

"If that consultative body agrees . . . the present life support system may be withdrawn and said action shall be without any civil or criminal liability therefore on the part of any participant, whether guardian, physician, hospital or others. . . ."

So the ethics committee was written into the decision. Dr. Karen Teel (*Baylor Law Review* 6:8-9, 1975) stated that many hospitals have an ethics committee made up not only of physicians but also social workers, attorneys, and theologians. In a report in the *Medical Tribune* (January 5, 1977) Dr. Teel later said, "I now have more and more reservations concerning the establishment of ethics committees. . . . I now believe that each case must be decided on its own merits."

[58]The United States Supreme Court had refused to be drawn into the Karen Quinlan case in its refusal to review the decision of the New Jersey Supreme Court. At the time of this writing, February 1979, Karen is still alive.

[59]Since the Karen Quinlan case, medical and other literature has been filled with "guidelines" for the physician in difficult situations. But see how easily guidelines for stopping life-prolonging treatments for dying or comatose patients (which is commonly practiced by reputable physicians all over the world) can readily be turned into directives for euthanasia. A perfect example is when the Swiss Academy of Medical Sciences issued such guidelines. As reported in *The New York Times* with a dateline of Basel, Switzerland: "A doctor said if the 'directives concerning euthanasia were applied in the United States, doctors would be permitted to end intravenous feedings of Karen Quinlan, the comatose New Jersey woman whose case set off an international debate.' " There are a number of misconceptions in this Swiss doctor's statement. First of all, the directives given by the Swiss Academy of Medical Sciences were not euthanasia guidelines, but he saw fit immediately to use that term as being synonymous with the Academy's statement. Second, Karen Quinlan is not being fed by intravenous feedings, but by feedings introduced via a nasogastric tube. We call attention to this difference because improper reporting in this instance could legitimately raise the question of whether feedings by tube were as "extraordinary" as intravenous feedings in the care of Karen Quinlan.

[60]Robert R. Durzon, administrator of HEW's new health-care financing administration, suggested in a memorandum to Joseph A. Califano, secretary of HEW, in June of 1977 that federal Medicare funds be withheld from states that do not enact living-will laws which permit terminally ill patients to have life-support

equipment withdrawn. The memorandum stated: "Encouraging states to pass such a law or, more strongly, withholding federal funds without passage would lower health spending when such wills are executed. . . . Over one-fifth of Medicare expenditures are for persons in their last year of life. Thus in fiscal year 1978, $4.9 billion dollars will be spent for such persons and if just one-quarter of these expenditures were avoided through adoption of living wills, the savings under Medicare alone would amount to $1.2 billion . . ." (reported Wednesday, June 22, 1977, in the *Washington Post*).

[61] An example of such a board's going beyond its proscribed boundaries by natural progression is found in the Human Rights Commission's assumption of abortion as one of its arenas of activity.

[62] *Medical Tribune,* October 10, 1973.

[63] Joseph Fletcher, "Ethics and Euthanasia," *American Journal of Nursing,* 73:670 (1973).

[64] Medically, Fletcher's example is not a good one. It is possible to have brain metastases revealed by a brain scan and not be in either pain or extremis.

[65] *Philadelphia Evening Bulletin,* August 13, 1977.

[66] *Time,* September 5, 1977, p. 29.

[67] *Philadelphia Evening Bulletin,* August 13, 1977.

[68] *Newsweek,* July 4, 1977.

[69] Richard L. Rubenstein, *The Cunning of History: Mass Death and the American Future* (New York: Harper & Row, 1975).

[70] Frederic Wertham in *A Sign for Cain: An Exploration of Human Violence* (New York: Macmillan, 1966, 1969) makes it quite clear that people of various classes in Germany surrendered their own individual will and conscience to that of the state. The dehumanization and depersonalization which followed in Germany—and this is the lesson for us—was not that the German people and the Nazis in particular were ideologically fanatical with hatred for their victims, but rather they were totally indifferent to their fate.

Those who carried out the killings in the euthanasia programs were academic physicians, many times professors in outstanding universities. They were not "mad" in the sense that we talk about mad scientists; they had fallen under the spell of utilitarianism and were more concerned about the cost of caring for a patient as opposed to killing him.

[71] Leo Alexander, "Medical Science Under Dictatorship," *New England Journal of Medicine,* 241:39-47, July 14, 1949. (This was also covered in *Newsweek,* July 9, 1973.)

[72] Ibid.

[73] Ibid.

[74] We believe that the "living will" will be one of the actual instruments which act as the *thin edge of the wedge* in opening up our society to the euthanasia movement. The living will is a document (now enacted as law in several of the states) which directs physicians concerning the maker's terminal illness and extraordinary care.

The first major stumbling block in any living will centers around the use of the word *terminal* when it refers to the patient's illness. The living will gives to the physician certain rights which might not be the intent of the patient, who may not know that his illness is terminal and/or whose death might not be imminent.

It is very difficult to say when death is imminent. The first patient for whom one of us [C. E. Koop] would have ever been able to sign an affadavit in reference to the imminence of death had what was thought to be a *terminal* neuroblastoma. The patient has graduated from law school and is alive more than thirty years later. This experience has been repeated time after time. In the language of the California Act, it is the physician's decision which makes death "imminent."

In the Arkansas legislation, Section 1 includes the terms *artificial, extraordinary, extreme* or *radical,* and *medical or surgical means or procedures* in the case of a patient unable to discuss this matter with his physician. Even a layman could see that this opens Pandora's box.

[75]Dr. Richard M. Hunt, "No Fault Guilt-Free History," *The New York Times,* February 16, 1976. Copyright © 1976 by The New York Times Company. Used by permission.

[76]Donald P. Warwich, "The Moral Message of Bucharest," *The Hastings Center Report,* December 19, 1974.

[77]One can say things accurately but obscurely, so that the true meaning is present but hidden. A fertilized egg is a zygote. Who would suspect that a postcoital antizygotic pill would prevent the implantation of the fertilized egg?

In 1965 the American College of Obstetricians and Gynecologists changed the definition of human pregnancy. Conception ceased to mean "fertilization"; conception thereafter meant "implantation."

In the American College of Gynecology Terminology *Bulletin* (September 1965) conception is redefined as the implantation of a fertilized ovum. "This definition has been selected deliberately because union of sperm and ovum cannot be detected clinically unless implantation occurs."

[78]"When Scientists Play the Role of God," *London Times,* November 16, 1978.

[79]H. J. Blackham, et al., *Objections to Humanism* (Riverside, Connecticut: Greenwood Press, 1967).

[80]We would like to include a word about rationalism. The Enlightenment was a revolution in thought which took place in the eighteenth century in Europe. One of its main ideas was that man is autonomous; that is, man starts out from himself and measures all things by himself. Thus, there was no place for revelation. The philosophers felt that *reason* (man's) should be supreme, rather than any communication from God.

Looked at from this viewpoint, this movement is called rationalism. This word means that its proponents assumed that man (though finite and limited) can begin from himself and gather all the information needed to explain all things. Rationalism rejects knowledge outside of man himself, especially any knowledge from God. Rationalism led naturally to the present predominant world view we have described at the beginning of this chapter: that is, *materialism* (only matter exists) or *naturalism* (no supernatural exists).

Having this as their world view, the rationalists had increasingly no place for things which were said to be "supernatural," such as miracles, the raising of the dead, and Christ's Transfiguration. These things were, therefore, first said to be beyond knowledge and thus of little or no value. Later they were arbitrarily said to be impossible. This view did not come because of scientific facts, but was rooted in the rationalist world view which they accepted.

Influenced by this thinking, the philosophers and rationalistic theologians made a division in the Bible between those things which fitted in with their rationalistic ideas and those which did not. Their attitude can be summed up simply: God cannot be known as One who acts in history. Therefore, they tried to divide the Bible roughly into natural and supernatural parts. They felt that the supernatural parts were unworthy to be accepted by "modern man," that they belonged necessarily to the realm of primitive superstition, that there was nothing objectively true about them.

An example of one who took this approach is the German scholar David Friedrich Strauss who wrote *The Life of Jesus* in 1835. In it he said that most of the material in the Gospels is "mythical." Speaking of the Transfiguration, he wrote, "It is impossible to maintain this historical, supernatural interpretation which the New Testament sanctions." So what he proposed was a thoroughgoing demythologizing of the Gospel story. The real history, he said, had to be separated from this mythology.

Strauss was not the first scholar to state such opinions, but you can see from the date of *The Life of Jesus*—1835—that the revolution took place a long time ago. The movement as a whole has been called "religious liberalism," because of its "free" approach to the Bible. It grew in momentum during the nineteenth century, and its assumptions are still the assumptions of many scholars in the Protestant world today and of an increasing number of Roman Catholic theologians, too.

What is most disturbing about this approach to the Bible is not that it disagrees with past traditions, but rather that it claims to be "scientific." We must be clear that Christianity has nothing to fear from modern science. Indeed, Christianity was instrumental in the origin of science. Tradition and authority should not be just blindly accepted, but examined to see if the things previously believed are indeed true. What *is* dangerous is the misuse of the claim to be "scientific." We do not think it is too strong to speak of this as "deception."

By using the word *scientific,* the religious liberalists gave the impression of the same type of certainty and objectivity that had become accepted in regard to the physical sciences. Using this claim, they proposed their various theories of how the Bible had actually come into existence, and on the basis of these theories altered the teaching that Christians had previously accepted. They rejected the Bible's accounts of miracles, such as the feeding of the 5,000 or Jesus' walking on the water. But they went much further than that. For example, they rejected the idea of a coming judgment for mankind, of salvation through the substitutionary work of Christ, of the divinity of Christ, of the Resurrection, of the Virgin Birth, and so on. What was left was a religion of morality, called by some the "Religion of the Sermon on the Mount" (though this itself was a serious misrepresentation, for the Sermon on the Mount, as well as teaching a very high moral code, also teaches quite explicitly such things as future judgment by Jesus Himself).

To ordinary people, these developments were bewildering. However, for many the radical conclusions of the scholars seemed to be irresistible, for they were presented as the result of careful and objective scientific scholarship. To disagree with the scholars was to be obscurantist. To maintain the traditional ideas simply indicated a refusal to follow the truth wherever the truth led.

From where we stand today, it is easy to see how naive these views really are.

For what has happened since that time is, first, that the internal weaknesses of the so-called scientific theories have become apparent. Second, literally tons of archaeological materials have been unearthed from the periods and the geographic locations covered by the Bible. Archaeology as a science has made huge strides in the last hundred years.

The scholars fail at this point because they are not scientific enough! They have fallen into the same trap which they accuse those who preceded them of falling into—of bringing preconceived ideas about God's revelation to bear on the discipline of biblical criticism. Because of their world view they refuse to accept the possibility that God could have communicated to man in such a way that what is contained in the Bible is reliable. They caricature this idea with such terms as the "dictation theory of inspiration." By this they act as though the scholars through the centuries (who have held that God has given us truth through the Bible) have taught (and must teach) that God used the human writers of the Bible like typewriters, simply typing out what He wanted man to understand. But, while some may have taught the dictation theory of inspiration, it was not the generally held concept.

The generally held concept was that God used people in the writing of the Bible without destroying their individuality and their significance. What they finally wrote, however, was what God knew was necessary for people to have as a written authority. Each writer was "himself," so to speak, but as each wrote—in a different style from others, in a different historical context, in different literary forms, and sometimes in different languages—he was led by God to write what God intended to be written. Thus, truth was given in all the areas the Bible touches upon.

The critics have continued the tradition received from the last century, which argued that God could not work into the world supernaturally. As Strauss said, "It is *impossible* to maintain as historical the supernatural interpretations the New Testament sanctions." Strauss was correct on one point here. What the New Testament (including the teaching of Christ) teaches about the supernatural happenings in observable history is exactly what Strauss and the other liberal theologians have denied.

It is this sort of thinking which still underlies so much liberal scholarship. Why is it impossible, for example, for God to have effected the Virgin Birth when Jesus was born? After all, since God designed the birth process in the first place, why can He not in one case interrupt the normal action of cause and effect that He created and initiate something different? In the same way, if God created everything at the beginning, why can He not also give life to the dead and raise up Jesus' body from the tomb? The only reason these things and others like them are so categorically denied is that the rationalist or naturalist world view has already been accepted.

When you hear people being critical about the Bible, remember that what seems to be scientific is not always so, and what are claimed to be the "assured results of scholarship" are not always so assured.

Let us give a recent example relating to the dating of the New Testament documents. For over a hundred years the idea has circulated among many scholars that the documents of the New Testament (or most of them) could not have been written at, or soon after, the time of Jesus' ministry. These scholars suggested in some cases that the Gospels were written about 150 years later and were therefore quite unreliable. In the same way, it was common for scholars to suggest that letters supposedly written by Paul or Peter or John were not written by them but by unknown writers who used the apostles' names many years after they died to gain acceptance for what they had written.

A New Testament scholar, the ex-Bishop of Woolwich, John Robinson, now dean of Trinity College, Cambridge, has written a book called *Redating the New Testament* (1976). What is striking is that previously this author had taken a very "liberal" position. At the outset of his book on the dating of the New Testament, he says he first began to question the late dates assigned to the New Testament writers when he realized how "much more than is generally recognised, the chronology of the New Testament rests upon presuppositions rather than facts." And he quotes the following from a letter from a famous New Testament scholar, C. H. Dodd: "I should agree with you that much of this late dating is quite arbitrary, even wanton, the offspring not of any argument that can be presented."

[81]Francis Bacon, *The New Organon and Related Writings* (Indianapolis: Bobbs-Merrill, 1960).

[82]René Descartes, *Meditations on First Philosophy* (Indianapolis: Bobbs-Merrill, 1960).

[83]H. J. Blackham, et al., *Objections to Humanism* (Riverside, Connecticut: Greenwood Press, 1967).

[84]Ibid.

[85]David Hume, *A Treatise of Human Nature* (New York: E. P. Dutton, 1956).

[86]Steven Weinberg, *The First Three Minutes: A Modern View of the Origin of the Universe* (New York: Basic Books, 1976).

[87]Aldous Huxley, *Brave New World* (New York: Harper & Row, 1932).

[88]Robert M. Pirsig, *Zen and the Art of Motorcycle Maintenance: An Inquiry Into Values* (New York: William Morrow, 1974).

[89]Two important arguments for Charles Darwin (1809-1882) and those he convinced have now been almost totally abandoned by evolutionists. The first involves vestigial organs, which (it was supposed) had served useful functions in an earlier stage of man's evolutionary development, but which later became literally useless by the changes brought about through natural selection. Vestigial organs are like crutches one uses after being injured in an accident. They serve a purpose for a time, but when the leg is better the crutches are no longer needed. Certain organs were said to be "vestiges," that is, leftovers from a previous stage in evolution. The simple problem with the argument is that as medical science has developed, most of these organs have been found to serve useful functions in the body.

A second important argument for Darwin and those he convinced is the dictum that "ontogeny recapitulates phylogeny." This idea is that the human embryo goes through the stages of evolution inside the mother's womb, resembling at one stage the fish and so on. The better we understand the embryo, however, the more dubious this argument is seen to be.

Yet, even if these two arguments have been largely given up, many still place their faith in the theory of an unbroken line from the molecule to man by chance. However, they are faced in modern discussions with at least two problems. First, the more fossil evidence we find, the more apparent it becomes that there have always been distinct breaks in the fossil record. Darwin admitted that the paleontological evidence in his day was slender, but, he said, as more is discovered the new evidence will support the hypothesis. This just has not happened.

The evidence of preman is sketchy, and recent discoveries in Africa and elsewhere have generated some difficult new problems in this area. But it is not just the so-called missing links between man and preman that constitute the problem, but *all* the missing links, right down the whole line. Not only are links missing; the chains themselves are missing. If one removes the speculative guesses, rather than links of different chains leading from simple to more complex organisms, one finds virtual explosions of mature life forms at different periods in geological time and many simple forms of life that remain unchanged for several millions of years up to their extinction or even to today.

The second major difficulty for today's evolutionist is that there is no sufficient mechanism to explain how lower life forms can be transformed into higher ones, no matter how much time is allowed. Natural selection cannot bear this weight. Current genetic theories seem even to point to natural selection as working *against* the direction of evolution. Despite the unlikely possibility of mutations that are advantageous, natural selection seems to simplify the genetic endowment of any group rather than lead it to higher orders of complexity.

[90]Pierre Teilhard de Chardin (1881-1955) is an example of this. He was a member of the Jesuit order and a French paleontologist and philosopher. His approach to evolution was an attempt to solve these problems through the use of mystical language, which did justice to neither clear Christian teaching nor scientific thought.

[91]Paul Hazard, *European Thought in the Eighteenth Century: From Montesquieu to Lessing* (Magnolia, Massachusetts: Peter Smith).

[92]Albert Camus, *The Myth of Sisyphus and Other Essays* (New York: Alfred A. Knopf, 1955).

[93]William Barrett, *Irrational Man: A Study in Existential Philosophy* (New York: Doubleday, 1958), p. 248.

[94]The site of the biblical city called Lachish is about thirty miles southwest of Jerusalem. This city is referred to on a number of occasions in the Old Testament. Imagine a busy city with high walls surrounding it, and a gate in front that is the only entrance to the city. We know so much about Lachish from archaeological studies that a reconstruction of the whole city has been made in detail. This can be seen at the British Museum in the Lachish Room in the Assyrian section.

There is also a picture made by artists in the eighth century before Christ, the Lachish Relief, which was discovered in the city of Nineveh in ancient Assyria. In this picture we can see the Jewish inhabitants of Lachish surrendering to Sennacherib, the king of Assyria. The details in the picture and the Assyrian writing on it give the Assyrian side of what the Bible tells us in Second Kings:

In the fourteenth year of King Hezekiah's reign, Sennacherib king of Assyria attacked all the fortified cities of Judah and captured them. So Hezekiah king of Judah sent this message to the king of Assyria at Lachish: "I have done wrong. Withdraw from me, and I will pay whatever you demand of me." The king of Assyria exacted from Hezekiah king of Judah three hundred talents of silver and thirty talents of gold. So Hezekiah gave him all the silver that was found in the temple of the LORD and in the treasuries of the royal palace.

At this time Hezekiah king of Judah stripped off the gold with which he had covered the doors and doorposts of the temple of the LORD, and gave it to the king of Assyria.

2 Kings 18:13-16

We should notice two things about this. First, this is a real-life situation—a real siege of a real city with real people on both sides of the war—and it happened at a particular date in history, near the turn of the eighth century B.C. Second, the two accounts of this incident in 701 B.C. (the account from the Bible and the Assyrian account from Nineveh) do not contradict, but rather confirm each other. The history of Lachish itself is not so important for us, but it does illustrate how the Bible can be, and is, confirmed historically even in some of its smaller historical details.

A much more dramatic story surrounds the discovery of the Dead Sea Scrolls in the present century. The Dead Sea Scrolls, some of which relate to the text of the Bible, were found at Qumran, about fifteen miles from Jerusalem.

Most of the Old Testament was originally written in Hebrew, and the New Testament in Greek. Many people have been troubled by the length of time that has elapsed between the original writing of the documents and the present translations. How could the originals be copied from generation to generation and not be grossly distorted in the process? There is, however, much to reassure confidence in the texts we have.

In the case of the New Testament, there are codes of the whole New Testament (that is, manuscripts in book form, like the Codes Sinaiticus and Codex Alexandrinus, dated around the fourth and fifth centuries respectively) and also thousands of fragments, some of them dating back to the second century. The earliest known so far is kept in the John Rylands Library in Manchester, England. It is only a small fragment, containing on one side John 18:31-33 and on the reverse, verses 37 and 38. It is important, however, both for its early date (about A.D. 125) and for the place where it was discovered, namely Egypt. This shows that John's Gospel was known and read in Egypt at that early time. There are thousands of such New Testament texts in Greek from the early centuries after Christ's death and resurrection.

In the case of the Old Testament, however, there was once a problem. There were no copies of the Hebrew Old Testament in existence which dated from before the ninth century after Christ. This did not mean that there was no way to check the Old Testament, for there were other translations in existence, such as the Syriac and the Septuagint (a translation into Greek from several centuries before Christ). However, there was no *Hebrew* version of the Old Testament from earlier than the ninth century after Christ—because to the Jews the Scripture was so holy it was the common practice to destroy the copies of the Old Testament when they wore out, so that they would not fall into any disrespectful use.

Then, in 1947, a Bedouin Arab made a discovery not far from Qumran, which changed everything. While looking for sheep, he came across a cave in which he discovered some earthenware jars containing a number of scrolls. (These jars are now in the Israeli Shrine of the Book in Jerusalem.) Since that time at least ten other caves in the same vicinity have yielded up other scrolls and fragments. Copies of all the Old Testament books except Esther have been discovered (in part or complete) among these remains. One of the most dramatic single pieces was a copy of the Book of Isaiah dated approximately a hundred years before Christ. What was particularly striking about this is the great closeness of the discovered text to the Hebrew text, which we previously had, a text written about a thousand years later!

On the issue of text, the Bible is unique as ancient documents go. No other book from that long ago exists in even a small percentage of the copies we have of the Greek and Hebrew texts which make up the Bible. We can be satisfied that we have a copy in our hands which closely approximates the original. Of course, there have been some mistakes in copying, and all translations lose something of the original language. That is inevitable. But the fact that most of us use translations into French, German, Chinese, English, and so on does not mean that we have an inadequate idea of what was written originally. We lose some of the nuances of the language, even when the translation is good, but we do not lose the essential content and communication.

We looked earlier at the city of Lachish. Let us return to the same period in Israel's history when Lachish was besieged and captured by the Assyrian King Sennacherib. The king of Judah at that time was Hezekiah.

Perhaps you remember the story of how Jesus healed a blind man and told him to go and wash in the Pool of Siloam. It is the same place known by King Hezekiah, approximately 700 years earlier. One of the remarkable things about the flow of the Bible is that historical events separated by hundreds of years took place in the same geographic spots, and, standing in these places today, we can feel that flow of history about us. The crucial archaeological discovery which relates to the Pool of Siloam is the tunnel which lies behind it.

One day in 1880 a small Arab boy was playing with his friend and fell into the pool. When he clambered out, he found a small opening about two feet wide and five feet high. On examination, it turned out to be a tunnel reaching back into the rock. But that was not all. On the side of the tunnel an inscribed stone (now kept in the museum in Istanbul) was discovered, which told how the tunnel had been built originally. The inscription in classical Hebrew reads as follows:

> The boring through is completed. And this is the story of the boring: while yet they plied the pick, each toward his fellow, and while there were yet three cubits [4¼ feet] to be bored through, there was heard the voice of one calling to the other that there was a hole in the rock on the right hand and on the left hand. And on the day of the boring through the workers on the tunnel struck each to meet his fellow, pick upon pick. Then the water poured from the source to the Pool 1,200 cubits [about 600 yards] and a 100 cubits was the height of the rock above the heads of the workers in the tunnel.

We know this as Hezekiah's Tunnel. The Bible tells us how Hezekiah made provision for a better water supply to the city: "As for the other events of Hezekiah's reign, all his achievements and how he made the pool and the tunnel by which he brought water into the city, are they not written in the book of the annals of the kings of Judah?" (2 Kings 20:20). We know here three things: the biblical account, the tunnel itself of which the Bible speaks, and the original stone with its inscription in classical Hebrew.

Fron he Assyrian side, there is additional confirmation of the incidents mentioned in the Bible. There is a clay prism in the British Museum called the Taylor Prism (British Museum, Ref. 91032). It is only fifteen inches high and was discovered in the Assyrian palace at Nineveh. This particular prism dates from about 691 B.C. and tells about Sennacherib's exploits. A section from the prism reads, "As for Hezekiah, the Jew, who did not submit to my yoke, forty-six of his strong walled cities, as well as small cities in their neighbourhood I have besieged and took . . . himself like a caged bird, I shut up in Jerusalem, his royal city. Earthworks I threw up against him." Thus, there is a three-way confirmation concerning Hezekiah's tunnel from the Hebrew side and this amazing confirmation from the Assyrian side.

There is also a confirmation of what the Bible says concerning the Egyptian King Tirhakah who came up to oppose the Assyrians. Confirmation of his reality is typified by a sphinx-ram in the British Museum (British Museum, Ref. B.B. 1779). The small figure between the legs of the ram is a representation of King Tirhakah. The Bible says that when Sennacherib heard that Tirhakah, king of Egypt, was coming to fight against him, he sent messengers to tell Hezekiah that help from Egypt would be of no use to him (see 2 Kings 19:9, 10 and Isaiah 37:9, 10).

The date of Sennacherib's campaign in Palestine is 701 B.C., and something which has often puzzled historians is the role of Tirhakah, who was not king of Egypt and Ethiopia until 690 B.C. But the solution to this problem is simple. In 701 B.C. Tirhakah was only a prince at the side of his military brother, the new Pharaoh Shebitku, who sent Tirhakah with an army to help Hezekiah fend off the Assyrian advance. But the story in Kings and Isaiah does not end in 701 B.C. It carries right through to the death of Sennacherib in 681 B.C., which is nine years after Tirhakah had become king of Egypt and Ethiopia. In other words, the biblical narrative, from the standpoint of 681 B.C., mentions Tirhakah by the title he bore at that time (that is, 681 B.C.), not as he was in 701 B.C. This is still done today, using a man's title as he is known at the time of writing even if one is speaking of a previous time in his personal history.

Unaware of the importance of these facts, and falling into wrong interpretations of some of Tirhakah's inscriptions, some Old Testament scholars have stumbled over each other in their eagerness to diagnose historical errors in the Books of Kings and Isaiah. But as the archaeological confirmation shows, they were quite mistaken. What is striking about these archaeological finds is the way they often converge; there is often not just one line of evidence but several in which the biblical account is confirmed. We do not have confirmation of every single detail in the biblical account, by any means. Nor do we need such total confirmation in view of the amount of evidence there is. To insist on confirmation at every point would be to treat the Bible in a prejudiced way, simply because it is the Bible. The fact that it is a religious book does not mean that it cannot also be true when it deals with history.

Not all archaeological finds have a convergence of many different interrelated lines like these around the life of Hezekiah, but they are no less striking. For example, take the "ration tablets" discovered in the ruins of Babylon. The Bible tells us that after the Assyrians had destroyed the northern kingdom of Samaria (around 721 B.C.), the southern kingdom, Judah, survived for almost another 150 years until approximately 586 B.C. By this time Assyria, one of the greatest military powers of the ancient world, had been defeated by Babylon, a neighboring state to the east. That was in 609 B.C. Four years later the Babylonian general, Nebuchadnezzar—then the crown prince—came west and completely defeated Necho II, king of Egypt, at the battle of Carchemish. As a result of this victory he laid claim to Judah, which had previously been within the sphere of influence of Egypt. King Jehoiakim of Judah thus now paid tribute to the Babylonians. The Bible tells us that Jehoiakim rebelled three years later: "During Jehoiakim's reign, Nebuchadnezzar king of Babylon invaded the land, and Jehoiakim became his vassal for three years. But then he changed his mind and rebelled against Nebuchadnezzar" (2 Kings 24:1).

The political background for this step can be understood from the Babylonian Chronicles (British Museum, Ref. 21946, records events from 597 B.C. down to 594). These were a compressed chronological summary of the principal events from the Babylonian court. There had been a crucial battle in 601 B.C. between the Egyptians and the Babylonians. This had left both sides weakened, and Jehoiakim took this opportunity to declare his independence of the Babylonian king. His independence, or rather Judah's independence, did not last long, for Jehoiakim himself died in 598 B.C., leaving his throne and the crisis to his son, Jehoiachin. Second Kings tells us what happened:

> At that time the officers of Nebuchadnezzar king of Babylon advanced on Jerusalem and laid siege to it, and Nebuchadnezzar himself came up to the city. . . . Jehoiachin king of Judah, his mother, his attendants, his nobles and his officials all surrendered to him.
> In the eighth year of the reign of the king of Babylon, he took Jehoiachin prisoner. . . . He made Mattaniah, Jehoiachin's uncle, king in his place and changed his name to Zedekiah.

2 Kings 24:10-12, 17

The story of Jehoiachin does not end there, however. The royal family were kept at the court of Nebuchadnezzar, and the Bible says that they, like other royal captives, were provided for by the king with rations of grain and oil:

> In the thirty-seventh year of the exile of Jehoiachin king of Judah, in the year Evil-Merodach [Nebuchadnezzar's successor] became king of Babylon, he released Jehoiachin from prison on the twenty-seventh day of the twelfth month. He spoke kindly to him and gave him a seat of honor higher than those of the other kings who were with him in Babylon. So Jehoiachin put aside his prison clothes and for the rest of his life ate regularly at the king's table. Day by day the king gave Jehoiachin a regular allowance as long as he lived.

2 Kings 25:27-30

The records of these allowances referred to in the Bible were unearthed in excavations in Babylon in basement storerooms of the royal palace (in Staat-Liches Museum, East Berlin, Vorderas Abteilung; Babylon 28122 and 28126). These are known as the "ration tablets" and they record who received such "rations." In these, Jehoiachin is mentioned by name.

We also have confirmation of the Babylonian advance towards Judah in Nebuchadnezzar's first campaign. Among the ruins of Lachish were discovered a number of ostraca. Ostraca are broken pieces of earthenware called potsherds, which were used for writing on in ink. (The Lachish ostraca are in the Palestinian Archaeological Museum, Jerusalem.) These brief letters reveal the increasing tensions within the growing state of Judah and tie in well with the picture given in the Bible by the Book of Jeremiah the Prophet. In Ostracon VI, the princes are accused of "weakening our hands" (that is, discouraging the writers), which is the very phraseology used in the Bible by the Judean princes against Jeremiah. Also, the use of fire beacons for signaling is found in both Ostracon IV and Jeremiah 6:1, each using the same terminology.

These events took place around the year 600 B.C. Events we considered earlier in relation to the capture of Lachish by Sennacherib during the reign of Hezekiah were around the year 700 B.C.

We now take a jump back in time to the middle of the ninth century before Christ, that is, about 850 B.C. Most people have heard of Jezebel. She was the wife of Ahab, the king of the northern kingdom of Israel. Her wickedness has become so proverbial that we talk about someone as a "Jezebel." She urged her husband to have Naboth killed, simply because Ahab had expressed his liking for a piece of land owned by Naboth, who would not sell it. The Bible tells us also that she introduced into Israel the worship of her homeland, the Baal worship of Tyre. This led to the opposition of Elijah the Prophet and to the famous conflict on Mount Carmel between Elijah and the priests of Baal.

Here again one finds archaeological confirmations of what the Bible says. Take for example: "As for the other events of Ahab's reign, including all he did, the palace he built and inlaid with ivory, and the cities he fortified, are they not written in the book of the annals of the kings of Israel?" (1 Kings 22:39).

This is a very brief reference in the Bible to events which must have taken a long time: building projects which probably spanned decades. Archaeological excavations at the site of Samaria, the capital, reveal something of the former splendor of the royal citadel. Remnants of the "ivory house" were found and attracted special attention (Palestinian Archaeological Museum, Jerusalem). This appears to have been a treasure pavilion in which the walls and furnishings had been adorned with colored ivory work set with inlays giving a brilliant decorative effect. Numerous fragments of these were found. This ties in well, too, with the denunciations revealed by the prophet Amos:

> "I will tear down the winter house
> along with the summer house;
> the houses adorned with ivory will be destroyed
> and the mansions will be demolished,"
> declares the LORD.
>
> Amos 3:15

Other archaeological confirmation exists for the time of Ahab. Excavations at Hazor and Megiddo have given evidence of the extent of fortifications carried out by Ahab. At Megiddo, in particular, Ahab's works were very extensive, including a large series of stables formerly assigned to Solomon's time.

On the political front, Ahab had to contend with danger from the Aramaeans just to the north (present-day Syria). Ben-hadad is named in 1 Kings 20:1 as the king of Syria who besieged Samaria, Ahab's capital. Ben-hadad's existence is attested by a stela (a column with writing on it) which has been discovered with his name written on it (Melquart Stela, Aleppo Museum, Syria). Again, a detail of history given in the Bible is shown to be correct.

Consider, too, the threat in the entire Middle East from the power of Assyria. In 853 B.C. King Shalmaneser III of Assyria came west from the region of the Euphrates River, only to be successfully repulsed by a determined alliance of all the states in that area of the Battle of Qarqar. Shalmaneser's record gives details of the alliance. In these he includes Ahab, who he tells us put 2,000 chariots and 10,000 infantry into the battle. However, after Ahab's death, Samaria was no longer strong enough to retain control, and Moab under King Mesha declared its independence, as 2 Kings 3:4, 5 makes clear: "Now Mesha king of Moab raised sheep, and he had to supply the king of Israel with a hundred thousand lambs and with the wool of a hundred thousand rams. But after Ahab died, the king of Moab rebelled against the king of Israel." The famous Moabite (Mesha) Stone, now in the Louvre, bears an inscription which testifies to Mesha's reality and of his success in throwing off the yoke of Israel. This is an inscribed black basalt stela, about four feet high, two feet wide, and several inches thick.

Ahab's line did not last long and was brutally overthrown by a man called Jehu. As one walks toward the Assyrian section in the British Museum, one of the first exhibits to be seen is the famous Black Obelisk. This stands about six feet high and was discovered at Nimrud (Calah) near the Assyrian capital at Nineveh. It describes how King Shalmeneser III compelled Jehu to submit to his authority and to pay him tribute. Here one can see a representation of the kneeling figure of either Jehu or his envoy before the Assyrian king. The inscription tells of Jehu's submission: "The tribute of Jehu, son of Omri: I received from him silver, gold, a golden bowl, a golden vase with pointed bottom, golden tumblers, golden buckets, tin, a staff for a king and purukhti fruits."

Jehu is referred to by the Assyrian records as son of Omri, not because he was literally his son, but because he was on the throne which had been occupied previously by the house of Omri. This event took place about 841 B.C.

Putting them all together, these archaeological records show not only the existence historically of the people and events recorded in the Bible but the great accuracy of the details involved.

If we take another hundred-year step backwards in time, we come to King Solomon, son of David. On his death the Jewish kingdom was divided into two sections as a result of a civil revolt: Israel to the north with Jeroboam as king and Judah (as it was called subsequently) to the south under Rehoboam, Solomon's son. In both the Books of Kings and Chronicles in the Bible we read how during Rehoboam's reign: "Shishak king of Egypt attacked Jerusalem" (1 Kings 14:25; 2 Chronicles 12:2), and how Shishak stripped Rehoboam of the wealth accumulated by his able father, Solomon. The reality of this event is confirmed by archaeology to a remarkable degree.

Shishak subdued not only Rehoboam but Jeroboam as well. The proof of this comes first from a fragment in a victory monument erected by Shishak and discovered at Megiddo, a city in the land of Israel. So the Egyptian king's force swept northwards, subdued the two Jewish kings, and then erected a victory monument to that effect. Traces of the destruction have also been discovered in such cities as Hazor, Gezer, and Megiddo. These confirm what was written in Second Chronicles:

> . . . he [Shishak] captured the fortified cities of Judah and came as far as Jerusalem.

Then the prophet Shemaiah came to Rehoboam and to the leaders of Judah who had assembled in Jerusalem for fear of Shishak, and he said to them, "This is what the LORD says, 'You have abandoned me; therefore, I now abandon you to Shishak.' "

The leaders of Israel and the king humbled themselves and said, "The LORD is just."

When the LORD saw that they humbled themselves, this word of the LORD came to Shemaiah: "Since they have humbled themselves, I will not destroy them but will soon give them deliverance. My wrath will not be poured out on Jerusalem through Shishak. They will, however, become subject to him, so that they may learn the difference between serving me and serving the kings of other lands."

When Shishak king of Egypt attacked Jerusalem, he carried off the treasures of the temple of the LORD and the treasures of the royal palace. He took everything, including the gold shields Solomon had made.

2 Chronicles 12:4-9

Further confirmation comes from the huge victory scene engraved on Shishak's order at the Temple of Karnak in Egypt. The figure of the king is somewhat obscured, but he is clearly named and he is seen smiting Hebrew captives before the god Amon, and there are symbolic rows of names of conquered towns of Israel and Judah.

Solomon is remembered also for his great wealth. The Bible tells us:

The weight of the gold that Solomon received yearly was 666 talents, not including the revenues from merchants and traders and from all the Arabian kings and the governors of the land.

King Solomon made two hundred large shields of hammered gold; six hundred bekas of gold went into each shield. He also made three hundred small shields of hammered gold, with three minas of gold in each shield. The king put them in the Palace of the Forest of Lebanon.

1 Kings 10:14-17

This wealth that the Bible speaks of has been challenged. Surely, some have said, these figures are an exaggeration. Excavations, however, have confirmed enormous quantities of precious metals, owned and distributed by kings during this period. For example, Shishak's son Osorkon I (statuette of Osorkon I, Brooklyn Museum, New York), the one who stood to gain from the booty carried off from Rehoboam's capital, is reported to have made donations to his god Amon totaling 470 tons of precious metal, gold, and silver, during only the first four years of his reign. This, of course, is much more than Solomon's 666 talents which equals approximately twenty tons of gold per annum. We also have confirmation of the Bible's reference to Solomon's gold as coming from Ophir. The location of Ophir is still unknown, but an ostracon dated a little later than Solomon's time actually mentions that thirty shekels of gold had come from Ophir for Beth-horon.

So the story goes on. We have stopped at only a few incidents in the sweep back to the year 1000 B.C. What we hope has emerged from this is a sense of the historical reliability of the Bible's text. When the Bible refers to historical incidents, it is speaking about the same sort of "history" that historians examine elsewhere in other cultures and periods. This is borne out by the fact that some of the incidents, some of the individuals, and some of the places have been confirmed by archaeological discoveries. Of course, not all the incidents, individuals, and places have been confirmed, but the tide of archaeological discoveries in the past hundred years has swept away the possibility of a naive skepticism about the Bible's history. And what is particularly striking is that the tide has built up concerning the time before the year 1000 B.C. Our knowledge about the years 2500 B.C. to 1000 B.C. has been vastly increased through discoveries sometimes of whole libraries and even of hitherto unknown people and languages.

There was a time, for example, when the Hittite people, referred to in the early parts of the Bible, were treated as fictitious by critical scholars. Then came the discoveries after 1906 at Boghaz Koi (Boghaz-köy) which not only gave us the certainty of their existence but stacks of details from their own archives! [95]Two things should be mentioned about the time of Moses in Old Testament history.

First, consider the archaeological evidence that relates to the period. True, it is not of the same explicitness that we have found, say, in relation to the existence of Ahab or Jehu or Jehoiakim. We have no inscription from Egypt which refers to Moses being taken out of the bulrushes and removed from the waterproof basket his mother had made him. But this does not mean that the Book of Exodus is a fictitious account, as some critics have suggested. Some say it is simply an idealized reading-back into history by the Jews under the later monarchy. There is not reason why these "books of Moses," as they are called, should not be treated as history, just as we have been forced to treat the Books of Kings and Chronicles dating 500 years later.

There is ample evidence about the building projects of the Egyptian kings, and the evidence we have fits well with Exodus. There are scenes of brickmaking (for example, Theban Tomb 100 of Rekhmire). Contemporary parchments and papyri tell of production targets which had to be met. One speaks of a satisfied official report of his men as "making their quota of bricks daily" (Papyrus Anastasi III vso, p. 3, in the British Museum. Also Louvre Leather Roll in the Louvre, Paris, col ii, mentions quotes of bricks and "taskmasters"). Actual bricks found show signs of straw which had to be mixed in with the clay, just as Exodus says. This matter of bricks and straw is further affirmed by the record that one despairing official complained, "There are no men to make bricks nor straw in my area."

We know from contemporary discoveries that Semites were found at all levels of Egypt's cosmopolitan society (Brooklyn Museum, New York, no. 35.1446. Papyrus Brooklyn). There is nothing strange therefore about Joseph's becoming so important in the pharaoh's court.

The store cities of Pithom and Raamses (Rameses) mentioned in Exodus 1:11 are well known in Egyptian inscriptions. Raamses was actually the east-Delta capital, Pi-Ramses (near Goshen), where the Israelites lived (to the east of the Nile Delta). It had fertile tracts, an area where the Israelites would have had ample experience of agriculture. Thus, the reference to agriculture found in the law of Moses would not have been strange to the Israelites even though they were in the desert at the time the law was given. Certainly there is no reason to say, as some critics do, that these sections on agriculture were an indication of a reading-back from a later period when the Jews were settled in Canaan.

The form of the covenant made at Sinai has remarkable parallels with the covenant forms of other people at that time. (On *covenants* and *parties to a treaty*, see C. F. A. Schaeffer, Ugaritica III Louvre, Paris; the Code of Hammurabi in the Louvre; and Treaty Tablet from Boghaz Koi [i.e., Hittite] in Turkey, Museum of Archaeology in Istanbul.) The covenant form at Sinai resembles covenants from that period but *not* from later in the first millennium B.C. Thus, just as the forms of letter writing of the first century after Christ (the types of introductions and greetings) are reflected in the letters of the apostles in the New Testament, it is not surprising to find the covenant form of the second millennium before Christ reflected in what occurred at Mount Sinai. God has always spoken to people within the culture of their time, which does not mean that God's communication is limited by that culture. It is God's communication but within the forms appropriate to the time.

The Pentateuch tells us that Moses led the Israelites up tne east side of the Dead Sea after their long stay in the desert. There they encountered the hostile kingdom of Moab. We have firsthand evidence for the existence of this kingdom of Moab—contrary to what has been said by critical scholars who have denied the existence of Moab at this time. It can be found in a war scene from a temple at Luxor (Al Uqsor). This commemorates a victory by Ramses II over the Moabite nation at Batora (Luxor Temple, Egypt).

Also, the definite presence of the Israelites in west Palestine (Canaan) no later than the end of the thirteenth century B.C. is attested by a victory stela of Pharaoh Merenptah (son and successor of Ramses II) to commemorate his victory over Libya (Israel Stela. Cairo Museum, no. 34025). In it he mentions his previous success in Canaan against Aschalon, Gize, Yenom, and *Israel;* hence there can be no doubt the nation of Israel was in existence at the *latest* by this time of approximately 1220 B.C. This is not to say it could not have been earlier, but it cannot be later than this date.

[96]We should take one last step back into the history of the Old Testament. In the previous note we looked first at the Dead Sea Scrolls, dating to around 100 B.C. Then we went back to the period of the Late Monarchy and looked first at the siege of Hezekiah in Jerusalem by Sennacherib in 701 B.C. and also at the last years of Judah down to about 600 B.C. Then we went further back to about 850 B.C., to Ahab and Jezebel, the ivory house, the Black Obelisk, the Moabite Stone and so on—then back again to about 950 B.C., to the time of Solomon and his son Rehoboam and the campaign by Shishak, the Egyptian pharaoh.

This should have built up in our minds a vivid impression of the historic reliability of the biblical text, including even the seemingly obscure details such as the ration tablets in Babylon. We saw, in other words, not only that the Bible gives us a marvelous world view that ties in with the nature of reality and answers the basic problems which philosophers have asked down through the centuries, but also that the Bible is completely reliable, *even on the historical level.*

The previous notes looked back to the time of Moses and Joshua, the escape from Egypt, and the settlement in Canaan. Now we will go back further—approximately 500 years before Moses—to the time of Abraham. We are now back as far as Genesis 12, near the beginning of the Bible.

Do we find that the narrative fades away to a never-never land of myths and legends? By no means. For we have to remind ourselves that although Genesis 12 deals with events a long time ago from our moment of history (about 2000

B.C. or a bit later), the civilized world was already not just old but ancient when Abram/Abraham left "Ur of the Chaldeans" (*see* Genesis 11:31).

Ur itself was excavated some fifty years ago. In the British Museum, for example, one can see the magnificent contents of a royal burial chamber from Ur. This includes a gold headdress still in position about the head of a queen who died in Ur about 2500 B.C. It has also been possible to reconstruct from archaeological remains what the streets and buildings must have been like at the time.

Like Ur, the rest of the world of the patriarchs (that is, of Abraham, Isaac, and Jacob) was firm reality. Such places as Haran, where Abraham went first, have been discovered. So has Shechem from this time, with its Canaanite stone walls, which are still standing, and its temple.

> He [Abram] took his wife Sarai, his nephew Lot, all the possessions they had accumulated and the people they had acquired in Haran, and they set out for the land of Canaan, and they arrived there.
>
> Abram traveled through the land as far as the site of the great tree of Moreh at Shechem. The Canaanites were then in the land, but the LORD appeared to Abram and said, "To your offspring I will give this land." So he built an altar there to the LORD, who had appeared to him.
>
> From there he went on toward the hills east of Bethel and pitched his tent, with Bethel on the west and Ai on the east. There he built an altar to the LORD and called on the name of the LORD. Then Abram set out and continued toward the Negev.
>
> Genesis 12:5-9

Haran and Shechem may be unfamiliar names to us but the Negev (or Negeb) is a name we have all read frequently in the news accounts of our own day.

Now we should turn to one of the most spectacular of modern archaeological discoveries, Ebla. While digging on an extensive mound forty-four miles south of Aleppo in Syria in 1974/75, an Italian archaeological expedition came across another of the vast libraries to which we referred earlier. A small room within the palace suddenly yielded up a thousand tablets and fragments, while another not far away a further fourteen thousand. There lay row upon row, just where they had fallen from the burning wooden shelves when the palace was destroyed about 2250 B.C.

What secrets did these tablets reveal? Without wishing to seem unnecessarily repetitive, we can say immediately that Ebla represents yet another discovery from the ancient past which does not make it harder for us to believe the Bible, but quite the opposite. And remember, these tablets date from well before the time of Abraham. The implications of this discovery will not be exhausted by even the turn of this century. The translation and publication of such a vast number of tablets will take years and years. It is important to understand that the information we now have from Ebla does not bear directly upon the Bible. As far as has been discovered, there is no certain reference to individuals mentioned in the Bible, though many names are similar, for example, Ishmael, Israel, and so forth. Biblical place names like Megiddo, Hazor, Lachish are also referred to. What *is* clear, however, is that certain individuals outside the Bible who previously had been considered fictitious by the critical scholars, simply because of their antiquity, are now quite definitely historic characters.

For example, the Assyrian King Tudiya (approximately 2500 B.C.) had already been known from the Assyrian king list composed about 1000 B.C. His name appeared at the head of the list, but his reality was dismissed by many scholars as "free invention, or a corruption." In fact, he was very much a real person and is known now from the Ebla records to have made a treaty with the king of Ebla. Thus, the genealogical tradition of the earlier parts of the Assyrian king list has been vindicated. It preserves faithfully, over a period of 1,500 years, the memory of real, early people who were Assyrian rulers. What we must learn from this is that when we find similar material in the Old Testament, such as the genealogical list in Genesis 7 or the patriarchal stories, we should be careful not to reject them out of hand, as the scholars have so often done. We must remember that these ancient cultures were just as capable of recording their histories as we are.

The most important aspect of the Ebla discoveries is undoubtedly their language. This has been found to be an ancient West-Semitic language to which such languages as Hebrew, Canaanite, Ugaritic, Aramaic, and Moabite are related. Thus we have now, for the first time, the whole "tradition" of West-Semitic language stretching over 2,500 years—something which was previously true only of Egyptian and Akkadian, to which Babylonian and Assyrian belong.

Up until quite recently, therefore, this meant that scholars could argue that many words which appeared in the Hebrew Old Testament were what they called "late." What they meant by this was that these words indicated a much later authorship than the time stated by the text itself. It would be as if one of us pretended to write a sixteenth-century book using such modern words as *automobile* and *computer*. In the case of the Pentateuch, for example, this was one of the arguments which led some scholars to suggest that it was not Moses who wrote these books, as the Bible says, but anonymous scribes from approximately 1,000 years later. The discoveries at Ebla have shown that many of these words were not late, but very early. Here is yet another example of a claimed "scientific" approach that merely reflects the philosophical prejudices of the scholars involved.

[97] A common assumption among liberal scholars is that because the Gospels are theologically motivated writings—which they are—they cannot also be historically accurate. In other words, because Luke, say (when he wrote the Book of Luke and the Book of Acts), was convinced of the deity of Christ, this influenced his work to the point where it ceased to be reliable as a historical account. The assumption that a writing cannot be both historical and theological is false.

The experience of the famous classical archaeologist Sir William Ramsay illustrates this well. When he began his pioneer work of exploration in Asia Minor, he accepted the view then current among the Tübingen scholars of his day that the Book of Acts was written long after the events in Paul's life and was therefore historically inaccurate. However, his travels and discoveries increasingly forced upon his mind a totally different picture, and he became convinced that Acts was minutely accurate in many details which could be checked.

What is even more interesting is the way "liberal" modern scholars today deal with Ramsay's discoveries and others like them. In *The New Testament: The History of the Investigations of Its Problems,* the German scholar Werner G.

Kümmel made no reference at all to Ramsay. This provoked a protest from British and American scholars, whereupon in a subsequent edition Kümmel responded. His response was revealing. He made it clear that it was his deliberate intention to leave Ramsay out of his work, since "Ramsay's apologetic analysis of archaeology [in other words, relating it to the New Testament in a positive way] signified no methodologically essential advance for New Testament research." This is a quite amazing assertion. Statements like these reveal the philosophic assumptions involved in much liberal scholarship.

A modern *classical* scholar, A. N. Sherwin-White, says about the Book of Acts: "For Acts the confirmation of historicity is overwhelming. . . . Any attempt to reject its basic historicity, even in matters of detail, must now appear absurd. Roman historians have long taken this for granted."

When we consider the pages of the New Testament, therefore, we must remember what it is we are looking at. The New Testament writers themselves make abundantly clear that they are giving an account of objectively true events.

[98]Acts is a fairly full account of Paul's journeys, starting in Pisidian Antioch and ending in Rome itself. The record is quite evidently that of an eyewitness of the events, in part at least. Throughout, however, it is the report of a meticulous historian. The narrative in the Book of Acts takes us back behind the missionary journeys to Paul's famous conversion on the Damascus Road, and back further through the Day of Pentecost to the time when Jesus finally left His disciples and ascended to be with the Father.

But we must understand that the story begins earlier still, for Acts is quite explicitly the second part of a continuous narrative by the same author, Luke, which reaches back to the birth of Jesus:

> In those days Caesar Augustus issued a decree that a census should be taken of the entire Roman world. (This was the first census that took place while Quirinius was governor of Syria.) And everyone went to his own town to register.
>
> So Joseph also went up from the town of Nazareth in Galilee to Judea, to Bethlehem the town of David, because he belonged to the house and line of David. He went there to register with Mary, who was pledged to be married to him and was expecting a child. While they were there, the time came for the baby to be born, and she gave birth to her firstborn, a son. She wrapped him in strips of cloth and placed him in a manger, because there was no room for them in the inn.
>
> Luke 2:1-7

In the opening sentences of his Gospel, Luke states his reason for writing:

> Many have undertaken to draw up an account of the things that have been fulfilled among us, just as they were handed down to us by those who from the first were eyewitnesses and servants of the word. Therefore, since I myself have carefully investigated everything from the beginning, it seemed good also to me to write an orderly account for you, most excellent Theophilus, so that you may know the certainty of the things you have been taught.
>
> Luke 1:1-4

In Luke and Acts, therefore, we have something which purports to be an adequate history, something which Theophilus (or anyone) can rely on as its pages are read. This is not the language of "myths and fables," and archeological discoveries serve only to confirm this.

For example, it is now known that Luke's references to the titles of officials encountered along the way are uniformly accurate. This was no mean achievement in those days, for they varied from place to place and from time to time in the same place. They were *proconsuls* in Corinth and Cyprus, *asiarchs* at Ephesus, *politarchs* at Thessalonica, and *protos* or "first man" in Malta. Back in Palestine, Luke was careful to give Herod Antipas the correct title of tetrarch of Galilee. And so on. The details are precise.

The mention of Pontius Pilate as Roman governor of Judea has been confirmed recently by an inscription discovered at Caesarea, which was the Roman capital of that part of the Roman Empire. Although Pilate's existence has been well known for the past 2,000 years by those who have read the Bible, now his governorship has been clearly attested outside the Bible.

BOOK FOUR: A CHRISTIAN MANIFESTO

Chapter 1: The Abolition of Truth and Morality

[1] *Humanist Manifestos I and II* (New York: Prometheus Books, 1973).

[2] This must not be confused with the humanistic elements which were developing slightly earlier in the Renaissance. Francis A. Schaeffer, *How Should We Then Live?* (Old Tappan, N.J.: Fleming H. Revell Co., 1976), pp. 58-78.

[3] See *How Should We Then Live?*, pp. 40 and 109.

[4] See Will and Ariel Durant's book, *The Lessons of History* (New York: Simon & Schuster, 1968), pp. 84-86.

[5] *American Law Review*, XIV, (1880), p. 233.

[6] *Harvard Law Review*, XL, (1918).

[7] Henry De Bracton, translation of *De Legibus et Consuetudinibus* (Cambridge, Mass.: Harvard-Belknap, 1968).

[8] See James L. Fisk, *The Law and Its Timeless Standard* (Washington: Lex Rex Institute).

[9] See Will and Ariel Durant's *The Lessons of History*, pp. 70-75

Chapter 2: Foundations for Faith and Freedom

[1] David Walker Woods, *John Witherspoon* (Old Tappan, N.J.: Fleming H. Revell Co., 1906).

[2] Edward Corwin, *The Supreme Court as National School Board*, Law and Contemporary Problems, 14, (1949), pp. 3, 11-12.

[3] Herbert W. Titus, Professor of Law, O. W. Coburn School of Law, *Education, Caesar's or God's: A Constitutional Question of Jurisdiction.*

[4] Ibid.

[5] Ibid.

[6] Ibid.

[7] Published by David C. Cook, Elgin, Illinois, 1982.

[8]Franky Schaeffer V, "The Myth of Neutrality," *Plan For Action* (Old Tappan, N.J.: Fleming H. Revell Co., 1980), p. 37. *Plan For Action* is an action handbook for *Whatever Happened to the Human Race?*

[9]Terry Eastland, "In Defense of Religious America," *Commentary* (June 1981), p. 39.

[10]Quoted in Perry Miller, editor, *The Legal Mind in America* (New York: Doubleday, 1962), p. 178.

[11]Eastland, p. 41.

Chapter 3: The Destruction of Faith and Freedom

[1]See *How Should We Then Live?*, p. 217.

[2]Ibid.

[3]William Bentley Ball is a partner of the law firm of Ball and Skelly of Harrisburg, Pennsylvania. He has been lead council in litigation in twenty states and has appeared before the Supreme Court in parental rights cases. He was chairman of the Federal Bar Association Committee on Constitutional Law, 1970-74.

[4]See *How Should We Then Live?*, chapters "The Rise of Modern Science" and "The Breakdown of Philosophy and Science," pp. 130-166.

[5]Durant, *The Lessons of History*, pp. 50 and 51.

[6]Ibid.

[7]See Jacques Monod, *Chance and Necessity* (New York: Alfred A. Knopf, 1971).

Chapter 4: The Humanist Religion

[1]*Humanist Manifestos I and II* (New York: Prometheus Books, 1973).

[2]John W. Whitehead, *The Second American Revolution.*

[3]William B. Provine, "The End of Ethics?" in *Hard Choices* (a magazine companion to the television series *Hard Choices*) (Seattle: KCTS-TV, channel 9, University of Washington, 1980), pp. 2, 3.

[4]Charles Peters, *How Washington Really Works* (Reading, Mass.: Addison-Wesley Pub. Co., 1980), p. 17.

[5]See *How Should We Then Live?*, pp. 239-243.

Chapter 5: Revival, Revolution, and Reform

[1]Howard A. Snyder, *The Radical Wesley* (Downers Grove, Ill.: InterVarsity Press, 1980), pp. 86, 87.

[2]Jeremy Rifkin, *Entropy* (New York: Viking, 1980), pp. 234-240.

[3]Francis A. Schaeffer, *Pollution and the Death of Man—The Christian View of Ecology* (Wheaton, Ill.: Tyndale House Publishers, 1970).

[4]Charles Finney, *Systematic Theology* (Minneapolis: Bethany Fellowship, Inc., 1976).

[5]Jonathan Kaufman, "Old Time Religion, An Evangelical Revival Is Sweeping the Nation But with Little Effect," *Wall Street Journal* (July 11, 1980).

[6]Franky Schaeffer V, *Addicted to Mediocrity* (Westchester, Ill.: Crossway Books, 1981), pp. 27, 28.

Chapter 6: An Open Window

[1]Eastland, p. 42.

[2]See pp. 224-254.

[3]Robert L. Toms, Editorial, *Theology, News and Notes* (December 1980), pp. 18, 19. Mr. Toms is a partner of Caldwell & Toms of Los Angeles. He is a former Corporations Commissioner of the State of California under Governor Reagan.
[4]Ibid.
[5]Samuel E. Ericsson, *Clergy Malpractice: Constitutional and Political Issues* (The Center for Law and Religious Freedom, Washington, D.C., May 1981). Mr. Ericsson is Special Counsel, Washington, D.C., office for the Center for Law and Religious Freedom. He is a graduate of Harvard Law School. Happily, since this book was written the church has won this case, but other cases of a somewhat like nature will certainly arise.

Chapter 7: The Limits of Civil Obedience
[1]Francis Legge, *Forerunners and Rivals of Christianity from 330 B.C. to 330 A.D.*, Vol. 1 (New Hyde Park, N.Y.: University Books, 1964), p. xxiv.
[2]Jasper Ridley, *John Knox* (New York: Oxford, 1968), p. 171.
[3,4]John Knox, *Works* (New York: AMS Press, Vol. vi, 1968), pp. 236-238.
[5]Samuel Rutherford, *Lex Rex, or, The Law and the Prince* (n.p., 1644), published in Vol. 3, *The Presbyterian Armoury* (1846), p. 34.

Chapter 8: The Use of Civil Disobedience
[1]Bob Dylan, *Slow Train Coming* (New York: Special Rider Music, CBS, Inc., 1979).
[2]Os Guinness, *The Dust of Death* (Downers Grove, Ill.: InterVarsity Press, 1973), pp. 177, 178.
[3]Eric von Kuehnelt-Leddihn, *Leftism: From de Sade and Marx to Hitler and Marcuse* (New Rochelle, N.Y.: Arlington House, 1974), p. 427.
[4]See *How Should We Then Live?*, pp. 120-124.

Chapter 9: The Use of Force
[1]"Seminary Students Arrested for Abortion Clinic Protests," *Bulletin Newsupplement* (Asheville, N.C.: Perspective Press for the Reformed Presbyterian Church, Evangelical Synod, April 15, 1980).
[2]Ibid.
[3]Jan Pit, *Persecution: It Will Never Happen Here?* (Orange, Calif.: Open Doors With Brother Andrew, 1981), pp. 42, 43.
[4]See *How Should We Then Live?*, chapter 6, "The Enlightenment," pp. 120-128 and pp. 154-160.
[5]See *How Should We Then Live?*, pp. 113-119.
[6]Perry Miller, *Nature's Nation* (Cambridge, Mass.: Harvard-Belknap, 1967), p. 110.
[7]Ibid.
[8]Isaiah 59:12-16a.
[9]Revelation 3:2 (combination of *King James Version* and *New International Version*).

List of Translated Editions and Publishers of the Books in Volume Five

POLLUTION AND THE DEATH OF MAN

First United States edition, Tyndale House, 1970.
First British edition, Hodder and Stoughton, 1970.
Polución y la Muerte del Hombre (Spanish), Casa Bautista de Publicaciones, 1973.
Milieuvervuiling en de dood van de mens (Dutch), Buijten & Schipperheijn Publishing Co., Amsterdam, 1973.
Das Programmierte ende (German), Haus der Bibel, Geneva, R. Brockhaus Verlag, Wuppertal, 1975.
Kristitty ja Saastuva Luonto (Finnish), Kansan Raamattuseuran Säätiö, Helsinki, 1973.
La Pollution et la Mort de L'Homme (French). Ligue Pour la Lecture de la Bible, Guebwiller, 1974.
Poluição e a Morte do Homem (Portuguese), Junta de Educacão Religiosa e Publicações, Rio de Janeiro, 1976.

HOW SHOULD WE THEN LIVE?

First United States, edition, Fleming H. Revell, 1976. (Documentary film series—ten one-half hour films—Gospel Films, 1976.)
First British edition, Marshall, Morgan and Scott, 1980.
Hoe Zouden Wijdan Leven? (Dutch), Uitgeverij G.F. Callenbach bv, Nijkerk, 1977.
Wie Können wir den Leben? (German), Hänssler Verlag, Neuhausen-Stuttgart, 1977.
Japanese edition, Word of Life Press, 1979.

WHATEVER HAPPENED TO THE HUMAN RACE?

First United States edition, Fleming H. Revell, 1979. (Documentary film
    series—five one hour films—Franky V Productions Inc., 1979.)
First British edition, Marshall, Morgan and Scott, 1980.
Människa-vad Är Du Värd (Swedish), Bokförlaget Libris Orebro, 1981.
Wat Ging Er Mis (Dutch), Elsevier Focus bv, Amsterdam, 1981.

A CHRISTIAN MANIFESTO

First United States edition, Crossway Books, 1981.
First British edition, Pickering & Inglis Ltd., 1982.

Acknowledgments

POLLUTION AND THE DEATH OF MAN

The articles which comprise the Appendix have been previously copyrighted as follows, and are used by special permission of the authors and publishers:

"The Historical Roots of Our Ecologic Crisis," by Lynn White, Jr.; *Science*, Vol. 155, pp. 1203-1207, 10 March 1967. Copyright © 1967 by the American Association for the Advancement of Science.

"Why Worry about Nature?" Richard L. Means, *Saturday Review*, December 2, 1967. Copyright © 1967 Saturday Review, Inc.

HOW SHOULD WE THEN LIVE?

In July 1974 my son, Franky, came to me with a suggestion.

The suggestion was that, given time, finances, and hard work by himself and others and by me, a major cultural and historical documentary film series and book could perhaps be produced. Using my study, over the past forty years, of Western thought and culture as a base, we could attempt to present the flow and development which have led to twentieth-century thinking, and by so doing hope to show the essential answers. After much thought, I agreed that we had the responsibility to try.

First of all, let me thank Billy Zeoli for his immediate recognition of the potential of this project and for his steadfast backing and support which made this project possible.

To begin with, I wrote the basic text as a foundation for both the film script and the book manuscript. This basic text was then divided into two separate projects: first, a film script, and second, an expanded version, this book. The book, of course, could utilize

537

the full basic text and thus gives more substantiating material than was possible within the time limits of even a lengthy film series.

For both book and film episodes to succeed, however, careful research was necessary, and I am therefore especially grateful to Dr. Jeremy Jackson, who was our chief historical researcher, for the hundreds of hours of research that he did on the basic text and on the indexes and bibliography of this book. His help and timely suggestions were a constant source of inspiration.

Doctor H. R. Rookmaaker, my longtime associate in the work of L'Abri Fellowship and professor of art history at the Free University in Amsterdam, was our chief art researcher. His expert knowledge of art history and his consistent concern for the project were invaluable to both the book and the film.

It was a privilege to have Jane Stuart Smith as a staunch friend and supporter to whom to appeal on all aspects of the text related to music. Jane was our chief music researcher and her knowledge on the subject was invaluable.

There was much research needed in areas not easily categorized. So it is with appreciation that I thank John and Sandra Bazlinton for the research they did as our general cultural researchers. Their suggestions often provided a source of clarification on many subjects.

Beyond these basic researchers there were a host of those who were involved in detailed areas of research, in typing and checking the succeeding versions of the text, in the thousands of details involved in the film, and in many other ways too numerous to be able to mention. Their time and effort were invaluable to the project, and I want to say "thank you" to them all.

James W. Sire was a great help on the editorial work of the book text; many thanks to him.

It was a pleasure working with all those at Fleming H. Revell Company; especially enjoyable were the friendship and support of Bill Barbour and Richard Baltzell. Richard Baltzell gave the final editorial touches to the book. He was also a great help in the final critical reading of the book manuscript, as were Udo Middelmann, Jeremy Jackson, and Franky Schaeffer.

I wish to express my gratitude to my co-workers at L'Abri Fellowship, whose work was increased during the two years I was working on this project, for the very practical help they often provided in addition to their moral support.

Acknowledgments would be totally incomplete without saying

"thank you" to Edith, my wife. She was patient beyond words through my tense periods, both while writing and filming. Without her constant encouragement, I simply would not have made it through this project.

I trust that the work and the vision of the people named or mentioned above will be rewarded in their being able to see a tangible change for the better brought about in our day and age by this book and its film counterpart.

Francis A. Schaeffer

Excerpts from the Francis Crick article "Why I Study Biology" which appeared in the Spring 1971 issue of *Washington University Magazine* are used by permission.

The Hans Arp poem "Für Theo Van Doesburg" is used by permission of Madame Marguerite Arp.

Excerpt from "The Waste Land" by T. S. Eliot is used by permission of the publishers, Harcourt Brace Jovanovich, Inc.

WHATEVER HAPPENED TO THE HUMAN RACE?

First we would like to thank Franky Schaeffer V Productions Inc., most particularly Franky Schaeffer and Jim Buchfuehrer, who worked with us in taking the ideas expressed in this book through every stage of development. Their company financed and arranged for the research and made many direct contributions to the text.

Franky Schaeffer wrote the screenplay for this book's accompanying film series and directed the episodes. Jim Buchfuehrer produced the series. As a team, together they made this project possible.

Another team, the general pediatric surgical staff of the Children's Hospital of Philadelphia and their paramedical personnel, made it possible for one of us to devote the necessary time to complete work on the book and film series.

A number of experts in various fields contributed greatly to the research and development necessary for this project. Professor Kenneth A. Kitchen, lecturer in Egyptian and Coptic at the School of Archaeology and Oriental Studies at the University of Liverpool, England, added much to our knowledge and research for the archaeological data. We had invaluable help from Ranald Macaulay in general research and through his special assistance with Chapters 4 and 5.

In addition we would thank the following for their contributions: Francis Ackerman, Jerram Barrs, Dr. James B. Hurley, Dr. Jeremy C. Jackson, Dick Keyes, Udo Middelmann, Oliver O'Donovan, John Sandri, and Dr. Joseph Stanton. Their time and efforts are greatly appreciated, as is the editorial work of James W. Sire and Evelyn Sendecke.

Francis A. Schaeffer
C. Everett Koop, M.D.

A CHRISTIAN MANIFESTO

"Seminary Students Arrested for Abortion Clinic Protests," *Bulletin Newsupplement,* April 15, 1980, © 1980.

A paper by William Ball, presented at a 1981 Christian Legal Society conference.

Humanist Manifestos I and II, edited by Paul Kurtz, copyright © 1973 by Prometheus Books, with permission of the publisher.

The Radical Wesley, by Howard A. Snyder, copyright © 1980 by Inter-Varsity Christian Fellowship of the USA; used by permission of InterVarsity Press, Downers Grove, Illinois 60515.

Holy Bible: New International Version, copyright © 1978 by the New York International Bible Society. Used by permission of Zondervan Bible Publishers.

"When You Gonna Wake Up," by Bob Dylan, copyright © 1979 by Special Rider Music.

Nature's Nation, by Perry Miller, copyright © 1967 by Harvard University Press.

"Where Is Science Taking Us? Gerald Holton Maps the Possible Routes," copyright © 1981 by The Chronicle of Higher Education, from May 18, 1981 issue.

"The End of Ethics?" by William B. Provine, reprinted from *Hard Choices* (a magazine companion to the television series *Hard Choices);* used by permission of KCTS-TV, Seattle and William B. Provine

Index to Volumes I-V